THE VICTORIAN NOVEL

Modern Essays in Criticism

The Victorian Novel

MODERN ESSAYS IN CRITICISM

Edited by IAN WATT

OXFORD UNIVERSITY PRESS
London   Oxford   New York
1971

OXFORD UNIVERSITY PRESS
Oxford London New York
Glasgow Toronto Melbourne Wellington
Cape Town Salisbury Ibadan Nairobi Lusaka Addis Ababa
Bombay Calcutta Madras Karachi Lahore Dacca
Kuala Lumpur Hong Kong Tokyo

Preface

Those who are reading these words presumably see no need to justify this particular addition to the vast and growing list of collections of critical essays. For one thing, the Victorian Age, having survived both the disgrace of being out-of-date and the hardly less dangerous glory of being antique, is now proudly and justifiably unfurling a banner with the strange device of relevance. It is also manifest that Victorian literature found its most typical and widely acknowledged voices among its novelists. And one of the most striking features in the scholarship and criticism of the last decades has undoubtedly been the way in which we have been enabled to attend to the Victorian novelists with a fuller understanding of their historical context and of their enduring literary greatness.

The particular selection of essays gathered here cannot, perhaps, so easily be justified. The anthologist finds himself the prey of many conflicting imperatives: the claims of the established versus the claims of the new; the need for breadth and the need for depth; the value of methodological variety and the value of direct literary illumination; the practical utility of reprinting what is not easily available as against making the selection representative even if it means reprinting essays that have already received the accolade of paperback publication; and finally there is the conflict between a personal literary commitment and an awareness of one's own fallibility. In attempting to mediate between all these imperatives the anthologist is likely to end up with something very different from what he originally expected or intended, especially when other intractable difficulties, whether personal or commercial, have been faced.

Still, despite all these difficulties, mitigated as they were by the advice of many friends who, despite my gratitude, I will not name because, invidiously, some are, and some are not, alas!, represented below, I hope that this collection of modern essays on the Victorian novel will be found to justify itself.

Textual Note

Though I have occasionally expanded footnote references and translated a few bits of Latin, I have refrained from regularizing the annotation, deeming that any possible peril to the authority of the *MLA Style Sheet* would be counterbalanced by exposure to the earlier, and especially British, casualness which it superseded. Short omissions in the text are indicated by single ellipses . . . ; longer ones by double ellipses . . . .

August 1970   I.W.

Contents

vii

THE VICTORIAN NOVEL

Modern Essays in Criticism

KATHLEEN TILLOTSON

Introductory

In the forties the author had several methods of getting his books into the hands of the public.[1] Three such methods are illustrated by [*Dombey and Son, Mary Barton, Vanity Fair,* and *Jane Eyre*], and a fourth by Kingsley's *Yeast.*

The commonest material form in which a reader of the eighteen-forties met a new novel, as at almost any time in the nineteenth century, was that taken by *"Jane Eyre: An Autobiography.* Edited by Currer Bell." This novel was in three small "post octavo" volumes—like David Copperfield's first novel, "compact in three individual wollumes"[2]—the usual format for novels since about 1830. By modern standards the volumes seem small and squat—like bound Penguins, but with better margins and more lead between the lines. Their most surprising feature is their price—a guinea and a half for the three. Surprising, until one realizes the dominance of the circulating libraries, and their interest in keeping book prices high.[3] Then as now, very few people *bought* new fiction in volume form; and of these, fewer still would feel inclined to buy a novel by an unknown writer—really unknown, for the poems of Currer, Ellis, and Acton Bell, published in the previous year, had only two buyers and three

From *Novels of the Eighteen-Forties* (Oxford: Clarendon Press, 1954), pp. 21-53. Copyright © 1954 by Kathleen Tillotson. Reprinted by permission of the publisher and author.

reviews. But after reading early reviews of *Jane Eyre,* the reader would probably order a copy of it from his circulating library.[4] By the eighteen-forties the circulating library was everywhere—Thackeray's verses were apt:

> In the romantic little town of Highbury
> My father kep a circulating library.[5]

And the subscription rates were very moderate—for new novels only one guinea a year. The separate volumes made for convenience of fireside reading, and for sharing among members of a family; though it would be exasperating to finish volume I, which ends at the point where Jane rescues Mr. Rochester from his blazing bed, when one's elder sister had not quite finished volume II. For the three-volume form matched a formal literary design: in many novels the structural divisions are as clear as the three acts of a play.

Less common were novels in two volumes. One of these was *Mary Barton.* It was included in a well-known series, "Chapman and Hall's Series of Original Works";[6] although anonymous, it might be more likely than *Jane Eyre* to take immediate buyers, for its sub-title, "A Tale of Manchester Life," was in 1848 highly topical; and its price was eighteen shillings.

The publication of a new novel in one volume was rare; the unpopularity of this form with publishers (again, thanks to the tyranny of the libraries) may have been one cause of the rejection of Charlotte Brontë's *The Professor.* The one-volume form normally signalized a cheap reprint, usually appearing two or three years after first publication;[7] it seems also to have been used for certain special types of novel, perhaps less likely to find favour with library subscribers—religious novels[8] and tales intended to appeal to younger as well as older readers.[9]

In the same year as *Mary Barton* another method of publication —that of the magazine serial—is illustrated by the fifth novel mentioned above. In the July number of *Fraser's Magazine for Town and Country,* a half-crown monthly of independent views, appeared anonymously the first instalment of *Yeast: or the Thoughts, Sayings and Doings of Lancelot Smith, Gentleman*; it was concluded in six instalments (rather less than Kingsley had intended) by December. So for fifteen shillings the reader had good value.

But if the would-be novel-reader had no library subscription, and took in no magazine, he could still have his new novels. In any month of 1847, he might see in the bookshops, in paper wrappers, greenish blue or bright yellow, for only one shilling, the current monthly parts of *Dealings* / *with the Firm of* / *Dombey and Son* / *Wholesale, Retail, and for Exportation* / *By Charles Dickens* and *Vanity Fair* / *Pen and Pencil Sketches of English Society* / *By W. M. Thackeray*. That was the form in which these two novels made their first appearance; and it was that form which so greatly extended the novel-reading public, by the simple device of spreading and lowering the cost—the total cost for a work equal in length to a "three-decker" came to £1. No wonder that a critic of 1851 remarked (prematurely, however) that the three-volume novel was "'going out with the tide,' being superseded by the periodical novel, a cheaper article."[10] In other ways these two forms of publication—magazine serial and part-issue—increased the popularity of the novel. The suspense induced by "making 'em wait" was intensified by being prolonged—to see what happened next the reader had to wait a month at a time. All novel-readers know the temptation to turn to the end: here is a confession of Thackeray's (a double confession):

> In the days of the old three-volume novels, didn't you always look at the end, to see that Louisa and the Earl (or young clergyman, as the case might be) were happy? If they died, or met with other grief . . . I put the book away.[11]

But during publication in parts there was no end to turn to—which some readers found an added pleasure: Disraeli's Lord Montfort, for instance:

> I like books that come out in numbers, as there is a little suspense, and you cannot deprive yourself of all interest by glancing at the last page of the last volume.[12]

Often the end was not even written, perhaps not predetermined: for this and other reasons, publication in parts induced, as I hope to show, a kind of contact between author and reader unknown today.

In the eighteen-forties neither of these forms of publication was quite new. The monthly part as a method of publishing new fiction had become established only in the late eighteen-thirties; but its ancestors are found in two very different types of part-issue common in the eighteenth and early nineteenth century. First, the very cheap part-issue of reprints of popular fiction now famous from Hazlitt's reference:

> The world I had found out in Cooke's edition of the British Novelists [1792] was to me a dance through life, a perpetual gala-day. The sixpenny numbers of this work regularly contrived to leave off just in the middle of a sentence, and in the nick of a story, where Tom Jones discovers Square behind the blanket. . . .[13]

Secondly, there was the expensive part-issue of new and finely illustrated works, often architectural and topographical. Fielding refers to such publications in *Joseph Andrews:*

> Homer was the first inventor of the art which hath so long lain dormant, of publishing by numbers; an art now brought to such perfection, that even dictionaries are divided and exhibited piecemeal to the public.[14]

If fiction was published with illustrations in this way—"raffish colour-plate books of the *Tom and Jerry* type,"[15] the emphasis was on the illustrations. It is an offshoot of this second type that we find when, late in 1835, the publishers Chapman and Hall planned with an artist called Seymour "a series of cockney sporting plates of a superior sort" to be accompanied by letter-press and published in monthly parts. The scheme hung fire for a while, until they thought of a young author who had written a series of sketches of cockney life in the *Monthly Magazine* and *Morning Chronicle,* and put before him the general notion of a "Nimrod club of sportsmen." The young author knew little about sport, and asked for a freer hand and a wider range of English scenes and people; as a concession he would keep the general idea of a club—"My views being deferred to, I thought of Mr. Pickwick"—and *The Posthumous Papers of the Pickwick Club* were accordingly begun.[16] The artist died suddenly after the second number, and his place was taken by Hablot K. Browne ("Phiz") who was to be long associated with Dickens. In this type of part-issue the artist is normally the dominating partner. But by the accidents of the publishers' choice of author and the first artist's death, the balance between writer and artist was changed, and it was not as a series of superior plates accompanied by letter-press that even its earliest readers thought of the *Pickwick Papers.* The letter-press so caught the public interest that it not only fairly launched Dickens on his career, but initiated a virtually new method of publishing fiction, and established in the public the habit of buying novels as well as borrowing them. Only a limited demand was expected: the binder prepared 400 copies of the first number, but by the time the fifteenth was reached, over 40,000 were required.[17] Dickens leapt into fame: everyone read *Pickwick*. Emily Eden, the sister of the Governor General, found it "the only fun in India," and read it in numbers "not more than ten times";[18] Alexander Bain read it in his Natural History class "out of the professor's sight";[19] Dr. Arnold complained to his neighbour Wordsworth that his boys at Rugby thought of nothing but "Bozzy's next number";[20] Captain Brown in *Cranford* was run over by a railway train while reading his copy of the current number.

After such success, it was natural that Dickens should retain this pattern of publication as a kind of trade-mark. For eight of his novels, the pattern is uniform—a shilling monthly part of thirty-two pages, generally with two plates,[21] the work completed in twenty monthly parts issued as nineteen, the concluding part being a double number at two shillings. Throughout the period of Dickens's working life, from 1836 to 1870, when he died after writing the sixth of the projected twelve numbers of *Edwin Drood,* the monthly part-issue was a fairly popular method of distribution.[22] The public liked it for its cheapness and perhaps also for its particular qualities of suspense. The publishers liked it for various financial reasons— high circulation, spreading and elasticity of costs, payments from advertisers (each part carried extra leaves of general advertisements), independence of lending libraries. The author liked it both for its large financial rewards—which reached him while he was writing—for reducing the risk of piracy, and for the warmth of contact with his readers.

In the end one cheap form of publication devoured the other; the part-issue was driven off the market by its rival the magazine serial. When *Macmillan's Magazine* and the *Cornhill,* costing a shilling[23] instead of half-a-crown, were founded in 1859–60, the doom of the part-issue was in sight; for the reader could now get his instalment of a novel and much else besides at the same price.[24]

The history of the magazine serial is a much longer one, extending through the eighteenth century to our own day and adorned by great names such as Meredith, Hardy, and Henry James. Reprinted

fiction had appeared in eighteenth-century magazines; the first new
novel to appear in that form was Smollett's *Sir Lancelot Greaves* in
The British Magazine (1760–1). Later, in the eighteen-thirties,
Marryat had several serials running; *Oliver Twist* ran through
twenty-four numbers of *Bentley's Miscellany*; and by 1840 serials
are usual in the half-crown monthlies; *Fraser's*, for example, had
Thackeray's *Catherine* (1839–40) and *The Luck of Barry Lyndon*
(1844). At first, they tend to be shorter works than the novels
issued in parts—may even, like Thackeray's *Shabby Genteel Story*
(1840), be long short-stories completed in about six instalments.
Cheaper and more specialized periodicals also carried serials; several
early tales and novels of Charlotte Yonge, for example, appear in
the monthly *Magazine for the Young*, the *Churchman's Companion*,
and a little later in the *Monthly Packet* under her own editorship.

At a still lower rate, the new popular weekly papers were providing serial fiction for the masses. At the price of a penny, the reader
could have his fill of serial romance, along with much improving
and informative matter, in (for example) the *Family Herald, Lloyd's
Penny Weekly Miscellany*, or *Reynolds' Miscellany*. The interest of
these serials may be mainly sub-literary;[25] but such periodicals
helped to prepare the way for Dickens's twopenny weekly *Household Words*, started in 1850, with Mrs. Gaskell as an early con-
tributor.[26]

So far as the reader was concerned, there was little difference between periodical serializing and monthly part-issue;[27] but the author
ran the risk of subservience to editorial policy. Later instances of
this will spring to mind—the trouble which led to the withdrawing
of Trollope's *Rachel Ray* from *Good Words*, Hardy's difficulties
with *Tess* in the *Graphic*. But the less strict standards of 1848 already provide one instance: the editor of *Fraser's* asked Kingsley to
shorten *Yeast*[28] because some readers were threatening to cancel
their subscription. Kingsley had to comply, but published the complete version in book form with further additions in 1851. There
was no such drawback when the editor wrote his own serials, as
Dickens did later when he ran *Hard Times* in *Household Words, A
Tale of Two Cities* and *Great Expectations* in *All the Year Round*.
(But Dickens was severe with contributors, and had particular difficulty with Mrs. Gaskell over *North and South* in 1855:[29]—"If I
were Mr. G. O Heaven how I would beat her!" The difficulty here
was aesthetic—Dickens's insistence that each weekly instalment

should end at an arresting point, a tough order especially for so leisurely an author.)

Serial publication, as I have said, induced a close relation between author and reader—in Thackeray's words, a "communion between the writer and the public . . . something continual, confidential, something like personal affection."[30] Dickens showed his own awareness of it in his prefatory note to the concluding number of *Dombey and Son*:

> I cannot forego my usual opportunity of saying farewell to my readers in this greeting-place, though I have only to acknowledge the unbounded warmth and earnestness of their sympathy in every stage of the journey we have just concluded.[31]

And so did Thackeray in his preface to *Pendennis* when it was published in book form:

> in his constant communication with the reader the writer is forced into a frankness of expression, and to speak out his own mind and feelings as they urge him. . . . It is a sort of confidential talk between writer and reader.

(This has an obvious bearing on Thackeray's apparent garrulity.) The prolonging of this intercommunication over eighteen months or more enforced the effect of contact; there was a sense of long familiar association—in which, as one reviewer said, a "sort of tenderness" came to be felt even for the "covers of the monthly instalments."[32]

The response of the public to each instalment was lively. Each number, said a contemporary critic,

> is anticipated with more anxiety than the Indian Mail, and is a great deal more talked about when it does come.[33]

Evidence of such talk exists abundantly; contemporary letters and memoirs testify to the buzz of excited discussion between the numbers in mansion and parsonage, college, and cottage. "Will Nelly die? I think she should," writes Lady Stanley to her daughter-in-law.[34] Some of this buzz reached the author in letters—it is the beginning of "fan mail."[35] One admirer wrote to Dickens, to "counsel him to develop the character [of Sam Weller] largely—to the utmost."[36] The original of Miss Mowcher in *David Copperfield* wrote to protest, so that the character is altered between chapters xxii and xxxii.[37] Thackeray received complaints that *Vanity Fair* contained too much Amelia, and entreaties that Laura in *Pendennis* might marry Warrington, and that Clive Newcome might marry Ethel. ("What could a fellow do? So many people wanted 'em married.")[38]

Publication in numbers also afforded evidence of fluctuating sales, and to this Dickens was especially alert. When sales fell for the early numbers of *Martin Chuzzlewit* (perhaps because he had lost readers over the previous experiment of *Master Humphrey's Clock*),[39] he sent Martin to America, and watched them revive a little; when they rose again after the introduction of Mrs. Gamp, he provided more of her. Thackeray cared less for such evidence, but was not less conscious of it. The fact that "subscribers left him" when Pendennis was shown as meeting temptation probably strengthened him in his determination. But to Dickens declining sales brought a sense of insecurity, not only financial but creative. The accounts after the second number of *Our Mutual Friend* showed a fall, and this left him, he said, "going round and round like a carrier pigeon, before swooping on number seven"[40] (the number he was then about to write). But the stimulus of rising sales was a much more usual experience, carrying him forward on a wave of confidence. It was not the mere desire for money, nor even the mere desire to please, though he felt both strongly; rather the sense of a sympathetic, applauding public seems to have been profoundly necessary to him. The editing of cheap weeklies, the producing and acting of plays (not for money but for charity), and above all, the public readings from his books, tell the same story. These readings, first thought of in 1846, were begun in 1853, and continued against all advice, friendly and medical, until the year of his death—for which they were at least partly to blame. Nothing could compete with the intoxication of actually *seeing* the audience responding, with laughter and tears, even swoons and fits, to Sam Weller and Mrs. Gamp, little Nell and Paul Dombey, Bill Sikes and Nancy. But though this became an almost morbid satisfaction, it sprang from a need he felt as a literary artist, a need of which I believe serial publication first made him conscious. In the serial-writer's relation to his public there is indeed something of the stimulating contact which an actor or a public speaker receives from an audience. Serial publication gave back to story-telling its original context of performance, the context that Chaucer, for example, knew and exploited (the units of his narrative are often like serial instalments, and his confiding yet reserved relation with his audience is often like Thackeray's). The creative artist, as R. G. Collingwood has said, requires an audience whose function is not merely receptive but collaborative, even "concreative." "It is a weakness of printed literature that this reciprocity between writer and reader is difficult to maintain."[41] Thanks partly to serial publication it was less difficult in the nineteenth century than now, and the novelists, especially Dickens, drew some of their strength from it.

It is obviously a condition of this reciprocity that the novel should be written, as well as read, in instalments, month by month; while his public is reading, the novelist is writing; each number comes to the reader fresh from the author's mind, glistening with baptismal ink. "The following pages" says Dickens in the preface to *Pickwick,* when this practice still had novelty "have been written from time to time, almost as the periodical occasion arose."[42] He had no need to say it later; it was assumed, as by the innumerable readers who wrote hopefully to beg a reprieve for little Nell. This hand-to-mouth method of composition, at first sight so perilous, was habitual with both Dickens and Thackeray (except in *Esmond*); it accounts of course for their both leaving novels unfinished at their death, *Edwin Drood* and *Denis Duval*—novels partly published, but with little more in the writer's desk than had been printed. Such a method made great demands on the novelist, and the letters of both Dickens and Thackeray are strewn with references to the agony of working against time. Dickens's more exacting contracts early in his career sometimes obliged him to be writing two serials in the month, devoting a fortnight to each; after 1843 he usually contrived to be writing hard for one fortnight and spending the other, not of course in rest (for he never rested) but on other activities. During the "writing" fortnight he would accept no engagements ("I am always a prisoner, more or less, at this time of the month")[43] and his iron will and rigorous method kept him invariably up to time. He wrote on uniform-sized "slips," and knew how many should go to a number;[44] on the few occasions when he miscalculated there was a last-minute dash to the printing-office—once at least from the Continent —to cut or to add. (The cancelled passages still exist in proof state, and a few have already been published.[45]) But the dread of failing outright in his obligations is rare. In the autumn of 1846 the double demands of the early numbers of *Dombey* and of the promised "Christmas Book" nearly defeated him. And he had once a bad moment of panic in a stationer's shop at Broadstairs when he overheard a lady inquire for the latest number of *David Copperfield;* she was told that it would appear at the end of the month; and he knew he had not as yet written a word of it; "Once, and but once only in my life, I was—frightened!"[46]

For Thackeray, on the other hand, panic was constant—he usually left his writing till the eleventh hour, having formed as a journalist the habit of working with the printer's boy at the door:

> Towards the end of the month I get so nervous that I don't speak to anybody scarcely.
>
> I always have a life-&-death struggle to get out my number of *Vanity Fair.*[47]

No wonder Charlotte Brontë refused her publisher's suggestion that she should write a serial on the grounds that she had neither the necessary confidence nor the "unflagging animal spirits."[48] Once only did Dickens and Thackeray fail their readers. Dickens suspended both *Pickwick* and *Oliver Twist* in 1837 when his young sister-in-law Mary Hogarth died; *Pendennis* ceased to appear for three months in 1849 during Thackeray's serious illness—anxious inquiries poured in, and the finished work is dedicated gratefully to his physician.

The practice of serial publication did not go uncriticized. "Art will not endure piecemeal generation"[49] is a judgement of the fifties; earlier, there were objections to "novel-writing in scraps against time"[50] and, more pungently, to "the monstrous anomaly of a twenty-month's labour and a piecemeal accouchement."[51] Reviewers were not quite disinterested; part-issue put them in a difficulty. If they reviewed the novel during publication, they risked premature judgement; if they waited for completion, their criticism might well be superfluous.

But it is too readily assumed that serial-writing is damaging to the artistic unity of the novel. There are advantages as well as disadvantages; novelists and critics were well aware of the problem. Trollope saw that serial publication at least prevented any "long succession of dull pages":

> The writer . . . should feel that he cannot afford to have many
> pages skipped out of the few which are to meet the reader's eye
> at the same time. Who can imagine the first half of the first vol-
> ume of *Waverley* coming out in shilling numbers?[52]

Here the advantage is clear: the serial novelist must arouse interest
and display his main characters in the opening number. With the
opening of *Waverley* we may contrast the opening numbers of
Dombey and Son and *Vanity Fair,* each of which presents a scene
showing the major characters at a crucial point in their lives, and
indicating the forces of the coming conflict. But Trollope also saw
the disadvantage to the novelist of being unable to revise an early
number in the light of later requirements. He himself wrote serials,
but was too cautious to do his writing month by month; he refused
to start publication until the whole was complete, giving as his
reason that:

> An artist should keep in his hand the power of fitting the begin-
> ning of his work to the end. . . . When some young lady at the
> end of a story cannot be made quite perfect in her conduct, that
> vivid description of angelic purity with which you laid down the
> first lines of her portrait should be slightly toned down.[53]

A commoner criticism, which came from authors as well as critics,
was that the design of the whole was apt to be sacrificed to the
number-unit, and especially to the need of an effective close to a
number. To "provide a certain number of these [closes] at regular
intervals," said Harriet Martineau, was "like breaking up the broad
lights and shadows of a great picture, spoiling it as a composition."[54]
In addition there was the danger of the too complete climax. After
the death of Paul which concluded the fifth number of *Dombey
and Son,* even Dickens's admirer, Francis Jeffrey, had his doubts:
"After this climax . . . what are you to do with the fifteen that are
to follow?"[55] This anxiety was certainly shared by Dickens. At the
head of his notes for the succeeding part he wrote: "Great point of
the No. to throw the interest of Paul, AT ONCE ON FLORENCE."[56]
Dickens had much more concern for the design of his novels than
he is commonly credited with; and so had contemporary critics—
"One of the great achievements in the art of the novel is unity."[57]
But the serial novelists in general were not careless of "unity"; they
did not expect to be forgotten when the instalments were complete;

they meant their novels to be read and reread in book form. *Pickwick* might be criticized as "a discursive rambling narrative";[58] but Dickens said in his preface that his care was to achieve two things; while every number should be

> to a certain extent complete in itself . . . yet . . . the whole twenty numbers, when collected, should form one tolerably harmonious whole, each leading to the other by a gentle and not unnatural process of adventure.[59]

As he went on, Dickens learned more and more how to keep the larger unit in mind. Although he wrote from month to month he was not improvising, except in detail. The whole pre-existed in his mind. "The design and purpose of [*The Old Curiosity Shop* was] distinctly marked in my mind from the commencement."[60] In *Martin Chuzzlewit,* he assured his readers that he had "endeavoured to resist the temptation of the current Monthly Number, and to keep a steadier eye upon the general purpose and design."[61] His letters show further that the creative period in the writing came some months before publication: he was "in the agonies of plotting and contriving" *Chuzzlewit* in November 1842. The first intimation of *Dombey* is characteristic:

> Vague thoughts of a new book are rife within me just now; and I go wandering about at night . . . according to my usual propensity at such a time, seeking rest, and finding none.[62]

This was in March 1846; in April, the "new book" was advertised for publication, to begin in October. Four months later he had written only the first number, but was able to outline the general plan of the whole novel in a letter to Forster, "this is what cooks call 'the stock of the soup.' All kinds of things will be added to it, of course."[63] Three months after that, the first number appears.

Dickens, it is clear, had for at least some of his novels the sort of prevision that Flaubert described:

> Un bon sujet de roman est celui qui vient tout d'une pièce, d'un seul jet. C'est une idée mère d'où toutes les autres découlent.[64]

Whether or not that prevision came to him so easily as Bagehot supposed of Scott is open to doubt:

> The procedure of the highest genius doubtless is scarcely a procedure; the view of the whole story comes at once upon its imagination like the delicate end and the distinct beginning of some long vista.[65]

His references in letters to "violent restlessness," "ghostly unrest," and "hideous state of mind" in the period of incubation suggest a more uncomfortable process. But they make it clear that he underwent the true creative agony, not the mere bustle of the pot-boiler.

Unfortunately where Thackeray is concerned we lack precise evidence on the early planning of his novels. But we know that an earlier version of the first eight chapters of *Vanity Fair* (then called simply "Pen and Pencil Sketches of English Society") was written early in 1845 and offered in vain to more than one publisher;[66] the design must therefore have been partly formed two years before publication.

The principle of design in single numbers, for both Dickens and Thackeray, is evident even without the testimony of Dickens's "number-plans" and Thackeray's letters. If a modern reader knows where the number divisions fall, he can readily find examples in plenty, and perceive their relation to the whole. It is part of the injustice done to Dickens and Thackeray that no modern edition supplies such information[67] [it is supplied by Mrs. Tillotson for *Dombey and Son* and *Vanity Fair* in *Novels of the Eighteen-Forties*, p. 318; and a good many editions of Dickens and others now supply it. Ed.].

Within a single number, the balance is held between varieties of narrative method—summary, description, and presentation—and also between the fortunes of different sets of characters. In the sixth number of *Dombey and Son*, for example, the interest is divided between Captain Cuttle and Walter Gay, Florence and her father: but with no loss of unity, for both Walter's departure and her father's neglect mark the decline of Florence's fortunes. In the eleventh number of *Vanity Fair*, the emphasis is first on the rise in Becky's fortunes, then on the fall in Amelia's; the close of chapter xxxvii, in which their two young sons meet by chance in the park, supplying the transition. A study of the way the numbers end is particularly rewarding. The sinister suggestion of Diogenes's attack on Mr. Carker at the close of the seventh number and of Mr. Carker's thoughts about Mr. Dombey's second marriage at the close of the ninth show Dickens's power of raising anticipation and using the emphasis of the number-ending to draw attention to a piece of the pattern that might be overlooked. Sometimes he places a clinching, almost epigrammatic sentence at the close, as in the first and (in the original edition)[68] the fifth numbers—"Here's to Dombey and Son—and Daughter!" says Walter, and Miss Tox echoes "And so Dombey and Son really is a daughter after all!"

It goes without saying that the endings do not deal in the grosser kinds of suspense, familiar in the old film serials. The surprises favoured belong to the refined sort which includes the fulfilment of what has been unconsciously expected. Perhaps the most magnificent curtain-line of all comes at the close of the fourth number of *Vanity Fair*. Becky is playing some deep game, which has not been clearly revealed; she has left Queen's Crawley and is staying in London with old Miss Crawley, with Rawdon in attendance on his aunt. Old Sir Pitt comes to visit her:

> "I say agin, I want you," Sir Pitt said, thumping the table. "I can't git on without you. I didn't see what it was till you went away. The house all goes wrong. It's not the same place. All my accounts has got muddled agin. You *must* come back. Do come back. Dear Becky, do come!"
>
> "Come—as what, Sir?" Rebecca gasped out.
>
> "Come as Lady Crawley, if you like," the baronet said, grasping his crape hat. "There! will that zatusfy you? Come back and be my wife. Your vit vor't. Birth be hanged. You're as good a lady as ever I see. You've got more brains in your little vinger than any baronet's wife in the country. Will you come? Yes or no?"
>
> "O Sir Pitt!" Rebecca said, very much moved.
>
> "Say yes, Becky," Sir Pitt continued. "I'm an old man, but a good'n. I'm good for twenty years. I'll make you happy, zee if I don't. You shall do what you like; spend what you like; and 'av it all your own way. I'd make you a zettlement. I'll do everything regular. Look year!" and the old man fell down on his knees and leered at her like a satyr.
>
> Rebecca started back a picture of consternation. In the course of this history we have never seen her lose her presence of mind; but she did now, and wept some of the most genuine tears that ever fell from her eyes.
>
> "O Sir Pitt!" she said. "O Sir—I—I'm *married already*."

After this the reader's instinct is to reread the April number to discover missed clues. Even if he guesses the identity of the man, he has a month in which to speculate on the likely results of the disclosure. At the beginning of the May number Thackeray teases the reader:

> Every reader of a sentimental turn (and we desire no other) must have been pleased with the *tableau* with which the last act of our little drama concluded: for what can be prettier than an image of Love on his knees before Beauty?

It is not until the end of the chapter that the name of Becky's husband is given. Unless the modern reader is aware of that month's wait, some of Thackeray's effect is lost.

Very different in its reverberation is another surprise ending, that of the ninth, the great Waterloo number. This number includes the farewells of Rawdon and George, the departure of the regiment, Amelia's suspicions of Becky's intrigue with her husband, the rumours that come about the battle, the comedy of Jos Sedley's plans of flight from Brussels, and the "most expensive half-hour of his life," when Becky sells him the horses. Only in the closing paragraphs of the number do we move from Brussels to the battlefield. The two last sentences of the number bring the field and city together:

> No more firing was heard at Brussels—the pursuit rolled miles away. The darkness came down on the field and city; and Amelia was praying for George, who was lying on his face, dead, with a bullet through his heart.[69]

In Dickens's farewell to his readers[70] at the close of *Dombey and Son* he acknowledged "the unbounded warmth and earnestness of their sympathy"; and he chose the obvious example:

> If any of them have felt a sorrow in one of the principal incidents on which this fiction turns, I hope it may be a sorrow of that sort which endears the sharers in it, one to another. This is not unselfish in me. I may claim to have felt it, at least as much as anybody else; and I would fain be remembered kindly for my part in the experience.

He was referring, of course, to the death of Paul Dombey. He had set out to "make 'em cry," and he had succeeded. Here is a well-known contemporary comment on the fifth number:

> Oh my dear dear Dickens! what a No. 5 you have given us! I
> have so cried and sobbed over it last night, and again this morn-
> ing; and felt my heart purified by those tears. . . . Since that di-
> vine Nelly . . . there has been nothing like it. Every trait so
> true and so touching . . . and yet lightened by that fearless
> innocence. . . .[71]

The writer is Lord Jeffrey, the same who had sacrificed Wordsworth's *Excursion* in the *Edinburgh Review*. Something may be discounted for his nationality, and something for his years—he was now seventy-five—but on the whole, this is the response typical of Dickens's first readers.[72] And it is certainly not the response of the modern reader. The question suggests itself, How far are we, or how far is Dickens at fault—and not only Dickens but his first public? Our response is not of course peculiar to our own century: among the Victorians there were a few dry-eyed resisters. Henry Hallam confessed himself "so hardened as to be unable to look on [the death of Paul] in any light but pure 'business.' "[73] Fitzjames Stephen complained that Dickens "gloats . . . touches, tastes, smells and handles as if [the death of Little Nell] were some savoury dainty"[74]; Walter Bagehot in 1858 criticized Dickens's "fawning fondness" for "dismal scenes"[75]; Ruskin in 1880 accused him of killing Little Nell as a butcher kills a lamb, for the market.[76] By the late nineteenth century the resistance seems to have been pretty general, judging from Gissing's cautious defence of Little Nell's death-bed in 1900: "This pathos was true for them and for their day."[77] His defence was on the right lines, the historical lines, for the response to such pathos must always be related to those changing things, manners and beliefs. In the eighteen-forties tears were shed more readily, and by men as well as by women. (Indeed any study of past literature soon discovers that the taboo on male tears is peculiar to our own century; and there are signs that it is even now on its way out.) At that time few would have agreed with Chesterton that while humour is of its nature expansive, pathos is in its nature confined.[78] We have also to bear in mind our other modern inhibitions, especially our inarticulateness on the subject of death (represented in "No flowers. No letters"). The absence of a context for death in modern life, the lack of a setting of common belief—all this must impoverish its treatment in literature and the social impact of any treatment it receives. All that our own fiction can put beside the death of little Paul is the long-drawn clinical horror of the death of little Phil from tubercular meningitis in Aldous Huxley's *Point Counter Point*.

Dickens suffered from his imitators; he was initiating, not continuing a tradition. To put a child at the centre of a novel for adults was virtually unknown when Dickens wrote *Oliver Twist* and *The Old Curiosity Shop*. Further, the sufferings of children at this time have social relevance. Many of his readers had read the five reports on Child Labour which appeared between 1831 and 1843. Part of Gissing's defence is on these lines:

> Such pathos is called "cheap" . . . in Dickens's day, the lives, the happiness of children were very cheap indeed, and . . . he had his purpose in insisting on their claims to attention.[79]

Some writers of the mid-century considered the age unduly sensitive—Bagehot, for example:

> The unfeeling obtuseness of the early part of this century was to be corrected by an extreme, perhaps an excessive, sensibility to human suffering.[80]

Dickens's pathos had its social purpose. Nell, Smike, Jo, even Paul are all in different ways social victims: as much as the Wilson twins in *Mary Barton*. With the pathos of their deaths is combined apportionment of particular blame:

> Dead, your Majesty. Dead, my lords and gentlemen. . . . And dying thus around us, every day.[81]

As it happens, in the case of Paul Dombey the historical grounds for defence are not the only ones to appeal to. There are also aesthetic grounds: stronger here than in *The Old Curiosity Shop*. Gissing was understating the case when he said, "If the situation is to be presented at all, it might be much worse done."[82] The pathos is in control because the scene is given from a limiting angle. We see with Paul's eyes, and not, until the close, with those of the author or the stricken onlookers. We see what Paul sees, the faces of friends appearing and disappearing through the more urgent visions of delirium; he is not self-conscious about his own death, he says goodbye, but—in contrast to Tennyson's "May Queen" and Charlotte Brontë's Helen Burns— he makes no farewell speeches.[83] Dickens's use of poetic imagery as

a means of releasing yet controlling emotion is the same sort as
Shakespeare's. (Indeed, in comparison with Constance's lament for
Arthur, Dickens is reserved.) The death of a child represents the extreme of pathos, but is incapable of treatment as tragedy; its expression, therefore, is found most appropriately in lyric, and when they
touch it narrative and drama aspire towards that kind. This is true of
the death of the child in Chaucer's *Prioress's Tale,* and in Spenser's
Daphnaida:

> She fell away in her first ages spring,
> Whil'st yet her leafe was greene, and fresh her rinde,
> And whil'st her braunch faire blossomes foorth did bring,
> She fell away against all course of kinde:
> For age to dye is right, but youth is wrong;
> She fel away like fruit blowne downe with winde:
> Weepe Shepheard weepe to make my undersong.

Dickens stands in less need of defence when he conveys pathos
indirectly by means of a chance detail. In the sixth number, Paul's
funeral passes down the street and is seen by the wife of a street
entertainer:

> The feathers are yet nodding in the distance, when the juggler
> has the basin spinning on a cane, and has the same crowd to ad-
> mire it. But the juggler's wife is less alert than usual with the
> money-box, for a child's burial has set her thinking that perhaps
> the baby underneath her shabby shawl may not grow up to be a
> man, and wear a sky-blue fillet round his head, and salmon-
> coloured worsted drawers, and tumble in the mud.

There, the method is nearer Thackeray's; and it was in this direction—away from "expansive" pathos—that Dickens moved in *David
Copperfield.*[84]

Thackeray did not attempt to describe the death of a child, unless
we count the episode in *Barry Lyndon*[85]—and this is removed from
pure pathos by the ironies of Barry's narration. He was himself
deeply moved by the fifth number of *Dombey;*[86] but in his writing
he was protected from Dickens's dangers by his view that pathos
should be "very occasional indeed in humorous works." (In "humorous works" he would include, as his lecture "On Charity and
Humour" shows, both Dickens's novels and his own.) He approved
of his own comparison of Amelia to Lady Jane Grey "trying the

axe" when she is determining to send little George to live with his grandfather, because "it leaves you to make your own sad pictures— We shouldn't do much more than that I think in comic books."[87] This comes well from Thackeray, whose own pathos has an economy which is rare in Dickens. At its finest (the death of George Osborne, the death of old Sedley) it is of no time; it has something nearer the "sad earnestness and vivid exactness" that Newman found in the classical poets. And it is seldom exclusive of other emotions—sometimes indeed armed against mockery by containing mockery. The rapidity of the transition might often be expressed in his own words—"with one eye brimming with pity, the other steadily keeping watch over the family spoons."[88] If he, too, is by modern standards "sentimental," he also, in Clough's words, "sees the silliness sentiment runs into, and so always tempers it by a little banter and ridicule."[89]

NOTES

1. Little attention has been paid to these—relatively little even by bibliographers. But see Michael Sadleir, *Trollope, a Bibliography* (1928), *XIXth Century Fiction* (2 vols., 1951), *Victorian Fiction* (catalogue of an exhibition arranged by John Carter and Michael Sadleir, 1947); Graham Pollard, *Serial Fiction* in *New Paths in Book Collecting* (1934). The *Cambridge Bibliography* is erratic in noting the original form of publication, especially for minor novelists.

2. Ch. li.

3. See Michael Sadleir, *Bibliographical Aspects of the Victorian Novel* (1937) (typescript in British Museum), and the sources referred to above.

4. It was advertised in the *Athenæum* (13 November 1847), p. 1162, as "Now ready at all the libraries"; a review in *Tait's Edinburgh Magazine* (May 1848), pp. 346-8, says that few circulating libraries are without it.

5. *Letters*, ed. Gordon Ray (1945-6), iv, 356.

6. This had originated in 1843, as "Chapman and Hall's Monthly Series," an interesting compromise between part-issue and volume publication; novels were announced, and a few published, in four monthly parts at three shillings each. Sadleir has shown that this was "a conscious attempt to break the conventional fiction-price and fiction-format," defeated, like earlier ventures, by the dominance of the libraries (*XIXth Century Fiction*, ii. 132).

7. The *Parlour Library* (1847-63), an early venture in cheap fiction

series, in shilling volumes of "about 320 pages," published monthly, included "works of fiction, by the most celebrated authors"; most of its early volumes were reprints or translations, but vol. i and vol. xi were new works by the Irishman William Carleton. It was advertised as "universally proclaimed by the press of Great Britain, the cheapest ever published" (*Athenæum,* 11 December 1847, p. 1284).

8. *Loss and Gain* (1848), *The Nemesis of Faith* (1849).
9. Examples are Harriett Mozley's *Louisa* (1842), Charlotte Yonge's *Abbeychurch* (1844) and *Scenes and Characters* (1847); these overlap with the first group and, like *Loss and Gain,* were published by Burns, who also included new religious fiction in his series, *The Englishman's Library.*
10. *Fraser's* (January 1851), p. 75.
11. *Philip,* ch. xxiii.
12. *Endymion* (1880), iii. 1.
13. "On Reading Old Books," *London Magazine* (February 1821); collected in *The Plain Speaker* (1826). Besides Cooke's series there was *Harrison's Novelist's Magazine* (1780-8), and in our period a well-known and remarkably cheap publication, the twopenny weekly *Romancist, and Novelist's Library* (1839-40, 1841-2). See further Pollard, op. cit., pp. 259-61, and Sadleir, *XIXth Century Fiction,* ii (Section 3), pp. 135-7, 141-5. Of these series, Edward Lloyd's weekly part-issues of sensational new fiction are the obvious descendants.
14. 1742; ii. 1. These continued throughout the nineteenth century; by the forties they were often of a cheap, "useful-knowledge" type, like Charles Knight's *New Orbis Pictus.*
15. Sadleir, *Bibliographical Aspects of Victorian Fiction* (unpaged).
16. Preface to cheap edition, 1847; quoted John Forster, *The Life of Dickens* (1872-4), i. 5.
17. Forster, ii. 1; T. Hatton and A. H. Cleaver, *A Bibliography of the Periodical Works of Charles Dickens* (1933), p. 6.
18. *Miss Eden's Letters,* ed. Violet Dickinson (1919), p. 298. She says, "there has been a Calcutta reprint, lithographs and all."
19. *Autobiography* (1904), p. 53; account of the winter session 1837-8 at Marischal College, Aberdeen.
20. *Letters of William and Dorothy Wordsworth: the Later Years,* ed. Eide Selincourt, (1939), iii. 1120; and cf. Arnold's letter to Cornish, 6 July 1839, in Stanley's *Life,* ch. ix.
21. Except for *Pickwick,* Nos. I-II.
22. Examples include a few novels of Mrs. Trollope, Ainsworth, Marryat; most of Surtees; Thackeray's *Vanity Fair* and *Pendennis.* After 1850 there are *The Newcomes* (1853-5) and *The Virginians* (1857-9), Trollope's *Can You Forgive Her?* (1864-5) and *The Way We Live Now* (1874-5). The failure of *The Vicar of Bullhampton* (1869-70) in this form marks the decline of the part-issue. A new modification

appears with George Eliot's *Middlemarch* (eight five-shilling parts at irregular intervals in 1871-2) and *Daniel Deronda* (1876). This form was imitated by Trollope's *Prime Minister* (1875-6).

Part-issue was not confined to novels; the greatest autobiography of the century, Newman's *Apologia,* was published in eight weekly parts, and Browning's *The Ring and the Book* in four monthly volumes, on the stated grounds that he wished people "not to turn to the end," but to have "time to read and digest . . . but not to forget what has gone before" (*William Allingham, A Diary,* 1907, p. 181).

23. An earlier venture in the field was *Douglas Jerrold's Shilling Magazine* (1845-8) with serials by Jerrold, R. H. Horne, and others, as well as articles, short stories, reviews, and poems. According to Jerrold's biographer (Blanchard Jerrold, *The Life and Remains of Douglas Jerrold,* 1859, ch. x) this was at first successful, but fell off later because Jerrold had so many other irons in the fire. But in any case it was probably too radical, and too "low," to offer a serious challenge to the half-crown monthlies in that period.

24. See Trollope, *Autobiography,* ch. xv. Serials in the *Cornhill* included *Framley Parsonage, Lovel the Widower, Philip, Romola,* and *Wives and Daughters;* in *Macmillan's,* Hughes's *Tom Brown at Oxford,* and Kingsley's *Water Babies.*

25. They tend to reflect fashions that were dying out in serious novels; many are historical, others "Gothic," like Reynolds's *Wagner, the Wehr-Wolf,* others again pseudo-Society like *Julia Tremaine.* But they should not be confused with the later "penny dreadfuls," deliberately aimed at the juvenile market. James Malcolm Rymer (identified in the British Museum catalogue) also wrote *Varney the Vampire* (published in weekly part-issues) but his several serials in *Lloyd's Penny Weekly Miscellany* are not particularly horrific. Of these, *Ada, the Betrayed* was a favourite of the schoolboy D. G. Rossetti, along with two historical serials by Pierce Egan—*Robin Hood* and *Wat Tyler* (W. M. Rossetti, *Dante Gabriel Rossetti, his Family-Letters, with a Memoir,* 2 vols., 1895, i. 82). The cheap romantic fiction of the forties and fifties offers a virtually unexplored field to bibliographers and literary and social historians. The competition between it and cheap instructive series is described by Charles Knight, in *The Old Printer and the Modern Press* (1854), and *Passages in a Working Life* (3 vols., 1864-5).

26. *Lizzie Leigh* (1850), *Cranford* (1851-3), *North and South* (1854-5).

27. The part-issue was of course longer than the monthly magazine instalment, and that was longer than the weekly instalment; and the shorter the unit, the greater the emphasis on "climax." Dickens often chafed at the restrictions of the weekly instalment.

28. *Charles Kingsley; his letters and memories of his life,* edited by his wife (1877), ch. vii; letter to John Conington, 19 December 1848.

29. See A. B. Hopkins, "Dickens and Mrs. Gaskell," *Huntington Library Quarterly*, ix. 4 (August 1946), pp. 366-76.

30. "A Box of Novels," *Fraser's* (February 1844); *Works*, vi. He is speaking, with his usual generosity, of Dickens.

31. Cf. Albert Smith's farewell in *The Pottleton Legacy* (1849), referring to "the continuous intercourse from month to month . . . establishing a tie which is not willingly broken."

32. Review of *Dombey* in *The Sun* (13 April 1848). George Eliot was "convinced that the slow plan of publication [of *Middlemarch*]" was "of immense advantage . . . in deepening the impression" (letter of 4 August 1872).

33. *Fraser's* (January 1851), p. 75.

34. *The Ladies of Alderley*, ed. N. Mitford (1938), p. 2; letter of 27 January 1841.

35. And like fan mail it is found at all literary levels. The author of *Ada, the Betrayed* thanked "over two hundred ladies and gentlemen" for their letters (*Lloyd's Penny Weekly Miscellany*, 1843, No. 52).

36. William Jerdan, *An Autobiography* (1852), iv. 364.

37. Cf. Forster, vi. 7, and K. J. Fielding in *The Listener* (9 July 1951) with new letters.

38. *Letters*, iii. 465 n.

39. Forster, iv. 2. A modern scholar has attributed the fall to *American Notes* (Ada B. Nisbet, "The Mystery of *Martin Chuzzlewit*," in *Essays . . . dedicated to Lily B. Campbell*, University of California Press, 1950).

40. Forster, ix. 5; letter of 10 June 1863.

41. *The Principles of Art* (1938), pp. 323-4; and see the whole chapter (xiv).

42. Preface to 1837 edition.

43. *Letters*, ii. 13; letter of 10 February 1847.

44. Dickens's methods were first studied by John Butt, "Dickens at Work," *Durham University Journal*, xl, No. 3 (June 1948); see also the same writer's "Dickens's Notes for his Serial Parts," *The Dickensian*, xlv. 3, No. 291 (June 1949).

45. John Butt and Kathleen Tillotson, "Dickens at Work on *Dombey and Son*," *Essays and Studies by Members of the English Association*, N.S., iv. (1951), pp. 77-78, 92; John Butt, "*David Copperfield*: From Manuscript to Print," *R.E.S.*, N.S., i. 3 (July 1950); *The Dickensian*, xlviii. 4, No. 304 (September 1952), xlix. 1-2, Nos. 305-6 (December 1952, March 1953).

46. W. Charles Kent, *Charles Dickens as a Reader* (1872), pp. 45-46.

47. *Letters*, ii. 311, 346.

48. *Shakespeare Head Brontë* (1932-8). ii. 161; letter of 14 December 1847.

49. *North British Review* (October 1855), p. 350; and see *Blackwood's* (April 1855), p. 455.

50. *Fraser's* (April 1840), p. 400.

51. *Fraser's* (January 1851), p. 75. In that outspoken age, this seems to have been a favourite figure; compare Douglas Jerrold's letter to Dickens in 1846: "You have heard, I suppose, that Thackeray is big with twenty parts, and, unless he is wrong in his time, expects the first instalment at Christmas" (Blanchard Jerrold, *Life and Remains of Douglas Jerrold,* 1859, p. 265).

52. *Autobiography,* ch. viii.

53. *Autobiography,* ch. viii. The exception to Trollope's rule of writing is *Framley Parsonage,* serialized in the *Cornhill* at Thackeray's request, and with characteristically inadequate notice.

54. *Autobiography,* iv. 4. Cf. Crabb Robinson, *Books and their Writers,* ed. E. J. Morley, ii. 578.

55. Lord Cockburn, *Life of Lord Jeffrey* (1852), ii. 407.

56. Butt and Tillotson, op. cit., p. 82; from the manuscripts in the Forster collection at the Victoria and Albert Museum.

57. *Fraser's* (October 1851), p. 382.

58. *Blackwood's* (April 1855), p. 455.

59. Preface to 1837 edition. Compare his advice to Mrs. Brookfield in 1866 (*Letters,* iii. 461-2): "notice how . . . the thing has to be planned for presentation in these fragments, and yet for afterwards fusing together as an uninterrupted whole."

60. *Letters,* i. 305.

61. Preface to 1844 edition.

62. *Letters,* i. 487, 740; for later novels see, for example, ii. 338, 649, 658.

63. Forster, vi. 2.

64. *Correspondance, quatrième série* (Paris, 1927), pp. 463-4: letter of 1861 [?].

65. *Literary Studies,* ii. 161 ("The Waverley Novels," 1858). Scott's methods are described by Sir Herbert Grierson, *Sir Walter Scott* (1938), pp. 128-9.

66. Gordon N. Ray, "Vanity Fair," in *Essays by Divers Hands,* Royal Society of Literature, N.S., xxv (1950), 92-93. The manuscript of these chapters is in the Pierpont Morgan Library.

67. A fairly close analysis of *Dombey and Son* from this point of view is given in Butt and Tillotson, op. cit., and of *David Copperfield* in John Butt's articles in *The Dickensian,* Nos. 294-6 (1950).

   The point at which a number begins is shown (for the novels in monthly numbers) in T. Hatton and A. H. Cleaver, *Bibliography of the Periodical Works of Charles Dickens* (1933).

68. See my note in *The Dickensian,* xlvii. 2 (March 1951), pp. 81 f.

69. I do not know how soon Thackeray revised this famous sentence, deleting the opening "The"; certainly by 1853.

70. This becomes the Preface to the first edition (1848).

71. Lord Cockburn, *Life of Lord Jeffrey* (1852), ii. 406-7.

72. "We envy not the man who can read for the first time the account of the death of little Paul Dombey with a heart unmoved and an eye tearless" (*The Sun,* 13 April 1848); and see n. 85.

73. C. and F. Brookfield, *Mrs. Brookfield and her Circle* (2 vols., 1905), i. 255. Henry Hallam was the son of the historian.

74. "The Relation of Novels to Life," *Cambridge Essays . . . 1855,* p. 175.

75. *Literary Studies,* ii. 188-9 ("Charles Dickens," 1858).

76. "Fiction Fair and Foul" in *Maemillan's Magazine; Works,* xxxiv.

77. *The Immortal Dickens* (1923), p. 199. (written as Preface for Rochester edition).

78. Introduction to *Pickwick* (Everyman edition).

79. *Charles Dickens, a critical study* (1898), p. 176.

80. *Literary Studies,* ii. 190 ("Charles Dickens," 1858).

81. *Bleak House,* ch. xlvii.

82. Loc. cit.

83. Dickens's one instance of sentimental piety in a sick child's speech is in *Oliver Twist,* ch. vii (Dick's farewell to Oliver).

84. Thackeray noted the change of manner in this novel: "I think he has been reading a certain yellow-covered book and with advantage too" (*Letters,* ii. 531); so did F. J. Hort, in a letter of August 1849; "exceedingly beautiful, with much extravagance pruned off. Without in the least ceasing to be Dickens, he has learnt much from Thackeray" (*Life and Letters,* 2 vols., 1896, i. 113).

85. Ch. xix.

86. *Letters,* ii. 266 n., quoting George Hodder, *Memoirs of my Time* (1870), p. 277.

87. *Letters,* ii. 424-5. See also "A Grumble about the Christmas Books" (*Fraser's,* January 1847; *Works,* vi. 581-609).

88. *Philip,* ch. xiv.

89. Letter of 3 January 1853; *Poems and Prose Remains* (1869), i. 191.

V. S. PRITCHETT

The Comic World of Dickens

Those who have written the best criticism of Dickens in the last twenty years are united in their belief that the serious and later Dickens is more important and has more meaning for the modern reader, than the comic Dickens; or, that, in any case, the comic Dickens has been overdone. I do not share this opinion, nor do I think that those intelligent readers who read for pleasure hold the opinion either. Dickens' reputation and achievement rest on his comic writing and above all on his comic sense of life. The comic world is a complete world in itself. It is, as Mr. Middleton Murry has said in a recent book on Swift, an orgiastic world, with only a dubious relation with the moral hierarchy. It is, in short, an alternative world to that of ordinary experience and as valid as the poetic which it often criticizes or inverts. It is true that, in the narrow sense of being humorous, Dickens is not continually comic; one can, more accurately, call him picturesque, theatrical, Gothic; even so, it is impossible to divide a writer into sections which have no relationship with each other. We cannot separate the comic from the indignant, sermonizing, melodramatic, revolutionary or murderous Dickens, for the comic, in him, was not mere comic relief. The

From *The Listener,* June 3, 1954, pp. 970-73. Copyright © 1954 by the British Broadcasting Corporation. Reprinted by permission of the author and publisher.

Wilfers are another way of laughing at the Veneerings, just as the Veneerings are a way of laughing at the obsession with money in Victorian society; and that laughter is joined to the hatred and despair Dickens felt about it. It is above all in the comic Dickens that we find the artist who has resolved, for a moment, the violent conflicts in his disorderly genius and who has found, what all the greatest artists have sought, the means of forgiving life. In these comic passages we find his poetry and a quality we can only call radiant. It is important to remember that, with the exception of *Edwin Drood,* where there is a change in prose style, the serious Dickens is *not* a realist. There are brilliantly funny things in *Edwin Drood,* but we notice how detachable they are from the realism of the background and the main story. The contrast between realism and fantasy becomes awkward in this book.

The early Dickens is, of course, soaked in Fielding, and Smollett. He can, at any period of his life, make use of their tradition when he wants to do so. The general, discursive, ironical tone of *Oliver Twist* is Fielding; the picaresque incident of *Pickwick* comes from him also. Sterne and the romantic movement have taught him the value of pathos, tears, changeableness, and the gestures against an unjust world. When I say that Fielding has had his effect, I refer to Fielding's Victorian novel *Amelia* rather than to the other novels. A very important difference is that Dickens is more violent than Fielding, yet far softer hearted—I mean violent in emotional temperament. Fielding's violence in *Jonathan Wild* is purely intellectual. We can explain this by saying that the sedate and abstract preconceptions of the eighteenth century have gone and that Man and Nature have been replaced by talkative men and women. There is also a class difference: the eighteenth-century writers were gentlemen or aspired to be men of the world of fashion. Dickens is plainly lower middle class—the most energetic, intelligent and insecure class of that society. Always on the defensive, they are the richest in fantasy life. They cannot afford the great passions, but demand to be judged by their dreams and sentiments. Oddity, being "characters," is their great solace.

If a debtor is thrown into prison in the eighteenth century, we know he is a rash *rentier:* he has simply behaved thoughtlessly as gentlemen and men of honor do. In Dickens, debt is an undeserved human misfortune which comes unreasonably to people who are trapped by character or circumstance despite all their conscientious efforts. Mild cadging and borrowing have entered the purview of satire, of sentiment and of the genteel world of euphemism. Skimpole, Micawber, the Marshalsea figures, are all debtors. Debts become tragic and comic at once. They lead to delicate moral casuistries, amusing hypocrisies and the evasions of middle-class life. Dickens, of course, got all this from his father who was a part source of the immense comedy of money and rhetoric which is basic in the novelist. Money and humbug—they are the new subjects of a commercial age. The father of the Marshalsea, that old professional borrower, says to his son who is angry because he is refused a loan:

> And is it Christian, let me ask you, to stigmatise and denounce an individual for begging to be excused this time when the same individual may—ha—respond with the required accommodation next time? Is it part of a Christian not to—hum—not to try again?

The old man (Dickens says) had worked himself into a religious fervor when he said this. Not (we notice) into the disdain of a gentleman.

We have moved from the eighteenth century's grandiloquent sense of Fortune, to the nineteenth century's sense of cash. Another change is that Dickens depends far more on *character* than on events, except perhaps in *Pickwick*. The horseplay is far less, the misadventures and knockabout have declined. The situations have become more subtle and depend on the characters themselves. Dickens' comedy is the comedy of people who *are* something, rather than the comedy of people who *do* something which leads to new plot, farces or messes. In the plot sense, Dickens stands still.

But the most important change is the dropping of sexual love. The ribald or sensual humor of the English tradition which puritanism did not really destroy, goes down before another enemy; the immense effort toward material progress which we call the industrial revolution or that great assertion of will which we call the Victorian age. Already in the eighteenth century there were many signs of a dichotomy: Hogarth contrasted *The Rake's Progress* with the story of *The Industrious Apprentice*. I need not go into the whole question of Victorianism and sex for it has often been done, except to say that the Victorian attitude is an aspect of the *violence* of Victorian society and Dickens was both a tender and a violent writer. Huge changes in the traditions of society produce their self-mutilations. It may well be that the violence, the rebellion, the histrionics,

the egotism and fantasy of Dickens, all of which are manifest in
his comedy just as they are in his social indignation, were deeply
affected by a willful impatience with love. Of course, love has
always been a stock comic subject: its illusions are irresistibly
funny. Some have traced the hardening of Dickens' heart to the
humiliation of his failure with Maria Beadnell. They have said this
was the point at which the poet was injured and turned into the
comedian. It seems to me more likely that his incredible and very
Victorian will to success had already done that much earlier in childhood. Against sex are built up the steadfast yet gentle defense of the
sentiments, the drama of a black and white morality, and Dickens'
personal feeling for power.

For the comic Dickens women are mainly of the insecure middle
class, soured by marriage, capricious sluts, and termagants, a terrible
sisterhood of scolds or frantic spinsters. This is essentially a boy's
view derived from a nagging home, or from a boy's vanity. He was
pretty enough and clever enough to want all attention for himself.
Women are also fools, in his comedy, pettish in love, tiresome in
childbirth, perpetually snuffling, continuously breeding. The hatred
of children is another fundamental Victorian theme. Dickens is full
of it and its natural daydream: the child-wife and the idealized
child. What replaced the sane eighteenth-century attitude to sex
in the comic writings of Dickens? I think probably the stress was
put on another hunger—the hunger for food, drink and security, the
jollity and good cheer. Domestic life means meals. Good food makes
people good. To our taste now this doesn't seem very amusing. Half
of Victorian England was disgustingly overfed, and since Dickens
was an extremist he pushed the note of jollity much too far. The
jolly Dickens is the one part of him that has become unreadable.

A more important change is in the *ground* or point of view of
comedy. In the eighteenth century, this ground is the experience of
the grown man. Even Sterne is a grown man. These writers are
secure. In Dickens, the ground is the high visual sense and sharp
ear of the experienced child who is insecure. The children of the
Victorian age are precisely in the situation of the poor, and get much
the same treatment: a huge, inevitable, sharp-witted and accusing
class. Dickens' grotesque sense of physical appearance is the kind of
sense the child has, and in the graver, later books, the sense that the
writer is on his *own* and *alone* is very strong. He has grown up from
the child *alone* into the man *alone*. Dickens is not following the

Way of the World, but, in his satire, he is a rebel attacking the Way from outside. In personal life, he was quite incapable of keeping up with worldly characters like Wilkie Collins.

The gallery of Dickens' comic characters is so huge that it is hard to know where to begin. Dickens was a city. He was chiefly London, just as Joyce was Dublin. We can call Dickens' comedy gothic, a thing of saints, gargoyles, fantastic disorderly carvings. We can call it *mad*. A large number of his comic characters can be called *mad* because they live or speak as if they were *the only self in the world*. They live alone by some private idea. Mrs. Gamp lives by the fiction of the approval of her imaginary friend Mrs. Harris. Augustus Moddle lives by the fixed idea of a demon and by the profound psychological, even metaphysical truth that, in this life, everyone seems to belong to a person whom he calls "another." In our time Moddle would be reading Kierkegaard. Mr. Gradgrind lives by the passionate superstition that only "Facts" exist, Mr. Dick by his obsession with King Charles's head. Mr. Micawber lives by the surveying of dreams. Mr. Pecksniff lives by metaphors; Mr. Sapsea thinks he is something called Mind and, in one special flight of fancy, gets himself described as "Oh thou" by his dead betrothed. These people are known to us because they are turned inside out: we know at once their inner life and the illusions they live by. An illusionist and a solitary himself, Dickens understands this immediately.

In Dickens, the comic characters who belong to what I call the *sane* tradition are comparatively few and they come notably early in his work. Mr. Pickwick, for example, is the standard unworldly, benevolent man of the eighteenth century. His chief troubles—the bedroom scene at Ipswich and the breach of promise case—seem to spring from being in an eighteenth-century situation with a nineteenth-century mind. If anyone gets into the wrong bedroom in the eighteenth century they either intend to do so or are prepared to fight their way out. Mr. Pickwick would never think of fighting and is genuinely shocked, as no eighteenth-century man could be, when his motives are impugned. Sam Weller is a sane character. But Tony Weller has the madness creeping on: the obsession with widows.

I shall have more to say about the madness of Dickens' characters later on. What I want to do first of all is to look at his method. The sketches by Boz start by being character sketches of types. We see for example a beadle. We see the election of a beadle. Here the characteristic thing happens. Dickens notes the fact that the job is

apt to be given to the most deserving candidate and the deserts are
reckoned by the number of children a man has. Dickens at once
turns this idea into fantasy. Bung with five children is only thirty
years old, therefore likely to surpass Mr. Spruggins in philoprogenitiveness, because Spruggins has the advantage of eleven children
but the disadvantage of being fifty years old. Once more, the Victorian joke about the wretched children, the swarm, the basis of
Dickens' idea that childbirth is funny; it is thought to be funny
because the idea of pain and poverty—more mouths to feed—is intolerable. A comic protest, not altogether indignant, against the horrors of the Victorian swarm. (Dickens couldn't stand the sight of his
own children after the age of two or three.) Dickens' comic method
is to take a real situation and to add an idea to it. There are four
spinsters, for example. Add the *idea* that a man is known to be paying court to one of them but none of the neighbors knows which.
Add to this the *idea* that for all the neighbors know he *may* have
married the whole four of them. This *"adding of an idea"* is the
basis of the simplest kind of humor and especially of farce. The
interesting thing is that Dickens started on the lowest rung of the
comic ladder. He is a comic who comes up from the vulgar or
facetious level.

The next fundamental element is that Dickens began his long
observation of human mannerisms in speech, as a parliamentary reporter. He noticed, as he listened to the awful speeches of politicians, that they are punctuated by mechanical emphasis and repetition. The following passage could very well be literal observation:

> Then would he be there to tell that honorable gentleman that
> the Circumlocution Office not only was blameless in this matter
> but was commendable in this matter, was extollable to the skies in
> this matter. Then would he be there to tell that honorable gentle-
> man that although the Circumlocution Office was invariably right
> and wholly right it never was so right as in this matter.

To this Dickens added the fantastic idea that people speak in a
public manner in private life.

> Jinkins is a man of superior talents. I have conceived a great re-
> spect for Jinkins. I take Jinkins' desire to pay polite attention to
> my daughters as an *additional* proof of the friendly feelings of
> Jinkins.

That is Mr. Pecksniff speaking, but in fact many of Dickens' characters of the pompous kind talk like that. Is it real observation or comic trick? We can only judge each case on its merits. In Mr. Pecksniff's case it *is* his character to be a phrase-maker, a lover of platitudes; but it is also in his character to be arch, affected and cold. Mr. Pecksniff is funny when he says that about Jinkins because we do not really believe anyone would talk privately in a parliamentary fashion; but there is reason to suspect that while we are laughing at Pecksniff, Pecksniff himself has invented this absurd way of speaking in order to mock at Jinkins in a cold, ironical, artificial way. For Pecksniff is not a simple black and white hypocrite, he has a very mannered detachment. His speech is that of a man amusing himself at someone else's expense.

There is also a double laughter, a laugh within a laugh, when for example Mr. Pecksniff says: "To draw a lamp post has a tendency to refine the mind and give it a *classical turn.*"

When he was charged with exaggeration Dickens replied that he simply saw and heard far more than most people. But it is also true that he added to the material given to him by one or two overwhelming characters and transformed people by presenting not only their characters, but their persona and their self-made myth. Dickens was a myth-maker when he said that "even Mr. Pecksniff's throat was moral."

Dickens certainly caught the comedy of English self-consequence but, in many cases, he *also* caught the fact that these people knew exactly what they were up to. Biographers tell us that he learned this, as I have said, from studying the large, oratorical manner of his father. His father's manner was like a farcical parliamentary manner transposed to private life. One can distinguish in Dickens I think between those repetitions of words which tend to caricature *from the outside* and those which fix a character by taking us into his *inner* fantasy world. The repetition of the word "fact" in the portrait of the Fact-Hound, Mr. Gradgrind, is a device of caricature, something discharged from a hostile position outside the character. It's the old, distorting formula of the dominant passion. But take another instance. The repetition of "the silent tomb" motif in the character of Mr. Pecksniff is more complex. Look at the passage at the end of *Martin Chuzzlewit* where Pecksniff takes his leave, shamed and exposed but not silenced:

"If you ever contemplate the silent tomb, Sir, which you will
excuse me for entertaining some *doubt* of your doing, after the
conduct into which you have allowed yourself to be betrayed this
day; if you ever contemplate the silent tomb, Sir, think of me. If
you find yourself *approaching* the silent tomb, Sir, think of *me*.
If you should wish to have anything *inscribed* upon your silent
tomb, Sir, let it be that I—ah, my remorseful Sir, that I—the humble individual who has now the honor of *reproaching* you *forgave*
you."

The repetition is done in different tones of voice and insinuation.
And this is a traditional device of comedy. Dickens was a considerable actor himself and he caught the actor in others and also the
highly emotional temper of Victorian society; he liked writing actable
lines; but Pecksniff is not only giving a polished performance, now
sarcastic, now threatening, now ironical and mocking his tormentors.
He is making himself ridiculous but he *thinks he is making fools of
his listeners*. He is also using an image—"silent tomb"—which may
be ludicrous but which also exactly corresponds to the condition of
the hypocritical mind. A life of hypocrisy can succeed on the condition that it reduces moral standards, moral words, and life itself to
meaninglessness. The hypocrite is indeed an empty tomb for he has
killed life with words. He is also called traditionally a "whited
sepulchre." It must have terrified the interminably talkative Pecksniff that the chief condition of tombs is their silence.

I know it is very dangerous to pay too close attention to a writer's
images and phrases. The fact is that to Dickens, as to all primitive
natures, there was something comic in death. Especially there was
something funny in dead wives. Mr. Sapsea's betrothed is idiotic in
the grave. Mr. Pecksniff drags the dead into his comedy. The height
of Dickens' comedy of birth and death is reached by Mrs. Gamp.

"Which Mr. Chuzzlewit" said Mrs. Gamp "is well-known to
Mrs. Harris as has one sweet infant (tho she do not wish it
known) in her own family by the mother's side, kep in spirits in
a bottle; and that sweet babe she see at Greenwich Fair, a travelling in company with the pink eyed lady Prooshan dwarf, and livin
skelinton, which judge her feeling when the barrel organ played
and she was showed her own dear sister's child, the same not being

expected from the outside picter, where it was painted quite con-
trairy in a living state, many sizes larger, and performing beautiful
on the arp, which never did that dear child know or do; since
breathe it never did, to speak on, in this wale."

The foetus in the bottle, the child with the harp. That is going
pretty far, but it is the fundamental, almost stock stuff of macabre
comedy.

Pecksniff, Mrs. Gamp and Micawber belong to what we call, in
a cliché, "the great comic characters"; that is to say they are part
human beings and part myth or projection of the characters' own
imaginative conception of themselves. Mrs. Gamp belongs to the
same order of character as the Wife of Bath, Juliet's nurse and Mrs.
Bloom. It is commonly said of Pecksniff that he is too hateful. The
same criticism is made of that great Russian hypocrite Iudushka in
The Golovlyov Family. Pecksniff is certainly superficially hateful.
The paradox of literature is that if a writer hates his hateful character too much he kills him; indeed it is the necessity of art that a
writer must delight imaginatively even in his hateful characters. The
art of the comic is to correct vice by laughter, because laughter is
living. Or it is an orgiastic alternative to living. And in the laughter,
the character was, as it were, reborn in a more tolerable dimension.
Pecksniff will never be lovable but that does not mean that his
author has not delighted in him. Dickens sees into the peculiarity
of Pecksniff's mind and it is in the comic movements of the mind
and inner life rather than in the comic events and plot—as I have
said—that Dickens reaches his heights. Of course there *are* comic
incidents in Pecksniff's career, the finest one being his drunkenness
and his love-making to Mrs. Todgers. He makes a speech with a
muffin stuck, butter side down, to the knee of his trousers. Dickens
is capable of the most delicate ironical comedy too—for example, the
scene in the Marshalsea in *Little Dorrit* where the penniless bankrupt, the father of the Marshalsea, makes a point of entertaining,
with aristocratic condescension, one of his even less fortunate friends.
This has an irony as fully drawn as anything in Cervantes. But
Dickens mainly goes *first* for mannerism; at the next stage, for mannerism that reveals the conflict between the inner and outer man;
at the *next* stage for that poetic clown—the inner consciousness itself.
The clown may be innocent as Mr. Dick is, or Betsy Trotwood or

Moddle, but he may be corrupt like Mr. Pecksniff and Mrs. Gamp.
If he is corrupt his inner life becomes grotesque.

> "My feelings, Mrs. Todgers, will not consent to be entirely
> smothered like the young children in the tower. They are grown
> up and the more I press the bolster on them, the more they look
> round the corner of it."

It has been said that if the comic characters of Dickens are not
exaggerations and caricatures, then at any rate, they are flat and
static. They circle round in the strange dog basket of their minds,
and never escape from their compulsions. But I cannot really agree
that the compulsive pattern in these characters makes *all* of them
static and flat. There is a considerable growth in Pecksniff. It is
true that he certainly does not move forward and develop very far
as a character in action in the maner of Iudushka or in the manner
of Oblomov; unless we say that Pecksniff begins by being a humbug
and ends by becoming a villain. And we must admit that the comic
or rather the fantastic characters are awkward when they have to
act within the terms of a realistic, dramatic plot. They are essentially
sedentary soliloquists, not people made for action.

The fact is that Dickens had a merely theatrical notion of evil.
He thought bad men became evil men merely by becoming theatrical
and non-comic; there is no need for Pecksniff to be a swindler; he
is evil enough in rendering life meaningless. Yet there is a moment
when Pecksniff does become permissibly evil and when his character
shows a terrifying side. I am thinking of the scene when he proposes
marriage of Mary Graham: a comic character dealing with a straight
character. No metaphors now, no clowning, but smooth, persistent,
planned and skillful tactics. Mr. Pecksniff is a cold hard libertine.
He is capable of lust and violence and actually has courage in this
scene. His courage makes him frightening and certainly shows a
development in his character. When Miss Graham turns Mr. Pecksniff down Dickens writes in a different tone:

> He seemed to be shrunk and reduced, to be trying to hide him-
> self within himself; and to be wretched at not having the power
> to do it. His shoes looked too large; his sleeves looked too long; his
> hair looked too limp; his features looked too mean; and his exposed
> throat looked as if a halter would have done it good. For a minute
> or two, he was hot and pale, mean and shy and slinking and conse-
> quently, not at all Pecksniffian.

You can see now why Dickens was so keen on Pecksniff's moral throat. That phrase, "not at all Pecksniffian," is a serious development in depth. Yet it is out of key. The great characters of Dickens grow inwardly, if they do happen to grow. If it is true that they move very little forward they grow larger on the spot where they stand, because they are worked over in detail. This detail is not analytical but is a further encrustation of foolery. We recognize the imaginative truth of Dickens' fantasies because, at their heart, lies the comic fact that men behave as if they were solitary animals. A large number of the comic characters of Dickens think they are totally alone.

How does Pecksniff compare with figures like Tartuffe or Iudushka? There can hardly be a correct analogy with Tartuffe simply because the theater has to simplify and intensify. Molière is more imaginative than Dickens in showing that Tartuffe not only gains his ends by pretending virtue, but gets out of the attacks made on him, by grandiloquently confessing, knowing no one will believe him. Tartuffe, in other words, exploits vice as well as virtue. Since Tartuffe embodies the idea of hypocrisy he cannot be loved. Iudushka also surpasses Pecksniff because he is grimmer. He is comical because he is a bore. And he is also shown as self-corrupting. He bores himself. Dickens is certainly not as perceptive as the Russian writer, nor does Dickens rise to the heights that the Russian reaches in the scenes describing Iudushka's old age. Dickens had no real sense of the mind diseased. Closer to reality, facing the dreadful *fact* not the poetic fantasy of human solitude, the Russian sees the pathos indeed the tragedy of the egotist. Pecksniff goes out of his comedy with a speech and a gesture; Iudushka goes out of the squalid comedy with a scream of loss, pain, terror.

There is of course a movement, in Dickens' work, away from the fantasy and the gothic to the realistic form of humor. The figure of Mr. Bounderby is an example from *Hard Times*. Mr. Bounderby has the absurd pride of the self-made man. He is proud of his own hard times and he is well worked out. That is to say "hard times" is an idea added to all the characters and seen, in his case, on the comic level. He is a figure out of social satire who is not visited by the grace of the comic forgiveness. The more blasting kind of comic realism is to be found in certain minor characters, and especially among the aggressive poor. Here Dickens reaches very fine points of social irony, for the poor are capable of looking after themselves.

They are not solitaries. They are not clowns. They speak out with
the skill of rival comic authors. There is that famous visit of Mrs.
Pardiggle to the poor man. There is nothing eccentric about him.

> "Is my daughter a-washing? Yes she is a-washing. Look at the
> water. Smell it. That's wot we drinks. How d'you like it and what
> d'you think of gin instead. Ain't my place dirty? Yes it is dirty;
> it's naturally dirty and it's naturally unwholesome and we've had
> five dirty and unwholesome children, as is all dead infants, and so
> much the better for them and for us besides. And how did my wife
> get that black eye? Why, I give it to her: an if she says I didn't
> she's a liar."

Let us turn from the individual comic characters to the mass
comic effects of Dickens, to that mode of comedy which generalizes
and which is commonly employed in satire. This satire becomes
harsher and I think cruder as Dickens grows older, as his nerves
became exacerbated by domestic unhappiness, by overwork, by
straining after money, and as Victorianism became more vulgar and
more blatant. There is an increase in hatred and violence as the
years go by. These are dulling to the poetic genius and the comic
portrait of Mr. Gradgrind, for example, is actually dull. There is a
point in Dickens where one catches the note of untransmuted hysteria and megalomania. In this sense one can understand the resentment of conservative critics like Walter Bagehot who thought,
with some justice, that the picture of the Circumlocution Office was
a libel. But of course Bagehot was wrong if he expected comic
writers to bow to a moral hierarchy. The essence of satire is its anger,
fantasy and untruth, and when Dickens describes a bureaucracy he
was creating a mythical institution. All bureaucracies are tyrannies
of the individual. Dickens' ridicule is the soliloquist's protest against
institutions.

The tradition of comic generalization is one of the strongholds
of English comedy. These generalizations are social rather than
intellectual. The comic generalizations in the eighteenth century
are concerned with man and human nature, vice and virtue and so
on; these ideas are indeed intellectual but realism pulls the idea
down into the roaring gutters and vulnerable bedrooms of everyday
life, so that "man in society," "man in the way of the world" are the
tests. From Scott and Jane Austen the elaborate English class system

replaces man, vice, virtue, etc., and quickly absorbs the comic genius. In Thackeray, in Trollope, in Meredith, in the very Dickensian Wells of *Tono-Bungay*, these festive social generalizations, stuffed with comical allusions to class, define our comic tradition.

But there is of course an anarchic and rebellious process continually going on against the pressure of society and the generalizations of Dickens are meant to reduce institutions to idiocy. He proceeds, in his usual way, to lift them off the ground, make them float absurdly in mid-air. The famous analysis of parliamentary government in *Bleak House* (which can be checked up in the acquiescent political comedies of Trollope) is an indignant lark. Dickens understood the art of calling people funny names and his ear for funny sounds is always splendid. The farce of the Circumlocution Office is not only funny itself, but, with deadly eye, Dickens sees that the place is not only a bureaucracy but is also a family stronghold. His comic genealogy of the Chuzzlewit family is not all of a piece. It satirizes many kinds of believers in genealogy. Beginning in the spacious manner of Fielding, in order to set a grave tone, it proceeds to irony about William the Conqueror; and at this point, by a stroke of genius, he has his brilliant idea that the Chuzzlewits must be descended from Guy Fawkes because there was a lady in the family known as "the matchmaker." Having run through the gamut of family snobbery he ends up with the superb statement of the outrageously common member of the family, that his grandfather was a nobleman called The Lord No Zoo. The generalizations about the Veneering Family have the same quality of irresponsible comic investigations, in depth.

When one reads the critics and hears this or that writer described as Dickensian, one very soon finds that this deeply important capacity for comic social generalization is missing. I rather think Wells was the last to have it—in the first part of *Tono-Bungay*. It has gone because the sense of the whole of a society has gone. The novel has become departmentalized. We now talk of novels of private life, and novels of public life. In Dickens, on the contrary, the private imagination, comic, poetical and fantastic, was inseparable from the public imagination and the operation of conscience and rebellion. This amalgamation was possible, I think, because he felt from childhood the sense of being outside society, because he was a sort of showman, not because he was a social or political thinker with a program.

HUMPHRY HOUSE

The Macabre Dickens

The present lively interest in Dickens has in it an element never before prominent in all his hundred years of popularity—an interest in his mastery of the macabre and terrible in scene and character. His understanding of and power of describing evil and cruelty, fear and mania and guilt; his overburdening sense, in the crises, of the ultimate loneliness of human life—things like these are now seen to be among the causes of his enigmatic hold on people's hearts. He has worked as much beneath the surface as above it; and he was possibly not himself fully conscious of what he was putting into his books. The floor of consciousness has been lowered. The awful area of human experience in which small cruelty and meanness and stupidity may swell and topple over into murder, insane revenge, sadistic, bloody violence and riot; the area where dream and reality are confused or swiftly alternating—these are now seen to be closer to ourselves and to common life than our grandfathers suspected. They thought that Dickens on his violent and evil side—when he wrote about Sikes and Jonas Chuzzlewit and Bradley Headstone—was writing about a special, separate class called criminals; that Miss Havisham, Mr. Dick and Miss Flite belonged to another separate class called lunatics—at most social problems; at least, wild exag-

From *All in Due Time* (London: Rupert Hart-Davis Ltd., 1955), pp. 183-89. Reprinted by permission of Granada Publishing Ltd. First delivered on the B.B.C. Third Programme, June 3, 1947.

gerated flights of fancy. We now see more plainly that John Jasper may be any one of us; that the murderer is not far beneath the skin; that the thickness of a sheet of paper may divide the proud successful man of the world from the suicide or the lunatic. We have also dived again into what used to be dismissed as melodrama.

Lord Acton once wrote in a letter that Dickens "knows nothing of sin when it is not crime." Within the narrow limits of theological pigeon-holes this is true; the word "sin" hardly occurs in the novels; wickedness is not regarded as an offence against a personal God. But if the judgment is that Dickens knows nothing of evil unless it is recognised and punishable by the law, it is quite false. The great black, ghastly gallows hanging over all, of which Dickens writes in the Preface to *Oliver Twist,* is not just the official retribution of society against those who break its rules; it is a symbol of the internal knowledge of guilt, the knowledge that makes Sikes wander back and forth in the country north of London, dogged not by fear of the police but by the phantom of Nancy, the knowledge that produces the last vision of her eyes which is the immediate cause of his death. Acton, with the logic of Catholicism, thought it a fault in Dickens that he "loved his neighbour for his neighbour's sake"; but, within the range of moral action that this allows, Dickens is continually dealing with the forms of evil which the absence or failure of love may breed, and with the more terrible effects of emotional greed, the exploitation of one person by another, which often overflows into cruelty and violence. His methods of dealing with these moral problems and the conflicts they involve are various, but they are always peculiar and oblique; they are rarely brought out openly on the main surface of the story; they are never analysed as the story goes along. They are sometimes displayed through a grotesque character in such a way that they become so sharp and hideous that it is hard to recognise their seriousness and truth. Such, for example, is Quilp's cruelty towards his wife, which seems a fantastic travesty of human action if one overlooks Mrs. Quilp's one phrase:

> Quilp has such a way with him when he likes, that the best-looking woman here couldn't refuse him if I was dead.

That one sentence goes to the core of Quilp: for all his grotesque exterior he has in him a secret and serious human *power:* he is no figure of fun.

Except in such sudden phrases as these, Dickens's imagination usually concentrates through all the greater part of a story now on the black, now on the white, exclusively: the two don't interpenetrate. It is only in the portraits of boyhood and adolescence, such as those of Pip and the early Copperfield, that the medley of moral direction is really convincing. The adult characters for most of their course drive headstrong forward, virtuously or villainously or in some grotesque neutral zone where moral decisions do not have to be made. It is as if Dickens was afraid of attempting to portray the full complexity of an adult. Then, quite suddenly, a portentous thing happens. It is worth noticing first what does *not* happen. I cannot think of a single instance in which one of the good characters suddenly reveals a streak of evil: the Jarndyces and Cheerybles and Brownlows persevere infallible and unsullied to the end. The startling thing that *does* happen is that the villains suddenly reveal, if not a streak of good, a streak of vivid power, and then an immense depth of intricate, confused and pitiable humanity. Suddenly their awakened sense of guilt, their fears, remorse, regrets, and above all their terrible loneliness strike out like lightning from the complex plot. As death comes upon them they are transformed, not by any crude magic of reformation such as works wonders with Scrooge, but by an understanding and sympathy, a knowledge of their fears and weakness, far more heart-rending than the moral judgments which convention and the plot pass against them. Examples of this are Fagin, Sikes, Jonas Chuzzlewit, even Quilp: but for the moment let us look closely at Mr. Carker in *Dombey and Son*.

Carker has most often been regarded as a typical villain out of melodrama. One critic at least has called his drive across France from Dijon to the coast a "masterpiece of melodrama." So persistent has this way of regarding it been that this same critic himself heightens the scene by speaking of Carker's "last journey through the *stormy* night." But Dickens makes no mention of any storm whatever; in fact he writes in quite a different mood of "a sigh of mountain air from the distant Jura, fading along the plain." It is nearer the truth to say that in this scene Carker shakes off the last suggestion of melodrama and becomes a figure of immense significance. I will quote a few paragraphs—not continuous—from the description of the later part of this drive:

> Gathered up moodily in a corner of the carriage, and only intent on going fast—except when he stood up, for a mile together, and

looked back; which he would do whenever there was a piece of open country—he went on, still postponing thought indefinitely, and still always tormented with thinking to no purpose. . . .

Shame, disappointment, and discomfiture gnawed at his heart; a constant apprehension of being overtaken, or met—for he was groundlessly afraid even of travellers, who came towards him by the way he was going—oppressed him heavily. The same intolerable awe and dread that had come upon him in the night, returned unweakened in the day. The monotonous ringing of the bells and tramping of the horses; the monotony of his anxiety, and useless rage; the monotonous wheel of fear, regret, and passion, he kept turning round and round; made the journey like a vision, in which nothing was quite real but his own torment. . . .

It was a fevered vision of things past and present all confounded together; of his life and journey blended into one. Of being madly hurried somewhere, whither he must go. Of old scenes starting up among the novelties through which he travelled. Of musing and brooding over what was past and distant, and seeming to take no notice of the actual objects he encountered, but with a wearisome exhausting consciousness of being bewildered by them, and having their images all crowded in his hot brain after they were gone.

Whatever language this is, it is not the language of melodrama; it is a tremendous analysis of the psychological effects of guilt, shame and thwarted vanity. It is only in the light of these great final scenes that Carker's character as shown earlier in the book becomes intelligible; it is then seen that he is not the motivelessly malignant villain of melodrama: he is a man of intellect, of great ambition and great sexual vitality; his worse flaws are self-centredness and vanity. It is exactly this sort of man who would be afflicted with a total blindness about what Edith Dombey, in a position, as he thinks, to satisfy both his ambition and his sexual desires, was really thinking and feeling. The final disclosure would have been bitter to Carker for many reasons, but bitterest perhaps because it showed him that he had been abysmally blind and *stupid*; yet he was too self-centred, intricate and cunning to allow reflection on his own stupidity to come uppermost in his tortured thoughts. There is much of Dickens himself in Mr. Carker: and it is starting to see the hopelessness of his wheels within wheels of thought: there is no solution but death.

One of the problems that face the critic of Dickens is to explain how this intimate understanding of morbid and near-morbid psy-

chology links on to his apparent optimism, and above all to his
humour. I think we can safely say that the countless scenes of
gregarious and hearty happiness, which seem to us so unconvincing,
seem so because they represent a revulsion from the abysses of evil,
a strenuous and ardent *wish* to achieve happiness, rather than the
realisation of it. But what of the great grotesque and humorous
characters—Mrs. Gamp, Pecksniff, Mr. Turveydrop and the rest?
One very fruitful suggestion was made by George Henry Lewes,
only two years after Dickens's death:

> In no other perfectly sane mind (Blake I believe was not per-
> fectly sane) have I observed vividness of imagination approaching
> so closely to hallucination. . . . Dickens once declared to me that
> every word said by his characters was distinctly *heard* by him; I
> was at first not a little puzzled to account for the fact that he could
> hear language so utterly unlike the language of real feeling; but
> the surprise vanished when I thought of the phenomena of hallu-
> cination.

Lewes applied this idea both to the speaking of certain characters
and also to the visual descriptions of persons and scenes. In each
case it was the definiteness and insistence of the image or the sound
which were abnormal. This idea is, I think, extremely useful in
helping to explain the impression one gets from the books of isolated
spells of intense imagination which then stop; it also helps to explain
the feeling of isolation about the characters: one almost hallucina-
tory experience succeeded by another, the two being mutually exclusive. There was no comprehensive, constructive, master imagination which held the diverse experiences together, except in very
rare instances, mostly to do with memories of childhood. The great
grotesque comic characters—Mrs. Gamp is the purest of the type—
are the best examples of this exclusive, one-track intense development and could not have their unique stature without it. In other
instances the form of hallucination was not that of something seen
or heard externally, but an internal illusion by which Dickens himself virtually assumed the character of which he was writing. His
daughter Mamie described how she saw him grimacing in a glass,
talking aloud the speeches of a character, completely unaware of his
actual surroundings, not even noticing that she was in the room.

If one starts by thinking of Dickens as a man with an imagination of this quality and intensity and exclusiveness, it helps to ex-

plain not only the recurrent treatment in the novels of various forms of mania and illusion, but also the preoccupation with evil. Similar processes of concentration, exclusion and distortion must have occurred in the mental part of his own life, as distinct from his written work. Edmund Wilson, in his essay *The Two Scrooges,* argued that Dickens was "the victim of a manic-depressive cycle, and a very uncomfortable person." His own life was, in a sense, far beyond what could be said of most men, acting out, or attempting to act out, his own imaginings. His passion for theatricals was only a symptom of the trouble, or an effort to work it off without serious consequences. In real living the concomitant of blindness, especially to the thoughts and feelings of other people, may be resentment and hatred, even to the point of imagining murder, against those who fail to conform to the policy or come up to the idea of themselves that it entails. But there will also be moments of terrible awakening when the illusion and the self-deceit it involved are ended, and there will be a great wave of remorse and guilt and shame for the evils imagined or other evils actually done. There is evidence enough to show that Dickens's personality was strong enough, especially over women, to project his own imagined policies upon others so that in general they conformed; at certain crises the attempt failed and a hideous major conflict came into the open. Lewes said he saw no traces of insanity in Dickens's life; nor would he; for Dickens normally had a very strong conscious control, and was able to work out many of his conflicts through his novels. But his daughter Kate, Mrs. Perugini, did significantly say to a friend that after his wife left their home Dickens behaved towards the children "like a madman," that all the worst in him came out; and she added that her father was "a very wicked man."

This is a very different matter from saying that he was a commonplace bounder; there is no need for Dickens's descendants to defend him against charges of being a dishonest drunken libertine: neither the charges nor the defence are relevant to a man of his size and complexity and importance. It is clear from the evidence of the novels alone that Dickens's acquaintance with evil was not just acquired *ab extra,* by reading the police-court reports (much as he loved them) and wandering about Seven Dials and the Waterside by night; it was acquired also by introspection. His own temptations and imaginings, isolated and heightened by the peculiar, narrowing, intense quality of his imagination, fed daily by the immense power which he felt himself to possess over others' personalities—these were the authentic sources of his great criminal characters. Their ultimate trembling loneliness, or hunted wanderings, or self-haunted hallucinations, or endless, destroying self-analysis, came also from himself. Our generation has come to recognise this by introspection, too.

NORTHROP FRYE

Dickens and the Comedy of Humors

Dickens presents special problems to any critic who approaches him in the context of a "Victorian novelist." In general, the serious Victorian fiction writers are realistic and the less serious ones are romancers. We expect George Eliot or Trollope to give us a solid and well-rounded realization of the social life, attitudes, and intellectual issues of their time: we expect Disraeli and Bulwer-Lytton, because they are more "romantic," to give us the same kind of thing in a more flighty and dilettantish way; from the cheaper brands, Marie Corelli or Ouida, we expect nothing but the standard romance formulas. This alignment of the serious and the realistic, the commercial and the romantic, where realism has a moral dignity that romance lacks, intensified after Dickens's death, survived through the first half of the twentieth century, and still lingers vestigially. But in such an alignment Dickens is hard to place. What he writes, if I may use my own terminology for once, are not realistic novels but fairy tales in the low mimetic displacement. Hence there has grown up an assumption that, if we are to take Dickens seriously, we must emphasize the lifelikeness of his characters or the shrewd-

From *Experience in the Novel: Selected Papers from the English Institute,* ed. by Roy Harvey Pearce (Columbia University Press: New York and London, 1968), pp. 49-81. Copyright © 1968 by Columbia University Press. Reprinted by permission of the author and the publishers.

ness of his social observation; if we emphasize his violently unplausible plots and his playing up of popular sentiment, we are
emphasizing only his concessions to an undeveloped public taste.
This was a contemporary view of him, expressed very lucidly by
Trollope in *The Warden,* and it is still a natural one to take.

A refinement of the same view sees the real story in Dickens's
novels as a rather simple set of movements within a large group of
characters. To this a mechanical plot seems to have been attached
like an outboard motor to a rowboat, just to get things moving faster
and more noisily. Thus our main interest, in reading *Little Dorrit,*
is in the straightforward and quite touching story of Clennam's love
for the heroine, of their separation through her suddenly acquired
wealth, and of their eventual reunion through her loss of it. Along
with this goes a preposterous melodrama about forged wills, identical
twins, a mother who is not a mother, skulking foreigners, and dark
mysteries of death and birth which seems almost detachable from
the central story. Similarly, we finish *Our Mutual Friend* with a
clear memory of a vast panoramic pageant of Victorian society, from
the nouveau-riche Veneerings to Hexam living on the refuse of
the Thames. But the creaky Griselda plot, in which John Harmon
pretends to be dead in order to test the stability of his future wife,
is something that we can hardly take in even when reading the
book, much less remember afterwards.

Some works of fiction present a clearly designed or projected plot,
where each episode seems to us to be logically the sequel to the
previous episode. In others we feel that the episode that comes next
does so only because the author has decided that it will come next.
In stories with a projected plot we explain the episode from its
context in the plot; in stories lacking such a plot, we are often
thrown back on some other explanation, often one that originates
in the author's wish to tell us something besides the story. This
last is particularly true of thematic sequences like the "Dream Play"
of Strindberg, where the succession of episodes is not like that of
a projected plot, nor particularly like a dream either, but has to be
accounted for in different terms. In Dickens we often notice that
when he is most actively pursuing his plot he is careless, to the
verge of being contemptuous, of the inner logic of the story. In
Little Dorrit, the mysterious rumblings and creakings in the Clennam house, referred to at intervals throughout, mean that it is about
to fall down. What this in turn means is that Dickens is going to

push it over at a moment when the villain is inside and the hero outside. Similarly, Clennam, after a good deal of detective work, manages to discover where Miss Wade is living on the Continent. She did not expect him to ferret out her address, nor had she anything to say to him when he arrived; but, just in case he did come, she had written out the story of her life and had kept it in a drawer ready to hand to him. The outrage on probability seems almost deliberate, as does the burning up of Krook in *Bleak House* by spontaneous combustion as soon as the author is through with him, despite Dickens's protests about the authenticity of his device. Dickens's daughter, Mrs. Pellegrini, remarked shrewdly that there was no reason to suppose that *The Mystery of Edwin Drood* would have been any more of an impeccable plot-structure than the novels that Dickens had already completed. But, because it is unfinished, the plot has been the main focus of critical attention in that story, usually on the assumption that this once Dickens was working with a plot which was not, like a fictional Briareus, equipped with a hundred arms of coincidence.

T. S. Eliot, in his essay on Dickens and Wilkie Collins, remarks on the "spurious fatality" of Collins's detective-story plots. This is no place to raise the question of why the sense of fatality in *The Moonstone* should be more spurious than in *The Family Reunion,* but we notice in Dickens how strong the impulse is to reject a logicality inherent in the story in favor of impressing on the reader an impatient sense of absolutism: of saying, in short, *la fatalité, c'est moi.* This disregard of plausibility is worth noticing, because everyone realizes that Dickens is a great genius of the absurd in his characterization, and it is possible that his plots are also absurd in the same sense, not from incompetence or bad taste, but from a genuinely creative instinct. If so, they are likely to be more relevant to the entire conception of the novel than is generally thought. I proceed to explore a little the sources of absurdity in Dickens, to see if that will lead us to a clearer idea of his total structure.

The structure that Dickens uses for his novels is the New Comedy structure, which has come down to us from Plautus and Terence through Ben Jonson, an author we know Dickens admired, and Molière. The main action is a collision of two societies which we may call for convenience the obstructing and the congenial society. The congenial society is usually centered on the love of hero and heroine, the obstructing society on the characters, often parental, who try to thwart this love. For most of the action the thwarting characters are in the ascendant, but toward the end a twist in the plot reverses the situation and the congenial society dominates the happy ending. A frequent form of plot-reversal was the discovery that one of the central characters, usually the heroine, was of better social origin than previously thought. This theme of mysterious parentage is greatly expanded in the late Greek romances, which closely resemble some of the plots of Menander. Here an infant of noble birth may be stolen or exposed and brought up by humble fosterparents, being restored to his original status at the end. In drama such a theme involves expounding a complicated antecedent action, and however skillfully done not all audiences have the patience to follow the unraveling, as Ben Jonson discovered to his cost at the opening of his *New Inn*. But in narrative forms, of course, it can have room to expand. Shakespeare gets away with it in *The Winter's Tale* by adopting a narrative-paced form of drama, where sixteen years are encompassed by the action.

Dickens is, throughout his career, very conventional in his handling of the New Comedy plot structure. All the stock devices, listed in Greek times as laws, oaths, compacts, witnesses, and ordeals, can be found in him. *Oliver Twist* and *Edwin Drood* are full of oaths, vows, councils of war, and conspiracies, on both benevolent and sinister sides. Witnesses include eavesdroppers like the Newman Noggs of *Nicholas Nickleby* or Morfin the cello-player in *Dombey and Son*. Ordeals are of various kinds: near-fatal illnesses are common, and we may compare the way that information is extracted from Rob the Grinder by Mrs. Brown in *Dombey and Son* with the maltreating of the tricky slave in Menander and Plautus. Many thrillers (perhaps a majority) use a stock episode of having the hero entrapped by the villain, who instead of killing him at once imparts an essential piece of information about the plot to him, after which the hero escapes, gaining his wisdom at the price of an ordeal of facing death. This type of episode occurs in *Great Expectations* in the encounter with Orlick.

Every novel of Dickens is a comedy (N.B.: such words as "comedy" are not essence words but context words, hence this means: "for every novel of Dickens the obvious context is comedy"). The death of a central character does not make a story tragic, any more than a similar device does in *The King and I* or *The Yeomen of the Guard*. Sydney Carton is a man without a social function who

achieves that function by sacrificing himself for the congenial society; Little Nell's death is so emotionally luxurious that it provides
a kind of muted festivity for the conclusion, or what *Finnegans
Wake* calls a "funferall." The emphasis at the end of a comedy is
sometimes thrown, not on the forming of a new society around the
marriage of hero and heroine, but on the maturing or enlightening
of the hero, a process which may detach him from marriage or full
participation in the congenial group. We find this type of conclusion in Shaw's *Candida*: Dickens's contribution to it is *Great Expectations*. Again, there is usually a mystery in Dickens's stories, and
this mystery is nearly always the traditional mystery of birth, in
sharp contrast to the mystery of death on which the modern who-
dunit is based. In Dickens, when a character is murdered, we
usually see it done, and if not the suspense is still perfunctory. A
detective appears in *Bleak House* to investigate the murder of Tulkinghorn, but his task is easy: Lady Dedlock keeps a French maid,
and French maids, being foreign, are emotionally unpredictable and
morally insensitive. The problem is much less interesting than the
problem of Lady Dedlock's guilty secret, which involves a birth.
Unless Edwin Drood was very unlike Dickens's other heroes, the
mystery about him is much more likely to have been a mystery of
how he got into the world than of how he disappeared from it.

The emergence of the congenial society at the conclusion of the
story is presented in the traditional New Comedy terms of festivity.
It usually holds several marriages; it dispenses money if it has
money, and it dispenses a good deal of food. Such features have remained unchanged in the New Comedy tradition since Greek times.
Dickens's predilection for feasting scenes needs no laboring: it may
be significant that his last written words are "falls to with an appetite." This feature accounts for his relentless plugging of Christmas,
always for him the central symbol of the congenial family feast.
The famous sentimentality of Dickens is largely confined to demon-
strations of family affection, and is particularly evident in certain set
scenes that immediately precede the dénouement, where the affection of brother and sister, of father and daughter, or more rarely of
mother and son, is the main theme. Examples are the housekeeping
of Tom and Ruth Pinch in *Martin Chuzzlewit,* the dinner of Kit
and his mother in *The Old Curiosity Shop,* the meetings of Bella
Wilfer with her father in *Our Mutual Friend.* Such relationships,
though occasionally described as marriages, are "innocent" in the

technical Victorian sense of not involving sexual intercourse, and if they seem to post-Freudian readers to be emotionally somewhat overcharged, it is because they contribute to, and anticipate, the final triumph of Eros at the end of the story. The disregard of plausibility, already mentioned, is another traditional feature, being part of the violent manipulation of the story in the direction of a happy ending. Those who object to such endings on the grounds of probability are often put in the position of questioning the ways of divine providence, which uses the author as its agent for vindicating virtue and baffling vice.

Most of the people who move across the pages of Dickens are neither realistic portraits, like the characters of Trollope, nor "caricatures," so far as that term implies only a slightly different approach to realistic portraiture. They are humors, like the characters in Ben Jonson, who formulated the principle that humors were the appropriate characters for a New Comedy plot. The humor is a character identified with a characteristic, like the miser, the hypochondriac, the braggart, the parasite, or the pedant. He is obsessed by whatever it is that makes him a humor, and the sense of our superiority to an obsessed person, someone bound to an invariable ritual habit, is, according to Bergson, one of the chief sources of laughter. But it is not because he is incidentally funny that the humor is important in New Comedy: he is important because his obsession is the feature that creates the conditions of the action, and the opposition of the two societies. In *The Silent Woman*, everything depends on Morose's hatred of noise; covetousness and gullibility set everything going in *Volpone* and *The Alchemist* respectively. Thus it is only the obstructing society which is "humorous," in the Jonsonian sense, as a society. In Dickens we find humors on both sides of the social conflict, genial, generous, and lovable humors as well as absurd or sinister ones. But the humors in the congenial society merely diversify it with amiable and harmless eccentricities; the humors of the obstructing society help to build up that society, with all its false standards and values.

Most of the standard types of humor are conspicuous in Dickens, and could be illustrated from *Bleak House* alone: the miser in Smallweed; the hypocrite in Chadband; the parasite in Skimpole and Turveydrop; the pedant in Mrs. Jellyby. The braggart soldier is not much favored: Major Bagstock in *Dombey and Son* is more of a parasite. Agreeably to the conditions of Victorian life, the braggart soldier is replaced by a braggart merchant or politician. An example, treated in a thoroughly traditional manner, is Bounderby in *Hard Times*. Another Victorian commonplace of the braggart-soldier family, the duffer sportsman, whose pretensions are far beyond his performance, is represented by Winkle in *The Pickwick Papers*. There are, however, two Winkles in *The Pickwick Papers*, the duffer sportsman and the pleasant young man who breaks down family opposition on both sides to acquire a pleasant young woman. The duality reflects the curious and instructive way that *The Pickwick Papers* came into being. The original scheme proposed to Dickens was a comedy of humors in its most primitive and superficial form: a situation comedy in which various stock types, including an incautious amorist (Tupman), a melancholy poet (Snodgrass), and a pedant (Pickwick), as well as Winkle, get into one farcical predicament after another. This form is frequent in stories for children, and was represented in my childhood by now obsolete types of comic strip and silent movie comedies. It must have left some descendants in television, but my impression is that contemporary children are deficient in this vitamin. But although traces of the original scheme persist throughout *The Pickwick Papers*, it quickly turns inside out into a regular New Comedy story, which leads up in the regular way to a recognition scene and a reversal of direction in the plot at its most serious point, in the debtors' prison. The pedant becomes a man of principle, and the humor of pedantry is transferred to the law which entraps him. Thus the comedy of humors takes root in society, as Dickens sees society, instead of merely extending from one incident to another.

The simplest form of humor is the tagged humor, who is associated with the repetition of a set phrase. Thus we have Mrs. Micawber, whose tag is that she will never desert Mr. Micawber, and Major Bagnet in *Bleak House*, who admires his wife but asserts that he never tells her so because "discipline must be maintained." We notice that our sense of superiority to such characters is edged with antagonism: when the repeated trait is intended to be endearing we are more likely to find it irritating, as E. M. Forster does Mrs. Micawber's. Jarndyce with his "east wind" tag and Esther Summerson's constant bewilderment that other people should find her charming do not stick in our minds in the way that Chadband and Mrs. Jellyby do. The humor is, almost by definition, a bore, and the technical skill in handling him consists in seeing that we get just enough but not too much of him. The more unpleasant he is, the easier this problem is to solve. Repetition which is excessive even by Dickensian standards, like the emphasis on Carker's teeth in *Dombey and Son,* is appropriate for a villain, as its effect is to dehumanize and cut off sympathy. We cannot feel much concern over the fate of a character who is presented to us mainly as a set of teeth, like Berenice in Poe. The "lifelikeness" of a humor depends on two things: on the fact that we are all very largely creatures of ritual habit, and on the strength of a perverse tendency in most of us to live up to our own caricatures. Pecksniff may be a humbug, but that can hardly be the whole of our feeling about him when he begins to sound like a member of my own profession attempting to extract a discussion from a group of clammed-up freshmen:

> "The name of those fabulous animals (pagan, I regret to say) who used to sing in the water, has quite escaped me."
>
> Mr. George Chuzzlewit suggested "Swans."
>
> "No," said Mr. Pecksniff. "Not swans. Very like swans, too. Thank you."
>
> The nephew with the outline of a countenance, speaking for the first and last time on that occasion, propounded "Oysters."
>
> "No," said Mr. Pecksniff, with his own peculiar urbanity, "nor oysters. But by no means unlike oysters: a very excellent idea; thank you, my dear sir, very much. Wait! Sirens. Dear me! sirens, of course."

Humors are, at least dramatically, "good" if they are on the side of the congenial society, "bad" or ridiculous if on the side of the obstructing one. Thus the humor comedy has an easy and natural connection with the morality play. We notice this in the allegorical names that Dickens often gives some of his minor characters, like the "Pyke" and "Pluck" who are the satellites of Sir Mulberry Hawk in *Nicholas Nickleby,* or the "Bar," "Bishop," and "Physician" who turn up at Merdle's dinners in *Little Dorrit.* We notice it also in Dickens's tendency to arrange his humors in moral pairs, whether both are in the same novel or not. As just indicated, we have a "good" major in *Bleak House* and a "bad" one with a very similar name in *Dombey and Son;* we have a villainous Jew in *Oliver Twist* and a saintly Jew in *Our Mutual Friend,* and so on. Within *Dombey and Son* itself the "bad" major is paired against a "good" navy man, Captain Cuttle. If characters change sides, there may be a metamorphosis of character, which is not difficult in the humor technique, because it simply means putting on a different mask. Thus the generous Boffin pretends to be a miser for a while; Scrooge goes through the reverse process; Mercy Pecksniff changes roles from the feather-head to the faithful ill-used wife, and so on. Many humors are really chorus characters, who cannot do anything in the plot unless they step out of their roles: an example is Lord Frederick Verisopht in *Nicholas Nickleby,* who has to harden up a good deal to make his tragic end appropriate. The commonest form of this metamorphosis, and the most traditional one, is the release of the humor from his obsession at the end of the story: through the experience gained in the story, he is able to break through his besetting fault. At the end of *Martin Chuzzlewit* there is a whole series of these changes: the hero escapes from his selfishness, Mark Tapley from his compulsion to search for difficult situations in order to "come out strong," and Tom Pinch from an innocence that Dickens recognizes to be more obsessive than genuine innocence, and which we should now think of as a streak of masochism.

The rhetoric of the tagged humor consists mainly of variations of the stock identifying phrase or phrases. Some humors acquire a personal rhetorical rhythm of a strongly associative kind, which because it is associative gives the effect of being obsessive. The disjointed phrases of Jingle and the asyntactic babble of Mrs. Nickleby and Flora Finching are perhaps the most consistently successful examples. Closer to the single identifying phrase are Uriah Heep's insistence on his "'umble" qualities, which reminds us a little of Iago's "honest" tag, and the repetitions that betray the hypocrisy of Casby, the squeezing landlord in *Little Dorrit*. Others develop parodies of standard types of oratory, like Chadband with his parsonical beggar's whine or Micawber with his Parliamentary flourishes.

More significant, for a reason that will meet us in a moment, is the humor of stock response, that is, the humor whose obsession it is to insist that what he or she has been conditioned to think proper and acceptable is in fact reality. This attitude gives us the Bouvard-et-Pécuchet type of humor, whose mind is confined within a dictionary of accepted ideas. Such humors, it is obvious, readily expand into cultural allegories, representatives of the kind of anxiety that caricatures an age. Thus our stereotypes about "Victorian prudery" are represented by Podsnap in *Our Mutual Friend* and Mrs. Gen-

eral (the prunes-and-prisms woman) in *Little Dorrit*. Martin Chuzzlewit finds that America is full of such humors: American shysters
are no better and no worse than their British counterparts, but there
is a more theoretical element in their lying, and bluster about their
enlightened political institutions is much more used as a cover for
swindling. In America, in other words, the complacent Podsnap and
the rascally Lammle are more likely to be associated in the same
person. The implication, which Dickens is not slow to press, is that
American life is more vulnerable than British life to character assassination, personal attacks, charges of being un-American, and
mob violence. A humor of this stock-response type is comic on
Freudian principles: he often says what more cautious people would
not say, but show by their actions that they believe. Thus Bumble's
remarks about "them wicious paupers" are funny, not as typical of
a Victorian beadle but as revealing the hatred and contempt for the
poor that official charity attempts to disguise.

Sometimes a humor's obsessed behavior and repetitive speech suggest a puppet or mechanical doll, whose response is invariable whatever the stimulus. We may feel with some of these characters that
the mechanical quality is simply the result of Dickens's not having
worked hard enough on them, but occasionally we realize that Dickens himself is encouraging us to see them as inanimate objects.
Wemmick the postbox in *Great Expectations*, Pancks the "tug" in
Little Dorrit, and several characters who are figuratively and to some
extent literally wooden, like Silas Wegg, are examples. The Captain
Cuttle of *Dombey and Son*, in particular, impresses us as an animated version of the Wooden Midshipman over the shop he so
often inhabits. In *The Old Curiosity Shop*, after we have been introduced to Quilp, Little Nell and her grandfather set out on their
travels and see a Punch and Judy show. It occurs to us that Quilp,
who is described as a "grotesque puppet," who lies, cheats, beats his
wife, gets into fistfights, drinks like a salamander, and comes to a
sticky end in a bog, *is* Punch, brought to life as a character. Wynd-
ham Lewis, in an essay on Joyce (another admirer of Ben Jonson),
notes the Dickensian ancestry of Bloom's interior monologue in the
speech of Jingle. He might have noted a similar connection between
Flora Finching's unpunctuated harangues in *Little Dorrit* and the
reverie of Molly Bloom. Lewis in his turn developed, mainly out of
Bergson, a theory of satire as a vision of human behavior in mechanical terms, where his main predecessor, if not one he recognized,

was Dickens. We notice also the reappearance of the Punch figure
in the center of *The Human Age*.

We noted that, while there are humors on both sides of the social
conflict in Dickens, it is only the obstructing society which is humorous as a society. This takes us back to the feature I mentioned
at the beginning which distinguishes Dickens from his major contemporaries in fiction. In most of the best Victorian novels, apart
from Dickens, the society described is organized by its institutions:
the church, the government, the professions, the rural squirearchy,
business, and the trade unions. It is a highly structured society, and
the characters function from within those structures. But in Dickens
we get a much more freewheeling and anarchistic social outlook. For
him the structures of society, as structures, belong almost entirely to
the absurd, obsessed, sinister aspect of it, the aspect that is overcome
or evaded by the comic action. The comic action itself moves toward
the regrouping of society around the only social unit that Dickens
really regards as genuine, the family. In other Victorian novelists
characters are regrouped within their social structures; in Dickens
the comic action leads to a sense of having broken down or through
those structures. Naturally there are limits to this: the same social
functions have to continue; but the sense that social institutions have
to reverse their relationship to human beings before society really
becomes congenial is very strong.

The law, for instance, as represented by the Chancery suit in
Bleak House and the Circumlocution Office in *Little Dorrit,* is a
kind of social vampire, sucking out family secrets or draining off
money through endless shifts and evasions. It is explicitly said in
both novels that the legal establishment is not designed to be an
instrument of society, but to be a self-perpetuating social parasite.
Education, again, is usually presented in Dickens as a racket, a
brutal and malignant racket with Squeers and Creakle, a force-feed-
ing racket in the "fact" school of *Hard Times* and the Classical cram
school of Dr. Blimber in *Dombey and Son.* Dickens's view of the
liberalizing quality of the Victorian Classical training is perhaps
symbolized in the grotesque scenes of Silas Wegg stumbling through
Gibbon's *Decline and Fall* to the admiration of the illiterate Boffins:
an unskillful performance which nobody understands. As for religion, even the respectable churches have little to do except marry
the hero and heroine, and the spokesmen of the chapel, Chadband
and Stiggins, are the same type of greasy lout as their ancestor in

Ben Jonson, Zeal-of-the-Land Busy. Politics, from the Eatanswill
election in *Pickwick* to the Parliamentary career of Veneering in
Our Mutual Friend, is a farce, only tolerable when an amusing one.
Industry is equally repulsive whether its spokesman is Bounderby or
the labor organizer Slackbridge. The amassing of a fortune in the
City, by Dombey, Ralph Nickleby, or Merdle in *Little Dorrit,* is an
extension of miserliness: it is closely associated with usury; the
debtor's prison is clearly the inseparable other side of it, and it
usually blows up a bubble of credit speculation with no secured
assets, ending in an appalling financial crash and endless misery.
Martin Chuzzlewit carefully balances the swindling of American
real estate speculators with the precisely similar activities of Montague's Anglo-Bengalee Company in London. In several of the novels
there are two obstructing societies, one a social establishment and
the other a criminal anti-establishment. When this occurs there is
little if anything morally to choose between them. We find the
Artful Dodger no worse than the respectable Bumble in his beadle's
uniform, and Pip discovers a human companionship with the hunted
convict on the marshes that the Wopsles and Pumblechooks of his
Christmas dinner exclude him from.

It is perhaps in *Little Dorrit* that we get the most complete view
of the obstructing society, a society which is shown to be a self-
imprisoning society, locking itself in to the invariable responses of
its own compulsions. At the beginning we are introduced to various
types of prison: the Marseilles prison with Blandois, the quarantine
prison with the discontented Tattycoram and her Lesbian familiar
Miss Wade, the prison-house of the paralyzed Mrs. Clennam, and
finally the Marshalsea. As the story goes on these external prisons
give place to internal ones. With the Circumlocution Office the
prison image modulates to a maze or labyrinth, a very frequent
sinister image in Dickens, and gradually a unified vision of the
obstructing society takes shape. This society is symbolized by the
Barnacles, who, as their name indicates, represent a social parasitism
inherent in the aristocracy, and operating through the political and
legal establishment. They are a family, but not a genuine family:
their loyalties are class or tribal loyalties cutting across the real structure of society. One of their members, Mrs. Gowan, even goes so
far as to speak of marriage as "accidental," and stresses the primary
necessity of defending the position of her class, or rather of her
private myth about her class. The fact that her son becomes the

husband of the only child of the Meagles family gives a most ambiguous twist to the happy ending of the novel. We may compare the disaster wrought by Steerforth in *David Copperfield,* whose mother is similarly obsessed with making her son into a symbol of class arrogance. We begin to understand how consistent the pitiful pretense of aristocracy that old Dorrit tries to maintain, first in the prison, then in prosperity, is with the general scheme of the story. Miss Wade's autobiography, headed "The History of a Self-Tormentor," however arbitrarily introduced into the story, has a genuine symbolic relevance to it, and one of the most sharply observed passages in the novel is the moment of self-awareness when Fanny Dorrit realizes that her own selfishness is implacably driving her into an endless, pointless, pleasureless game of one-upmanship with Mrs. Merdle. Similarly in *Great Expectations* the "gentleman's" world which entraps Pip is symbolized by the decaying prison-house where all the clocks have been stopped at the moment of Miss Havisham's humiliation, the rest of her life consisting only of brooding on that moment.

The obstructing society in Dickens has two main characteristics: it is parasitic and it is pedantic. It is parasitic in the sense of setting up false values and loyalties which destroy the freedom of all those who accept them, as well as tyrannizing over many of those who do not. Dickens's implicit social vision is also radical, to an extent he hardly realized himself, in dividing society between workers and idlers, and in seeing in much of the leisure class a social sanctioning of parasitism. As for its pedantry, it is traditional in New Comedy to set up a pragmatic standard, based on experience, as a norm, and contrast it with the theoretical approaches to life typical of humors who cannot escape from their reflex responses. Like Blake, like every writer with any genuine radicalism in him, Dickens finds the really dangerous social evils in those which have achieved some acceptance by being rationalized. Already in *Oliver Twist* the word "experience" stands as a contrast to the words "experimental" and "philosophical," which are invariably pejorative. This contrast comes into Bumble's famous "the law is a ass" speech. In *Hard Times* the pedantry of the obstructing society is associated with a utilitarian philosophy and an infantile trust in facts, statistics, and all impersonal and generalized forms of knowledge. We may wonder why Dickens denounces this philosophy so earnestly and caricatures it so crudely, instead of letting its absurdities speak for themselves. But

it is clear that *Hard Times,* of all Dickens's stories, comes nearest
to being what in our day is sometimes called the dystopia, the book
which, like *Brave New World* or *1984,* shows us the nightmare
world that results from certain perverse tendencies inherent in society getting free play. The most effective dystopias are likely to be
those in which the author isolates certain features in his society that
most directly threaten his own social function as a writer. Dickens
sees in the cult of facts and statistics a threat, not to the realistic
novelist, and not only to a life based on concrete and personal relations, but to the unfettered imagination, the mind that can respond
to fairy tales and fantasy and understand their relevance to reality.
The insistence on the importance of fairy tales, nursery rhymes, and
similar genres in education often meets us in Dickens, and implies
that Dickens's fairy-tale plots are regarded by Dickens himself as
an essential part of his novels.

The action of a comedy moves toward an identity which is usually
a social identity. In Dickens the family, or a group analogous to a
family, is the key to social identity. Hence his recognition scenes
are usually genealogical, concerned with discovering unknown fathers and mothers or articulating the correct family relationships.
There are often three sets of parental figures attached to a central
character, with several doubles of each. First are the actual parents.
These are often dead before the story begins, like the fathers of
Nicholas Nickleby and David Copperfield, or stagger on weakly for
a few pages, like David Copperfield's mother, or are mysterious and
emerge at the end, sometimes as bare names unrelated to the story,
like Oliver Twist's father or the parents of Little Nell. The father
of Sissy Jupe in *Hard Times* deserts her without ever appearing in
the novel; the first things we see in *Great Expectations* are the
tombstones of Pip's parents. Pip himself is brought up by a sister
who is twenty years older and (as we learn on practically the last
page of the book) has the same name as his mother. Next come the
parental figures of the obstructing society, generally cruel or foolish,
and often descended from the harsh step-parents of folktale. Murdstone and his sister, Pip's sister, the pseudo-mothers of Esther Summerson and Clennam, belong to this group. One very frequent device which combines these two types of relationship is that of the
preternaturally loving and hard-working daughter who is the sole
support of a weak or foolish father. We have, among others, Little
Dorrit, Little Nell, whose grandfather is a compulsive gambler,

Jenny Wren in *Our Mutual Friend* with her drunken "child," Madeline Bray in *Nicholas Nickleby*, and, in a different way, Florence Dombey. Naturally the marriage of such a heroine, following on the death of the parent, transfers her to the more congenial society. Finally we have the parental or avuncular figures of the congenial society itself, those who take on a protective relation to the central characters as the story approaches its conclusion. Brownlow in *Oliver Twist*, who adopts the hero, Jarndyce in *Bleak House*, Abel Magwitch in *Great Expectations*, the Cheeryble brothers in *Nicholas Nickleby*, the Boffins in *Our Mutual Friend*, are examples. Abel Magwitch, besides being the ultimate father of Pip, is also the actual father of Estella, which makes Estella in a sense Pip's sister: this was doubtless one reason why Dickens so resisted the conventional ending of marriage for these two. The more realistic developments of New Comedy tend to eliminate this genealogical apparatus. When one of the girls in *Les Précieuses Ridicules* announces that being so interesting a girl she is quite sure that her real parents are much more interesting people than the ones she appears to have, we do not take her very seriously. But Dickens is always ready to cooperate with the lonely child's fantasies about lost congenial parents, and this marks his affinity with the romantic side of the tradition, the side related to Classical romance.

I have used the word "anarchistic" in connection with Dickens's view of society, but it is clear that, so far as his comic structure leads to any sort of vision of a social ideal, that ideal would have to be an intensely paternalistic society, an expanded family. We get a somewhat naïve glimpse of this with the Cheeryble brothers in *Nicholas Nickleby*, giving a party where the faithful servitors are brought in at the end for a drink of champagne, expressing undying loyalty and enthusiasm for the patronizing social arrangements. The reader gets the uneasy feeling that he is listening to the commercial. When in *Little Dorrit* Tattycoram runs away from the suffocating geniality of the Meagles family she has to be brought back repentant, though she may well have had much more of the reader's sympathy than Dickens intended her to have. Even the Dedlock ménage in *Bleak House*, hopeless social anachronism as Dickens clearly recognizes it to be, is still close enough to a family to gather a fair amount of the society of the novel around it at the end. In contrast, social parasites often assume the role of a false father. Examples include the Marquis in *A Tale of Two Cities* whose assassin is technically guilty of parricide, Sir Joseph Bowley, the Urizenic friend and father of the poor in *The Chimes,* and the elder Chester in *Barnaby Rudge.*

In New Comedy the obstructing humors absorb most of the character interest: the heroes and heroines are seldom individualized. Such characters as Bonario in *Volpone* or Valère in *Tartuffe* are only pleasant young men. In Dickens too the heroes and heroines resemble humors only in the fact that their responses are predictable, but they are predictable in terms of a norm, and they seldom if ever appear in the ridiculous or self-binding role of the humor. Such characters, who encourage the reader to identify with them, and who might be called norm-figures, could not exist in serious twentieth-century fiction, which belongs to the ironic mode, and sees all its characters as affected in some degree by hampering social forces. But they have some validity in nineteenth-century low mimetic conventions, which present only what ·is conventionally presentable, and whose heroes and heroines may therefore logically be models of presentability.

Comedy usually depicts the triumph of the young over the old, but Dickens is unusual among comic writers in that so many of his heroes and heroines are children, or are described in ways that associate them with childhood. Nobody has described more vividly than Dickens the reactions of a sensitive child in a Brobdingnagian world dominated by noisome and blundering adults. And because nearly all these children are predestined to belong to the congenial society, they can only be hurt, not corrupted, by the obstructing society. The one striking exception is Pip, whose detachment from the false standards of the obstructing group forms the main theme of *Great Expectations.* But David Copperfield is only superficially affected by his environment, and Oliver Twist escapes from the activities of the Fagin gang as miraculously as Marina does from the brothel in Shakespeare's *Pericles.* Usually this predestined child-figure is a girl. Many of the heroines, even when grown women, are described as "little" or are compared to fairies. A frequent central theme in Dickens is the theme of *Alice in Wonderland:* the descent of the invulnerable girl-child into a grotesque world. In the preface to *The Old Curiosity Shop* Dickens speaks of his interest in the beauty-and-beast archetype, of the girl-child surrounded by monsters, some of them amiable like Kit, others sinister like Quilp. Little Nell descends to this grotesque world and then rejoins the angels; the other heroines marry into the congenial society. The girl-child among grotesques recurs in Florence Dombey's protection by Captain Cuttle, in Little Dorrit's mothering of Maggie, and in many similar scenes. Sometimes an amiable grotesque, Toots or Kit or Smike or Chivery, will attach himself to such a girl-child figure, not good enough to marry her but protesting eternal devotion nonetheless, a kind of late farcical vestige of the Courtly Love convention. Nobody turns up in *The Old Curiosity Shop* good enough to marry Little Nell, which is doubtless one reason why she dies. We may also notice the role of the old curiosity shop itself: it plays little part in the story, but is a kind of threshold symbol of the entrance into the grotesque world, like the rabbit-hole and mirror in the Alice books. Its counterparts appear in the Wooden Midshipman shop in *Dombey and Son,* the Peggotty cottage in *David Copperfield,* the bone-shop of Venus in *Our Mutual Friend,* and elsewhere.

Many of the traditional features of romantic New Comedy reached their highest point of development in nineteenth-century Britain, making it the obvious time and place for a great genius in that form to emerge. One of these, already glanced at, is the domination of narrative genres, along with a moribund drama. Dickens had many dramatic interests, but his genius was for serial romance and not for the stage. Another is the Victorian assumption of moral standards shared between author and reader. This feature makes for melodrama, where the reader emotionally participates in the moral conflict of hero and villain, or of virtue and temptation. The rigidity, or assumed rigidity, of Victorian sexual mores is a great help to a nineteenth-century plot, as it enables an author, not only to make a Wagnerian noise about a woman's extramarital escapade, but to make the most frenzied activity on her part plausible as an effort to conceal the results of it. But the relation of melodrama to the foreground action is far more important than this.

A realistic writer in the New Comedy tradition tends to work out his action on one plane: young and old, hero and humor, struggle for power within the same social group. The more romantic the writer, the more he tends to set over against his humorous world another kind of world, with which the romantic side of his story is associated. In a paper presented to the English Institute nearly twenty years ago, I spoke of the action of romantic Shakespearean comedy as divided between a foreground world of humors and a background "green world," associated with magic, sleep and dreams, and enchanted forests or houses, from which the comic resolution comes. Dickens has no green world, except for a glint or two here and there (e.g., the pastoral retreats in which Smike and Little Nell end their days, Jenny Wren's paradisal dreams, the "beanstalk" abode of Tartar in *Edwin Drood*, and the like), but he does have his own way of dividing his action. I have spoken of the nineteenth-century emphasis on the presentable, on the world of public appearance to which the nineteenth-century novelist is almost entirely confined. Behind this world lies a vast secret world, the world of privacy, where there is little or no communication. For Dickens this world is associated mainly with dreams, memories, and death. He describes it very eloquently at the opening of the third "Quarter" of *The Chimes*, and again in the first paragraph of the third chapter of *A Tale of Two Cities*, besides referring frequently to it throughout his work.

Few can read Dickens without catching the infection of his intense curiosity about the life that lies in the dark houses behind the lights of his loved and hated London. We recognize it even at second hand: when Dylan Thomas's *Under Milk Wood* opens on a night of private dreams we can see an unmistakably Dickensian influence. For most of the ironic fiction of the twentieth century, this secret world is essentially the bedroom and bathroom world of ordinary privacy, as well as the world of sexual drives, perversions, repressions, and infantile fixations that not only complements the public world but conditions one's behavior in it at every point. Characters in twentieth-century fiction have no privacy: there is no distinction between dressing-room and stage. Dickens is by no means unaware of the importance of this aspect of the hidden world, but it is of little use to him as a novelist, and he shows no restiveness about being obliged to exclude it. This is because he is not primarily an ironic writer, like Joyce or Flaubert. What he is really curious about is a hidden world of *romantic* interest, not a world even more squalid and commonplace than the visible one. His detective interest in hidden life is comparable to other aspects of Victorian culture: one thinks of the pre-Raphaelite paintings where we are challenged to guess what kind of story is being told by the picture and its enigmatic title, or of all the poems of Browning that appeal to us to deduce the reality hidden behind what is presented.

In following the main action of a Dickens novel we are frequently aware of a second form of experience being held up to it like a mirror. Sometimes this is explicitly the world of the stage. The kind of entertainment afforded by the Vincent Crummles troop in *Nicholas Nickleby* parallels the uninhibited melodrama of the main story: the dance of the savage and the Infant Phenomenon, in particular, mirrors the Dickensian theme of the girl-child in the monster-world. In *Hard Times,* where the relation is one of contrast, a circus company symbolizes an approach to experience that Gradgrind has missed out on. The Punch and Judy show in *The Old Curiosity Shop,* one of several popular dramatic entertainments in that book, has been mentioned, and in *Great Expectations* Pip, haunted by the ghost of a father, goes to see Mr. Wopsle in *Hamlet.* Then again, Dickens makes considerable use of the curious convention in New Comedy of the doubled character, who is often literally a twin. In *The Comedy of Errors* the foreground Ephesus and the background Syracuse, in *Twelfth Night* the melancholy courts of Orsino and Olivia, are brought into alignment by twins. Similarly, the foreground action of *Little Dorrit* is related to the background action partly through the concealed twin brother of Flintwinch. In *A Tale of Two Cities,* where the twin theme is at its most complicated, the resemblance of Darnay and Carton brings the two cities themselves into alignment. In *Dombey and Son* the purse-proud world of Dombey and the other social world that it tries to ignore are aligned by the parallel, explicitly alluded to, between Edith Dombey and Alice Brown. There are many other forms of doubling, both of characters and of action, that I have no space here to examine.

The basis for such a dividing of the action might be generalized as follows. There is a hidden and private world of dream and death, out of which all the energy of human life comes. The primary manifestation of this world, in experience, is in acts of destructive violence and passion. It is the source of war, cruelty, arrogance, lust, and grinding the faces of the poor. It produces the haughty lady with her guilty secret, like Lady Dedlock or Edith Dombey or Mrs. Clennam, the lynching mobs that hunt Bill Sikes to death or proclaim the charity of the Protestant religion in *Barnaby Rudge,* the flogging schoolmasters and the hanging judges. It also produces the courage to fight against these things, and the instinctive virtue that repudiates them. In short, the hidden world expresses itself most directly in melodramatic action and rhetoric. It is not so much better or worse than the ordinary world of experience, as a world in which good and evil appear as much stronger and less disguised forces. We may protest that its moods are exaggerated, its actions unlikely, its rhetoric stilted and unconvincing. But if it were not there nothing else in Dickens would be there. We notice that the mainspring of melodramatic action is, like that of humorous action, mainly obsession. We notice too that Dickens's hair-raising descriptions, like that of Marseilles at the opening of *Little Dorrit* with its repetition of "stare," are based on the same kind of associative rhetoric as the speech of the humors.

From this point of view we can look at the foreground action of the humors in a new light. Humors are, so to speak, petrified by-products of the kind of energy that melodrama expresses more directly. Even the most contemptible humors, the miserly Fledgeby or the hypocritical Heep, are exuberantly miserly and hypocritical: their vices express an energy that possesses them because they cannot possess it. The world they operate in, so far as it is a peaceable and law-abiding world, is a world of very imperfectly suppressed violence. They never escape from the shadow of a power which is at once Eros and Thanatos, and are bound to a passion that is never satisfied by its rationalized objects, but is ultimately self-destructive. In the earlier novels the emotional focus of this self-destroying passion is usually a miser, or a person in some way obsessed with money, like Ralph Nickleby, Dombey, Little Nell's grandfather, or Jonas Chuzzlewit. The folktale association of money and excrement, which points to the psychological origin of miserliness, appears in the "Golden Dustman" theme of *Our Mutual Friend*, and is perhaps echoed in the names Murdstone and Merdle. In the later novels a more explicitly erotic drive gives us the victim-villain figures of Bradley Headstone and Jasper Drood. Food and animals are other images that Dickens often uses in sexual contexts, especially when a miser aspires to a heroine. Arthur Gride in *Nicholas Nickleby* speaks of Madeline Bray as a tasty morsel, and Uriah Heep is compared to a whole zoo of unpleasant animals: the effect is to give an Andromeda pattern to the heroine's situation, and suggest a demonic ferocity behind the domestic foreground. The same principle of construction causes the stock-response humors like Podsnap or Gradgrind to take on a peculiar importance. They represent the fact that an entire society can become mechanized like a humor, or fossilized into institutions. This could happen to Victorian England, according to *Hard Times*, if it takes the gospel of facts and statistics too literally, and did happen to prerevolutionary France, as described in *A Tale of Two Cities,* dying of what Dickens calls "the leprosy of unreality," and awaiting the melodramatic deluge of the Revolution.

The obstructing humors cannot escape from the ritual habits that they have set up to deal with this disconcerting energy that has turned them into mechanical puppets. The heroes and heroines, however, along with some of the more amiable humors, have the power to plunge into the hidden world of dreams and death, and, though narrowly escaping death in the process, gain from it a renewed life and energy. Sometimes this plunge into the hidden world is symbolized by a distant voyage. The incredible Australia that makes a magistrate out of Wilkins Micawber also enables the hunted convict Magwitch to become an ambiguous but ultimately genuine fairy godfather. Walter Gay in *Dombey and Son* returns from the West Indies, remarkably silent, long after he has been given up for dead, and the reader follows Martin Chuzzlewit into a place, ironically called Eden, where he is confidently expected to die and nearly does die, but where he goes through a metamorphosis of character that fits him for the comic conclusion. Other characters, including Dick Swiveller, Pip, and Esther Summerson, go into a delirious illness with the same result. *Our Mutual Friend* has a complex pattern of resurrection imagery connected with dredging the Thames, reviving from drowning, finding treasure buried in dust-heaps, and the like; a similar pattern of digging up the dead in *A Tale of Two Cities* extends from the stately Dr. Manette to the grotesque Jerry Cruncher. We notice too that the sinister society is often introduced in a kind of wavering light between sleep and waking: the appearance of the faces of Fagin and Monks at Oliver Twist's window and the alleged dreams of Abbie Flintwinch in *Little Dorrit* are examples. The most uninhibited treatment of this plunge into the world of death and dreams occurs, as we should expect, in the Christmas Books, where Scrooge and Trotty Veck see in vision a tragic version of their own lives, and one which includes their own deaths, then wake up to renewed festivity. It seems clear that the hidden world, though most of its more direct expressions are destructive and terrible, contains within itself an irresistible power of renewing life.

The hidden world is thus, once again in literature, the world of an invincible Eros, the power strong enough to force a happy ending on the story in defiance of all probability, pushing all the obstructing humors out of the way, or killing them if they will not get out of the way, getting the attractive young people disentangled from their brothers and sisters and headed for the right beds. It dissolves all hardening social institutions and reconstitutes society on its sexual basis of the family, the shadowy old fathers and mothers being replaced by new and livelier successors. When a sympathetic character dies, a strongly religious projection of this power often appears: the "Judgment" expected shortly by Miss Flite in *Bleak House,* for instance, stands in apocalyptic contrast to the Chancery court. Dickens's Eros world is, above all, a designing and manipulating power. The obstructing humor can do only what his humor makes him do, and toward the end of the story he becomes the helpless pawn of a chess game in which black can never ultimately win.

The victorious hidden world is not the world of nature in the Rousseauistic context of that word. The people who talk about this kind of nature in Dickens are such people as Mrs. Merdle in *Little Dorrit,* Mrs. Chick in *Dombey and Son,* and Wackford Squeers—not an encouraging lot. Like most romancers, Dickens gives a prominent place to the fool or "natural"—Smike, Mr. Dick, Barnaby Rudge—whose instincts make up for retarded intelligence. But such people are privileged: elsewhere nature and *social* education, or human experience, are always associated. To say that Dora Copperfield is an unspoiled child of nature is also to say that she is a spoiled child. Dickens's nature is a human nature which is the same kind of thing as the power that creates art, a designing and shaping power. This is also true of Shakespeare's green world, but Dickens's Eros world is not the conserving force that the green world is, which revitalizes a society without altering its structure. At the end of a Shakespeare comedy there is usually a figure of authority, like Prospero or the various dukes, who represents this social conservation. We have nothing in Dickens to correspond to such figures: the nearest to them are the empty Santa Claus masks of the Cheerybles, Boffin, and the reformed Scrooge. For all its domestic and sentimental Victorian setting, there is a revolutionary and subversive, almost a nihilistic, quality in Dickens's melodrama that is post-Romantic, has inherited the experience of the French Revolution, and looks forward to the world of Freud, Marx, and the existential thriller.

I used the word "absurd" earlier about Dickens's melodramatic plots, suggesting that they were creatively and not incompetently absurd. In our day the word "absurd" usually refers to the absence of purpose or meaning in life and experience, the so-called metaphysical absurd. But for literary criticism the formulating of the theory of the absurd should not be left entirely to disillusioned theologians. In literature it is design, the forming and shaping power, that is absurd. Real life does not start or stop; it never ties up loose ends; it never manifests meaning or purpose except by blind accident; it is never comic or tragic, ironic or romantic, or anything else that has a shape. Whatever gives form and pattern to fiction, whatever technical skill keeps us turning the pages to get to the end, is absurd, and contradicts our sense of reality. The great Victorian realists subordinate their storytelling skill to their representational skill. Theirs is a dignified, leisurely vehicle that gives us time to look at the scenery. They have formed our stock responses to fiction, so that even when traveling at the much higher speed of drama, romance, or epic we still keep trying to focus our eyes on the incidental and transient. Most of us feel that there is something else in Dickens, something elemental, yet unconnected with either realistic clarity or philosophical profundity. What it is connected with is a kind of story that fully gratifies the hope expressed, according to Lewis Carroll, by the original of Alice, that "there will be nonsense in it." The silliest character in *Nicholas Nickleby* is the hero's mother, a romancer who keeps dreaming of impossible happy endings for her children. But the story itself follows her specifications and not those of the sensible people. The obstructing humors in Dickens are absurd because they have overdesigned their lives. But the kind of design that they parody is produced by another kind of energy, and one which insists, absurdly and yet irresistibly, that what is must never take final precedence over what ought to be.

JOHN BUTT

The Serial Publication of Dickens's Novels
Martin Chuzzlewit and *Little Dorrit*

Nowadays we are accustomed to novels being published in single volumes, but 120 years ago this form of publication was unusual. In the eighteenth century novels had appeared in five, or even in nine volumes, and by the time of Scott and Jane Austen the favourite number was three or four. The prices varied; but it was not uncommon to charge as much as half-a-guinea a volume, which made novel-reading exceedingly expensive for those who did not belong to a circulating library. These were the conditions ruling when Dickens began to write. His first novel, *Pickwick Papers,* shows him attempting to reach a larger number of readers by cutting the price to suit their pockets, and the method he chose was to publish in serial.

During the course of his career he tried several types of serial. Thus *Oliver Twist* was published monthly in *Bentley's Miscellany; The Old Curiosity Shop* and *Barnaby Rudge* were published weekly in *Master Humphrey's Clock; Hard Times* and *Great Expectations* appeared weekly, the first in *Household Words* and the second in *All The Year Round;* while for *A Tale of Two Cities* he adopted a

From *Pope, Dickens and Others: Essays and Addresses* (Edinburgh: Edinburgh University Press; and Chicago: Aldine Publishing Company, 1969), pp. 149-64. Copyright © by Mrs. E. M. Butt. Reprinted by permission of Mrs. Butt and the publishers. The essay was originally read at Cambridge in 1958.

70

simultaneous publication of weekly and monthly issues. For the remainder of his novels he chose the monthly serial part, which he had first used in *Pickwick*. It is with this form only that I shall concern myself.

The serial form of the monthly part was determined during the writing of *Pickwick*. Dickens himself tells us of the decision to increase the number of pages after the first two issues from twenty-four a month (or three half-sheets) to thirty-two (or two whole-sheets); and thirty-two pages was always thereafter to be his monthly stint. This provided enough room for three or four chapters; never more, except in the final "double" number, though in *Pickwick*, nos. x and xii, and *Chuzzlewit*, nos. ii, iv, v, and vii there are only two. There are no monthly numbers consisting of a single chapter; and the six I have named are the only numbers with two. The appeal of three or four chapters seems originally to have been that they gave the opportunity for the diversity of material which Dickens was accustomed to supplying in the magazine. Thus the third number of *Pickwick* (chapters vi-viii), which was the first of thirty-two pages, is designedly miscellaneous in content, with Mr. Tupman's amorous adventure, the sporting humour of Mr. Winkle's shooting and the cricket match, some comic oratory, a set of verses ("The Ivy Green"), and a grim short story of "The Convict's Return." Few numbers in the later novels so obviously imitate a magazine's contents, though in *Chuzzlewit* he will still offer his readers a magazine sketch from time to time. "Town and Todgers's" (chapter ix) in no. iv clearly recalls the original Boz, and that manner is seen only a little less clearly in the proceedings of the Anglo-Bengalee Disinterested Loan and Life Assurance Company of no. xi (chapters xxvii-xxix). Sketches of this kind disappear from the novels after *Chuzzlewit*, a sign that Dickens by that time was making a clearer distinction between the novel and the magazine.

But though these sketches disappear in the interests of a more closely integrated novel, Dickens still usually likes to see his three or four chapters as an opportunity for variety of incident and manner. He will occasionally give us homogeneous numbers; and the three American numbers, vii, ix, and xiii (chapters xvi-xvii, xxi-xxiii, xxxiii-xxxv), are notable instances, for these instalments are solely concerned with the experiences of Martin and Mark Tapley in the United States; but in contrast with these there is the variety offered by such a number as viii (chapters xviii-xx), which contains the death of Anthony Chuzzlewit, the first introduction of Mrs. Gamp, and Jonas's engagement to Mercy Pecksniff. Scarcely less diverse is no. xviii (chapters xlviii-l), which begins with Young Martin's early morning visit to Tom Pinch and the revelations of Lewsome, goes on to Mrs. Gamp's quarrel with Mrs. Prig, and ends with Old Martin announcing himself to Tom Pinch as his employer.

In *Little Dorrit* the only number to match the American numbers of *Chuzzlewit* in homogeneity is no. xviii (Book ii, chapters xxvii-xxix), which is devoted to Arthur Clennam's experiences in the Marshalsea. Diversity, then, would seem to be Dickens's policy, as he faced the writing of the great majority of his monthly instalments; and though he may have begun by aiming at variety in imitation of the magazine, he was induced to continue to keep this end in view by the varied strands of his plots.

Though nowadays we normally read Dickens's novels without paying attention to their serial divisions, it is important for us to recognize that that was impossible for his first readers. They were originally confined to their thirty-two pages, which they could easily read on the evening of publication. Their reading was therefore subject to long and frequent interruptions; and though they must certainly have had the impression of watching the development of a single work of art, to which each instalment made its contribution, they must also have been aware that each number had its identity —its physical identity, obviously, when bound by its green paper covers, but its identity as a structural unit as well. This would have been at its clearest on the rare occasions when the contents were homogeneous; but elsewhere there would have been the impression of a slow, gradual unfolding of the plot. And Dickens helps his readers to accept the identity of the unit by paying attention to the manner in which it begins and ends. He seems to have felt that the ending was the more important, for he never panders to readers' forgetfulness by summarizing past events, he rarely even refers to them, and he never uses such a phrase as "last month" or "in the last number." I quote a few instances from *Chuzzlewit* to show the utmost he is prepared to do in helping his reader pick up the thread after a month's interval:

> No. ix. The knocking at Mr Pecksniff's door, though loud enough, bore no resemblance whatever to the noise of an American railway train at full speed. It may be well to begin the present chapter with

this frank admission, lest the reader should imagine that the sounds now deafening this history's ears have any connection. . . .[1]

No. XII. As the surgeon's first care after amputating a limb is to take up the arteries the cruel knife has severed, so it is the duty of this history, which in its remorseless course has cut from the Pecksniffian trunk its right arm, Mercy, to look to the parent stem, and see how in all its various ramifications it got on without her.[2]

No. XVII. Tom Pinch and his sister having to part, for the dispatch of the morning's business, immediately after the dispersion of the other actors in the scene upon the wharf with which the reader has already been acquainted, had no opportunity of discussing the subject at that time. But Tom, in his solitary office. . . .[3]

But the *conclusion* of each number is a different matter. In the first number of *Pickwick*, Dickens had been constrained to bring the number to a close in the middle of a chapter; but elsewhere he always contrived that the end of a number and the end of a chapter should coincide. But the end of the final chapter of a number necessarily involves a longer pause than the end of any other chapter provides, and how is that to be treated? It is popularly believed that the serial writer tries to reach a moment of apprehension, that he suspends his narrative at an emotional climax, leaving his readers in anxiety for what is to come. There are some instances of these melodramatic endings in *Chuzzlewit*, notably VIII, where Tom Pinch announces the arrival of old Martin in Mr. Pecksniff's village, while Jonas is in his house:

> "Dear, dear!" cried Tom, "what have I done? I hoped it would be a pleasant surprise, sir. I thought you would like to know."
> But at that moment a loud knocking was heard at the hall-door.[4]

And X, where Chuffey greets the newly-married Mercy:

> "You are not married?" he said, eagerly. "Not married?"
> "Yes. A month ago. Good Heaven, what is the matter?"
> He answered nothing was the matter; and turned from her. But in her fear and wonder, turning also, she saw him raise his trembling hands above his head, and heard him say:
> "Oh! woe, woe, woe, upon this wicked house!" It was her welcome,—HOME.[5]

More grossly melodramatic is the conclusion of XVII with Jonas's return to London after the murder of Montague Tigg:

> Whether he attended to their talk, or tried to think of other things, or talked himself, or held his peace, or resolutely counted the dull tickings of a hoarse clock at his back, he always lapsed, as if a spell were on him, into eager listening. For he knew it must come; and his present punishment, and torture, and distraction, were, to listen for its coming.
> Hush![6]

There is nothing equivalent to that in *Little Dorrit*. The closest in excitement is the end of IX, where at last Pancks reveals to Clennam the result of his researches:

> "We've been at it, night and day, for I don't know how long. Mr Rugg, you know how long? Never mind. Don't say. You'll only confuse me. You shall tell her, Mr Clennam. Not till we give you leave. Where's that rough total, Mr Rugg? Oh! Here we are! There, sir! That's what you'll have to break to her. That man's your Father of the Marshalsea!"[7]

But whereas the three *Chuzzlewit* numbers were terminated in a mood of apprehension, the *Dorrit* number ends on a climax of excitement. It would take too long to classify all the terminations, and would not serve much purpose. There are those which, while clearly pointing to future action, arrive at an acceptable moment of rest; such is Mark Tapley's view of the Land of Liberty at the conclusion of the bad Atlantic crossing in no. VIII. There is the picturesque ending of *Dorrit,* no. III, where we see in the light of dawn John Baptist Cavalletto running away from his patron (Book 1, chapter xi), or the more contrived grouping of Little Dorrit and Maggy sleeping in St. George's vestry at the end of no. IV (chapter xiv), and John Chivery's new inscription for his gravestone at the end of V (chapter xviii). My point is that the end is recognized and designed in various ways as a suitable point of rest, even though the rest is sometimes charged with apprehension.

Yet though each number had its separate identity, it was planned to make a contribution to a larger whole. In the 1837 Preface to *Pickwick,* Dickens describes what he was attempting to do:

The publication of the book in monthly numbers, containing only thirty-two pages in each, rendered it an object of paramount importance that, while the different incidents were linked together by a chain of interest strong enough to prevent their appearing unconnected or impossible, the general design should be so simple as to sustain no injury from this detached and desultory form of publication, extending over no fewer than twenty months. In short, it was necessary—or it appeared so to the Author—that every number should be, to a certain extent, complete in itself, and yet that the whole twenty numbers, when collected, should form one tolerably harmonious whole, each leading to the other by a gentle and not unnatural progress of adventure.

It is obvious that in a work published with a view to such considerations, no artfully interwoven or ingeniously complicated plot can with reason be expected.

So far as organization was concerned, he was not setting himself a very exacting task in *Pickwick*. One number more or less than twenty for that novel would not have mattered very much. But still, twenty numbers had been stipulated, perhaps for no better reason than that twenty shillings make one pound, and he was determined not to alter the decision. The original advertisement had specified "about twenty numbers," and an Address prefaced to *Pickwick* no. x declared his "intention to adhere to his original pledge."

The length of *Pickwick* determined the length of every subsequent monthly novel, except *Edwin Drood,* designed for completion in twelve, and this exact prescription became an important factor as soon as he began to pay more attention to plot. This happened in the very next novel, *Nicholas Nickleby*. Although the preface still shows him thinking in terms of the periodical essay and using the words of an eighteenth-century periodical essayist to justify his work, it was during the progress of that novel that he began to meditate a plot. It is certainly neither "artful" nor "ingenious," and it in no way corresponds to the theme of the book; but there it is, manifest for the first time in no. xiv (chapters xliii-xlv), when Dickens has only six months more in front of him, and must devise some means of bringing the book to a close.

In *Martin Chuzzlewit* and in each of the later novels, Dickens set out with a theme in mind and devised a plot to help him in expounding that theme. His success in *Chuzzlewit* is not so striking as in the later novels, but there is no doubting his intentions: "I set out, on this journey which is now concluded, with the design of exhibiting, in various aspects, the commonest of all vices"; so he writes in the original preface, and the last words of the first Number explain what that commonest of all vices is: " 'Oh self, self, self! Every man for himself, and no creature for me!' Universal self! Was there nothing of its shadow in these reflections, and in the history of Martin Chuzzlewit, on his own showing?"[8] And that Dickens has kept that theme before him, we have at least his word in the original preface, written after completing the novel:

> I have endeavoured in the progress of this Tale, to resist the temptation of the current Monthly Number, and to keep a steadier eye upon the general purpose and design. With this object in view, I have put a strong constraint upon myself from time to time, in many places; and I hope the story is the better for it, now.

The theme demanded more attention to design than he had paid in *Pickwick* and *Nickleby*. It was not merely a question of illustrating aspects of selfishness in such characters as Pecksniff, Jonas, and the two Martins, and of unselfishness in Mark Tapley, John Westlock, and Tom Pinch, but the action must also serve to punish Pecksniff and Jonas, and to work a cure upon the two Martins. The punishment of Pecksniff requires the deception played upon him by Old Martin, and preparations are made for that as early as chapter vi, the first chapter of no. iii, where Pecksniff arranges to go up to London with his daughters at Old Martin's behest.

At what point Dickens decided upon the manner of Jonas's punishment, it is difficult to determine; but if he foresaw the murder of Montague Tigg as soon as Jonas became involved in the Anglo-Bengalee, we must place it no earlier than no. xi (chapters xxvii-xxix). But the murder of Tigg is no more than an exacerbation of Jonas's offences. The death of Anthony occurs in no. viii, and the first indications of Jonas's distaste for his father appear in chapter xi, the first chapter of no. v, but not, I think, any earlier. It is also part of Jonas's function to ruin Pecksniff, his father-in-law, and this he does in no. xvi, in a scene which Thackeray especially admired, where Jonas triumphs at the very moment when Pecksniff thinks he is achieving his masterpiece of dissembling (chapter xliv). But for Jonas to be placed in the necessary relationship with Pecksniff, the marriage with Mercy must be arranged, and that takes us back to no. IV (chapters ix-x).

Now to speak of these incidents being designed implies some premeditation on Dickens's part; yet Forster tells us that Dickens began his work hurriedly, altered his course at the opening, and saw little at that moment of the main track of his design. The letters substantiate Forster in part at least. There was no prolonged period of incubation. Throughout the late summer and autumn of 1842, he was fully occupied with *American Notes,* which was not disposed of until the end of October. He then immediately went upon a short trip to Cornwall to look for the opening scene of a new book. Whatever his scheme was, it was found impracticable. His correspondence with John Leech in the first week of November shows him in the process of considering it and turning it down. Yet as early as 12 November he writes to Miss Coutts that he is "in the agonies of plotting and contriving a new book," by 8 December the first Number was "nearly done," and on 31 December it was published.[9] There was certainly little enough time for premeditation. But, as I have already said, the theme of self is propounded in the first Number, and there Pecksniff opens his designs on Old Martin. Old Martin's plans are laid in no. III (chapters vi-viii), and Jonas plans to marry Mercy in no. IV (chapters ix-x). There is room enough for growth under his hands in the very process of writing, and I feel doubtful whether, for example, he foresaw the possibilities of Jonas deceiving Pecksniff in no. XVI (chapters xlii-xliv) when he chose a wife for Jonas in IV. But my point is this, that from an early stage in the novel he has to take his decisions knowing he has about 624 pages at his disposal, divided into twenty monthly parts. Obviously Old Martin must reveal himself to Pecksniff in his true colours in the last Number. How much should be disposed of before then? Young Martin should be cured, should seek to reconcile himself with his grandfather, and should be rebuffed by Pecksniff. Therefore Young Martin must be brought back from America soon enough to allow for that. In fact he returns in XIII (in chapter xxxv), though that may have been less because he needed Martin in England, than because he had grown tired of America.

The unfolding of the subplot relating to Jonas may well have caused more trouble. Though the Anglo-Bengalee complications are opened as early as no. XV (in chapter xxvii), there is no room to develop them until the end of XIV (chapters xxxvi-xxxviii), partly because Martin has to be brought back from America, but largely because Dickens has allowed Tom Pinch to become a pet character and to steal more than his share of space. But once the Anglo-Bengalee is resumed in xiv, there is obviously little time to spare. In xv (chapters xxxix-xli) Jonas is stopped from making off to the Continent, in xvi (chapters xlii-xliv) he goes down to Wiltshire to seduce Pecksniff, in xvii (chapters xlv-xlvii) he murders Montague Tigg, in xviii (chapters xlviii-l) Lewsome reveals what he knows, and in the first chapter (li) of xix/xx Jonas commits suicide. It looks as though Dickens has kept a sharp eye on the decreasing number of pages at his disposal from no. xiv onwards.

If he had lived in the previous generation, I suspect that he would have found his task a little easier, since the convention of the three-volume novel acted as a constant reminder to a novelist of the point which he had reached in his story. We can observe even so comparatively reckless a novelist as Scott taking his bearings as he moves from one volume to the next. But a novel of 624 large octavo pages is an unwieldy size; and even when divided into units of thirty-two it seems to require some larger grouping to make its form felt. After *Martin Chuzzlewit* Dickens was to write three more novels with no other division than chapter and number. These were *Dombey and Son, David Copperfield,* and *Bleak House.* But during the writing of his next novel, *Hard Times,* a weekly serial, he made a note in his memoranda, which reads "Republish in three books? 1. Sowing. 2. Reaping. 3. Garnering." The device of dividing into books was not a new one. Fielding had adopted it from the epic in *Joseph Andrews,* and many novelists had followed him. What perhaps attracted Dickens's attention was Thackeray's refinement in *Esmond* (1852) of not merely numbering his books, as the custom was, but of naming them too. At any rate when *Hard Times* was reissued in volume form, it was divided into three books with the titles I have mentioned; and except for *Edwin Drood,* every subsequent novel was divided into books, even in the serial issue.

The most attractive example is *Great Expectations,* which is divided into three equal parts of nineteen chapters, representing the three stages of Pip's expectations. The first stage ends with the announcement of his expectations and his move to London, and the second ends with the return of Pip's unknown benefactor, the convict Magwitch. Who can doubt that the reader's sense of the larger movements in the story is assisted by these divisions; and who can doubt, as he contemplates this threefold structure, that all was carefully planned from the beginning?

Little Dorrit[10] is also divided into books, "Book the First. Poverty," "Book the Second. Riches," but this was not part of the original conception of the novel. Professor Kathleen Tillotson[11] has shown that the original title of the novel, *Nobody's Fault,* was abandoned, in all probability, during the writing of chapter xii, the first chapter of no. iv, not long before the publication of no. i, and a new title, *Little Dorrit,* was substituted. The sub-title, "Book the First. Poverty," was added in proof. It could not, of course, have had any relevance to the original title, *Nobody's Fault*; but once the change to *Little Dorrit* was made, probably in the middle of September 1855, Dickens could afford to reconsider his bearings in the light of the new title, and adopt a notion expressed to Forster in a letter of 16 September, when he was beginning to work upon no. iii (chapters ix-xi):

> There is an enormous outlay in the Father of the Marshalsea chapter, in the way of getting a great lot of matter into a small space. I am not quite resolved, but I have a great idea of overwhelming that family with wealth. Their condition would be very curious. I can make Dorrit [he means Little Dorrit] very strong in the story, I hope.[12]

In its timing the decision is comparable to that major decision in *Chuzzlewit* to entangle Pecksniff in Old Martin's toils, and one might argue what difference the comparative lateness of the decision had upon the earlier numbers already written. But irrespective of that, I think it is clear that once the decision has been made and "Book the First. Poverty" inscribed in proof, Old Dorrit will be released from the Marshalsea at the end of no. x (in chapter xxxvi), and Dickens must take up his dispositions accordingly. On this we have additional evidence for *Little Dorrit* denied to us for *Martin Chuzzlewit*, and that is the so-called "Number-Plans," the memoranda which Dickens wrote to assist him in designing each Number. They show this recognition of a turning-point in no. x. In the Number-Plan for no. vii, chapter xxiii, we read "Pancks. Pave the way for his discovery, and the end of book [the] 1st"; in viii, chapter xxix, "Glimpse of Little Dorrit and Pancks, to carry through"; and in ix (chapters xxx-xxxii), the general direction reads "Tip?-Fanny?-Father and Uncle?-Carry through, except the Uncle-Family Spirit— working up to what they are likely to be in a higher station," and

for chapter xxxii, where Clennam visits Little Dorrit in the Marshalsea, the note reads, "Prepare for the time to come, in that room,
long afterwards. Pancks, immensely excited—strong preparation for
the end of the book."

There are two advantages of the division into two books, which
these memoranda seem to me to indicate. One is that dispositions
can be taken with a nearer end in view and with a more manageable quantity of numbers in hand. Instead of that distant and
crowded no. xix-xx, there is the more immediate climax in no. x to
plan for. And on the other side of that dividing line, planning can
be carried on within more manageable limits. With Clennam and
Little Dorrit to be married in xix-xx and the end of the old house
and Rigaud, Flintwinch, and Mrs. Clennam, it seems suitable to
place Clennam in prison in the penultimate number. Accordingly I
am inclined to read as a fairly early decision, taken well before the
writing of xviii, the two general memoranda in that Number-Plan
for Contents:

> Clennam in the Marshalsea, and lodged in the old room. Little
> Dorrit comes to him in the old dress, and attended by Maggy in
> the old way. The Merdle Image smashed?

And I am fortified in the view that those plans, though written in
the Number-Plan for xviii, were made well in advance of no. xviii,
by a reply to the Merdle question: "Done last Number." Yes, of
course; most of no. xvii (chapters xxiii-xxvi) had been given to
smashing "The Merdle Image." Dickens could not possibly have
forgotten it; and the only explanation of this curious entry in the
xviiith Number-Plan must be that Dickens had at one time resolved
that the smash should occur there, not reflecting perhaps (or not
deciding) that since Arthur Clennam was to be involved in the
smash, the smash must occur before he is shown in the Marshalsea,
to which of course he was sent as a bankrupt.

But whether we agree with these speculations or not at least
we may allow that this long-term miscalculation about the death
of Merdle, slight as it is, provides evidence of foresight directed
to the planning of the novel, number by number. The Merdle entries in this second book, in particular, show the deliberate march
of controlled events. They begin in xii (chapters v-vii) with "Pave
the way—with the first stone—to Mr. Merdle's ruining everybody?
Yes." In xiii (Chapters viii-xi) he is merely reviewed with the mem-

orandum "Mr. Merdle? Next time." And next time, that is, in xiv (chapters xii-xiv), he is triumphantly entered with a "Yes," triply underlined, and the note "Mr. Merdle's Barnacle dinner, for the great patriotic purpose of making Young Sparkler a Lord of the Treasury." The first memorandum for xv (chapters xv-xviii) reads "Mr. Dorrit to come to London, Invest his property with Mr. Merdle, and return full of plans, never to be accomplished. Tone on to his dying in next Number." xvi (chapters xix-xxii) merely notes "Pave on to Mrs. Merdle's great dinner," which is of course accomplished in xvii (chapters xxiii-xxvi), where the memorandum reads "Merdles? Yes. His suicide and demolition."

The second advantage in the division of the novel into two books, is that it permits some contrasted movements, some parallel scenes, and contrived ironies. The most obvious is the passage from poverty to riches in Book 1, and from riches to poverty in Book 2. We must surely also notice the assembly of travellers gathered at Marseilles in the opening scene of Book 1 matched by the assembly of travellers at the Great St. Bernard in the opening scene of Book 2, and Clennam bringing comfort to Little Dorrit in the Marshalsea at the end of Book 1 matched by the reversal of roles at the end of Book 2 where it is Clennam that is in the Marshalsea and Little Dorrit that brings him comfort there. No less obvious is the irony of Mr. Dorrit's being freed from imprisonment in the first Book, only to become the prisoner of polite society in the Second, with Mrs. General as jailer.

Certainly the pointing of these contrasts and ironies is assisted by the two-book structure. But there are themes which appear to be unaffected by that structure and to be developed irrespective of it. The fall of the old house and the discovery of Mrs. Clennam's secret are pursued over the full range of twenty numbers rather than within the limited scope of two books of ten numbers each. Some continuity must be expected; but perhaps we all wish that Dickens could have devised something a little more memorable for the connecting thread. At any rate there is some satisfaction that Dickens himself could not trust himself to recollect all the relevant details. The Number-Plans show that before he sat down to write the final double number, he had to set out the whole Clennam-Flintwinch-Dorrit entanglement in note form with page references back to his printed text. These he called his "Memoranda for working the Story round," "Retrospective" and "Prospective." Ironically his last enquiry reads "What was the appeal to Mrs. Clennam. Do Not Forget?"

NOTES

1. Chapter xxi.
2. Chapter xxx.
3. Chapter xlv.
4. Chapter xx.
5. Chapter xxvi.
6. Chapter xlvii.
7. Book I, Chapter xxxii.
8. Chapter iii.
9. Letters, I, 487, 493, 497.
10. A fuller account of the serial publication of this novel may be found in "Dickens' Monthly Number Plans for *Little Dorrit,*" Paul D. Herring, *Modern Philology,* 64 (August 1966), 22-63.
11. [In John Butt and Kathleen Tillotson,] *Dickens at Work* (1957), 231.
12. *Life,* viii, i.

ROBERT ALAN DONOVAN

Structure and Idea in *Bleak House*

> I propose therefore that we enquire into the
> nature of justice and injustice, first as they appear
> in the State, and secondly in the individual, pro-
> ceeding from the greater to the lesser and com-
> paring them.
>
> —PLATO, *The Republic,* trans. Jowett

If anything can supply an intelligible principle of Dickens's development as a novelist, it is the constant strengthening and focusing
of his protest against social injustice. This pervasive concern with
social justice is the link connecting the otherwise light-hearted and
high-spirited meanderings of Pickwick in a world of coaching inns
and manor farms to the sinister events which are preparing in the
dark world of Chancery in *Bleak House* or of the Marshalsea in
Little Dorrit. Speaking of this last novel, Shaw remarked in his
often quoted preface to *Great Expectations* that it "is a more sedi-
tious book than *Das Kapital*. All over Europe men and women are
in prison for pamphlets and speeches which are to *Little Dorrit* as
red pepper to dynamite."[1] Shaw had, like Macaulay, his own heightened and telling way of putting things, but to a world which persisted in regarding Dickens as the great impresario of soap opera,
Shaw's comments needed to be made. The indifference of society to
the suffering of its members; the venality, brutishness, or sheer in-

From *English Literary History,* Vol. 29 (1962), 175-201. Copyright © 1962
by The Johns Hopkins Press. Reprinted by permission of The Johns Hopkins
Press.

eptitude of its public servants; its perverse substitution of the virtues of the head for those of the heart; the hopeless inadequacy of its political and philanthropic institutions: these are the recurring motifs of Dickens's novels, from the scenes in the Fleet Prison in *Pickwick* to the symbolic dust heap in *Our Mutual Friend*.

Dickens's aroused social conscience has of course led some of his critics into seeing his work as more doctrinaire, more rigorously ordered than it is. Thus T. A. Jackson and Jack Lindsay have tried in vain to assimilate Dickens's "line" to the orderly fabric of Marxism,[2] and Shaw, of course, tended to exaggerate the explosive force of the novels as propaganda. Nevertheless, in spite of Dickens's reluctance to make common cause with any philosophically grounded reform movement, it is possible to abstract from the novels a more or less consistent point of view toward society and its ills. This ground has been covered so often, and there is such substantial agreement on the articles of Dickens's creed, that I shall limit myself to the briefest summary.

The first point to be observed is that Dickens is not a radical who wants to tear society apart and rebuild it according to first principles. With all its anomalies and incidental absurdities, Dickens never really questioned the basic class structure of English society. It is certainly sounder to align him with the "conservative" tradition exemplified by Carlyle and Ruskin, for he shares with them a kind of perpetual and indignant astonishment that human beings should so far surrender their own nature as to consign their most fundamental interests to machines. The machines, of course, are the literal ones which were reshaping England into something brutal and ugly, but they are also the ones, figuratively speaking, represented by such doctrinaire systems of thought as Benthamism or the political economy of the Manchester School, or by the social or political institutions which assumed that human beings could be administered to by systematic processes in which the basic fact of man's spirituality might be conveniently ignored—democratic government, for example, or evangelical religion.

Dickens's distrust of institutions and of intellectual systems is not the product of experience, for this distrust is clearly evident in *Pickwick*, and though it accumulates emotional charge, it is not really deeper in the late novels. His anti-intellectualism is revealed, in part, by a kind of instinctive response to any attempt to stifle or destroy the irrational part of man's nature; hence Dickens's affectionate regard for the weak-minded, and the prominent symbolic role given to the nonrational entertainments of Sleary's Circus in *Hard Times* (the logical culmination of a series, beginning with Mr. Vincent Crummles and Mrs. Jarley). The only forces of social amelioration to which Dickens gives his unqualified assent are man's native impulses of benevolence and self-sacrifice. At first he is prepared to believe that these impulses are strong enough in normal human beings to combat the various evils of society. Pickwick's benevolence is irrepressible and unconquerable. But either because the evils have grown greater, or because Dickens's faith in the humanity of ordinary people has grown less, the early optimism fades and is replaced by a heavy and virtually impenetrable gloom, lightened only occasionally, and inadequately, by acts of private charity and self-sacrifice. The fierce indignation that breaks out in the early novels becomes a kind of brooding melancholy as Dickens looks at the world in the ripeness of his age.

Though Dickens's social criticism runs through all his novels, it gathers to its greatest clarity and intensity in the six novels which comprise the bulk of his later work: *Dombey and Son, Bleak House, Hard Times, Little Dorrit, Great Expectations,* and *Our Mutual Friend.* Of these *Bleak House* is the most comprehensive criticism of society and may fairly be taken to represent Dickens's mature diagnosis of, and prognosis for, his age. *Bleak House* is also one of his most artful books, and unlike *Hard Times,* another very artful book, it is quintessentially Dickensian in spirit and technique. In the present essay I propose to examine *Bleak House,* both as an embodiment of Dickens's social protest and as a narrative structure, in an effort to see how structure and idea engage each other.

I

The main theme of *Bleak House* is responsibility. The content of the book may most succinctly be described as a series of studies in society's exercise (more often the evasion or abuse) of responsibility for its dependents. In his earlier novels Dickens characteristically locates the source of evil in specific human beings, the villains in his typically melodramatic plots. Sometimes he makes evil grow out of sheer malignity (Quilp), but even when the evil represented is of a predominantly social character it is generally personified, in the acquisitiveness of a Ralph Nickleby, for example, or the officious cruelty of a Bumble. But *Bleak House* has no villain. It offers a jungle without predators, only scavengers. Evil is as impersonal as the fog which is its main symbol. The Court of Chancery, the main focus of evil in the novel and the mundane equivalent of hell, harbors no devil, only a rather mild and benevolent gentleman who is sincerely desirous of doing the best he can for the people who require his aid. Esther describes the Lord Chancellor's manner as "both courtly and kind," and remarks at the conclusion of her interview, "He dismissed us pleasantly, and we all went out, very much obliged to him for being so affable and polite; by which he had certainly lost 'no dignity, but seemed to us to have gained some."[3] This is not irony; by an inversion of Mephistopheles's paradox, the Lord Chancellor is "ein Teil von jener Kraft, die stets das Gute will und stets das Böse schafft."

Dickens found in the Court of Chancery specifically, and in the law generally, the true embodiment of everything that was pernicious. The law touched Dickens often enough in his private life, and the actual cases of victims of legal proceedings always roused his indignation even when he was not personally involved. The result was a vein of legal satire beginning with the Bardell-Pickwick trial and running throughout the novels, but it is not Dickens's private grievance against the law that I am here concerned with. The law was to become for him a means by which as an artist he could most faithfully and effectively image a world gone wrong. Like Jeremy Bentham, Dickens was appalled by the chaos of the British law; its random accumulation of statute law, common law, and precedents in equity; its overlapping and conflicting jurisdictions; its antiquated and mysterious rituals and procedures. But Bentham was only appalled by the lack of intelligible system, not by the law itself, and he accordingly set out to put things right. Dickens, on the other hand, who shared with such other Victorian writers as Browning, Trollope, and W. S. Gilbert a profound misunderstanding and distrust of the legal mind, was as much disturbed by legal system as the lack thereof. It is perhaps suggestive that Dickens's satire does not merely attack abuses of the law, it attacks the fundamental postulates of the British legal system. Dodson and Fogg are contemptible less because they are lawyers than because they are grasping, mean, and hypocritical human beings. Dickens aims a subtler shaft at Perker, Mr. Pickwick's solicitor, an amiable and seemingly harmless man who cannot restrain his admiration for the acuity of Dodson and Fogg, and it is Perker, not his opponents, who is the prototype of the lawyers of *Bleak House*: Tulkinghorn, Vholes, and Conversation Kenge. None of these proves to be guilty of anything approaching sharp practice; on the contrary, they are all offered as examples of capable and conscientious legal practitioners, and the evil they give rise to is not a consequence of their abusing their functions but of their performing them as well as they do. Conversation Kenge may be taken as expressing the opinion of the legal fraternity at large when he holds up for Esther's admiration that "monument of Chancery practice," Jarndyce and Jarndyce, the case in which "every difficulty, every contingency, every masterly fiction, every form of procedure known in that court, is represented over and over again" (ch. 3). To Dickens this is a little like a surgeon's describing a newly sutured incision as "beautiful." He despised lawyers (and here Vholes is his principal example) because they drew their living from human misery without contributing significantly to alleviate it. But Dickens's feeling toward the cannibalistic Vholes is only incidental to the main point, which is the concept of the law implied by Kenge's rhapsody.

The law, especially British law, is an instrument of justice which often seems to the layman to put a higher value on consistency and orderly procedure than on justice itself. That in any given instance the law is capable of doing manifest injustice, no one would deny, but that the elaborate body of procedures, fictions, and precedents is the safest guarantee against capricious or arbitrary judgment, and in the long run, in the majority of cases, the most efficient mechanism of seeing justice done is the common ground for the defense of systems of jurisprudence. Justice becomes a by-product of law, and the law itself, by a kind of natural descent from the primitive trial by combat, assumes the character of an intellectual contest in which attack and counterattack, the play of knowledge, ingenuity, and skill, are of transcendent interest, even when the result is a matter of indifference. It amounts to no paradox, then, to say that the lawyer cares nothing for justice; he cares only for the law. Of the justice, that is to say, of the social utility, of his professional activity he is presumably convinced antecedently to his engaging in it, but he goes about his business secure in the knowledge that justice will best be served by his shrewdness in outwitting his adversary. To the lawyer the law is intellectual, abstract, and beautiful, like a

game of chess, and it is just here that the fundamental ground of
Dickens's quarrel with him lies. Justice for Dickens was generally
open and palpable. He couldn't understand why man's natural emotional response to injustice wasn't a sufficient impetus to lead him to
correct it if he could. With the abstract and intellectual approach to
the evils of life Dickens had no sympathy and no patience at all,
and the law, therefore, became for him a comprehensive symbol of
an attitude toward life that seemed to him perverse and wrong.
Dickens's anti-intellectualism is concentrated and brought to bear
in his satire on the law.

But there is special point and relevance to the attack on Chancery
in *Bleak House*. In the first place, Chancery exemplifies more perfectly than the law courts properly so-called the characteristically
slow and circuitous processes of British jurisprudence. Its ritual was
more intricate, its fictions more remote from actualities, its precedents more opaque, than those of the Queen's Bench, or the Ex-
chequer, or the Court of Common Pleas. And of course the slowness of Chancery proceedings was legendary. Holdsworth emphasizes this point neatly by quoting Lord Bowen: "Whenever any
death occurred, bills of review or supplemental suits became necessary to reconstitute the charmed circle of the litigants which had
been broken. . . . It was satirically declared that a suit to which
fifty defendants were necessary parties . . . could never hope to
end at all, since the yearly average of deaths in England was one
in fifty, and a death, as a rule, threw over the plaintiff's bill for at
least a year."[4] The High Court of Chancery, then, provided a microcosm of the legal world of nineteenth-century England, magnifying
the law's essential features and reducing its flaws to absurdity. In the
second place, Chancery is specially appropriate as an image of
the kind of responsibility that *Bleak House* is really about. The Lord
Chancellor's legal responsibility is of a curious and distinctive character. The law courts, with their various ramifications and subdivi-
sions, civil, criminal, and ecclesiastical, exist to provide a bar where
anyone who believes himself injured according to the common or
statute law may plead his case. But the law has many loopholes, and
it is desirable that some provision be made to redress wrongs which
are not covered by any existing law. Moreover a considerable body
of potential litigants—chiefly widows and orphans—being unable to
plead in their own behalf, must be protected against injustice. The
Lord Chancellor's Court was devised for just such a purpose, to

provide relief where the ordinary channels of legal procedure offered none. The origin of the Lord Chancellor's judicial function is described by Blackstone:

> When the courts of law, proceeding merely upon the ground of the king's original writs, and confining themselves strictly to that bottom, gave a harsh or imperfect judgment, the application for redress used to be to the king in person assisted by his privy council . . . and they were wont to refer the matter either to the chancellor and a select committee, or by degrees to the chancellor only, who mitigated the severity or supplied the defects of the judgments pronounced in the courts of law, upon weighing the circumstances of the case.[5]

From a court of appeals the Chancellor's Court developed into an ordinary court of equity in which a plaintiff could sue for redress by the presentation of a bill, and which claimed, furthermore, exclusive jurisdiction in supervising the proper administration of trusts and wills. It must be remembered, too, that antecedent to his judicial responsibility the Lord Chancellor bore a responsibility which was ecclesiastical and eleemosynary. Let me quote Blackstone once more on the Chancellor's office:

> Being formerly usually an ecclesiastic, (for none else were then capable of an office so conversant in writings,) and presiding over the royal chapel, he became keeper of the king's conscience; visitor, in right of the king, of all hospitals and colleges of the king's foundation; and patron of all the king's livings under the value of twenty marks *per annum* in the king's books. He is the general guardian of all infants, idiots, and lunatics; and has the general superintendance of all charitable uses in the kingdom. [III, 48]

Incorporating in his single office all the "charitable uses in the kingdom," the Lord Chancellor furnishes Dickens with a compendious symbol of all the ways in which one human being can be charged with the care of another: he is a father to the orphan, a husband to the widow, a protector to the weak and infirm, and an almoner to the destitute. What better focus of attention in a book about human responsibility could Dickens find than a suit in Chancery?

At one end of the scale is the Lord Chancellor in Lincoln's Inn Hall, at the other is Jo, society's outcast, with no proper place of his own, "moving on" through the atrocious slum of Tom-All-Alone's,

itself a "monument of Chancery practice," for its dismal and neglected appearance proclaims its connection with Chancery. Who
will take responsibility for Jo? Not government, engaged in an endless wrangle over the proper emolument for the party faithful; not
religion, in the person of Mr. Chadband sermonizing over Jo's invincible ignorance; not law, concerned only with Jo's "moving on";
not organized charity, which finds the natives of Borrioboola-Gha or
the Tockahoopo Indians a great deal more interesting than the
dirty home-grown heathen. Jo subsists entirely on the spasmodic generosity of Snagsby, who relieves his own feelings by compulsively
giving half-crowns to Jo, or on the more selfless generosity of Nemo,
who supplies Jo's only experience of human companionship until
Esther and George and Allan Woodcourt come to his aid. Jo's function as an instrument of Dickens's social protest is clear. In his life
and in his death he is a shattering rebuke to all those agencies of
church and state which are charged with the care of the weak and
the helpless and the poor, from the Lord Chancellor's court down
to the Society for the Propagation of the Gospel in Foreign Parts.
And Jo's experience throws a strong glare on the causes of their inadequacy; they fail conspicuously and utterly because they are
nothing more than machines, because they are illuminated from the
head, never from the heart, because, ultimately, they fail to acknowledge Dickens's most important moral and social maxim, that
human beings can live together only on terms of mutual trust and
love.

Between the Lord Chancellor and Jo, Dickens illustrates every
relation of dependency which is possible in civilized society, in
every one of which, as we have seen, the Lord Chancellor himself
participates by a species of legal fiction. Consider, for example, the
condition of parenthood. Every child begets a responsibility in his
parents; in *Bleak House* Dickens examines a wide range of cases in
order to trace the extent to which that responsibility is successfully
discharged. Only a very few parents in the sick society of this novel
manage to maintain a healthy and normal relation with their children; one must contrive to get as far from the shadow of Chancery
as Elephant and Castle, to find a domestic happiness like the Bagnets'. The virtuous mean of parental devotion is the exception;
more often we have the excess, like Mrs. Pardiggle's ferocious bullying of her children, or still oftener the deficiency, instanced by Mrs.
Jellyby's total neglect of her family, or Harold Skimpole's similar

behavior toward his. But the real symptom of disease is the frequency with which we find the normal relation between parent and child inverted. Skimpole is, as he frequently avers, a child, but the engaging qualities which this pose brings to the surface are quickly submerged again in his reckless self-indulgence, and his avocations, harmless or even commendable in themselves, the pursuit of art and beauty, become like the flush of fever, a sign of decay when we recognize that they are indulged at the expense of his responsibilities as the head of a family, and that his existence is so thoroughly parasitical. But just as there are parents who turn into children, a few children turn into parents. Charley Neckett, for example, at the death of her father is rudely thrust into maturity at the age of thirteen with a brother of five or six and a sister of eighteen months to care for. Esther describes her as "a very little girl, childish in figure but shrewd and older-looking in the face—pretty-faced too—wearing a womanly sort of bonnet much too large for her, and drying her bare arms on a womanly sort of apron. Her fingers were white and wrinkled with washing, and the soap-suds were yet smoking which she wiped off her arms. But for this, she might have been a child, playing at washing, and imitating a poor working-woman with a quick observation of the truth" (ch. 15). Even Esther herself exhibits a kind of reversal of roles. Like Charley (and a good many other characters in the story) she is an orphan, and her relations with the other inmates of Bleak House are curiously ambiguous and ill-defined. She is ostensibly the companion of Ada Clare and the ward of Mr. Jarndyce, both of which offices confer upon her a dependent status, yet in this household she assumes the moral leadership, a leadership which is explicitly recognized by the others' use of such nicknames as Little Old Woman, Mrs. Shipton, Mother Hubbard, and Dame Durden. Esther's relation with Mr. Jarndyce (whom she calls "Guardian") is further complicated by their betrothal; for as long as this lasts she stands toward him simultaneously as mother, daughter, and fiancée. In the Smallweed family the children all appear unnaturally old; only the senile display the attributes of childhood: "There has been only one child in the Smallweed family for several generations. Little old men and women there have been, but no child, until Mr. Smallweed's grandmother, now living, became weak in her intellect, and fell (for the first time) into a childish state" (ch. 21). The most complete and perfect inversion of all, however, is to be seen in the Tur-

veydrop household, where young Prince labors unceasingly to maintain his father in the style to which he has become accustomed as
an imitation Regency beau. The selfish old parasite, who sends his
son off to his dancing school in Kensington while he goes himself
to dine comfortably at the French House in the Opera Colonnade,
is absolutely stunned by Prince's "ingratitude" at thinking of marriage with Caddy Jellyby, and the young couple must sue on their
knees for Mr. Turveydrop's consent:

> "My dear father," returned Prince, "we well know what little
> comforts you are accustomed to, and have a right to; and it will
> always be our study, and our pride, to provide those before any-
> thing. If you will bless us with your approval and consent, father,
> we shall not think of being married until it is quite agreeable to
> you; and when we *are* married, we shall always make you—of
> course—our first consideration. You must ever be the Head and
> Master here, father; and we feel how truly unnatural it would be
> in us, if we failed to know it, or if we failed to exert ourselves in
> every possible way to please you."
>
> Mr. Turvydrop underwent a severe internal struggle, and came
> upright on the sofa again, with his cheeks puffing over his stiff
> cravat; a perfect model of parental deportment.
>
> "My son!" said Mr. Turveydrop. "My children! I cannot resist
> your prayer. Be happy!" [ch. 23]

The irony is enforced by the fact that from this marriage can
come only a stunted, malformed, deaf-mute child. Generally speaking, the society of *Bleak House* is one in which the normal responsibility of parent for child has most often been abused or shirked.

The pattern of inversion reasserts itself when we turn our attention to another relation of dependency—marriage. Of course there
are obvious instances of the neglect of marital (as well as maternal)
responsibility like Mrs. Jellyby's high-minded disregard of her family, and there are equally obvious instances of abuse of the obedience enjoined by the marriage sacrament, like the abject submission of the brick-makers' wives to their husbands' brutality. Esther
and Ada find one of these women furtively bringing comfort to the
bereaved mother of a dead child, but with one eye always on the
door of the public house:

> "It's you, young ladies, is it?" she said, in a whisper. "I'm
> a-watching for my master. My heart's in my mouth. If he was to

> catch me away from home he'd pretty near murder me."
>
> "Do you mean your husband?" said I.
>
> "Yes, miss, my master." [ch. 8]

But setting these instances aside, we are confronted in *Bleak House* by a stereotype of marriage in which the normal economic and social functions of husband and wife are reversed. Mr. Snagsby's deference to his wife remains within the bounds of conventional Dickensian social comedy and by itself is neither morbid nor especially significant:

> Mr. Snagsby refers everything not in the practical mysteries of the business to Mrs. Snagsby. She manages the money, reproaches the Tax-gatherers, appoints the time and places of devotion on Sundays, licenses Mr. Snagsby's entertainments, and acknowledges no responsibility as to what she thinks fit to provide for dinner; insomuch that she is the high standard of comparison among the neighboring wives, a long way down Chancery Lane on both sides, and even out in Holborn. [ch. 10]

But, as in the case of Skimpole, what begins in the light-hearted vein of comedy quickly darkens, and the relation assumes an unhealthy taint. Mrs. Snagsby, who enters as the conventional loud-voiced shrew, becomes, before her final exit, a shrinking paranoiac, "a woman overwhelmed with injuries and wrongs, whom Mr. Snagsby has habitually deceived, abandoned, and sought to keep in darkness. . . . Everybody it appears . . . has plotted against Mrs. Snagsby's peace" (ch. 54). And the Snagsby menage is further significant in that it provides a pattern of the marriage relation that is disturbingly common. Mr. Bayham Badger's uxoriousness far surpasses Mr. Snagsby's. It extends so far, in fact, that he is willing to suffer total eclipse in favor of his predecessors, Mrs. Badger's former husbands. And even the happy and amiable Bagnets display a domestic arrangement which, in spite of Matthew's stoutly (though not very convincingly) maintained fiction that "discipline must be preserved," places Mrs. Bagnet firmly in command of the family fortunes and policy. There is special meaning and pathos, however, in the union of Rick Carstone and Ada Clare, perhaps the only truly romantic pairing in the whole story (for, it must be noted in passing, some of the most admirable characters either are denied or deliberately evade the responsibilities of marriage—Mr. Jarndyce, Captain Hawdon, Boythorn, and Trooper George). This couple, the epitome of youth and hope and beauty, is doomed to frustration and tragedy because they take the contagion of Chancery, but that infection is itself made possible by the fact that the moral resources in their marriage, the courage, strength, and devotion, all belong to Ada. The corruption that marks the society of *Bleak House* may find its center and aptest symbol in Lincoln's Inn Hall, but its true origin is in the decay of the most fundamental social institution, the family. When parents will not or cannot take care of their children, when husbands refuse to be masters in their own houses, above all when these relations are not illuminated and softened by love, it is useless to expect those public institutions in which the relations of the family are mirrored to supply their defects.

But Dickens does not limit himself to the family. His novel is an intricate, if not always very systematic, study of the bonds which link human beings together. The very shape of his imaginative vision is perhaps given by the invariability with which people are seen as demonstrating potential or actual relations of responsibility or dependency toward one another. Here are masters and servants, landlords and tenants, employers and employees, professional men and clients, officers and men, all enforcing the inescapable truth that men and women share a common destiny. I do not propose to examine these various relations in detail; examples will suggest themselves to every reader of *Bleak House*. I believe that the breadth and the closeness of Dickens's analysis of society imply both his conviction that man cannot evade the consequences of his brotherhood with every other man, and his belief that human brotherhood can never be adequately affirmed or practiced through agencies which are the product of the intellect alone.

II

Edmund Wilson long ago hailed *Bleak House* as inaugurating a new genre, the novel of the "social group."[6] The term is both apt and suggestive, but it defines the inner form of the novel without explaining how Dickens imposed structural form upon it. The tendency of recent criticism has been to seek the novel's main structural principal in patterns of diction, imagery, or symbolism which are essentially verbal. This approach has led to some interesting and valuable insights,[7] but they have sometimes been achieved at the expense of ignoring other, more obvious and palpable features. The

art of the novel, as Dickens conceived and practiced it, was still a
story-telling art, and though it is certainly true that his language, especially, in the mature works, is richly charged and implicative, I
do not believe that we can understand the structure of *Bleak House*
without reference to those ingredients which are constituted by its
participation in a story-telling tradition—I mean, specifically, plot
and the closely related layers of character and point of view.

First the plot. "Plot" here means the record of events, organized
according to some intelligible principle of selection and arrangement. The narration of unrelated (even though sequential) events
does not give rise to plot; time sequence alone does not organize
experience in any meaningful way. The loosest kind of organization is supplied by character; events may be related in that they
happen to the same person, whether or not they reveal any growth,
either in the character himself, or in our understanding of him. A
somewhat more complicated structure arises when events are related to each other by their common illustration of a single idea or
of several related ideas. Finally, events may be organized according
to a causal sequence in which each successive event is in some way
caused by the one which precedes it. Now only in the last sense does
plot function as the unifying element in a story, for though it is
possible for a story to have a plot in either of the first two senses,
we would, in those cases, probably refer the story's unity to, respectively, character or theme.

It is virtually impossible to put all the events of *Bleak House* into
a single causal sequence, or even into several, as long as we understand by "events" what that word normally signifies, that is, births,
deaths, betrothals, marriages, whatever, in short, is likely to be entered in the family Bible, and perhaps also such other occurrences
(of a less public and ceremonial nature) as quarreling, making love,
eating, drinking, working, etc., which may have an interest of their
own. *Bleak House* is full enough of "events" in this sense; I count
nine deaths, four marriages, and four births. The difficulty is in
assigning their causes or their consequences. What are we to make
of the death of Krook for example? The question is not one of phys-
iology; I don't propose to reopen the question of spontaneous combustion. The question is properly one of psychology: how is Krook's
death related to the play of human motives and purposes? The answer, of course, is that it is not so related at all; it is a simple *deus ex
machina* whose only artistic justification is to be sought at the level

of symbolism. Rick Carstone's death, by contrast, is integrated with plot, for though its physiological causes may be as obscure as those of Krook's death, its psychological causes are palpable and satisfying. Or take Esther's marriage to Allan Woodcourt. Is it the inevitable culmination of a pattern of events or merely a concession to popular sentiment, like the second ending of *Great Expectations?* A great many, perhaps most, of the "events" of *Bleak House* consist of such hard and stubborn facts—stubborn in that they are not amenable to the construction of any intelligible law; they exist virtually uncaused, and they beget effects which are quite disproportionate to their own nature or importance. Events have a way of taking us by surprise, for even though Dickens is careful to create an appropriate atmosphere whenever he is about to take someone off, the time and manner of death are generally unpredictable.

The artistic center of the novel is generally taken to be Chancery, but if so it seems to me that Chancery functions as a symbol, not as a device of plot. We are permitted glimpses from time to time of what "happens" in Chancery, but Jarndyce and Jarndyce obviously follows no intelligible law of development, and so it is meaningless to talk about a Chancery plot or subplot. Furthermore, though Chancery affects the lives of many, perhaps all, of the characters in *Bleak House,* it does not do so in the sense that significant events take place there. The only event in the Court of Chancery that proves to have significant consequences for the people outside is the cessation of Jarndyce and Jarndyce when the whole property in dispute has been consumed in legal costs. But this is itself a conclusion reached by the stern requirements of economics rather than by the arcane logic of the law. Chancery affects men's lives the way God does, not by direct intervention in human affairs, but by commanding belief or disbelief.

In a few instances events align themselves in something approaching a genuine causal sequence. The story of Rick Carstone, for example, who undergoes a slow moral deterioration because he is gradually seduced into believing in Chancery, provides an example of a meaningful pattern of events. But Rick's story is neither central, nor altogether satisfying, principally, I believe, because it is observed only at intervals, and from without.[8] It remains true that it is all but impossible to describe what happens in *Bleak House* by constructing a causal sequence of events.

The difficulty largely disappears, however, when we stop trying to discover a more or less systematic pattern of events, and try instead to define the organization of the book in terms of discovery, the Aristotelian anagnorisis. The plot, in this case, is still woven of "events," but the word now signifies some determinate stage in the growth of awareness of truths which are in existence, potentially knowable, before the novel opens. Events, in the original sense of that term, become important chiefly as the instrumentalities of discovery. Krook's death, for example, leads to the unearthing of an important document in Jarndyce and Jarndyce, and incidentally to the disclosure of a complex web of relations involving the Smallweed, Snagsby, and Chadband families. The murder of Tulkinghorn and the arrest of Trooper George are red herrings, designed to confuse the issue, but ultimately they make possible the complete unveiling of the pattern of human relations that it is the chief business of the novel to disclose. The progressive discovery of that pattern is, then, the "plot" of the novel, and it constitutes a causal sequence, not in that each discovery brings about the next, but in that each discovery presupposes the one before. We need to know that Lady Dedlock harbors a secret which she regards as shameful before we can discover the existence of some former connection between her and Nemo, and we need to be aware of that connection before we can add to it the more important discovery that Esther is the daughter of Nemo and Lady Dedlock. And so on, until the whole complicated web stands clearly revealed.

This kind of structure is, as everyone knows, the typical pattern of the detective story. Such fundamentally human concerns as crime and punishment lie outside the scope of detective fiction, in which the murder may take place before the story begins, and the retribution may finally catch up with the murderer after it ends. The plot of the detective story consists simply in the discovery—withheld, of course, as long as possible—of the one hypothesis which will account for all the disparate facts or "events" that make up the story. The interest is centered, in classical specimens of the genre, not in the events but in the process by which the events are rendered meaningful, ordinarily in the activity of the detective as he proceeds toward a solution. *Bleak House,* of course, has many detectives. Not counting the unforgettable Inspector Bucket "of the Detective," a great many characters are at work throughout the novel at unraveling some private and vexing problem of their own: Mr. Tulkinghorn, stalking Lady Dedlock's secret with fearful persistency, or

Mr. Guppy, approaching the same mystery from Esther's side, or Mrs. Snagsby, endeavoring to surprise her husband's guilty connections, or even Esther herself, troubled by the riddle of her own mysterious origin and still more mysterious participation in the guilt of her unknown mother. But the presence or activity of a detective is incidental to the main scheme of such fiction, from *Oedipus Tyrannus* onward, to present a mystery and then solve it. The beginning, middle, and end of such an action can be described only in terms of the reader's awareness; the beginning consists of the exposition in which the reader is made aware of the mystery, that is of the facts that require explanation; the end consists of his reaching a full understanding of the mystery which confronted him, for when all is known the story must come to an end. The middle, then, is comprised of his successive states of partial or incorrect knowledge.

The mystery presents itself, in the typical detective novel, with crystalline purity. Someone has been murdered; the problem is to discover, in the graphic but ungrammatical language of the usual cognomen, Who done it? In *Bleak House* the problem is somewhat different. It is true that there is a murder, and that the murderer must subsequently be picked out of three likely suspects, but the main mystery, the one that sustains the motion of the whole book and gives it a unity of plot, is not a question of determining the agent of some past action (though the mystery may be formulated in these terms) so much as it is a question of establishing the identity of all the characters involved, and in the world of *Bleak House* one's identity is defined according to his relations to other people. Two recent writers, James H. Broderick and John E. Grant, consider that the novel is given its shape by Esther's successful quest for identity, or place, in the society of the book,[9] and I see no reason why the establishment of identity, not merely for Esther, but for all or most of the characters may not provide a workable principle of structure. Esther's identity is secure when she discovers who her parents are, and this is certainly the heart of *Bleak House*'s mystery, but that discovery comes shortly after the middle of the book, when Lady Dedlock discloses herself to Esther. The novel is not complete until all the relations of its various characters are recognized and established (or re-established) on some stable footing. Sir Leicester Dedlock must adjust his whole view of the world to conform to the discovery he makes about his wife; harmony must be restored between Mr. Jarndyce and Rick; Esther must discover her true relation

to Mr. Jarndyce—and to Allan Woodcourt. Even the minor characters must be accounted for: Trooper George must become once again
the son of Sir Leicester's housekeeper and the brother of the iron-
master; Mr. and Mrs. Snagsby must be reconciled as man and wife;
all misunderstandings, in short, must be cleared away.

One of the most curious features of *Bleak House*, one of the attributes which is most likely to obtrude itself and bring down the
charge of staginess is Dickens's careful husbandry of characters.
That he disposes of so many may perhaps be worthy of remark, but
still more remarkable is the fact that he makes them all, even the
most obscure, serve double and triple functions. Mr. Boythorn, for
example, the friend of Mr. Jarndyce who is always at law with his
next-door neighbor, Sir Leicester Dedlock, doubles as the rejected
suitor of Miss Barbary, Esther's aunt. And it is surely a curious
coincidence which sends Rick, when he is in need of a fencing
teacher, to Trooper George, who is not only related to the Chesney
Wold household through his mother, but also deeply in debt to
Grandfather Smallweed (Krook's brother-in-law), and of course he
has served under Captain Hawdon, Esther's father. Mrs. Rachael,
Miss Barbary's servant, turns up again as the wife of the oily Mr.
Chadband, and even Jenny, the brickmaker's wife, appears for-
tuitously to change clothes with Lady Dedlock. These examples,
which might easily be multiplied, irresistibly create the impression,
not of a vast, chaotic, utterly disorganized world, but of a small,
tightly ordered one. That the novel thus smacks of theatrical artifice
constitutes a threat to the "bleakness" of *Bleak House*, for we are
never confronted, in this world, by the blank and featureless faces
of total strangers, the heart-rending indifference of the nameless
mob; all the evils of this world are the work of men whose names
and domestic habits we know, and for that reason, it would appear,
are deprived of most of their terrors.

Perhaps the most serious charge that can be brought against the
artistry of *Bleak House* grows out of some of the characteristic features which I have been discussing. How can the discerning reader
avoid being offended, it will be argued, by a novel which obviously
wants to say something serious and important about society, but at
the same time contrives to say it in the most elaborately artificial
way possible? How can we be serious about social criticisms which
come to us through the medium of the most sensational literary
genre, and are obscured by every artifice of melodrama? The objec-

tion seems to be a damaging one, but I wonder if Dickens's employment of the techniques of the detective story and of melodrama may
not enforce, rather than weaken, his rhetorical strategy. The plot, as
I conceive it, consists of the progressive and relentless revelation of
an intricate web of relations uniting all the characters of the novel,
by ties of blood or feeling or contract. And Dickens's assignment of
multiple functions to the minor characters is merely a means of rein-
forcing and underscoring our sense that human beings are bound
to each other in countless, often unpredictable ways. It is difficult
to see how Dickens could have found a clearer, more emphatic way
of drawing up his indictment against society for its failure to exercise responsibility than by his elaborate demonstration of human
brotherhood.

The bleakness of *Bleak House* is the sense of hopelessness inspired
by the knowledge that men and women, subjected to the common
shocks of mortality, will nevertheless consistently repudiate the
claims which other people have on them. The sense of hopelessness
is intensified and made ironic by the closeness, figuratively speaking,
of their relations to other people (sometimes, of course, the closeness
is literal, as in the hermetic little community of Cook's Court, Cursi-
tor Street). It is appropriate that the novel should be shaped by
discoveries rather than by events, for the sense of hopelessness, or
bleakness, can hardly be sustained in a world that can be shaped to
human ends by human will. The events of this novel are accidental
in a double sense; most of them are unplanned and unpredictable,
and they are moreover nonessential to the view of human experience
that Dickens is concerned to present. Human relations, the ones that
are important, are not constituted by events (though they may be
revealed by events—Esther's smallpox, for example), because events
just happen, they follow no intelligible law either of God or man.
Human relations are inherent in the nature of society, and the duty
of man is therefore not something arbitrary and intrinsically meaningless which can be prescribed and handed down to him by some
external authority (like law); it is discoverable in, and inferable
from, his social condition and only needs to be seen to command
allegiance. The tragedy of *Bleak House* is that awareness of human
responsibility invariably comes too late for it to be of any use.
Nemo's, or Coavinses's, or Jo's membership in the human race is
discovered only after his death, and Sir Leicester Dedlock awakens
to recognition of the true nature of the marriage bond only when

his wife has gone forth to die. Still, it is important to have that awareness, and the most effective way to produce it, surely, is to make its slow growth the animating principle of the novel.

III

If we choose to talk about the plot of *Bleak House* as constituted by a growing awareness of human relations and human responsibilities, sooner or later we must raise the question, *Whose* awareness? The problem of point of view is so important in the detective story, in fact, that it is most often met by the creation of a special point-of-view character. The classical instance, of course, is Dr. Watson, but Dr. Watson has had countless avatars. *Bleak House* is enough of a detective story so that it must reckon with some, at least, of the problems that Dr. Watson was invented to solve. The mystery must be preserved, so the narrator's perspicacity must have rather clearly defined limits, but at the same time the mystery must take hold of the reader, so the narrator must possess lively human sympathies and be capable of moral insights which are as just and true as his practical judgments are absurd. Such considerations impose limits on the choice of a narrative perspective for *Bleak House,* but there are other considerations which affect that choice too. The mystery whose solution dominates the novel is not such a simple, or at any rate such a limited problem as identifying a particular character as the criminal; Dickens's villain is a whole society, and its guilt cannot be disclosed by a sudden dramatic unveiling. Furthermore Dickens is only partly concerned with the disclosure of the truth to the reader; a more fundamental matter is the discovery by the agents themselves of the relations in which they stand toward all the other members of society. It is the story of Oedipus on a large scale.

Because of the staggering breadth of Dickens's design the selection of a narrative point of view is extraordinarily difficult. If he chooses an omniscient, third-person point of view a good deal of the emotional charge is lost, particularly if the narrator remains (as he must) sufficiently aloof from the actions and events he describes to avoid premature disclosures. On the other hand, a first person narrator suffers equally important disabilities. The most immediately obtrusive of these is physical and practical. How can a single character be expected to participate directly in all the relations the novel is about? How can one character contribute evidence (as opposed to hearsay) of events which take place in London, in Lincolnshire, and in Hertfordshire, sometimes simultaneously? The difficulty could be partly met by the selection of one of those numerous characters like Tulkinghorn or Mr. Guppy or young Bart Smallweed who seem to be always on the "inside," in control of events simply because they know about them, yet one difficulty yields only to be replaced by another. Characters like Tulkinghorn obviously lack the "lively human sympathies" which give to the first person point of view its special value, and as narrator Tulkinghorn (who is in any case disqualified on the more fundamental ground that he is killed) would offer no advantage over the omniscient point of view. The obvious solution to this dilemma is to have both points of view, alternating the narration between them.

The dual point of view in *Bleak House* has always served as a speck of grit around which the commentators have secreted their critical pearls. E. M. Forster regards it as a blemish, though he thinks Dickens's talent can make us forget it: "Logically, *Bleak House* is all to pieces, but Dickens bounces us, so that we do not mind the shiftings of the view point."[10] Others defend the double point of view as artistically appropriate.[11] I regard the device as a concession to a necessity that I can see no other way of circumventing, but there are perhaps one or two things to be said about it.

Bleak House is a novel without a center. There is no single character to whom the events of the story happen, or with reference to whom those events are significant. It is not even possible (as I have already argued) to understand the novel as a unified system of coordinate plots or of plot and subplots. Except for this want of a center the novel might be compared to a spider web in which each intersection represents a character, connected by almost invisible but nonetheless tenacious filaments to a circle of characters immediately surrounding him and ultimately, of course, to all the other characters. But the spider web has a center (and a villain), so a more appropriate comparison might be made to a continuous section of netting, or better still, to the system of galaxies which make up the universe. It appears to a terrestrial observer that all the other galaxies are receding from him at an unthinkable rate of speed, implying that his own post of observation constitutes the center of things. Yet the centrality of his own position is merely a function of his special point of view. So with *Bleak House*. Esther is, in this special sense, the "center" of the novel, not because she so regards herself, but because she supplies the central observation point, because relations are measured according to their nearness or farness from her just as astronomical distances are measured in parsecs—heliocentric parallax (in seconds of arc) as recorded for a terrestrial observer. To pass, for example, from Esther to Nemo (or some other intermediate character) to George to Matthew Bagnet is to move, so to speak, from the center outward. But Esther is not really the center of the novel. To think of her as such is to destroy or at least to do serious violence to Dickens's view of the world and transform his indictment of society into a sentimental fable. To deprive the novel of its specious center, to provide it with a new perspective which, like stereoscopic vision, adds depth, is an important function of the omniscient point of view.

Dickens's handling of that portion of the narrative which is related by the omniscient observer (roughly half of the novel) is, on the whole, masterly. I do not know that any critic denies the full measure of praise for things like the opening paragraph or two of the novel, that magnificent evocation of the London fog which has been quoted so often that I may be excused from doing so here. The laconic, unemotional style, with its sentence fragments and present participles in place of finite verbs, the roving eye, which, like the movie camera mounted on an overhead crane, can follow the action at will, are brilliantly conceived and deftly executed. It is a descriptive style emancipated from the limitations of time and space, and accordingly well-suited to its special role in the novel. But Dickens's control of this narrator is uneven. Superbly fitted for the descriptive passages of the novel, his tight-lipped manner must give way to something else in passages of narration, or, still more conspicuously, in those purple rhetorical passages that Dickens loves to indulge in. As a narrator, the omniscient persona (now speaking in finite verbs in the present tense) suffers somewhat from a hollow portentousness, a lack of flexibility, and a rather pointless reticence which can become annoying, as in the narration of Tulkinghorn's death (though here again the descriptive powers get full play). The requirements of consistency do not seem to trouble Dickens when it is time to step forward and point the finger at the object of his satire. The narrative persona is dropped completely when Dickens speaks of Buffy and company, or apostrophizes the "right" and "wrong" reverends whom he holds responsible for the death of Jo. But these passages win us by their obvious sincerity, and we need not trouble ourselves over the fact that the mask has been inadvertently dropped. To insist on a rigorous consistency here is to quibble over trifles, for generally speaking the third person narration is adroit and effective.

The focus of discontent with the manipulation of point of view in *Bleak House* is Esther Summerson. Fred W. Boege writes: "There is nothing necessarily wrong with the idea of alternating between the first and third persons. The fault lies rather with Dickens' choice of a medium for the first-person passages. *David Copperfield* demonstrates that the conventional Victorian hero is not a commanding figure in the center of a novel. Esther Summerson proves that the conventional heroine is worse; for the hero is hardly more than colorless, whereas she has positive bad qualities, such as the simpering affectation of innocence."[12] I think it is essential to distinguish carefully between Esther's qualities as "heroine" and Esther's qualities as narrator, for though the two functions are not wholly separate, it ought to be possible to have a bad heroine who is a good narrator and vice versa. As a heroine she clearly belongs to a tradition that we tend to regard as hopelessly sentimental and out-of-date. She is sweet-tempered and affectionate, and she is also capable and strong and self-denying. The first two qualities almost invariably (at least within the conventions of Victorian fiction) render their possessor both unsympathetic and unreal. One thinks of Amelia Sedley or Dinah Morris or Dickens's own Agnes Wickfield, and prefers, usually, the society of such demireps as Becky Sharp or Lizzie Eustace. Still, Esther's strength of character ought to save her and give her a genuine hold on our regard, except for the fact that as narrator she is faced with the necessity of talking about herself, and her modest disclaimers ring false. When she tells us that she is neither good, nor clever, nor beautiful, she forfeits a good deal of the regard that her genuinely attractive and admirable qualities demand. Esther the heroine is in a sense betrayed by Esther the narrator into assuming a posture that cannot be honestly maintained.

Whatever one thinks of Esther as a person, the important question at the moment is her discharge of the narrator's responsibility. The sensibility which is revealed by her attributes as a character (the term "heroine" is somewhat misleading) is of course the same one which will determine the quality of her perceptions and insights as narrator, and it is here, I think, that some confusion arises, for it is generally assumed that Esther's simplicity, her want of what might be called "diffractive" vision, the power of subjecting every experience to the play of different lights and colors, is held to undermine or even destroy her value as narrator. We have become so used to accepting the Jamesian canons of art and experience that we refuse validity to any others. The attitude is unfortunate, not to say parochial. For James "experience" (the only kind of experience that concerned the artist) was constituted by the perception of it. "Experience," he writes in "The Art of Fiction," "is never limited, and it is never complete; it is an immense sensibility, a kind of huge spider-web of the finest silken threads suspended in the chamber of consciousness, and catching every air-borne particle in its tissue. It is the very atmosphere of the mind; and when the mind is imaginative . . . it takes to itself the faintest hints of life, it converts the very pulses of the air into revelations."[13] This conception of experience is at the root of James's conception of the art of the novel, for it prescribes that the simplest kind of happening may be converted to the stuff of art by a sufficiently vibrant and sensitive point of view character. To a Lambert Strether the relations of Chad Newsome and Mme. de Vionnet are subtle, complex, and beautiful, because he is; but to another observer the same liaison is common and vulgar. Strether possesses what I have chosen to call diffractive vision, the ability to see a whole spectrum where the vulgar can see only the light of common day.

How can poor little Esther Summerson manage to perform the same function as a character with the depth and resonance of Lambert Strether? The answer, obviously, is that she can't. But I must hasten to add that she doesn't have to. The ontological basis of James's fiction is radically different from that of Dickens's; for in James what seems is more important than what is, and he accordingly requires a perceiving intelligence of the highest order. In Dickens, on the other hand, though he too is concerned with the characters' awareness, the relations which they are to perceive have a "real" existence which is not contingent on their being seen in a certain way. For this reason Esther does not have to serve as the instrument of diffraction; the light is colored at its source. To the sensitive Jamesian observer a single human relation appears in almost an infinite number of lights, and a single act may be interpreted in many ways. But Dickens does not work that way, at least not in *Bleak House*. Here the richness and infinite variety of human experience are suggested by the sheer weight of example, by the incredible multiplication of instances, and the narrator's chief function is simply to record them.

When Socrates and his friends Glaucon and Adeimantus differed over the nature of justice and injustice, Socrates proposed to settle the dispute, in the passage of the *Republic* from which my epigraph is taken, by constructing an imaginary and ideal state in order to see how justice originates. The method is not at all unlike that of Dickens, who proposes to investigate the abstraction "injustice" by seeing how it arises in an imaginary replica of the real world. Both methods assume that what is universal and abstract is rendered most readily intelligible by what is particular and concrete, and furthermore that the particular and concrete establish a firmer hold on our feelings than the universal and abstract. For both Plato and Dickens are concerned not only with making justice and injustice understood, but with making them loved and hated, respectively. The method is perhaps suggestive of allegory, but it differs in important ways from any technique of symbolic representation. It is a species of definition which proceeds by attempting to specify the complete denotation of the thing to be defined. To the question, "What is Justice?" Plato replies by showing us his republic, perfect in all its details, and saying, "Justice is here." To a similar question about injustice Dickens need only reply by unfolding the world of *Bleak House*.

Let me particularize briefly. One of the important ethical abstractions the novel deals with is charity (a useful check list of such abstractions might be derived from the names of Miss Flite's birds). Dickens nowhere provides a statement of the meaning of this concept except by supplying a wide range of instances from which the concept may be inferred. Mrs. Jellyby (for example), Mrs. Pardiggle, Mr. Quale, and Mr. Chadband demonstrate various specious modes of the principal Christian virtue, and Captain Hawdon, Mr. Snagsby, Mr. Jarndyce, and Esther provide glimpses of the genuine article. None of these characters, and none of the acts by which they reveal their nature can be said to *stand for* the general idea, charity; collectively they *are* charity, which is thus defined by representing, on as ample a scale as possible, its denotation. So with the whole spectrum of moral ideas and human relations in *Bleak House;* Dickens offers his main commentary, not by names or labels, certainly not by analysis, and not even by symbolic analogues (though he uses them). His principal technique is the multiplication of instances. To say that in a novel which is as richly and palpably symbolic as *Bleak House* symbolism is unimportant would be absurd, and I have no intention of going so far. I wish only to direct attention toward a narrative method which seems to me to have been strangely neglected by comparison with the symbolism which has proved so fruitful of insight.

At any rate, I think Esther is vindicated as narrator. The narrative design of the novel really requires only two qualities of her, both of which she exemplifies perfectly. In the first place, she should be as transparent as glass. The complex sensibility which is a characteristic feature of the Jamesian observer would be in Esther not simply no advantage, it would interfere with the plain and limpid narration she is charged with. We must never be allowed to feel that the impressions of characters and events which we derive from her are significantly colored by her own personality, that the light from them (to revert to my optical figure) is diffracted by anything in her so as to distort the image she projects. One partial exception to this generalization implies the second of the two characteristics I have imputed to her. In the second place, then, we require of Esther sufficient integrity, in a literal sense, to draw together the manifold observations she sets down. The most complex and elaborate act of synthesis is reserved for the reader, but to Esther falls the important choric function of suggesting the lines along which that synthesis should take place by drawing her observations together under a simple, traditional, and predictable system of moral values. If Esther occasionally strikes us as a little goody-goody, we must recall her function to provide a sane and wholesome standard of morality in a topsy-turvy world.

No critic, surely, can remain unimpressed by the richness of *Bleak House,* a quality which is both admirable in itself and characteristically Dickensian. But the quality which raises the novel to a class by itself among Dickens's works is its integrity, a product of the perfect harmony of structure and idea. Edmund Wilson located the peculiar achievement of *Bleak House* in its establishment of a new literary form, "the detective story which is also a social fable," but he provided no real insight into the method by which these radically unlike forms were made to coalesce. The secret, I believe, is partly in that instinctive and unfathomable resourcefulness of the artist, which enables him to convert his liabilities into assets, to make, for example, out of such an unpromising figure as Esther

Summerson, just the right point of view character for the first-person portion of the novel. But the real greatness of *Bleak House* lies in the happy accident of Dickens's hitting upon a structural form (the mystery story) and a system of symbols (Chancery) which could hold, for once, the richness of the Dickensian matter without allowing characters and incidents to distract the reader from the total design. The mysterious and sensational elements of the plot are not superimposed on the social fable; they are part of its substance. The slow but relentless disclosure of the web of human relations which constitutes the novel's inner form makes a superb mystery, but what makes it a monumental artistic achievement is that it is also and simultaneously one of the most powerful indictments of a heartless and irresponsible society ever written. *Bleak House* is the greatest of Dickens's novels because it represents the most fertile, as well as the most perfectly annealed, union of subject and technique he was ever to achieve.

NOTES

1. Edinburgh, 1937. Reprinted in *Majority, 1931-52*, ed. Hamish Hamilton (London, 1952).
2. Thomas A. Jackson, *Charles Dickens* (New York, 1938); Jack Lindsay, *Charles Dickens* (New York, 1950).
3. *Bleak House* (The Nonesuch Dickens; Bloomsburg, 1938), ch. 3. All quotations follow the text of this edition.
4. William S. Holdsworth, *Dickens as a Legal Historian* (New Haven, 1929), p. 91.
5. Sir William Blackstone, *Commentaries on the Laws of England* (London, 1800), III, 50-51.
6. Edmund Wilson, "Dickens: The Two Scrooges," *The Wound and the Bow* (Boston, 1941), p. 34.
7. See, for example, Norman Friedman, "The Shadow and the Sun: Notes toward a Reading of *Bleak House*," *Boston University Studies in English*, III (1957), 147-66; J. Hillis Miller, *Charles Dickens: The World of His Novels* (Cambridge, Mass., 1958), pp. 160-224; Louis Crompton, "Satire and Symbolism in *Bleak House*," *Nineteenth-Century Fiction*, XII (1957-58), 284-303.
8. As Edgar Johnson has argued, Dickens was not to do justice to the theme of the moral deterioration of the hero until *Great Expectations* (*Charles Dickens: His Tragedy and Triumph* [New York, 1952], p. 767).

9. "The Identity of Esther Summerson," *Modern Philology*, LV (1958), 252-58.

10. *Aspects of the Novel* (London, 1927), p. 108.

11. For example, M. E. Grenander, "The Mystery and the Moral: Point of View in Dickens's 'Bleak House,'" *Nineteenth-Century Fiction*, X (1955-56), 301-305.

12. "Point of View in Dickens," *PMLA*, LXV (1950), 94.

13. *Partial Portraits* (London, 1888), p. 388.

G. ROBERT STANGE

Expectations Well Lost:
Dickens' Fable for His Time

Great Expectations is a peculiarly satisfying and impressive novel. It is unusual to find in Dickens' work so rigorous a control of detail, so simple and organic a pattern. In this very late novel the usual features of his art—proliferating sub-plots, legions of minor grotesques—are almost entirely absent. The simplicity is that of an art form that belongs to an ancient type and concentrates on permanently significant issues. *Great Expectations* is conceived as a moral fable; it is the story of a young man's development from the moment of his first self-awareness, to that of his mature acceptance of the human condition.

So natural a theme imposes an elemental form on the novel: the over-all pattern is defined by the process of growth, and Dickens employs many of the motifs of folklore. The story of Pip falls into three phases which clearly display a dialectic progression. We see the boy first in his natural condition in the country, responding and acting instinctively and therefore virtuously. The second stage of his career involves a negation of child-like simplicity; Pip acquires his "expectations," renounces his origins, and moves to the city. He rises in society, but since he acts through calculation rather than

From *College English*, XVI (1954-55), 9-17. Copyright © 1954 by the National Council of Teachers of English. Reprinted by permission of the author and publishers.

through instinctive charity, his moral values deteriorate as his social graces improve. This middle phase of his career culminates in a sudden fall, the beginning of a redemptive suffering which is dramatically concluded by an attack of brain fever leading to a long coma. It is not too fanciful to regard this illness as a symbolic death; Pip rises from it regenerate and percipient. In the final stage of growth he returns to his birthplace, abandons his false expectations, accepts the limitations of his condition, and achieves a partial synthesis of the virtue of his innocent youth and the melancholy insight of his later experience.

Variants of such a narrative are found in the myths of many heroes. In Dickens' novel the legend has the advantage of providing an action which appeals to the great primary human affections and serves as unifying center for the richly conceived minor themes and images which form the body of the novel. It is a signal virtue of this simple structure that it saves *Great Expectations* from some of the startling weaknesses of such excellent but inconsistently developed novels as *Martin Chuzzlewit* or *Our Mutual Friend*.

The particular fable that Dickens elaborates is as interesting for its historical as for its timeless aspects. In its particulars the story of Pip is the classic legend of the nineteenth century: *Great Expectations* belongs to that class of education or development-novels which describe the young man of talents who progresses from the country to the city, ascends in the social hierarchy, and moves from innocence to experience. Stendhal in *Le Rouge et le Noir,* Balzac in *Le Père Goriot* and *Les Illusions perdues,* use the plot as a means of dissecting the post-Napoleonic world and exposing its moral poverty. This novelistic form reflects the lives of the successful children of the century, and usually expresses the mixed attitudes of its artists. Dickens, Stendhal, Balzac communicate their horror of a materialist society, but they are not without admiration for the possibilities of the new social mobility; *la carrière ouverte aux talents* had a personal meaning for all three of these energetic men.

Pip, then, must be considered in the highly competitive company of Julien Sorel, Rubempré, and Eugène de Rastignac. Dickens' tale of lost illusions, however, is very different from the French novelists'; *Great Expectations* is not more profound than other development-novels, but it is more mysterious. The recurrent themes of the genre are all there: city is posed against country, experience against innocence; there is a search for the true father; there is the exposure to crime and the acceptance of guilt and expiation. What Dickens' novel lacks is the clarity and, one is tempted to say, the essential tolerance of the French. He could not command either the saving ironic vision of Stendhal or the disenchanted practicality and secure Catholicism of Balzac. For Dickens, always the Victorian protestant, the issues of a young man's rise or fall are conceived as a drama of the individual conscience; enlightenment (partial at best) is to be found only in the agony of personal guilt.

With these considerations and possible comparisons in mind I should like to comment on some of the conspicuous features of *Great Expectations*. The novel is interesting for many reasons: it demonstrates the subtlety of Dickens' art; it displays a consistent control of narrative, imagery, and theme which gives meaning to the stark outline of the fable, and symbolic weight to every character and detail. It proves Dickens' ability (which has frequently been denied) to combine his genius for comedy with his fictional presentation of some of the most serious and permanently interesting of human concerns.

The principal themes are announced and the mood of the whole novel established in the opening pages of *Great Expectations*. The first scene with the boy Pip in the graveyard is one of the best of the superbly energetic beginnings found in almost all Dickens' mature novels. In less than a page we are given a character, his background, and his setting; within a few paragraphs more we are immersed in a decisive action. Young Pip is first seen against the background of his parents' gravestones—monuments which communicate to him no clear knowledge either of his parentage or of his position in the world. He is an orphan who must search for a father and define his own condition. The moment of this opening scene, we learn, is that at which the hero has first realized his individuality and gained his "first most vivid and broad impression of the identity of things." This information given the reader, the violent meeting between Pip and the escaped convict abruptly takes place.

The impression of the identity of things that Pip is supposed to have received is highly equivocal. The convict rises up like a ghost from among the graves, seizes the boy suddenly, threatens to kill him, holds him upside down through most of their conversation, and ends by forcing the boy to steal food for him. The children of Dickens' novels always receive rather strange impressions of things, but Pip's epiphany is the oddest of all, and in some ways the most ingenious. This encounter in the graveyard is the germinal scene of the novel. While he is held by the convict Pip sees his world upside down; in the course of Dickens' fable the reader is invited to try the same view. This particular change of viewpoint is an ancient device of irony, but an excellent one: Dickens' satire asks us to try reversing the accepted senses of innocence and guilt, success and failure, to think of the world's goods as the world's evils.

A number of ironic reversals and ambiguous situations develop out of the first scene. The convict, Magwitch, is permanently grateful to Pip for having brought him food and a file with which to take off his leg-iron. Years later he expresses his gratitude by assuming in secrecy an economic parenthood; with the money he has made in Australia he will, unbeknownst to Pip, make "his boy" a gentleman. But the money the convict furnishes him makes Pip not a true gentleman, but a cad. He lives as a flâneur in London, and when he later discovers the disreputable source of his income is snobbishly horrified.

Pip's career is a parable which illustrates several religious paradoxes: he can gain only by losing all he has; only by being defiled can he be cleansed. Magwitch returns to claim his gentleman, and finally the convict's devotion and suffering arouse Pip's charity; by the time Magwitch has been captured and is dying Pip has accepted him and come to love him as a true father. The relationship is the most important one in the novel: in sympathizing with Magwitch Pip assumes the criminal's guilt; in suffering with and finally loving the despised and rejected man he finds his own real self.

Magwitch did not have to learn to love Pip. He was naturally devoted to "the small bundle of shivers," the outcast boy who brought him the stolen food and the file in the misty graveyard. There is a natural bond, Dickens suggests, between the child and the criminal; they are alike in their helplessness; both are repressed and tortured by established society, and both rebel against its incomprehensible authority. In the first scene Magwitch forces Pip to commit his first "criminal" act, to steal the file and food from his sister's house. Though this theft produces agonies of guilt in Pip, we are led to see it not as a sin but as an instinctive act of mercy. Magwitch, much later, tells Pip: "I first become aware of myself, down in Essex, a thieving turnips for my living." Dickens would have us, in some obscure way, conceive the illicit act as the means of self-realization.

In the opening section of the novel the view moves back and
forth between the escaped criminal on the marshes and the harsh
life in the house of Pip's sister, Mrs. Joe Gargery. The "criminality"
of Pip and the convict is contrasted with the socially approved
cruelty and injustice of Mrs. Joe and her respectable friends. The
elders who come to the Christmas feast at the Gargerys' are pleased
to describe Pip as a criminal: the young are, according to Mr. Hub-
ble, "naterally wicious." During this most bleak of Christmas dinners the child is treated not only as outlaw, but as animal. In Mrs.
Joe's first speech Pip is called a "young monkey"; then, as the spirits
of the revellers rise, more and more comparisons are made between
boys and animals. Uncle Pumblechook, devouring his pork, toys
with the notion of Pip's having been born a "Squeaker":

> "If you had been born such, would you have been here now?
> Not you. . . ."
> "Unless in that form," said Mr. Wopsle, nodding towards the
> dish.
> "But I don't mean in that form, sir," returned Mr. Pumble-
> chook, who had an objection to being interrupted; "I mean, enjoy-
> ing himself with his elders and betters, and improving himself
> with their conversation, and rolling in the lap of luxury. Would he
> have been doing that? No, he wouldn't. And what would have
> been your destination?" turning on me again. "You would have
> been disposed of for so many shillings according to the market
> price of the article, and Dunstable the butcher would have come
> up to you as you lay in your straw, and he would have whipped
> you under his left arm, and with his right he would have tucked
> up his frock to get a penknife from out of his waistcoat-pocket,
> and he would have shed your blood and had your life. No bring-
> ing up by hand then. Not a bit of it!"

This identification of animal and human is continually repeated
in the opening chapters of the novel, and we catch its resonance
throughout the book. When the two convicts—Pip's "friend" and the
other fugitive, Magwitch's ancient enemy—are captured, we experience the horror of official justice, which treats the prisoners as if
they were less than human: "No one seemed surprised to see him,
or interested in seeing him, or glad to see him, or sorry to see him,
or spoke a word, except that somebody in the boat growled as if to

dogs, 'Give way, you!'" And the prison ship, lying beyond the mud of the shore, looked to Pip "like a wicked Noah's ark."

The theme of this first section of the novel—which concludes with the capture of Magwitch and his return to the prison ship—might be called "the several meanings of humanity." Only the three characters who are in some way social outcasts—Pip, Magwitch, and Joe Gargery the child-like blacksmith—act in charity and respect the humanity of others. To Magwitch Pip is distinctly not an animal, and not capable of adult wickedness: "You'd be but a fierce young hound indeed, if at your time of life you could help to hunt a wretched warmint." And when, after he is taken, the convict shields Pip by confessing to have stolen the Gargerys' pork pie, Joe's absolution affirms the dignity of man:

> "God knows you're welcome to it—so far as it was ever mine," returned Joe, with a saving remembrance of Mrs. Joe. "We don't know what you have done, but we wouldn't have you starved to death for it, poor miserable fellow-creatur.—Would us, Pip?"

The next section of the narrative is less tightly conceived than the introductory action. Time is handled loosely; Pip goes to school, and becomes acquainted with Miss Havisham of Satis House and the beautiful Estella. The section concludes when Pip has reached early manhood, been told of his expectations, and has prepared to leave for London. These episodes develop, with variations, the theme of childhood betrayed. Pip himself renounces his childhood by coming to accept the false social values of middle-class society. His perverse development is expressed by persistent images of the opposition between the human and the non-human, the living and the dead.

On his way to visit Miss Havisham for the first time, Pip spends the night with Mr. Pumblechook, the corn-chandler, in his lodgings behind his shop. The contrast between the aridity of this old hypocrite's spirit and the viability of his wares is a type of the conflict between natural growth and social form. Pip looks at all the shopkeeper's little drawers filled with bulbs and seed packets and wonders "whether the flower-seeds and bulbs ever wanted of a fine day to break out of those jails and bloom." The imagery of life repressed is developed further in the descriptions of Miss Havisham and Satis House. The first detail Pip notices is the abandoned brewery where the once active ferment has ceased; no germ of life is to be found in Satis House or in its occupants:

> . . . there were no pigeons in the dove-cot, no horses in the stable, no pigs in the sty, no malt in the storehouse, no smells of grains and beer in the copper or the vat. All the uses and scents of the brewery might have evaporated with its last reek of smoke. In a by-yard, there was a wilderness of empty casks. . . .

On top of these casks Estella dances with solitary concentration, and behind her, in a dark corner of the building, Pip fancies that he sees a figure hanging by the neck from a wooden beam, "a figure all in yellow white, with but one shoe to the feet; and it hung so, that I could see that the faded trimmings of the dress were like earthy paper, and that the face was Miss Havisham's."

Miss Havisham *is* death. From his visits to Satis House Pip acquires his false admiration for the genteel; he falls in love with Estella and fails to see that she is the cold instrument of Miss Havisham's revenge on human passion and on life itself. When Pip learns he may expect a large inheritance from an unknown source he immediately assumes (incorrectly) that Miss Havisham is his benefactor; she does not undeceive him. Money, which is also death, is appropriately connected with the old lady rotting away in her darkened room.

Conflicting values in Pip's life are also expressed by the opposed imagery of stars and fire. Estella is by name a star, and throughout the novel stars are conceived as pitiless: "And then I looked at the stars, and considered how awful it would be for a man to turn his face up to them as he froze to death, and see no help or pity in all the glittering multitude." Estella and her light are described as coming down the dark passage of Satis House "like a star," and when she has become a woman she is constantly surrounded by the bright glitter of jewelry.

Joe Gargery, on the other hand, is associated with the warm fire of the hearth or forge. It was his habit to sit and rake the fire between the lower bars of the kitchen grate, and his workday was spent at the forge. The extent to which Dickens intended the contrast between the warm and the cold lights—the vitality of Joe and the frigid glitter of Estella—is indicated in a passage that describes the beginnings of Pip's disillusionment with his expectations:

> When I woke up in the night . . . I used to think, with a
> weariness on my spirits, that I should have been happier and bet-
> ter if I had never seen Miss Havisham's face, and had risen to
> manhood content to be partners with Joe in the honest old forge.
> Many a time of an evening, when I sat alone looking at the fire,
> I thought, after all, there was no fire like the forge fire and the
> kitchen fire at home.
>
> Yet Estella was so inseparable from all my restlessness and dis-
> quiet of mind, that I really fell into confusion as to the limits of
> my own part in its production.

At the end of the novel Pip finds the true light on the homely
hearth, and in a last twist of the father-son theme, Joe emerges as a
true parent—the only kind of parent that Dickens could ever fully
approve, one that remains a child. The moral of this return to Joe
sharply contradicts the accepted picture of Dickens as a radical
critic of society: Joe is a humble countryman who is content with
the place in the social order he has been appointed to fulfill. He
fills it "well and with respect"; Pip learns that he can do no better
than to emulate him.

The second stage of Pip's three-phased story is set in London, and
the moral issues of the fiction are modulated accordingly. Instead of
the opposition between custom and the instinctive life, the novelist
treats the conflict between man and his social institutions. The
topics and themes are specific, and the satire, some of it wonderfully
deft, is more social than moral. Not all Dickens' social message is
presented by means that seem adequate. By satirizing Pip and his
leisure class friends (The Finches of the Grove, they call themselves) the novelist would have us realize that idle young men will
come to a bad end. Dickens is here expressing the Victorian Doctrine of Work—a pervasive notion that both inspired and reassured
his industrious contemporaries.

The difficulty for the modern reader, who is unmoved by the
objects of Victorian piety, is that the doctrine appears to be the
result, not of moral insight, but of didactic intent; it is presented
as statement, rather than as experience or dramatized perception,
and consequently it never modifies the course of fictional action or
the formation of character. The distinction is crucial: it is between
the Dickens who *sees* and the Dickens who *professes*; often between
the good and the bad sides of his art.

The novelist is on surer ground when he comes to define the nature of wealth in a mercantile society. Instead of moralistic condemnation we have a technique that resembles parable. Pip eventually learns that his ornamental life is supported, not by Miss Havisham, but by the labor and suffering of the convict Magwitch:

> "I swore arterwards, sure as ever I spec'lated and got rich, you should get rich. I lived rough, that you should live smooth; I worked hard that you should be above work. What odds, dear boy? Do I tell it fur you to feel a obligation? Not a bit. I tell it, fur you to know as that there dunghill dog wot you kept life in, got his head so high that he could make a gentleman—and, Pip, you're him!"

The convict would not only make a gentleman but own him. The blood horses of the colonists might fling up the dust over him as he was walking but, "I says to myself, 'If I ain't a gentleman, nor yet ain't got no learning, I'm the owner of such. All on you owns stock and land; which on you owns a brought-up London gentleman?' "

In this action Dickens has subtly led us to speculate on the connections between a gentleman and his money, on the dark origins of even the most respectable fortunes. We find Magwitch guilty of trying to own another human being, but we ask whether his actions are any more sinful than those of the wealthy *bourgeois*. There is a deeper moral in the fact that Magwitch's fortune at first destroyed the natural gentleman in Pip, but that after it was lost (it had to be forfeited to the state when Magwitch was finally captured) the "dung-hill dog" did actually make Pip a gentleman by evoking his finer feelings. This ironic distinction between "gentility" and what the father of English poetry meant by "gentilesse" is traditional in our literature and our mythology. In *Great Expectations* it arises out of the action and language of the fiction; consequently it moves and persuades us as literal statement never can.

The middle sections of the novel are dominated by the solid yet mysterious figure of Mr. Jaggers, Pip's legal guardian. Though Jaggers is not one of Dickens' greatest characters he is heavy with implication; he is so much at the center of this fable that we are challenged to interpret him—only to find that his meaning is ambiguous. On his first appearance Jaggers strikes a characteristic note of sinister authority:

He was a burly man of an exceedingly dark complexion, with an exceedingly large head and a correspondingly large hand. He took my chin in his large hand and turned up my face to have a look at me by the light of the candle. . . . His eyes were set very deep in his head, and were disagreeably sharp and suspicious. . . .

"How do you come here?"

"Miss Havisham sent for me, sir," I explained.

"Well! Behave yourself. I have a pretty large experience of boys, and you're a bad set of fellows. Now mind!" said he, biting the side of his great forefinger, as he frowned at me, "you behave yourself."

Pip wonders at first if Jaggers is a doctor. It is soon explained that he is a lawyer—what we now ambiguously call a *criminal* lawyer—but he is like a physician who treats moral malignancy, with the doctor's necessary detachment from individual suffering. Jaggers is interested not in the social operations of the law, but in the varieties of criminality. He exudes an antiseptic smell of soap and is described as washing his clients off as if he were a surgeon or a dentist.

Pip finds that Jaggers has "an air of authority not to be disputed . . . with a manner expressive of knowing something secret about every one of us that would effectually do for each individual if he chose to disclose it." When Pip and his friends go to dinner at Jaggers' house Pip observes that he "wrenched the weakest parts of our dispositions out of us." After the party his guardian tells Pip that he particularly liked the sullen young man they called Spider: "'Keep as clear of him as you can. But I like the fellow, Pip; he is one of the true sort. Why if I was a fortune-teller. . . . But I am not a fortune-teller,' he said. . . . 'You know what I am don't you?'" This question is repeated when Pip is being shown through Newgate Prison by Jaggers' assistant, Wemmick. The turnkey says of Pip: "Why then . . . he knows what Mr. Jaggers is."

But neither Pip nor the reader ever fully knows what Mr. Jaggers is. We learn, along with Pip, that Jaggers has manipulated the events which have shaped the lives of most of the characters in the novel; he has, in the case of Estella and her mother, dispensed a merciful but entirely personal justice; he is the only character who knows the web of secret relationships that are finally revealed to Pip. He dominates by the strength of his knowledge the world of guilt and sin—called *Little Britain*—of which his office is the center. He has, in brief, the powers that an artist exerts over the creatures of his fictional world, and that a god exerts over his creation.

As surrogate of the artist, Jaggers displays qualities of mind—complete impassibility, all-seeing unfeelingness—which are the opposite of Dickens', but of a sort that Dickens may at times have desired. Jaggers can be considered a fantasy figure created by a novelist who is forced by his intense sensibility to re-live the sufferings of his fellow men and who feels their agonies too deeply.

In both the poetry and fiction of the nineteenth century there are examples of a persistent desire of the artist *not to care.* The mood, which is perhaps an inevitable concomitant of Romanticism, is expressed in Balzac's ambivalence toward his great character Vautrin. As arch-criminal and Rousseauistic man, Vautrin represents all the attitudes that Balzac the churchman and monarchist ostensibly rejects, yet is presented as a kind of artist-hero, above the law, who sees through the social system with an almost noble cynicism.

Related attitudes are expressed in the theories of art developed by such different writers as Flaubert and Yeats. While—perhaps because—Flaubert himself suffered from hyperaesthesia, he conceived the ideal novelist as coldly detached, performing his examination with the deft impassivity of the surgeon. Yeats, the "last Romantic," found the construction of a mask or anti-self necessary to poetic creation, and insisted that the anti-self be cold and hard—all that he as poet and feeling man was not.

Dickens' evocation of this complex of attitudes is less political than Balzac's, less philosophical than Flaubert's or Yeats'. Jaggers has a complete understanding of human evil but, unlike the living artist, can wash his hands of it. He is above ordinary institutions; like a god he dispenses justice, and like a god displays infinite mercy through unrelenting severity:

> "Mind you, Mr. Pip," said Wemmick, gravely in my ear, as he took my arm to be more confidential; "I don't know that Mr. Jaggers does a better thing than the way in which he keeps himself so high. He's always so high. His constant height is of a piece with his immense abilities. That Colonel durst no more take leave of *him,* than that turnkey durst ask him his intentions respecting a case. Then between his height and them, he slips in his subordinate—don't you see?—and so he has 'em soul and body."

Pip merely wishes that he had "some other guardian of minor abilities."

The final moral vision of *Great Expectations* has to do with the nature of sin and guilt. After visiting Newgate Pip, still complacent and self-deceived, thinks how strange it was that he should be encompassed by the taint of prison and crime. He tries to beat the prison dust off his feet and to exhale its air from his lungs; he is going to meet Estella, who must not be contaminated by the smell of crime. Later it is revealed that Estella, the pure, is the bastard child of Magwitch and a murderess. Newgate is figuratively described as a greenhouse, and the prisoners as plants carefully tended by Wemmick, assistant to Mr. Jaggers. These disturbing metaphors suggest that criminality is the condition of life. Dickens would distinguish between the native, inherent sinfulness from which men can be redeemed, and that evil which destroys life: the sin of the hypocrite or oppressor, the smothering wickedness of corrupt institutions. The last stage of Pip's progression is reached when he learns to love the criminal and to accept his own implication in the common guilt.

Though Dickens' interpretation is theologically heterodox, he deals conventionally with the ancient question of free will and predestination. In one dramatic paragraph Pip's "fall" is compared with the descent of the rock slab on the sleeping victim in the Arabian Nights tale: Slowly, slowly, "all the work, near and afar, that tended to the end, had been accomplished; and in an instant the blow was struck, and the roof of my stronghold dropped upon me." Pip's fall was the result of a chain of predetermined events but he was, nevertheless, responsible for his own actions; toward the end of the novel Miss Havisham gravely informs him: "You have made your own snares. *I* never made them."

The patterns of culpability in *Great Expectations* are so intricate that the whole world of the novel is eventually caught in a single web of awful responsibility. The leg-iron, for example, which the convict removed with the file Pip stole for him is found by Orlick and used as a weapon to brain Mrs. Joe. By this fearsome chain of circumstance Pip shares the guilt for his sister's death.

Profound and suggestive as is Dickens' treatment of guilt and expiation in this novel, to trace its remoter implications is to find something excessive and idiosyncratic. A few years after he wrote *Great Expectations* Dickens remarked to a friend that he felt always as if he were wanted by the police—"irretrievably tainted." Compared to most of the writers of his time the Dickens of the later novels seems to be obsessed with guilt. The way in which his development-novel differs from those of his French compeers emphasizes an important quality of Dickens' art. The young heroes of *Le Rouge et le Noir* and *Le Père Goriot* proceed from innocence, through suffering to learning. They are surrounded by evil, and they can be destroyed by it. But Stendhal, writing in a rationalist tradition, and Balzac displaying the worldliness that only a Catholic novelist can command, seem astonishingly cool, even callous, besides Dickens. *Great Expectations* is outside either Cartesian or Catholic rationalism; profound as only an elementally simple book can be, it finds its analogues not in the novels of Dickens' English or French contemporaries, but in the writings of that other irretrievably tainted artist, Fyodor Dostoevski.

J. HILLIS MILLER

Our Mutual Friend

Our Mutual Friend is about "money, money, money, and what money can make of life." This theme plays an important part in Dickens' earlier fiction, too, but never does Dickens so concentrate his attention on the power of money as in this last of his completed novels. The central intrigue of the Harmon murder shows the inheritance of a great fortune apparently corrupting its inheritors, Noddy Boffin, and his ward, Bella Wilfer, just as the desire to "become respectable in the scale of society" corrupts Lizzie Hexam's brother, Charley. Money, one source of each character's station in life, separates Eugene Wrayburn and Lizzie Hexam. In this part of the story, as in others, Dickens is acutely conscious of the difference in people made by class distinctions. "How can I think of you as being on equal terms with me?" asks Lizzie of Eugene. "If my mind could put you on equal terms with me, you could not be yourself." Eugene's class status is an inextricable part of himself and stands between him and Lizzie as an almost palpable barrier. Class distinctions are shown in *Our Mutual Friend* to be closely intertwined with the power of money. The opposition of the "Voice of Society" to Eugene's marriage is as much based on the fact that Lizzie has

The afterword by J. Hillis Miller to *Our Mutual Friend* by Charles Dickens. Afterword copyright © 1964 by The New American Library, Inc., New York. Reprinted by permission of the author and publishers.

no money as on the fact that she is "a female waterman, turned factory girl." In the England of *Our Mutual Friend* inherited rank is in the process of giving way to the universal solvent of money, and most of the characters set their hearts on "money, money, money."

Mr. Podsnap's value in Mr. Podsnap's eyes is exactly determined by the amount of money he has, just as his possessions are valuable to him only because they are worth so much cash. Greed motivates Silas Wegg and Rogue Riderhood, characters from the bottom of society, as much as it motivates the Veneerings, the Lammles, Fascination Fledgeby, and other characters near the top of society. A minor character like Twemlow has been rendered ineffectual for life by the gift of a small annuity from his cousin, Lord Snigsworth, and another character, Mortimer Lightwood, says, "My own small income . . . has been an effective Something, in the way of preventing me from turning to at Anything."

The good characters are obsessed with money, too. John Harmon's purpose in life is to find some way to take the curse from the Harmon fortune, and the same desire secretly motivates Mr. Boffin. Old Riah suffers in the false position of being taken as the miserly head of Pubsey and Co. Even Betty Higden concentrates her waning energy on avoiding the workhouse and on protecting the burial money she has sewn in her dress. Her central aim is a desire for financial independence. From the top to the bottom of society most of the characters in *Our Mutual Friend* have their lives determined in one way or another by money, and think of little else.

What *is* money, for Dickens, and what has it "made of life"? Money, he sees, is the attribution of value to what is without value in itself: paper, gold, dust, earth, mud. The Harmon fortune has come from dust, the dust that rises in manmade geological formations around Boffin's Bower. Noddy Boffin is "the Golden Dustman." In one remarkable passage dust, the material source of money, is shown to be present everywhere in the city, along with a kindred mystery, the paper which is the basis of another form of currency:

> The grating wind sawed rather than blew; and as it sawed, the sawdust whirled about the sawpit. Every street was a sawpit, and there were no top-sawyers; every passenger was an under-sawyer, with the sawdust blinding him and choking him.
>
> That mysterious paper currency which circulates in London when the wind blows gyrated here and there and everywhere.

Whence can it come, whither can it go? It hangs on every bush, flutters in every tree, is caught flying by the electric wires, haunts every enclosure, drinks at every pump, cowers at every grating, shudders upon every plot of grass, seeks rest in vain behind the legions of iron rails.

If money is the ascribing of value to valueless matter, the basis of its power for evil over man is his forgetting of this fact. *Our Mutual Friend* is about a whole society which has forgotten. Instead of seeing that man has made money of dust and is the source of its value, this society takes money as the ultimate value-in-itself, the measure and source of all other value. As one of the Voices of Society says, "A man may do anything lawful for money. But for no money! Bosh!" The novel is a brilliant revelation of the results of this false worship of money.

When money is detached both from its material basis and from its human origin, it takes on a power of infinite self-multiplication. Cut off from reality and yet treated by men as the final criterion of worth, its infinity is like that reached when any number is divided by zero. "Money makes money," says Mr. Boffin, "as well as makes everything else." Such a false absolute are those "Shares," which, in their inexhaustible power to duplicate themselves and make everything of nothing, Dickens describes as the virtual god of a moneyed society. Like the mysterious paper currency blown everywhere in London, Shares pervade every corner of the nation's life and determine its nature:

As is well known to the wise in their generation, traffic in Shares is the one thing to have to do with in this world. Have no antecedents, no established character, no cultivation, no ideas, no manners; have Shares. Have Shares enough to be on Boards of Direction in capital letters, oscillate on mysterious business between London and Paris, and be great. Where does he come from? Shares. Where is he going to? Shares. What are his tastes? Shares. Has he any principles? Shares. What squeezes him into Parliament? Shares. Perhaps he never of himself achieved success in anything, never originated anything, never produced anything! Sufficient answer to all; Shares. O mighty Shares!

Money in its proliferation is hopelessly separated from any authentic human value. Its infinity is nothingness. The human beings who measure themselves and one another by such a yardstick become nothing themselves.

This emptying out of human beings as they become more and more alienated from reality can be seen everywhere in *Our Mutual Friend*.

Most obvious is the hollowness of society people like the Veneerings, the Lammles, and their "friends" the "Fathers of the Scrip-Church." As the Veneerings' name suggests, such people are a false surface with nothing beneath it. If people in "Society" are worth exactly the amount of money (or Shares) they possess, and if money is a human fiction, then the appearance of money is as good as really possessing it, as long as one is not found out. The real possession of money is nothing in itself, and the pretended possession of money is a nothing to the second power, which is neither worse nor better. The Veneering dinner parties are an elaborate theatrical ceremony resting on nothing, and the people who come to these parties have been so dehumanized by their submission to money that they exist not as individuals, but as their abstract roles, "Boots," "Brewer," and so on.

In one sense it is true to say that Dickens shows people turned into objects by money. Instead of being a unique and therefore infinitely valuable individual, each person becomes his monetary worth, an object interchangeable with others. To Mr. Podsnap it seems that his daughter can "be exactly put away like the plate, brought out like the plate, polished like the plate, counted, weighed, and valued like the plate." One of the potentates of Society describes Lizzie Hexam as a mere engine, fueled by so many pounds of beefsteak and so many pints of porter, and deriving therefrom power to row her boat. Bella Wilfer has been "willed away, like a horse, or a dog, or a bird," or "like a dozen of spoons." She suspects John Rokesmith of "speculating" in her. Her involvement in the Harmon mystery has alienated her from herself, and "made [her] the property of strangers."

Such objectifying is not the end of the malign magic performed on men by money. Money turns people into objects which are, like the Podsnap plate, valued only according to the money they are worth. This monetary measure of man might more properly be called a subjectifying. Money is an absolute value which has been generated by people in their living together. Another way to put this is to say that its value is entirely subjective. This value lies only in the collective hallucination of an existence where nothing exists, like the emperor's clothes. A piece of paper currency is worthless scrip. Its value is entirely *mediated*, that is, it is valued not for what it is in itself, but only as it is valued by others. In *Our Mutual Friend* all things and people have the mediated worth of a piece of paper money.

The title of the novel may be taken as an allusion to one form of this mediation. John Rokesmith exists not only for himself, but as he appears in the eyes of other people, and Bella Wilfer is guided at first in her response to him not by her own honest reaction, but by what other people think. Many characters in *Our Mutual Friend* are powerless to confront another person or thing directly. Like the unregenerate Bella, they can see others only through the haze which money casts over everything. This means that they value other people only as society values them, according to their worth in pounds, shillings, and pence. But money has reality only when it is based on some solid human or material reality. The characters in *Our Mutual Friend*, in their failure to see this and in their acceptance of money as intrinsically valuable, have come to live in a collective mirage. This mirage is a closed circuit in which nothing is reflected by nothing. Veneering's election to Parliament is a good example of this. The Veneerings, who are nothing in themselves, give value to the Lammles, Lady Tippins, and the rest, who are nothing in themselves, the Lammles give value to the Veneerings, and so back and forth, in a vain mirroring of nothing by nothing.

The motif of a literal mirroring occurs at crucial points in *Our Mutual Friend*. Poor little Miss Podsnap has derived her early views of life from "the reflections of it in her father's boots, and in the walnut and rosewood tables of the dim drawing-rooms, and in their swarthy giants of looking-glasses." She confronts life indirectly, as it is mediated by the massive presence of her father and his possessions. To see a Veneering dinner party reflected in "the great looking-glass above the sideboard," to see the vain Bella admiring herself in her mirror, or to see Fledgeby secretly watching Riah's reflection in the chimney-glass is to witness a concrete revelation of the way the lives of such people are self-mirroring. The reflection in the mirror is emptied of its solidity and presented as a thin surface of appearance hiding fathomless depths of nullity. Mirroring brings to light the vacuity of people whose lives are determined by money. Each such character is reflected in the blankness of the glass, and can see others only as they are mediated by a reflected image.

When this detachment from solidity is complete, human beings have only one opening for their energies: the attempt to dominate others by rising in the unreal scale which is generated in a society dominated by money. The image of a vertical scale permeates *Our Mutual Friend*. The characters feel themselves higher or lower on this scale as they possess more or less money, or as they can cheat others out of money in the perpetual poker game which society sustains. Mr. Boffin invokes the primary law of an acquisitive society in his defense of miserliness: "Scrunch or be scrunched." The Lammles, when they find that each has married the other under the mistaken impression that he is rich, decide to cooperate in fleecing society. Fascination Fledgeby seeks the secret control of others money gives, and Silas Wegg, exulting in the power he thinks the Harmon will gives him, declares he is one hundred, no, five hundred times the man Noddy Boffin is. The unrecognized emptiness of money makes it an unlimited instrument of man's will to power.

A society in which personal relations reduce themselves to a struggle for dominance develops that drama of *looks* and *faces* which is so important in *Our Mutual Friend*. Scenes in the novel are frequently presented as a conflict of masks. Each person tries to hide his own secret and to probe behind a misleading surface and find the secrets of others. The prize of a successful uncovering is the power that goes with knowing and not being known. Bella Wilfer finds that the Boffin household has become a confrontation of stealthy faces: "What with taking heed of these two faces, and what with feeling conscious that the stealthy occupation must set some mark on her own, Bella soon began to think that there was not a candid or a natural face among them all but Mrs. Boffin's." In the same way the Lammles exchange hidden looks over the heads of their unconscious victim, Georgiana Podsnap, and Silas Wegg and Mr. Venus trade glances as Wegg reads stories about misers to Mr. Boffin. In this case, as in the others, the master of the situation is the man whose face is an opaque nonreflector and remains unread.

In *Our Mutual Friend* the unreality of money has spread out to define the lives of most of the characters and to dissolve them in its emptiness. Master or slave, high on the scale or low, such characters float free in an unsubstantial realm of subjective fantasy. This quality is the chief source of the comedy of the novel. As in Dickens' earlier fiction, this comedy has its source in the incongruity of a mind enclosed in its own grotesque vision of things. In *Our Mutual Friend* this detachment has a special linguistic expression, partly a matter of the language used by the characters themselves and partly a matter of the way the narrator describes them. Both narrator and characters speak in metaphors which have separated themselves from their material basis, and hover in a verbal realm, a realm which perfectly defines the deracinated existence of the characters. What begins as a *jeu d'esprit*, a vivid way of describing a character or event, undermines the human reality it names and infects it parasitically with its own inane unreality. The Veneerings' butler is first *"like* a gloomy Analytical Chemist," but the figure of speech soon displaces the reality, and the butler becomes simply "the Analytical." In the same way Mrs. Podsnap is a rocking horse, Gaffer Hexam is a bird of prey, Mr. Wilfer is a cherub, and so on. Sometimes a whole scene is pervaded by a figure of speech and is transformed into a surrealistic nightmare, as in the case of a Podsnap soirée which is described as a steam bath of dinner smells:

> And now the haunch of mutton vapour-bath, having received a gamey infusion and a few last touches of sweets and coffee, was quite ready, and the bathers came. . . . Bald bathers folded their arms and talked to Mr. Podsnap on the hearth-rug; sleek-whiskered bathers, with hats in their hands, lunged at Mrs. Podsnap and retreated; prowling bathers went about looking into ornamental boxes and bowls as if they had suspicions of larceny on the part of the Podsnaps and expected to find something they had lost at the bottom; bathers of the gentler sex sat silently comparing ivory shoulders.

In such passages Dickens admirably exposes the hollowness of his people by describing them in language which affirms that a fantastic metaphor is as real here as anything else. The characters themselves use language which is hilariously detached from reality, like the poetry Wegg ludicrously misapplies to any situation. Dickens' characters, even stupid ones, have an extraordinary gift of speech. The comic characters in *Our Mutual Friend* unwittingly use this power to reveal their own vacuity. The weird scenes between Wegg and Venus, or the gammon and spinach of the Voices of Society, or the gorgeous nonsense of the colloquies between Mrs. Wilfer and Lavinia are triumphs of this mode of comedy. Such characters are cut off from any anchor of substantial feeling and release a splendid linguistic energy which expands inexhaustibly in the void. Speech, like money, has become in *Our Mutual Friend* a traffic in counterfeit coin.

If the novel demonstrates what money can make of life, it also shows what lies behind money, and it shows characters who escape from the collective dream it creates. If the personages are mostly bewitched by a false god, the novel as a whole is a work of demystification.

This is accomplished first through the language of the narrator. The voice the reader hears is cool and detached, very different, for example, from the emotionally involved voice of David Copperfield as he tells his own story. This is especially apparent in the scenes of the Veneering dinner parties. These are described in the present tense, in language that is cold and withdrawn, terse, with an elliptical economy new in Dickens. Sometimes verbs and articles are omitted, and the reader confronts a series of nouns with modifiers which produces the scene before his mind's eye as if by magical incantation: "Dining-room no less magnificent than drawing-room; tables superb; all the camels out, and all laden. Splendid cake, covered with Cupids, silver, and true-lovers' knots. Splendid bracelet, produced by Veneering before going down, and clasped upon the arm of bride." The ironic detachment of such language makes the consciousness of the narrator (and of the reader) into a mirror uncovering the emptiness of the characters. The reader himself becomes the great looking-glass above the sideboard which shows what money has made of life. This mirrorlike detachment to a greater or lesser degree is the narrative perspective of the entire novel. It allows the reader to escape from the enchantment which holds the characters.

Escape to what? What waking reality, for Dickens, lies behind the dream? Dickens gives unusual attention in this novel to elemental matter. If money is in one sense unreal, in another sense the paper or metal of which it is made has a solidity which mediated subjectives can never possess. Mr. Podsnap's hideous epergne reflects no value on its owner, but his desire not to have beautiful things on his table has inadevertently made it possible to see in his silver and plate the sheer, massive inertia of matter—heavy, impenetrable, meaningless, alien to man:

> Hideous solidity was the characteristic of the Podsnap plate. Everything was made to look as heavy as it could and to take up as much room as possible. Everything said boastfully, "Here you

have as much of me in my ugliness as if I were only lead; but I am so many ounces of precious metal worth so much an ounce—wouldn't you like to melt me down?" A corpulent straddling epergne, blotched all over as if it had broken out in an eruption rather than been ornamented, delivered this address from an unsightly silver platform in the centre of the table.

The otherness of elemental matter, brought to the surface in this passage, is kept constantly before the reader throughout *Our Mutual Friend*. It is the substance which lies behind or beneath the hollowness of an avaricious society. This substance is there on the literal level of the novel: in the fire where Lizzie Hexam sees pictures of her life, in the wind which blows the dust through the streets, creating a wild disorder in the clouds, and making the pitiful little tumults in the streets of no account. Elemental matter is present in the dust of the Harmon Mounds, in the mud of the river, in the dunghills where Noddy Boffin's misers hid their gold, in the gold itself in the Bank of England—in which Bella would like to have "an hour's gardening, with a bright copper shovel." Elemental matter is present in the river which flows through all the novel and is the scene of much of its action. All four elements are unobtrusively gathered together when Charley Hexam says of a glow in burning coal: "That's gas, that is, coming out of a bit of a forest that's been under the mud that was under the water in the days of Noah's Ark."

These material elements are not "symbols," if that means expressions of some reality which transcends them, and for which they stand. The river, the dust, the wind, and the fire are what they are: mere matter. *Our Mutual Friend* differs in this from Dickens' earlier novels. In *Dombey and Son* or *David Copperfield* the sea is a symbol of transcendent spiritual reality. The river of *Our Mutual Friend* is, in most of the passages describing it, only water, but, like the other material elements, it has a substantiality which the Voice of Society lacks. The narrator keeps this reality before the reader throughout the novel, not only in the literal scene, but in metaphors, overt and covert, in a thousand subtle linguistic touches which refer back to it, as the mutton vapor bath links the Podsnap drawing rooms to the Thames, or as Fascination Fledgeby, after his thrashing by Lammle, is shown "plunging and gambolling all over his bed, like a porpoise or dolphin in its native element."

The various dramatic actions of the novel show characters breaking through illusion to confront material reality. Such a confrontation takes two forms. There is first the literal descent into matter, Silas Wegg's plunge into a garbage cart, the drownings or near drownings of John Harmon, George Radfoot, Gaffer Hexam, Rogue Riderhood, Bradley Headstone, and Eugene Wrayburn. These entries into matter are also encounters with death, and dispersion into dust to which we shall all come at last. In addition, a human and inward form of substantial reality plays an important role in *Our Mutual Friend:* emotions, the affective depths of the self. Alienated, unreal people are incapable of authentic feeling. Their emotions are falsified or betrayed by their conscious behavior. The story of Bradley Headstone shows a man of strong repressed emotions destroyed when these feelings rise from his inner depths. Bradley's feelings are explicitly associated with the sea, those outer depths of water. "No man knows till the time comes, what depths are within him," Bradley tells Lizzie. "To me you brought it; on me, you forced it; and the bottom of this raging sea . . . has been heaved up ever since."

Only the characters who confront material and emotional depths, and then return to live their surface lives in terms of those depths can reconcile "Society" and reality. Eugene Wrayburn returns from his near death in the river to reject class distinctions, marry Lizzie Hexam, and conquer the boredom which has undermined his life, making him "like one cast away, for the want of something to trust in, and care for, and think well of." Bella Wilfer, who, like Eugene, has been "giddy for want of the weight of some sustaining purpose," renounces her desire for money and chooses to become the "Mendicant's Bride." This proves that "she's the true golden gold at heart." Gold does not measure the value of man. Man's heart, golden or empty, gives value to money and makes it a force for good or for evil. In the hands of Bella and John Harmon the Harmon fortune "turns bright again, after a long, long rust in the dark, and at last begins to sparkle in the sunlight." Just as Mr. Boffin's change to a miser is only apparent, just as Rogue Riderhood is not changed by his near death in the Thames, and just as Eugene Wrayburn has been a good fellow all along, so Bella Wilfer does not really change. Her true nature is brought to the surface. Even in this last of his finished novels, a novel with so many apparent transformations of character, Dickens remains true to his feeling that each man or woman has a fixed nature, a selfhood which may be obscured or distorted but never essentially altered.

T. S. ELIOT

Wilkie Collins and Dickens

It is to be hoped that some scholarly and philosophic critic of the present generation may be inspired to write a book on the history and æsthetic of melodrama. The golden age of melodrama passed, it is true, before any person living was aware of its existence: in the very middle of the last century. But there are many living who are not too young to remember the melodramatic stage before the cinema replaced it; who have sat entranced, in the front stalls of local or provincial theatres, before some representation of *East Lynne*, or *The White Slave*, or *No Mother to Guide Her*; and who are not too old to have observed with curious interest the replacement of dramatic melodrama by cinematographic melodrama, and the dissociation of the elements of the old three-volume melodramatic novel into the various types of the modern 300-page novel. Those who have lived before such terms as "high-brow fiction," "thrillers" and "detective fiction" were invented realize that melodrama is perennial and that the craving for it is perennial and must be satisfied. If we cannot get this satisfaction out of what the publishers present as "literature," then we will read—with less and less pretence of concealment—what we call "thrillers." But in the golden age of melodramatic fiction there was no such distinction. The best novels *were* thrilling; the distinction of genre between such-and-such a profound "psychological" novel of to-day and such-and-such a masterly "detective" novel of to-day is greater than the distinction of genre between *Wuthering Heights,* or even *The Mill on the Floss,* and *East Lynne,* the last of which "achieved an enormous and instantaneous success, and was translated into every known language, including Parsee and Hindustani." We believe that several contemporary novels have been "translated into every known language"; but we are sure that they have less in common with *The Golden Bowl,* or *Ulysses,* or even *Beauchamp's Career,* than *East Lynne* has in common with *Bleak House.*

In order to enjoy and to appreciate the work of Wilkie Collins, we ought to be able to reassemble the elements which have been dissociated in the modern novel. Collins is the contemporary of Dickens, Thackeray, George Eliot; of Charles Reade and almost of Captain Marryat. He has something in common with all of these novelists; but particularly and significantly with Dickens. Collins was the friend and sometimes the collaborator of Dickens; and the work of the two men ought to be studied side by side. There is, unhappily for the literary critic, no full biography of Wilkie Collins; and Forster's *Life of Dickens* is, from this point of view, most unsatisfactory. Forster was a notable biographer; but as a critic of the work of Dickens his view was a very narrow view. To anyone who knows the bare facts of Dickens's acquaintance with Collins, and who has studied the work of the two men, their relationship and their influence upon one another is an important subject of study. And a comparative study of their novels can do much to illuminate the question of the difference between the dramatic and the melodramatic in fiction.

Dickens's "best novel" is probably *Bleak House;* that is Mr. Chesterton's opinion, and there is no better critic of Dickens living than Mr. Chesterton. Collins's best novel—or, at any rate, the only one of Collins's novels which everyone knows—is *The Woman in White.* Now *Bleak House* is the novel in which Dickens most closely approaches Collins (and after *Bleak House, Little Dorrit* and parts of *Martin Chuzzlewit*); and *The Woman in White* is the novel in which Collins most closely approaches Dickens. Dickens excelled in character; in the creation of characters of greater intensity than human beings. Collins was not usually strong in the creation of

character; but he was a master of plot and situation, of those elements of drama which are most essential to melodrama. *Bleak House*
is Dickens's finest piece of construction; and *The Woman in White*
contains Collins's most real characterization. Everyone knows Count
Fosco and Marion Halcombe intimately; only the most perfect Collins reader can remember even half a dozen of his other characters
by name.

Count Fosco and Marion are indeed real personages to us; as
"real" as much greater characters are, as real as Becky Sharp or
Emma Bovary. In comparison with the characters of Dickens they
lack only that kind of reality which is almost supernatural, which
hardly seems to belong to the character by natural right, but seems
rather to descend upon him by a kind of inspiration or grace. Collins's best characters are fabricated, with consummate skill, before
our eyes; in Dickens's greatest figures we see no process or calculation. Dickens's figures belong to poetry, like figures of Dante or
Shakespeare, in that a single phrase, either by them or about them,
may be enough to set them wholly before us. Collins has no phrases.
Dickens can with a phrase make a character as real as flesh and
blood—"What a life young Bailey's was"—like Farinata

> Chi fur gli maggior tui?

or like Cleopatra,

> I saw her once
> Hop forty paces through the public street.

Dickens's characters are real because there is no one like them; Collins's because they are so painstakingly coherent and lifelike.
Whereas Dickens often introduces a great character carelessly, so
that we do not realize, until the story is far advanced, with what a
powerful personage we have to do, Collins, at least in these two
figures in *The Woman in White,* employs every advantage of dramatic effect. Much of our impression of Marion is due to the words
in which she is first presented:

> The instant my eyes rested on her I was struck by the rare
> beauty of her form, and by the unaffected grace of her attitude.
> Her figure was tall, yet not too tall; comely and well developed,
> yet not fat; her head set on her shoulders with an easy, pliant firm-
> ness; her waist, perfection in the eyes of a man, for it occupied its

natural place, it filled out its natural circle, it was visibly and de-
lightfully undeformed by stays. She had not heard my entrance
into the room, and I allowed myself the luxury of admiring her
for a few moments before I moved one of the chairs near me as
the least embarrassing means of attracting her attention. She
turned towards me immediately. The easy elegance of every movement of her limbs and body, as soon as she began to advance from
the far end of the room, set me in a flutter of expectation to see
her face clearly. She left the window—and I said to myself, The
lady is dark. She moved forward a few steps—and I said to myself,
The lady is young. She approached nearer, and I said to myself
(with a sense of surprise which words fail me to express), The
lady is ugly!

The introduction of Count Fosco—too long to quote in full—requires
many more small strokes; but we should observe, Marion Halcombe
being already given, that our impression of the Count is made very
much stronger by being given to us as Marion's impression of him:

> There are peculiarities in his personal appearance, his habits,
> and his amusements, which I should blame in the boldest terms,
> or ridicule in the most merciless manner, if I had seen them in
> another man. What is it that makes me unable to blame them, or
> to ridicule them in *him*?

After this who can forget the white mice or the canaries, or the way
in which Count Fosco treated Sir Percival's sulky bloodhound? If
The Woman in White is the greatest of Collins's novels, it is so
because of these two characters. If we examine the book apart from
Marion and Fosco, we must admit that it is not Collins's finest work
of construction, and that certain of his peculiar melodramatic gifts
are better displayed in other books. The book is dramatic because
of two characters; it is dramatic in the way in which the dramatic
differs from the melodramatic. Sir Percival Glyde is a figure of
pasteboard, and the mystery and the plot of which he is the centre
are almost grotesque. The one of Collins's books which is the most
perfect piece of construction, and the best balanced between plot
and character, is *The Moonstone*; the one which reaches the greatest
melodramatic intensity is *Armadale*.

The Moonstone is the first and greatest of English detective novels.
We say *English* detective novels, because there is also the work of Poe,

which has a *pure* detective interest. The detective story, as created by Poe, is something as specialized and as intellectual as a chess problem; whereas the best English detective fiction has relied less on the beauty of the mathematical problem and much more on the intangible human element. In detective fiction England probably excels other countries; but in a genre invented by Collins and not by Poe. In *The Moonstone* the mystery is finally solved, not altogether by human ingenuity, but largely by accident. Since Collins, the best heroes of English detective fiction have been, like Sergeant Cuff, fallible; they play their part, but never the sole part, in the unravelling. Sherlock Holmes, not altogether a typical English sleuth, is a partial exception; but even Holmes exists, not solely because of his prowess, but largely because he is, in the Jonsonian sense, a humorous character, with his needle, his boxing, and his violin. But Sergeant Cuff, far more than Holmes, is the ancestor of the healthy generation of amiable, efficient, professional but fallible inspectors of fiction among whom we live to-day. And *The Moonstone,* a book twice the length of the "thrillers" that our contemporary masters write, maintains its interest and suspense at every moment. It does this by devices of a Dickensian type; for Collins, in addition to his particular merits, was a Dickens without genius. The book is a comedy of humours. The eccentricities of Mr. Franklin Blake, the satire on false philanthropy in the character of Mr. Godfrey Ablewhite (to say nothing of the Life, Letters and Labours of Miss Jane Ann Stamper), Betteridge with his *Robinson Crusoe,* and his daughter Penelope, support the narrative. In other of Collins's novels, the trick of passing the narration from one hand to another, and employing every device of letters and diaries, becomes tedious and even unplausible (for instance, in *Armadale,* the terrific villain, Miss Gwilt, commits herself to paper far too often and far too frankly); but in *The Moonstone* these devices succeed, every time, in stimulating our interest afresh just at the moment when it was about to flag.

And in *The Moonstone* Collins succeeds in bringing into play those aids of "atmosphere" in which Dickens (and the Brontës) exhibited such genius, and in which Collins has everything except their genius. For his purpose, he does not come off badly. Compare the description of the discovery of Rosanna's death in the Shivering Sands—and notice how carefully, beforehand, the *mise-en-scène* of the Shivering Sands is prepared for us—with the shipwreck of Steerforth in *David Copperfield.* We may say "There is no comparison!" but there *is* a comparison; and however unfavourable to Collins, it must increase our estimation of his skill.

There is another characteristic of Wilkie Collins which also brings him closer to Dickens, and it is a characteristic which has very great melodramatic value: compare the work of Collins with the work of Mrs. Henry Wood, already mentioned, and one sees how important for melodrama is the presence or absence of this. Forster, in his *Life of Dickens,* observes:

> On the coincidences, resemblances and surprises of life Dickens liked especially to dwell, and few things moved his fancy so pleasantly. The world, he would say, was so much smaller than we thought it; we were all so connected by fate without knowing it; people supposed to be far apart were so constantly elbowing each other; and tomorrow bore so close a resemblance to nothing half so much as to yesterday.

Forster mentions this peculiarity early in the life of Dickens, long before Dickens became acquainted with Collins. We may take it that this feeling was common to Dickens and Collins, and that it may have been one of the causes of their being drawn so sympathetically together, once they had become acquainted. The two men had obviously in common a passionate feeling for the drama. Each had qualities which the other lacked, and they had certain qualities in common. It is perfectly reasonable to believe that the relations of the two men—of which Forster gives us only the barest and most unsatisfactory hints—affected profoundly the later work of each. We seem to find traces of it in *Little Dorrit* and *The Tale of Two Cities.* Collins could never have invented Durdles and Deputy; but Durdles and Deputy were obviously to play their part in a whole, *bien charpenté* as Collins's work is, and as the work of Dickens prior to *Bleak House* is not.

One of the minor works of Collins which illustrates especially this insistence upon the "coincidences, resemblances and surprises of life" is *The Frozen Deep.* The story, as we read it, was patched up from the melodrama which Collins wrote first; which was privately performed with great success on several occasions, and in which Dickens took the leading part. Collins was the cleverer at writing stage pieces; but we may imagine that Dickens was the cleverer at acting them; and Dickens may have given to the rôle of

Richard Wardour, in acting it, an individuality which it certainly lacks in the story. This story, we may add for the benefit of those who have not read it, depends upon coincidence with a remarkably long arm; for the two men who ought not to meet—the accepted and the rejected lover—do meet, and under the most unlikely conditions they join, without knowing each other's identity, the same Polar Expedition.

In *The Frozen Deep* Collins wrote a piece of pure melodrama. That is to say, it is nothing but melodrama. We are asked to accept an improbability, simply for the sake of seeing the thrilling situation which arises in consequence. But the frontier of drama and melodrama is vague; the difference is largely a matter of emphasis; perhaps no drama has ever been greatly and permanently successful without a large melodramatic element. What is the difference between *The Frozen Deep* and *Œdipus the King*? It is the difference between coincidence, set without shame or pretence, and fate—which merges into character. It is not necessary, for high drama, that accident should be eliminated; you cannot formulate the proportion of accident that is permissible. But in great drama character is always felt to be—not more important than plot—but somehow integral with plot. At least, one is left with the conviction that if circumstances had not arranged the events to fall out in such and such a way, the personages were, after all, such that they would have ended just as badly, or just as well, and more or less similarly. And sometimes the melodramatic—the accidental—becomes for Collins the dramatic—the fatal. There is one short tale, not one of his best known, and far from being his best—a tale with an extremely improbable ghost—which nevertheless is almost dramatic. It is called *The Haunted Hotel*; what makes it better than a mere readable second-rate ghost story is the fact that fatality in this story is no longer merely a wire jerking the figures. The principal character, the fatal woman, is herself obsessed by the idea of fatality; her motives are melodramatic; she therefore compels the coincidences to occur, feeling that she is compelled to compel them. In this story, as the chief character is internally melodramatic, the story itself ceases to be merely melodramatic, and partakes of true drama.

There is another characteristic of certain tales of Collins's, which may be said to belong to melodrama, or to the melodramatic part of drama. It consists in delaying, longer than one would conceive it possible to delay, a conclusion which is inevitable and wholly for-

seen. A story like *The New Magdalen* is from a certain moment
merely a study in stage suspense; the *dénouement* is postponed,
again and again, by every possible ingenuity; the situations are in
the most effective sense theatrical, without being in the profounder
sense dramatic. They are seldom, as in *The Woman in White*, situations of conflict between significant personalities; they are more often
conflicts between chessmen which merely occupy hostile positions on
the board. Such, for instance, is the prolonged battle between Captain Wragge and Mrs. Lecomte at Aldburgh, in *No Name*.

The one of Collins's novels which we should choose as the most
typical, or as the best of the more typical, and which we should
recommend as a specimen of the melodramatic fiction of the epoch,
is *Armadale*. It has no merit beyond melodrama, and it has every
merit that melodrama can have. If Miss Gwilt did not have to bear
such a large part of the burden of revealing her own villainy, the
construction would be almost perfect. Like most of Collins's novels,
it has the immense—and nowadays more and more rare—merit of
being never dull. It has, to a very high degree, the peculiar Collins
merit above mentioned, which we might call the air of spurious
fatality. The machinery of the book is operated by the Dream. The
mind of the reader is very carefully prepared for acceptance of the
Dream; first by the elaborately staged coincidence of the two cousins
getting marooned on the wreck of the ship on which the father of
the one had long before entrapped the father of the other; secondly
by the way in which the Dream is explained away by the doctor.
The doctor's explanation is so reasonable that the reader immediately
reacts in favour of the Dream. Then, the character of the dreamer
himself is made plausibly intuitive; and the stages by which the
various parts of the Dream are realized are perfectly managed. Particularly is this true of the scene in which, after some excellent
comedy of humours on the boating party, Miss Gwilt arrives at sun-
set on the desolate shore of the Norfolk Broads. By means of the
Dream, we are kept in a state of tension which makes it possible to
believe in characters which otherwise we should find preposterous.

The greatest novels have something in them which will ensure
their being read, at least by a small number of people, even if the
novel, as a literary form, ceases to be written. It is not pretended
that the novels of Wilkie Collins have this permanence. They are
interesting only if we enjoy "reading novels." But novels are still
being written; and there is no contemporary novelist who could not

learn something from Collins in the art of interesting and exciting the reader. So long as novels are written, the possibilities of melo-drama must from time to time be re-explored. The contemporary "thriller" is in danger of becoming stereotyped; the conventional murder is discovered in the first chapter by the conventional butler, and the murderer is discovered in the last chapter by the conven-tional inspector—after having been already discovered by the reader. The resources of Wilkie Collins are, in comparison, inexhaustible.

And even if we refused to take Collins very seriously by himself, we can hardly fail to treat him with seriousness if we recognize that the art of which he was a master was an art which neither Charles Reade nor Dickens despised. You cannot define Drama and Melo-drama so that they shall be reciprocally exclusive; great drama has something melodramatic in it, and the best melodrama partakes of the greatness of drama. *The Moonstone* is very near to *Bleak House*. The theft of a diamond has some of the same blighting effect on the lives about it as the suit in Chancery; Rosanna Spearman is de-stroyed by the diamond as Miss Flite is destroyed by Chancery. Col-lins's novels suggest questions which no student of "the art of fic-tion" can afford to neglect. It is possible that the artist can be too conscious of his "art." Perhaps Henry James—who in his own prac-tice could be not only "interesting," but had a very cunning mastery of the finer melodrama—may have had as a critic a bad influence. We cannot afford to forget that the first—and not one of the least difficult—requirements of either prose or verse is that it should be interesting.

RAYMOND WILLIAMS

The Industrial Novels

Our understanding of the response to industrialism would be incomplete without reference to an interesting group of novels, written at the middle of the century, which not only provide some of the most vivid descriptions of life in an unsettled industrial society, but also illustrate certain common assumptions within which the direct response was undertaken. There are the facts of the new society, and there is this structure of feeling, which I will try to illustrate from *Mary Barton, North and South, Hard Times, Sybil, Alton Locke,* and *Felix Holt.*

Mary Barton (1848)

Mary Barton, particularly in its early chapters, is the most moving response in literature to the industrial suffering of the 1840s. The really impressive thing about the book is the intensity of the effort to record, in its own terms, the feel of everyday life in the working-class homes. The method, in part, is that of documentary record, as may be seen in such details as the carefully annotated reproduction of dialect, the carefully included details of food prices in the ac-

From *Culture and Society 1780-1950* (London: Chatto and Windus; and New York: Columbia University Press, 1958), pp. 87-109. Copyright © 1958 by Raymond Williams. Reprinted by permission of the author and publishers.

count of the tea-party, the itemized description of the furniture of the Bartons' living-room, and the writing-out of the ballad (again annotated) of *The Oldham Weaver*. The interest of this record is considerable, but the method has, nevertheless, a slightly distancing effect. Mrs. Gaskell could hardly help coming to this life as an observer, a reporter, and we are always to some extent conscious of this. But there is genuine imaginative re-creation in her accounts of the walk in Green Heys Fields, and of tea at the Bartons' house, and again, notably, in the chapter *Poverty and Death* where John Barton and his friend find the starving family in the cellar. For so convincing a creation of the characteristic feelings and responses of families of this kind (matters more determining than the material details on which the reporter is apt to concentrate) the English novel had to wait, indeed, for the early writing of D. H. Lawrence. If Mrs. Gaskell never quite manages the sense of full participation which would finally authenticate this, she yet brings to these scenes an intuitive recognition of feelings which has its own sufficient conviction. The chapter *Old Alice's History* brilliantly dramatizes the situation of that early generation brought from the villages and the countryside to the streets and cellars of the industrial towns. The account of Job Legh, the weaver and naturalist, vividly embodies that other kind of response to an urban industrial environment: the devoted, lifelong study of living creatures—a piece of amateur scientific work, and at the same time an instinct for living creatures which hardens, by its very contrast with its environment, into a kind of crankiness. In the factory workers walking out in spring into Green Heys Fields; in Alice Wilson, remembering in her cellar the ling-gathering for besoms in the native village that she will never again see; in Job Legh, intent on his impaled insects—these early chapters embody the characteristic response of a generation to the new and crushing experience of industrialism. The other early chapters movingly embody the continuity and development of the sympathy and cooperative instinct which were already establishing a main working-class tradition.

The structure of feeling from which *Mary Barton* begins is, then, a combination of sympathetic observation and of a largely successful attempt at imaginative identification. If it had continued in this way, it might have been a great novel of its kind. But the emphasis of the method changes, and there are several reasons for this. One reason can be studied in a curious aspect of the history of the writing of the book. It was originally to be called *John Barton*. As Mrs. Gaskell wrote later:

> Round the character of John Barton all the others formed them-selves; he was my hero, *the* person with whom all my sympathies went.[1]

And she added:

> The character, and some of the speeches, are exactly a poor man I know.[2]

The change of emphasis which the book subsequently underwent, and the consequent change of title to *Mary Barton,* seem to have been made at the instance of her publishers, Chapman and Hall. The details of this matter are still obscure, but we must evidently allow something for this external influence on the shape of the novel. Certainly the John Barton of the later parts of the book is a very shadowy figure. In committing the murder, he seems to put himself not only beyond the range of Mrs. Gaskell's sympathy (which is understandable, but, more essentially, beyond the range of her powers. The agony of conscience is there, as a thing told and sketched, but, as the crisis of "my hero; *the* person with whom all my sympathies went," it is weak and almost incidental. This is be-cause the novel as published is centred on the daughter—her inde-cision between Jem Wilson and "her gay lover, Harry Carson"; her agony in Wilson's trial; her pursuit and last-minute rescue of the vital witness; the realization of her love for Wilson: all this, the familiar and orthodox plot of the Victorian novel of sentiment, but of little lasting interest. And it now seems incredible that the novel should ever have been planned in any other way. If Mrs. Gaskell had written "round the character of Mary Barton all the others formed themselves," she would have confirmed our actual impression of the finished book.

Something must be allowed for the influence of her publishers, but John Barton must always have been cast as the murderer, with the intention perhaps of showing an essentially good man driven to an appalling crime by loss, suffering and despair. One can still see the elements of this in the novel as we have it, but there was evi-dently a point, in its writing, at which the flow of sympathy with which she began was arrested, and then, by the change of emphasis which the change of title records, diverted to the less compromising figure of the daughter. The point would be less important if it were not characteristic of the structure of feeling within which she was working. It is not only that she recoils from the violence of the murder, to the extent of being unable even to enter it as the experience of the man conceived as her hero. It is also that, as compared with the carefully representative character of the early chapters, the murder itself is exceptional. It is true that in 1831 a Thomas Ashton, of Pole Bank, Werneth, was murdered under somewhat similar circumstances, and that the Ashton family appear to have taken the murder of Carson as referring to this. Mrs. Gaskell, disclaiming the reference in a letter to them, turned up some similar incidents in Glasgow at about the same time. But in fact, taking the period as a whole, the response of political assassination is so uncharacteristic as to be an obvious distortion. The few recorded cases only emphasize this. Even when one adds the cases of intimidation, and the occasional vitriol-throwing during the deliberate breaking of strikes, it remains true, and was at the time a subject of surprised comment by foreign observers, that the characteristic response of the English working people, even in times of grave suffering, was not one of personal violence. Mrs. Gaskell was under no obligation to write a representative novel; she might legitimately have taken a special case. But the tone elsewhere is deliberately representative, and she is even, as she says, modelling John Barton on "a poor man I know." The real explanation, surely, is that John Barton, a political murderer appointed by a trade union, is a dramatization of the *fear of violence* which was widespread among the upper and middle classes at the time, and which penetrated, as an arresting and controlling factor, even into the deep imaginative sympathy of a Mrs. Gaskell. This fear that the working people might take matters into their own hands was widespread and characteristic, and the murder of Harry Carson is an imaginative working-out of this fear, and of reactions to it, rather than any kind of observed and considered experience.

The point is made clearer when it is remembered that Mrs. Gaskell planned the murder herself, and chose, for the murderer, "my hero, *the* person with whom all my sympathies went." In this respect the act of violence, a sudden aggression against a man contemptuous of the sufferings of the poor, looks very much like a projection, with which, in the end, she was unable to come to terms. The imagina-

tive choice of the act of murder and then the imaginative recoil from
it have the effect of ruining the necessary integration of feeling in
the whole theme. The diversion to Mary Barton, even allowing for
the publishers' influence, must in fact have been welcome.

Few persons felt more deeply than Elizabeth Gaskell the sufferings of the industrial poor. As a minister's wife in Manchester, she
actually saw this, and did not, like many other novelists, merely
know it by report or occasional visit. Her response to the suffering is
deep and genuine, but pity cannot stand alone in such a structure
of feeling. It is joined, in *Mary Barton,* by the confusing violence
and fear of violence, and is supported, finally, by a kind of writing-
off, when the misery of the actual situation can no longer be en-
dured. John Barton dies penitent, and the elder Carson repents of
his vengeance and turns, as the sympathetic observer wanted the
employers to turn, to efforts at improvement and mutual understanding. This was the characteristic humanitarian conclusion, and
it must certainly be respected. But it was not enough, we notice,
for the persons with whom Mrs. Gaskell's sympathies were engaged. Mary Barton, Jem Wilson, Mrs. Wilson, Margaret, Will,
Job Legh—all the objects of her real sympathy—end the book far removed from the situation which she had set out to examine. All are
going to Canada; there could be no more devastating conclusion. A
solution within the actual situation might be hoped for, but the
solution with which the heart went was a cancelling of the actual
difficulties and the removal of the persons pitied to the uncompro-
mised New World.

North and South (1855)

Mrs. Gaskell's second industrial novel, *North and South,* is less interesting, because the tension is less. She takes up here her actual
position, as a sympathetic observer. Margaret Hale, with the feelings
and upbringing of the daughter of a Southern clergyman, moves
with her father to industrial Lancashire, and we follow her reactions, her observations and her attempts to do what good she can.
Because this is largely Mrs. Gaskell's own situation, the integration
of the book is markedly superior. Margaret's arguments with the
mill-owner Thornton are interesting and honest, within the political
and economic conceptions of the period. But the emphasis of the
novel, as the lengthy inclusion of such arguments suggests, is al-

most entirely now on attitudes *to* the working people, rather than on the attempt to reach, imaginatively, their feelings about their lives. It is interesting, again, to note the manner of the working-out. The relationship of Margaret and Thornton and their eventual marriage serve as a unification of the practical energy of the Northern manufacturer with the developed sensibility of the Southern girl: this is stated almost explicitly, and is seen as a solution. Thornton goes back to the North

> to have the opportunity of cultivating some intercourse with the hands beyond the mere "cash nexus."[3]

Humanized by Margaret, he will work at what we now call "the improvement of human relations in industry." The conclusion deserves respect, but it is worth noticing that it is not only under Margaret's influence that Thornton will attempt this, but under her patronage. The other manufacturers, as Thornton says, "will shake their heads and look grave" at it. This may be characteristic, but Thornton, though bankrupt, can be the exception, by availing himself of Margaret's unexpected legacy. Money from elsewhere, in fact —by that device of the legacy which solved so many otherwise insoluble problems in the world of the Victorian novel—will enable Thornton, already affected by the superior gentleness and humanity of the South, to make his humanitarian experiment. Once again Mrs. Gaskell works out her reaction to the insupportable situation by going—in part adventitiously—outside it.

Hard Times (1854)

> Ordinarily Dickens's criticisms of the world he lives in are casual and incidental—a matter of including among the ingredients of a book some indignant treatment of a particular abuse. But in *Hard Times* he is for once possessed by a comprehensive vision, one in which the inhumanities of Victorian civilization are seen as fostered and sanctioned by a hard philosophy, the aggressive formulation of an inhumane spirit.[4]

This comment by F. R. Leavis on *Hard Times* serves to distinguish Dickens's intention from that of Mrs. Gaskell in *Mary Barton. Hard Times* is less imaginative observation than an imaginative judgement. It is a judgement of social attitudes, but again it is something more than *North and South*. It is a thorough-going and creative examination of the dominant philosophy of industrialism—of the hardness that Mrs. Gaskell saw as little more than a misunderstanding, which might be patiently broken down. That Dickens could achieve this more comprehensive understanding is greatly to the advantage of the novel. But against this we must set the fact that in terms of human understanding of the industrial working people Dickens is obviously less successful than Mrs. Gaskell: his Stephen Blackpool, in relation to the people of *Mary Barton,* is little more than a diagrammatic figure. The gain in comprehension, that is to say, has been achieved by the rigours of generalization and abstraction; *Hard Times* is an analysis of Industrialism, rather than experience of it.

The most important point, in this context, that has to be made about *Hard Times* is a point about Thomas Gradgrind. Josiah Bounderby, the other villain of the piece, is a simple enough case. He is, with rough justice, the embodiment of the aggressive money-making and power-seeking ideal which was a driving force of the Industrial Revolution. That he is also a braggart, a liar and in general personally repellent is of course a comment on Dickens's method. The conjunction of these personal defects with the aggressive ideal is not (how much easier things would be if it were) a necessary conjunction. A large part of the Victorian reader's feelings against Bounderby (and perhaps a not inconsiderable part of the twentieth-century intellectual's) rests on the older and rather different feeling that trade, as such, is gross. The very name (and Dickens uses his names with conscious and obvious effect), incorporating *bounder,* incorporates this typical feeling. The social criticism represented by *bounder* is, after all, a rather different matter from the question of aggressive economic individualism. Dickens, with rough justice, fuses the separate reactions, and it is easy not to notice how one set of feelings is made to affect the other.

The difficulty about Thomas Gradgrind is different in character. It is that the case against him is so good, and his refutation by experience so masterly, that it is easy for the modern reader to forget exactly *what* Gradgrind is. It is surprising how common is the mistake of using the remembered name, Gradgrind, as a class-name for the hard Victorian employer. The valuation which Dickens actually asks us to make is more difficult. Gradgrind is a Utilitarian: seen by Dickens as one of the *feeloosofers* against whom Cobbett

thundered, or as one of the *steam-engine intellects* described by
Carlyle. This line is easy enough, but one could as easily draw another: say, Thomas Gradgrind, Edwin Chadwick, John Stuart Mill.
Chadwick, we are told, was "the most hated man in England," and
he worked by methods, and was blamed for "meddling," in terms
that are hardly any distance from Dickens's Gradgrind. Mill is a
more difficult instance (although the education of which he felt
himself a victim will be related, by the modern reader, to the Gradgrind system). But it seems certain that Dickens has Mill's *Political
Economy* (1849) very much in mind in his general indictment of
the ideas which built and maintained Coketown. (Mill's reaction, it
may be noted, was the expressive "that creature Dickens."[5]) It is
easy now to realize that Mill was something more than a Gradgrind.
But we are missing Dickens's point if we fail to see that in condemn-
ing Thomas Gradgrind, the representative figure, we are invited also
to condemn the kind of thinking and the methods of enquiry and
legislation which in fact promoted a large measure of social and
industrial reform. One wonders, for example, what a typical Fabian
feels when he is invited to condemn Gradgrind, not as an individual
but as a type. This may, indeed, have something to do with the
common error of memory about Gradgrind to which I have referred. Public commissions, Blue Books, Parliamentary legislation—
all these, in the world of *Hard Times*—are Gradgrindery.

For Dickens is not setting Reform against Exploitation. He sees
what we normally understand by both as two sides of the same coin,
Industrialism. His positives do not lie in social improvement, but
rather in what he sees as the elements of human nature—personal
kindness, sympathy, and forbearance. It is not the model factory
against the satanic mill, nor is it the humanitarian experiment
against selfish exploitation. It is, rather, individual persons against
the System. In so far as it is social at all, it is the Circus against
Coketown. The schoolroom contrast of Sissy Jupe and Bitzer is a
contrast between the education, practical but often inarticulate,
which is gained by living and doing, and the education, highly ar-
ticulated, which is gained by systemization and abstraction. It is a
contrast of which Cobbett would have warmly approved; but in so
far as we have all (and to some extent inevitably) been committed
to a large measure of the latter, it is worth noting again what a
large revaluation Dickens is asking us to make. The instinctive, un-
intellectual, unorganized life is the ground, here, of genuine feel-

ing, and of all good relationships. The Circus is one of the very few ways in which Dickens could have dramatized this, but it is less the circus that matters than the experience described by Sleary:

> ". . . that there ith a love in the world, not all Thelf-interetht after all, but thomething very different . . . it hath a way of ith own of calculating or not calculating, which thomehow or another ith at leatht ath hard to give a name to, ath the wayth of the dogth ith."[6]

It is a characteristic conclusion, in a vitally important tradition which based its values on such grounds. It is the major criticism of Industrialism as a whole way of life, and its grounds in experience have been firm. What is essential is to recognize that Dickens saw no social expression of it, or at least nothing that could be "given a name to." The experience is that of individual persons. Almost the whole organization of society, as Dickens judges, is against it. The Circus can express it because it is not part of the industrial organization. The Circus is an end in itself, a pleasurable end, which is instinctive and (in certain respects) anarchic. It is significant that Dickens has thus to go outside the industrial situation to find any expression of his values. This going outside is similar to the Canada in which *Mary Barton* ends, or the legacy of Margaret Hale. But it is also more than these, in so far as it is not only an escape but a positive assertion of a certain kind of experience, the denial of which was the real basis (as Dickens saw it) of the hard times.

It was inevitable, given the kind of criticism that Dickens was making, that his treatment of the industrial working people should have been so unsatisfactory. He recognizes them as objects of pity, and he recognizes the personal devotion in suffering of which they are capable. But the only conclusion he can expect them to draw is Stephen Blackpool's:

> "Aw a muddle!"[7]

This is reasonable, but the hopelessness and passive suffering are set against the attempts of the working people to better their conditions. The trade unions are dismissed by a stock Victorian reaction, with the agitator Slackbridge. Stephen Blackpool, like Job Legh, is shown to advantage because he will not join them. The point can be gauged by a comparison with Cobbett, whose criticism of the System is in many ways very similar to that of Dickens, and rests on so many similar valuations, yet who was not similarly deceived, even when the trade unions came as a novelty to him. The point indicates a wider comment on Dickens's whole position.

The scathing analysis of Coketown and all its works, and of the supporting political economy and aggressive utilitarianism, is based on Carlyle. So are the hostile reactions to Parliament and to ordinary ideas of reform. Dickens takes up the hostility, and it serves as a comprehensive vision, to which he gives all his marvellous energy. But his identification with Carlyle is really negative. There are no social alternatives to Bounderby and Gradgrind: not the time-serving aristocrat Harthouse; not the decayed gentlewoman Mrs. Sparsit; nowhere, in fact, any active Hero. Many of Dickens's social attitudes cancel each other out, for he will use almost any reaction in order to undermine any normal representative position. *Hard Times,* in tone and structure, is the work of a man who has "been through" society, who has found them all out. The only reservation is for the passive and the suffering, for the meek who shall inherit the earth but not Coketown, not industrial society. This primitive feeling, when joined by the aggressive conviction of having found everyone else out, is the retained position of an adolescent. The innocence shames the adult world, but also essentially rejects it. As a whole response, *Hard Times* is more a symptom of the confusion of industrial society than an understanding of it, but it is a symptom that is significant and continuing.

Sybil, or The Two Nations (1845)

Sybil can be read now as the production of a future Conservative Prime Minister, and hence in the narrow sense as a political novel. The elements of political pleading are indeed evident in any reading of it. Their curiosity, their partisanship and their opportunism are matched only by their brilliance of address. The novel would be fascinating if it were only political. The stucco elegance of Disraeli's writing has a consonance with one kind of political argument. What is intolerable in his descriptions of persons and feelings becomes in his political flights a rather likeable panache. The descriptions of industrial squalor are very like those of Dickens on Coketown: brilliant romantic generalizations—the view from the train, from the hustings, from the printed page—yet often moving, like all far-seeing rhetoric. There are similar accounts of the condi-

tions of the agricultural poor which need to be kept in mind against
the misleading contrasts of *North and South*. Again, in a quite different manner, there is in *Sybil* the most spirited description of the
iniquities of the tommy-shop, and of the practical consequences of
the system of truck, to be found anywhere. Disraeli's anger—the
generalized anger of an outsider making his way—carries him often
beyond his formal text. The hostile descriptions of London political
and social life are again generalization, but they have, doubtless, the
same rhetorical significance as those of the forays among the poor.
Anyone who is prepared to give credit to Disraeli's unsupported authority on any matter of social fact has of course mistaken his man,
as he would similarly mistake Dickens. But Disraeli, like Dickens, is
a very fine generalizing analyst of cant, and almost as fine a generalizing rhetorician of human suffering. Both functions, it must be
emphasized, are reputable.

In terms of ideas, *Sybil* is almost a collector's piece. There is this,
for instance, from Coleridge:

> But if it have not furnished us with abler administration or a more
> illustrious senate, the Reform Act may have exercised on the coun-
> try at large a beneficial influence? Has it? Has it elevated the tone
> of the public mind? Has it cultured the popular sensibilities to
> noble and ennobling ends? Has it proposed to the people of Eng-
> land a higher test of national respect and confidence than the de-
> basing qualification universally prevalent in this country since the
> fatal introduction of the system of Dutch finance? Who will pre-
> tend it? If a spirit of rapacious covetousness, desecrating all the hu-
> manities of life, has been the besetting sin of England for the last
> century and a half, since the passing of the Reform Act the
> altar of Mammon has blazed with triple worship. To acquire, to
> accumulate, to plunder each other by virtue of philosophic phrases,
> to propose a Utopia to consist only of WEALTH and TOIL, this has
> been the breathless business of enfranchised England for the last
> twelve years, until we are startled from our voracious strife by the
> wail of intolerable serfage.[8]

It is true that this is political, a part of the grand assault on Whiggery. But the terms of the assault are familiar, as part of a much
wider criticism. Or again this, which was to reappear in our own
century with an air of original discovery:

". . . There is no community in England; there is aggregation, but aggregation under circumstances which make it rather a dissociating than a uniting principle. . . . It is a community of purpose that constitutes society . . . without that, men may be drawn into contiguity, but they still continue virtually isolated."

"And is that their condition in cities?"

"It is their condition everywhere; but in cities that condition is aggravated. A density of population implies a severer struggle for existence, and a consequent repulsion of elements brought into too close contact. In great cities men are brought together by the desire of gain. They are not in a state of cooperation, but of isolation, as to the making of fortunes; and for all the rest they are careless of neighbours. Christianity teaches us to love our neighbour as ourself; modern society acknowledges no neighbour."[9]

These views of the Chartist Stephen Morley were the common element in a number of varying political positions. They have remained the terms of a basic criticism of Industrialism.

The two nations, of rich and poor, have of course become famous. The basis of the attempt to make one nation of them is the restoration to leadership of an enlightened aristocracy. For,

"There is a change in them, as in all other things," . . . said Egremont.

"If there be a change," said Sybil, "it is because in some degree the people have learnt their strength."

"Ah! dismiss from your mind those fallacious fancies," said Egremont. "The people are not strong; the people never can be strong. Their attempts at self-vindication will end only in their suffering and confusion."[10]

It is, of course, the familiar injunction, in Cobbett's words, to "be quiet," and the familiar assumption of the business of regeneration by others—in this case "the enlightened aristocracy." Disraeli shared the common prejudices about the popular movement: his account of the initiation of Dandy Mick into a Trade Union—

". . . you will execute with zeal and alacrity . . . every task and injunction that the majority of your brethren . . . shall impose upon you, in furtherance of our common welfare, of which they are the sole judges: such as the chastisement of Nobs, the assassination of oppressive and tyrannical masters, or the demolition of

> all mills, works and shops that shall be deemed by us incor-
> rigible."[11]

—is characteristically cloak-and-dagger. This must be acknowledged
alongside the shrewder assessment:

> The people she found was not that pure embodiment of unity of
> feeling, of interest, and of purpose which she had pictured in her
> abstractions. The people had enemies among the people: their own
> passions; which made them often sympathize, often combine, with
> the privileged.[12]

This shrewdness might well have been also applied to some of Disraeli's other abstractions, but perhaps that was left for later, in the
progress of his political career.

The passages quoted are near the climax of that uniting of Egremont, "the enlightened aristocrat," and Sybil, "the daughter of the
People," which, in the novel, is the symbolic creation of the One
Nation. This, again, is the way the heart goes, and it is the novel's
most interesting illustration. For Sybil, of course, is only theoretically
"the daughter of the People." The actual process of the book is the
discovery that she is a dispossessed aristocrat, and the marriage bells
ring, not over the achievement of One Nation, but over the uniting
of the properties of Marney and Mowbray, one agricultural, the
other industrial: a marriage symbolical, indeed, of the political development which was the actual issue. The restored heiress stands,
in the general picture, with Margaret Thornton's legacy, with Canada, and with the Horse-Riding. But it is significant of Disraeli's
shrewdness that, through the device, he embodied what was to
become an actual political event.

Alton Locke, Tailor and Poet (1850)

In part, Alton Locke is in the orthodox sense an "exposure": an informed, angry and sustained account of sweated labour in the
"Cheap and Nasty" clothing trade. Much of it can still be read in
these terms, with attention and sympathy. It is fair to note, however,
that in respect of this theme the Preface is more effective than the
novel, and for the unexpected reason that it is more specific.

The wider intention of the book is rather different. It is really a
story of conversion: of the making of a Chartist in the usual sense,

and of his remaking in Kingsley's sense. This is the basic movement in a book which is extremely discursive in mood. The earlier chapters are perhaps the most effective: the caricature of the Baptist home; the indignant realism of the apprenticeship in the sweating-rooms; the generalized description of the longing from the "prison-house of brick and iron" for the beauty apprehended as knowledge and poetry. The beginnings of Alton Locke in political activity are also, in general outline, convincing. With them, however, begins also the major emphasis on argument, on prolonged *discussion* of events, which is evidently Kingsley's motive and energy. Often this discussion is interesting, particularly as we recognize the familiar popularization of Carlyle and of the ideas which Carlyle concentrated. This merges, from the time of the conversion (the curious chapter *Dreamland*), into the Christian Socialist arguments with which Kingsley's name is commonly identified. It is doubtful whether much attention of a different kind, attention, that is, other than to the genealogy of ideas, can be given to all these parts of the book. A very large part of it is like reading old newspapers, or at least old pamphlets. The issues are there, but the terms are arbitrary and the connexions mechanical. The book is not an "autobiography" but a tract.

We need note here only the conclusion, alike of the story and of the argument. Once again, the motive to Chartism, to a working-class political movement, has been sympathetically set down (it was on this score that Kingsley and others were thought of as "advanced" or "dangerous" thinkers). But again the effort is seen finally as a delusion: in effect—"we understand and sympathize with your sufferings which drove you to this, but what you are doing is terribly mistaken":

> "Ay," she went on, her figure dilating, and her eyes flashing, like an inspired prophetess, "that is in the Bible! What would you more than that? That is your charter; the only ground of all charters. You, like all mankind, have had dim inspirations, confused yearnings after your future destiny, and, like all the world from the beginning, you have tried to realise, by self-willed methods of your own, what you can only do by God's inspiration, God's method. . . . Oh! look back, look back, at the history of English Radicalism for the last half-century, and judge by your own deeds, your own worlds; were you fit for those privileges which you so

frantically demanded? Do not answer me, that those who had
them were equally unfit; but thank God, if the case be indeed so,
that your incapacity was not added to theirs, to make confusion
worse confounded. Learn a new lesson. Believe at last that you are
in Christ, and become new creatures. With those miserable, awful
farce tragedies of April and June, let old things pass away, and all
things become new. Believe that your kingdom is not of this world,
but of One whose servants must not fight."[13]

It is not surprising after this that the destiny of the hero is—once
again—emigration. Alton Locke dies as he reaches America, but his
fellow-Chartist, Crossthwaite, will come back after seven years.

The regeneration of society, according to Kingsley's Cambridge
preface to the book, will meanwhile proceed under the leadership
of a truly enlightened aristocracy. It will be a movement towards
democracy, but not to that "tyranny of numbers" of which the dangers have been seen in the United States. For:

> As long, I believe, as the Throne, the House of Lords, and the
> Press, are what, thank God, they are, so long will each enlargement
> of the suffrage be a fresh source not of danger, but of safety; for
> it will bind the masses to the established order of things by that
> loyalty which springs from content; from the sense of being appre-
> ciated, trusted, dealt with not as children, but as men.[14]

Felix Holt (1866)

Felix Holt was not published till 1866, but we can set beside it a
passage from a letter of George Eliot's, written to J. Sibree in 1848,
just after the French Revolution of that year:

> You and Carlyle . . . are the only two people who feel just as I
> would have them—who can glory in what is actually great and
> beautiful without putting forth any cold reservations and incredu-
> lities to save their credit for wisdom. I am all the more delighted
> with your enthusiasm because I didn't expect it. I feared that you
> lacked revolutionary ardour. But no—you are just as *sans-culottish*
> and rash as I would have you. . . . I thought we had fallen on
> such evil days that we were to see no really great movement—that
> ours was what St. Simon calls a purely critical epoch, not at all an
> organic one; but I begin to be glad of my date. I would consent,

however, to have a year clipt off my life for the sake of witnessing
such a scene as that of the men of the barricades bowing to the
image of Christ, "who first taught fraternity to men." One trembles to look into every fresh newspaper lest there should be something to mar the picture. . . . I should have no hope of good
from any imitative movement at home. Our working classes are
eminently inferior to the mass of the French people. In France the
mind of the people is highly electrified; they are full of ideas on
social subjects; they really desire social *reform*—not merely an acting out of Sancho Panza's favourite proverb, "Yesterday for you,
today for me." The revolutionary animus extended over the whole
nation, and embraced the rural population—not merely, as with
us, the artisans of the towns. Here there is so much larger a proportion of selfish radicalism and unsatisfied brute sensuality (in
the agricultural and mining districts especially) than of perception
or desire of justice, that a revolutionary movement would be simply destructive, not constructive. Besides, it would be put down.
. . . And there is nothing in our Constitution to obstruct the slow
progress of *political* reform. This is all we are fit for at present.
The social reform which may prepare us for great changes is more
and more the object of effort both in Parliament and out of it. But
we English are slow crawlers.[15]

The distinctions in this are doubtful, but the tone indicates an intelligence of a different order from the other novelists discussed. We
are interested in Mrs. Gaskell or Kingsley or Disraeli because of
what they testified; with George Eliot there is another interest, because of the quality of the witness.

This quality is evident in *Felix Holt*, which as a novel has a quite
different status from those previously discussed. It has also, however, much in common with them. The formal plot turns on the
familiar complications of inheritance in property, and Esther, with
her inherited breeding showing itself in poor circumstances, has
something in common with Sybil. As with Sybil, her title to a great
estate is proved, but there the comparison with Disraeli ends. Harold Transome is, like Egremont, a second son; like him, he turns to
the reforming side in politics. But George Eliot was incapable of
resting on the image of an Egremont, the figurehead of the enlightened gentleman. Harold Transome is a coarser reality, and it is
impossible that Esther should marry him. She renounces her claim

and marries Felix Holt. It is as if Sybil had renounced the Mowbray estates and married Stephen Morley. I do not make any claim
for the superior reality of George Eliot's proceedings. The thing is as
contrived, in the service of a particular image of the desirable, as
Disraeli's very different dénouement. George Eliot works with a
rather finer net, but it is not in such elements of the novel that her
real superiority is apparent.

Nor again is there much superiority in her creation of Felix Holt
himself. He is shown as a working-man radical, determined to stick
to his own class, and to appeal solely to the energies of "moral
force." He believes in sobriety and education, argues for social rather
than merely political reform, and wants to be

> a demagogue of a new sort; an honest one, if possible, who will
> tell the people they are blind and foolish, and neither flatter them
> nor fatten on them.[16]

It is not easy, at any time, to say whether a character "convinces."
We are all apt, in such questions, to impose our own conceptions
both of the probable and the desirable. But one can usually see,
critically, when a character comes to existence in a number of aspects, forming something like the image of a life; and, alternatively,
when a character is fixed at a different and simpler stage: in the
case of Felix Holt, at a physical appearance and a set of opinions.
Mrs. Gaskell could conceive the early John Barton in much these
terms, but, because other substance was lacking, she had virtually
to dismiss him as a person when the course of action found necessary on other grounds went beyond the limits of her sympathy. Felix
Holt, like Alton Locke, is conceived as a more probable hero: that is
to say, as one whose general attitude is wholly sympathetic to the
author, and who is detached from him only by a relative immaturity.
Like Alton Locke, Felix Holt becomes involved in a riot; like him,
he is mistaken for a ringleader; like him, he is sentenced to imprisonment. This recurring pattern is not copying, in the vulgar sense.
It is rather the common working of an identical fear, which was
present also in Mrs. Gaskell's revision of John Barton. It is at root
the fear of a sympathetic, reformist-minded member of the middle
classes at being drawn into any kind of mob violence. John Barton
is involved in earnest, and his creator's sympathies are at once withdrawn, to the obvious detriment of the work as a whole. Sympathy
is transferred to Jem Wilson, mistakenly accused, and to Margaret's

efforts on his behalf, which have a parallel in Esther's impulse to speak at the trial of Felix Holt. But the basic pattern is a dramatization of the fear of being involved in violence: a dramatization made possible by the saving clause of innocence and mistaken motive, and so capable of redemption. What is really interesting is that the conclusion of this kind of dramatization is then taken as proof of the rightness of the author's original reservations. The people are indeed dangerous, in their constant tendency to blind disorder. Anyone sympathizing with them is likely to become involved. Therefore (a most ratifying word) it can be sincerely held that the popular movements actually under way are foolish and inadequate, and that the only wise course is dissociation from them.

Of course, that there is inadequacy in any such movement is obvious, but the discriminations one would expect from a great novelist are certainly not drawn in *Felix Holt*. Once again Cobbett is a touchstone, and his conduct at his own trial after the labourers' revolts of 1830 is a finer demonstration of real maturity than the fictional compromises here examined. Cobbett, like nearly all men who have worked with their hands, hated any kind of violent destruction of useful things. But he had the experience and the strength to enquire further into violence. He believed, moreover, what George Eliot so obviously could not believe, that the common people were something other than a mob, and had instincts and habits something above drunkenness, gullibility and ignorance. He would not have thought Felix Holt an "honest demagogue" for telling the people that they were "blind and foolish." He would have thought him rather a very convenient ally of the opponents of reform. George Eliot's view of the common people is uncomfortably close to that of Carlyle in *Shooting Niagara*: "blockheadism, gullibility, bribeability, amenability to beer and balderdash." This was the common first assumption, and was the basis for the distinction (alike in her 1848 comment and in *Felix Holt*) between "political" and "social" reform. The former is only "machinery"; the latter is seen as substance. The distinction is useful, but consider this very typical speech by Felix Holt:

> "The way to get rid of folly is to get rid of vain expectations, and of thoughts that don't agree with the nature of things. The men who have had true thoughts about water, and what it will do when it is turned into steam and under all sorts of circumstances, have

made themselves a great power in the world: they are turning the
wheels of engines that will help to change most things. But no
engines would have done, if there had been false notions about
the way water would act. Now, all the schemes about voting, and
districts, and annual Parliaments, and the rest, are engines, and
the water or steam—the force that is to work them—must come out
of human nature—out of men's passions, feelings, and desires.
Whether the engines will do good work or bad depends on these
feelings."[17]

But the "engines" mentioned are, after all, particular engines, proposed to do different work from the engines previously employed.
It is really mechanical to class all the engines together and to diminish their importance, when in fact their purposes differ. The new
proposals are an embodiment of "passions, feelings, and desires":
alternative proposals, supported by alternative feelings, so that a
choice can properly be made. The real criticism, one suspects, is of
"thoughts that don't agree with the nature of things," and this "nature of things" can either be a supposedly permanent "human nature," or else, as probably, the supposedly immutable "laws of society." Among these "laws," as Felix Holt's argument continues, is
the supposition that among every hundred men there will be thirty
with "some soberness, some sense to choose," and seventy, either
drunk or "ignorant or mean or stupid." With such an assumption
it is easy enough to "prove" that a voting reform would be useless.
George Eliot's advice, essentially, is that the working men should
first make themselves "sober and educated," under the leadership of
men like Felix Holt, and then reform will do some good. But the
distinction between "political" and "social" reform is seen at this
point at its most arbitrary. The abuses of an unreformed Parliament
are even dragged in as an argument against parliamentary reform—
it will only be more of the same sort of thing. The winning through
political reform of the means of education, of the leisure necessary
to take such opportunity, of the conditions of work and accommodation which will diminish poverty and drunkenness: all these and
similar aims, which were the purposes for which the "engines" were
proposed, are left out of the argument. Without them, the sober responsible educated working man must, presumably, spring fully
armed from his own ("drunken, ignorant, mean and stupid") head.
It has passed too long for a kind of maturity and depth in ex-

perience to argue that politics and political attachments are only
possible to superficial minds; that any appreciation of the complexity of human nature necessarily involves a wise depreciation of these
noisy instruments. The tone—"cold reservations and incredulities to
save their credit for wisdom"—is often heard in *Felix Holt:*

> Crying abuses—"bloated paupers," "bloated pluralists," and other
> corruptions hindering men from being wise and happy—had to be
> fought against and slain. Such a time is a time of hope. After-
> wards, when the corpses of those monsters have been held up to
> the public wonder and abhorrence, and yet wisdom and happiness
> do not follow, but rather a more abundant breeding of the foolish
> and unhappy, comes a time of doubt and despondency. . . .
> Some dwelt on the abolition of all abuses, and on millennial bless-
> edness generally; others, whose imaginations were less suffused
> with exhalations of the dawn, insisted chiefly on the ballot-box.[18]

The wise shake of the head draws a complacent answering smile.
But what I myself find in such a passage as this, in the style ("suf-
fused with exhalations of the dawn"; "millennial blessedness generally") as in the feeling ("a more abundant breeding of the foolish
and unhappy"), is not the deep and extensive working of a generous
mind, but rather the petty cynicism of a mind that has lost, albeit
only temporarily, its capacity for human respect.

Felix Holt's opinions are George Eliot's opinions purged of just
this element, which is a kind of intellectual fatigue. It is the mood
of the 'sixties—of *Shooting Niagara* and *Culture and Anarchy*—
holding an incompetent post-mortem on the earlier phases of Radicalism. Felix Holt himself is not so much a character as an imper-
sonation: a rôle in which he again appears in the *Address to Working Men, by Felix Holt,* which George Eliot was persuaded to write
by her publisher. Here the dangers of active democracy are more
clearly put:

> The too absolute predominance of a class whose wants have been
> of a common sort, who are chiefly struggling to get better and more
> food, clothing, shelter, and bodily recreation, may lead to hasty
> measures for the sake of having things more fairly shared which,
> even if they did not fail . . . would at last debase the life of the
> nation.[19]

Reform must proceed

> not by any attempt to do away directly with the actually existing
> class distinctions and advantages . . . but by the turning of Class
> Interests into Class Functions. . . . If the claims of the unen-
> dowed multitude of working men hold within them principles
> which must shape the future, it is not less true that the endowed
> classes, in their inheritance from the past, hold the precious ma-
> terial without which no worthy, noble future can be moulded.[20]

George Eliot, in this kind of thinking, is very far from her best.
Her position, behind the façade of Felix Holt, is that of a Carlyle
without the energy, of an Arnold without the quick practical sense,
of an anxiously balancing Mill without the intellectual persistence.
Yet it is clear that, inadequate as her attempt at a position may be,
it proceeds, though not fruitfully, from that sense of society as a
complicated inheritance which is at the root of her finest work. In
Felix Holt, this sense is magnificently realized at the level of one set
of personal relationships—that of Mrs. Transome, the lawyer Jer-
myn and their son Harold Transome. In *Middlemarch,* with almost
equal intensity, this realization is extended to a whole representative
section of provincial society. Always, at her best, she is unrivalled
in English fiction in her creation and working of the complication
and consequence inherent in all relationships. From such a position
in experience she naturally sees society at a deeper level than its
political abstractions indicate, and she sees her own society, in her
own choice of word, as "vicious." Her favourite metaphor for society is a network: a "tangled skein"; a "tangled web"; "the long-
growing evils of a great nation are a tangled business." This, again,
is just; it is the ground of her finest achievements. But the metaphor, while having a positive usefulness in its indication of complexity, has also a negative effect. For it tends to represent social
—and indeed directly personal—relationships as passive: acted upon
rather than acting. "One fears," she remarked, "to pull the wrong
thread, in the tangled scheme of things." The caution is reasonable,
but the total effect of the image false. For in fact every element in
the complicated system is active: the relationships are changing, constantly, and any action—even abstention; certainly the impersona-
tion of Felix Holt—affects, even if only slightly, the tensions, the
pressures, the very nature of the complication. It is a mark, not of
her deep perception, but of the point at which this fails, that her

attitude to society is finally so negative: a negativeness of detail which the width of a phrase like "deep social reform" cannot disguise. The most important thing about George Eliot is her superb control of particular complexities, but this must not be stated in terms of an interest in "personal" relationships as opposed to "social" relationships. She did not believe, as others have tried to do, that these categories are really separate: "there is no private life which has not been determined by a wider public life," as she remarks near the beginning of *Felix Holt*. Yet it is a fact that when she touches, as she chooses to touch, the lives and the problems of working people, her personal observation and conclusion surrender, virtually without a fight, to the general structure of feeling about these matters which was the common property of her generation, and which she was at once too hesitant to transcend, and too intelligent to raise into any lively embodiment. She fails in the extension which she knows to be necessary, because indeed there seems "no right thread to pull." Almost any kind of social action is ruled out, and the most that can be hoped for, with a hero like Felix Holt, is that he will in the widest sense keep his hands reasonably clean. It is indeed the mark of a deadlock in society when so fine an intelligence and so quick a sympathy can conceive no more than this. For patience and caution, without detailed intention, are very easily converted into acquiescence, and there is no right to acquiesce if society is known to be "vicious."

These novels, when read together, seem to illustrate clearly enough not only the common criticism of industrialism, which the tradition was establishing, but also the general structure of feeling which was equally determining. Recognition of evil was balanced by fear of becoming involved. Sympathy was transformed, not into action, but into withdrawal. We can all observe the extent to which this structure of feeling has persisted, into both the literature and the social thinking of our own time.

NOTES

1. Cit. *Elizabeth Gaskell: her life and work*, A. B. Hopkins, 1952, p. 77.
2. Ibid.
3. *North and South*, E. Gaskell (1889 edn.), Ch. li, p. 459.

4. *The Great Tradition,* F. R. Leavis, London, 1948, p. 228.

5. Cit. *Life of John Stuart Mill,* M. St. J. Packe, 1954, p. 311.

6. *Hard Times,* C. Dickens, Book the Third—*Garnering,* Ch. viii.

7. Ibid., Ch. vi.

8. *Sybil, or the Two Nations,* B. Disraeli, repr. Penguin edn., 1954, p. 40.

9. Ibid., pp. 71-72.

10. Ibid., p. 267.

11. Ibid., pp. 216-217.

12. Ibid., p. 280.

13. *Alton Locke, Tailor and Poet, an Autobiography,* C. Kingsley (1892 edn.), Ch. xxxvii, pp. 285-287.

14. Ibid., *Preface to the Undergraduates of Cambridge,* p. xxxiv.

15. Letter to J. Sibree, February 1848, in *George Eliot's Life, as related in her letters and journals,* ed. Cross; "New Edition" (n.d.), pp. 98-99.

16. *Felix Holt the Radical,* G. Eliot (1913 edn.), 2 vols., Vol. 2, p. 41 (Ch. xxvii).

17. Ibid., Vol. 2, p. 89 (Ch. xxx).

18. Ibid., Vol. 1, pp. 266-267 (Ch. xvi).

19. *Address to Workingmen, by Felix Holt,* George Eliot, Blackwood's, 1868; repr. *Essays and Leaves from a Notebook,* Blackwood, 1884, pp. 341-342.

20. Ibid., pp. 333 and 348.

ROBERT B. HEILMAN

Charlotte Brontë's "New" Gothic

In that characteristic flight from cliché that may plunge him into the recherché the critic might well start from *The Professor* and discover in it much more than is implied by the usual dismissal of it as Charlotte Brontë's poorest work. He might speculate about Charlotte's singular choice of a male narrator—the value of it, or even the need of it, for her. For through William Crimsworth she lives in Héger, making love to herself as Frances Henri: in this there is a kind of ravenousness, inturning, splitting, and doubling back of feeling. Through Crimsworth she experiences a sudden, vivid, often graceless mastery. But these notes on the possible psychology of the author are critically useful only as a way into the strange tremors of feeling that are present in a formally defective story. Pelet identifies "a fathomless spring of sensibility in thy breast, Crimsworth." If Crimsworth is not a successful character, he is the channel of emotional surges that splash over a conventional tale of love: the author's disquieting presence in the character lends a nervous, off-center vitality. The pathos of liberty is all but excessive (as it is later in Shirley Keeldar and Lucy Snowe): Crimsworth sneers,

From *From Jane Austen to Joseph Conrad* ed. by Robert C. Rathburn and Martin Steinmann, Jr. (Minneapolis: University of Minnesota Press, 1958), pp. 71-85. Copyright © 1958 by the University of Minnesota. Reprinted by permission of the author and publishers.

". . . I sprang from my bed with other slaves," and rejoices, "Liberty I clasped in my arms . . . her smile and embrace revived my life." The Puritan sentiment (to be exploited partially in Jane Eyre and heavily in Lucy Snowe) becomes tense, rhetorical, fiercely censorious; the self-righteousness punitive and even faintly paranoid. Through the frenetically Protestant Crimsworth and his flair for rebuke Charlotte notes the little sensualities of girl students ("parting her lips, as full as those of a hot-blooded Maroon") and the coquettish yet urgent sexuality of Zoraide Reuter perversely responding to Crimsworth's ostensible yet not total unresponsiveness to her: "When she stole about me with the soft step of a slave, I felt at once barbarous and sensual as a pasha."

Charlotte looks beyond familiar surfaces. In Yorke Hunsden she notes the "incompatibilities of the 'physique' with the 'morale.'" The explosive Byronic castigator has lineaments "small, and even feminine" and "now the mien of a morose bull, and anon that of an arch and mischievous girl." In this version of the popular archetype, "rough exterior but heart of gold," Charlotte brilliantly finds a paradoxical union of love and hate; she sees generosity of spirit sometimes appearing directly but most often translated into antithetical terms that also accommodate opposite motives—into god-like self-indulgence in truth-telling; almost Mephistophelian cynicism; sadism and even murderousness in words.

Charlotte's story is conventional; formally she is for "reason" and "real life"; but her characters keep escaping to glorify "feeling" and "imagination." Feeling is there in the story—evading repression, in author or in character; ranging from nervous excitement to emotional absorption; often tense and peremptory; sexuality, hate, irrational impulse, grasped, given life, not merely named and pigeonholed. This is Charlotte's version of Gothic: in her later novels an extraordinary thing. In that incredibly eccentric history, *The Gothic Quest*, Montague Summers asserts that the "Gothic novel of sensibility . . . draws its emotionalism and psychology . . . from the work of Samuel Richardson." When this line of descent continues in the Brontës, the vital feeling moves toward an intensity, a freedom, and even an abandon virtually non-existent in historical Gothic and rarely approached in Richardson. From Angria on, Charlotte's women vibrate with passions that the fictional conventions only partly constrict or gloss over—in the center an almost violent devotedness that has in it at once a fire of independence, a spiritual energy, a vivid sexual responsiveness, and, along with this, self-righteousness, a sense of power, sometimes self-pity and envious competitiveness. To an extent the heroines are "unheroined," unsweetened. Into them there has come a new sense of the dark side of feeling and personality.

The Professor ventures a little into the psychic darkness on which *Villette* draws heavily. One night Crimsworth, a victim of hypochondria, hears a voice saying, "In the midst of life we are in death," and he feels "a horror of great darkness." In his boyhood this same "sorceress" drew him "to the very brink of a black, sullen river" and managed to "lure me to her vaulted home of horrors." Charlotte draws on sex images that recall the note of sexuality subtly present in other episodes: ". . . I had entertained her at bed and board . . . she lay with me, . . . taking me entirely to her death-cold bosom, and holding me with arms of bone." The climax is: "I repulsed her as one would a dreaded and ghastly concubine coming to embitter a husband's heart toward his young bride. . . ." This is Gothic, yet there is an integrity of feeling that greatly deepens the convention.

From childhood terrors to all those mysteriously threatening sights, sounds, and injurious acts that reveal the presence of some malevolent force and that anticipate the holocaust at Thornfield, the traditional Gothic in *Jane Eyre* has often been noted, and as often disparaged. It need not be argued that Charlotte Brontë did not reach the heights while using hand-me-down devices, though a tendency to work through the conventions of fictional art was a strong element in her make-up. This is true of all her novels, but it is no more true than her counter-tendency to modify, most interestingly, these conventions. In both *Villette* and *Jane Eyre* Gothic is used but characteristically is undercut.

Jane Eyre hears a "tragic . . . preternatural . . . laugh," but this is at "high noon" and there is "no circumstance of ghostliness"; Grace Poole, the supposed laugher, is a plain person, than whom no "apparition less romantic or less ghostly could . . . be conceived"; Charlotte apologizes ironically to the "romantic reader" for telling "the plain truth" that Grace generally bears a "pot of porter." Charlotte almost habitually revises "old Gothic," the relatively crude mechanisms of fear, with an infusion of the anti-Gothic. When Mrs. Rochester first tried to destroy Rochester by fire, Jane "baptized"

Rochester's bed and heard Rochester "fulminating strange anathemas at finding himself lying in a pool of water." The introduction of comedy as a palliative of straight Gothic occurs on a large scale when almost seventy-five pages are given to the visit of the Ingram-Eshton party to mysterious Thornfield; here Charlotte, as often in her novels, falls into the manner of the Jane Austen whom she despised. When Mrs. Rochester breaks loose again and attacks Mason, the presence of guests lets Charlotte play the nocturnal alarum for at least a touch of comedy: Rochester orders the frantic women not to "pull me down or strangle me"; and "the two dowagers, in vast white wrappers, were bearing down on him like ships in full sail."

The symbolic also modifies the Gothic, for it demands of the reader a more mature and complicated response than the relatively simple thrill or momentary intensity of feeling sought by primitive Gothic. When mad Mrs. Rochester, seen only as "the foul German spectre—the Vampyre," spreads terror at night, that is one thing; when, with the malicious insight that is the paradox of her madness, she tears the wedding veil in two and thus symbolically destroys the planned marriage, that is another thing, far less elementary as art. The midnight blaze that ruins Thornfield becomes more than a shock when it is seen also as the fire of purgation; the grim, almost roadless forest surrounding Ferndean is more than a harrowing stage-set when it is also felt as a symbol of Rochester's closed-in life.

The point is that in various ways Charlotte manages to make the patently Gothic more than a stereotype. But more important is that she instinctively finds new ways to achieve the ends served by old Gothic—the discovery and release of new patterns of feeling, the intensification of feeling. Though only partly unconventional, Jane is nevertheless so portrayed as to evoke new feelings rather than merely exercise old ones. As a girl she is lonely, "passionate," "strange," "like nobody there"; she feels superior, rejects poverty, talks back precociously, tells truths bluntly, enjoys "the strangest sense of freedom," tastes "vengeance"; she experiences a nervous shock which is said to have a lifelong effect, and the doctor says "nerves not in a good state"; she can be "reckless and feverish," "bitter and truculent"; at Thornfield she is restless, given to "bright visions," letting "imagination" picture an existence full of "life, fire, feeling." Thus Charlotte leads away from standardized characterization toward new levels of human reality, and hence from stock responses toward a new kind of passionate engagement.

Charlotte moves toward depth in various ways that have an immediate impact like that of Gothic. Jane's strange, fearful symbolic dreams are not mere thrillers but reflect the tensions of the engagement period, the stress of the wedding-day debate with Rochester, and the longing for Rochester after she has left him. The final Thornfield dream, with its vivid image of a hand coming through a cloud in place of the expected moon, is in the surrealistic vein that appears most sharply in the extraordinary pictures that Jane draws at Thornfield: here Charlotte is plumbing the psyche, not inventing a weird *décor*. Likewise in the telepathy scene, which Charlotte, unlike Defoe in dealing with a similar episode, does her utmost to actualize: "The feeling was not like an electric shock; but it was quite as sharp, as strange, as startling: . . . that inward sensation . . . with all its unspeakable strangeness . . . like an inspiration . . . wondrous shock of feeling. . . ." In her flair for the surreal, in her plunging into feeling that is without status in the ordinary world of the novel, Charlotte discovers a new dimension of Gothic.

She does this most thoroughly in her portrayal of characters and of the relations between them. If in Rochester we see only an Angrian-Byronic hero and a Charlotte wish-fulfillment figure (the two identifications which to some readers seem entirely to place him), we miss what is more significant, the exploration of personality that opens up new areas of feeling in intersexual relationships. Beyond the "grim," the "harsh," the eccentric, the almost histrionically cynical that superficially distinguish Rochester from conventional heroes, there is something almost Lawrentian: Rochester is "neither tall nor graceful"; his eyes can be "dark, irate, and piercing"; his strong features "took my feelings from my own power and fettered them in his." Without using the vocabulary common to us, Charlotte is presenting maleness and physicality, to which Jane responds directly. She is "assimilated" to him by "something in my brain and heart, in my blood and nerves"; she "must love" and "could not unlove" him; the thought of parting from him is "agony." Rochester's oblique amatory maneuvers become almost punitive in the Walter-to-Griselda style and once reduce her to sobbing "convulsively"; at times the love-game borders on a power-game. Jane, who prefers "rudeness" to "flattery," is an instinctive evoker of passion: she learns "the pleasure of vexing and soothing him by turns" and pursues a "system" of working him up "to considerable irritation" and coolly leaving him; when, as a result, his caresses become grimaces, pinches, and tweaks, she records that, sometimes at least, she "decidedly preferred these fierce favors." She reports, "I crushed his hand . . . red with the passionate pressure"; she "could not . . . see God for his creature," and in her devotion Rochester senses "an earnest, religious energy."

Charlotte's remolding of stock feeling reaches a height when she sympathetically portrays Rochester's efforts to make Jane his mistress; here the stereotyped seducer becomes a kind of lost nobleman of passion, and of specifically physical passion: "Every atom of your flesh is as dear to me as my own. . . ." The intensity of the pressure which he puts upon her is matched, not by the fear and revulsion of the popular heroine, but by a responsiveness which she barely masters: "The crisis was perilous; but not without its charm. . . ." She is "tortured by a sense of remorse at thus hurting his feelings"; at the moment of decision "a hand. of fiery iron grasped my vitals . . . blackness, burning! . . . my intolerable duty"; she leaves in "despair"; and after she has left, "I longed to be his; I panted to return . . ."—and for the victory of principle "I abhorred myself . . . I was hateful in my own eyes." This extraordinary openness to feeling, this escape from the bondage of the trite, continues in the Rivers relationship, which is a structural parallel to the Rochester affair: as in Rochester the old sex villain is seen in a new perspective, so in Rivers the clerical hero is radically refashioned; and Jane's almost accepting a would-be husband is given the aesthetic status of a regrettable yielding to a seducer. Without a remarkable liberation from conventional feeling Charlotte could not fathom the complexity of Rivers—the earnest and dutiful clergyman distraught by a profound inner turmoil of conflicting "drives": sexuality, restlessness, hardness, pride, ambition ("fever in his vitals," "inexorable as death"); the hypnotic, almost inhuman potency of his influence on Jane, who feels "a freezing spell," "an awful charm," an "iron shroud"; the relentlessness, almost the unscrupulousness, of his wooing, the resultant fierce struggle (like that with Rochester), Jane's brilliantly perceptive accusation, ". . . you almost hate me . . . you would kill me. You are killing me now"; and yet her mysterious near-surrender: "I was tempted to cease struggling with him—to rush down the torrent of his will into the gulf of his existence, and there lose my own."

Aside from partial sterilization of banal Gothic by dry factuality and humor, Charlotte goes on to make a much more important—indeed, a radical—revision of the mode: in *Jane Eyre* and in the other novels, as we shall see, that discovery of passion, that rehabilitation of the extra-rational, which is the historical office of Gothic, is no longer oriented in marvelous circumstance but moves deeply into the lesser known realities of human life. This change I describe as the change from "old Gothic" to "new Gothic." The kind of appeal is the same; the fictional method is utterly different.

When Charlotte went on from *Jane Eyre* to *Shirley*, she produced a book that for the student of the Gothic theme is interesting precisely because on the face of things it would be expected to be a barren field. It is the result of Charlotte's one deliberate venture from private intensities into public extensities: Orders in Council, the Luddites, technological unemployment in 1811 and 1812, a social portraiture which develops Charlotte's largest cast of characters. Yet Charlotte cannot keep it a social novel. Unlike Warren, who in the somewhat similar *Night Rider* chose to reflect the historical economic crisis in the private crisis of the hero, Miss Brontë loses interest in the public and slides over into the private.

The formal irregularities of *Shirley*—the stop-and-start, zig-zag movement, plunging periodically into different perspectives—light up the divergent impulses in Charlotte herself: the desire to make a story from observed outer life, and the inability to escape from inner urgencies that with centrifugal force unwind outward into story almost autonomously. Passion alters plan: the story of industrial crisis is repeatedly swarmed over by the love stories. But the ultimate complication is that Charlotte's duality of impulse is reflected not only in the narrative material but in two different ways of telling each part of the story. On the one hand she tells a rather conventional, open, predictable tale; on the other she lets go with a highly charged private sentiency that may subvert the former or at least surround it with an atmosphere of unfamiliarity or positive strangeness: the Gothic impulse.

For Charlotte it is typically the "pattern" versus the "strange." She describes "two pattern young ladies, in pattern attire, with pattern deportment"—a "respectable society" in which "Shirley had the air of a black swan, or a white crow. . . ." When, in singing, Shirley "poured round the passion, force," the young ladies thought this "strange" and concluded: "What was *strange* must be *wrong*; . . ."

True, Charlotte's characters live within the established "patterns" of life; but their impulse is to vitalize forms with unpatterned feeling, and Charlotte's to give play to unpatterned feeling in all its forms. She detects the warrior in the Reverend Matthew Helstone; reports that Malone the curate "had energy enough in hate"; describes Shirley weeping without apparent reason; recounts Mrs. Yorke's paranoid "brooding, eternal, immitigable suspicion of all men, things, creeds, and parties"; portrays Hiram Yorke as scornful, stubborn, intolerant of superiors, independent, truculent, benevolent toward inferiors, his virtues surrounding an aggressive *amour propre*.

Shirley is given a vehement, sweeping, uninhibited criticalness of mind; in her highly articulate formulations of incisive thought is released a furious rush of emotional energy. Within the framework of moral principles her ideas and feelings are untrammeled. She vigorously debunks clichés against charity, but against the mob she will defend her property "like a tigress"; to Yorke's face she does a corrosive analysis of his personality; she attacks Milton in a fiery sweeping paean to Eve, the "mother" of "Titans"; in an almost explosive defense of love she attacks ignorant, chilly, refined, embarrassed people who "blaspheme living fire, seraph-brought from a divine altar"; when she insists that she must *"love"* before she marries, her "worldly" Uncle Sympson retorts, "Preposterous stuff!—indecorous—unwomanly!"

Beside the adults who in ways are precocious are the precocious children—the Yorkes who have their parents' free-swinging, uninhibited style of talk; Henry Sympson, having for his older cousin Shirley an attachment that borders on sexual feeling; and most of all Martin Yorke, aged fifteen, to whose excited pursuit of Caroline, almost irrelevant to plot or theme, Charlotte devotes two and a half zestful chapters. Martin is willing to help Caroline see Robert Moore, "her confounded sweetheart," to be near her himself, and he plans to claim a reward "displeasing to Moore"; he thinks of her physical beauties. Once he gets between Robert and Caroline at good-bye time; "he half carried Caroline down the stairs," "wrapped her shawl round her," and wanted to claim a kiss. At the same time he feels "power over her," he wants her to coax him, and he would like "to put her in a passion—to make her cry." Charlotte subtly conveys the sexuality of his quest—a rare feat in the nineteenth-century novel.

In Robert Moore, the unpopular mill-owner, Charlotte finds less social rightness or wrongness than his strength, his masculine appeal; her sympathy, so to speak, is for the underside of his personality. It "agreed with Moore's temperament . . . to be generally hated"; "he like a silent, sombre, unsafe solitude"; against the vandals his "hate is still running in such a strong current" that he has none left for other objects; he shows "a terrible half" of himself in pursuing rioters with "indefatigable, . . . relentless assiduity"; this "excitement" pleases him; sadistically he likes to "force" magistrates to "betray a certain fear." He is the great lover of the story; he almost breaks Caroline's heart before he marries her, and he even has a subtle impact on Shirley, teasingly communicated, though officially denied, by Charlotte. What Caroline yields to is his "secret power," which affects her "like a spell." Here again Charlotte records, as directly as she can, simple sexual attractiveness. From the problem novel she veers off into "new Gothic"; in old Gothic, her hero would have been a villain.

True to convention, the love stories end happily. But special feelings, a new pathos of love, come through. Louis Moore demands in a woman something "to endure, . . . to reprimand"; love must involve "prickly peril," "a sting now and then"; for him the "young lioness or leopardess" is better than the lamb. There is that peculiarly tense vivacity of talk between lovers (the Jane-Rochester style), who discover a heightened, at times stagey, yet highly communicative rhetoric, drawing now on fantasy, now on moral conviction, verging now on titillating revelation, now on battle; a crafty game of love, flirting with an undefined risk, betraying a withheld avowal, savoring the approach to consummation, as if the erotic energy which in another social order might find a physical outlet were forcing itself into an electric language that is decorous but intimately exploratory. Between Louis Moore, who has "a thirst for freedom," and Shirley, to whom finding love is the Quest for the Bridle (for "a *master* [whom it is] impossible not to love, and very possible to fear"), there is an almost disturbingly taut struggle, a fierce intensification of the duel between Mirabel and Millamant, complex feelings translated into wit, sheer debate, abusiveness of manner, and a variety of skirmishings; Louis, the lover, adopting the stance of power and consciously playing to fright; the pursuit of an elusive prey ending in a virtual parody of "one calling, Child!/ And I replied, My Lord"; over all of this a singular air of strained excitement, of the working of underlying emotional forces that at the climax leads to a new frenetic intensification of style in Louis's notebook:

> "Will you let me breathe, and not bewilder me? You must not smile at present. The world swims and changes round me. The sun is a dizzying scarlet blaze, the sky a violet vortex whirling over me."
>
> I am a strong man, but I staggered as I spoke. All creation was exaggerated: colour grew more vivid: motion more rapid; life itself more vital. I hardly saw her for a moment; but I heard her voice— pitilessly sweet. . . . Blent with torment, I experienced rapture.

Nor does Charlotte's flair for "unpatterned feeling" stop here: Shirley, the forceful leader who has already been called "a gentleman" and "captain," languishes under the found bridle of the masterful lover, whom she treats chillily and subjects to "exquisitely provoking" postponements of marriage; he calls her a "pantheress" who "gnaws her chain"; she tells him, "I don't know myself," as if engagement had opened to her eyes a previously undetected facet of her nature. Though "these freaks" continue, she is "fettered" at last; but not before the reader is radically stirred by the felt mysteries of personality. Before Charlotte, no love story tapped such strange depths, no consummation was so like a defeat.

Here Charlotte is probing psychic disturbance and is on the edge of psychosomatic illness. The theme draws her repeatedly. When Caroline thinks Robert doesn't love her, she suffers a long physical decline, described with painful fullness. She "wasted," had a "broken spirit," suffered "intolerable despair," felt the "utter sickness of longing and disappointment," at night found "my mind darker than my hiding-place," had "melancholy dreams," became "what is called nervous," had "fears I never used to have," "an inexpressible weight on my mind," and "strange sufferings," believed at times "that God had turned His face from her" and sank "into the gulf of religious despair." Charlotte divines this: "People never die of love or grief alone; though some die of inherent maladies which the tortures of those passions prematurely force into destructive action." Caroline lingers in illness, has fancies "inscrutable to ordinary attendants," has a hallucination of talking to Robert in the garden. Shirley, having been bitten by a dog which she believes to be mad, becomes seriously ill; psychosomatic illness springs directly from Charlotte's special sensitivity to the neurotic potential in human nature. A complementary awareness, that of the impact of the physical on the psychic, appears when she observes the "terrible depression," the "inexpressible—dark, barren, impotent" state of mind of Robert when he is recovering from a gunshot wound.

To give so much space to a lesser work is justifiable only because some of its contents are of high historico-critical significance. Though *Shirley* is not pulled together formally as well as *Jane Eyre* or even the more sprawling *Villette,* and though the characters are as wholes less fully realized, still it accommodates the widest ranging of an extraordinarily free sensibility. Constantly, in many different directions, it is in flight from the ordinary rational surface of things against which old Gothic was the first rebel in fiction; it abundantly contains and evokes, to adapt Charlotte's own metaphor, "unpatterned feeling." It turns up unexpected elements in personality: resentfulness, malice, love of power; precocities and perversities of response; the multiple tensions of love between highly individualized lovers; psychic disturbances. And in accepting a dark magnetic energy as a central virtue in personality, Charlotte simply reverses the status of men who were the villains in the sentimental and old Gothic modes.

Of the four novels, *Villette* is most heavily saturated with Gothic —with certain of its traditional manifestations (old Gothic), with the undercutting of these that is for Charlotte no less instinctive than the use of them (anti-Gothic), and with an original, intense exploration of feeling that increases the range and depth of fiction (new Gothic).

As in *Jane Eyre,* Charlotte can be skillful in anti-Gothic. When Madame Beck, pussyfooting in espionage, "materializes" in shocking suddenness, Lucy is made matter-of-fact or indignant rather than thrilled with fright. "No ghost stood beside me . . ." is her characteristic response to a Beck surprise. Once the spy, having "stolen" upon her victims, betrays her unseen presence by a sneeze; Gothic yields to farce. Technically more complex is Charlotte's use of the legend of the nun supposedly buried alive and of the appearances of a visitant taken to be the ghost of the nun; Charlotte coolly distances herself from this by having Lucy dismiss the legend as "romantic rubbish" and by explaining the apparitions as the playful inventions of a giddy lover. True, she keeps the secret long enough to get a few old Gothic thrills from the "ghost," but what she is really up to is using the apparitions in an entirely new way; that is, for responses that lie beyond the simplicities of terror.

First, the apparitions are explained as a product of Lucy's own psychic state, the product, Dr. John suggests, of "long-continued mental conflict." In the history of Gothic this is an important spot, for here we first see the shift from stock explanations and responses to the inner human reality: fiction is slowly discovering the psychic depths known to drama for centuries.

Then, when Lucy next sees the nun, she responds in a way that lies entirely outside fictional convention: "I neither fled nor shrieked . . . I spoke . . . I stretched out my hand, for I meant to touch her." Not that Lucy is not afraid, but that she is testing herself—an immense change from the expectable elementary response: the *frisson* disappears before the complexer action that betokens a maturing of personality.

Finally, Paul and Lucy both see the spectre and are thus brought closer together: they have had what they call "impressions," and through sharing the ghost they assume a shared sensibility. Paul says, "I was conscious of rapport between you and myself." The rapport is real, though the proof of it is false; the irony of this is a subtle sophistication of Gothic.

The responsiveness, the sensitivity, is the thing; many passages place "feeling" above "seeing" as an avenue of knowledge. Reason must be respected, for it is "vindictive," but at times imagination must be yielded to, like a sexual passion at once feared and desired. There is the summer night when the sedative given by Madame Beck has a strange effect:

> Imagination was roused from her rest, and she came forth impetuous and venturous. With scorn she looked on Matter, her mate—
> "Rise!" she said; "Sluggard! this night I will have *my* will; nor shalt thou prevail."
> "Look forth and view the night!" was her cry; and when I lifted the heavy blind from the casement close at hand—with her own royal gesture, she showed me a moon supreme, in an element deep and splendid.
> . . . She lured me to leave this den and follow her forth into dew, coolness, and glory.

There follows the most magnificent of all Charlotte's nocturnes: that vision of the "moonlit, midnight park," the brilliance of the fete, the strange charm of places and people, recounted in a rhythmical, enchanted style (the "Kubla Khan" mode) which at first reading gives the air of a dream mistaken for reality to what is in fact reality made like a dream. This is a surrealistic, trance-like episode which makes available to fiction a vast new territory and idiom. The surrealistic is, despite Montague Summers, one of the new phases of Gothic, which in its role of liberator of feeling characteristically explores the non-naturalistic: to come up, as here, with a profounder nature, or a nature freshly, even disturbingly, seen.

The surrealism of Lucy's evening is possible only to a special sensitivity, and it is really the creation of this sensitivity, in part pathological, that is at the apex of Charlotte's Gothic. In *The Professor* the tensions in the author's contemplation of her own experience come into play; in *Shirley* various undercurrents of personality push up into the social surfaces of life; in *Jane Eyre* moral feeling is subjected to the remolding pressures of a newly vivid consciousness of the diverse impulses of sexuality; and in *Villette* the feeling responses to existence are pursued into sufferings that edge over into disorder. The psychology of rejection and alienation, first applied to Polly, becomes the key to Lucy, who, finding no catharsis for a sense of desolation, generates a serious inner turmoil. She suffers from "a terrible oppression" and then from "anxiety lying in wait on enjoyment, like a tiger crouched in a jungle . . . his fierce heart panted close against mine; . . . I knew he waited only for sundown to bound ravenous from his ambush." Depression is fed by the conflict between a loveless routine of life and her longings, which she tried to put down like "Jael to Sisera, driving a nail through their temples"; but this only "transiently stunned" them and "at intervals [they] would turn on the nail with a rebellious wrench: then did the temples bleed, and the brain thrill to its core."

These strains prepare us for the high point in Charlotte's new Gothic—the study of Lucy's emotional collapse and near breakdown when vacation comes and she is left alone at the school with "a poor deformed and imbecile pupil." "My heart almost died within me. . . . My spirits had long been gradually sinking; now that the prop of employment was withdrawn, they went down fast." After three weeks, storms bring on "a deadlier paralysis"; and "my nervous system could hardly support" the daily strain. She wanders in the street: "A goad thrust me on, a fever forbade me to rest. . . ." She observes a "growing illusion" and says, ". . . my nerves are getting overstretched. . . ." She feels that "a malady is growing upon" her mind, and she asks herself, "How shall I keep well?" Then come "a peculiarly agonizing depression"; a nine-days storm: "a strange fever of the nerves and blood"; continuing insomnia, broken only by a terrifying nightmare of alienation. She flees the house, and then comes the climactic event of her going to a church and despite the intensity of her Protestant spirit entering the confessional to find relief.

From now on, overtly or implicitly, hypochondria and anxiety keep coming into the story—the enemies from whose grip Lucy must gradually free herself. At a concert she spotted the King as a fellow-victim of "that strangest spectre, Hypochondria," for on his face she saw its marks, whose meaning, "if I did not *know*, at least I *felt*. . . ." When, after her return to Beck's on a rainy night, things are not going well, a letter from Dr. John is "the ransom from my terror," and its loss drives her almost to frenzy. She describes night as "an unkindly time" when she has strange fancies, doubts, the "horror of calamity." She is aware of her "easily-deranged temperament." Beyond this area of her own self-understanding we see conflicts finding dramatic expression in her almost wild acceptance of Rachel's passionate acting of Phèdre ("a spectacle low, horrible, immoral"), which counterbalances her vehement condemnation of a fleshy nude by Rubens (one of the "materialists"). Paul identifies her, in a figure whose innocence for him is betrayed by the deep, if not wholly conscious, understanding that leads Charlotte to write it: "a young she wild creature, new caught, untamed, viewing with a mixture of fire and fear the first entrance of the breaker in."

There is not room to trace Lucy's recovery, especially in the important phase, the love affair with Paul which is related to our theme by compelling, as do the Jane-Rochester and Louis Moore-Shirley relationships in quite different ways, a radical revision of the feelings exacted by stereotyped romance. What is finally noteworthy is that Charlotte, having chosen in Lucy a heroine with the least durable emotional equipment, with the most conspicuous neurotic element in her temperament, goes on through the history of Lucy's emotional maturing to surmount the need for romantic fulfillment and to develop the aesthetic courage for a final disaster—the only one in her four novels.

Some years ago Edmund Wilson complained of writers of Gothic who "fail to lay hold on the terrors that lie deep in the human soul and that cause man to fear himself" and proposed an anthology of horror stories that probe "psychological caverns" and find "disquieting obsessions." This is precisely the direction in which Charlotte Brontë moved, especially in Lucy Snowe and somewhat also in Caroline Helstone and Shirley Keeldar; this was one aspect of her following human emotions where they took her, into many depths and intensities that as yet hardly had a place in the novel. This was the finest achievement of Gothic.

Gothic is variously defined. In a recent book review Leslie Fiedler implies that Gothic is shoddy mystery-mongering, whereas F. Cudworth Flint defines the Gothic tradition, which he considers "nearly central in American literature," as "a literary exploration of the avenues to death." For Montague Summers, on the other hand, Gothic was the essence of romanticism, and romanticism was the literary expression of supernaturalism. Both these latter definitions, though they are impractically inclusive, have suggestive value. For originally Gothic was one of a number of aesthetic developments which served to breach the "classical" and "rational" order of life and to make possible a kind of response, and a response to a kind of thing, that among the knowing had long been taboo. In the novel it was the function of Gothic to open horizons beyond social patterns, rational decisions, and institutionally approved emotions; in a word, to enlarge the sense of reality and its impact on the human being. It became then a great liberator of feeling. It acknowledged the nonrational—in the world of things and events, occasionally in the realm of the transcendental, ultimately and most persistently in the depths of the human being. (Richardson might have started this, but his sense of inner forces was so overlaid by the moralistic that his followers all ran after him only when he ran the wrong way.) The first Gothic writers took the easy way: the excitement of mysterious scene and happening, which I call old Gothic. Of this Charlotte Brontë made some direct use, while at the same time tending toward humorous modifications (anti-Gothic); but what really counts is its indirect usefulness to her: it released her from the patterns of the novel of society and therefore permitted the flowering of her real talent—the talent for finding and giving dramatic form to impulses and feelings which, because of their depth or mysteriousness or intensity or ambiguity, or of their ignoring or transcending everyday norms of propriety or reason, increase wonderfully the sense of reality in the novel. To note the emergence of this "new Gothic" in Charlotte Brontë is not, I think, to pursue an old mode into dusty corners but rather to identify historically the distinguishing, and distinguished, element in her work.

THOMAS MOSER

What Is the Matter With Emily Jane?
Conflicting Impulses in *Wuthering Heights*

I

Ever since C. P. Sanger,[1] over thirty years ago, charted the elaborate time scheme of *Wuthering Heights*[2] and showed the symmetrical arrangement of characters, commentators have been writing in awe-struck terms of the novel's design. Even Dorothy Van Ghent, the most perceptive of its critics, calls *Wuthering Heights* "highly wrought."[3] Others have drawn analogies to music and have—inevitably—invoked the sacred name of Beethoven. Moreover, critics have generally insisted that the structure is truly artful; it supports the meaning. The form fits the subject—in Lord David Cecil's homely phrase—"like a glove."[4]

I would suggest that the nineteenth-century view of *Wuthering Heights* as a powerful and imperfect book comes closer to the truth than recent assertions of its exquisite shape. I would suggest, too, that Charlotte Brontë's frequently maligned description of her sister as a most unconscious artist bears rereading:

> Her imagination, which was a spirit more sombre than sunny, more powerful than sportive, found in such traits material whence

From *Nineteenth-Century Fiction*, Vol. XVII, No. 1, 1-19. © 1962 by the Regents of the University of California. Reprinted by permission of the Regents of the University of California and the author.

it wrought creations like Heathcliff, like Earnshaw, like Catherine. Having formed these beings, she did not know what she had done. If the auditor of her work, when read in manuscript, shuddered under the grinding influence of natures so relentless and implacable, of spirits so lost and fallen; if it was complained that the mere hearing of certain vivid and fearful scenes banished sleep by night, and disturbed mental peace by day, Ellis Bell would wonder what was meant, and suspect the complainant of affectation. . . .

Whether it is right or advisable to create things like Heathcliff, I do not know: I scarcely think it is. But this I know; the writer who possesses the creative gift owns something of which he is not always master—something that at times strangely wills and works for itself. [Pp. 180, 181.]

The two most distinctive features of the design of *Wuthering Heights* are its multiple narrators (who cause the chronological involutions) and its two generations of love triangles. The narrative method is indeed a brilliant invention. Mrs. Van Ghent reveals two of its uses: the narratives of Nelly Dean and Lockwood place the drama "in the context of the psychologically familiar"; the displacement "into past time and into the memory of an old woman functions in the same way as dream displacements: it both censors and indulges, protects and liberates."[5] Even more important, it seems to me, these narrators, the epicene Lockwood and the prudent Nelly, are obtuse; they misinterpret the action and in their characters act as ironic contrasts to Heathcliff and Cathy. But in the second half of the novel the method essentially breaks down: the narrators cease to serve as ironic screens and the novel suffers seriously. Mark Schorer's stimulating and complex interpretation of *Wuthering Heights* relies not only upon the narrative perspective but also upon the continuance of the story through another generation. "One of the most carefully constructed novels in the language," it is carried on long enough to show that convention and the "cloddish world" survive and that Heathcliff's passion is "meaningless at last." But *is* this what the novel shows? Does not the creation of the second generation serve chiefly to mar the structure by contradicting the novel's true subject. Probably Emily Brontë at no time consciously accepted her true subject; in the closing pages of *Wuthering Heights* she certainly rejects it—to the obvious detriment of her art. How does one determine a novel's "true subject"? To try to discuss this in a few sentences is absurd; yet an oversimplified answer may help to clarify the problems posed by *Wuthering Heights*. A novel's true subject is the one that, regardless of the novelist's conscious intention, actually informs the work, the one that elicits the most highly energized writing. To put it another way, a novelist has found the true subject of his book when he dramatizes the truth he cannot escape rather than the illusion he longs to make true."[6]

Lord David Cecil's account of the true subject of *Wuthering Heights* ("philosophy," he terms it) has been conspicuously influential. He calls Emily Brontë a "mystic" who views the cosmos as the "expression of certain living spiritual principles . . . the principle of storm . . . and the principle of calm." These principles do not conflict. "They are the component parts of a harmony." The final impression that *Wuthering Heights* leaves is one of "cosmic order . . . harmonious, complete."[7] Despite the ingenuity of this reading, it hardly describes the common reader's response to *Wuthering Heights*, or his recollection of it. One admires and rereads the novel for the grand passion of Heathcliff and Cathy. Lord David's discussion must be seen then as rationalization rather than interpretation. Most commentators, in fact, evince a longing to tame the novel, to make their pleasure in it somehow respectable. This would explain the reiterated references to Emily Brontë as a mystic, and the evident comfort that enthusiasts take in the notion that Cathy and Heathcliff's love is "sexless," meaning, presumably, that intercourse is not even implied.

II

Lord David's essay commands assent at least in its stress on the characters as representative of universal forces. It is rather the vagueness of his definitions and their generality of application which seem dubious. Mrs. Van Ghent and Richard Chase give, I think, much more persuasive symbolic readings. The former describes Heathcliff as "essentially, anthropomorphized primitive energy,"[8] and the latter calls him "sheer dazzling sexual"[9] force. I would be even more specific. Over a century ago Emily Brontë dramatized what Freud subsequently called the id. She discovered and symbolized in Heathcliff and, to a lesser extent, in Cathy that part of us we know so little about, the secret well-spring of vitality, the child that lurks within everyone, even within so ordinary a person as Nelly Dean or one so weak as Lockwood. Somehow, Emily Brontë penetrated to that most obscure part of the psyche and "characterized" it. The primary traits which Freud ascribed to the id apply perfectly to Heathcliff: the source of psychic energy; the seat of the instincts (particularly sex and death); the essence of dreams; the archaic foundation of personality—selfish, asocial, impulsive.

I do not mean to say that *Wuthering Heights* is a sport, a modern novel born by chance in the nineteenth century. It clearly belongs to the tradition of tales of overwhelming, self-consuming love described in Denis de Rougemont's *Love in the Western World*. More particularly, it has close affinities in terms of character, situation, and recurrent imagery with *Clarissa;* both novels come from the same kind of imagination—English, Puritan, essentially feminine. Nor do I wish by a Freudian reading of symbols to exclude mythic interpretations. By stressing a perhaps restrictive reading, I hope to throw into sharper relief the novel's weaknesses—and strengths.

The basic childishness of Cathy and Heathcliff and their impulse to lose themselves in the world of external nature need no analysis. Mrs. Van Ghent's brilliant essay makes these quite clear. But Heathcliff as the embodiment of sexual energy requires detailed explanation not only because critics have largely ignored this role but also because Emily Brontë apparently tried to disguise the truth from herself. The large body of evidence suggesting that Emily Brontë felt Heathcliff to be pure sexual force lies just beneath the surface, in a series of scenes involving Heathcliff, Cathy, and, in most cases, an ineffectual male. Each scene dramatizes a dispute of some sort over entrance through a door or window. Heathcliff always wins, and the images suggest that the victory is a sexual conquest.[10]

The *locus classicus* for this pattern is the eleventh chapter. Edgar has just learned that Heathcliff intends to marry Edgar's sister Isabella, and he determines to throw Heathcliff out of the house. To this end he orders three servants to wait in the passage while he enters the kitchen where Heathcliff and Cathy converse. When he demands Heathcliff's "instant departure," the latter responds in a way calculated to cast doubt on Edgar's masculinity: "Cathy, this lamb of yours threatens like a bull!" Edgar tries to signal the servants for help, but Cathy slams the door to the passage and locks it, saying that she will swallow the key before Edgar shall get it and that she wishes that Heathcliff may flog Edgar sick:

> It did not need the medium of a flogging to produce that effect on
> the master. He tried to wrest the key from Catherine's grasp; and
> for safety she flung it into the hottest part of the fire; whereupon
> Mr. Edgar was taken with a nervous trembling, and his counte-
> nance grew deadly pale. For his life he could not avert that access
> of emotion—mingled anguish and humiliation overcame him com-
> pletely. He leant on the back of a chair, and covered his face.
> [P. 53.]

Notice here that Cathy throws the key into the fire, which throughout the novel is associated with Heathcliff and Cathy, and opposed
to Edgar. (Cathy says earlier of Heathcliff, "Whatever our souls are
made of, his and mine are the same, and Linton's is as different as a
moonbeam from lightning, or frost from fire.") Notice too that Edgar's response to the defeat at Cathy's hands far exceeds the apparent
danger of a beating by Heathcliff. It is almost as if Edgar senses in
this defeat his sexual inferiority to Heathcliff and Cathy. Certainly
Cathy views the situation in these terms: "Oh! Heavens! In old days
this would win you knighthood! . . . We are vanquished! we are
vanquished! Heathcliff would as soon lift a finger at you as the king
would march his army against a colony of mice."

In the ensuing action, Edgar appears to put Heathcliff to rout; he
strikes him across the throat, taking his breath momentarily, and
walks out the back door, through the yard, to summon the servants
from the front of the house. Heathcliff vows immediate vengeance:
"I'll crush his ribs in like a rotten hazel-nut!" But Nelly, to prevent
violence, tells one of her white lies. Edgar, she says, has sent only
his servants to the back door and is himself in hiding. Heathcliff
thus finds himself trapped by Cathy's earlier stratagem against Edgar. The front door of the kitchen remains locked, the key in the
fire. But Heathcliff does not tremble; he quickly remedies the loss
of the key by seizing from the fireplace a poker, smashing the lock,
and making his escape through the "inner door."

Cathy's response to the drama has sexual overtones. "Very much
excited," she hastens upstairs to the parlor, throwing herself on the
sofa: "A thousand smiths' hammers are beating in my head!" She
directs Nelly not to permit Isabella to approach and lies in wait for
Edgar. She tells Nelly to remind Edgar of her "passionate temper,
verging, when kindled, on frenzy," and to "dismiss that apathy" out
of her face. Edgar appears, not in anger but in sorrow. His lack of

fire enrages Cathy. She stamps her foot: "Your cold blood cannot be worked into a fever—your veins are full of ice-water—but mine are boiling, and the sight of such chilliness makes them dance." When Edgar asks her to choose between him and Heathcliff, she tells him to leave her and rings the bell until it breaks with a twang. Then she lies on the sofa dashing her head against the arm and gnashing her teeth. Edgar and Nelly cannot understand her feelings, and she rushes into her bedroom, locks the door, and remains alone for three days. When she finally lets Nelly in, it is clear that she is dying. Her description of her first night alone in the bedroom dramatizes her complete absorption with Heathcliff. She had fallen unconscious and had not begun to awaken until dawn.

> "I thought as I lay there, with my head against that table leg, and my eyes dimly discerning the grey square of the window, that I was enclosed in the oak-panelled bed at home. . . . I was a child; my father was just buried, and my misery arose from the separation that Hindley had ordered between me and Heathcliff—I was laid alone, for the first time, and, rousing from a dismal doze after a night of weeping—I lifted my hand to push the panels aside, it struck the tabletop!" [P. 58.]

Cathy asks Nelly to open the window for her, Nelly refuses, and Cathy throws it open herself and leans out, "careless of the frosty air that cut about her shoulders as keen as a knife." Finally Edgar appears. Shocked by her haggard countenance, he takes her in his arms. "Ah! you are come, are you, Edgar Linton? . . . You are one of those things that are ever found when least wanted, and when you are wanted, never!" She goes on to make what seems a most curious remark, in view of the fact that Edgar is embracing her: "What you touch at present, you may have; but my soul will be on that hill-top before you lay hands on me again. I don't want you, Edgar, I'm past wanting you."

These three scenes—the kitchen, the upstairs parlor, and Cathy's bedroom three days later—need little comment. In the kitchen battle over the key, Cathy reveals her contempt for Edgar's masculinity by seizing the key and locking the door, and Heathcliff shows himself master by breaking the lock with the poker. When Cathy hurries up to the parlor to lie on the sofa, her longing for love gives Edgar another chance. All may be well between them if he will come, not blaming her but loving and wanting her. Instead, he shows no feeling at all while she, raging at his utter inadequacy, breaks the bell pull. Sexual frustration clearly contributes to her collapse after Edgar's failure. Cathy's dream of the time Hindley first removed Heathcliff from her bed (he was thirteen and she twelve) reaffirms that only her foster brother and childhood lover can alleviate her suffering. Edgar is useless, she tells him, and his masculine attentions are no longer wanted. Heathcliff must come through that window to satisfy Cathy. (Since Emily Brontë cannot let this happen, on the literal level—because Heathcliff and Cathy are "one"? because Emily Brontë wrote under some kind of incest taboo? because she would have curtailed her story?—she has Heathcliff snatch Isabella away from Thrushcross Grange at the very time that Cathy is calling for him through the window and telling Edgar that she'll be dead "before you lay hands on me again.")

III

The kitchen scene offers the most vivid example of Heathcliff as sexual force, but it is far from unique. In fact, it is only one of many following the same pattern. Emily Brontë repeatedly portrays Heathcliff as breaking through a barrier, identified with Cathy, which an ineffectual male either attempts to break and cannot or attempts futilely to defend. Sometimes a fourth party is present, chiefly as a witness to narrate the scene later to the reader. (Mrs. Van Ghent interprets windows in *Wuthering Heights* as symbolic of the barrier between the "human" and the "other" world;[11] windows and doors seem also to admit of another more specific reading.)

The early scenes of this type all show, as might be expected, Edgar as the ineffectual male. In the first, Heathcliff appears only as a potential invader of Thrushcross Grange the night he and Cathy, still children, are caught peeking through the windows at Edgar and Isabella. The Lintons take in Cathy and send away Heathcliff. But he lurks outside and later tells Nelly: "If Catherine had wished to return, I intended shattering their great glass panes to a million of fragments." The next such scene occurs three years after Heathcliff's departure (a departure signalized by a huge bough falling across the roof of Wuthering Heights and knocking stones into the kitchen fire). Heathcliff returns in September 1783. Here is Nelly's and the reader's first view of him, on the porch of Thrushcross Grange:

"He leant against the side, and held his fingers on the latch, as if intending to open for himself." Instead he opens it for Nelly to take his message upstairs; Cathy joins him immediately and later flies up the stairs "breathless and wild" with the wonderful news of his return. For the next three months Heathcliff visits more and more frequently until the violent scene in the kitchen, after which he steals Isabella away. The last of the invasion scenes during Cathy's life occurs two months later, when Heathcliff has returned to learn that she lies on the point of death. He tells Nelly he will fight his way into Thrushcross Grange if she will not let him in. As usual she gives in so as to prevent violence. Actually, Heathcliff manages alone, walking past the watchdog and into the house. "He did not hit the right room directly; she motioned me to admit him; but he found it out, ere I could reach the door, and in a stride or two was at her side, and had her grasped in his arms." He and Cathy embrace tumultuously; Cathy collapses, not from the power of Heathcliff's love but from despair at the sound of Edgar's approaching step. Heathcliff at last withdraws to the garden and Cathy never regains consciousness.

Cathy dies in childbirth early Monday morning, March 20, 1784, and is buried the following Friday. That night Heathcliff enacts his most violent invasion, this time into Wuthering Heights with Hindley acting as the ineffectual male striving to bar the door. The latter may seem a strange choice for this role; nevertheless, not only is he no match for Heathcliff, but he is also less than the master of women. Some years earlier, Nelly, virtually his foster sister, renders him, literally and symbolically, harmless by taking "the shot out of the master's fowling piece." Hindley, drunk, seizes a carving knife and orders Nelly to open her mouth:

> He held the knife in his hand, and pushed its point between my teeth: but, for my part, I was never much afraid of his vagaries. I spat out, and affirmed it tasted detestably—I would not take it on any account.
> "Oh!" said he, releasing me. . . . [P. 34.]

The night after Cathy's funeral finds Hindley similarly armed, holding a "curiously constructed pistol, having a double-edged spring knife attached to the barrel" which he normally carries concealed in his waistcoat. Isabella admires the pistol:

> I surveyed the weapon inquisitively; a hideous notion struck me. How powerful I should be possessing such an instrument! I took it from his hand, and touched the blade. He looked astonished at the expression my face assumed during a brief second. It was not horror, it was covetousness. He snatched the pistol back, jealously. . . . [P. 65.]

Heathcliff returns from the cemetery and finds the kitchen door locked. As he walks around the house through the snow, Hindley and Isabella agree to keep him out. "Do!" says Isabella. "Put the key in the lock, and draw the bolts." Hindley determines to murder Heathcliff and asks silence of Isabella. But although she wants Heathcliff dead, Isabella, like all the other characters in the novel, cannot finally see harm done him. Impulsively, she shouts a warning through the lattice. Heathcliff knocks the casement to the floor and, when Hindley rushes forward to shoot, reaches through and wrenches the weapon away. It goes off harmlessly and the spring knife closes, not on Heathcliff's, but on Hindley's wrist. Heathcliff "then took a stone, struck down the division between two windows, and sprung in."

The scene seems incomplete. Why should Heathcliff bother to break through simply to get at Isabella, whom he detests? Sixteen chapters and eighteen years later the reader finally discovers Heathcliff's mission that night. He had been digging up Cathy's newly filled grave when he felt her warm breath upon him:

> "Her presence was with me; it remained while I re-filled the grave, and led me home. . . . Having reached the Heights, I rushed eagerly to the door. It was fastened; and, I remember, that accursed Earnshaw and my wife opposed my entrance. I remember stopping to kick the breath out of him, and then hurrying upstairs, to my room, and hers—I looked round impatiently—I felt her by me—I could *almost* see her. . . ." [Pp. 131-32.]

Clearly, Heathcliff's victory over Hindley, like those over Edgar, is part of his quest for Cathy.

Even Lockwood, with his minimal role in the lives of the lovers, is permitted to play the ineffectual male once. His lack of masculinity needs no documentation. The only time a woman ever responded to him, Lockwood, as he himself admits, "shrunk icily into myself, like a snail; at every glance retired colder and farther."

While calling on his landlord, Heathcliff, Lockwood is snowbound and spends the night. The housekeeper puts him, unbeknownst to Heathcliff, in the old paneled bed where Cathy and Heathcliff had slept as children. Here Lockwood dreams his memorable dream: that the waif Cathy knocks on the window to be let in and that he tries to silence the cry by unhasping the casement but cannot because the "hook was soldered into the staplè, a circumstance observed by me when awake." In his dream he breaks the glass and finds his hand clasped by a tiny hand; terrified, he scrapes the wrist on the broken pane and finally screams so loudly as to waken himself and arouse Heathcliff. When he tells Heathcliff the dream, he is sent out of the room. But Lockwood surreptitiously observes Heathcliff: "He got on to the bed, and wrenched open the lattice, bursting, as he pulled at it, into an uncontrollable passion of tears. 'Come in! come in!' he sobbed. 'Cathy, do come. Oh do—*once* more!'"

This is the last time Heathcliff violently removes a barrier between himself and Cathy. And Lockwood's role is obviously more that of witness than opponent. There are, however, two other occasions at the end of Heathcliff's life when no other male is present and opposition is only implied. When the sexton is digging another grave, Heathcliff has Cathy's coffin uncovered. He strikes that side of the coffin loose which will be next to his: "and I bribed the sexton to pull it away, when I'm laid there, and slide mine out too." Eight months later Nelly finds Heathcliff lying dead in his and Cathy's paneled bed, with the window swinging to and fro and with eyes that "would not shut." Nelly reports that Heathcliff was buried as he had wished. Presumably, then, Heathcliff's intention was fulfilled, that "by the time Linton gets to us, he'll not know which is which!"

Not only is Heathcliff a consistently successful invader, but he also bars the way to others and establishes himself as sole keeper of the keys. The first page of the novel shows Heathcliff leaning over the gate, hands in his waistcoat, while Lockwood burbles a request to enter. This image of Heathcliff standing menacingly at the entrance to Wuthering Heights recurs frequently throughout the novel. Even more striking is Heathcliff's tenacity when Isabella and later the younger Cathy try to deprive him of house keys. Isabella, coming to Wuthering Heights for the first time since her marriage, wanders through the house looking for the bedroom she will share with her husband. Joseph warns her that Heathcliff's is just the one she cannot see, so she sleeps in a chair in Hareton's room until Heathcliff finds her. Isabella reports to Nelly his reaction: "I told him the cause of my staying up so late—that he had the key of our room in his pocket. The adjective *our* gave mortal offense. He swore it was not, nor ever should be mine. . . ."

Although Emily Brontë refers frequently to Heathcliff's violent treatment of the children in the second half of the novel, she dramatizes it only once. This is the time when Heathcliff captures the younger Cathy in order to force her to marry his son Linton. The subsequent action makes an interesting contrast to Edgar's battle for the kitchen key with the other Cathy many years before. Her daughter, black eyes flashing, says, "Give me that key—I will have it!" She snatches at the "instrument" and almost gets it out of Heathcliff's loosened fingers. He warns her to stand off, but she ignores the warning and applies her teeth to his hand. (Her mother, in the earlier battle, had threatened to swallow the key to keep it from Edgar.) Heathcliff suddenly and deliberately releases the key. But he shows none of Edgar's humiliation. For when Cathy goes to secure the key, he seizes her, pulls her on his knee, and administers a "shower of terrific slaps on both sides of the head." A touch on the chest stops Nelly when she tries to interfere; Heathcliff picks the key off the floor and, "perceiving us all confounded, rose, and expeditiously made the tea himself."

The actions and the language of the scenes examined above—surely the most memorable scenes in the novel—indicate that, whether she "knew" it or not, Emily Brontë was writing a passionate paean to Eros. The novel moves relentlessly toward its necessary end—the complete physical union of Cathy and Heathcliff. Moreover, although Emily Brontë frustrates this union on the literal level until both are buried, and thus makes a "story," symbolically she accomplishes it in almost every scene Cathy and Heathcliff play together. At the same time she soundly defeats all the other characters (particularly the Thrushcross Grange inmates) whenever they attempt to curb Heathcliff in his quest for Cathy.

IV

E. M. Forster says that *Wuthering Heights* is one of those novels that asks of the reader the "suspension of the sense of humour."[12] This comment applies with much more force to the second half (with the exception of a few scenes) than it does to the first. The violence of the scenes just discussed does not seem laughably melodramatic. It is perfectly in keeping with the characters. As Mrs. Van Ghent says, "Heathcliff might *really* be a demon."[13] Again, Cathy's wild speeches to Nelly and Edgar in her bedroom after three days of isolation are completely appropriate to her. And these are perhaps the loveliest pages of the novel.

That Emily Brontë loses control of the second half of her novel and writes insincerely is suggested by her attempts to endow the thin-blooded Thrushcross Grange people with the emotional language of Heathcliff and Cathy. This occurs in Isabella's account of Heathcliff to Nelly immediately after Cathy's death and almost precisely in the middle of the novel:

> "I gave him my heart, and he took and pinched it to death; and flung it back to me—people feel with their hearts, Ellen, and since he has destroyed mine, I have not power to feel for him, and I would not, though he groaned from this, to his dying day; and wept tears of blood for Catherine!" [P. 79.]

From Cathy's lips a speech like this would be convincing. But there is no evidence that Isabella's love for Heathcliff is anything but self-infatuation or that she ever had a heart to feel with, let alone to give. The younger Cathy employs the same kind of inappropriately emotional language to express sympathy for Linton Heathcliff, whom even Nelly Dean scorns. The scene, like many of the later ones, parodies an earlier. Hareton locks out Linton and Cathy, and Linton shrieks in helpless rage until he falls in a fit. Cathy expostulates: "Ellen, I was ready to tear my hair off my head! I sobbed and wept so that my eyes were almost blind." Had her mother said this about her lover, we would be convinced. But not here.

Emily Brontë at first persuades the reader when she consistently and movingly implies that a future of ecstasy will reward Heathcliff's and Cathy's quest for each other. The second half of the book promises a resolution on the realistic level through a younger generation, with Cathy playing her mother's role, Hareton playing Heathcliff's, and Linton playing Edgar's. The reader, however, will hardly accept the new terms of the perfect relationship between the sexes. Emily Brontë asks us to admire the younger Cathy's quest, first for a patient, in Linton, and then for a pupil, in Hareton. And both boys desire, not union with an equal, but unsexed bliss with a mother.

Cathy from the beginning is related to Linton like a sentimental nurse to a sickly child, "stroking his curls, and kissing his cheek, and offering him tea in her saucer, like a baby." Later she arranges his pillows, offers her shoulder or her knee as support for his head. She views marriage with him as perpetuating this relationship.

> "I'm a woman—and I'm certain Linton would recover quickly if he had me to look after him—I'm older than he is, you know, and wiser, and less childish, am I not? And he'll soon do as I direct him, with some slight coaxing—He's a pretty little darling when he's good. I'd make such a pet of him, if he were mine." [P. 110.]

Linton's saccharine speeches (quite out of character) suggest that Emily Brontë actually feels Cathy praiseworthy in her attitude toward him: "Believe that if I might be as sweet, and as kind, and as good as you are, I would be, as willingly and more so, than as happy and healthy. And believe that your kindness has made me love you deeper than if I deserved your love. . . ." On this Cathy modestly comments: "I felt he spoke the truth." Love, which in the older generation is the expression of vital energy, dwindles, in the younger, to the pleasure of nursing and to gratitude at being mothered.

Also characteristic of the younger Cathy are her stirring debates with Heathcliff in which she plays either the little heroine of Victorian stage melodrama spurning the cruel villain or the embattled champion of woman's rights castigating the dissolute male:

> "Mr. Heathcliff, *you* have *nobody* to love you; and, however miserable you make us, we shall still have the revenge of thinking that your cruelty arises from your greater misery! You *are* miserable, are you not? Lonely, like the devil, and envious like him? *Nobody* loves you—*nobody* will cry for you, when you die! I wouldn't be you!" [P. 130.]

Such speeches recur with alarming frequency in the last fifty pages of the book and suggest, painfully, Emily Brontë's identification with her moralizing heroine.

While Linton is made for his part, Hareton apparently needs the rough edges rubbed off before he can be Cathy's next suitable minion. The roughness is only apparent, however, since Hareton early tries to ingratiate himself with Cathy. Heathcliff, it is true, had marked him for his own: "Now, my bonny lad, you are mine! And we'll see if one tree won't grow as crooked as another, with the same wind to twist it!"[14] Hareton, however, proves himself no oak of the Heathcliff-Cathy variety. After Linton's death, Emily Brontë and the second Cathy speedily deprive him of his male sexual force. First he is incapacitated for the masculine sport of hunting. Not only does his gun burst but his arm is injured and he is "condemned to the fireside and tranquility," which, Nelly tells us, "suited Catherine." Hareton has recourse to his other masculine sport, smoking, but Cathy, like her mother with Edgar's key, takes Hareton's pipe from his mouth, breaks it, and throws it behind the fire. Although Hareton swears and takes another pipe, his smoking is never mentioned again, and a few minutes later we see him accept from Cathy a handsome book wrapped in white paper and tied with a bit of ribbon. Hareton trembles, his face glows, and soon his lessons have begun, Cathy's hand upon his shoulder. Presently all Wuthering Heights suffers feminization. Under Cathy's tutelage Hareton clears out Joseph's black currant trees for a flower bed while she puts primroses in her beloved's porridge.

How Lord David and most other Brontë critics can take seriously the affair between Cathy and Hareton remains a mystery. Their love story belongs with countless pieces of subliterary fiction in women's magazines; it is simply a superficial stereotyped tale of feminine longings. Emile Brontë gives her heroine first a spoiled and then a tractable child to play with—a "love affair" without any of the concomitant inconveniences of sex. As the novel loses its force, the reader's mind inevitably wanders away from the work of art to its creator, the intense, inhibited spinster of Haworth. Her careful arrangement of symmetrical sets of characters, rather than signifying her continuing involvement with her subject, denotes simply that she has abandoned it.

V

For the structure that is organic form comes neither from intricate time schemes nor the neat repetition of character types. It rises from deep within the artist and relates directly to his felt awareness of life. Yet there is one aspect of the *Wuthering Heights* chronology that does express Emily Brontë's sense of Heathcliff's magical sexual power. Let us look with the eye of a month-counting neighborhood gossip at three important marriages and subsequent blessed events. A little calendar work reveals that Heathcliff's presence was vital to the conception of all three children of the second generation.

No one knew where Hindley met Frances or when they married. Certain it is that Hindley brought her with him when he returned from college for his father's funeral in October 1777; the next June, the ninth month after their arrival at Wuthering Heights, saw the birth of Hareton, last of the Earnshaws. Heathcliff has, of course, little personal impact upon Hindley's relations with Frances, and one could attribute Hareton's conception after their arrival to the potent atmosphere of Wuthering Heights. But Emily Brontë shows in detail the immense effect Heathcliff has on relations between Cathy and Edgar. They marry in April 1783, and "for the space of half a year, the gunpowder lay as harmless as sand, because no fire came near to explode it." However, "on a mellow evening in September," Heathcliff finally returns. Cathy glows with delight at his appearance, and he flashes glances at her, his "eyes full of black fire," while Edgar grows "pale with pure anoyance." That night Edgar cries in bed. At first Cathy is irritated, but Heathcliff's return has wiped out the "misery" of her marriage and has reconciled her "to God, and humanity." She makes peace with Edgar; the morrow finds her exuberantly vivacious and Edgar no longer peevish. He permits her to visit Wuthering Heights that afternoon with Isabella; "she rewarded him with such a summer of sweetness and affection, in return, as made the house a paradise for several days, both master and servants profiting from the perpetual sunshine." This one blissful period in their marriage ends soon with the quarrel over Heathcliff and Isabella. But clearly within those few days when Heathcliff's fire first nears Cathy's gunpowder, Cathy and Edgar conceive their child. The second Cathy is born on March 20, 1784, in the seventh month after Heathcliff's appearance, "a puny, seven months' child."

Heathcliff proves himself as potent a literal as symbolic father. He carries Isabella away in January 1784, and within twenty-four hours she wants to be back in Thrushcross Grange. Apparently Emily Brontë imagines them sleeping together only the first night. Certainly she stresses the fact that Heathcliff never permits the detested Isabella to enter his Wuthering Heights bedroom. Nevertheless, the following September, in the ninth month after their elopement, Isabella gives birth to Linton Heathcliff.

When E. M. Forster said that Emily Brontë tried to hide the clock in her book, he did not mean, one trusts, all this! Of course it is

impossible to know whether Emily Brontë consciously arranged the
births of Hareton and Cathy so that Heathcliff could influence their
conceptions and whether she meant that Linton was conceived at
Heathcliff's and Isabella's first and only sexual encounter. My own
guess is that Emily Brontë did not consciously manipulate the time
scheme here, but that her vision of Heathcliff as the energy that in-
vests the universe, together with her woman's sense of the biological
rhythms of life, produced these strangely appropriate results.

Her sense of Heathcliff's potency does not wholly desert her during the second half of the novel. Only this can explain all the improbable circumstances that "cause" the second Cathy to be drawn
time after time, against the wills of her father, Nelly, and herself, to
Wuthering Heights. Only Heathcliff's power can account for Isabella's half-conscious longing, after he has driven her away, for him
to follow her, give her a new wedding ring, and take her back. Why
else should Nelly fail to shout when help is near, and why should
she irrationally blame herself rather than Heathcliff when she and
Cathy are captured? In the later pages, he looms over Wuthering
Heights like the source of a gigantic magnetic field; fitfully, reluc-
tantly, unconsciously, its victims acknowledge that its power is good.

From Heathcliff as energy, however, to the words of Lockwood
that close the book is a long step indeed; so, too, is the shift from the
Lockwood and Nelly of the opening pages to their roles at the end.
At the beginning both exist as ironic and, at times, ludicrous contrasts to the principals. Lockwood's sexual timidity effectively enhances Heathcliff's vigor, and Nelly's prudent complacency puts into
strong relief Cathy's passion, but Emily Brontë's handling of her two
narrators in the second half partakes of the general decline in quality. Nelly Dean becomes more and more an official voice of the
author. No irony intervenes as she sings the younger Cathy's praises
to Linton. Even worse are Lockwood's coyly banal observations on
the love play of Cathy and Hareton. He hears her voice, "sweet as
a silver bell," threatening Hareton with a hairpulling if he mispro-
nounces, and Hareton in "softened tones," demanding a kiss if he
speaks correctly. Cathy leans over him, her "light shining ringlets
blending, at intervals, with his brown locks," as she superintends
his studies. "The task was done," says Lockwood, "not free from
further blunders, but the pupil claimed a reward and received at
least five kisses, which, however, he generously returned." (P. 140.)

The first Cathy and Heathcliff are pretty well distilled out of the novel by its last page. Country people insist that Heathcliff "walks," but Nelly shows little sign of uneasiness. The novel ends with these words, much quoted and highly praised, spoken by Lockwood at the graves of the lovers:

> I lingered round them, under that benign sky, watched the moths fluttering among the heath and hare-bells; listened to the soft wind breathing through the grass; and wondered how anyone could ever imagine unquiet slumbers, for the sleepers in that quiet earth. [P. 153.]

In view of what we know of Heathcliff, perpetually vibrant with passion, and of Cathy ceaselessly haunting him, we must find this passage profoundly ironic. There is, however, no evidence that Emily Brontë perceived that irony.

Mark Schorer's reading of the novel describes what may well have been Emily Brontë's ultimate conscious attitude toward her creation. He suggests that she "begins by wishing to instruct her narrator, the sentimental dandy Lockwood, in the nature of a grand passion, and and that somehow she ends by instructing herself in the vanity of human wishes." She tries to take Cathy and Heathcliff at their own valuation, to exalt the moral magnificence of unmoral passion. "Her novelistic art had to evaluate her world." It is through her arrangement of the generations, "as neat and tidy as the cupboard of a spinster," and by screening the narrative through the perspectives of two conventional people, that she sees "what her unmoral passions come to. Moral magnificence? Not at all; rather, a devastating spectacle of human waste: ashes." Probably Mr. Schorer is right in saying that this was Emily Brontë's conscious response to her work. Yet, as her sister said, she did not really understand what she was writing. Otherwise, she could not have tried to pass off as real and important those illusory figures, Hareton and the younger Cathy. Surely the authentic Emily Brontë does not believe that real love can be exemplified by this couple, so oblivious to the primitive forces that underlie life. The authentic Emily Brontë who wrote the masterpiece we return to is the creator of Heathcliff, vibrating with energy, and Cathy, scorning the pusillanimous Edgar to cry across the moors to her demon lover.

NOTES

1. "The Structure of *Wuthering Heights*," *The Hogarth Essays*, No. XIX (London, 1926).
2. New York, 1950. All citations made in the text will be from this edition, the Rinehart. It includes the preface Charlotte Brontë wrote to the second edition (1850) as well as an interpretive introduction by Mark Schorer.
3. Van Ghent, *The English Novel: Form and Function* (New York, 1953), p. 153. I should here like to acknowledge a considerable debt both to Mrs. Van Ghent and to Albert J. Guerard for suggestions concerning this paper.
4. Cecil, *Early Victorian Novelists* (London, 1934), p. 185.
5. Van Ghent, pp. 155, 160.
6. *As I Lay Dying* provides an example of a novel in which the author's intention conflicts with the true subject. Addie Bundren's long, explicitly philosophical monologue gives the intended subject: the cleavage between thought and action. Faulkner apparently wishes in this novel to rank his characters according to the ability of each to unite thought and action, and in these terms, Addie comes first, Anse last. But whatever the intended subject, *As I Lay Dying* succeeds primarily as a comic novel, the dramatization of man enduring amid a welter of absurd disasters. This is what energizes the novel, and the central figure is Anse—almost the type of the comic hero—selfish, amoral, buffeted on all sides, but, somehow, always landing on his feet.
7. Cecil, pp. 151, 152, 167, 164.
8. Van Ghent, p. 154.
9. Chase, "The Brontës, or Myth Domesticated," *Forms of Modern Fiction*, ed. William Van O'Connor (Minneapolis, 1948), p. 109.
10. I first noticed this pattern while studying a similar and recurrent scene in the novels of Joseph Conrad: an older man attempts to kill the hero at the door of the heroine's boudoir, but the heroine intervenes, disarms the older man, and drops the weapon at the hero's feet. Conrad seems unconsciously to imagine the older man as an impotent voyeur; the disarming figures as a symbolic statement of his impotence. But since the hero frequently identifies himself with the older man, the heroine's contemptuous gesture of dropping the weapon at the hero's feet tends to cast doubt on his masculinity too. Emily Brontë's scene differs from Conrad's in the important respect that although females may assist Heathcliff and may help to disarm his opponents, they never disarm him nor is there ever any implication that he really needs help.

Other affinities between Conrad and Emily Brontë have been noticed, particularly their common use of multiple narrators and involuted chronology. I suspect that the resemblance in the present instance reflects chiefly the uneasiness of both about sexual matters. In Conrad's early, major novels, the scene plays an unimportant part, but in the later, inferior works, it is crucial, betraying Conrad's doubts about his intended theme of "affirmation." In *Wuthering Heights,* this scene lies at the very heart of the novel's meaning. I need not say, I trust, that only a few novels will respond to this kind of examination—those in which unconscious creation plays a large part and in which sex is a central subject. Although characters in *Middlemarch* stand in doorways, hold objects, and even drop them, the novel will yield no extra meaning by undergoing this kind of analysis. In *Middlemarch,* everything is held up to the light; George Eliot requires no second guessing.

11. Van Ghent, pp. 160-163.
12. Forster, *Aspects of the Novel* (New York, 1927), p. 211.
13. Van Ghent, p. 154.
14. Heathcliff's tree metaphor is appropriate since both he and the first Cathy are consistently associated with trees. The pine bough scratching the window, in Lockwood's dream, becomes Cathy's fingers, and her marriage to Edgar resembles putting "an oak in a flower-pot" (p. 163). When Heathcliff leaves Wuthering Heights a branch strikes the roof, and he beats his head bloody against a tree trunk at Cathy's death. The lovers become a single tree in Cathy's image: whoever tries to separate them will "meet the fate of Milo" (p. 85), the Greek athlete caught by the tree he was trying to split and torn to death by wolves.

ARNOLD KETTLE

Emily Brontë: *Wuthering Heights* (1847)

Wuthering Heights, like all the greatest works of art, is at once concrete and yet general, local and yet universal. Because so much nonsense has been written and spoken about the Brontës and because Emily in particular has been so often presented to us as a ghost-like figure surrounded entirely by endless moorland, cut off from anything so banal as human society, not of her time but of eternity, it is necessary to emphasize at the outset the local quality of the book.

Wuthering Heights is about England in 1847. The people it reveals live not in a never-never land but in Yorkshire. Heathcliff was born not in the pages of Byron, but in a Liverpool slum. The language of Nelly, Joseph and Hareton is the language of Yorkshire people. The story of *Wuthering Heights* is concerned not with love in the abstract but with the passions of living people, with property-ownership, the attraction of social comforts, the arrangement of marriages, the importance of education, the validity of religion, the relations of rich and poor.

There is nothing vague about this novel; the mists in it are the mists of the Yorkshire moors; if we speak of it as having an ele-

From *An Introduction to the English Novel* (London: Hutchinson Publishing Group, Ltd., 1951), pp. 139-55. Copyright © 1951 by Hutchinson Publishing Group Ltd. Reprinted by permission of the author and publisher.

mental quality it is because the very elements, the great forces of nature are evoked, which change so slowly that in the span of a human life they seem unchanging. But in this evocation there is nothing sloppy or uncontrolled. On the contrary the realization is intensely concrete: we seem to smell the kitchen of Wuthering Heights, to feel the force of the wind across the moors, to sense the very changes of the seasons. Such concreteness is achieved not by mistiness but by precision.

It is necessary to stress this point but not, of course, to force it to a false conclusion. The power and wonder of Emily Brontë's novel does not lie in naturalistic description, nor in a detailed analysis of the hour-by-hour issues of social living. Her approach is, quite obviously, not the approach of Jane Austen; it is much nearer to the approach of Dickens. Indeed, *Wuthering Heights* is essentially the same kind of novel as *Oliver Twist*. It is not a romance, not (despite the film bearing the same title) an escape from life to the wild moors and romantic lovers. It is certainly not a picaresque novel and it cannot adequately be described as a moral fable, though it has a strong, insistent pattern. But the pattern, like that of Dickens's novel, cannot be abstracted as a neat sentence: its germ is not an intellectualized idea or concept.

Emily Brontë works not in ideas but in symbols, that is to say concepts which have a significance and validity on a level different from that of logical thought. Just as the significance of the workhouse in *Oliver Twist* cannot adequately be conceived in merely logical terms but depends on a host of associations—including its physical shape and colour—which logical analysis may penetrate but is unlikely adequately to convey, so the significance of the moors in *Wuthering Heights* cannot be suggested in the cold words of logic (which does not mean that it is illogical). The symbolic novel is an advance on the moral fable just in the sense that a symbol can be richer—can touch on more of life—than an abstract moral concept.

The opening sentence of the *Social Contract* gives a simple example: "Man was born free, but everywhere he is in chains." Of the two statements in this sentence the first is abstract, the second symbolic. And the impact of the second on our imagination is greater than that of the first for this very reason. (If one were concerned to go deeper into the matter one might suggest that Rousseau *knew* that man was in chains but merely speculated that he had been born free.) Now, whereas the symbolism of the moral fable (and the fable is itself a kind of extended symbol) is inherently limited by the abstract concept behind it, the symbolism of *Wuthering Heights* or the good part of *Oliver Twist* is the expression of the very terms in which the novel has been conceived.* In fact, it *is* the novel and the novel stands or falls by its validity, its total adequacy to life.

Wuthering Heights is a vision of what life in 1847 was like. Whether it can be described as a vision of what life as such—all life—is like is a question we will consider later. It is, for all its appearance of casualness and the complexity of its family relationships, a very well-constructed book, in which the technical problems of presentation have been most carefully thought out. The roles of the two narrators, Lockwood and Nelly Dean, are not casual. Their function (they the two most "normal" people in the book) is partly to keep the story close to the earth, to make it believable, partly to comment on it from a common-sense point of view and thereby to reveal in part the inadequacy of such common sense. They act as a kind of sieve to the story, sometimes a double sieve, which has the purpose not simply of separating off the chaff, but of making us aware of the difficulty of passing easy judgments. One is left always with the sense that the last word has not been said.

The narrators do not as a rule talk realistically, though sometimes Nelly's part is to slip into a Yorkshire dialect that "places" what she is describing and counteracts any tendency (inherent in symbolic art) to the pretentious. At critical points in the narrative we are not conscious of their existence at all; there is no attempt at a limiting verisimilitude of speech. They do not impose themselves between us and the scene. But at other times their attitudes are important.

One of the subtleties of the book is the way these attitudes change and develop; Lockwood and Nelly, like us, learn from what they experience, though at first their limitations are made use of, as in the very first scene when the expectations of the conventional Lockwood are so completely shocked by what he finds at Wuthering

---

* A simple, though not infallible, indication of the kind of novel one is dealing with is given by the naming of characters. In allegory and the novel of "humours" names always denote character—e.g., Faithful and Squire Allworthy. In totally non-symbolic novelists like Jane Austen the names are quite without significance: Emma Woodhouse might equally well be called Anne Elliot. In novels which have a certain symbolic quality the names of characters generally have a peculiar rightness of their own: Heathcliff, Noah Claypole, Henry James's characters.

Heights. He goes there, he the normal Victorian gentleman, expecting to find the normal Victorian middle-class family. And what he finds—a house seething with hatred, conflict, horror—is a shock to us, too. The attack on our complacency, moral, social and spiritual, has already begun.

The centre and core of the book is the story of Catherine and Heathcliff. It is a story which has four stages. The first part, ending in the visit to Thrushcross Grange, tells of the establishing of a special relationship between Catherine and Heathcliff and of their common rebellion against Hindley and his régime in Wuthering Heights. In the second part is revealed Catherine's betrayal of Heathcliff, culminating in her death. The third part deals with Heathcliff's revenge, and the final section, shorter than the others, tells of the change that comes over Heathcliff and of his death. Even in the last two sections, after her death, the relationship with Catherine remains the dominant theme, underlying all else that occurs.

It is not easy to suggest with any precision the quality of feeling that binds Catherine and Heathcliff. It is not primarily a sexual relationship. Emily Brontë is not, as is sometimes suggested, afraid of sexual love; the scene at Catherine's death is proof enough that this is no platonic passion, yet to describe the attraction as sexual is surely quite inadequate. Catherine tries to express her feelings to Nelly (she is about to marry Linton).

> "My great miseries in this world have been Heathcliff's miseries, and I watched and felt each from the beginning: my great thought in living is himself. If all else perished, and *he* remained, *I* should still continue to be; and if all else remained, and he were annihilated, the universe would turn to a mighty stranger: I should not seem a part of it. My love for Linton is like the foliage in the woods: time will change it, I'm well aware, as winter changes the trees. My love for Heathcliff resembles the eternal rocks beneath: a source of little visible delight, but necessary. Nelly, I *am* Heathcliff! He's always, always in my mind: not as a pleasure, any more than I am always a pleasure to myself, but as my own being."[1]

and Heathcliff cries, when Catherine is dying: "I *cannot* live without my life, I *cannot* live without my soul."[2] What is conveyed to us here is the sense of an affinity deeper than sexual attraction, something which it is not enough to describe as romantic love.

This affinity is forged in rebellion and, in order to grasp the

concrete and unromantic nature of this book, it is necessary to recall
the nature of that rebellion. Heathcliff, the waif from the Liverpool
slums, is treated kindly by old Mr. Earnshaw but insulted and degraded by Hindley. After his father's death Hindley reduces the boy
to the status of a serf. "He drove him from their company to the
servants, deprived him of the instructions of the curate, and insisted
that he should labour out of doors instead; compelling him to do so
as hard as any other hand on the farm."[3] The situation at Wuthering Heights is wonderfully evoked in the passage from Catherine's
journal, which Lockwood finds in his bedroom:

> "An awful Sunday!" commenced the paragraph beneath. "I
> wish my father were back again. Hindley is a detestable substitute
> —his conduct to Heathcliff is atrocious—H. and I are going to
> rebel—we took our initiatory step this evening.
>
> "All day had been flooding with rain; we could not go to church,
> so Joseph must needs get up a congregation in the garret, and,
> while Hindley and his wife basked downstairs before a comfortable
> fire—doing anything but reading the Bibles, I'll answer for it—
> Heathcliff, myself, and the unhappy plough-boy, were commanded
> to take our Prayer-books, and mount: were ranged in a row, on a
> sack of corn, groaning and shivering, and hoping that Joseph
> would shiver too, so that he might give us a short homily for his
> own sake. A vain idea! The service lasted precisely three hours:
> and yet my brother had the face to exclaim, when he saw us de-
> scending, 'What, done already?' On Sunday evenings we used to
> be permitted to play, if we did not make much noise; now a mere
> titter is sufficient to send us into corners!
>
> "'You forget you have a master here,' says the tyrant. 'I'll de-
> molish the first who puts me out of temper! I insist on perfect
> sobriety and silence. Oh, boy! was that you? Frances darling, pull
> his hair as you go by: I heard him snap his fingers.' Frances pulled
> his hair heartily, and then went and seated herself on her hus-
> band's knee: and there they were, like two babies, kissing and
> talking nonsense by the hour—foolish palaver that we should be
> ashamed of. We made ourselves as snug as our means allowed in
> the arch of the dresser. I had just fastened our pinafores together,
> and hung them up for a curtain, when in comes Joseph on an
> errand from the stables. He tears down my handiwork boxes my
> ears and croaks—

" 'T' maister nobbut just buried, and Sabbath no o'ered, and t' sound o' t' gospel still i' yer lugs, and ye darr be laiking! Shame on ye! Sit ye down, ill childer! There's good books enough if ye'll read em! sit ye down, and think of yer sowls!'

"Saying this, he compelled us so to square our positions that we might receive from the far-off fire a dull ray to show us the text of the lumber he thrust upon us. I could not bear the employment. I took my dingy volume by the scroop, and hurled it into the dog-kennel, vowing I hated a good book. Heathcliff kicked his to the same place. Then there was a hubbub!

" 'Maister Hindley!' shouted our chaplain. 'Maister, coom hither! Miss Cathy's riven th' back of "Th' Helmet O Salvation," un Heathcliffs pawsed his fit into t' first part o' "T' Brooad Way to Destruction." It's fair flaysome, that ye let 'em go on this gait. Ech! th' owd man wad ha' laced 'em properly—but he's goan!'

"Hindley hurried up from his paradise on the hearth, and seizing one of us by the collar, and the other by the arm, hurled both into the back kitchen, where, Joseph asseverated, 'owd Nick' would fetch us as sure as we were living, and, so comforted, we each sought a separate nook to await his advent."[4]

This passage reveals, in itself, a great deal of the extraordinary quality of *Wuthering Heights*. It is a passage which, in the typical manner of the novel, evokes, in language which involves the kind of attention we give to poetry, a world far larger than the scene it describes, and evokes it through the very force and concreteness of the particular scene. The rebellion of Catherine and Heathcliff is made completely concrete. They are not vague romantic dreamers. Their rebellion is against the régime in which Hindley and his wife sit in fatuous comfort by the fire whilst they are relegated to the arch of the dresser and compelled for the good of their souls to read the *Broad Way to Destruction* under the tutelage of the canting hypocrite Joseph. It is a situation not confined, in the year 1847, to the more distant homesteads of the Yorkshire moors.

Against this degradation Catherine and Heathcliff rebel, hurling their pious books into the dog-kennel. And in their revolt they discover their deep and passionate need of each other. He, the outcast slummy, turns to the lively, spirited, fearless girl who alone offers him human understanding and comradeship. And she, born into the world of Wuthering Heights, senses that to achieve a full humanity, to be true to herself as a human being, she must associate herself totally with him in his rebellion against the tyranny of the Earnshaws and all that tyranny involves.

It is this rebellion that immediately, in this early section of the book, wins over our sympathy to Heathcliff. We know he is on the side of humanity and we are with him just as we are with Oliver Twist, and for much the same reasons. But whereas Oliver is presented with a sentimental passivity, which limits our concern, Heathcliff is active and intelligent and able to carry the positive values of human aspiration on his shoulders. He is a conscious rebel. And it is from his association in rebellion with Catherine that the particular quality of their relationship arises. It is the reason why each feels that a betrayal of what binds them together is in some obscure and mysterious way a betrayal of everything, of all that is most valuable in life and death.

Yet Catherine betrays Heathcliff and marries Edgar Linton, kidding herself that she can keep them both, and then discovering that in denying Heathcliff she has chosen death. The conflict here is, quite explicitly, a social one. Thrushcross Grange, embodying as it does the prettier, more comfortable side of bourgeois life, seduces Catherine. She begins to despise Heathcliff's lack of "culture." He has no conversation, he does not brush his hair, he is dirty, whereas Edgar, besides being handsome, "will be rich and I shall like to be the greatest woman of the neighbourhood, and I shall be proud of having such a husband."[5] And so Heathcliff runs away and Catherine becomes mistress of Thrushcross Grange.

Heathcliff returns, adult and prosperous, and at once the social conflict is re-emphasized. Edgar, understandably, does not want to receive Heathcliff, but Catherine is insistent:

> "I know you didn't like him," she answered, repressing a little the intensity of her delight. "Yet, for my sake, you must be friends now. Shall I tell him to come up?"
>
> "Here," he said, "into the parlour?"
>
> "Where else?" she asked.
>
> He looked vexed, and suggested the kitchen as a more suitable place for him. Mrs. Linton eyed him with a droll expression—half angry, half laughing at his fastidiousness.
>
> "No," she added after a while; "I cannot sit in the kitchen. Set two tables here, Ellen: one for your master and Miss Isabella,

being gentry, the other for Heathcliff and myself, being the lower orders. Will that please you, dear? . . ."[6]

And from the moment of Heathcliff's reappearance Catherine's attempts to reconcile herself to Thrushcross Grange are doomed. In their relationship now there is no tenderness, they trample on each other's nerves, madly try to destroy each other; but, once Heathcliff is near, Catherine can maintain no illusions about the Lintons. The two are united only in their contempt for the values of Thrushcross Grange. "There it is," Catherine taunts Edgar, speaking of her grave, "not among the Lintons, mind, under the chapel roof, but in the open air, with a headstone."[7] The open air, nature, the moors are contrasted with the world of Thrushcross Grange. And the contempt for the Lintons is a *moral* contempt, not a jealous one. When Nelly tells Heathcliff that Catherine is going mad, his comment is:

> "You talk of her mind being unsettled. How the devil could it be otherwise in her frightful isolation? And that insipid paltry creature attending her from *duty* and *humanity!* From *pity* and *charity!* He might as well plant an oak in a flower pot, and expect it to thrive, as imagine he can restore her to vigour in the soil of his shallow cares!"[8]

The moral passion here is so intense, so deeply imbedded in the rhythm and imagery of the prose, that it is easy to be swept along without grasping its full and extraordinary significance. Heathcliff at this point has just perpetrated the first of his callous and ghastly acts of revenge, his marriage to Isabella. It is an act so morally repulsive that it is almost inconceivable that we should be able now to take seriously his attack on Edgar Linton, who has, after all, by conventional, respectable standards, done nobody any harm. And yet we *do* take the attack seriously because Emily Brontë makes us. The passion of the passage just quoted has the quality of great poetry. Why?

We continue to sympathize with Heathcliff, even after his marriage with Isabella, because Emily Brontë convinces us that what Heathcliff stands for is morally superior to what the Lintons stand for. This is, it must be insisted, not a case of some mysterious "emotional" power with which Heathcliff is charged. The emotion be-

hind his denunciation of Edgar is *moral* emotion. The words "duty"
and "humanity," "pity" and "charity" have precisely the kind of
force Blake gives such words in his poetry.*

They are used not so much paradoxically as in a sense inverted
but more profound than the conventional usage. Heathcliff speaks,
apparently paradoxically, of Catherine's "frightful isolation," when
to all appearances she is in Thrushcross Grange less isolated, more
subject to care and society, than she could possibly be with him.
But in truth Heathcliff's assertion is a paradox only to those who
do not understand his meaning. What he is asserting with such
intense emotional conviction that we, too, are convinced, is that
what he stands for, the alternative life *he* has offered Catherine is
more natural (the image of the oak enforces this), more social and
more moral than the world of Thrushcross Grange. Most of those
who criticize Heathcliff adversely (on the grounds that he is un-
believable, or that he is a neurotic creation, or that he is merely the
Byronic satan-hero revived) fail to appreciate his significance because they fail to recognize this moral force. And as a rule they fail
to recognize the moral force because they are themselves, consciously or not, of the Linton party.

The climax of this inversion by Heathcliff and Catherine of the
common standards of bourgeois morality comes at the death of
Catherine. To recognize the revolutionary force of this scene one
has only to imagine what a different novelist might have made of it.

The stage is all set for a moment of conventional drama. Catherine is dying, Heathcliff appears out of the night. Two possibilities
present themselves: either Catherine will at the last reject Heathcliff, the marriage vow will be vindicated and wickedness meet its
reward; or true love will triumph and reconciliation proclaim the
world well lost. It is hard to imagine that either possibility ever
crossed Emily Brontë's mind, for either would destroy the pattern
of her book, but her rejection of them is a measure of her moral
and artistic power. For instead of its conventional potentialities the
scene acquires an astonishing moral power. Heathcliff, confronted

---

* E.g. Pity would no more
        If we did not make somebody Poor;
        And Mercy no more could be
        If all were as happy as we

   or

        Was Jesus humble? or did he
        Give any proofs of Humility.

with the dying Catherine, is ruthless, morally ruthless: instead of
easy comfort he offers her a brutal analysis of what she has done.

> "You teach me now how cruel you've been—cruel and false.
> *Why* did you despise me? *Why* did you betray your own heart
> Cathy? I have not one word of comfort. You deserve this. You
> have killed yourself. Yes, you may kiss me, and cry: and wring
> out my kisses and tears: they'll blight you—they'll damn you. You
> loved me—then what *right* had you to leave me? What right—an-
> swer me—for the poor fancy you felt for Linton? Because misery
> and degradation, and death, and nothing that God or Satan could
> inflict would have parted us, *you,* of your own will, did it. I have
> not broken your heart—*you* have broken it; and in breaking it you
> have broken mine. So much the worse that I am strong. Do I want
> to live? What kind of living will it be when you—oh, God! would
> *you* like to live with your soul in the grave?"[9]

It is one of the harshest passages in all literature, but it is also one
of the most moving. For the brutality is not neurotic, nor sadistic,
nor romantic. The Catherine-Heathcliff relationship, standing as it
does for a humanity finer and more morally profound than the
standards of the Lintons and Earnshaws has to undergo the kind of
examination Heathcliff here brings to it. Anything less, anything
which smudged or sweetened the issues involved, would be inadequate, unworthy. Heathcliff knows that nothing can save Catherine
from death but that one thing alone can give her peace, a full and
utterly honest understanding and acceptance of their relationship
and what it implies. There is no hope in comfort or compromise.
Any such weakness would debase them both and make a futile waste
of their lives and death. For Heathcliff and Catherine, who reject
the Lintons' chapel roof and the consolations of Christianity, know,
too, that their relationship is more important than death.

In the section of the book that follows Catherine's death Heathcliff continues the revenge he has begun with his marriage to Isabella. It is the most peculiar section of the novel and the most difficult because the quality of Heathcliff's feeling is of a kind most
of us find hard to comprehend. All normal and healthy human
feeling is rejected. He cries:

> "I have no pity! I have no pity! The more the worms writhe,
> the more I yearn to crush out their entrails! It is a moral teething;

and I grind with greater energy, in proportion to the increase of pain."[10]

"It is a moral teething"—the phrase is both odd and significant, giving as it does the answer to our temptation to treat this whole section as a delineation of pathological neurosis. Heathcliff becomes a monster: what he does to Isabella, to Hareton, to Cathy, to his son, even to the wretched Hindley, is cruel and inhuman beyond normal thought. He seems concerned to achieve new refinements of horror, new depths of degradation. And we tend to feel, perhaps, unless we read with full care and responsiveness, that Emily Brontë has gone too far, that the revenge (especially the marriage of Cathy and Linton Heathcliff) has o'erflown the measure.

And yet it is only one side of our minds, the conscious, limited side that refers what we are reading to our everyday measures of experience that makes this objection. Another side, which is more completely responding to Emily Brontë's art, is carried on. And the astonishing achievement of this part of the book is that, despite our protests about probability (protests which, incidentally, a good deal of twentieth-century history makes a little complacent), despite everything he does and is, we continue to sympathize with Heathcliff—not, obviously, to admire him or defend him, but to give him our inmost sympathy, to continue in an obscure way to identify ourselves with him *against* the other characters.

The secret of this achievement lies in such a phrase as "it is a moral teething" and in the gradually clarifying pattern of the book. Heathcliff's revenge may involve a pathological condition of hatred, but it is not at bottom merely neurotic. It has a moral force. For what Heathcliff does is to use against his enemies with complete ruthlessness their own weapons, to turn on them (stripped of their romantic veils) their own standards, to beat them at their own game. The weapons he uses against the Earnshaws and Lintons are their own weapons of money and arranged marriages. He gets power over them by the classic methods of the ruling class, expropriation and property deals. He buys out Hindley and reduces him to drunken impotency, he marries Isabella and then organizes the marriage of his son to Catherine Linton, so that the entire property of the two families shall be controlled by himself. He systematically degrades Hareton Earnshaw to servility and illiteracy. "I want the triumph of seeing *my* descendant fairly lord of *their* estates! My child hiring their children to till their father's lands for wages."[11] (This is a novel which, some critics will tell you, has nothing to do with anything as humdrum as society or life as it is actually lived.) And what particularly tickles Heathcliff's fancy is his achievement of the supreme ruling-class triumph of making Hareton, the boy he degrades, feel a deep and even passionate attachment towards himself.

Heathcliff retains our sympathy throughout this dreadful section of the book because instinctively we recognize a rough moral justice in what he has done to his oppressors and because, though he is inhuman, we understand *why* he is inhuman. Obviously we do not approve of what he does, but we understand it; the deep and complex issues behind his actions are revealed to us. We recognize that the very forces which drove him to rebellion for a higher freedom have themselves entrapped him in their own values and determined the nature of his revenge.

If *Wuthering Heights* were to stop at this point it would still be a great book, but a wholly sombre and depressing one. Man would be revealed as inevitably caught up in the meshes of his own creating; against the tragic horror of Heathcliff's appalling rebellion the limited but complacent world of Thrushcross Grange would seem a tempting haven and the novel would resolve itself into the false antithesis of Thrushcross Grange/Wuthering Heights, just as in *Oliver Twist* the real antithesis becomes sidetracked into the false one of Brownlow/Fagin. But *Wuthering Heights*, a work of supreme and astonishing genius, does not stop here. We have not done with Heathcliff yet.

For at the moment of his horrible triumph a change begins to come over Heathcliff.

"It is a poor conclusion, is it not?" he observed, having brooded a while on the scene he had just witnessed: "an absurd termination to my violent exertions? I get levers and mattocks to demolish the two houses, and train myself to be capable of working like Hercules, and when everything is ready and in my power, I find the will to lift a slate off either roof has vanished! My old enemies have not beaten me; now would be the precise time to revenge myself on their representatives: I could do it, and none could hinder me. But where is the use? I don't care for striking; I can't take the trouble to raise my hand! That sounds as if I had been labouring the whole time only to exhibit a fine trait of magnanim-

ity. It is far from being the case: I have lost the faculty of enjoying their destruction, and I am too idle to destroy for nothing.
    "Nelly, there is a strange change approaching: I'm in its
shadow at present."[12]

and he goes on to speak of Cathy and Hareton, who "seemed a
personification of my youth, not a human being. Hareton's aspect
was the ghost of my immortal love; of my wild endeavour to hold
my right; my degradation, my pride, my happiness and my anguish."
When Nelly asks "But what do you mean by a *change,* Mr. Heathcliff?" he can only answer "I shall not know that till it comes," he
said "I'm only half conscious of it now." Once more the stage is
set for a familiar scene, the conversion of the wicked who will in the
final chapter turn from his wickedness. And once more the conventional must look again.

The change that comes over Heathcliff and the novel and leads
us on to the wonderful, quiet, gentle, tentative evocation of spring
of the final sentence, is a very subtle one. It has something of the
quality of the last two acts of *The Winter's Tale* but is much less
complete, less confident. Mr. Klingopulos in his interesting essay on
Wuthering Heights[13] has commented on the ambiguous nature of
this final tranquillity. I do not agree with his analysis but he has
caught the tone most convincingly. Heathcliff, watching the love of
Cathy and Hareton grow, comes to understand something of the
failure of his own revenge. As Cathy teaches Hareton to write and
stops laughing at his ignorance we too are taken back to the first
Catherine.

Cathy and Hareton are not in the novel an easy re-creation of
Catherine and Heathcliff; they are, as Mr. Klingopulos remarks, different people, even lesser people, certainly people conceived on a
less intense and passionate scale than the older lovers. But they do
symbolize the continuity of life and human aspirations, and it is
through them that Heathcliff comes to understand the hollowness
of his triumph. It is when Hareton, who loves him, comes to Cathy's
aid when he strikes her that the full meaning of his own relationship with Catherine comes back to him and he becomes aware that
in the feeling between Cathy and Hareton there is something of
the same quality. From the moment that Cathy and Hareton are
drawn together as rebels the change begins. For now for the first
time Heathcliff is confronted not with those who accept the values

of Wuthering Heights and Thrushcross Grange but with those who share, however remotely, his own wild endeavours to hold his right.

Heathcliff does not repent. Nelly tries to make him turn to the consolations of religion.

> "You are aware, Mr. Heathcliff," I said, "that from the time you were thirteen years old, you have lived a selfish, unchristian life; and probably hardly had a Bible in your hands during all that period. You must have forgotten the contents of the Book, and you may not have space to search it now. Could it be hurtful to send for some one—some minister of any denomination, it does not matter which—to explain it, and show you how very far you have erred from its precepts; and how unfit you will be for its heaven, unless a change takes place before you die?"
>
> "I'm rather obliged than angry, Nelly," he said, "for you remind me of the manner in which I desire to be buried. It is to be carried to the churchyard in the evening. You and Hareton may, if you please, accompany me: and mind, particularly, to notice that the sexton obeys my directions concerning the two coffins! No minister need come; nor need anything be said over me.—I tell you I have nearly attained my heaven, and that of others is altogether unvalued and uncoveted by me."[14]

One sentence here, in its limpid simplicity, especially evokes the state of mind Heathcliff has come to. He speaks of the manner in which he wishes to be buried. "It is to be carried to the churchyard in the evening." The great rage has died in him. He has come to see the pointlessness of his fight to revenge himself on the world of power and property through its own values. Just as Catherine had to face the full moral horror of her betrayal of their love, he must face the full horror of his betrayal too. And once he has faced it he can die, not nobly or triumphantly, but at least as a man, leaving with Cathy and Hareton the possibility of carrying on the struggle he has begun, and in his death he will achieve again human dignity, "to be carried to the churchyard in the evening."

It is this re-achievement of manhood by Heathcliff, an understanding reached with no help from the world he despises, which, together with the developing relationship of Cathy and Hareton and the final sense of life reborn in springtime, gives to the last pages of Wuthering Heights a sense of positive and unsentimental hope.

The Catherine-Heathcliff relationship has been vindicated. Life will go on and others will rebel against the oppressors. Nothing has been solved but much has been experienced. Lies, complacencies and errors, appalling errors, have been revealed. A veil has been drawn from the conventional face of bourgeois man; he has been revealed, through Heathcliff, without his mask.

Above all, the quality of the feeling that binds Catherine and Heathcliff has been conveyed to us. Their love, which Heathcliff can without idealism call immortal, is something beyond the individualist dream of two soul-mates finding full realization in one another; it is an expression of the necessity of man, if he is to choose life rather than death, to revolt against all that would destroy his inmost needs and aspirations, of the necessity of all human beings to become, through acting together, more fully human. Catherine, responding to this deep human necessity, rebels with Heathcliff but in marrying Edgar (a "good" marriage if ever there was one) betrays her own humanity; Heathcliff, by revenging himself on the tyrants through the adoption of their own standards makes more clear those standards but betrays too his humanity and destroys his relationship with the dead Catherine whose spirit must haunt the moors in terror and dismay.

Only when the new change has come over Heathcliff and he again recognizes through Hareton (and remotely, therefore, through Catherine herself) the full claims of humanity can Catherine be released from torment and their relationship re-established. Death is a matter of little importance in *Wuthering Heights* because the issues the novel is concerned with are greater than the individual life and death. The deaths of Catherine and Heathcliff are indeed a kind of triumph because ultimately each faces death honestly, keeping faith. But there is no suggestion that death itself is a triumph: on the contrary it is life that asserts itself, continues, blossoms again.

Mr. David Wilson in his excellent essay on Emily Brontë[15] to which I am deeply indebted (though I do not agree with all of his interpretation) suggests an identification, not necessarily conscious in Emily Brontë's mind, of Heathcliff with the rebellious working men of the hungry "forties" and of Catherine with that part of the educated class which felt compelled to identify itself with their cause. Such a formulation, suggestive as it is, seems to me to be too far removed from the actual impact of *Wuthering Heights* as a novel, to be satisfactory. But Mr. Wilson has done a valuable service in rescuing *Wuthering Heights* from the transcendentalists and in insisting on the place of Haworth (generally assumed to be a remote country village) in the industrial revolution and its attendant social unrest.* The value of his suggestion with regard to Heathcliff and Catherine seems to me in the emphasis it gives to the concrete, local particularity of the book.

It is very necessary to be reminded that just as the values of Wuthering Heights and Thrushcross Grange are not simply the values of *any* tyranny but specifically those of Victorian society, so is the rebellion of Heathcliff a particular rebellion, that of the worker physically and spiritually degraded by the conditions and relationships of this same society. That Heathcliff ceases to be one of the exploited is true, but it is also true that just in so far as he adopts (with a ruthlessness that frightens even the ruling class itself) the standards of the ruling class, so do the human values implicit in his early rebellion and in his love for Catherine vanish. All that is involved in the Catherine-Heathcliff relationship, all that it stands for in human needs and hopes, can be realized only through the active rebellion of the oppressed.

Wuthering Heights then is an expression in the imaginative terms of art of the stresses and tensions and conflicts, personal and spiritual, of nineteenth-century capitalist society. It is a novel without idealism, without false comforts, without any implication that power over their destinies rests outside the struggles and actions of human beings themselves. Its powerful evocation of nature, of moorland and storm, of the stars and the seasons is an essential part of its revelation of the very movement of life itself. The men and women of *Wuthering Heights* are not the prisoners of nature; they live in the world and strive to change it, sometimes successfully, always painfully, with almost infinite difficulty and error.

This unending struggle, of which the struggle to advance from class society to the higher humanity of a classless world is but an episode, is conveyed to us in *Wuthering Heights* precisely because the novel is conceived in actual, concrete, particular terms, because the quality of oppression revealed in the novel is not abstract but concrete, not vague but particular. And that is why Emily Brontë's novel is at the same time a statement about the life she knew, the

* One of the most interesting exhibits in the Haworth museum today is a proclamation of the Queen ordering the reading of the Riot Act against the rebellious workers of the West Riding.

life of Victorian England, and a statement about life as such. Virginia Woolf, writing about it, said:

> That gigantic ambition is to be felt throughout the novel, a struggle half thwarted but of superb conviction, to say something through the mouths of characters which is not merely "I love" or "I hate" but "we, the whole human race" and "You, the eternal powers . . ." the sentence remains unfinished.[16]

I do not think it remains unfinished.

NOTES

1. *Wuthering Heights,* Chap. IX.
2. Ibid., Chap. XVI.
3. Ibid., Chap. VI.
4. Ibid., Chap. III.
5. Ibid., Chap IX.
6. Ibid., Chap. X.
7. Ibid., Chap. XII.
8. Ibid., Chap. XIV.
9. Ibid., Chap. XV.
10. Ibid., Chap. XIV.
11. Ibid., Chap. XX.
12. Ibid., Chap. XXXIII.
13. *Scrutiny,* Vol. XIV, No. 4.
14. *Wuthering Heights,* Chap. XXXIV.
15. *Modern Quarterly,* Miscellany No. 1 (1947).
16. *The Common Reader* (Pelican ed.), p. 158.

JOHN GROSS

Mrs. Gaskell

Mrs. Gaskell, as everyone knows, has charm. It was not a very common quality among early Victorian writers, and it is what keeps her work fresh while that of so many of her contemporaries has grown musty. But in literature charm can often be a dubious asset: it has also led to her being treated as a lightweight, automatically consigned to the ranks of the miniaturists and minor talents. No one would claim that she was a great writer, least of all Mrs. Gaskell herself; on the contrary, she is one of those novelists, like Peacock or E. M. Forster, whose strength partly comes from a firm refusal to have greatness thrust upon them. Her sureness of touch and her good sense are inseparably bound up with her modesty, her unassuming manner; and writing when she did, we may well be grateful that she was so rarely hectoring or loquacious, so sparing with the *vox humana* and the purple peroration. But one should be careful not to make too much of her purely negative virtues: it is what has led to her remaining generally under-valued, even though her reputation has held steady for a hundred years.

From *The Novelist as Innovator,* ed. by Walter Allen (London: British Broadcasting Corporation, 1965), pp. 49-63. Copyright © 1965 by the British Broadcasting Corporation. Reprinted by permission of the author and publisher. Originally given as a talk on the B.B.C. Third Programme on January 18, 1965.

That reputation rests chiefly on *Cranford,* of course, and to a lesser extent on *Wives and Daughters.* She has often been described as a belated and diminished Jane Austen (although there is no evidence that she ever read Jane Austen, incidentally). She was essentially a backward-looking writer, at her happiest portraying the bygone modes and manners of genteel society in a small country-town; her best work is in the vein of demure comedy, half idyllic, half tinged with pathos. As for the books with an industrial setting, *Mary Barton* and *North and South,* they represent a noble response to the social crisis of early Victorian England, and they are still of value to the historian; but they carried her out of her depth as an artist. It took courage to write them, but they are raw and often unconvincing.

This is the conventional view, and like most conventional views it has a good deal of truth in it. I don't think it does Mrs. Gaskell justice, however. Up to a point I can sympathize with those critics who see the industrial novels, for all their shortcomings, as her most original and impressive achievement, while treating the domestic stories, though excellent of their kind, as smaller and safer, an indulgence to which Mrs. Gaskell had earned the right. But this is not really an adequate view of the case, either. To appreciate Mrs. Gaskell fully one must try to see her work as a whole, to understand how *Cranford,* with its muslins and bonnets and filigree sugar-tongs, came to be sandwiched in between *Mary Barton* and *North and South*—novels full of gloom and violence, set against a background of typhoid epidemics and vitriol-throwing and strike-breaking.

Not that there is any mystery about the source of the contrast in Mrs. Gaskell's own life. Born in Cheyne Walk during the Napoleonic Wars, when Chelsea was still an outer suburb, brought up in the comfortable little town of Knutsford, educated in Stratford-on-Avon at the most ladylike of establishments for young ladies, she might reasonably have looked forward to an easy unruffled existence. Instead, through marrying William Gaskell, she found herself plunged into the Manchester of the stormy Thirties and Hungry Forties—transplanted without warning from the world of Mary Russell Mitford to the world of Friedrich Engels. It was an experience with which she constantly tried to cope as a writer, and one which was to colour much of her finest work.

There is no question of her being an innovator in the narrow technical sense: she had the natural story-teller's cunning and she stuck to traditional methods. Her skill in handling a plot developed considerably in the course of her career, but she showed almost no interest in narrative devices for their own sake. Nor did she have a consciously worked-out aesthetic. But then very few novelists do. Originality in fiction is far more likely to be a question of making new types of subject-matter amenable to traditional treatment for the first time, or of being forced to look at conventional subject-matter with fresh eyes. And Mrs. Gaskell's originality comes about in both these ways, as the result of a collision between temperament and material.

Certainly she created a great stir in her own time. There had been industrial novels before, long-forgotten books like Mrs. Trollope's *Michael Armstrong the Factory Boy*, but none of them had made anything like the impact of *Mary Barton*. The one exception is *Sybil*, where Disraeli's skill in drawing working-class scenes (I'm thinking of things like the riot at the tommy-shop) is often passed over simply because it is so unexpected, because we know that he relied on blue-books and second-hand sources for describing the poor while his gorgeous operatic fantasies of high life came to him unprompted. Still, in the end there is no denying that he wrote as an outsider, and that he saw his characters as case-histories, illustrations of a predetermined thesis. Mrs. Gaskell's great virtue was that she was interested in the People as people, that she had a gossipy curiosity about their daily lives. And she kept a cool head—the first thing which strikes one about *Mary Barton* is its composure.

This in itself was unusual. The condition-of-England debate which had already been going on for a decade and more had generally been marked by a note of hysteria: understandably, perhaps, since the early Victorians were bearing the brunt of unprecedented social change, but it meant that the working-class usually appear in the literature of the period bathed in a lurid artificial light. Think of *Locksley Hall*—

> Slowly comes a hungry people, as a lion creeping
>   nigher,
> Glares at one that nods and winks behind a slowly
>   dying fire

or the frenzied glimpse of the Chartists in *The Old Curiosity Shop*, or the apocalyptic thunderings of Carlyle—

sooty Manchester, it too is built upon the infinite abysses!

By contrast, Mrs. Gaskell opens her "tale of Manchester life" with
a country outing, a family row, a tea-party: instead of the infinite
abysses, she shows us the curtains and the crockery. All this leads
on the unresisting reader, as cajolery or exhortation never could, to
terrible scenes like the Davenport family huddled in their pestilence-
ridden cellar: "the very smoke seemed purifying and healthy in the
thick clammy air." We are never allowed to forget that human
beings remain human beings under the most harsh or harrowing
circumstances. There are always feelings to be hurt as well as bodies
to be starved: how truthful is the flicker of self-pity, even reproach,
which comes between the woman and her dying husband, or the
tiny consolation which she gets from going to his funeral in a bor-
rowed black dress—"a satisfaction to her poor heart in the midst of
her sorrow." Never was irony less complacent: Mrs. Gaskell is talking about human needs, not human weaknesses. Her express purpose was to win respect for her characters: "the vices of the poor
sometimes astound us *here;* but when the secrets of all hearts shall
be made known, their virtues will astound us in far greater degree."
That sounds as though she might be in danger of turning maudlin,
but she knew the importance of keeping her eye on the object. There
are no flights of polychrome angels at Davenport's funeral, only a
portable wooden gravestone which does duty while the soil is shov-
elled in and is then carried off to the next hole where it is needed.

No doubt, *Mary Barton* survives chiefly as a documentary: it belongs on the same shelf with Samuel Bamford rather than with—shall
we say?—Percy Lubbock. Nowadays the documentary element in
fiction is usually belittled, or taken as the sign of a second-rate talent,
although we are surely deluding ourselves if we suppose that one of
the main attractions of the novel isn't still what it has always been,
sheer information. (Mary McCarthy has made the point very well
in her essay on "The Fact in Fiction.") At any rate, Mrs. Gaskell
herself certainly felt that she was opening up new territory, and the
main requirement was simply to tell truth. Because of her obvious
honesty, it is remarkable how little she was hampered by the purely
verbal reticence which was mandatory at the time; italics speak
louder than words when, describing a slum street, she says that
"women from their doors tossed household slops of *every* description
into the gutter." But one can make too much of her as a direct on-
the-spot reporter; she also tried to provide perspective.

It is worth looking at her attitude to dialect in this respect. Whenever a character uses an unfamiliar Lancashire word or construction, she supplies a footnote citing a parallel, as often as not from Chaucer, but also from Shakespeare, *Piers Plowman,* the Book of Common Prayer. This is more than antiquarianism; it serves to remind the middle-class reader that Manchester isn't on another planet, that there is a continuity—and a dignity—in human affairs. The most striking use made of common speech is in the chapter (often singled out for praise, and rightly) where Job Legh recalls his visit to London, many years before. He had gone there together with his son-in-law's father in order to see his daughter and her husband; on arrival they found the young couple dead, and brought their baby back to Manchester. It could easily be a mawkish episode —in most Victorian novels a name like Job would already be a warning signal. But in fact it is utterly convincing, and no less poignant for being darkened by a quarrel between the old men, or stiffened with some tough humour:

> My heart were very sore for the little one, as it groped about wi'
> its mouth; but for a' this I could scarce keep fra' smiling at th'
> thought o' us two oud chaps, th' one wi' a woman's nightcap on,
> sitting on our hinder ends for half the night, hushabying a babby
> as wouldn't be hushabied.

This is the kind of speech which Shakespeare understood, but which very few novelists at that time had learned to listen to. Scott, perhaps: but Scott didn't write about mill-hands and factory operatives.

Mrs. Gaskell originally intended to call the book *John Barton,* and she certainly weakened it by shifting the emphasis on to his daughter: it ends up at the level of well-managed melodrama. (Not quite fair: with Mrs. Gaskell the truth is always liable to keep breaking through, and there are individual passages, like the one where the mill-owner's pampered daughters learn that their brother has been murdered, which could scarcely be bettered.) John Barton himself is an impressive figure; to begin with his bitterness and bewilderment are seen from the inside, until he finds himself assigned the role of assassin—though even then he commands a certain degree of Mrs. Gaskell's sympathy. She has been criticized for turning a representative type into a special case, but given her general position she could hardly have done otherwise. She advocated a change of heart, not a change of the social order; and consequently there came a point at which the revolutionary, however sympathetic, shaded over into the criminal. It was precisely this which was meant to be John Barton's tragedy.

Nevertheless the book was widely regarded as subversive at the time. The second Manchester novel, *North and South,* which appeared seven years later, was deliberately much closer to the masters' point of view. Thornton the manufacturer learns a measure of humility through financial failure, and realizes that he should have cultivated "some intercourse with the hands beyond the mere 'cash nexus.'" But he still makes the right husband for Margaret, the sensitive heroine, who not only marries him but also lends him the money he needs to set himself up in business again. North and South are reconciled to the tune of £1,857—Mrs. Gaskell hasn't forgotten the virtue of being circumstantial.

As a social document, then, *North and South* is more cautious, more evasive than *Mary Barton.* But as a novel it is more revolutionary, since the author has a deeper personal stake in it, and deliberately uses a more sophisticated narrative technique. She is no longer the detached observer, the well-disposed district visitor; through the consciousness of Margaret she allows the world which she describes to impinge directly upon her. Indeed, the book often gives the effect of someone being exposed: there are those long walks of Margaret's down endless dingy streets, past the factory gates:

> She did not mind meeting any number of girls, loud spoken and boisterous though they might be. But she alternately dreaded and fired up against the workmen, who commented not on her dress, but on her looks, in the same open, fearless manner.

Margaret is fastidious, well bred, a Southerner who turns up her nose at "trade"; nothing in her past has prepared her for life in "Milton Northern"—Manchester, that is:

> The heavy smoky air hung about her bedroom, which occupied the long narrow projection at the back of the house. The window, placed at the side of the oblong, looked to the blank wall of a similar projection, not above ten feet distant. It loomed through the fog like a great barrier to hope.

Milton Northern might have been devised by Lewis Mumford to illustrate the desolation of the unplanned industrial city. And Margaret herself, stranded in the North like a friendless immigrant, is an early study in cultural dislocation. The book is resolutely modern, particularly in its insistence that "you can't go home again." One of best chapters, near the end, shows Margaret returning to the Hampshire village where she had grown up. She has only been away three years, but there is change everywhere: "slight, yet pervading all." Her disappointment is subtly handled; for example, she shivers away from the pain which she knows she must feel when she revisits her old home, but she finds it so altered and "improved," inside and out, that the real pain is less than she had anticipated. But in the end, she is overpowered by "a sense of change, of individual nothingness, of perplexity and disappointment." Other people's lives go on; while just in case Margaret is still in danger of idealizing country customs, she is forced to hear about a grisly local superstition which involves roasting a cat alive.

There is very little idealizing Milton Northern, either. John Thornton and his iron-willed old mother speak the language of harsh self-assertion. By comparison the well-to-do Carsons in *Mary Barton* were mere ciphers. Mrs. Gaskell has learned about power, and the trappings of power: the Thornton drawing-room, for instance, is a miniature essay in conspicuous consumption:

> There was no one in the drawing room. It seemed as though no one had been in it since the day when the furniture was bagged up with as much care as if the house was to be overwhelmed with lava, and discovered a thousand years hence. The walls were pink and gold; the pattern on the carpet represented bunches of flowers on a light ground, but it was carefully covered up in the centre by a linen drugget, glazed and colourless. The window-curtains were lace; each chair and sofa had its own particular veil of netting or knitting. . . . In the middle of the room, right under the bagged-up chandelier, was a large circular table, with smartly bound books arranged at regular intervals round the circumference of its polished surface, like gaily coloured spokes of a wheel. Everything reflected light, nothing absorbed it. The whole room had a painfully spotted, spangled, speckled look about it, which impressed Margaret so unpleasantly that she was hardly conscious of the peculiar cleanliness required to keep everything so white and pure in such an atmosphere, or the trouble that must be willingly expended to secure that effect of icy, snowy discomfort.

The master of this unprepossessing house is a walking embodiment of the business ethic at its most ruthless. The Protestant ethic, too; "Their merchants be like princes," his mother had read out to him as a boy, and if he has a hero it is Oliver Cromwell. ("Cromwell would have made a capital mill-owner, Miss Hale. I wish we had him to put down this strike for us.") Yet Thornton *is* a master, and Margaret is secretly attracted by his dynamism: in the end she gives herself to him, proud and combative though she is. The most original feature of *North and South,* although Mrs. Gaskell wasn't equipped to do more than hint at it, is the idea of sexual excitement being entwined with social antagonism. John Thornton undoubtedly exercises sexual magnetism: in some ways he is a preposterous figure, especially if taken at face value. But he makes more sense if one thinks of Gerald Crich in *Women in Love.* There is even a suggestion of race-antagonism in his relationship with Margaret, as Elizabeth Bowen has pointed out—it is as if the couple are divided by a Mason-Dixon line as well as by social barriers. Thornton has a touch of the domesticated Nordic hero: "You're worshippers of Thor," Margaret's father tells him. One can see a partial parallel with Disraeli's fanciful distinction between an energetic Saxon middle-class and an effete Norman aristocracy.

Set against the clanking machinery and the grime and the hard faces of the industrial novels, *Cranford* looks frailer than ever. Exquisite workmanship, yes, but if it is inspected too closely won't the charm evaporate? In fact the reverse is true. *Cranford* is indestructible: it has the confidence, the grace, the rightness which can only come when an author is writing out of an unimpeded imagination, and writing about the things which matter most to him. One doesn't want to be portentous about a work of such airy good humour, but those dainty Hugh Thomson illustrations give the wrong idea: *Cranford* is something more than a superior *Quality Street.* In its delicate oblique way it is as much a comment on the condition of England as *Mary Barton* or *North and South.*

Yet it seems at first as though the ladies of Cranford are living in an inviolable dream-world, static and self-contained—a world with the firm outlines and vivid colours of a unique never-to-be-repeated childhood recollection. Everything has its right name and its right place: the settings have a nursery-rhyme neatness, household objects look as enticing as toys. A timeless world, too—the clock has stopped but Cranford doesn't know it. The inhabitants are impressive because they never suspect that they are quaint, never think of themselves as museum-pieces. And they never ask themselves whether Cranford has a future, although the town "is in possession of the Amazons: all the holders of houses above a certain rent are women." Men are dangerous intruders: they trample on the Cranford proprieties, and disrupt the prevailing calm. When Captain Brown arrives, he speaks openly of being poor—as though he had never heard of Elegant Economy; and he has the gall to prefer Dickens to Dr. Johnson. But he doesn't live to trouble Cranford for long: he is knocked down by a train while reading the latest number of *Pickwick*.

Still, even Cranford can't remain sealed off for ever. At the other end of the railway line, a mere twenty miles away, is the roaring industrial city of Drumble. Drumble is the home of the narrator, Mary Smith, and she can only manage occasional trips to Cranford. In a sense the book is about Mary's changing vision of the little town. True, it was not originally planned as a full-length book; Mrs. Gaskell created it episode by episode for *Household Words* (Dickens called her his Scheherezade). But there is a distinct pattern of development. At the outset Cranford is summed up more than anyone else by Deborah Jenkyns. The elder daughter of the former rector, she is a formidable upholder of dignity and decorum, with the heavy manner and decided views of an eighteenth-century bluestocking. As such she is a source of piquant comedy in the eyes of the narrator. All the Cranford ladies have settled immovably into their own particular eccentricities, but Miss Jenkyns is the recognized leader of opinion. She completely overshadows her timid self-effacing sister Miss Matty, and it is only after her death—how subtly Mrs. Gaskell suggests the sense of relief which it brings—that Miss Matty gradually emerges as the true heroine of the book. The crucial scene—perhaps Mrs. Gaskell's finest—is the one where she learns about the failure of the Town and Country Bank, where all her savings are invested. She is out shopping with Mary, buying some silk for a new gown. They hesitate over the crimson and the silver grey, the lilac with yellow spots and the sage green: it is Cranford at its prettiest. Then suddenly the blow falls: they overhear the shop assistant refusing a farmer who is paying for his goods with a five-pound note from the Town and Country. Miss Matty obeys her first instinct, which is to give the farmer five sovereigns in exchange for the worthless note, and though Mary remonstrates with her—does she plan to make good everybody's loss?—she insists that she had to do her duty as she saw it. She can't grasp the principles of Joint-stock finance; she lives exclusively in a world of personal responsibilities and direct obligations. Later, when she has been set up in a little shop, she has scruples of conscience about selling tea when there is already another shop in the town supplying it, Mr. Johnson's; so she trots round and asks him whether it is likely to injure his trade. Mary's father, a bustling Drumble businessman who has been helping to straighten out Miss Matty's affairs, calls this idea of hers "great nonsense," and wonders how tradespeople are to get on

> "if there is to be a continual consulting of each other's interests, which would put a stop to all competition directly." And perhaps it would not have done in Drumble, but in Cranford it answered very well; for not only did Mr. Johnson put at rest all Miss Matty's scruples and fear of injuring his business, but I have reason to know he repeatedly sent customers to her, saying that the teas he kept were of a common kind, but that Miss Jenkyns had all the choice sorts.

Miss Matty's triumph is Cranford's; her unselfishness and good faith bring out the same qualities in others. The ladies may be parochial and prim, but they know where their duty lies, and they all rally round. Elegant economy, in spite of its pretences, has a sounder heart than political economy, and Mary Smith comes to value Cranford at its true worth. But she herself belongs as irrevocably to Drumble as Margaret Hale eventually does to Milton Northern; and her admiration is tempered by a little quiet cynicism:

> Miss Matty almost made me angry by dividing her sympathy between the directors of the bank (whom she imagined overwhelmed by self reproach for the mismanagement of other people's affairs) and those who were suffering like her. Indeed, of the two she seemed to think poverty a lighter burden than self-reproach; but privately I doubted if the directors would agree with her.

Mrs. Gaskell does not make any simple assertions about the absolute superiority of Cranford over the modern world; in fact, the book is full of delicate strokes and counter-strokes, and if Cranford means Miss Matty's sense of honour it also means the Honourable Mrs. Jamieson's vanity, or Deborah Jenkyns' narrow-mindedness. Indeed,

the more we learn to appreciate Miss Matty, the less amusing (retrospectively) Deborah becomes. She isn't just a comical old dragon: it
is hard to forgive her for ruining Matty's one chance of real happiness by preventing her from what would supposedly have been marrying beneath her. Cranford can be sterile as well as innocent.

In the end this is a sad book, for all its high spirits. The last
chapter is called "Peace to Cranford"—a happy ending, but also an
epitaph. For Cranford, seemingly fixed for ever in bright perfection,
is already half-way to becoming a ghost-town. The assembly room,
for instance:

> The old room was dingy; the salmon-coloured paint had faded
> into a drab; great pieces of plaster had chipped off from the white
> wreaths and festoons on its walls; but still a mouldy odour of aris-
> tocracy lingered about the place, and a dusty recollection of the
> days that were gone made Miss Matty and Mrs. Forrester bridle
> up as they entered, and walk mincingly up the room, as if there
> were a number of genteel observers, instead of two little boys with
> a stick of toffy between them with which to beguile the time.

Like other mid-century novelists (Thackeray especially), Mrs.
Gaskell is acutely aware of the passage of time. It might almost be
said that Drumble and Cranford are living by different time-scales
(one is reminded of Sybil, where the favourite boast of the Manchester workers is that they "know the time of day"). Early Victorian nostalgia was a by-product of accelerating social change, of
urban sprawl and railway time-tables. It could often be a sickly
thing, but Mrs. Gaskell knew how to handle it tactfully. Here she
stands almost alone; few if any of her contemporaries could have
produced a requiescat for the eighteenth century so finely balanced
between humour and regret as the wonderful chapter where Mary
and Miss Matty sort out old family letters before burning them.

In the last years of her life Mrs. Gaskell gave up writing about
current social problems. But they still make their presence felt off-
stage. Cousin Phillis, her most accomplished short novel apart from
Cranford, is a simple traditional story about an inexperienced country girl who is taken up by a man of the world and is unable to
forget him when he drops her; but what lends it force, and makes
the pastoral atmosphere of Phillis's world so convincing, so Words-
worthian, is that the man is an engineer working on the new railway
line: once again, it is a clash between two worlds, two rhythms of

life. In Mrs. Gaskell's masterpiece, *Wives and Daughters,* on the other hand, the "new fangled railways" are only a rumour overheard in the closing pages. The mellow roundedness of the book, the sense which the reader has, in Henry James's words, of "a new arbitrary world being reared over his heedless head, a world marvellously inclusive of him"—these things depend on the fact that Mrs. Gaskell stays firmly inside the period of her youth. It can scarcely be called the work of an innovator. But by this time Mrs. Gaskell had the satisfaction of knowing that her early work had helped to pave the way for the leading novelist of the next generation:

> I was conscious, while the question of my power was still un-decided for me, that my feeling towards life and Art had some affinity with the feeling which had inspired *Cranford* and the earlier chapters of *Mary Barton.*

These were the words of George Eliot—a witness whose testimony gives one some idea of the place which Mrs. Gaskell ought to have in the history of the English novel.

G. ARMOUR CRAIG

On the Style of *Vanity Fair*

. . . there is still a very material difference of
opinion as to the real nature and character of the
Measure of Value in this country. My first question, therefore, is, what constitutes this Measure
of Value? What is the significance of that word
"a Pound"?

> Speech of Sir Robert Peel on
> the Bank Charter Acts (6 May 1844)

Perhaps I might be a heroine still, but I shall
never be a good woman, I know.

> Mrs. Gaskell, *Wives and Daughters* (1866)

"Among all our novelists his style is the purest, as to my ears it is
also the most harmonious. Sometimes it is disfigured by a slight
touch of affectation, by little conceits which smell of the oil;—but
the language is always lucid." The judgment is Anthony Trollope's
and the lucidity he praises is Thackeray's: "The reader, without
labour, knows what he means, and knows all that he means."[1] The
judgment has been shared by many, perhaps even by Thackeray

From *Style in Prose Fiction: English Institute Essays,* ed. by Harold C. Martin
(New York: Columbia University Press, 1959), pp. 87-113. Copyright © 1959
by Columbia University Press. Reprinted by permission of the author and
publisher.

himself, for he was vigilant in detecting "fine writing" or "claptraps" in the work of others,[2] and for himself he insisted that "this person writing strives to tell the truth. If there is not that, there is nothing."[3] Yet some reconciling is necessary, for the truth is not always lucid and lucidity may not always be quite true.

There is at any rate a passage in chapter 42 of Vanity Fair[4] for Trollope's judgment of which the modern reader—at least this reader —would give a good deal. It describes the life of Jane Osborne keeping house for her father: her sister is now the fashionable Mrs. Frederick Bullock, her brother, disowned by their father for his marriage to Amelia Sedley, has been killed at Waterloo, and Jane now lives in idle spinsterhood in the great glum house in Russell Square.

> It was an awful existence. She had to get up of black winter's mornings to make breakfast for her scowling old father, who would have turned the whole house out of doors if his tea had not been ready at half-past eight. She remained silent opposite to him, listening to the urn hissing, and sitting in tremor while the parent read his paper, and consumed his accustomed portion of muffins and tea. At half-past nine he rose and went to the City, and she was almost free till dinner-time, to make visitations in the kitchen and to scold the servants: to drive abroad and descend upon the tradesmen, who were prodigiously respectful: to leave her cards and her papa's at the great glum respectable houses of their City friends; or to sit alone in the large drawing-room, expecting visitors; and working at a huge piece of worsted by the fire, on the sopha, hard by the great Iphigenia clock, which ticked and tolled with mournful loudness in the dreary room. The great glass over the mantle-piece, faced by the other great console glass at the opposite end of the room, increased and multiplied between them the brown holland bag in which the chandelier hung; until you saw these brown holland bags fading away in endless perspectives, and this apartment of Miss Osborne's seemed the centre of a system of drawing-rooms. When she removed the cordovan leather from the grand piano, and ventured to play a few notes on it, it sounded with a mournful sadness, startling the dismal echoes of the house. [pp. 441-42]

Thackeray's prose is seldom better than this. The passage comes from a paragraph that comments on the difference between Jane

Osborne's life and that of her sister: "One can fancy the pangs" with which Jane regularly read about Mrs. Frederick Bullock in the "Morning Post," particularly the account of her presentation at the Drawing-room. The reader, characteristically, is invited to supply from his own observation the sort of vulgar envy that feeds upon accounts of "Fashionable Reunions" in the newspaper and to look down on Jane Osborne's suffering as no more than the deprivation of the snobbish pleasures of elegant society. The passage begins, then, easily enough: "It was an awful existence." And "awful" is at first simply a colloquial affectation. It becomes something more, however, as we move into the account of Jane's routine and ascend from the tremors of the breakfast table to the solitude of the drawing room with its covered chandelier "fading away in endless perspectives": the conversational pitch turns momentarily solemn with the vision of "this apartment of Miss Osborne's" as "the centre of a system of drawing-rooms"—including perhaps even that most august of all such apartments where her sister has been received. It would be hard to find this an example of the "little conceits which smell of the oil," for even here Thackeray does not lose his customary confidential hold upon the reader. The vision is kept close to us by his usual resource: the opposing mirrors "increased and multiplied between them the brown holland bag in which the chandelier hung; until *you* saw these brown holland bags fading away in endless perspectives." The "you" is no doubt as unobtrusive as an idiom. But it is not inconsistent with Thackeray's constant and fluent address to his reader, an address at its best as easy as idiom. In this very short passage Thackeray has moved from an example of the snobbery he loved to detect to a memorable symbol of the society in which snobbery flourishes. It is a society of endless perspectives, a system of drawing rooms whose center is everywhere, whose circumference is nowhere.

But is this what Thackeray meant? And is it the "all" that he meant? Certainly the symbol is not characteristic—it is indeed unique in *Vanity Fair*. Usually, or at any rate perhaps too often, Thackeray renders the barren routines of high life in mock genealogies or in the kind of mildly allegorical guest list that follows this passage. We are told that twice a month the solitary dinners of Mr. and Miss Osborne are shared with "Old Dr. Gulp and his lady from Bloomsbury Square, . . . old Mr. Frowser the attorney, . . . old Colonel Livermore, . . . old Serjeant Toffy, . . . sometimes old Sir

Thomas Coffin." *Vanity Fair*, we recall, began as "Pen and Pencil
Sketches of English Society," as an extension of *The Book Of Snobs*.
Yet Thackeray seems to have felt the need of some larger, more inclusive presiding idea. In the early stages of writing the first few
numbers he "ransacked" his brain for another title, and "Vanity
Fair," he said, came to him suddenly in the middle of the night.[5]
It seems to have summed up for him a position from which he
could confidently go on with his "Novel without a Hero," but a
position of course very different from John Bunyan's. The original
Vanity Fair as described by Evangelist is the dwelling place of
abominations. But it is after all only one more obstacle on the road
to the Celestial City, and all such obstacles are rewards in disguise.
"He that shall die there," says Evangelist, "although his death will
be unnatural, and his pain perhaps great, he will yet have the better
of his fellow." While there are some unnatural and painful deaths
in Thackeray's Fair, there seems to be no act of resistance or sacrifice
by which anyone can get the better of anyone else, and the irony
of the title has no doubt been lively in the minds of many readers.
But Evangelist lays down a more poignantly ironical prescription:
"he that will go to the [Celestial] City, and yet not go through this
Town [where Vanity Fair is kept], *must* needs *go out of the
World*."[6] If there is no Celestial City beyond Thackeray's Fair, and
if there is no hero determined to fight on to a heavenly peak, it is
even more certain that none of Thackeray's characters shall go out
of this world. On every page of *Vanity Fair* we find description, exposure, comment, from a position much less elevated and secure
than that of an evangelist, yet one from which we do see into an
"all" as large as a whole society.

Certainly the style of all this commenting and exposing is this-
worldly to a degree that would have puzzled Bunyan as much as it
has troubled some of his descendants. In the preface to *Pendennis*
Thackeray speaks of his work as "a sort of confidential talk between
reader and writer," and it was the excess of this conception of himself—"the little earmark by which he is most conspicuous"—that
Trollope found "his most besetting sin in style." The "sin" is "a
certain affected familiarity"; Thackeray "indulges too frequently in
little confidences with individual readers, in which pretended allusions to himself are frequent. 'What would you do? what would
you say now, if you were in such a position?' he asks."[7] Yet for
Trollope, although this familiarity might breed occasional contempt,

it did not finally compromise the great virtue of Thackeray's lucidity. "As I have said before, the reader always understands his words without an effort, and receives all that the author has to give."[8] But to know what, and to know all, a writer means is to be in his confidence indeed, and it would be a serious lapse of style that his confidence should break down in affectation or something worse.

In "Before the Curtain," the preface he wrote in 1848 for the completed novel, Thackeray promises his reader "no other moral than this tag to the present story," that after wandering with him through the Fair, "When you come home, you sit down, in a sober, contemplative, not uncharitable frame of mind, and apply yourself to your books or your business." He raises no literary expectations, he promises no carefully graduated feast of human nature, he does not even excuse himself to those who find all Fairs "immoral" and hence refuse to enter this one. The stern moralists may be quite right in withholding their custom, but those "of a lazy, or a benevolent, or a sarcastic mood, may perhaps like to step in for half an hour and look at the performance." This casualness, the queer juxtaposition of "lazy," "benevolent," and "sarcastic," may seem like the very height of good breeding. It does sum up the uncomfortable collocation of responses that any reader must make to some stretches of the novel. But it also promises that this writer will keep us free from violent emotions as we read. It is the guarantee of a special detachment.

Such detachment is often suggested by a coy version of one of Fielding's comic devices. When we witness the departure of Becky and Amelia from Chiswick Mall, the last flurry of farewells is recounted thus: "Then came the struggle and the parting below. Words refuse to tell it. . . ." The congregation of servants and pupils, the hugging and kissing and crying are such "as no pen can depict, and as the tender heart would fain pass over" (chap. 1, p. 6). Or, on the morning after the fatal excursion to Vauxhall, Joseph Sedley lies "groaning in agonies which the pen refuses to describe" (chap. 6, p. 55) while he suffers the aftermath of rack punch. Becky, disappointed in her attempt to capture Joseph, goes away from the Sedley house to her duties as governess: "Finally came the parting with Amelia, over which I intend to throw a veil" (chap. 6, p. 61). Such mild affectations as these amuse a good deal less than their frequency suggests they should, however obliquely they may glance at sentimental explorations of young female affection or the tract-writer's interest in the heavy repentance of the drunkard. But they are the simplest and the least interesting form of a larger kind of detachment.

About other episodes the narrator is more artfully silent. Perhaps the most interesting is the courtship of Rawdon Crawley, which extends over several chapters and is concealed in the narrative of Becky's ministrations to old Miss Crawley. It will be recalled that the success of Becky's attentions to this lady, the old aunt whose wealth is the object of all the Crawleys' envy and scheming, alarms Mrs. Bute Crawley—whose portrait, incidentally, as well as that of her family and of her husband the Rector, make one wonder that Thackeray could have quarreled with Jerrold's anticlericalism.[9] Mrs. Bute's scheming to secure Miss Crawley's money for her own leads her to warn Rawdon that when his stepmother dies, old Sir Pitt will marry Becky. Rawdon's response sets the level of intrigue exactly:

> "By Jove, it's too bad," thought Rawdon, "too bad, by Jove! I do believe the woman wants the poor girl to be ruined, in order that she shouldn't come into the family as Lady Crawley." [chap. 14, p. 133]

He proceeds to the recommended seduction, but is outguessed by the frank and outraged role that Becky adopts when he "rallie[s] her in his graceful way about his father's attachment." The game goes on, Miss Crawley recovers from her surfeit under Becky's assiduous care, and shortly news comes that the meek Lady Crawley is dead. Rawdon and his aunt discuss the matter while Becky stands by.

> Rebecca said nothing. She seemed by far the gravest and most impressed of the family. She left the room before Rawdon went away that day; but they met by chance below, as he was going away after taking leave, and had a parley together. [chap. 14, p. 143]

And the next thing we know, old Sir Pitt has come to town and is down on his knees to ask for the hand of Becky. The narrator comments:

> In the course of this history we have never seen her lose her presence of mind; but she did now, and wept some of the most genuine tears that ever fell from her eyes. [chap. 14, p. 144]

But what does "genuine" mean here? Or "they met by chance" in the passage above? Are we to infer that during their "parley" Becky uses the threat of a proposal from the father to make sure of the son? Are we to infer that the tears are genuine because she has planned too well—the threat she has used to get one husband has turned out to be prophetic, and she might have had the father? Are they tears of rage? of regret? As we move on to the next chapter we certainly find no circumstantial report of when and how Becky and Rawdon are married; instead there is a good deal of indirect veiling of the scene and refusing of the pen. "How they were married is not of the slightest consequence to anybody." Perhaps, it is conjectured, they went off one afternoon when Becky was presumed to be visiting Amelia. But the matter is left in uncertainty. On the one hand, "Who needs to be told, that if a woman has a will, she will assuredly find a way?" And on the other: "who on earth, after the daily experience we have, can question the probability of a gentleman marrying anybody?" (chap. 16, p. 153).

The concealment of the circumstances of the marriage may appeal to the lazy, may satisfy the benevolent, and it may give the sarcastic something to work on too. But its most important effect is that the narration here, clustered about with confidential comments and dismissive questions, sets before us a way of knowing the world. It is a way so inferential, so dependent upon unfinished implications, that it comes close to the character of gossip. And a good gossip, while its unfinished sentences and its discreet and indiscreet omissions may keep us from the exhilaration of indignation or rhapsody, can suggest values and insights superior to the vocabulary of the purveyor or the listener. Here, whatever the meaning of that "by chance" that modifies the meeting of Becky and Rawdon, or whatever the meaning of that "genuine" that modifies her tears, we can only infer that the marriage is the result neither of grand passion nor of mean seduction. The veiling of the secret here means that we can only accept Becky's marriage as a convenience. Even the grossness of Mrs. Bute's plotting is lost in the shadows.

The questions with which Thackeray disposes of this affair— "Who needs to be told . . . who can question the probability . . ." —are of course the most conspicuous earmark of his detachment in *Vanity Fair*. There is the issue of who made the first move in Becky's first romance, with the young Reverend Mr. Crisp who came infatuated to tea at Chiswick Mall: after a parenthetical cloud of hints and counter-hints the narrator concludes, "But who can tell you the real truth of the matter?" (chap. 2, p. 14). Just as when the pen refuses to tell, the implication here is only coy. But a good many hundred pages later, in what is called "A Vagabond Chapter" (chap. 64), this kind of coyness can exasperate. It comes in a passage summarizing Becky's career after her fall from polite society in London: "When she got her money she gambled; when she had gambled it she was put to shifts to live; who knows how or by what means she succeeded? . . . The present historian can give no certain details regarding the event" (p. 681). The detachment inculcated here is vast and affluent indeed; it is perhaps matched only by the elaborate veiling of the circumstances of Joseph Sedley's death. But the most puzzling questions in the book are those that comment upon its crucial passage.

Every reader of *Vanity Fair* remembers the "discovery scene" of chapter 53—the scene in which Becky suffers exposure and isolation after her husband and Lord Steyne violently clash. And every student of the novel knows that this scene is a battleground upon which the judgments of a number of Thackeray's critics have collided. Rawdon, having been freed from the spunging house, hurries "across the streets and the great squares of Vanity Fair, and bursts in upon his wife and Lord Steyne in something less than *flagrante delicto* though ready for embarrassment."

> Steyne was hanging over the sofa on which Becky sate. The wretched woman was in a brilliant full toilette, her arms and all her fingers sparkling with bracelets and rings; and the brilliants on her breast which Steyne had given her. He had her hand in his, and was bowing over it to kiss it, when Becky started up with a faint scream as she caught sight of Rawdon's white face. At the next instant she tried a smile, a horrid smile, as if to welcome her husband; and Steyne rose up, grinding his teeth, pale, and with fury in his looks.
>
> He, too, attempted a laugh—and came forward holding out his hand. "What, come back! How d'ye do, Crawley?" he said, the nerves of his mouth twitching as he tried to grin at the intruder.
>
> There was that in Rawdon's face which caused Becky to fling herself before him. "I am innocent, Rawdon," she said "before God, I am innocent." She clung hold of his coat, of his hands; her own were all covered with serpents, and rings, and baubles.

"I am innocent. —Say I am innocent," she said to Lord Steyne.

He thought a trap had been laid for him, and was as furious with the wife as with the husband. "You innocent! Damn you!" he screamed out. "You innocent! Why, every trinket you have on your body is paid for by me. I have given you thousands of pounds which this fellow has spent, and for which he has sold you. Innocent, by—! You're as innocent as your mother, the ballet-girl, and your husband the bully. Don't think to frighten me as you have done others. Make way, sir, and let me pass"; and Lord Steyne seized up his hat, and, with flame in his eyes, and looking his enemy fiercely in the face, marched upon him, never for a moment doubting that the other would give way.

But Rawdon Crawley springing out, seized him by the neck-cloth, until Steyne, almost stangled, writhed, and bent under his arm. "You lie, you dog!" said Rawdon. "You lie, you coward and villain!" And he struck the Peer twice over the face with his open hand, and flung him bleeding to the ground. It was all done before Rebecca could interpose. She stood there trembling before him. She admired her husband, strong, brave, and victorious.

"Come here," he said. —She came up at once.

"Take off those things." —She began, trembling, pulling the jewels from her arms, and the rings from her shaking fingers, and held them all in a heap, quivering, and looking up at him. "Throw them down," he said, and she dropped them. He tore the diamond ornament out of her breast, and flung it at Lord Steyne. It cut him on his bald forehead. Steyne wore the scar to his dying day. [pp. 554-55]

The theatricality of the passage—Becky's clinging and quivering, the serpents and baubles on her hands, Rawdon's springing out and his terse manifesto, the flame in the eyes of the wicked nobleman and the lifelong scar on his head—all such features suggest that the creator of Punch's Prize novelists is once again engaged in something like parody.[10] On the other hand it has been asserted that far from a joke, the scene "is the chief ganglion of the tale; and the discharge of energy from Rawdon's fist [sic] is the reward and consolation of the reader."[11] The most extensive criticism of the scene finds it unprepared for and conveyed by a dramatic technique foreign to Thackeray's genius,[12] but this judgment has in turn been disposed of by another critic who finds Thackeray's usual stamp upon it and some other felicities as well. He suggests that one of these is the way in which "Steyne wore the scar" echoes "Steyne wore the star."[13] By the same sort of reasoning we might infer from "He tore the diamond ornament out of her breast" that Becky's heart is surpassing hard; and certainly Thackeray tells us that the battle takes the heart out of her. But the one touch upon which Thackeray himself is known to have commented is Becky's response to the sudden burst of energy from Rawdon: "She stood there trembling before him. She admired her husband, strong, brave, and victorious." Of this observation Thackeray is reported to have said that it was a touch of genius,[14] and it does consort well with his special genius in the rest of the book.

For although the battle seems to be the expression of outraged honor, it is a collision that misses its main issue and prize. As the resistless masses meet, Becky stands off to one side, and although her admiration is unacceptable or even unknown to Rawdon, and although we are told that her life seems so "miserable, lonely, and profitless" after Rawdon has silently departed that she even thinks of suicide, there is still a profound irrelevance in this violent scene. Becky's maid comes upon her in her dejection and asks the question that is in every reader's mind: *"Mon Dieu,* madame, what has happened?" And the "person writing" concludes this crucial chapter with an enlargement of the same question:

> What *had* happened? Was she guilty or not? She said not; but who could tell what was truth which came from those lips; or if that corrupt heart was in this case pure? All her lies and her schemes, all her selfishness and her wiles, all her wit and her genius had come to this bankruptcy. [p. 556]

Becky lies down, the maid goes to the drawing room to gather up the pile of trinkets, and the chapter ends. If Thackeray has not risen to a cruel joke on those readers who find consolation and reward in the discharge of energy from Rawdon, he has at least interrupted their satisfaction.

Lord Steyne's meaning of "guilty"—"He thought a trap had been laid for him" by Becky and Rawdon—is of course quite false, though it corroborates the characterization of Steyne as one experienced in double-dealing. "Guilty" from Rawdon's point of view of course means, as he tells Pitt next day, that "it was a regular plan between that scoundrel and her" to get him out of the way (chap.

54, p. 559). And Thackeray goes to as great lengths to make it impossible for us to know that this interpretation is true as he does to conceal the timing and motives of Becky's marriage. To see the entangling and displacing of any clear answer, we need only ask "guilty of what?" The usual answer is of course "guilty of adultery" (or guilty of getting ready for it),[15] and Thackeray's silence is commonly attributed to his awareness of the "squeamishness" of his public. Indeed he himself lends real authority to this account of the matter. In 1840, writing on Fielding, he complains that the world no longer tolerates real satire. "The same vice exists now, only we don't speak about it; the same things are done, but we don't call them by their names."[16] And in *Vanity Fair* he complains that he must be silent about some events in Becky's later career because he must satisfy "the moral world, that has, perhaps, no particular objection to vice, but an insuperable repugnance to hearing vice called by its proper name" (chap. 64, p. 671). There may well be evidence in Thackeray's personal history to suggest in addition that he was, perhaps even before the separation from his mad wife, evasive and unclear on the subject of sexual behavior. But however complicated the tensions of Thackeray's own emotional experience, and however rigid the scruples of his audience, the answer to the questions with which he comments on this most important episode cannot be a single "name" or possess any "proper name." For he has led us here, however uneasily, with mingled attitudes of parody and outrage, to a startling though incomplete vision of a new social world, a vision exactly proportioned to the irrelevance of the violence we have witnessed.

The words of the passage that command our moral response are precisely those that most clearly approach parody: Becky responds to a nameless "that" in Rawdon's face by exclaiming "I am innocent." If the reader trained in melodrama scoffs at the response and turns Becky into a consummate villain, he will have some trouble getting through the rest of the novel, and it is likely that he will long since have become exasperated with Thackeray's tone, his silences and implications. The same is true, moreover, of the sentimental reader who throws down the volume and declares that Becky has been monstrously wronged and victimized by wicked men in a bad world. But the reader who says, in effect, "it is impossible to tell whether or of what she is guilty" is exactly in the difficult position of one who accepts Thackeray's narrative as it is given. And what such a reader sees from this position must fill him with wonder if not dismay. For he sees that while he wants to answer these questions, he cannot do so, and he can only conclude that he is looking at a situation before which his moral vocabulary is irrelevant. Becky in her isolation has finally gone out of this world, and it will take a new casuistry to bring her back. Thackeray uses some strong moral words in his comment, it is true: "who could tell what was truth which came from those lips; or if that corrupt heart was in this case pure?" But while we know that Becky has lied heartily to Steyne, and to his hearty admiration, we cannot know that she is lying to Rawdon when she insists on her innocence. Whatever corruption we may have seen, the question this time is in earnest. The qualities named in the final statement, and especially by its last word, tell us where we are: "All her lies and her schemes, all her selfishness and her wiles, all her wit and her genius had come to this bankruptcy." For these are the terms not so much of moral as of financial enterprise, and "this bankruptcy" is the real touch of genius in the passage. Thackeray's questions and his comment express neither indignation nor sympathy. Rather, they bring before us the terrible irresolution of a society in which market values and moral values are discontinuous and separate. And Thackeray will not—he can not—support us as we revolt from such a spectacle.

The ghostly paradigm upon which human nature plays in *Vanity Fair* is the credit economy that in Thackeray's own lifetime finally developed from a money economy. Even the constant gambling in Thackeray's Fair, historically appropriate as it may be to his Regency setting (and much of his own early experience as it may reflect), suggests the unpredictability of the system. Distant though the gambler may be from respectability, his luck is only a little less mysterious than the power his winnings confer upon him. However it may be in the most famous conversation recorded in modern literary history, it is all too true in *Vanity Fair* that rich people are different because they have more money. Thackeray exposed himself to some high-minded criticism from George Henry Lewes when he published the number containing Becky's famous reflection, "I think I could be a good woman if I had five thousand a year." For he had commented, "And who knows but Rebecca was right in her speculations—and that it was only a question of money and fortune which made the difference between her and an honest woman?"

(chap. 41, p. 436). In its interrogative form the comment is much more precise than the declaration Thackeray wrote to Lewes. The latter called it "detestable" to say that "honesty is only the virtue of abundance." Thackeray replied that he meant "only that he in the possession of luxuries . . . should be very chary of despising poor Lazarus on foot, and look very humbly and leniently upon the faults of his less fortunate brethren." This is of course no answer; or if it is, it asks for a curious forbearance towards Becky Sharp. But Thackeray qualifies at once: "I am quite aware of the dismal roguery . . . [which] goes all through the Vanity Fair story—and God forbid that the world should be like it altogether: though I fear it is more like it than we like to own."[17] The likeness to "the world" is in the belief that money is magic and in the frightening awareness, no doubt recently reinforced by the financial crisis of 1847, that no theory had yet been devised to control it. Walter Bagehot, in the *Economic Studies* he was composing in the 1870s, confessed to "a haze" in the language in which he described the growth of capital, and he remarked too with admiration that "a very great many of the strongest heads in England spend their minds on little else than on thinking whether other people will pay their debts."[18] For him that system was "marvellous" by which "an endless succession of slips of written promises should be turned into money as readily as if they were precious stones"—so marvelous indeed that it "would have seemed incredible in commerce till very recent times."[19] Thackeray's attitude, doubtless shaped by the short period he spent as a bill broker in 1833—an episode he apparently tried hard to forget[20]—was not so admiring. His Fair, at any rate, is a market the movements of which are perplexing in the extreme.

The first mention of the "guilt" or "innocence" of Becky's relations to Lord Steyne comes in a passage about the "awful kitchen inquisition" of the servants of Vanity Fair. We are told that Raggles, the retired butler of Miss Crawley, who owns the house in Curzon Street where Becky and Rawdon live well on nothing a year, is ruined by his extension of credit to them. But he is the victim of something more than the simple excess of liabilities over assets. The "*Vehmgericht* of the servants'-hall" early pronounces Becky guilty:

> And I shame to say, she would not have got credit had they not believed her to be guilty. It was the sight of the Marquis of Steyne's carriage-lamps at her door, contemplated by Raggles,

burning in the blackness of midnight, "that kep him up," as he afterwards said; that, even more than Rebecca's arts and coaxings. [chap. 44, pp. 461-62]

The question of guilt here is quite subordinate to the question of credit, and Raggles is ruined not because he is right about Becky's guilt but because he believes in a strict correlation between Becky's moral and financial status. The last of Raggles is seen at the drunken party of the servants on the morning after the battle; our last glimpse of him is not as he suffers in ruin but as he looks at his fellows "with a wild surprise" upon hearing from Becky that Rawdon "has got a good appointment" (chap. 55, p. 565). It is no wonder that Thackeray should have said in a letter to his mother written during the very month when the "discovery scene" appeared,

> I can't find the end of the question between property and labour. We want something almost equal to a Divine Person to settle it. I mean if there is ever to be an elucidation of the mystery it is to be solved by a preacher of such novelty and authority, as will awaken and convince mankind—but O how and when?[21]

Whatever the fate of the larger question, Thackeray does do some novel preaching upon bankruptcy in one section of *Vanity Fair*. John Sedley, we recall, is ruined in the uncertainties following Napoleon's escape from Elba (chap. 18, pp. 170 ff.), and Thackeray's extended portrait of the "business and bustle and mystery of a ruined man" (chap. 20, p. 195) seems at first sight disproportionate. Of course the bankruptcy accounts for the career of Amelia, but not for all of it. For old Osborne, who also emerges from the background just here, is described as behaving towards his former friend Sedley "with savageness and scorn." Our attitude is shaped precisely by Osborne's insisting that as a bankrupt Sedley must be wicked—that he is both out of business and out of the circle of decency. "From a mere sense of consistency, a persecutor is bound to show that the fallen man is a villain—otherwise he, the persecutor, is a wretch himself" (chap. 18, p. 173). And Osborne is characterized more grossly still by his opposition to Amelia for his son, by his insistence that George marry the rich mulatto Miss Schwarz, and by his vast self-righteousness. Osborne is perhaps an inept caricature of the City man who has succumbed completely to the superstitions of money, but he is a new kind of portrait, and one not less complicated than

Dickens's portrait of another hard businessman whose adventures were being issued in installments at the same time.

While Thackeray's Mr. Osborne is a crude warning to those who identify bankruptcy and corruption, Dickens's Mr. Dombey is an astonishing testimonial to the degree of violence that must be exerted to link the experience of bankruptcy with moral reform. In the same month, March of 1848,[22] in which they read of the collision between Rawdon and Lord Steyne, readers who followed both authors were shaken by a passage of dreadful violence that describes a collision between Mr. Dombey's manager, Carker, and a railway engine (chap. 55). Dombey witnesses the event and faints at the sight—it is not an "accident" but the physical embodiment of a terrible obsession. When we next encounter Dombey (chap. 58) he is superintending the bankruptcy of his firm which results from Carker's secret machinations and which he will do nothing to avert. He is alone in the world, for he has driven away his gentle daughter Florence, and he is a "ruined man." With gruesome immediacy he thinks of suicide, but just before the knife strikes, his daughter rushes in, a great reconciliation and redemption occurs, and Mr. Dombey, no longer worth five thousand or very much of anything a year, is at last a good man. For all his inventive energy Dickens cannot make clear the relation between the departure of Carker from this world and the moral conversion that Mr. Dombey then undergoes. But this number of *Dombey and Son* together with the contemporaneous number of *Vanity Fair* suggests the extreme lengths to which two of the most sensitive minds of the mid-century were driven in their effort to reconcile the mysterious power of finance capitalism with the requirements of private morality. "Sell yourself" still meant the worst degradation, but the time was approaching when it would become a formula for "success."

In *Vanity Fair* at any rate Becky's bankruptcy offers no clearer connection between villainy—or goodness—and loss of credit than does the situation of Old John Sedley that Osborne so ruthlessly categorizes. The thoroughness with which Thackeray has covered his tracks suggests that no single transaction, not even payment by adultery, is at issue here. The kind of credit upon which the Crawleys lived so well in London and Paris is beyond the power of any act or value to overtake, for it is the social version of that system in which the perpetual promise to pay is taken for the perpetual fact of payment. "The truth is, when we say of a gentleman that he lives

well on nothing a year, we use the word 'nothing' to signify something unknown" (chap. 36, p. 374). It may be that Rawdon and
Becky are "wicked," but their wickedness will not account for their
credit as they pursue the fashionable life. Just as the war that so
mysteriously yet inevitably ruined John Sedley was, as Thackeray
tells us, a lucky accident interrupting the endless double- and triple-
dealing among nations (chap. 28, pp. 279–80), so for Becky an accident interrupts the double-dealing and counter double-dealing of the
scramble for social power. The perspectives here are indeed almost
endless; they are certainly beyond the limits of innocence or guilt.
Even Rawdon, who experiences something like conversion or reform
as Becky's career reaches its height, is not quite secure. His one assertion to Becky after the battle is an ironic fulfillment of Steyne's
accusation: "You might have spared me a hundred pounds, Becky,
out of all this—I have always shared with you" (chap. 53, p. 556).[23]
And the last words he speaks in the novel are as ambiguous as any
question from the narrator:

> "She has kep money concealed from me these ten years," he said.
> "She swore, last night only, she had none from Steyne. She knew
> it was all up, directly I found it. If she's not guilty, Pitt, she's as
> bad as guilty, and I'll never see her again, never." [chap. 55,
> p. 579]

It is hardly possible to find the outrage of manly honor in these
exactly struck last words. The distinction between "guilty" and "as
bad as guilty" would be the final viciousness if it were not the final
irrelevance.

But, again, is this what Thackeray means, and is it the *all* that he
means? We can believe so only by acknowledging that the easy
confidence between reader and writer promised at the beginning has
been renounced, for we are here outside the domain of laziness,
benevolence, or sarcasm. If the renunciation were the deliberate
act of a supreme ironist who turns and rends us for our naive acceptance of his confidential detachment, Thackeray would indeed
have created a masterpiece. But in the crucial scene and in portions
of the chapters that lead to it Thackeray has exposed us to violent
emotions that no politeness can conceal. The enmity between Little
Rawdy and Lord Steyne, for example, is an extension of Becky's
neglect of her child that erupts into physical violence: Becky boxes
his ears for listening to her on the stairs as she entertains Lord

Steyne (chap. 44, p. 460). The child indeed makes his first speaking appearance in the same chapter as that in which Lord Steyne also first appears, grinning "hideously, his little eyes leering towards Rebecca" (chap. 37, p. 389). The juxtaposition is emphasized when little Rawdon is apostrophized:

> O thou poor lonely little benighted boy! Mother is the name for God in the lips and hearts of little children; and here was one who was worshipping a stone. [p. 392]

The appeal is no mere instance of competing with the creator of little Paul Dombey, as everyone who has read Thackeray's letters to his own mother will know. It is an appeal similar to many others in the narrative of Amelia, although there Thackeray is more characteristically reticent. When Amelia and her mother are reunited after her marriage, though Thackeray begins by referring to "How the floodgates were opened," he adds, "Let us respect Amelia and her mamma whispering and whimpering and laughing and crying in the parlour and the twilight." And when Amelia retreats to meditate in "the little room" with its "little white bed" in her old home, Thackeray desists:

> Have we a right to repeat or to overhear her prayers? These, brother, are secrets, and out of the domain of Vanity Fair, in which our story lies. [chap. 26, pp. 262, 264]

Even—especially—if we construe this scene and its secrets as an expression of Amelia's first awareness that she is to be a mother herself, it still involves relationships and sentiments outside the "domain" that Thackeray so thoroughly explored. It is a domain bounded by the "politeness" invoked in that early address to the reader in which the narrator promises "to love and shake by the hand" his "good and kindly" characters, "to laugh confidentially in the reader's sleeve" at the "silly" ones, but "to abuse in the strongest terms that politeness admits of" all those who are "wicked and heartless" (chap. 8, p. 79). Such terms of abuse for the wicked and love for the good are for the most part so polite that we accept them with all the detachment guaranteed by the Manager of the Performance. But the limits of this detachment—its very bankruptcy—can be shown only as we glimpse the howling wilderness outside, where the secrets of private feelings are violently confused with public forces of huge and mysterious dimensions, and where there is neither lucidity nor truth.

What Thackeray does then exhibit within the domain of the Fair is the impossibility of self-knowledge and, in the fullest sense, dramatic change. The most intimate experiences of the self, whether in prayer or in love, in disappointment or in outrage, must be kept outside. Becky's "I am innocent" is no more an articulation of the truth than it is the lucid exposure of a lie. But to put us where we cannot know "What *had* happened" and to face us with the bewildering irrelevance of our polite detachment, Thackeray was driven to an extreme that no style of his could control. He could not be clear without being untruthful, and he could not be truthful without being obscure. He tried to recover himself, it is true, in the subsequent chapters by returning to the conception of Becky that most saves his book. The most interesting feature of her characterization is not that she begins from the ambiguous social position of the orphan and governess—"'I don't trust them governesses, Pinner,' says the Sedley housekeeper with enormous assurance, 'they're neither one thing nor t'other. They give themselves the hairs and hupstarts of ladies, and their wages is no better than you nor me'" (chap 6, p. 60). Thackeray is concerned with much more than the favorite Victorian example of social mobility. The greater truth about Becky is that she is a mimic, that she trades on the difference between fantasy and society, between the role and the fact. But the truth of endless mimicry is much too large for the domain of the lucid. It is larger than any drawing room, park, or square of Vanity Fair, and it could be forced in only by an act of violence that darkened lucidity and concealed truth. The casuistry upon which *Vanity Fair* rests is unique, and the responses of many thousands of readers for a hundred years to this much-read book must constitute one of the most erratic subterranean currents of our moral history.

NOTES

1. *An Autobiography,* ed. by Frederick Page (London, 1950), p. 244.
2. See, e.g., his review of "A New Spirit Of The Age," *Works—The Oxford Thackeray,* ed. by George Saintsbury (17 vols.; London, 1908), VI, 424; or some advice on "fine writing" in *The Letters and Private Papers of William Makepeace Thackeray,* ed. by Gordon N. Ray (4 vols.; Cambridge, Mass., 1945), II, 192.

3. Preface to *Pendennis*.

4. References are to the Modern Library College Editions reprint (New York, 1950), which is based on the edition of 1864.

5. Gordon N. Ray, *Thackeray: The Uses of Adversity: 1811-1846* (New York, 1955), pp. 384-85.

6. *The Pilgrim's Progress . . .* , ed. by Edmund Venables, rev. by Mabel Peacock (Oxford, 1925), pp. 82 ff.

7. Anthony Trollope, *Thackeray* (London, 1879), pp. 197-98.

8. *Ibid.*, p. 198.

9. See Ray, *Uses of Adversity*, pp. 370-71.

10. As has been suggested by Kathleen Tillotson, *Novels of the Eighteen-Forties* (Oxford, 1954), pp. 233-34.

11. Robert Louis Stevenson, "A Gossip on Romance," *Memories and Portraits* (New York, 1910), p. 239 (Vol. 17 of the Biographical Edition of the *Works*). Stevenson's judgment is endorsed by Professor Ray in *Uses of Adversity*, p. 410.

12. Percy Lubbock, *The Craft of Fiction* (London, 1954), pp. 101 ff. Lubbock's argument has been criticized by Professor Ray (*Uses of Adversity*, pp. 409-10) and by Geoffrey Tillotson, *Thackeray the Novelist* (Cambridge, Eng., 1954), pp. 82 ff.

13. G. Tillotson, *Thackeray the Novelist*, p. 84.

14. See Ray, *Uses of Adversity*, p. 500, n. 19; and *Letters and Private Papers*, II, 352 *n*.

15. See, e.g., Ray, *Uses of Adversity*, p. 502, n. 14.

16. *Works*, III, 385.

17. *Letters and Private Papers*, II, 353-54.

18. *The Works and Life of Walter Bagehot*, ed. by Mrs. Russell Barrington (10 vols.; London, 1915), VII, 248, 131.

19. *Ibid.*, p. 251.

20. See *Uses of Adversity*, pp. 159-60.

21. *Letters and Private Papers*, II, 356.

22. See K. Tillotson, *Novels of the Eighteen-Forties*, p. 318.

23. For a quite different interpretation, see K. Tillotson, *Novels of the Eighteen-Forties*, pp. 248, 251.

GORDON N. RAY

Vanity Fair: One Version of the Novelist's Responsibility

My title, I am afraid, has an old-fashioned ring. The novelists of today who best know their job believe with André Gide that "the moral
issue for the artist is not that he should present an idea that is useful
but that he should present an idea well."[1] They have relinquished
their ethical role by eliminating themselves, and therefore the question of responsibility to their readers, from their books. Their credo
is summed up by Evelyn Waugh in an article on Graham Greene's
The Heart of the Matter. Greene's style is functional, not at all "specifically literary," he writes. "The words are simply mathematical
symbols for his thought. Moreover, no relation is established between
writer and reader. The reader has not had a conversation with a third
party such as he enjoys with Sterne or Thackeray." There is not even
an observer through whose eyes events are seen. The technique employed is that of the cinema, with Greene as director and producer.
"It is the modern way of telling a story."[2]

Victorian novelists, on the other hand, cherished the relation of
writer to reader and pondered very seriously their moral obligation to
their audience. Of them all Thackeray has been most severely re-
proached by later critics for intruding upon his stories in the charac-

From *Essays by Divers Hands: Being the Transactions of the Royal Society of
Literature by the United Kingdom*, New Series, XXV (1950), pp. 342-56.
Reprinted by permission of the author and publisher.

ter of guide, philosopher and friend. But perhaps it has been too
hastily assumed that the advantage in this particular must lie with
the modern novelist. At any rate, instead of taking it for granted that
Thackeray's penchant for moral commentary is an excrescence, unhappily all too common among the naïve and primitive novelists who
lived before Henry James, I propose to inquire how he came to entertain his conception of the novelist's responsibility, how his work
was altered by it, how it affected his standing with his readers, and
how it is related to his intellectual position in his age.

I

When the first monthly number of *Vanity Fair* appeared in January,
1847, Thackeray had for ten years earned his living by his pen; yet
what reputation he had achieved hardly extended beyond his fellow-
writers and a small audience of discriminating readers. Because they
were either anonymous or written over one or another of his various
noms de plume, his long series of brilliant contributions to *Fraser's
Magazine, Punch* and the *Morning Chronicle* had little cumulative effect. The "great stupid public,"[3] as he called it, passed him by
indifferent. "Mrs. Perkins's [Ball] is a great success—the greatest I
have had—very nearly as great as Dickens," he remarked of the first
of his Christmas books in December of 1846, "that is Perkins 500,
Dickens 25,000—only that difference!"[4]

The reception accorded the yellow-wrappered parts of *Vanity Fair*
was at first hardly more encouraging. But gradually they began to
be talked about. Friendly paragraphs underlined their excellence in
Fraser's Magazine, the *Scotsman* and the *North British Review.* In
July, after the seventh monthly number had appeared, the *Sun*
hailed Thackeray as "the Fielding of the nineteenth century."[5] By
September Mrs. Carlyle was convinced that *Vanity Fair* "beats Dickens out of the world."[6] A long panegyric by Abraham Hayward in
the *Edinburgh Review* of January, 1848, sealed the success of the
novel. "There is no use denying the matter or blinking it now,"
Thackeray wrote a few days later. "I am become a sort of great man
in my way—all but at the top of the tree: indeed there if the truth
were known and having a great fight up there with Dickens."[7]

How is one to account for this sudden and splendid elevation to
eminence of a writer who had been regarded a year earlier, so Henry
Kingsley relates, as "a man known certainly to some extent, but who

was thought to have had sufficient trial, and to have found his métier as a clever magazine writer"?[8] What was the element hitherto lacking in Thackeray's books which explains the immense prestige of *Vanity Fair* with Victorian readers? A glance at his career before 1847 may answer these questions.

Connop Thirlwall said of the England of Thackeray's youth: "Society possesses two or three strong, stiff frames, in which all persons of liberal education who need or desire a fixed place and specific designation must consent to be set."[9] Thackeray obstinately sought success outside these frames. Abandoning the university after five terms and the Inns of Court after a few months, he tried his fortune as an artist and as a journalist, both employments then well beyond the social pale. He discovered before long that he could not draw well enough to succeed as a painter; and he later confessed that *"what I wrote was bad and poor stuff for many years."*[10] Meanwhile, not wholly by his own fault, he had lost the modest fortune on which he had relied for a competence while he pursued his unconventional path. He was consequently exposed for many years to the distresses and humiliations of shabby gentility. When a happy marriage and recognition as a periodical writer began to promise compensation for earlier misfortunes, his wife became insane. It is not surprising that Thackeray accumulated from these experiences what Taine calls "a treasure of mediated hatred."

His history as a writer was hardly more propitious. Coming to literary maturity in the eighteen-thirties, an age of uncertain taste and uninspiring example, he turned decisively away from prevailing formulas for the novel, which seemed to him either childish or unwholesome. It was his endeavour, he said in a rare statement of purpose, "to work as an artist telling the truth and morbidly perhaps eschewing humbug."[11]

Telling the truth to Thackeray meant describing life as he had seen it during the bitter years since he came of age. "He was created," he told Dr. John Brown, "with a sense of the ugly, the odd, of the meanly false, of the desperately wicked; he laid them bare: them under all disguises he hunted to death."[12] The first readers of *The Yellowplush Papers, Catherine, Denis Haggarty's Wife,* and *Barry Lyndon* not unnaturally found the themes that Thackeray's experience suggested to him low and sordid.

The second part of his programme, even morbidly to eschew humbug, led him to tell his stories substantially without commentary; for as a young man he was inclined to identify humbug with moralizing. Whenever he could, he adopted a dramatic disguise. The opinion of Yellowplush, George Fitz-Boodle and Barry Lyndon are intended for the most part to characterize these worthies; not to convey Thackeray's judgments. In more than one of his critical essays of the middle eighteen-forties, Thackeray explicitly stated that it is not the novelist's business to teach.

> If we want instruction [he wrote of Lever's "St. Patrick's Eve"], we prefer to take it from fact rather than from fiction. We like to hear sermons from his reverence at church; to get our notions of trade, crime, politics and other national statistics from the proper papers and figures; but when suddenly, out of the gilt pages of a pretty picture book, a comic moralist rushes forward, and takes occasion to tell us that society is diseased . . . persons who wish to lead an easy life are inclined to remonstrate against this literary ambuscadoe.[13]

To a public eager for guidance from its literary mentors, this attitude recommended Thackeray hardly more than did his subject matter.

Moreover, the disappointments of Thackeray's life sometimes goaded him to savage and devil-may-care protest. We find him resolving to contribute to *Punch* in 1842, at a time when that magazine was still identified in the public mind with the notorious *Age* and *Satirist* newspapers, because it offered him "a great opportunity for unrestrained laughing, sneering, kicking and gambadoing."[14] He made little effort, indeed, to ensure success by conciliating his audience. *The Book of Snobs* was designed from beginning to end to prick its readers out of their complacency. And none of Thackeray's earlier books lacks many passages in the same vein, of which the following imaginary after-dinner conversation from *The Irish Sketch-Book* may stand as an example:

> One word more regarding the Widow Fagan's house. When Peggy brought in coals for the drawing-room fire, she carried them—in what do you think? "In a coal-scuttle, to be sure," says the English reader, down on you as sharp as a needle.
>
> No, you clever Englishman, it wasn't a coal-scuttle.
>
> "Well, then, it was in a fire-shovel," says that brightest of wits, guessing again.

No, it *wasn't* a fire-shovel, you heaven-born genius; and you
might guess from this until Mrs. Snooks called you up to coffee,
and you would never find out. It was in something which I have
already described in Mrs. Fagan's pantry.

"Oh, I have you now, it was the bucket where the potatoes
were: the thlatternly wetch!" says Snooks.

Wrong again—Peggy brought up the coals—in a CHINA PLATE!
Snooks turns quite white with surprise, and almost chokes himself with his port. "Well," says he, "of all the *wum* countwith
that I ever wead of, hang me if Ireland ithn't the *wummetht*.
Coalth in a plate! Mawyann, do you hear that? In Ireland they
alwayth thend up their coalth in a plate!"[15]

Stung by such taunts as this, it mattered little to the average Englishman that none of Thackeray's works after 1840 was without
many touches of profound insight and tenderness. Such mitigations
were forgotten, and the reader was left with the prevailing impression of a brilliant but forbidding talent which made him uneasy
while it amused him. He regarded Thackeray as a writer for whom
he could feel no affection and with whom he could achieve little
solidarity.

II

If Thackeray had continued in this vein, he would hardly have
written *Vanity Fair*. But late in 1846 he experienced a change of
heart, the culmination of a progressive reconciliation to life, which
can be compared with John Stuart Mill's awakening from Bentham-
ite Utilitarianism twenty years earlier. Attention is directed to it
by a letter which Thackeray wrote to Mark Lemon, the editor of
Punch, in February of 1847. His subject was the last paragraph of
"The Snobs of England": "To laugh at such is Mr. Punch's business. May he laugh honestly, hit no foul blow, and tell the truth
when at his very broadest grin—never forgetting that if Fun is good,
Truth is still better, and Love is best of all."[16]

What I mean [he explained to Lemon], applies to my own case
and that of all of us—who set up as Satirical-Moralists—and
having such a vast multitude of readers whom we not only amuse
but teach. . . . A few years ago I should have sneered at the

idea of setting up as a teacher at all, and perhaps at this pompous and pious way of talking about a few papers of jokes in *Punch*—but I have got to believe in the business, and in many other things since then. And our profession seems to me to be as serious as the Parson's own.[17]

What happened to Thackeray in the eighteen-forties affords at least a partial explanation of his altered attitude towards the writer's task. After the break-up of his marriage he fell into a life of Bohemian bachelorhood, living in lodgings and finding his amusement in taverns, clubs, or the homes of his friends. It was a hectic, rootless existence, which he was by no means self-sufficient enough to enjoy. In June of 1845 family circumstances at last made it possible for his mother to bring his two daughters to visit him in London. They stayed only a few days, and after their departure, Thackeray wrote to his mother:

> I wish you had never come that's the truth—for I fancied myself perfectly happy until then—now I see the difference: and what a deal of the best sort of happiness it is God's will that I should lose. Whitebait dinners are all very well but—hang the buts—it is those we are always sighing after.[18]

He set his heart on re-establishing his home; and fourteen months later he realized his desire. The society of his daughters, aged nine and six, brought him to an attitude of mind quite different from that which he had displayed among his rough and sometimes raffish "companions . . . over the bottle."[19] He wrote to his mother in December, 1846:

> Now they [his daughters] are with me I am getting so fond of them that I can understand the pangs of the dear old mother who loses them. . . . Continual thoughts of them chase I don't know how many wickednesses out of my mind: Their society makes many of my old amusements seem trivial and shameful. What bounties are there of Providence in the very instincts which God gives us. . . . Remember the children are in their natural place: with their nearest friend working their natural influence: getting and giving the good let us hope, which the Divine Benevolence appointed to result from the union between parents and children.[20]

The revolution that Thackeray's reunion with his family worked in his scale of values radically altered his conception of what fiction ought to be. By good fortune the fragmentary manuscript of the early chapters of *Vanity Fair* survives in the Pierpont Morgan Library to show exactly what happened. It would appear that Thackeray began his novel early in 1845 and soon completed enough for two monthly parts. These eight chapters he wrote in his slanting hand. When Colburn and two or three other publishers refused *Pen and Pencil Sketches of English Society*, as the story was first called, Thackeray laid his manuscript temporarily aside. By March of 1846 Bradbury and Evans had accepted it; but other work intervened, and Thackeray did not return to his novel until the last months of that year. The changes that he made at this time are readily identifiable, for they were entered, perhaps at the printer's request, in his more legible upright hand.

Thackeray's revisions everywhere bear the mark of his new view of fiction. For the noncommittal *Pen and Pencil Sketches of English Society* he substituted the pregnant phrase *Vanity Fair,* in itself a judgment on the life that he was describing. Here and there in his earlier narrative, which was almost as devoid of authorial intrusion as *Barry Lyndon,* he introduced passages of moral commentary. The next to the last chapter of *Pen and Pencil Sketches of English Society,* for example, had originally been devoted entirely to Becky's first letter to Amelia from Queen's Crawley. In his revision Thackeray added six concluding paragraphs which sum up the serious and responsible view that he had come to take of novel-writing.

> And, as we bring our characters forward [he wrote], I will ask leave, as a man and a brother, not only to introduce them, but occasionally to step down from the platform, and talk about them: if they are good and kindly, to love them and shake them by the hand: if they are silly, to laugh at them confidentially in the reader's sleeve: if they are wicked and heartless, to abuse them in the strongest terms which politeness admits of.
>
> Otherwise you might fancy it was I who was sneering at the practice of devotion, which Miss Sharp finds so ridiculous; that it was I who laughed good-humouredly at the reeling old Silenus of a baronet—whereas the laughter comes from one who has no reverence except for prosperity, and no eye for anything beyond success. Such people there are living and flourishing in the world—

Faithless, Hopeless, Charityless; let us have at them, dear friends, with might and main. Some there are, and very successful too, mere quacks and fools: and it was to combat and expose such as those, no doubt, that laughter was made.[21]

Similarly, in the chapter following Thackeray inserted after his portraits of old Sir Pitt Crawley and his wife passages underlining the fashion in which each of these characters exemplifies the theme of his novel. Of Sir Pitt he wrote:

Vanity Fair—Vanity Fair! Here was a man, who could not spell, and did not care to read—who had the habits and the cunning of a boor: whose aim in life was pettifogging: who never had a taste, or emotion, or enjoyment, but what was sordid and foul: and was a dignitary of the land, and a pillar of the state. He was high sheriff, and rode in a golden coach. Great ministers and statemen courted him; and in Vanity Fair he had a higher place than the most brilliant genius or spotless virtue.[22]

As Thackeray went on from the point where his 1845 narrative ended, he was able to avoid the relatively crude and awkward patchwork of these earlier insertions. He moved with increasing ease from narrative to commentary and back again. His theme sufficiently stated, he no longer found it necessary to insist heavily on its explicit formulation. Nevertheless, he did not lose his guiding vision of the world as "Vanity Fair," and all his effects were planned to emphasize it. His letters everywhere reveal his concentration upon the ethical issues raised by the action of his novel. In July of 1847, for example, he told his mother:

Of course you are quite right about Vanity Fair and Amelia, it is mentioned in this very number. My object is not to make a perfect character or anything like it. Don't you see how odious all the people are in the book (with the exception of Dobbin)—behind whom all there lies a dark moral I hope. What I want is to make a set of people living without God in the world (only that is a cant phrase) greedy pompous mean perfectly self-satisfied for the most part and at ease about their superior virtue.[23]

And after his novel was completed, he explained to Robert Bell, who had protested against the "foul atmosphere" of Vanity Fair:

If I had put in more fresh air as you call it my object would have been defeated—It is to indicate, in cheerful terms, that we are for the most part an abominably foolish and selfish people "desperately wicked" and all eager after vanities. . . . I want to leave everybody dissatisfied and unhappy at the end of the story— we ought all to be with our own and all other stories. Good God don't I see (in that may-be cracked and warped looking glass in which I am always looking) my own weaknesses wickednesses lusts follies shortcomings? . . . We must lift up our voices about these and howl to a congregation of fools: so much at least has been my endeavour.[24]

III

Thackeray's contemporaries were profoundly impressed, as we are to-day, by "the generalizing eye, the penetrative humor, and the genial breadth of sympathy"[25] which enabled him to present convincingly the immense panorama of English life that one finds in *Vanity Fair*. No doubt these qualities in themselves suffice to explain his emergence to popularity after ten years of relative neglect. But Thackeray's novel brought him prestige as well as popularity; and this prestige derived from his capacity to judge the social scene as well as to portray it. Indeed, the conception of the novelist's responsibility which informs *Vanity Fair* was the chief factor in establishing Thackeray's contemporary reputation. It freed him from the diffidence and scoffing aloofness that had previously prevented him from giving his talent free play; and it provided him with an organizing idea, about which to arrange the wealth of impressions that he had accumulated.

The proof that Thackeray's novel earned him a position, not merely as one more accomplished entertainer of the calibre of Ainsworth, Disraeli, or Bulwer-Lytton, but as a great moralist, is not far to seek. Charlotte Brontë wrote, in dedicating the second edition of *Jane Eyre* to Thackeray:

There is a man in our own days whose words are not framed for delicate ears; who, to my thinking, comes before the great ones of society, much as the son of Imlah came before the throned Kings of Judah and Israel; and who speaks truth as deep, with a power as prophet-like and as vital. . . . I see in him an intellect profounder and more unique than his contemporaries have yet recognized; because I regard him as the first social regenerator of the day—as the very master of that working corps who would restore to rectitude the warped system of things.[26]

To-day these phrases sound almost ludicrously overstrained. But we are deficient in historical understanding if we dismiss them as merely Miss Brontë's excited way. There is abundant corroborative testimony to the powerful effect of Thackeray's novel upon its first readers, from which I cite the recollections of John Cordy Jeaffreson:

Men read those much-abused yellow pamphlets that came out month after month; and strong men, men not given to emotion, least of all to religious excitement, laid them down with tearful eyes and full hearts; and they were not a few who prayed earnestly to the Almighty for mercy and help, and rose from their knees with a determination to be men of charity.[27]

The early reviews of *Vanity Fair* everywhere reveal sluggish consciences stirred by the evidence of social corruption that Thackeray had amassed and interpreted. Harriet Martineau left *Vanity Fair* unfinished, unable to go on from "the moral disgust it occasions";[28] Miss Rigby, who persisted, declared in the *Quarterly Review* that it was "one of the most distressing books we have read for many a long year."[29] John Forster in the *Examiner* was appalled by its "exhalations of human folly and wickedness."[30] Robert Bell in *Fraser's Magazine* found it a "revolting reflex of society," which forced its readers "to look into the depths of a loathsome truth." Hogarth's "Gin Lane" did not seem to him a far-fetched comparison.[31] An anonymous reviewer in a magazine published on the continent, where the lessons of the revolutionary year 1848 loomed large for all to read, went further still. Observing that *Vanity Fair* portrays "naked and prosaic actuality which is often hideous of aspect but always true to life," he asked anxiously: "Is it advisable to raise so ruthlessly the veil which hides the rottenness pervading modern society?"[32]

IV

To inquire why Thackeray's contemporaries took *Vanity Fair* and its author so seriously is to ask in effect what was his intellectual position in his age. A modest and unassertive man, Thackeray did not regard himself as a prophet. In the words "I have no head above my eyes,"[33] he once emphatically disclaimed any capacity for abstract thought. But conceivably the very fact that his unsystematic mind found expression in attitudes rather than in theories made his opinions the more acceptable to his Victorian readers. They found in him a teacher who provided a loose but temporarily tenable synthesis of ultimately irreconcilable social standards.

This point can best be illustrated by comparing his view of fashionable society, the epitome of the small class in whose interest England was then organized and governed, with that of two fellow novelists, Disraeli and Dickens. A quarter of a century before *Vanity Fair* was written, members of the upper world hardly troubled to justify their monopoly of privilege. They displayed instead a superb disdain of conflicting interests neatly summed up in Lord Melbourne's remark that he liked the Garter, because "there was no damned merit about it." Consider, for example, Lord Orford's reply to an invitation to become President of the Norwich Bible Society in 1824:

> Sir,—I am surprised and annoyed by the contents of your letter. *Surprised,* because my well-known character should have exempted me from such an application; and *annoyed* because it compels me to have even this communication with you.
>
> I have long been addicted to the gaming table. I have lately taken to the Turf. I fear I frequently blaspheme. But I have never distributed religious tracts. All this was known to you and your society. Notwithstanding which you think me a fit person to be your President. God forgive your hypocrisy.[34]

Disraeli adopted without reserve the aristocratic attitude illustrated in the letter of this Regency grandee. Like Lockhart he thought that there was no greater pleasure than "the calm contemplation of that grand spectacle denominated 'the upper world.' It is infinitely the best of theatres, the acting is incomparably the first, the actresses the prettiest."[35] To him society was opportunity, the embodiment of the career open to the talents.

Disraeli's picture of fashionable society in *Coningsby* is cool and detached, devoid of emotional colouring or moral implications. Here is a characteristic vignette of Lord Monmouth, modelled upon the same Marquess of Hertford whom Thackeray was later to portray as Lord Steyne:

> Lord Monmouth beheld his grandson. His comprehensive and penetrating glance took in every point with a flash. There stood before him one of the handsomest youths he had ever seen, with a mien as graceful as his countenance was captivating; and his whole air breathing that freshness and ingenuousness which none so much appreciates as the used man of the world. And this was his child; the only one of his blood to whom he had been kind. It would be exaggeration to say that Lord Monmouth's heart was touched; but his good-nature effervesced, and his fine taste was deeply gratified. He perceived in an instant such a relation might be a valuable adherent; an irresistible candidate for future elections: a brilliant tool to work out the Dukedom. All these impressions and ideas, and many more, passed through the quick brain of Lord Monmouth ere the sound of Coningsby's words had seemed to cease, and long before the surrounding guests had recovered from the surprise which they had occasioned them, and which did not diminish, when Lord Monmouth, advancing, placed his arms round Coningsby with a dignity of affection that would have become Louis XIV, and then, in the high manner of the old Court, kissed him on each cheek.[36]

Disraeli is delighted by the scene and by the actors in it. Without illusions as to Monmouth's moral worth, he yet savours all the refinements of his character, and is at pains to communicate them with delicacy. "It would be exaggeration to say that Lord Monmouth's heart was touched; but his good nature effervesced and his fine taste was deeply gratified." The sentence is that of an artist who loves his subject.

In Dickens's *Little Dorrit* we find the reverse of the medal. Dickens's radicalism had been counterbalanced in his early books by a pervasive optimism; as late as *David Copperfield* the edge of his social criticism was blunted by farce. When Mrs. Waterbrook announces over the dinner table that if she has a weakness, it is Blood, Dickens intends us to be amused, not indignant. By the time that he wrote *Little Dorrit*, however, he meant mischief. The book is an attack on "the Society business"[37] as the organizing principle of the Victorian social hierarchy. Dickens shows society bowing and scraping before "the great and wonderful Merdle," a financier whose vast

operations have raised him suddenly from obscurity to celebrity.
Early in the story Dickens describes a dinner party given by the
great man:

> There were magnates from the Court and magnates from the
> City, magnates from the Commons and magnates from the Lords,
> magnates from the bench and magnates from the bar, Bishop
> magnates, Treasury magnates, Horse Guard magnates, Admiralty
> magnates—all the magnates that keep us going, and sometimes
> trip us up.
> "I am told," said Bishop magnate to Horse Guards, "that Mr.
> Merdle has made another enormous hit. They say a hundred
> thousand pounds."
> Horse Guards had heard two.
> Treasury had heard three.
> Bar, handling his persuasive double eye-glass, was by no means
> clear but that it might be four. It was one of those happy strokes
> of calculation and combination, the result of which it was difficult
> to estimate. It was one of those instances of a comprehensive
> grasp, associated with habitual luck and characteristic boldness,
> of which an age presented us but few. . . .
> Admiralty said Mr. Merdle was a wonderful man. Treasury
> said he was a new power in the country, and would be able to buy
> up the whole House of Commons. Bishop said he was glad to
> think that this wealth flowed into the coffers of a gentleman who
> was always disposed to maintain the best interests of Society.[38]

Everyone is delighted with Merdle's success, everyone expands in
its presence, except the great man himself, who is haunted by an
undefined *malaise,* by a complaint for which his physician can find
no cure. Not until Merdle has cut his throat in his bath near the
end of the novel does Dickens reveal what has troubled this idol of
"Society."

> The late Mr. Merdle's complaint had been, simply, Forgery
> and Robbery. He, the uncouth object of such widespread adula-
> tion, the sitter at great men's feasts, the roc's egg of great ladies'
> assemblies, the subduer of exclusiveness, the leveller of pride, the
> patron of patrons, the bargain driver with a Minister for Lord-
> ships of the Circumlocution Office, the recipient of more acknowl-
> edgment within some ten or fifteen years, at most, than had been

bestowed in England upon all peaceful, public benefactors, and upon all the leaders of all the Arts and Sciences, with all their works to testify for them, during two centuries at least—he, the shining wonder, the new constellation to be followed by the wise men bringing gifts, until it stopped over certain carrion at the bottom of a bath and disappeared—was simply the greatest Forger and the greatest Thief that ever cheated the gallows.[39]

The same society which delighted Disraeli bored and disgusted Dickens. Too impatient to analyse it in detail, to explore its refinements, he summed it up in terms of types and general impressions, judged it and dismissed it.

In *Vanity Fair* Thackeray steers a middle course between two extremes. Equally repugnant to him were Disraeli's amoral acceptance of the *status quo* and Dickens's destructive radicalism. His response to high life was ambivalent, his picture of it oblique. He was fascinated by the aristocratic outlook—no attitude is more often explored in his books—but he could not identify himself with it in the manner of Disraeli, for he recognized that it had become an anachronism in a prevailingly middle-class world. In describing fashionable society he took refuge in irony, which permitted him to convey at once his attraction and his repulsion, or in a professed ignorance of its ways, which made it necessary for him to rely for information on what other persons, not always reliable witnesses, had told him.

The masterly chapter entitled "Gaunt House," for example, is composed chiefly of gossip about Lord Steyne and his family communicated by sardonic old Tom Eaves, "who has no part in this history," says Thackeray, "except that he knew all the great folks in London, and the stories and mysteries of each family."[40] To complete Eaves's revelations we are accommodated with a cross-section of London opinion as to the propriety of attending Lord Steyne's entertainments:

> "Lord Steyne is really too bad," Lady Slingstone said, "but everybody goes, and of course I shall see that my girls come to no harm." "His lordship is a man to whom I owe much, everything in life," said the Right Reverend Doctor Trail, thinking that the archbishop was rather shaky; and Mrs. Trail and the young ladies would as soon have missed going to church as to one of his lordship's parties. "His morals are bad," said little Lord Southdown to

his sister, who meekly expostulated, having heard terrific legends
from her mamma with respect to the doings at Gaunt House;
"but hang it, he's got the best dry sillery in Europe!" And as for
Sir Pitt Crawley, Bart.—Sir Pitt that pattern of decorum, Sir Pitt
who had led off at missionary meetings,—he never for one moment thought of not going too. "Where you see such persons as
the Bishop of Ealing and the Countess of Slingstone, you may be
pretty sure, Jane," the baronet would say, "that *we* cannot be
wrong. The great rank and station of Lord Steyne put him in a
position to command people in our station in life. The Lord Lieutenant of a county, my dear, is a respectable man."[41]

Adopting the guise of "Rumour painted full of tongues," Thackeray
presents Lord Steyne and Gaunt House in perspective, with no less
wit and delicacy than Disraeli displays in portraying Lord Monmouth, with no more attempt at palliation than Dickens employs in
describing Merdle.

The resulting picture of high society was precisely what the intelligent Victorian reader desired. He still had, in Gladstone's phrase,
"a sneaking kindness for a lord"; but he had lost his assurance in the
essential rightness of the aristocratic system. Thackeray satisfied both
his taste and his conscience. "Thackeray's *Vanity Fair* is pathetic in
its name, and in his use of the name," Emerson wrote; "an admission
it is from a man of fashion in the London of 1850 that poor old
Puritan Bunyan was right in his perception of the London of 1650.
And yet now in Thackeray is the added wisdom, or skepticism, that,
though this be really so, he must yet live in tolerance of, and practically in homage and obedience to, these illusions."[42]

What comment on the validity of Gide's formula that "the moral
issue for the artist is not that he should present an idea that is useful
but that he should present an idea well" is suggested by the account
which I have given of Thackeray's acceptance of moral obligation
towards his readers and of the consequences of this acceptance in
his career? The hazards latent in Thackeray's conflicting views became only too evident in his later work. In 1908, when Galsworthy
published *Fraternity,* Conrad wrote to him of the novel:

> . . . before all it is the work of a moralist . . . a humanitarian
> moralist. . . . This fact which you cannot help, and which may
> lead you yet to become the Idol of the Public—if I may so express
> myself—arises as the greatest danger in the way of your art. It

may prevent the concentration of effort in one simple direction—
because your art will always be trying to assert itself against the
impulse of your moral feelings.[43]

In the eighteen-fifties Thackeray's critics increasingly urged similar
counsels upon him, but he was as incapable as Galsworthy of following such advice. And indeed, *The Virginians, Lovel the Widower* and *Philip*—whatever their other merits—oppress the reader by
their tired rehearsal of moral commonplaces. In these stories the
figure that Thackeray cuts as a moralist almost inclines one to regard
Gide's statement as axiomatic.

But a consideration of Thackeray's finer work redresses the balance. To reread *Vanity Fair, Pendennis, Esmond* and *The Newcomes* is to understand why Henry James placed Thackeray among
the novelists whom he thought of "primarily as great consciences
and great minds,"[44] why James Hannay admired in him "the broad
sagacity, sharp insight, large and tolerant liberality, which marked
him as one who was a sage as well as a story-teller, and whose stories
were valuable because he was a sage."[45] In *Vanity Fair* above all
Thackeray's acceptance of the novelist's responsibility was a lib-
erating decision that immeasurably deepened his capacity for social
judgment. The moral fervour which fills *Vanity Fair* with the ur-
gency of a fresh revelation gives it a unity and intensity attained by
few novels of comparable scope. Confronted by the complexity of
contemporary life and by general disagreement regarding ethical
presuppositions, the modern writer must no doubt leave the task of
moral judgment to his readers; but he suffers as a novelist by doing
so.

NOTES

1. Quoted by François Mauriac, *God and Mammon* (London, 1936),
   p. 58.
2. "Felix Culpa," *Commonweal*, XLVIII (July 16, 1948), p. 323.
3. *Cornhill Magazine*, XIII (January, 1866), 48.
4. *The Letters and Private Papers of William Makepeace Thackeray*,
   ed. Ray, 4 volumes (Cambridge, Mass., 1945-46), II, 258. Cited
   hereafter as *Letters*.
5. *Letters*, II, 312n.
6. *Letters and Memorials of Jane Welsh Carlyle*, ed. James Anthony
   Froude, 3 volumes (London, 1883), II, 3.

7. *Letters*, II, 333.
8. "Thackeray," *Macmillan's Magazine*, IX (February, 1864), 356.
9. *Letters Literary and Theological* (London, 1881), p. 93.
10. Rowland Grey, "Thackeray and France (With an Unpublished Thackeray Letter)," *Englishwoman*, XXXVII (May, 1918), 112-13.
11. *Letters*, II, 316.
12. *Horae Subsecivae, Third Series* (Edinburgh, 1884), p. 180.
13. "Lever's St. Patrick's Eve—Comic Politics," *Morning Chronicle*, April 3, 1845.
14. *Letters*, II, 54.
15. *Works*, ed. Saintsbury, 17 volumes (London, 1908), V, 91-92.
16. *Works*, IX, 493.
17. *Letters*, II, 282.
18. *Letters*, II, 197.
19. *Letters*, II, 210.
20. *Letters*, II, 255.
21. *Works*, XI, 96.
22. *Works*, XI, 102-03.
23. *Letters*, II, 309.
24. *Letters*, II, 423-24.
25. H. D. Trail, *The New Fiction and Other Essays on Literary Subjects* (London, 1897), p. 169.
26. Two volumes (Oxford, 1931), I, ix-x.
27. *Novels and Novelists from Elizabeth to Victoria*, 2 volumes (London, 1858), II, 279.
28. *Autobiography*, ed. Maria Webster, 2 volumes (Boston, 1877), II, 60.
29. "Vanity Fair—and Jane Eyre," LXXXIV (December, 1848), 155.
30. "Vanity Fair," July 22, 1848, 468.
31. "Vanity Fair," XXXVIII (September, 1848), 321-22.
32. Quoted from the *Magazin für die Litteratur des Auslandes* in the Readers' Classics edition of *Vanity Fair* (Bath, 1919), p. 61.
33. Reported by George Curtis, *Harper's Magazine*, VIII (May, 1854), 840.
34. Quoted by Sir Algernon West, *Recollections*, 2 volumes (London, 1899), I, 26-27.
35. Quoted by Andrew Lang, *The Life and Letters of John Gibson Lockhart*, 2 volumes (London, 1897), II, 82-83.
36. Book Four, chapter 6; *Works*, 12 volumes (London, 1927), VIII, 195-96.
37. *Letters of Charles Dickens*, ed. Walter Dexter, 3 volumes (London, 1938), II, 766.
38. Book the First, chapter 21; *Complete Works* (London, 1901-02), XVI, 300-01.

39. Book the Second, chapter 25; *Complete Works*, XVI, 835.
40. *Works*, XI, 90.
41. *Works*, XI, 597.
42. *Journals*, ed. E. W. Emerson and W. E. Forbes, 10 volumes (London, 1913), VIII, 113-14.
43. Quoted by H. V. Marrot, *Life and Letters of John Galsworthy* (London, 1935), p. 229.
44. *French Poets and Novelists* (London, 1878), p. 113.
45. *Brief Memoir of the Late Mr. Thackeray* (Edinburgh, 1864), p. 22.

GEORG LUKÁCS

Making History Private: *Henry Esmond*

. . . [The] tendency to make history private is a general characteristic of the nascent decline of great realism. It is true, naturally,
of the contemporary novel as well, even where important contemporary events have a direct bearing on the action. The change in the
relation of such events to the private experiences of the main characters not only alters their function in the action itself, but also
their appearance in the whole structure of the novel's world. The
classical historical novel—and following it the great realistic contemporary novel—chooses central figures who despite their "middle
of the road" personalities, which we have analysed at length, are
nevertheless suited to stand at the meeting-point of great social-
historical collisions. The historical crises are direct components of
the individual destinies of the main characters and accordingly form
an integral part of the action itself. In this way the individual and
the social-historical are inseparably connected in regard to both
characterization and action.

From *The Historical Novel,* trans. from the German by Hannah and Stanley
Mitchell (London: Merlin Press, 1962; Boston: Beacon Press, 1963), pp. 200-
206. Copyright © 1962, 1963 by Merlin Press and Beacon Press. Reprinted by
permission of the author, translators, and publishers. This extract concludes
the section entitled "Making Private, Modernization and Exoticism," from a
division of the book entitled "The Historical Novel and the Crisis of Bourgeois
Realism." (Editor's title.)

266

This manner of portrayal is simply the artistic expression of that genuine historicism—the conception of history as the destiny of the people—which motivated the classics. The more this historicism breaks down, the more everything social appears simply as *"milieu,"* as picturesque atmosphere or immobile background etc., against which supposedly purely private histories are unfolded. Generalization takes the form both of making the main figures "sociological" average men and of inserting "symbols" from outside into the characterization and action. Obviously the greater the social events, the more visible their historical interest, the more inevitable is this kind of portrayal. The portrayal of the outbreak of the Franco-Prussian war in Zola's *Nana* and of the historical events in *Marie Grubbe* are fundamentally no different in their general conception, however much they may differ technically and stylistically.

There is perhaps even more to be learned in this respect from the important English realists of the transition period, for Maupassant and Jacobsen belong already to a more advanced stage of this development. We wish briefly to take the example of Thackeray. Thackeray is an outstanding critical realist. He has deep ties with the best traditions of English literature, with the great social canvases of the eighteenth century, which he treated at length in several interesting critical studies. Consciously, he has no interest in separating the historical from the social-critical novel, that is in turning the historical novel into a genre of its own, which was generally the objective result of this development. However, he does not base himself on the classical form of the historical novel, that is on Scott; instead, he attempts to apply the traditions of the eighteenth century social novel to a new type of historical novel. We have said before that eighteenth century historical events were included in the English realist novel particularly in Fielding and Smollett, however only insofar as they came into direct contact with the personal lives of the heroes; thus from the standpoint of the general conception and artistic tendencies of this period, only episodically and never really affecting the chief problems of the novels.

Thackeray, then, consciously takes over this manner of portrayal in his historical novels, but his outlook and artistic aim are quite different from those of the eighteenth century realists. *The approach of the latter towards historicism* grew in a natural way out of their social-critical, realist tendencies. It was one of the many steps towards that realistic conception of history, of social and natural life, which reached its apex in Scott or Pushkin. In the case of Thackeray this *return* to the style and structure of the novels of the eighteenth century stems from a quite different ideological cause, from a deep and bitter disillusionment with the nature of politics, with the relations between social and political life in his own time. This disillusionment expresses itself satirically. By resuming the style of the eighteenth century Thackeray wishes to expose contemporary apologetics.

He, therefore, sees the dilemma in the portrayal of historical events as a choice between public pathos and private manners, the glorification of the one or the realistic depiction of the other. Thus when his hero, Henry Esmond, telling his own story—at the turn of the seventeenth to eighteenth centuries—polemically counters the official histories with the novels of Fielding, when in a discussion with Addison he defends the rights of realism in describing war against poetic embellishment, his language—the language of the memoir—captures the tone of the period beautifully, yet at the same time it expresses Thackeray's own artistic convictions. The basis of this style is the exposure of false heroism, in particular the reputed heroism fostered by historical legend. Esmond speaks of this, too, very vividly and finely: "What spectacle is more august than that of a great king in exile? Who is more worthy of respect than a brave man in misfortune? Mr. Addison has painted such a figure in his noble piece of *Cato*. But suppose fugitive Cato fuddling himself at the tavern with a wench on his knee, a dozen faithful and tipsy companions of defeat, and a landlord calling out for his bill; and the dignity of misfortune is straightway lost." Thackeray requires this exposure in order to strip history of its periwig, in order to deny that English and French history took place only at the courts of Windsor and Versailles.

Of course, it is Esmond who says all this and not Thackeray himself, and the novel is not meant to be an objective picture of the time, but simply the hero's autobiography. But apart from the fact that this relationship between private manners and historical events is very similar, say, to that in *Vanity Fair,* with a writer as important and conscious as Thackeray the composition of *Henry Esmond* cannot be accidental. The memoir is an appropriate form for Thackeray's exposure of pseudo-greatness. Everything can be seen from the proximity of everyday private life and, shown in this microscopic way, the false pathos of the artificial, self-imagined hero collapses. And this is what is intended. The hero has seen Louis XIV in old age. Louis, says Esmond, was perhaps a hero for a book, for a statue, for a mural, "but what more than a man for Madame Maintenon, or the barber who shaved him, or Monsieur Fagon, his surgeon?" Proximity destroys the alleged greatness of Marlborough, the Stuart Pretender and many others. And when every great man swindle of history has been exposed, there remains just the honesty of simply, slightly above average men capable of real sacrifice like the hero himself.

This picture is remarkably consistent. But is it a real picture of the time, as Thackeray intended? Thackeray's answer to his own dilemma is right enough. But the dilemma itself is narrow and wrong. There is a third way: what, in fact, the classical historical novel does. Admittedly, the epoch following the "Glorious Revolution" and ending with the establishment of the House of Hanover on the throne of England is certainly not one of the most heroic of periods; especially as regards the behaviour and activity of the supporters of Stuart Restoration. But we recall that Scott, too, had portrayed these Stuart restoration attempts (in *Waverley* and, for a later period, in *Rob Roy* and *Redgauntlet*), and had neither idealized nor indeed spared either the dynasty or its followers. Nevertheless, the picture of history he produced was grand, dramatic and rife with deep conflict in every phase. The secret of these grand dimensions is easily discoverable. Scott gives a broad and *objective* picture both of the historical forces which lead to the Stuart rebellions and of those which inevitably foredoom them. At the centre of this picture are the Scottish clans, driven to desperation by economic and social circumstances and misled by adventurers. The fate of the Pretender himself is tragi-comic in Scott, the fate of his English adherents either comic or pathetic. The latter are dissatisfied with the Hanoverian régime, yet keep quiet because they are too cowardly and irresolute to act, because they do not dare jeopardize their material well-being; because the growth of capitalism in England has levelled out the former distinctions between feudal and capitalist land-ownership. But since the background to the action is the real suffering and real heroism (however untimely and misguided) of a people, the events lose all their trivial, mean and haphazard qualities, all that is purely individual and private about them.

Thackeray, however, does not see the people. He reduces his story to the intrigues of the upper classes. Of course, he knows perfectly well that these trivialities are confined to the class he describes and tell us nothing of the real historical process. It is not by chance that every so often the Cromwell age, the heroic period of the English people, casts its shadow in discussions. But this period seems to have wholly disappeared, and the life which is described is given over entirely to trivial and private goings-on. The people's attitude to what happens is never revealed. Yet it was at this time that those who had fought the battles of the Civil War, above all the middle farmers, yeomanry and city plebeians were undergoing economic and moral ruin as a result of the tempestuous development of capitalism. Only much later did the new heroes, the Luddites and Chartists, arise from the soil made fertile by their blood. Of this tragedy, which is the real basis of the tragi-comedies and comedies occurring "on top" Thackeray sees nothing.

But he thereby dispels historical objectivity, and the more compellingly he motivates his characters psychologically, the subtler this private psychology, the more haphazard it all appears in an historical perspective. The psychology is not wrong, on the contrary it very subtly shows the accidental nature of the political standpoints of the characters. But this accidentality can only appear truly false, if placed within an objective class context where it becomes a factor of historical necessity. Scott's Waverley also joins the Stuart Rebellion by accident; but he is simply there as a foil to those for whom the revolt is a social-historical necessity. The perspective in which Thackeray shows Marlborough, however, is purely private. His hero, he says, has become a bitter enemy rather than an enthusiastic follower of Marlborough simply because of bad treatment at a levée. The resulting caricature is such that Thackeray himself feels compelled to counter his own subjectivism with supplementary corrections and notes to his memoirs. But these corrections lessen the onesidedness only theoretically, they cannot give the figure of Marlborough any objective-historical relief.

This subjectivism degrades all the historical figures who appear in the novel. We see only the "all-too-human" side of Swift, so that we should have to regard him as a petty intriguer and careerist, if we did not have a different picture of him from *his own* works. But even characters whom Esmond describes with obvious sympathy, such as Steele and Addison, the well-known writers of the epoch, are objectively degraded, because their personalities reveal no more than the normal, sociable habits of everyday private life. What made them into important representatives of the epoch, into ideologists of big social changes is excluded from the story by Thackeray's general conception. The influence of their journal *The Spectator,* which extended over the whole of educated bourgeois Europe, is sufficiently well-known in both history and the history of literature, as well as the fact that it was largely due to the use of everyday events as a basis for arguing and demonstrating the new, triumphant morality of the rising bourgeoisie. *The Spectator* turns up in *Henry Esmond,* too; the hero uses his personal friendship with the editors in order to ridicule the frivolous coquetry of the woman with whom he is in love and so exert a beneficial moral influence upon her. No doubt such articles did appear in the journal. But to reduce its historical role to private episodes of this kind means, objectively, the distortion of history, its degradation to the level of the trivial and the private.

Thackeray undoubtedly suffered as a result of this discrepancy. In another historical novel (*The Virginians*) he gives voice to his dissatisfaction. He argues that it is not possible for the present-day writer to show his characters in the context of their professional lives, their actual work etc. The writer has to confine himself to the passions—love or jealousy—on the one hand and to outward forms of social life (in the superficial "worldly" sense) on the other. Thackeray herewith states very tersely the decisive failing of the period of the nascent decline of realism—though without understanding the real social causes and their artistic consequences. He does not see this failing as the result of a narrowed-down and one-sided conception of man, of the fact that characters have come adrift from the main currents of popular life and hence from the really important problems and forces of the age.

The classic realist writers were able to portray these sides of human life poetically and plastically, because in their works all social forces still took the form of human relationships. An important reversal such as the threatened bankruptcy of old Osbaldiston in *Rob Roy* enables Scott to draw from the social-human drama of the situation the various commercial practices of the Glasgow merchants without any ponderous descriptions of *milieu.* In Tolstoy, the different attitudes to professional army life on the part of Andrei Bolkonsky, Nikolai Rostov, Boris Drubetskoy, Berg etc., the differing views on agriculture and serfdom on the part of old and young Bolkonsky are organic integral components of the story, and of the human and psychological development of these characters.

As attitudes towards society and history become more and more private, so such vividly seen connections vanish. Professional life appears dead; everything human is submerged under the desert sands of capitalist prose. The later naturalists—even Zola—seize upon the prose and place it at the centre of literature, but they only fix and perpetuate its withered features, limiting their picture to a description of the "thing-like" *milieu*. What Thackeray, with the right instinct, though from a false situation, declared unportrayable, they leave as it is, replacing portrayals by mere descriptions—supposedly scientific, and brilliant in detail—of things and thing-relationships.

Thackeray is too conscious a realist, too strongly tied to the traditions of true realism for him to take this naturalist way out. Hence he escapes back beyond the classical and for him unattainable form of the historical novel to an artificial renewal of the style of the English Enlightenment. This archaism, however, can only lead to problematic results, as it does elsewhere. The quest for a style leads to stylization, bringing the weaknesses in Thackeray's general conception of social life garishly to the surface, stressing them much more strongly than he would consciously intend. His only wish is to expose false greatness, pseudo-heroism, yet the effect of his stylization, as we have seen, is to show every historical figure, whatever his importance, in a disparaging and sometimes thoroughly destructive light. He wishes to counter this with the genuine, inner nobility of simple morality, but his stylization turns his positive characters into tedious, insufferable paragons of virtue. True, the literary traditions of the eighteenth century lend cohesion to his works and this has a beneficial effect at a time when naturalism is beginning to break up narrative form. Still, this cohesion is only a stylistic one, it does not touch the depths of the portrayal; hence at most it can only cover up the "problematic" which arises from the making private of history, but not solve it.

U. C. KNOEPFLMACHER

On *Adam Bede*

The Value of Hindsight: Adam's Fortunate Fall

In *Adam Bede,* as in the *Scenes of Clerical Life,* the past imparts
meaning to the uncertainties of the present and the future. Though
Mrs. Poyser intimidates her servant with a "Dantean picture of her
future" and later causes little Tommy to fear "the dreadful picture
she had made of the possible future" ([all citations are to the Cab-
inet edition, Edinburgh, N.D.] chap. 6, p. 109; chap. 20, p. 344),
her dire predictions are always founded on past experience. Adam
Bede, likewise, on catching his "imagination leaping forward" checks
his tendency to make "arrangements for an uncertain future." Experience and tradition have given him principles which he regards as
"knowledge to be acted on" (chap. 19, p. 316). He is therefore unlike Mr. Craig, the gardener, whose "calkilations" lead him to make
weather forecasts as faulty as those made by the astronomer in *Ras-
selas.* More important, Adam is unlike Arthur and Hetty whose
irresponsibility leads them to deny the "tyrannous memories" of the

From *George Eliot's Early Novels: The Limits of Realism* (Berkeley and Los
Angeles: University of California Press, 1968), pp. 108-27. Copyright 1968 by
the Regents of the University of California. Reprinted by permission of the
Regents of the University of California and the author. The selection com-
prises the last two parts of a four-part chapter entitled "Pastoralism and the
Justification of Suffering: *Adam Bede.*"

past (chap. 29, p. 32). Yet he will nonetheless be drawn into the tragedy created by Hetty.

Like Milton's Eve, Hetty wants to cast her past life behind her; but her "narrow bit of an imagination" only leads her to make "ill-defined pictures" of the future (chap. 15, p. 230). Whereas Dinah's sympathetic intuition is based on her awareness of biblical history, Hetty's mind has never adopted "a single Christian idea or Christian feeling" (chap. 37, p. 144). She is guided only by her current sensual responses. In *Paradise Lost*, Eve's appetite is aroused "by the smell/So savory of that Fruit" as she approaches the Tree of Knowledge (IX, 740-741). Similarly, Hetty is stimulated by the "sweet languid odours of the garden at the Chase" where she will lose her innocence (chap. 13, 202). Eve wants to be immortal, to rise in station. She fancies herself heightened "through expectation high / Of knowledge, nor was God-head from her thought" (IX, 789–790). Hetty, who will later crave "the means of living as long as possible" (chap. 37, p. 139), also flutters between "memory and dubious expectation" as she passes the gates of the forbidden Fir-Tree Grove (chap. 13, p. 200):

> That was the foreground of Hetty's picture; behind it lay a bright hazy something—days that were not to be as the other days of her life had been. It was as if she had been wooed by a river-god, who might at any time take her to his wondrous halls below a watery heaven. [Chap. 13, p. 202.]

Eve indulges in a pagan worship of the tree of which she has eaten. Arthur mythologizes the wood in which he seduces Hetty as a "sacred grove" immune to time:

> His arm is stealing round the waist again, it is tightening its clasp; he is bending his face nearer and nearer to the round cheek, his lips are meeting those pouting child-lips, and for a long moment time has vanished. He may be a shepherd in Arcadia for aught he knows, he may be the first youth kissing the first maiden, he may be Eros himself, sipping the lips of Psyche—it is all one. [Chap. 13, p. 204.]

But Hetty is not a Keatsian goddess; the stasis of this garden is but a figment of Arthur's imagination. The novelist's mythological references are every bit as ironic as those Milton uses to describe Adam and Eve's lovemaking after the Fall. If Adam and Eve soon feel ashamed in their nakedness, Arthur, too, becomes uncomfortable, suddenly conscious that "something bitter had begun to mingle itself with the fountain of sweets." Adam and Eve are reminded of God's rule; Arthur is reminded of time. He pulls out his watch and wonders "how late it is." He hopes that his watch is too fast. It is later than he thinks.

In *Paradise Lost,* man's loss of innocence is momentous: all Nature groans, and time is born. In *Adam Bede,* the repercussions are less earthshaking. Still, Hetty's crime will alter the world around her; Loamshire life will never be the same. Social bonds are to be broken: Adam Bede and Martin Poyser will find, contrary to their own predictions, that the young squire has made their bread bitter to them. The bonds of family and friendship are violated: the Poysers feel disgraced by their niece, and the rector regrets his blind trust in Arthur. The microcosm George Eliot has created becomes as disturbed as Milton's gigantic universe. The fall of Adam and Eve leads to the murder of Abel, their son; Arthur must share the blame for the murder of his child. In each case, error could have been avoided and "tomorrow would have been a life hardly conscious of a yesterday" (chap. 12, pp. 193–194). Yet, both authors want characters and readers to be conscious of this yesterday, if truth is to come out of error and faith out of despair.

Hetty's crime forces Adam to reconsider his confident belief in an ordered world. He questions "if there's a just God" at all (chap. 41, p. 203). An idealized portrait of Robert Evans, George Eliot's father, he is more sinned against than sinning. But, like Milton's more culpable Adam, he too must overcome despair by recognizing the paradox of a fortunate fall. For Milton, this recognition is based on Adam's understanding of the mercy promised by Christ; for George Eliot, it is predicated on Adam's acceptance of the creed of love which Ludwig Feuerbach had attributed to his Man of Sorrows. Milton's Son of God identifies himself with Adam on recognizing the "contrition in his heart" (XI, 27); similarly, Adam Bede is elevated as soon as his heart leads his imagination. In *The Essence of Christianity,* Feuerbach had asserted:

> Christianity is distinguished from other religions by this, that in other religions the heart and imagination are divided, in Christianity they coincide. Here the imagination does not wander, left

to itself; it follows the leadings of the heart; it describes a circle, whose center is feeling . . . in brief, it has, at least generally, a practical concentric tendency, not a vagrant, merely poetic one. . . . With the Orientals, with the Greeks, imagination, untroubled by the wants of the heart, revelled in the enjoyment of earthly splendour and glory; in Christianity it descended from the palace of the gods into the abode of poverty, where only want rules,—it humbled itself under the sway of the heart.[1]

It is in the "abode of poverty," his narrow chamber at Stoniton, that Adam Bede becomes capable of joining the heart and imagination in the fashion of Feuerbach's Christ. Hetty's trial has forced him to "look back on all the previous years as if they had been a dim sleepy existence" (chap. 42, p. 209). So far, he has shown the "practical" imagination Feuerbach describes: " 'There's nothing but what's bearable as long as a man can work,' he said to himself: 'the natur o' things doesn't change, though it seems as if one's life was nothing but change. The square o' four is sixteen, and you must lengthen your lever in proportion to your weight'" (chap. 11, p. 171). But Adam had lacked "fellow-feeling with weakness that errs in spite of foreseen consequences" (chap. 19, p. 316). Sure of his own course, he had been intolerant of his father's failings. Rejecting his mother's solicitous offers of food, he had worked on the coffin that Thias was to have finished, rigidly fixing his thoughts on "the sad present and probably sad future." But Adam had been unaware of that future's immediacy; only after he found his drowned father the next morning did his memory check his former harshness: "Adam's mind rushed back over the past in a flood of relenting and pity" (chap. 4, p. 76).

Now, at Stoniton, with a watch before him, "as if he were counting his long minutes," Adam rejects the food proffered by Bartle Massey. The "brave active man" feels himself like a Samson blinded by Delilah, powerless to contemplate "irremediable evil." His father's death so far only has taught him the "alphabet" of the lesson he is about to learn, namely, that men must share the outward consequences of the errors committed by others, as well as their "inward suffering" (chap. 19, p. 316). At first, Adam is conscious only of his own helplessness. Soon, however, he sees his own lot in relation to that of others through Bartle's vivid description of Hetty's misery, her uncle's shame, and the rector's charity. His imagination finally follows the leadings of the heart: "We hand folks over to God's mercy, and show none ourselves. I used to be hard sometimes: I'll never be hard again. I'll go, Massey—I'll go with you." By accepting the cup of wine and the loaf of bread pushed on him by the school-teacher who is himself a sufferer, Adam becomes a celebrant in George Eliot's religion of humanity. The new Adam and "the Adam Bede of former days" have at last become one (chap. 42, p. 214).

Adam still must forgive Hetty and her seducer in order to signify his new-found compassion. But he has been initiated "into a new state." It is Arthur who now must be made sadder and wiser. Possessed of the "vagrant" fancy that George Eliot, like Feuerbach, dislikes, he must be confronted with the "concentric tendency" that will end the wanderings of his mind. Adam has been renovated through his acceptance of the yoke of suffering; Arthur, however, informed of his grandfather's death, envisions a "renovated life" without sorrow. He bursts out of his room and gallops to Loamshire, yielding to his habitual tendency of "speculating what might happen in the future" (chap. 16, p. 259). With consummate irony, George Eliot follows the new squire on his ride from Liverpool. His thoughts are as panoramic as the countryside; though "not quite at ease about the past" (chap. 44, p. 228), Arthur confidently charts a future without Hetty.

Anticipating a new meeting with the girl, Arthur orders his thoughts. He assures himself of his present chastening and contemplates his possible reactions on seeing Hetty once again: "It was the exaggerating effect of imagination that made his heart still beat a little more quickly at the thought of her. When he saw the little thing again as she really was, as Adam's wife, at work quite prosaically in her new home, he should perhaps wonder at the possibility of his past feelings. Thank heaven it had turned out so well" (chap. 44, p. 230). Arthur's precarious manipulation of the future recalls his rationalization on deserting Hetty: "She would owe the advantage of his care for her in future years to the sorrow she had incurred now. So good comes out of evil. Such is the beautiful arrangement of things!" (chap. 29, p. 36). But his airy anticipations are dashed to pieces when a second letter informs him of Hetty's trial. Only now does he see her "as she really was." And, more important, he is also forced to see himself correctly for the first time. On his way to Hayslope, he had hoped that "his real life was beginning." His real life *has* begun, but it is a life that will be spent in recollection, shaded by guilt. The disparager of Wordsworth has become one of the outcasts of *Lyrical Ballads*.

For George Eliot, as for Wordsworth, memory lends meaning to the present. But the temporal ironies of *Adam Bede* are closer to Milton than to Wordsworth. Just as Satan's magnificent taunts are completely undermined by our having witnessed, beforehand, the very outcome of the archangel's defiance, so are Arthur's intentions to "show the Loamshire people what a fine country gentleman he was" presented only after we have already been apprised of their futility. The distortion in time allows the reader to exercise hindsight, to perceive that the characters cannot halt the sequence of events which they have unleashed. In chapter thirty-nine, "The Tidings," the novelist plays with the incompleteness of both Adam's and the rector's knowledge. A messenger is speaking to Mr. Irwine, and Adam is asked to wait. Staring absently "at the clock on the opposite wall," he becomes engrossed in his own thoughts: "he could not care about other people's business" (chap. 39, pp. 175, 176). Yet their business proves to be his very own. The rector has just been informed of Hetty's pregnancy, crime, and capture; he is pained to think that Adam is about to confess having fathered Hetty's child. Adam, however, thinking that Hetty has joined Arthur, has come to identify her seducer. Skillfully, George Eliot plays with each man's ignorance of what the other man knows. Adam's allusion to Arthur staggers Mr. Irwine: "No, Adam, no—don't say it, for God's sake!" Yet Adam completes his revelation. The rector, now in possession of the total truth we have already suspected, makes his own revelation: Hetty has been seized for child-murder. Adam's disbelief echoes that of the clergyman: "It isn't possible. She never had a child" (chap. 39, pp. 178, 181). Adam is forced to review his past relationship with his intended bride, to reject his false interpretation of her motives in wanting to marry him. The rector likewise must recall his earlier fastidiousness in intruding on Arthur's secret: "He saw the whole history now by that terrible illumination which the present sheds back upon the past" (chap. 39, p. 180). Adam becomes bent on revenge against Arthur; but Mr. Irwine knows what has to be done: "there are others to think of, and act for, besides yourself. . . . I expect it from your strength of mind, Adam—from your sense of duty to God and man—that you will try to act as long as action can be of any use" (p. 185).

The rector's words introduce the somewhat melancholy creed that

Adam and Dinah will ultimately adopt. Pain must be transformed into sympathy, and sympathy into action. Adam likes to read about Moses in the Old Testament because, as he puts it, "He carried a hard business well through, and died when other folks were going to reap the fruits: a man must have courage to look at life so, and think what'll come of it after he's dead and gone" (chap. 50, p. 298).[2] Even Dinah the spiritualist knows that men can "live only a moment at a time" (chap. 3, p. 51). Adam and Dinah come to bear an "easy yoke" with "steadfast patience."[3] They learn "to strengthen each other in all labour, to rest on each other in all sorrow, to minister to each other in all pain, to be one with each other in silent unspeakable memories at the moment of the last parting" (chap. 54, p. 369). Labor, sorrow, pain, and death: Adam and Dinah must be allowed to retain their earthly paradise, for in George Eliot's view there can be no "happier life" such as that vouchsafed, in another world, to the couple which Milton had banned east of Eden.

Adam thus finds a way of bridging past and future through his Carlylean gospel of work. *Past and Present* ends with a poetic salvo:

> The future hides in it
> Good hap and sorrow;
> We press still thorow,
> Nought that abides in it
> Daunting us,—onward.

Adam the carpenter also presses onward. He is not a historical figure like those magnified in *On Heroes*; his actions are less imposing than those of Tennyson's forward-looking Ulysses. Yet he is celebrated for his Puritan belief in salvation through work: like Carlyle's ineloquent "man of practice" or the Telemachus who civilizes the Ithacans, he brings stability and direction to the social order. Adam promises Arthur that he will carry out the improvements which the squire had wanted to introduce: "It's all I've got to think of now— to do my work well, and make the world a bit better place for them as can enjoy it" (chap. 48, p. 277). Arthur—a follower of the "undivine Ignavia," Idleness—has not been a "valiant Abdiel, found faithful still."[4] In *Adam Bede,* as in *Past and Present,* it is up to the man of practice whose heart is "full of sorrow, of unspoken sadness, seriousness,"[5] to regenerate the flowery world that others must vacate.

The Dilemma of Hetty Sorrel

The determined Adam becomes the vehicle for the novelist's attempt to reconcile the discrepant realities of a material and a moral order. In a chapter entitled "The Reconciliation of Realism and Moralism," Bernard J. Paris states that George Eliot demanded that all her characters view reality scientifically but that, at the same time, she recognized that a purely objective view of reality could provide no morality or sense of purpose. Hence, though rejecting "the subjective approach as a means of arriving at truth," she also regarded it as "the only way of comprehending the significance of human values." Mr. Paris continues: "Her procedure is to view the cosmos first objectively, as it is presented by science, and then, without losing sight of its true nature, to seek its moral implications."[6]

Mr. Paris' statement about George Eliot's general intentions certainly applies to *Adam Bede*, where she tried, far more arduously than in her three *Scenes of Clerical Life*, to create a "cosmos" containing both natural and moral laws. Yet intentions are not necessarily achievements: *Adam Bede* is hardly free from the serious difficulties which this philosophical novelist met throughout her career in her desire to be faithful to two essentially opposed criteria of truth. Though far less crude than in her *Scenes*, these difficulties are quite palpable in her first full-length novel. The combination of "realism" and moralism did not come as easily as Mr. Paris' statement would suggest; George Eliot herself complained in the novel's seventeenth chapter that "Falsehood is so easy, truth so difficult." In *Adam Bede*, that "falsity, which despite one's best efforts, there is reason to dread," manifests itself in two ways: in the narrator's ambivalence towards the "Nature" whose sway and power he interprets and in the disproportionate castigation of Hetty Sorrel. It is in her characterization of the latter that George Eliot seriously infringes on the artistic "quality of truthfulness" that she maintains so superbly through most of the novel.

Adam Bede is ruled by a power as absolute as Milton's God. "Nature," the narrator informs us, knits men together "by muscle and bone, and divides us by the subtler web of our brains; blends yearning and repulsion; and ties our heartstrings to beings that jar us at every moment" (chap. 4, p. 55). This Nature stamps the personality of all men (chap. 12, p. 186) and "has a language of her own, which she uses with strict veracity" (chap. 15, p. 228). Those who dare to "extract the very opposite of her real meaning" (p. 229) will suffer for their mistakes; even those who submit to her buffets soon learn, as small children do, "not to expect that our hurts will be made much of" (chap. 27, p. 5). Though equally harsh and demanding, Milton's God had been just; moreover, His justice was tempered by the Son's mercy. By comparison, the exacting Nature whose ways George Eliot's narrator tries to justify seems capricious and indifferent. It shows as little awareness of love as that power which Tennyson had depicted in the earlier portions of *In Memoriam*.

The novelist's trust in love and goodness consequently becomes a check, a defense, against this unperturbed temporal power. Like Dinah, the narrator must plead that we trust intuitions: "I am of the opinion that love is a great and beautiful thing too; and if you agree with me, the smallest signs of it will not be chips and sawdust to you: they will rather be like those little words, 'light' and 'music,' stirring the long-winding fibres of your memory, and enriching your present with your most precious past" (chap. 50, p. 311). But Nature herself yields few such signs. She remains unsentimental. As in "Mr. Gilfil's Love-Story," the landscape is unmoved by the "blighting sorrow" that can befall man. It reveals no omens to those who would be guided by it: "For if it be true that Nature at certain moments seems charged with a presentiment of one individual lot, must it not also be true that she seems unmindful, unconscious of another?" (chap. 27, p. 4.)

It is noteworthy that, in the novel's scheme, these opposing moods of a two-faceted Nature should correspond exactly to the figures of Dinah and Hetty. Dinah, capable of "presentiment," always cares for the lot of her fellow men; Hetty remains so "unmindful" and "unconscious" of others that, in her instinct to survive, she rids herself of her own child as soon as it is born. Both are incomplete halves. In chapter fifteen, where George Eliot contrasts the two women, she comes close to explicitly allegorizing them by calling them "higher" and "lower nature," respectively (p. 240). Dinah, she implies, can be made whole again "by a good deal of hard experience"; but Hetty must remain undeveloped and incomplete. Dinah can give up "the art of vision" and readjust her sights by taking Hetty's place in Adam's material world. Hetty, however, will remain blind. Throughout the novel, the girl whom Arthur idealizes as

Psyche is uncomprehending and devoid of soul. Dinah's "treble tones"—like Milly Barton's deathbed perception of angelic music—are meant to signify the awareness of a higher rhythm than that which punctuates the purely physical world. Hetty, on the other hand, is noted for her "limited range of music." Her cousin's "sweet clear voice" is irritating to her, "mingling with her own peevish vexation like music with jangling chains" (p. 238). Far more than Arthur, Hetty is chained to the sensory world.

Beyond her brief confession to Dinah, there is no evidence that Hetty ever understands the full import of her actions. Even the donkey-like Bessy Cranage, that other recusant who is so slow and unresponsive, is declared to be Hetty's superior "in the matter of feeling" (chap. 5, p. 415). Arthur's rationalizations are always treated with ironic understanding; he is tolerated as a well meaning, if foolish, young man. But Hetty is indicted from the start; even her initial innocence, we are told, has a "false air" about it (chap. 7, p. 122). The hardness which Mrs. Poyser has noticed in her niece comes to the fore during Hetty's flight: "A hard and even fierce look had come in the eyes, though their lashes were as long as ever, and they had all their dark brightness. And the cheek was never dimpled with smiles now. It was the same rounded pouting, childish prettiness, but with all love and belief in love departed from it—the sadder for its beauty, like that wondrous Medusa-face, with the passionate, passionless lips" (chap. 37, p. 145). Unlike Caterina or Maggie Tulliver, Hetty learns nothing from her flight. The author's pretended pity for this seventeen-year old child introduces the only discordant notes in the novel: only a few lines after the narrator has professed that his "heart bleeds for her as I see her toiling along on weary feet," George Eliot makes sure to remind us that Hetty's "objectless" pilgrimage is still "apart from all love." The girl clings to life instinctively, "only as the hunted wounded brute clings to it" (p. 153).

Yet Hetty is denied even the good instincts of a beast. Though repeatedly linked to animals throughout the novel, these associations are never in her favor. Arthur pretends to go to the Hall Farm in order "to look at the whelps Poyser is keeping for me" (chap. 5, p. 90), though he really wants to see his tenant's niece. She, by not keeping his own "whelp," will later belie Arthur's intention to bring about a "better practice of husbandry" (chap. 24, p. 400). The birth of a litter of "unnecessary babbies" to Bartle Massey's bitch Vixen, causes her misogynist master to inveigh against the uselessness of all the human laws devised to deal with women ever since Eve's fall. Yet the laws which Vixen follows are natural: she is as tender to her pups as to the master who has rescued her from drowning; her "conscience" is "all run to milk" (chap. 2, pp. 359, 370). Hetty, however, is devoid of conscience. She is so narcissistic that she denies the most basic instincts of motherhood; she kisses her own limbs before giving birth to her child and then promptly looks for a spot to drown the unwanted "babby." After the infant dies of exposure and starvation, she is found by a peasant, with a "big piece of bread on her lap" (chap. 43, p. 222).

Some critics still insist, after the manner of Leslie Stephen, that Hetty is "thoroughly charming."[7] If so, her charm is the perverse result of George Eliot's excessive efforts to denigrate her character. For her creator has made this unnatural child of nature far too repulsive. The only explanations advanced to account for the homely Marian Evans' treatment of beautiful Hetty Sorrel have been biographical surmises: "It is almost as though Hetty's very prettiness is scored up as a bad mark against her."[8] It is true that, as the landlady in Windsor remarks, "It 'ud have been a good deal better for her if she'd been uglier and had more conduct" (chap. 36, p. 134). But ugliness is not necessarily a safeguard against misconduct. Some other critics have surmised, that George Eliot used this pretty, but dumb creature to chastise herself for her own sexual lapses.[9] Yet Hetty's beauty also serves a far more explicit function: the narrator repeatedly suggests that the girl's loveliness is analogous to that of her physical surroundings. Loamshire needs the "image of a great agony" to stir men into superior feelings that can find no ready source in nature. Hetty, whose surname corresponds to the plant which in "Mr. Gilfil's Love-Story" had been a part of the natural cycle so impervious to Tina's suffering, is forced by her creator to wear a crown of thorns. Unlike Dinah, she has refused to "vibrate in the least under a touch that fills others with a tremulous rapture of quivering agony" (chap. 9, p. 141). She must be made to suffer.

The motives for George Eliot's inclemency are hardly to be found in any personal resentment against her creation's beauty. The beautiful egoists of her later novels, figures like Esther Lyon or Gwendolen Harleth, respond like Arthur Donnithorne to the moral vision with which they are confronted. Even the unresponsive Rosamond Lydgate in *Middlemarch* (who, like Hetty, is responsible for losing a child) is not castigated so severely as the "hardhearted hussy" whom Mrs. Poyser likens to a fruit "wi' a hard stone inside it." The reasons for George Eliot's fierceness are to be found elsewhere. At one point in the story, Rector Irwine asks Arthur if it is "some danger of your own that you are considering in this philosophical, general way?" (chap. 16, p. 258). The same question might be asked of the novelist. The "general way" in which she disposes of Hetty's "lower nature" reveals that, far from being reconciled, her moralism and the "realism" with which she beholds an amoral natural order still are in conflict.

In the urban setting of "Janet's Repentance," George Eliot had tried to overcome the moral blindness of Milby by playing Lawyer Dempster against Mr. Tryan. In the rural world of *Adam Bede,* Hetty's resistance to the love represented by Dinah's "higher nature" epitomizes the novelist's fear of the indifference of the natural order. Poor Hetty is made to stand for all that is inhuman in "Nature." Her characterization is almost totally devoid of those touches which the novelist had used to soften Dempster's malevolence: Mrs. Poyser's children delight in the birds they encounter on their walks, but "Hetty could not be got to give any heed to these things" (chap. 18, p. 289). Adam identifies his exertions with those of the workerants, but Hetty is impassive, "not caring to know the difficulties of ant-life" (chap. 20, p. 333). Instead, she is destructive, careless: she plucks "leaves from filbert-trees" and tears them up in her hand (chap. 30, p. 49). In the chapter which George Eliot significantly entitles "Hetty's World," she strongly hints that this world is devoid of soul.

In "Janet's Repentance," George Eliot had identified Dempster's unreceptiveness with the negativism of an entire town. Hetty, however, stands apart from the Loamshire rustics. She is too frail a target for her creator's Miltonic artillery. Whereas Gwendolen Harleth can stand for an entire social order in need of purpose, Hetty's "world" is, after all, merely that of her tiny dairy. George Eliot's wrath at this Perdita-like "queen of curds and creams" seems disproportionate. The expiation she allows to Arthur is denied to a creature who is made to seem far more culpable than the original Eve had been. In *Romola,* the unthinking Tessa, seduced by Tito Melema, is left unscathed; it is Tito, a more malignant Arthur Donnithorne, who in the course of the novel alters his shape from archangel to fiendish "Satanasso." In *Adam Bede,* however, Hetty almost becomes

Eve and Serpent rolled into one. Bartle Massey claims at one point that only in Paradise was man exempt from the treachery of woman, "though you see what mischief she did as soon as she'd an opportunity" (chap. 21, p. 361). Yet the first Eve's "mischief" seems slighter than Hetty Sorrel's; left unprotected by Adam, deluded by Satan, she showed nobility in her disgrace. In *her* disgrace, however, Hetty merely wants Dinah to remove her fears. Whereas the God of *Paradise Lost* refused to create "another Eve" for the equally guilty Adam, the novelist of *Adam Bede* conveniently places Dinah in Hetty's stead.

The contrast between Dinah and Hetty is indebted to that between Jeanie and Effie Deans in Scott's *The Heart of Mid-Lothian,* a novel which also contains deliberate links to Wordsworth's "The Thorn."[10] Scott, too, professes to be a "realist" in the role of historian. But he is less interested in chastising the "lower nature" of Effie Deans than in vindicating the beliefs of her spirited sister. It is Jeanie's actions which are at the center of his book. If Hetty's pilgrimage is one of despair, Jeanie's is one of trust. Dinah's powers of presentiment cannot prevent the "thorny ticket" which George Eliot weaves for Hetty; though rescued from human justice, Hetty is executed by her moralistic creator. Jeanie Deans, however, successfully defies the laws of probability to save her sister. Though she is "no heroine of romance," Scott admits that there is nonetheless "something of romance in Jeanie's venturous resolution" (chap. 27). Her resolution substantiates her belief—and the author's—in a justice higher than those of the fallible Scottish courts.

Scott's belief in such justice allows him to be kindlier to Effie than George Eliot can afford to be to Hetty Sorrel. Hetty dreams of becoming a lady by marrying her seducer. Yet the novelist denounces her presumption; not only Adam but even Arthur deserves a better lot. Effie Deans, on the other hand, becomes Lady Staunton; her sister is surprised to see the refinements she has acquired. Although Effie loses both her husband and her child, she lives on, aware of her faults. Hetty's own understanding matters little to George Eliot. Her "lower nature" remains an obstacle in the way of the novelist's desire to demonstrate the rationality of universal love in a universe no longer ordered by a providential dispensation. Not until *Silas Marner,* where she, like Scott, would allow the illogic of the fairy tale, would George Eliot be able to dispense justice in her fictional world.

The only link between Hetty and the other characters in the novel is provided by the common denominator of suffering. In *Adam Bede*, as in the poems about guilt and sorrow in the *Lyrical Ballads* or in Emily Brontë's *Wuthering Heights*, the recognition of sorrow triggers an awareness of a higher order of reality. Like Martha Ray, the Ancient Mariner, and Heathcliff, Hetty must face the terror of isolation, the "horror of this cold, and darkness, and solitude—out of all human reach" (chap. 37, p. 147). In "The Thorn," the implications of Martha's story are impressed upon a Gulliver-like "captain of a small trading vessel"; the agonies of the Ancient Mariner and Heathcliff are sufficient to disrupt the complacency of their witnesses —the Wedding Guest and Lockwood, the city dweller. In *Adam Bede*, likewise, the death of Hetty's child and the girl's trial widens the understanding of all major characters, if not Hetty's own. It is the acceptance of Adam—a Wedding Guest turned titular hero— which chiefly concerns George Eliot. Yet Dinah, the Poysers, Rector Irwine, must also readjust their aims; the solitude first experienced by Hetty and then by the outcast Arthur leads them to regroup and close their ranks. The gaps left by the two exiles are filled: Adam carries out Arthur's improvements, and Dinah takes Hetty's place. To a greater extent than in "Amos Barton" or "Janet's Repentance," there is a sense of completion and restoration. Suffering *has* yielded purpose; though not as Arthur intended, good *has* come out of evil.

George Eliot's predecessors had used the stereotype of the guilty sufferer to imply the existence of an essentially benevolent universe. Martha Ray's suffering and the Ancient Mariner's expiation suggest that they have committed infractions against an order which is essentially harmonious; Heathcliff's Satanism is belied by the wholesome relation which springs up in the next generation of lovers; even Effie Deans's skeptical view of earthly and divine justice is undermined by her sister's unflagging faith in a reasonable Providence which sorts out error from truth. In all these cases, the tribulations merely confirm the existence of a purposeful design. George Eliot likewise means to chasten her Adam into giving his assent to a universe which she—like Wordsworth, Coleridge, Brontë, and Scott— wants to infuse with the intuition of love. But her predecessors had relied on an aura of the supernatural to validate this intuition: even the unsentimental Jeanie Deans embarks on a pilgrimage in which the various stages correspond to those encountered by Bunyan's

Christian. The supernatural spirits of "The Ancient Mariner," the shaking earth which refuses to yield up Martha's buried child, Lockwood's surrealistic dreams, and the fantasies of the demented Madge Wildfire create atmospheres in which we can suspend our disbelief and envision an order beyond the ordinary reality represented by the Wedding Guest, the sea captain and the villagers, Lockwood and Nelly Dean, and the unimaginative courts of Scotland.

In *Adam Bede* George Eliot repeatedly hints that there is such a higher order behind the visible, temporal world of Loamshire. Yet the autumn haze which envelops her pastoral world hides only a recognition of the universality of human misery. The narrator of "The Thorn" ends his account by recollecting Martha's piercing cry: "Oh misery! oh misery! / Oh woe is me! oh misery!" The cry, like the thorn, attests to the existence of a reality more extraordinary than that grasped by the fact-finding villagers. In *Adam Bede,* on the other hand, this same cry of misery must by itself compel men to love each other. Despite her Miltonic efforts, George Eliot could not bring herself to impress mind and conscience on an order that remained unmindful and unconscious to higher feeling.

In "Janet's Repentance," the novelist had already expressed her revulsion over this material order: "When our life is a continuous trial, the moments of respite seem only to substitute the heaviness of dread for the heaviness of actual suffering: the curtain of cloud seems parted an instant only that we may measure all its horror as it hangs low, black and imminent, in contrast with the transient brightness" (chap. 5, pp. 112–113). In *Adam Bede,* both Dinah and Hetty must recognize that they are living in "this solid world of brick and stone." Dinah must give up her yearning for transcendence; Hetty must abandon her dreamy tendency to see "all things through a soft, liquid veil" (chap. 9, p. 146). It is significant that immediately after the publication of *Adam Bede* George Eliot should turn to the romantic horror tale of "The Lifted Veil." In that fantasy she examined the trances of a seer unable to bear the heavy world of actuality. Gifted with powers of foresight far stronger than those of Dinah Morris, Latimer unveils terrors unsuspected by Dinah or Adam. George Eliot's "mental phases" were far from over. Clearly this Victorian "realist" had not yet reconciled her acceptance of objective truth with her reservations about her right to imagine a reality that might also be true to a better world.

NOTES

1. *The Essence of Christianity,* trans. George Eliot (New York, 1957), pp. 148-149.
2. Cf. George Eliot's Miltonic poem "The Death of Moses," which ends: "He has no tomb, / He dwells not with you dead, but lives as Law."
3. The words belong to a hymn by John Wesley which Dinah sings.
4. *Past and Present,* Book IV, chap. 6, p. 279. Carlyle's condemnation of the landed gentry who seek others to do their work, is echoed by George Eliot's treatment of Arthur. She sent Jane Welsh Carlyle a copy of *Adam Bede,* hoping unsuccessfully to give "the philosopher" the same sort of pleasure she had from the beginning of *Sartor Resartus* (GEL, III, 23).
5. *Ibid.,* Book III, chap. 5, p. 161.
6. Paris, *Experiments in Life* (Detroit, 1965), pp. 242-244.
7. *George Eliot* (London, 1902), p. 76. Robert Speaight regards Hetty as "the *femme moyenne sensuelle* at her most attractive" and finds "no judgment in George Eliot's tracing of her fortunes" (*George Eliot* [London, 1954], p. 45). Gerald Bullett detects no differences between the author's attitudes towards Arthur and Hetty; theirs, he says, is "an idyll of first love, presented with delicacy and understanding" (*George Eliot* [London, 1947], p. 175).
8. Walter Allen, *George Eliot* (New York and Toronto, 1964), p. 102. Joseph Warren Beach is more explicit: "This great bluestocking . . . this scholar with a face like a horse" cannot sympathize with a creature "so pretty as Hetty Sorrel" (*The Twentieth-Century Novel: Studies in Technique* [New York, 1960], p. 19).
9. Cf. V. S. Pritchett, *The Living Novel* (New York, 1957), p. 92: "George Eliot was punishing herself and Hetty has to suffer for the 'sins' George Eliot had committed, and for which, to her perhaps unconscious dismay, she herself was never punished."
10. In Scott's novel, Madge Wildfire becomes deranged, like Martha Ray, after the loss of her child; it is she who steals Effie's son. When Jeanie finds her, Madge sits on "a variegated hillock of wild flowers and moss, such as the poet of Grasmere has described in his verses on the Thorn" (*The Heart of Mid-Lothian,* ed. John H. Raleigh [Boston, 1966], p. 298).

BARBARA HARDY

Implication and Incompleteness:
George Eliot's *Middlemarch*

Harry Richmond is a rambling novel, concentrated in its moral
subject and point of view, expansive in action, symbolism and
imagery. *Middlemarch* provides us with a model for the expansive
form, in its large scope, multiple variations, and freedom from the
restrictions of either aesthetic or ideological form. Many of its structural features—antithesis and parallelism, anticipation and echo,
scenic condensation—are those we also find in Meredith and indeed
in Henry James, but in a restricted range. Not only is the organization of *Middlemarch* much less conspicuous and indeed less ele-
gantly symmetrical than that of a novel by James, but there is never
any sacrifice of truthfulness to the achievement of aesthetic ends.
The form is the means to the ends of good story, moral argument,
and the imitation of life. It is much more naturally plotted than the
ideological novels, less dependent on coincidence and less restricted
to crisis, and it shapes its moral argument tentatively through character and action, instead of shaping character and action in accord-
ance with dogma. There are no strong climaxes like those at the end
of *The Ambassadors* and *Jane Eyre* which complete a pattern or
clinch an argument but distort the appearances of life.

From *The Appropriate Form: An Essay on the Novel* (London: Athlone Press,
1964), pp. 105-31. Copyright © 1964 by the Athlone Press. Reprinted by
permission of the author and publisher.

The act of comparison is a dangerous tool in criticism. We may too easily select the material for comparison in order to back our prejudices and preferences, and if we shift the comparison, and put *Middlemarch* beside *Le Rouge et le Noir,* or *Anna Karenina,* or *Lady Chatterley's Lover,* we must modify our sense of its expansiveness and truthfulness. *Middlemarch* is a large, free, and truthful novel (to keep fairly close to James's terms but to reverse his judgement) but it has its own special restrictions. If we compare it with the novels I have just mentioned, novels which resemble it in social and psychological material to a sufficient extent to make the comparison viable, then we should use the word "realism" more warily in our praise of George Eliot.

Middlemarch is only restrictedly truthful in its treatment of sexuality. The consequence is not only to make us use the word "realism" warily but also to look hard at our praise of its formal unity. For one of the interesting features of this restriction is that it is uneven. The novel does not reveal a consistent restriction but a lop-sided one.

This restriction is present in George Eliot's early novels, too. It is, for instance, possible to argue that although the sexual desires of Maggie and Stephen, in *The Mill on the Floss,* are frankly dramatized, in general conception and in tense detail, the sexual implications of Maggie's relationship with Philip Wakem would have been more moving and incisive if they had gone beyond hints and implications. The sexual *lacunae* in *Adam Bede* are even plainer. Hetty's seduction by Arthur is dramatized in minute psychological detail, through the point of view of both characters. Arthur's desires are presented largely by implication and in symbol, but such symbols as the violent ride away from temptation and the unthinking ride back towards it are sufficient to give them substance. I do not have in mind an absence of physical detail but an absence of relevant emotional statement when I suggest that this sexual embodiment of Arthur throws into high relief what remains unsubstantial in Hetty. Her brilliantly recorded fantasy-life is remarkably lacking in sexual detail, but nowhere does George Eliot draw our attention to this conspicuous absence, or comment on its causes and effects, as she does with all other dramatized aspects of Hetty's mind and feelings. She tells us that Hetty is hard, but not that she is cold. The lack of sexuality seems to be the product of omission rather than of reticence, and it will not do, I think, to excuse the omissions on the ground that they are conventional or historically necessary. Hetty and Arthur are not a shadowy idyllic couple, but are subjected to the persistent analysis of both irony and sympathy. And Arthur is by no means a hero without sexuality.

It would be difficult to complain that the staled passions and live humiliations of Mrs. Transome lose anything by being portrayed in a Victorian novel, though we may notice that her "past" is shown retrospectively, in the novel's past, which possibly removes some of the difficulties of sexual delineation. The important thing, as I have already stressed, is not the absence of sexual realism achieved through a detailed clinical report, but the absence or presence of that psychological realism which makes the characters appear as sexual beings. And in spite of conventions of reticence, I would claim that George Eliot writes about Maggie and Mrs. Transome and Gwendolen, Arthur, Stephen and Grandcourt, as creatures of sexual vitality, desire, and commitment. It is because of their sexuality that they are vulnerable, moved, aggressive, or threatened: sex enters not only into the "portraits" but into the causality of the action. The passions and conflicts of these characters are sufficiently vivid and particular to make her moral argument meaningful despite changes in sexual morality.

In the earlier novels she handles sexual situations which she is able to make fairly explicit. There is no doubt that Janet is driven to drink by a sadistic drunkard, no doubt that Hetty is seduced and becomes pregnant, no doubt that Mrs. Transome has committed adultery, even though George Eliot does not always give names to the situations and relationships. Her refusal to give names is probably less a matter of social decorum than a matter of dramatic effect. Our curiosity and tension, and our troubled identification with secrecy, privacy, or anxiety, is brought about by local evasiveness and lack of explicit naming. We do not know immediately what Mrs. Transome has done, nor do we know immediately that Hetty is pregnant. Our lack of information is justified by their furtiveness or pride. Our mere suspicion matches their understandable retreat from the subject. In these instances George Eliot withholds information in order to create tension and shock or decorously follows the reticence and evasiveness implicit in the situation.

In *Middlemarch* George Eliot is dealing with a situation which she cannot even name, and her evasiveness and suggestiveness, her retreat and approach, deserves close attention. Her refusal to be explicit is so marked that many readers do not even notice that there

is anything which she is refusing to be explicit about. She is reticent—not, I claim, silent—about the Casaubon marriage. This reticence, because it is not silence, is compatible with a truthful and
complete account of what it was like for Dorothea to be married
to Casaubon, and what it was like for Casaubon to be married to
Dorothea. We may not see the point at once, but when we do, I
suggest, everything fits. But the novel's truthfulness is not sustained.
In Dorothea's relationship with Will we have much more than a
refusal to name the passions. We have a refusal even to suggest
them. She is reticent about Dorothea and Casaubon, but she leaves
things out in her treatment of Dorothea and Will. The omission is
both an unrealistic element in an unusually realistic novel and the
cause of imbalance. We can make the criticism in terms of truth
and in terms of form. *Middlemarch* has often been praised as a great
realistic novel and, more latterly, as a triumph of unified organization, but both its realism and its unity are flawed.

This flaw has to be uncovered in some detail. There have been
many commentaries on the novel, but its delineation of sexuality
has been glanced at very shyly or neglected utterly. Critics may have
sometimes assumed that the sexual implications of the Casaubon
marriage are obvious. It is true that they form only a part of the
moral and psychological action and are easily subsumed in a general
account of the great trials and smaller triumphs of Dorothea Brooke.
I do not want to give the impression that the novel has been mis-
understood because critics have not recognized the impotence of
Casaubon. This is a part of the story, but not the whole. But I want
to bring out this part, and for several reasons. Some readers interpret
this reticence as omission, and their view is encouraged by a generalized notion about the absence of sex in Victorian fiction, and in
turn encourages this notion to persist: only in a Victorian novel
could we have such an asexual view of a marriage. Some readers
think that the omission is there, but is unimportant: the question
does not come up, the failure of the marriage has nothing to do with
sex. Some even respond rather perversely to what clues and cues we
are given, and see Casaubon as physically repulsive, like Hardy's
Phillotson, or even sadistic, like Grandcourt in *Daniel Deronda*.
These are some of the views I have met—though not in print. One
published view is that of John Hagan, in an article in *Nineteenth
Century Fiction*: "*Middlemarch*: Narrative Unity in the Story of
Dorothea Brooke" (June, 1961). Mr. Hagan calls Casaubon "a ster-

ile ascetic." We can all agree as to his sterility, but I think George Eliot tells us something about its cause. Calling Casaubon "ascetic," however, seems as appropriate as calling Sir Clifford Chatterley ascetic. Neither of them has to make any effort to subdue the flesh.

George Eliot never tells us that Casaubon is impotent. Like most English novelists of her time, she is reticent, sometimes evasive, about sex. *Middlemarch* appeared twenty years before *Jude the Obscure,* and if we compare it with contemporary novels in France and Russia, it leaves out a lot. Everybody knows that Dickens was interested in the social aspects of sex, but contrived to write at length about a prostitute, in *Oliver Twist,* without giving her a local habitation or a name which would be unpalatable in family reading. Sex as an aspect of personal relations scarcely comes into Dickens, but George Eliot is plainly giving her action some sexual substance in *Adam Bede, The Mill on the Floss,* and *Daniel Deronda.* Her domestic drama seems restrained when we compare her with Tolstoy, but restraint is not the same thing as omission, and if we confuse the two when discussing *Middlemarch* we are surely imprecise when we proffer the favourite words of praise like "adult" and "realistic." I am not claiming sexual realism for George Eliot. D. H. Lawrence allows himself total explicitness and is moreover interested in aspects of sexual behaviour which do not concern *Middlemarch* in any way. George Eliot writes within a restricted convention of reticence, and is emphasizing sensibility rather than sexuality. But if we look at the sexual implications of Casaubon, and see what they contribute to the moral and social pattern of the novel, George Eliot's dramatization of the conflict between life-values and death-values—Eros and Thanatos—will appear to have a good deal in common with *Lady Chatterley's Lover.* Certain Iliads, as Carlyle reminds us in *Sartor Resartus,* acquire new extrinsic significance over the years, and it is possible that the twentieth-century reader of *Middlemarch* sees this correlation of sexual and social values with exaggerated clarity. When we isolate a theme we invariably appear to exaggerate its prominence, but I hope I am isolating something which is an important and neglected part of the novel. *Middlemarch* uses the sexual theme not merely in order to confront life more truthfully, but in a significant bracketing of social criticism and individual moral affirmation. The rescue into love, which is a theme in many novels besides *Middlemarch* and *Lady Chatterley's Lover,* involves some social diagnosis of personal failures in feeling and relationship. It makes a symbolic equation of social and sexual energy in ways which hold both terms in equal tension. The virile rescuer can be a vivid symbol of social revolution; the decadent society can be seen as a cause of individual sterility; the failure of love can be explored causally—in the condensed causality of symbolism— and generalized. Such symbolism is condensed: it is not necessarily true that reactionaries are sexually impotent, and in these novels their impotence functions as metaphor. But this is more than rhetoric. There is some literal truth in relating the capacity for loving individuals to the capacity for loving humanity, and although the sexually impotent may be capable of love, the novelist can use both kinds of impotence and energy as mutual reinforcements. Unfortunately, *Middlemarch* does not make this reinforcement in a sufficiently complete fashion. The rescue and its implications are blurred and softened by an inadequate rescuer. One of the many reasons for discussing the Casaubon marriage is the light it has to throw on the character and role of Will Ladislaw. But this is to anticipate. The first thing to look at is the Casaubon marriage itself.

It would be misleading to say that the first real crisis in Dorothea's development is the sexual failure of her marriage. George Eliot's main emphasis is emotional, not physical, and though this emphasis may be in part attributable to the reticent treatment of sex, it is mainly caused by George Eliot's chosen situation—the frustration and collapse of a general marital failure. Casaubon's impotence is part of a larger incapacity for life, an incapacity we also find in Sir Clifford Chatterley. There is, however, one important difference between the two characters. In both the novelist is using physical impotence—I suppose "unrealistically"—as a sign of basic sterility. Sir Clifford's impotence, caused by a war-wound, is made the cause of his imaginative and emotional failure. Lawrence uneasily combines an account of psychological causality with a metaphor. George Eliot avoids this causal account. Casaubon's physical impotence is seen neither as cause or effect of his general impotence. It is one of many symptoms. And even if we recognize that its appearance in the cluster of other symptoms is metaphorical and not realistic—there are presumably intellectual egoistic failures, incapable of proper human relations, who are sexually potent—his impotence is a fine stroke, which does more than complete a total picture of failure. It brings out Dorothea's ignorance and ardour, and society's irresponsibility in "smiling on propositions of marriage from a sickly man to a girl less than half his own age" (1st edition, 1871–2; dropped in later editions).

Unless we see the sexual implications of Dorothea's crisis in Rome, George Eliot must seem to be vainly expending much of her satire and her sympathy. The author's reticence finds dramatic reason (or excuse) in the character's reserve: "No one would ever know what she thought of a wedding journey to Rome." But by the time we reach this enigmatic comment on Dorothea's reticence we have heard many frankly explicit doubts and fears about her marriage. Such doubts are voiced by several characters, though never to Dorothea. Each point of view is isolated and tempered by the prejudice of the speaker into a local effect of vagueness or ambiguity. Such ambiguity disappears as the impressions converge.

Let us look at some of these separate but converging points of view, noticing that they appear in several ways. There is the author's analysis of Dorothea's consciousness, ironically neighboured by an analysis of Casaubon's which is deliberately non-committal on first appearance. There is the spirited commentary of some biassed and unreliable spectators.

Dorothea has been frequently analysed and I will therefore merely pick out one or two relevant features. She is healthy, ardent, idealistic, young enough to be Casaubon's daughter, and very innocent. Her innocence is brought out strongly in her misunderstanding of the motives and affections of Sir James Chettam and in the explicit contrast between her and her sister, the more knowing and "worldly-wise" Celia. It is Dorothea, not Casaubon, who tries to be an ascetic. She tries to renounce and rationalize her response to the glow of jewels and the joys of riding. Like Maggie, she knows too little about her own instincts to be able to adopt the ascetic role with safety. She has theoretical ideals of marriage ominously expressed in references to fathers and teachers, Milton and Hooker. She creates an image of her own nature and an image of ideal marriage which matches Casaubon's with fatal perfection. She defends his "great soul" against Celia's distaste for his looks and habits. There is, of course, the additional irony that even measured by this theoretical ideal of marriage, Casaubon falls short: he is not a Hooker or a Milton in intellect or scholarship, and his soul is a little one, if we can fall into George Eliot's way of measuring souls. But this irony is not immediately relevant to my argument, and I mention it only to stress the selective analysis I am making. If Dorothea were right about her own emotional needs—which she is not—she would still be in for intellectual and moral disillusion. It is the emotional and physical shock which I want to bring out here.

When we see her in Rome, through Naumann's shrewd perception, she is standing in her Quakerish garb beside the statue of Ariadne, then thought to be the Cleopatra. George Eliot deliberately reminds us of both Ariadne and Cleopatra, and the association with Ariadne, forsaken after all her efforts in her maze, is as relevant as the sensual association with Cleopatra which gives extra point to Naumann's comment on the "fine bit of antithesis." The girl and the statue are not as different as all that, despite appearances.

Next we see her weeping, feeling a tendency of "fits of anger and repulsion," disturbed by the violence and incoherence of Rome and by Casaubon's deficiencies of sensibility and explanation. Both she and Casaubon are irritable and nervous, and when she begs him to let her help in his work, "in a most unaccountable, darkly-feminine manner . . . with a slight sob and eyes full of tears," she explains that she "can be of no other use." She asks if he is "thoroughly satisfied with our stay—I mean, with the result as far as your studies are concerned." Before Ladislaw's scepticism has made her doubt the value of Casaubon's research she has already begun to feel doubts about the future years "in her own home," realizing that "the way in which they might be filled with joyful devotedness was not so clear to her as it had been." The main action of disillusionment is expressed in the response to Rome, which startles and bewilders her, while Casaubon comments "in a measured official tone," quoting authoritative opinions on Raphael, for instance, with Cupid and Psyche picked out for special illustration. There is direct comment too, when George Eliot observes, with meticulous qualification, that this frustration and disappointment might have "remained longer unfelt" if there had been ardour and tenderness:

> If he would have held her hands between his and listened . . . or if she could have fed her affection with those childlike caresses which are the bent of every sweet woman, who has begun showering kisses on the hard pate of her bald doll, creating a happy love within that woodenness from the wealth of her own love. That was Dorothea's bent. With all her yearning to know what was afar from her and to be widely benignant, she had ardour enough for what was near, to have kissed Mr. Casaubon's

coat-sleeve, or to have caressed his shoe-latchet, if he would have made any other sign of acceptance than pronouncing her, with his unfailing propriety, to be of a most affectionate and truly feminine nature, indicating at the same time by politely reaching a chair for her that he regarded these manifestations as rather crude and startling. [ch. xx]

This describes a failure in feeling, and though there seem to be physical implications, it is certainly no clear indication of impotence. But this account is set in a context of highly critical comment which is frankly physical, and not primarily concerned with Casaubon's failures in tenderness or sensibility. The initial physical contrast between Dorothea and Casaubon is presented in descriptive detail: Dorothea's health, her "grand woman's frame" and—at a significant point, just before Mr. Brooke is to announce Casaubon's proposal—"maternal hands," contrast with Casaubon's poor physique, white moles with hairs, and so forth. The inequality of the physical match is not left to the reader's inferences. Almost everyone who comments on the marriage reacts in protest and disgust. The exceptions are the over-tolerant and detached Cadwallader, and vague, self-engrossed Mr. Brooke, who feels that the complications of women are equalled only "by the revolutions of irregular solids." Brooke's own reasons for never marrying are scarcely calculated to evoke respect and his hints about "the noose" and a husband's desire for mastery are carefully placed in a very personal context. The fastidious Celia shrinks, but we see her responsive in the context of her limited egoism and superficial common sense. Sir James Chettam, as the Cadwalladers point out, speaks with the partiality of a young, handsome, and rejected suitor: "Good God! It is horrible! He is no better than a mummy," and "What business has an old bachelor like that to marry? He has one foot in the grave," and "He must be fifty and I don't believe he could ever have been more than the shadow of a man. Look at his legs." Later he calls him "a parchment code" and claims that "he has got no good red blood in his body." The outspoken Mrs. Cadwallader, connoisseur of "blood and breeding," calls Casaubon "A great bladder for dried peas to rattle in." She reassures Sir James that Celia will now be the better match, since "this marriage to Casaubon is as good as going to a nunnery," and winds up her comment on his blood, "Somebody put a drop under a magnifying glass, and it was all semi-colons and parentheses." Will's early hostility to Dorothea makes him conclude that there "could be no sort of passion in a girl who would marry Mr. Casaubon," but he soon comes to rival the jealous eloquence of Sir James and thinks of Casaubon as "having got this adorable young creature to marry him, and then passing his honeymoon away from her, groping after his mouldy futilities." He calls him "a cursed white-blooded coxcomb," thinks of "beautiful lips kissing holy skulls," and sees the marriage as "the most horrible of virgin-sacrifices." Will's reaction is the only one based on some comprehension of Dorothea's motives in marriage, and he uses the word "fanatic" to cover both these and her rejections of art.

The implications of this chorus of disapproval go beyond a distaste for mere outward disparity of body and age. Incidentally, Casaubon is no obvious case of senile impotence,[1] and he may even be nearer forty-five than Sir James's suggested fifty. Mr. Brooke tells Dorothea that "He is over five-and-forty, you know." Mrs. Cadwallader is unambiguously thinking of sterility, from whatever cause, and although this aspect of the Casaubon marriage is dealt with reticently, it is an important thread in the pattern. It is much less prominent than it would be in the life of a heroine who had staked less on marriage as an education and a vocation, and it is true that nowhere does Dorothea long for children or lament their lack. But the subject is present everywhere except in Dorothea's actual words. It is alive, for instance, in the ironical contrast of her frustration with Celia's maternal complacency and Rosamond's miscarriage. It is alive, too, in imagery: there is the image of the elfin child withered in its birth, the strong image of the judgement of Solomon, in which Dorothea figures as the true mother and Rosamond as the false, and perhaps in this image used on one occasion for Casaubon's unresponsiveness to Dorothea: "It is in these acts called trivialities that the seeds of joy are for ever wasted" (ch. xiii). Dorothea's lament is vague—it is for "objects who could be dear to her, and to whom she could be dear." On one occasion she is thinking of Casaubon's will, which has provided for issue, but at no point in her innocent scheming for sharing the estate with Will, nor in Casaubon's reactions, nor in her discussion with Lydgate about having nothing to do with her money, does the obvious question of heirs come up. It is a marriage without ardour, without children, and, most significantly, without the expectation of children.

Casaubon does contemplate his possible heirs in drawing up his

will, "made at the time of their marriage" as we are told in Chapter
xxxvii. It is now time to consider his expectations and reactions to
marriage. George Eliot endows him with "chilling rhetoric," both
in love-letter and speech, but draws our attention to the possibility
that this may not mean "that there is no good work or fine feeling in
him." She also warns us of the unreliability of Casaubon's critics,
forcing us to keep pace with the slow development of her action by
her usual omniscient author's disclaimer of omniscience. But as soon
as we enter the mind of Casaubon her irony and her pity confirm
suspicion.

Casaubon, like many lovers, is looking forward to "the happy
termination of courtship," but for his own peculiar reasons—he will
then be able to get on with his work. He has expected more from
courtship. Relying, as later in Rome, on the appropriate authorities,
he "determined to abandon himself to the stream of feeling, and
perhaps was surprised to find out what an exceedingly shallow rill
it was." Authority is discredited in the sad ridiculous conclusion,
"that the poets had much exaggerated the force of masculine passion."[2] His own deficiency is the only uncanvassed explanation: "It
had once or twice crossed his mind that there was possibly some
deficiency in Dorothea to account for the moderation of his aban-
donment; but he was unable to discern the deficiency, or to figure
to himself a woman who would have pleased him better; so that
there was clearly no reason to fall back upon but the exaggerations
of human tradition." Doubt continues:

> For in truth, as the day fixed for his marriage came nearer, Mr.
> Casaubon did not find his spirits rising . . . though he had won
> a lovely girl he had not won delight. . . . Poor Mr. Casaubon
> had imagined that his long studious bachelorhood had stored up
> for him a large compound interest of enjoyment, and that large
> drafts on his affections could not fail to be honoured. . . . There
> was nothing external by which he could account for a certain
> blankness of sensibility which came over him just when his ex-
> pectant gladness should have been most lively. . . . [ch. x]

The imagery of low vitality covers his egocentric feeling for his
wife and his work, his marital and his scholarly jealousies—a cloudy
damp engenders all. George Eliot turns from such satirical comment
to a straight unironical account of his conflict. He cannot tell Mr.
Brooke that he would like Ladislaw to leave Middlemarch because

this would be a public admission of deficiency: "To let anyone know that he was jealous would be to admit their (suspected) view of his disadvantages: to let them know that he did not find marriage particularly blissful would imply his conversion to their (probably) earlier disapproval . . . on the most delicate of all personal subjects, the habit of proud suspicious reticence told doubly" (ch. xxxvii).

Although the self-regard is still the same, a new note has entered since his earlier assumptions that the failure in delight was attributable to poetic exaggeration. Even though Casaubon now has rather more grounds for blaming the failure on Dorothea, who has proved unexpectedly critical and independent, it is in fact hinted that he at least sees the possibility of other people thinking in terms of his "disadvantages."

This is the failure of ardour seen from his point of view. The question of issue is touched on only once in his internal commentary. This is in Chapter xxix, after their marriage, when George Eliot interrupts the expected sympathetic analysis of Dorothea to consider instead the "intense consciousness" of Casaubon. Included in his marital balance-sheets are thoughts which go back to his previous expectations:

> On such a young lady he would make handsome settlements, and he would neglect no arrangements for her happiness: in return, he should receive family pleasures and leave behind him that copy of himself which seemed so urgently required of a man —to the sonneteers of the sixteenth century. Times had altered since them, and no sonneteer had insisted on Mr. Casaubon's leaving a copy of himself; moreover, he had not yet succeeded in issuing copies of his mythological key; but he had always intended to acquit himself by marriage. . . .

This account, moving backwards and forwards in time, is interesting in its ellipsis and juxtaposition. Casaubon's failure to leave a copy of his mythological key is ironically placed between the lack of any demand for him to leave another kind of copy and his (past) intention to acquit himself in marriage. It is a suggestive item, at least, and it is followed by an account of his lack of capacity for joy, which is in part a physiological explanation:

> To know intense joy without a strong bodily frame, one must have an enthusiastic soul. Mr. Casaubon had never had a strong

bodily frame, and his soul was sensitive without being enthusiastic: it was too languid to thrill out of self-consciousness into
passionate delight; it went on fluttering in the swampy ground
where it was hatched. . . .

George Eliot insists on the lack of passion, claiming pity, not contempt, for such a "small hungry shivering self," and ending with the
mention of "the new bliss" which "was not blissful to him":

> And the deeper he went in domesticity the more did the sense
> of acquitting himself and acting with propriety predominate over
> any other satisfaction. Marriage, like religion and erudition, nay,
> like authorship itself, was fated to become an outward require-
> ment, and Edward Casaubon was bent on fulfilling unimpeach-
> ably all requirements.

Whatever ambiguity and evasion may at times come from the convention of reticence, the double emphasis on emotional and physical
deficiency, on the one hand, and sterility, on the other, appear to
converge in only one possible explanation. It may be that the adult
Victorian reader found the suggestion more plainly pronounced than
the modern reader, having fewer cases of sexual frankness before him,
being more accustomed to implicit rather than explicit sexual themes,
and having no hardened prejudices about the limitations of the
Victorian novel.[3] Our expectations and prejudices may well blind us
to the implications of this reticent mode of suggestion, but if we look
carefully at these implications I think we must say that Casaubon is
sexually very inadequate. We cannot definitely say that the marriage
is never consummated, but since Dorothea's nervous misery begins
in Rome, this seems highly probable.

As I said at the beginning of this chapter, I do not think that the
truthfulness of *Middlemarch* is impaired because George Eliot does
not tell us outright that Casaubon is impotent. The very technique
of implication has dramatic advantages. Mrs. Cadwallader might be
expected to talk to Sir James in knowing metaphor. Casaubon might
be expected to avoid naming his deficiencies. Dorothea would only
weep in silence. On the other hand, I do not want to exaggerate this
dramatic decorum. It could have been combined with explicit naming, by the author or one of the characters, and there is no doubt that
social and literary restraint governs the novel's reticence. There is no
doubt, too, that the sexual failure is only a part of Casaubon's gen-

eralized failure of mind and feeling. But the author does not distort
the facts of nature and marriage: if we do not see the point, all is
not lost, and the novel makes sense. If we do, then many of the small
hints and details, as well as the larger tensions, make better sense,
are more coherent and complete.

But where the novel shows the unhappy consequences of restricted treatment of sex is in Dorothea's relation with Will Ladislaw.
Here is the psychological and structural flaw in *Middlemarch*. It is a
psychological flaw because of a failure in truthfulness, a structural
flaw because of the vivid presence of truthfulness elsewhere. I do
not insist on describing the flaw in psychological and structural terms
merely because of an interest in structure, but because I think the
successes and failures which are combined in *Middlemarch* afford an
interesting model for the formal critic. If we limit our definitions of
form in fiction, as we so often do, to the organization of symbols,
imagery, and ideas, then we may well pass over this failure. Recognition of this kind of failure forces us to review our ideas of form,
especially our ideas of unity. It is possible to demonstrate the thematic
and poetic unity of the novel: the themes cohere and persist throughout, and there is a mobile unity of imagery and symbol which has
been analysed by several critics. But if we regard form in the largest
sense, and think not merely of unity but of a more useful and less
popular word, completeness, then we have to qualify our praise of the
form of this novel.

The structural relationship of Casaubon and Ladislaw takes us
back to James, and suggests that there is some point in his "law" that
the antithesis should be direct and complete. Up to a point the fable
which lies at the heart of *Middlemarch* is clear enough. The three
main characters are Casaubon, Dorothea, and Ladislaw. The fable
may be called the rescue into love, and it has many forms in fiction.
It is present in James's *The Bostonians,* in Gissing's neglected novel
The Emancipated, in E. M. Forster's *A Room With a View* and
Where Angels Fear to Tread, in several of D. H. Lawrence's stories
and novels, and in Meredith's *Lord Ormont and his Aminta* and
perhaps in *The Egoist.* In all these novels the sexual rescue—from an
old man, a woman, a sterile aesthete—has social implications. The
rescuer is something of the Noble Savage and something of the Outsider, representing not only personal passion and fertility but the
new blood needed and feared by the old establishment. Casaubon is,
like Sir Clifford Chatterley, a cluster of different kinds of impotence.

His futile mythological research, his nominal clerical function, his birth and property, all combine with his physical and emotional deficiencies to give him a significant place in the unreformed society. Like Sir Clifford, his assumption of Providential grace and favour for self and class gives him more than a merely personal deadness and egoism, though both in *Middlemarch* and *Lady Chatterley's Lover,* this is only an indirect generalization in a novel containing a great deal of overt political and social discussion. George Eliot's advantage over Lawrence, despite her sexual reticence, is that she creates an individual as well as a symbol, a man who feels the internal strain and loneliness of his position, a man torn by doubt and anxiety and pride, a man capable of stepping briefly outside this clearly marked moral category and on one occasion speaking to Dorothea with surprise and humility and recognition, capable of responding as a human being and certainly created out of sympathy and fellow-feeling. There is no possibility of an even identification with the characters in *Lady Chatterley's Lover* because they are not evenly animated, but Casaubon is presented as part of his environment, having a history, having the register of his differentiated consciousness, made of the same stuff as everyone else though warped, hardened, and self-regarding.

Ladislaw completes and answers these social implications. He is "a kind of gypsy," defiantly declassé, grandson of a woman who rebelled against the Casaubon values of class and money, son of a woman who rebelled against the Bulstrode values of a Nonconformist respectable thieving line. His father is a musician, his mother an actress, and he is a dilettante and a Radical. As a Radical, of course, he also rejects the superficial and feeble liberalism of Brooke. Like Matey Weyburn in *Lord Ormont and his Aminta,* and Mellors in *Lady Chatterley,* he is a social misfit, a man seeking his vocation, and the poor man who wins the lady. But the mere absurdity of the comparison with Mellors or with Forster's Gino makes his deficiencies plain. As a Noble Savage he is a little fragile.

It may be objected that the very comparison itself is artificial, that I am complaining that Ladislaw fails to meet a standard set up by other novels and inappropriately applied to *Middlemarch.* Though I think the social implications of the love-story in *Middlemarch* are usefully brought out by this classification I am not judging Ladislaw by the general and external standards I may have implied, but by the expectations set up within the novel itself. Ladislaw and Casaubon make an excellent social antithesis in their roles, but an unequal sexual one.

The pattern is worked out very satisfactorily in terms of symbol and image. Dorothea is imprisoned in the stone prison of melancholy Lowick, in the labyrinth, in the dark tomb. Casaubon is the winter-worn husband, and the Minotaur. Ladislaw has a godlike brightness, is irradiated by images of light, is the natural daylight from which Dorothea is shut off. Images of darkness and light, aridity and water, enclosure and space, are strong. If Mellors turns up in the grounds of dismal Wragby in answer to Connie's question, "What next?", Ladislaw is the unexpected "someone quite young" found painting in the garden of Lowick. The generalized fertility symbols and more precise Persephone motifs are very subdued in *Middlemarch* when we compare it with *Lady Chatterley's Lover,* but they are present.

But poetic unity is not enough. The unity and antithetical completeness of the imagery and symbolism of place and weather and appearances are not endorsed by the characters. Ladislaw is presented in terms of sensibility, not sensuality. The sexual implications of the imagery are substantiated in Casaubon—of course he can only refer to the opinions of *cognoscenti* when he shows Dorothea *Cupid and Psyche*—but not in the rescuing hero. At times, indeed, the imagery itself takes on and contributes to Ladislaw's idyllic colouring: there is a sexual implication when Casaubon concludes that the poets have overrated the force of masculine passion which is sadly lacking when we find Will "verifying in his own experience that higher love-poetry which had charmed his fancy" (ch. xlvii). Those "tall lilies" which he associates with Dorothea are more like a romantic detail from a Pre-Raphaelite painting, disturbing in their chastity, than like the shooting daffodils of *Lady Chatterley's Lover.* When the Cupid and Psyche symbol finds its antithetical completion, after Casaubon's death, the image is delicate and innocent, not strongly passionate:

> She did not know then that it was Love who had come to her briefly, as in a dream before awaking, with the hues of morning on his wings—that it was Love to whom she was sobbing her farewell as his image was banished by the blameless rigour of irresistible day. [ch. lv]

The appropriate comment seems to be that at this point in the story she should have known. There are some Victorian novels in which it might seem captious not to accept such a lack of self-knowledge but *Middlemarch* is not one of them. George Eliot spends a fair amount of energy criticizing Dorothea's ignorance and short-sightedness but here remains romantically identified with this innocence.

Henry James is one of the few critics of Ladislaw to discuss his "insubstantial character" in the appropriate terms. If his meaning is ambiguous when he complains in his review of *Middlemarch* (*Galaxy*, March 1873) "He is really, after all, not the ideal foil to Mr. Casaubon which her soul must have imperiously demanded, and if the author of the *Key to all Mythologies* sinned by lack of ardour, Ladislaw too has not the concentrated fervour essential in the man chosen by so nobly strenuous a heroine," it is clear that he is not merely thinking of Dorothea's soul when he later says more outspokenly, in the person of Constantius, "If Dorothea had married anyone after her misadventure with Casaubon, she would have married a trooper" ("*Daniel Deronda*: A Conversation," *Atlantic Monthly*, December 1876).

I do not mean to suggest that our impression of Will is entirely romantic, innocent, and radiant. In his private thoughts about Dorothea's marriage, in his discussions with Naumann, in his excellently convincing relationship with Lydgate (especially where their masculine solidarity puts Rosamond's narrow femininity in its place), in his quarrels with Bulstrode and his differences with Brooke, he is detached, honest, and touchy. The relationship between Dorothea and Casaubon is presented in terms of sexuality, but that between Dorothea and Ladislaw is shown as denying it, and it is here that his masculinity falters. George Eliot is not hampered by the difficulties of describing actual love-making, though it is worth noticing that when Dorothea and Will touch each other they are at their most innocent and childlike. In the relationship between Maggie and Stephen, or the relationship between Lydgate and Rosamond, in this same novel, tension and desire are conveyed without physical detail.

In this novel sensibility acts as a surrogate for sensuality. This comes out in the presentation of Will as an artist, less marked by his ability than by impressionability. It comes out too in the sustained aesthetic debate which is the beginning of Dorothea's acquaintance with Will, and which has many implications. Dorothea is presented as a Puritan, and this makes for a special irony in her marriage—her self-abnegation has made the innocent blunder possible, but her ardour is there to suffer. It is Will who points out this ignorance and

sees the paradox, as Philip did for Maggie. He preaches ardently on
behalf of the art he loves, which Dorothea distrusts, because of its
obscure relation to the hard realities, because of its apparently trivial
delight in beauty. Will's attempt to convert her to the aesthetic attitude is most ironically placed in Rome, on her wedding-journey.
Will is presented as an aesthete of a special kind. His impressionability is both praised and doubted: if it shows itself in his response to
art and in his restless trials as poet and painter, it shows itself also in
his sensitivity to other people—to Lydgate, for instance, as well as to
Casaubon and Dorothea, where his understanding is less impartial.
But although he is carefully seen as a creature "of uncertain promise"
(like Fred Vincy), he is given much more than an effeminate aestheticism. His arguments in defence of beauty are largely realistic
attempts to persuade Dorothea into "a sturdy delight in things as
they are." Implicit in Dorothea's first bewildered impressions of Rome
is, I suggest, a reaction to sensuality, though this is muted if we
compare it with Strether's response to the sensuality of Paris or the
reactions of Forster's heroines in his Italian novels. A neglected novel
which probably owes much to *Middlemarch* and which makes a
very explicit use of the landscape and art of Italy in the education of
the senses is George Gissing's *The Emancipated* where Miriam, the
Puritan heroine, is prepared for her rescue into love by the sensual
challenge of painting. Miriam, like Dorothea, changes her views on
art, but after Mallard, the Bohemian hero, realizes that she is still
alarmed by sculpture, there comes an interestingly explicit dialogue
between Mallard and another male character in which this is expressly accounted for by the mention of nudity. Mallard rejects
Philistinism in a brave picture of a domestic circle where family reading will involve "no skipping or muttering or frank omissions" and
where "casts of noble statues . . . shall stand freely about." Journeys
to Italy in the last century presented special problems to Podsnaps
and others.

Middlemarch was written twenty years before *The Emancipated,*
but there are more than aesthetic implications in Dorothea's reaction
to Rome:

> Ruins and basilicas, palaces and colossi, set in the midst of a
> sordid present, where all that was living and warm-blooded
> seemed sunk in the deep degeneracy of a superstition divorced
> from reverence; the dimmer but yet eager Titanic life gazing and

struggling on walls and ceilings; the long vistas of white forms whose marble eyes seemed to hold the monotonous light of an alien world: all this vast wreck of ambitious ideals, sensuous and spiritual, mixed confusedly with the signs of breathing forgetfulness and degradation, at first jarred with an electric shock, and then urged themselves on her with that ache belonging to a glut of confused ideas which check the flow of emotion. Forms both pale and glowing took possession of her young sense, and fixed themselves in her memory even when she was not thinking of them, preparing strange associations which remained through her after-years. [ch. xx]

The vague sensual implications here, and elsewhere, are related to her "tumultous preoccupations with her personal lot," but not picked up in the ensuing debate with Will. This debate is indeed not continued throughout the novel, and lacks the clearer suggestions to be found in James or Gissing, who both correlate aestheticism with sensuality in their Bohemian characters. Will's Bohemianism[4] and his political activity are both related clearly enough, by opposition, to Casaubon's class-values, to Bulstrode's respectable Nonconformity, and to Brooke's brand of Radicalism, but they are less convincingly related to each other. If the idyllic and romantic innocence of Will's love for Dorothea is one weakness, his movement from art to politics is another aspect of his character which does not ring quite true. There is a slackening in the novel with the disappearance of the aesthetic debate which has carried so much of the antithetical play of social and sexual values. Will's political activity alone has a slighter reference, leaving his role as lover conspicuous and inadequate. We can see why the debate drops out. Once Dorothea sees her error in marriage, once she sees exactly where her fanaticism and self-ignorance have led her, the aesthetic debate is no longer required, and there are other ways of showing her aversion to her marriage. Her problem ceases to be one of bewilderment and becomes one of clear vision. Once she sees her marriage for what it is—which takes some time—her problem is chiefly that of accepting it, and living with it in activity and not mere resentment and despair. Dorothea cannot find Connie's solution, and has to live with her sterile marriage until her author provides the solution with Casaubon's death. Death often has to provide a substitute for divorce in Victorian fiction.

The weakness of the novel, and the weakness of Will Ladislaw,

are located in his relationship with Dorothea. It is when they are together, physically or in thoughts of each other, that the romantic
glow seems false and the childlike innocence implausible and inappropriate. In Will's other relations George Eliot can scarcely be accused of romantic softness, or of glossing over sexual problems. She
keeps her heroine clear of any emotional conflict in her feeling for
her husband and her feeling for Ladislaw, and here the moral scheme
strikes the modern reader as being worked out at the expense of
truthfulness. But although Will is shown as romantically rejoicing in
the purity of Dorothea and in the impossibility of his love—"What
others might have called the futility of his passion, made an additional delight for his imagination" (ch. xlvii)—this is only a part of
the analysis of Will's emotions. In his relations with Rosamond the
"romantic" glow is strikingly absent.

His rejection of Rosamond is violent, shocked and fearful, and he
deals a hard blow to her strong sexual vanity when he tells her that
he loves Dorothea: "I never had a *preference* for her, any more than
I have a preference for breathing. No other woman exists by the side
of her." His declaration is a fine example of George Eliot's psychological truthfulness at its best, and it is neither exclusive nor obsessed,
as declarations of love tend to be in many Victorian novels. George
Eliot shows us the present, in William James's words, as more like
a saddle-back than a razor-edge, for Will's confident rejection and
words of love and loyalty are darkened by the shadow of the possible
future. He looks over the edge of the present, though with pain and
not with desire. Feeling, moral commitment, and time, are truthfully
confused:

> When Lydgate spoke with desperate resignation of going to
> settle in London, and said with a faint smile, "We shall have you
> again, old fellow," Will felt inexpressibly mournful, and said
> nothing. Rosamond had that morning entreated him to urge this
> step on Lydgate; and it seemed to him as if he were beholding in
> a magic panorama a future where he himself was sliding into that
> pleasureless yielding to the small solicitations of circumstance,
> which is a commoner history of perdition than any single mo-
> mentous bargain.
>   We are on a perilous margin when we begin to look passively
> at our future selves, and see our own figures led with dull consent
> into insipid misdoing and shabby achievement. [ch. lxxix]

Those critics who find Will Ladislaw a weak romantic conception, the under-distanced product of the author's fantasy, might reflect on the fact that few Victorian heroes are shown as contemplating adultery, and so coolly and miserably, in the moment of passionate commitment to the pure heroine. George Eliot is restricted in her handling of the central relationship in this story, but her treatment of the relations of Will and Rosamond, like her treatment of the Casaubon marriage, shows not merely her ability to admit realities commonly left out of the novels of her time, but to recognize uncomfortable truths often evaded or denied outside literature.

Middlemarch is full of such uncomfortable admissions. There is Mary Garth's moment of fantasy about Farebrother, when she glimpses possibilities of a relationship which might have advantages which marriage with Fred, whom she loves, will lack. There is the extreme irritability of Dorothea, punctuated by her impulse to love, but not removed by it. There is the hard truth which Caroline learns in *Where Angels Fear to Tread*, "that wicked people are capable of love," shown with much less explicitness and fuss in the extreme case of Bulstrode. This kind of acceptance of the mixture of things is not confined to the hard truth. There is the comforting truth that we recognize with Lydgate, that even in the moment of passion, "some of us, with quick alternate vision, see beyond our infatuations, and even while we rave on the heights, behold the wide plain where our persistent self pauses and awaits us" (ch. xv). If Will is capable of tolerating his vision of adultery with Rosamond, there is another shift of mobile moral category when Rosamond for one brief moment responds to Dorothea, or when Casaubon recognizes Dorothea's gesture of patient love. The recognition of human complexity blurs the clearly established moral categories, if temporarily, and can work in the interest of moral optimism and pessimism. George Eliot's choice of the tentative word "meliorism" is clearly illustrated in her sense of the close neighbourhood, in human nature, of possibilities of the good and the bad.

Middlemarch, like most novels, has its formal simplifications and omissions which are determined by social and personal factors, but its expansiveness allows for many moments of surprising truth. We cannot say that there is a strict organization of category, of parallels and antitheses, which breaks down in the free admission of change and complexity. In describing the form of the novel we have to confront not a neat symmetry and clear unity which has additional details which seem to be added on, like grace-notes (if we admire them) or as wasteful and arbitrary strokes (if we do not approve), but a highly complex and mobile pattern. But this does not mean that we are left with no standards with which to judge formal success, and in at least one respect, as I have tried to show, it is necessary to criticize *Middlemarch* for a lack of balance and completeness. The demand for unity and the demand for truth should be inseparable. The inadequacy of the word "unity" is suggested in this attempt to analyse form and truth as inseparable constituents of the good novel, for it would be true to say that *Middlemarch* would be a satisfactory unity if the asexual presentation of Dorothea's relation with Will were matched by a similar omission in the presentation of her relation with Casaubon. Completeness seems to be a better word than unity, including as it does the formal concept of equality of strengths with the concept of truthfulness. Who would exchange the flawed *Middlemarch* with its omissions made conspicuous by its suggestive reticence, for a novel where truth were reduced and mere aesthetic balance retained?

NOTES

1. The actual age of characters who strike the modern reader as old is often surprising in earlier novels. Adam Verver, in *The Golden Bowl* (1905), is only 47 though he makes a more elderly impression and Charlotte says that he is responsible for the infertility of their marriage.
2. The motto for this chapter (vii) is "Piacer e popone, Vuol la sua stagione."
3. Since writing this I have seen David Daiches's little book on *Middlemarch* in which he discusses Casaubon's impotence, making the comment that "no doubt the Victorian reader failed to see in the relationship between these two the matching of impotence and sublimation" (*Studies in English Literature*, No. 11, p. 21). This conclusion strikes me as very odd.
4. George Eliot's use of art to express social value owes much, I suspect, to *Culture and Anarchy*.

W. J. HARVEY

The Intellectual Background of the Novel:
Casaubon and Lydgate

I

Scholarship in the humanities, as in the sciences, often seems to conform to a dialectic in which piecemeal and apparently random analysis of particular points is followed by the appearance of a general, synthetic study which aims to chart the whole field. But no sooner has the map been drawn than the process of detailed investigation starts again; contours are modified, landmarks are imperceptibly altered, a new minor tributary is followed to its source.

So it is with George Eliot. For more than thirty years the study of her intellectual *milieu* has been fixed and determined by P. Bourl'honne's *George Eliot: essai de biographie intellectuelle et morale, 1819–1854*.[1] There have, of course, been a number of useful essays on particular topics and much valuable work remains in the form of unpublished theses. But, by and large, Bourl'honne's was the

Note. This essay was completed before *A Middlemarch Miscellany* by J. C. Pratt became available (Princeton University Ph.D. thesis, 1965). This valuable edition of George Eliot's 1868-71 notebook contains material that extends the argument of my essay, modifying it in detail but not, I think, contradicting any important point.
From *Middlemarch: Critical Approaches to the Novel*, ed. by Barbara Hardy (London: Athlone Press, 1967), pp. 25-37. Copyright © 1967 by the Athlone Press. Reprinted by permission of the publishers.

full, general book to which one had to return. This—leaving aside the intrinsic merit of Bourl'honne's study—has had many disadvantages. It has sometimes been difficult to assimilate the subsequent accession of knowledge (one thinks of the great store of primary material in G. S. Haight's edition of George Eliot's letters). Most writers have accepted the implication contained in the very title of Bourl'honne's book, that George Eliot's intellectual development was complete by the mid-fifties—a very questionable assumption. And, most damagingly, it sometimes follows from this general assumption that George Eliot had worked out a formulated philosophy of life and theory of fiction which she then simply transferred to her creative work. The result of this has been some crude and over-simple equations between the ideas of her novels and the artistic forms which embodied them.

With some honourable exceptions, these assumptions were not challenged by post-war critics, whose main concern was to redefine the nature of George Eliot's artistic powers and to defend her against the charge of being *merely* a disguised philosopher. This led to an emphasis on the formal properties of her work, an emphasis valuable at the time, but one which served to postpone the question of the relation of philosophy to fiction. Clearly this is a complicated question since in one way George Eliot is not an "intellectual" novelist at all; she never produced a "novel of ideas" in the sense that, say, *Robert Elsmere* is a novel of ideas. But in most other senses she clearly has the best mind of all English novelists. Hence for some time the question of how ideas *work* in her fiction became more and more urgent until, in 1965, two new synthetic studies appeared which, taken together, may fairly be said to have advanced the problem well beyond the stage reached by Bourl'honne.[2]

Like Bourl'honne's, these are general studies, maps of the whole territory. Some dangers in intellectual history are constant and universal—the temptation, for example, to regard the individual as a kind of Aeolian harp, passively responding to the intellectual breezes of his age, or the temptation to assert too narrow a cause-and-effect relationship between the *milieu* and the person. But there are further dangers in generality; the maps may be too neat or precise to delineate the twists and turns, the labyrinths and metamorphoses of something so protean as the thought of an individual. There is the temptation to tease out into precision and order what is true only when left as part of that confused web of thoughts, emotions, doubts, hopes, attitudes, allegiances and prejudices which makes up a person's total and unique response to life. It is part of George Eliot's greatness that she gives us with so little falsification so much of that total response; it is only in these terms and not in those so useful to the intellectual cartographer that one can finally talk of her "philosophy." For all the acuteness, force and rigour of her intellect, George Eliot's outlook is not philosophic in the class-room sense of the word; it is really much closer to the sort of thing ordinary men mean when they talk of having a "philosophy of life." As such it is much more tolerant of muddle, contradiction and paradox; it is precisely George Eliot's recognition of this tangle that lends so much conviction to the "world-view" implicit in her novels.

There is one further complication. Although George Eliot's novels embody a total response she may, for dramatic purposes, allow only a small part of her intellectual range to be represented in a particular work. One has, very often, the feeling that she is working well within the limits of her mind and that what is left, as it were, unwritten in the margin affects that which is there on the printed page. Hence this essay, in which I wish to attempt something that may well seem tedious and irrelevant and which is certainly no more than a footnote to the large, synthetic studies I have already mentioned. It may seem tedious because it involves summarizing information extrinsic to the fiction; it may seem irrelevant because it involves exploring distant and sometimes dingy corridors of intellectual history. Yet the question of relevance is precisely the point of the essay. What light, we must ask, is thrown on *Middlemarch* by the remote, extrinsic and sometimes bizarre information in the margins of George Eliot's creative mind? This is a general problem but *Middlemarch* is a good test-case because it is so ample and well-documented a novel that it might at first seem a fully autonomous work, in the sense that it contains within itself all the information about it that we need to know.

II

I shall concentrate on Lydgate and Casaubon. The contrast between these two men, a contrast which contains many obvious points of similitude, is clearly one of the chief features of the novel's structure. Yet, at first glance, there would seem to be a striking disparity in George Eliot's treatment of them. Most of us, I think, would say

that Lydgate is much more fully and carefully documented in terms
of his social and intellectual background. His *milieu* is very thoroughly explored and his intellectual interests expounded in some
detail. Casaubon's social position is taken for granted and his intellectual interests, though insistently referred to, figure in the novel as
no more than a matter of hint and allusion, of casual mention of
Lowth or Warburton or Bryant.

Why should this be so? One general answer might be that George
Eliot realized that if she documented Casaubon in the same detail
as Lydgate the novel would be overburdened with a mass of exposition difficult to assimilate to the narrative flow. This is true but it
only pushes the problem back one stage so that we must now ask
why she favours Lydgate and not Casaubon or why she does not take
the background to *both* characters equally for granted. If we look at
the evidence of her letters and journals or of the Quarry for *Middlemarch* we find that George Eliot did a great deal of research necessary
to the creation of Lydgate—writing to doctors, reading back-files of
the *Lancet* and so on—whereas she did little for Casaubon. Yet this
proves nothing since, as we shall see, George Eliot was so familiar
with the body of intellectual interests figured by Casaubon that she
had no *need* to do fresh research; had she wished she could have
documented him out of thirty years' experience of the life he represents. Of course, Casaubon's social position was so familiar, not only
to George Eliot but also to her audience, as not to need documentation. The Anglican cleric, in all his doctrinal variety, was an extremely common figure in fiction. But this is not true of Casaubon's
peculiar intellectual interests. Moreover, the doctor was also a familiar fictional figure—thus we must ask what was so novel about
Lydgate as to demand fuller documentation?[3]

Here we must note one important difference between the two
characters. Casaubon's intellectual life has nothing at all to do with
either his religious life—which is even more non-existent than Mr.
Cadwallader's—or with his position in society. It is this divorce between the different aspects of the man that gives a particular ironic
weight to the futility of Dorothea's "eagerness for a binding theory
which could bring her own life and doctrine into strict connection
with that amazing past, and give the remotest sources of knowledge
some bearing on her actions" (Ch. 10) or—and here the irony is
heavier—her idea that "perhaps even Hebrew might be necessary—
at least the alphabet and a few roots—in order to arrive at the core

of things, and judge soundly on the social duties of the Christian" (Ch. 7).

In strong contrast we are told that Lydgate "carried to his studies in London, Edinburgh and Paris, the conviction that the medical profession as it might be was the finest in the world; presenting the most perfect interchange between science and art; offering the most direct alliance between intellectual conquest and the social good" (Ch. 15).

Between "the social good" and the "intellectual conquest," between his medical practice and his private researches, there is initially no divorce for Lydgate. They are tragically sundered by his marriage. And, because initial connection and subsequent divorce needs more demonstration than simple divorce, George Eliot must treat Lydgate in greater detail than Casaubon.

In one of his essays John Stuart Mill commented that: "In every religious record handed down from remote ages there is always much which, to advanced culture, seems inappropriate or false; but men do not pass suddenly from one system of thought to another; they first exhaust every imaginable expedient for reconciling the two."[4] While Mill's remark is appropriate to Casauban's age it is not appropriate to Casaubon himself. This is indeed perhaps the main point to be grasped about his scholarship; that it is in no sense an expedient for reconciling a system of thought to religious belief—as I have said Casaubon exhibits *no* religious life in any real sense of the phrase; indeed his researches are an escape route rather than an exploration, an attempt to disguise from others and even from himself the sense of human failure, the cold vacuum at the core of his being. Moreover, as the novel insists, his labours are misdirected, anachronistic and futile. To see why this is so we must explore his intellectual context and unravel two strands which cross and tangle in the late eighteenth and early nineteenth centuries—the development of the Higher Criticism and the interest in Mythography. If in following these clues, I seem to turn into a Casaubon myself, I apologize; the subject has a certain mouldering fascination and, if labyrinthine, does eventually lead back to the novel.

Let us dispose first of the Higher Criticism. I have already said that George Eliot had no need to do special research on this aspect of intellectual background; so familiar was she with the subject that she could in a sense have echoed Flaubert—"Casaubon, c'est moi." Of course, Hennell's *Inquiry concerning the Origin of Christianity* had played a crucial part in her own development, but I think the two primary documents for our purpose are her review of R. W. Mackay's *The Progress of the Intellect* in the *Westminster Review* (January 1851) and her translation, some years earlier, of Strauss's *Das Leben Jesu*. I shall lean heavily on the latter for my account of the Higher Criticism since we can thus be sure we are dealing with material George Eliot knew by heart.

Strauss begins with the same point as Mill, with the clash between ancient or sacred records taken literally and interpretations put upon them by more intellectually sophisticated ages. This is especially true of allegedly divine records which purport to tell of "the immediate intervention of the divine in human affairs," since intellectual progress "consists mainly in the gradual recognition of a chain of causes and effects connecting natural phenomena with each other," so that the rational mind will come to see ancient records only as "mediate links" and not as the literal word of God.

Given this clash, Strauss postulates two possible reactions: (1) The divine cannot have happened as recorded; (2) The records are true but that which has so happened cannot have been divine.

That being so men will adopt one of two methods of resolving the clash: (1) They will find allegorical meanings in the records, e.g. the Gods will represent forces of nature or will have some ethical signification; (2) They will take the records as history but will see them as the records of ancient men, not of gods.

Strauss points out that the Greeks reacted in both ways to the writings of Hesiod and Homer and he finds the same thing happening very early in the interpretation of Hebrew records. Thus Philo, when the story seems unworthy of God, when it is overtly anthropomorphic or self-contradictory, takes refuge in allegory. Thus Origen recognizes the divine in the records but denies it actually manifested itself in so immediate a manner. The modern representative of this reaction for Strauss is Kant, who sees divine records as allegories of the ethical ideas and imperatives which interested him. One offshoot of the reaction towards allegory which was later developed by German critics was the doctrine of Accommodation; this is the idea that writers of divine records accommodate their meaning to the limitations of their audience; when this audience is ignorant or barbarous the result may seem unedifying or untrue to later ages. As one German theologian, Semler, puts it: "Do not the better informed often find it expedient, when dealing with ignorant persons, to adopt their ideas and language; and do not priests habitually resort to the arts of the rhetorician?"

So much for the allegorical approach. The other mode of interpretation acknowledges the events recorded to be historically true but assigns them to a human and not to a divine origin; this naturally is the line taken in early days by heretics or by enemies of Christianity; it recurs again with some of the deists and free-thinkers of the eighteenth century—Toland, Bolingbroke, Wollaston—who apply it not merely to the Old Testament but also to the miracles of Jesus. It develops also in eighteenth-century Germany; for example, in the so-called Wolfenbuttel fragments published by Lessing in 1774, in which divine communication is attacked as mere pretence and miracles dismissed as illusions, "practised with the design of giving stability and efficiency" to Hebrew laws and institutions.

A mild proponent of this view might allow that the Deities of popular worship were probably once good and benevolent people who were later deified by posterity; a hostile proponent, on the other hand, would argue that divine records stem from artful imposters and cruel tyrants who "had veiled themselves in a nimbus of divinity for the purpose of subjugating the people to their dominion." It is this kind of approach George Eliot deplores in her review of Mackay:

> The introduction of a truly philosophic spirit into the study of mythology—an introduction for which we are chiefly indebted to the Germans—is a great step in advance of the superficial Lucian-like tone of ridicule adopted by many writers of the eighteenth century.

As George Eliot notes, those German scholars who lay the foundations of the Higher Criticism—Eichhorn, Paulus, Baur and Strauss himself—while anxious to find natural origins for divine records are also concerned to stress that the processes involved are morally blameless. Eichhorn's great contribution is to stress that Hebrew history must be treated in the same way as pagan history; the records are due to the different phraseology and habits of mind of a primitive age which we must now translate into our own idiom.

> The deistic idea of imposture could only occur to those refusing to interpret ancient records in the spirit of their age. Had those records been composed at this day, we should certainly be driven to

the alternative of miracle or intentional deceit; but the fact is otherwise; we have here the produce of simple uncritical minds unreservedly using their own conceptions and phraseology.

This growth of the historical sport of interpretation—with its study, for example, of the processes of oral transmission—leads to a view of divine records as myths, as the natural process of time and change.[5] The study of religion is assimilated to the study of mythology in general. Whereas the Renaissance treatment of mythology was concerned primarily with the adjusting of pagan fables to the Christian faith, this process is now reversed; the structure of both Old and New Testament are seen as examples of mythical structure and the groundwork is laid for a comparative study of religion.

Where does Casaubon's attempt to find the key to all Mythologies fit into this? It has often been assumed that when Ladislaw in Chapter 21 tells Dorothea that "If Mr. Casaubon read German he would save himself a great deal of trouble" he is referring to those pioneers of the Higher Criticism I have already mentioned. (It should be noticed that if this were the case Mr. Casaubon's ignorance was shared by practically all his fellow Anglicans.)[6] But it is not precisely so. Casaubon's efforts must, alas, be referred to a much less dignified context.

When an intellectual upheaval such as the one I have described takes place it is a long and confused process and often throws up many lunatic by-products. One such by-product of the attempt to treat Christianity in a philosophical and historical manner was the pseudo-science of mythography, which has indeed, deep roots, but which flourished in the late eighteenth and early nineteenth centuries. This is the dingy niche in which Casaubon, I fear, must be placed.[7]

Eighteenth-century mythography begins by opposing the prevailing tendency to reduce the Bible to myth and, in a sense, continues the Renaissance approach. But whereas the Renaissance generally reconciles pagan fable to Christianity by allegory the mythographer starts by trying to explain pagan myth as a corruption of facts recorded in the Bible; in other words he, too, uses an historical method though one which, as we shall see, needed an unusually large dose of ingenuity and imagination. There are later and more fantastic developments of mythography; one relatively sane approach was to find a rational basis for myth by seeing it as the embodiment of natural forces; another saw myth as symbolic particularly of the pro-creative powers. This led in the early nineteenth century to a flood of phallic symbol hunting, of the most comprehensive, hair-raising kind. But it is mainly with the historical mythographer that we are concerned. George Eliot in her review of Mackay notes that the Higher Criticism is superior not only to eighteenth-century rational-ism but also to "the orthodox prepossessions of writers such as Bryant, who saw in the Greek legends simply misrepresentations of the authentic history given in the book of Genesis."

Casaubon, of course, is characterized by Ladislaw as "crawling a little way after men of the last century—men like Bryant." But Jacob Bryant, whose *A New System, or an Analysis of Ancient Mythology* (1774–6) was amazingly popular, was relatively late in the traditions of historical mythography.

All the mythographers, like Casaubon, were seeking for a single key. Faced with a great diversity of race, custom, creed and fable they attempt to trace all these back to a single origin and square events and myths with the Bible. The single original culture is the world before the Flood; and the process of corruption and diversifica-tion is seen as a result of the scattering of peoples after the destruc-tion of the tower of Babel.

I will not attempt to describe in detail the extreme fringes of what is in itself a lunatic fringe; such speculations involve a great deal about the Druids—the Celts are a favourite candidate for one of the lost tribes of Israel—and about the sunken city of Atlantis. This mish-mash is not unimportant—some of it filters down into Mormonism, for example—but even Casaubon does not go to such extremes.

Rather, like Jacob Bryant, he would be concerned to reduce all myths into variants of the Bible story. Like Bryant he would have been plastic in adjusting inconvenient chronologies and like Bryant he would have supposed a single original language which was lost with the Tower of Babel. This concern with philology is important; George Eliot herself tells us that Casaubon's theories "floated among flexible conjectures no more solid than those etymologies which seemed strong because of likeness in sound, until it was shown that likeness in sound made them impossible."

This is indeed true of the mythographers—the attempt to trace every word back to a supposed Hebrew root which was diversified by the Tower of Babel led to a great deal of etymological confusion. Light began to dawn at the end of the eighteenth century when Sir

William Jones founded the Asiatic Society in 1784 and suggested that Sanskrit might be the common link between European languages. In 1816 a German scholar, Franz Bopp, elaborated the idea of an Indo-European family of languages, and in 1819 Jacob Grimm demonstrated the linguistic connections of diverse languages.

Thus when in Chapter 22 Ladislaw points out that Casaubon, unlike the German, "is not an Orientalist," he is merely underlining the backwardness and futility of Casaubon's scholarship. Casaubon's whole attempt—though he does not know it because he cannot read German—has been exploded in 1825 by the publication of Otfried Muller's *Prolegomena to a Scientific Mythology,* a work referred to by George Eliot in her review of Mackay. Muller ruled out all so-called etymological proofs that tried to relate diverse myths to a Hebrew origin and showed conclusively that mythologies developed independently; there was no chance of resolving the Many into the One. Thus Casaubon, through ignorance, is a complete anachronism, lost in the labyrinth of an exploded pseudo-science. What George Eliot explicitly says in the novel is fully confirmed by plumbing the intellectual history which lies beyond or beneath her fiction.

I shall not attempt to deal with the context of Lydgate's researches at such tedious length. Though George Eliot did a great deal of research on Lydgate's background she would, through G. H. Lewes, have met at first hand most of the men and ideas who go to form this historical context.

It has often been pointed out that the intellectual aspirations of Casaubon and Lydgate run parallel—both of them are seeking for a key, both of them are trying to resolve diversity and plurality into a basic unity. It is agreed that whereas Casaubon's activities are futile Lydgate's are noble, and it is commonly assumed that his life illustrated the blighting effects of his marriage on intellectual hopes that would otherwise have been fulfilled. But this last assumption is not strictly true; we know that George Eliot was generally suspicious of anything in the nature of *a* key to the meaning of life and in fact she carries the parallel between Casaubon and Lydgate a stage further by insisting that *both* of them are fundamentally mistaken in the nature of their research. The evidence is obvious with Casaubon but with Lydgate it resides in one brief remark which tends, I think, to get overlooked. The passage occurs in Chapter 15 in which George Eliot discusses Lydgate in relation to the great French physiologist, Bichat.

This great seer did not go beyond the consideration of the tissues as ultimate facts in the living organism, marking the limit of anatomical analysis; but it was open to another mind to say, have not these structures some common basis from which they have all started, as your sarsnet, gauze, net, satin and velvet from the raw cocoon? . . . What was the primitive tissue? In that way Lydgate put the question—not quite in the way required by the awaiting answer; but such missing of the right word befalls many seekers.

The comment is light because George Eliot does not wish us to think of Lydgate's endeavours as futile in the same way as Casaubon's. Indeed, they are not futile; for as T. H. Huxley said in an essay on cell-theory on which George Eliot made notes in the *Middlemarch* Quarry: "There are periods in the history of every science when a false hypothesis is not only better than none at all, but is a necessary forerunner of, and preparation for, the true one." This comment places Lydgate; it is in this sense that George Eliot can make it quite clear, without detracting from him, that he was mistaken in the direction of his research.

The problem then is—how precisely can we define Lydgate's mistake? One possible answer is in philosophical terms—that Lydgate may, in Huxley's terms, be confusing the familiar "Matter" with a real entity. Both Huxley in "The Physical Basis of Life" (an essay remarkably close in so many ways to George Eliot's own outlook) and Lewes in *Problems of Life and Mind* dilate on this fallacy.

But I suspect that George Eliot is thinking here in more specifically biological terms—that what is missing from Lydgate's question is any reference to cell-theory. Without going into the history of nineteenth-century biological thought I think we can say this is the right answer because it functions in terms of the novel itself.[8] In this way while the irony of Casaubon is that he is in ignorance of the real work already done by German scholars in the near-past, the irony of Lydgate is that he is just too soon for the real work to be done, again by German scholars, in the near future. This gives a particular emphasis to "the awaiting answer." Casaubon's mistake is his own fault, Lydgate's mistake is an accident of history. In his day his microscope would not have been good enough for the work to be done; Robert Brown—mentioned elsewhere by Lydgate—only did his vital work on the cell nucleus in 1831; the crucial break-through by the German

biologists, Schwann and Scheider, was to come a few years later in
1838–9. By that time Lydgate had dwindled to a fashionable practice
and a treatise on Gout. Poor Lydgate—his research, like his medical
practice, is just a little too premature. And there is, incidentally, one
final irony, disconnected with the novel, that George Eliot was herself limited in her biological knowledge, that biochemistry has, after
all, brought us back from cell-theory as she knew it to something like
Lydgate's notion of primitive tissue.

III

One function of this essay has been to show that George Eliot's mind
is like the National Gallery; for every canvas on display there are two
stored away in the basement. Granted that the full range of her mind
does not always display itself in her fiction the question of relevance
reasserts itself. This is something every reader must decide for himself. For my part, whereas the documentation of Lydgate's status as
a practising doctor is vital, since it affects the social pressures which
circumvent him, the delineation of his and Casaubon's purely intellectual *milieux* is relatively marginal. Nevertheless, it seems to me to
brace and support the novel while remaining largely invisible; the
comforting sense of amplitude, solidity or density that we derive from
the actual novel is thereby reinforced. Moreover, it does put Lydgate's research aspirations in a slightly different perspective and it
does help to define more precisely those overlapping areas of similitude and difference which he shares with Casaubon, so that we can
adapt to these two characters what Henry James once said of Lydgate
and Dorothea: "The mind passes from one to the other with that
supreme sense of the vastness and variety of human life, under aspects apparently similar, which it belongs only to the greatest novels
to produce."[9]

NOTES

1. Paris, 1933.
2. U. C. Knoepflmacher, *Religious Humanism and the Victorian Novel*
   (Princeton, 1965); B. J. Paris, *Experiments in Life; George Eliot's
   Quest for Values* (Detroit, 1965).
3. The point, briefly, is that George Eliot is delineating in Lydgate the
   emergence of a new kind of doctor, with new status and new ideas of

medical practice. Consequently he arouses the jealousy of his more traditional colleagues. For a fuller consideration of this aspect of Lydgate see my edition of *Middlemarch* (Penguin Books, 1965).

4. "Early Grecian History and Legend," *Edinburgh Review,* October 1846. Collected in the second volume of *Discussions and Dissertations,* the whole essay is a striking, if oblique, commentary on many aspects of Victorian religious thought.

5. One by-product of this was the attempt to treat the Bible as literature. A pioneer in this field was Robert Lowth in his *De sacra poesi Hebraeorum* (1753). Casaubon asks Dorothea to read him some pages of Lowth in Chapter 37.

6. "Writing to Julius Hare in 1835—the year of the publication of Strauss's *Das Leben Jesu*—Thomas Arnold notes as one of the objects of a proposed theological review: 'To make some beginnings of Biblical Criticism, which, as far as relates to the Old Testament, is in England almost nonexistent.'" W. O. Raymond, *The Infinite Moment* (Toronto, 1965), pp. 20-1.

7. The fullest treatment of mythography is E. B. Hungerford's *Shores of Darkness* (New York, 1941). Much relevant material is also contained in E. Neff's *The Poetry of History* (New York, 1947). I am deeply indebted to both these books.

8. On the general background of biological thought *see* C. J. Singer's *A History of Biology* (London, 1959).

9. Henry James, review of *Middlemarch* in *The Galaxy* (March 1873); reprinted in *The House of Fiction,* ed. L. Edel (London, 1957).

DOROTHY VAN GHENT

On *The Egoist*

With Meredith's *The Egoist* we enter into a critical problem. . . .
That is the problem offered by a writer of recognizably impressive
stature, whose work is informed by a muscular intelligence, whose
language has splendor, whose "view of life" wins our respect, and yet
for whom we are at best able to feel only a passive appreciation
which amounts, practically, to indifference. We should be unjust to
Meredith and to criticism if we should, giving in to the inertia of
indifference, simply avoid dealing with him and thus avoid the problem along with him. He does not "speak to us," we might say; his
meaning is not a "meaning for us"; he "leaves us cold." But do not
the challenge and the excitement of the critical problem as such lie
in that ambivalence of attitude which allows us to recognize the
intelligence and even the splendor of Meredith's work, while, at the
same time, we experience a lack of sympathy, a failure of any enthusiasm of response?

The difficulty is not that the Meredithian prose places too much
demand upon the reader's attentiveness. There is no "too much" of
this kind that a work of art can require of us. *Tristram Shandy* requires as much or more. Even *Pride and Prejudice,* for all its sim-

plicity of surface, asks that we read with as alert an attentiveness to the word. Henry James offers more sinuous verbal paths than Meredith, paths that demand more of concentration inasmuch as they may be marked only by commas or question marks or dots that signify a suspension or attenuation of the track of communication, where Meredith would set up crusty substantives for the mind's grasp to help it around corners. "The enjoyment of a work of art," James said,

> the acceptance of an irresistible illusion, constituting, to my sense, our highest experience of "luxury," the luxury is not greatest, by my consequent measure, when the work asks for as little atten- tion as possible. It is greatest, it is delightfully, divinely great, when we feel the surface, like the thick ice of the skater's pond, bear without cracking the strongest pressure we throw on it.[1]

And, indeed, it seems to be precisely where Meredith offers the toughest stylistic going that we enjoy him the most. This is true at least of *The Egoist,* if not of later work. Curiously, our very sense of a *virtue* of excrescence in the style is symptomatic of that failure of thoroughly significant communication which we feel in Meredith. It is symptomatic, but let us insist that it is not the failure itself; for to be felt as excrescence, even fine excrescence, style must be related to *something else* in the work to which it seems to be perilously appended—just as building ornament is sensed as excrescent only as we see it in relation to the building.

Nor is the difficulty a lack of sensitive craft and pattern. *The Egoist* is a beautifully planned novel. Its pace is assured and power- ful; from the opening incident, when Willoughby, on the terrace with Constantia Durham, snubs the marine lieutenant and tosses off, "I'll send him a check," to the last, when he deliciously misfires his revenge in all directions at once, events march their complicated route with a large inevitability. The spatial, or plastic, conception of the book is as fine as its movement in time: Willoughby's fantastic rigidity is set around, like a Maypole, with a gay and urgent dance on ribbons; the flat-footed, muscle-bound, blown-jowled monolith of his self-importance is host to a lawn festival of delicate searchings, bright scurryings, mobile strategies of the intelligences whose living occasions he has tried to halter at his center.

Nor should we confuse Meredith's failure with his deliberate limi- tation of the comic drama to the scope of a lawn festival, or, as he says, in his "Prelude" on the Comic Spirit, to human nature in the drawing-room of civilized men and women, where we have no dust of the struggling outer world, no mire, no violent crashes. . . .

In this "Prelude," he merely puts into manifesto a limitation which Jane Austen made; . . . he confines his interest to "human nature in the drawing-room." Human nature is as human there as anywhere else, its opportunities as full and as menacing as in a slum or a coal mine or a dust bowl or a snake pit. It is perhaps strategic to remind ourselves of this fact again here, before we go on to Henry James, for our understanding of James would indeed be stultified if we retained still any facile notion that "life" is deeper and thicker in certain material conditions than in others, among the masses than among the classes, on a street corner than in a drawing room, in a chamber pot than in a porcelain cup.

Mr. Wilson Follett, in his introduction to the Modern Library edition of *The Egoist,* approaches Meredith's dwindled reputation in another way, from the point of view of certain vast generational changes in philosophical and psychological assumptions as to the nature of personality. He says,

> The central fact, the change behind all changes, is the modern annihilation of the Will, both as a valid concept and as a working tool. Up to our own generation man had embraced the belief . . . that he was at least partly the master of his own fate; and, acting on that belief, he had often made his conviction actually work. It had the important pragmatic sanction that it made him feel at home in his world, a world of moral choice. It is among the ruins of that world that we now grope. We see ourselves as lost and rootless in a universe without meaning—victims of malevolently blind forces, in and outside ourselves, that predetermine our actions and reduce our will and our vaunted reason to mere delusive reflexes, behavioristic phenomena. Meredith represents a world of Will, a society of lives modifiable by Will; and that fact alone is enough to give our time the sensation of being divided from him by a span computable in nothing less than light-years.[2]

How, then, are we to understand the fact that George Eliot's universe, where moral choice traces its significant reign, is not similarly divided from us? Or, to use a modern example, how are we to justify our response of excited intelligence and conviction to a book like

Albert Camus's *La Peste*, where the vocation of man, even man in despair, is seen as altruistic *willing*? It might, indeed, be argued that, in a world denuded of values and meanings, dramas in which the will is an operative factor would have a greater poignancy of significance—at least potentially—than they could have in a world which took for granted the measurable effects of willing. It might be argued that, as the conception of the will has become more complicated, complicated by our knowledge that we act under "blind forces" which are our will while yet we will against them, dramas of human relationships under the aspect of personally willed modification would have a more intense interest for us because we would find in them a more complex significance, a greater ambiguity, than would be possible if the personal will were thought of as morally univocal and psychologically undivided. The fiction that has attracted us most in an "absurd" world whose expressive signature is the concentration camp is fiction in which the will, though viewed variously, is still the moral center of the composition: this is true—to take extreme cases— of those fictions in which the personal will is defeated, "absurdly" defeated, as in Kafka and Hardy; it is true of Hemingway's fictions, where the very meagerness of the area within the Nothing where the will can operate is the sign of its tragic nobility; it is true of those fictions that explore the possibilities of self-knowledge (knowledge of what it is that we "will," or of the will's capacity for modification, or of its need for reteaching by experience of the emotions and instincts it has neglected or denied), as in Conrad and James and much of Thomas Mann; it is true of those that explore the epic corruption of the will, as in Melville and Dostoevski. Generational changes in assumptions as to what the will is, how it works, whether it is practically operative or not, do not explain our distance from Meredith, for—so far as moral significance in fiction is concerned—our interest is still intensely in the concept of the will. It is probable that indifference to a work of art (after we have considered the work well) is never explained by the *kind* of "world view" or "life view" that it holds, no matter how alien from our own, but only by the lack of self-substantial coherency of that view of things as represented in the aesthetic form.

In connection with Meredith's view of the human world as a place where choices made by the personal will perceptibly affect reality, *The Egoist* offers, in its major elements, special reasons for a rapport with the modern reader which is nevertheless lacking. There are, in

the book, two chief modes in which the effective will appears, represented by Willoughby's immalleable self-will, aspiring to a simplifica-
tion of the universe on his own measure, and by Clara Middleton's
delicate, mobile, searching will, aspiring to air, opportunity, multi-
plicity. As for Willoughby's effectiveness,

> *Through very love of self himself he slew,*

as his epitaph has it—certainly a pronounced victory of volition. The
"comic drama of the suicide" illustrated by Willoughby's career is a
drama that, in clinical rather than in English country-house materials, is fairly obsessive to modern interest. It is a drama that Dr.
Karl Menninger has traced, uncomically, in *Man against Himself.*
We find the note of it in W. H. Auden's poem "September 1, 1939."

> The windiest militant trash
> Important Persons shout
> Is not so crude as our wish:
> What mad Nijinsky wrote
> About Diaghilev
> Is true of the normal heart;
> The error bred in the bone
> Of each woman and each man
> Craves what it cannot have,
> Not universal love,
> But to be loved alone.[3]

Of the craving "to be loved alone" Meredith's Willoughby makes the
necessary conversion into self-love, since we cannot be loved alone
by anybody but ourselves. With Clara,

> He dragged her through the labyrinths of his penetralia, in his
> hungry coveting to be loved more and still more, more still, until
> imagination gave up the ghost, and he talked to her plain hearing
> like a monster.

Willoughby is the fetus in full panoply, clothing himself "at others'
expense," enjoying, or seeking to enjoy, "without incurring the immense debtorship for a thing done," possessing "without obligation to
the object possessed." These phrases are Meredith's description of the
sentimentalist, Willoughby being the prime example; they are also
descriptive of an embryo. Willoughby is the monster of the womb,
imposing on drawing room and lawn his unearned adulthood, his

fetal vaporousness supported by name, wealth, and "a leg," and his demands for osmotic nourishment as if society were but one huge placenta designed for his shelter and growth. With Willoughby we *should* have the utmost rapport, for we have learned fiercely to understand him, through our so broadly ramified education in the fetal and infantile proclivities of the adult.

Willoughby must be delivered, but unfortunately not as in a normal birth, from the womb to the world, for he has been wearing the world as a custom-made womb. His delivery is the delivery of other people from him, from the extravagance of their courtesy in allowing him to occupy them. Willoughby is the difficult occasion for other people to dis-entrail themselves, by the exercise of intelligence, from a strangling, homomorphic Cause; he is the occasion in revolt against which individuality and variety of will are realized. By courtesy, faith, habit, and social exigency Clara Middleton and Vernon Whitford and Laetitia Dale find themselves in the kissing arms of this octopus, fanned on by the aunts, by Dr. Middleton's taste in port, and by a society of submarine fantasies and chattering twilight expectations. They extricate themselves, with difficulty, by learning to recognize meaning in experience and by acting on the recognition. "The drama of Meredith's characters," Ramon Fernandez says,

> is always and essentially the drama of an exacting sensibility. They begin by going straight ahead, in the direction of life, along the road of action. Their first acts, however rich and generous they may be, are simple, normal, not to say conventional. . . . Since they can live only by acting, they act at first in perfect harmony with the circle in which tradition has caused them to be born. But then sensibility, at the first collision, is awakened. They feel confusedly that they can no longer live in the conditions which at first they accepted. And there they are, thrown back upon themselves, attentive, on the alert, seeking anxiously among the echoes of experience the key to the enigma which shall deliver them. To live for them is to seek to think, but to think in order to be able afresh to breathe, act, and bloom.[4]

The nobility, the interest, the viability of this conception of character we cannot but acknowledge, and we make the acknowledgment the more readily as Meredith's view of life touches off with electric irony,

and almost as if allegorically, certain grim features, both psychological and political, of our own condition.

Why, then, do we find ourselves indifferent? "Not a difficulty
met," James said of Meredith, speaking as a novelist about a novelist,

> not a figure presented, not a scene constituted—not a dim shadow
> condensing once into audible or visible reality—making you hear
> for an instant the tap of its feet on the earth.[5]

This is perhaps to go too far, particularly between novelists who are
so much akin—in respect at least of stylistic elaboration, the social
setting, the delicate development of a consciousness of values—as
James is to Meredith in *The Egoist*. But it is indicative. Willoughby
is a victim in wax model, Virginia Woolf said, not flesh and blood:
he "is turned slowly round before a steady fire of scrutiny and criticism which allows no twitch on the victim's part to escape it"[6]—a
process that, on description, looks as unfair as other destructive
magical rites, as unfair as torture for confession. The fact is that
Willoughby is treated as a perfectly lonely aberration, a freak; nobody (neither we as readers nor anyone in the book) knows how he
came about, how he happened, what he is for, what connection there
might be between his psychological peculiarities and the human soul
at large. We do not really supply the connections when we say,
"There is a Willoughby in each of us," for though the statement
seems valid enough, its validity lies outside the book and not struc-
turally within it: *within* the book there are no Willoughbys except
Willoughby. Meredith makes similarly extraneous statements about
Willoughby's human representativeness, but they remain dogmatic,
without internal aesthetic corroboration. From the earliest note we
have of his youth,

> "When he was a child he one day mounted a chair, and there he
> stood in danger, would not let us touch him, because he was taller
> than we, and we were to gaze. Do you remember him, Eleanor?
> 'I am the sun of the house!' It was inimitable!"

he is uncaused, a prodigy; and his career in maturity has only an
external relatedness—a relatedness of exploitation—to other people; he
is an obstacle to them, an ingratiating and portentous obstacle, but
quite definitively outside of them, not inside. That we are not,

aesthetically, given any insight as to what subtle internal bonds there might be between Willoughby and society—what, in the social soul, was itself Willoughby in order to fertilize this monster—or as to what taint of identity there might be between the soul of Willoughby and the soul of anybody else, makes us restless with his image, powerfully as that image is drawn, for he has evidently much too important a symbolic potential to be left so without spiritual relations, so unproliferative of the possible meanings he might have either for the constitution of the body politic or for that of the private psyche.

Like the giant of *Jack and the Beanstalk,* he is an external menace only, not a suffered portion of self or of the cultural conditions of self. That giant's feet did not touch the earth, because, after the scramble of escape, the stalk was cut down at a single blow. At the end of *The Egoist,* a dozen people—all the world—take whacks with free conscience at the beanstalk. Jane Austen's Mr. Collins, in *Pride and Prejudice,* is a monster quite in the fetal style of Willoughby, but Mr. Collins has the spiritual support of a society of other monsters with common economic causes, and the menace that he offers is one that, graded from grotesque obviousness to inconspicuous subtlety, is distributed through the social organism, pervasive in the private soul, providing the common stuff of the very language—thus truly dangerous because unconsciously environing. Mr. Collins—that is, the representative qualities of Mr. Collins, the complacencies of egoism backed by desperations of economic footing and caste, in a culture contracted to their measure—cannot really be escaped, even by happy marriages and removals, but must be dealt with alertly at every moment as the condition of existence.

Henry James's Osmond, in *The Portrait of a Lady,* also affords parallels with Willoughby, and again the difference in treatment is significant of Meredith's failure to give his egoist a spiritual context. *The Egoist* is of the year 1877; *The Portrait of a Lady,* 1881. We should not wish to force an unwarranted meaning upon these dates, but they do provide a curious comment on the parallels between the two books, particularly in view of James's opinion of Meredith. Health, wealth, and beauty are the qualifications Willoughby demands in his bride; she must also

> come to him out of cloistral purity . . . out of an egg-shell, somewhat more astonished at things than a chick . . . and seeing him with her sex's eyes first of all men.

It is a note sounded also by Osmond, in James's *Portrait,* and we hear
in it almost the same comic exaggeration. He asks, concerning Isabel,
who has been suggested to him as a possible bride,

> "Is she beautiful, clever, rich, splendid, universally intelligent and
> unprecedentedly virtuous? It's only on those conditions that I care
> to make her acquaintance."

Contempt for "the world" is the breath of life to both Willoughby
and Osmond; their need to scorn it and set themselves and their
possessions apart from it is the inspiration of their existence, on the
principle that "the world" must admire where it is scorned and pay
to the scorner the tribute of its own helpless vulgarity. For Willoughby,

> The breath of the world, the world's view of him, was partly his
> vital breath, his view of himself. . . . [He was] born to look
> down upon a tributary world, and to exult in being looked to. Do
> we wonder at his consternation in the prospect of that world's
> blowing foul upon him? Princes have their obligations to teach
> them they are mortal, and the brilliant heir of a tributary world
> is equally enchained by the homage it brings him. . . .

And for Osmond,

> To surround his interior with a sort of invidious sanctity, to tanta-
> lise society with a sense of exclusion, to make people believe his
> house was different from every other, to impart to the face that he
> presented to the world a cold originality—this was the ingenious
> effort of the personage to whom Isabel had attributed a superior
> morality . . . under the guise of caring only for intrinsic values
> Osmond lived exclusively for the world. . . .

These parallelisms—and others—almost suggest that James deliberately used the pattern conceived by Meredith. But how much more
he discovered in it! The difference lies in a sense of spiritual context. Willoughby appears without "internal relations" with the society he dominates or with the individuals whose self-development
he attempts to suffocate; he is, moreover, personally valueless, a formal abstraction of conceit without any other palpable qualification
than a "leg." Osmond is incomparably a subtler evil, for he does represent values, and when he says—in the magnificent scene in which
he forbids Isabel to go to England—

> "I think we should accept the consequences of our actions, and
> what I value most in life is the honour of a thing!"

the gravity of his sincerity, speaking, as Isabel realizes, in the name of
"something sacred and precious," is in perfect measure with his blas-
phemy against *precisely the same values* as his wife interprets them.
The menace that he offers is a menace within Isabel herself, in her
recognition of the spiritual density and integrity of a man so corrupt.
Osmond speaks her own language, for it is in "the honour of a thing"
and in accepting "the consequences of her actions" that she finds her
own moral identity; the menace, the confusion that cripples decision,
lies in the formal similarity of their moral aspirations and the appalling dissimilarity of the interpretations these yield to each. Osmond has roots and ramifications: he is supported not only by human accomplices in his peculiarly subtle guilt, but by ages of value
growth thoroughly intelligential, by Rome itself, by Europe, by Isabel's own passion for a finer experience. It is Osmond's spiritual context, his "internal relations" with society and with individuals, that
make him so meaningful a figure. It is Willoughby's lack of such
context that makes him a *bibelot* of literature.

The prose style of *The Egoist,* intensely nervous and packed, constantly inventive, has somewhat the same status of an abnormal and
eccentric growth as does Willoughby, and in this sense Siegfried
Sassoon's remark that the phraseology of the book "is an artifice
which seems appropriate"[7] has an unintended rightness. The style
is beautifully wrought, as is the figure of Willoughby himself; we
cannot deny it its qualities of virtu. Again and again the vivid and
witty image concretizes a state of mind. There is Willoughby's agony
over the threatened defection of Clara.

> The fact that she was a healthy young woman returned to the
> surface of his thoughts like the murdered body pitched into the
> river, which will not drown, and calls upon the elements of dis-
> solution to float it.

Or the quality of his pathos with Laetitia:

> As his desire was merely to move her without an exposure of him-
> self, he had to compass being pathetic as it were under the im-
> pediments of a mailed and gauntleted knight, who can not easily
> heave the bosom, or show it heaving.

Or his torments of decision:

> Laocoon of his own serpents, he struggled to a certain magnificence of attitude in the muscular net of constrictions he flung round himself.

It is of this kind of stylistic virtuosity that Ramon Fernandez speaks when he says that Meredith's "artifice" consists

> in representing the most concrete possible equivalent for a mental movement. . . . Meredith fills in the intervals of the action with little symbolical actions because he is anxious above all not to let his thought and that of the reader lose their dramatic rhythm.[8]

His images, Fernandez says, thus constitute "a defense system against abstraction." Since the definitive and suicidal characteristic of the egoist is his abstraction from the living world, a style so full of concrete images and tough little verbal dramas has its peculiar logic here, for it keeps the egoist within our ken; he might otherwise lose his liveliness and dissolve into his own sentimental vapor. Yet, attractive as is this rationalization of style, one asks if there is not a fallacy in throwing so much of the burden of concreteness upon style and if the concreteness most necessary to fiction does not lie in that spiritual *contextualism* of lives which we have noticed as lacking in *The Egoist*. Where such context strongly exists and style subserves it, is not the concreteness there too—the concreteness that makes the created world of a novel excitedly meaningful "for us"? Where it does not exist, and style is called upon to substitute for it by energy and picture, is not style forced into an unnatural position where it figures as a kind of "egoist" itself—a separated, self-willed, self-regarding element? In what is surely one of the most abstract vocabularies in fiction, and one of the least "image-making" of styles, Jane Austen evoked a concrete world that is meaningful "for us" because, like a world, it exists in the autonomy of its own internal relations.

On Meredith's style is imposed a somewhat desperate function of keeping author, characters, and reader in a state of awareness, not so much of what is going on, but of each other, a function of keeping us awake to the fact that we are reading a brilliant book by an exceptionally intelligent author about highly burnished characters—all of which the style makes us ever so ready to admit. One thinks of Milton here, for Meredith's style has its brilliance as Milton's has its "grandness," and in reading Milton one has to hang on by the words and the astonishing verbal manipulation if sometimes by nothing else. What Desmond McCarthy said of Meredith might be said of Milton: "It must be remembered in reading Meredith that half his touches are not intended to help you to realize the objects so much as to put power into the form."[9] The statement applied to Meredith makes only a fumbling kind of sense, inasmuch as it divides the "form" from the "object," and what we see as failure in Meredith is just this division of form and object, the division of the elegant pattern and splendid style of the book from potential meaning, from potential relationships between characters and thus potential relationships with ourselves. Applied to Milton, it has a good deal more sense, and the difference lies here. One feels that, in a highly special and deeply meaningful way, the Miltonic style *is* "the object"; one feels that the verbal manipulation is the mind's desperate exhibition of its independence and strength, working on the plastic stuff of the world in a frightful vacuum of other stuff adequately tough to reward the worker's gift and exertion—the mind is with its "back to the wall," so to speak, in the position of Lucifer; one feels that this is the moral kinetics which, in Milton, is profoundly "the object," and that the "power" of Milton's language is the same as that satanic power which moved a causeway through empty space from hell to earth. We cannot say so much of Meredith. Style is here a brilliant manner, and, with some embarrassment—for we would not be without the pleasures Meredith provides—we would quote Dr. Middleton on style in the author's own admirably intelligent style:

> "You see how easy it is to deceive one who is an artist in phrases. Avoid them, Miss Dale; they dazzle the penetration of the composer. That is why people of ability like Mrs. Mountstuart see so little; they are bent on describing brilliantly."

NOTES

1. In *The Art of the Novel,* James's Critical Prefaces edited by R. P. Blackmur (New York: Charles Scribner's Sons, 1934), p. 304.
2. New York: 1947, pp. xii-xiii. Reprinted with permission.
3. *The Collected Poetry of W. H. Auden* (New York: Random House, Inc., 1945), p. 58.

4. *Messages* (New York: Harcourt, Brace & Company, Inc., 1927), p. 175.
5. Quoted by Siegfried Sassoon, in *Meredith* (New York: The Viking Press, Inc., 1948), p. 232.
6. *The Second Common Reader* (New York: Harcourt, Brace & Company, Inc., 1932), pp. 252-253.
7. Sassoon, *op. cit.*, p. 208.
8. *Messages, op. cit.*, p. 171.
9. Quoted by Siegfried Sassoon, *op. cit.*, p. 210.

M. A. GOLDBERG

Trollope's *The Warden*:
A Commentary on the "Age of Equipoise"

Anthony Trollope, like his contemporary, Walter Bagehot, has frequently been viewed as the perfect exponent of the Victorian era. References to an "age of Trollope" or an "age of Bagehot" are numerous. Yet, almost invariably, historians have turned to Trollope's later political novels—*The Way We Live Now, Phineas Redux, The Prime Minister*—rather than to the earlier works, *The Warden* or *Barchester Towers,* the two books on which Trollope's literary reputation seems to rest today. *The Warden,* especially, seems so nonpolitical, that critics appear to have limited themselves to discussing the charm of Trollope's characterization or to echoing Hawthorne's appraisal that, like all of Trollope's volumes, this is "just as English as beef-steak."

Early in *The Warden,* the author describes the position assumed by the Reverend Septimus Harding, precentor of Barchester Cathedral, toward the controversy raging about him. As warden of Hiram's Hospital, Mr. Harding is the recipient of funds attendant to his position. When distribution of the funds is challenged, Mr. Harding appears as the passive and innocent victim, caught between the bat-

From *Nineteenth-Century Fiction,* Vol. XVII, No. 4, 381-90. © 1962 by the Regents of the University of California. Reprinted by permission of the Regents and the author.

tles of conservative church dignitaries (represented by his son-in-law, Archdeacon Grantly) and the radicals (represented by his prospective son-in-law, John Bold). In his analysis of the warden's situation, Trollope writes:

> Different feelings kept him silent; he was as yet afraid of differing from his son-in-law—he was anxious beyond measure to avoid even a semblance of rupture with any of his order, and was painfully fearful of having to come to an open quarrel with any person on any subject. His life had hitherto been so quiet, so free from strife; his little early troubles had required nothing but passive fortitude; his subsequent prosperity had never forced upon him any active cares—had never brought him into disagreeable contact with any one. He felt that he would give almost anything . . . could he by so doing have quietly dispelled the clouds that were gathering over him—could he have thus compromised the matter between the reformer and the conservative, between his possible son-in-law, Bold, and his positive son-in-law, the archdeacon.[1]

This is not just a problem of characterization which we encounter here with the kindly old warden; nor is it wholly a matter of Trollope's political conservatism or his desire for ecclesiastical reform. True, we can interpret Mr. Harding's passivity, his anxiety to avoid quarrels, his desire for peace and quiet, as essential characteristics of his personality; or, like Bradford A. Booth, who views this as a social drama which anticipates Ibsen by several decades, we can examine that personality in relation to the ethical problems posed, the larger moral dilemma.[2] But another and larger dimension is added to the novel if we grasp the characterization and the ethical problem within the framework of the age—in particular the 1850's, when the novel first appeared, and which historians increasingly have called the "age of compromise" or the "age of equipoise."

These were the middle Victorian years, the calm that followed the bitter dissensions of the 1840's with open talk of imminent revolution and class war, and the hostilities of the 1880's when English history was being molded by Irish nationalism and Victorian radicalism was merging into twentieth-century socialism. It is in this middle period, with the Great Exhibition of 1851 at one pole and the Second Reform Bill of 1867 at the other, that Asa Briggs discerns a "superficially secure and comfortable England," preaching its gospel of work and peace, while rallying round a banner marked "Rest and be thankful."[3]

G. M. Young perceives "the great peace of the fifties" by contrasting the starkness of James Mill's earlier political dogmas with Bagehot's humorous wisdom in the *English Constitution,* where large allowances were made for stupidity, idleness, and the good nature of mankind. Life was too secure and too leisurely for agitation at this point, the reforms of the prior decades having temporarily satisfied both the conscience of the rich and the aspirations of the impoverished, according to Young. Following the surges of an impetuous and demanding youth, Victorianism was preparing to settle down to a comfortable middle-age, one that was to reach fulfillment with the Education Act of 1870, the Public Health Act of 1874, the Municipal Conference summoned in 1875, or the Factory Acts of 1878.[4]

It is understandable why the tide of Trollope's literary affairs turned with the publication of *The Warden* in 1855. Here, for the first time, Trollope managed to capture the spirit of his age: peace, quietude, equipoise, stability, compromise. We see this spirit most clearly in the warden himself. Throughout the novel he prefers compromise to strife, quietude to upheaval. Early in the text, for example, when the first murmurs of discontent are heard, that hospital funds have not been fairly divided between the warden and his twelve bedesmen, Mr. Harding declares his intention of adding to each man's pittance twopence a day from his own pocket, thus raising the daily stipend to one shilling and sixpence. This appears as a munificent gesture, but it is aimed more at quelling dissension than at removing an evil, as the author himself insists:

> That he himself was overpaid with his modest eight hundred pounds;—he who, out of that, voluntarily gave up sixty-two pounds eleven shillings and fourpence a year to his twelve old neighbours;—he who, for the money, does his precentor's work as no precentor has done it before, since Barchester Cathedral was built;—such an idea has never sullied his quiet, or disturbed his conscience [p. 11].

Though later the archdeacon urges him to dissuade the bedesmen from petitioning for a larger share of funds available, the warden prefers to "remain quiet in the matter" (p. 46). He is "in quiet possession of the good things he had" and would willingly have "compromised the matter" out of his "sheer love of quiet" (p. 51).

The situation demands some kind of change in the peace-loving warden, yet he remains adamant to the close—reinforced by Eleanor, his unmarried daughter who hopes her father "would escape all this dreadful turmoil" (p. 124); and also by his friend, the old bishop, who "wanted peace on the subject" (p. 80). To capitulate to the conservatives—the Archdeacon and Mrs. Grantly, Sir Abraham Haphazard, Mr. Chadwick, and Messrs. Cox and Cumming—demands that Mr. Harding deny the allegations of the newspapers, reject the petition of the bedesmen, and affirm the supremacy of the church militant. To accede to the reformers—John Bold, Tom Towers, the *Jupiter*, Dr. Anticant and Mr. Sentiment—demands that Mr. Harding involve himself with the problem of justice, deny the supremacy of his order, and initiate some plan to distribute the funds more equitably. Mr. Harding does neither. Instead, he slips quietly out of the dilemma by resigning. True, he speaks of an awakened conscience more nudged than aroused, for his resignation is aimed at removing himself from attack, not at alleviating wrongs. When he returns to his hotel, following his resignation, it is with no great moral exaltation, but "quietly, and with a palpitating heart; he almost longed to escape round the corner, and delay the coming storm." Chastised by his son-in-law, he feels small need to defend his stand; instead, we are told, his mind is chiefly engaged in reflecting "how he could escape to bed." His formal resignation, casting no aspersion upon the position being vacated, concedes that he will regard his successor "as enjoying a clerical situation of the highest respectability." And in his last farewell, urging his bedesmen "to raise no further questions among yourselves as to the amount of his [the new warden's] income," he admits, "I cannot say what should be the disposition of these moneys, or how they should be managed, and I have therefore thought it best to go" (pp. 166-191).

The quiet passivity of Mr. Harding is somewhat determined by his worship of St. Cecilia, who provides him with "the divine source of all his melodious joy" (p. 36). As editor of *Harding's Church Music* and director of the Barchester choir, the warden, affectionately named "old Catgut" by several of his bedesmen, is known to play the violoncello daily, honoring his friends with "strains which were to him so full of almost ecstatic joy; and he used to boast that such was the air of the hospital, as to make it a precinct specially fit for the worship of St. Cecilia" (p. 23).

Significantly, this is not the St. Cecilia of Dryden, the saint who has the power to draw an angel down to earth with music that can "untune the sky." Nor is this Pope's Cecilia, whose powers can "lift the soul to heaven."[5] For Pope and Dryden, the dynamic harmony between the temporal and the eternal, a balance between the terrestrial and the celestial is embodied in the music of St. Cecilia. The resultant order is cosmic—but for Mr. Harding, music is an escape from the demands of both the mortal and the divine. For Mr. Harding, Cecilia is the embodiment of personal peace, quiet and passivity. When John Bold comes to explain his projected attack upon the wardenship, Mr. Harding removes himself from the troublesome matter by playing rapidly on his imaginary violoncello (p. 26). When the archdeacon arrives to counsel him on his role in the ensuing battle, the warden creates "an ecstatic strain of perfect music, audible to himself and to St. Cecilia" (p. 44). Forced to hear the legal equivocations of Sir Abraham Haphazard, he escapes by "playing sad dirges on invisible stringed instruments in all manner of positions" (p. 82). In London, while awaiting an audience with Sir Abraham, his dreams turn the coffee-house clock "into a violoncello, with piano accompaniments"; and throughout his interview with the eminent barrister, to whom he first announces his resignation, the warden consistently plays "a slow tune on an imaginary violoncello" (pp. 158-165).

Throughout, Trollope certainly handles the warden with a sympathy and a gentleness of satire, much as Fielding handles Parson Adams or as Goldsmith treats his benevolent Vicar. Both Parson Adams and Dr. Primrose, however, are representative of the excesses of simple benevolence; they are Shaftesburian extremists who fail to recognize the prevalence of deceit and artifice in the world around them. For all his kindness and gentleness, though, Mr. Harding is no advocate of Shaftesburian principle. At his advanced age, he can only advocate snugness and security. Clearly, his world is far removed from the doubts and affirmations of Mill and Carlyle, Newman and Hardy, Arnold and Ruskin.

In his *Autobiography*, Trollope outlines his initial intentions for the novel. At first glance, these appear more consonant with the political and ecclesiastical reforms of the thirties and forties. "I had been struck by two opposite evils,—or what seemed to me to be evils, and . . . I thought that I might be able to expose them, or rather to describe them both in one and the same tale," Trollope announces:

> The first evil was the possession by the Church of certain funds and endowments which had been intended for charitable pur-

poses, but which had been allowed to become incomes for idle Church dignitaries. There had been more than one such case brought to public notice at the time [1851], in which there seemed to have been an egregious malversation of charitable purposes. The second evil was its very opposite. Though I had been much struck by the injustice above described, I had also often been angered by the undeserved severity of the newspapers towards the recipients of such incomes, who could hardly be considered to be the chief sinners in the matter.

Though this may represent a polemical statement of the author's original intentions, we are told almost immediately of the novel that "it failed altogether in the purport for which it was intended."[6]

This disparity between thematic intent and artistic fulfillment is made all the more clear when we examine Trollope's satiric techniques in exposing the "two opposite evils" with which he was initially concerned:

> In former times great objects were attained by great work. When evils were to be reformed, reformers set about their heavy task with grave decorum and laborious argument. . . . We get on now with a lighter step, and quicker: ridicule is found to be more convincing than argument, imaginary agonies touch more than true sorrows, and monthly novels convince, when learned quartos fail to do so [pp. 143-144].

By elevating Mr. Harding's two antagonists to the nobility and grandeur of epic heroes, while proportionately diminishing the value of their attendant actions, Trollope succeeds in mounting his ridicule of Archdeacon Grantly whose "great fault is an overbearing assurance of the virtues and claims of his order" and whose "great foible is an equally strong confidence in the dignity of his own manner and the eloquence of his own words"; and of John Bold who is "too much imbued with the idea that he has a special mission for reforming" (pp. 14-17). The satire is made all the more propitious by providing the antagonists with the non-heroic, cello-playing warden as the object of their struggles.

Trollope's satiric techniques are clearly suggestive of Pope's *Rape of the Lock,* and certainly within the tradition of Boileau's *Le Lutrin* and Dryden's *MacFlecknoe.* This is not to suggest that Trollope is offering here a mock-epic, or even that the mock-epic devices are sustained throughout the text. Within a limited degree, however, the novelist develops his ridicule of the "two opposite evils" through a series of epic allusions scattered throughout the book. These are especially concentrated in four significant chapters. "The Warden's Tea Party" (chap. vi), "The Jupiter" (chap. vii), "Iphigenia" (chap. xi), and "Mount Olympus" (chap. xiv).

Archdeacon Theophilus Grantly, whose praenomen satirizes his temporal concerns, is very vigilant to the slightest attack upon the power and wealth of the church. A Virgilian simile describes the archdeacon girding himself for battle against the petitioning bedesmen: "As the indomitable cock preparing for the combat sharpens his spurs, shakes his feathers, and erects his comb, so did the archdeacon arrange his weapons for the coming war, without misgiving and without fear" (p. 41). Similarly, when the archdeacon indulges in a short game of whist during the warden's tea party, the scene is presented in the same mock-heroic manner. From one side of the room, to the sound of music, a black-coated corps engaged in terpsichorean skirmishes with the muslin ranks:

> One by one they creep forth, and fire off little guns timidly, and without precision. Ah, my men, efforts such as these will take no cities, even though the enemy should be never so open to assault. At length a more deadly artillery is brought to bear; slowly, but with effect, the advance is made; the muslin ranks are broken, and fall into confusion; the formidable array of chairs gives way; the battle is no longer between opposing regiments, but hand to hand, and foot to foot with single combatants, as in the glorious day of old, when fighting was really noble [pp. 58-59].

Simultaneously, at the other side of the room arises another combat, more serious and more sober, for Archdeacon Grantly is engaged in the perils and enjoyments of whist against two prebendaries. Parallels with the famous card game in *The Rape of the Lock* are obvious:

> See how the archdeacon, speechless in his agony, deposits on the board his cards, and looks to heaven or to the ceiling for support. . . . With care precise he places every card, weighs well the value of each mighty ace, each guarded king, and comfort-giving queen; speculates on knave and ten, counts all his suits, and sets his price upon the whole. . . . Thrice has constant fortune favoured the brace of prebendaries, ere the archdeacon rouses him-

self to the battle; but at the fourth assault he pins to the earth a prostrate king, laying low his crown and sceptre, bushy beard, and lowering brow, with a poor deuce [p. 59].

Precisely the same transvaluating techniques are perceptible in Trollope's handling of John Bold and his reforming friends. Recognizably "the Barchester Brutus," Bold has initiated the attack upon the guardians of Hiram's Hospital. Confident that the warden's daughter, whom he loves, will not condemn him for doing what he thinks to be his duty, he bolsters himself "with the consolation of a Roman." The daily *Jupiter* has taken up the cause, and from its seat at Mount Olympus brought the affair under public notice "in one of its leading thunderbolts" (pp. 56-65).

At Mount Olympus, "the workshop of the gods," labors Tom Towers, a "heaven-sent messenger" who has been intimate with Bold and often discussed with him the affairs of the hospital.

> Who has not heard of Mount Olympus,—that high abode of all the powers of type, that favoured seat of the great goddess Pica, that wondrous habitation of gods and devils, from whence, with ceaseless hum of steam and never-ending flow of Castalian ink, issue forth fifty thousand nightly edicts for the governance of a subject nation?

Here, "Tom Towers compounded thunderbolts for the destruction of all that is evil and for the furtherance of all that is good, in this and other hemispheres." Tom Towers, who appears "as though he were a mortal man, and not a god dispensing thunder-bolts from Mount Olympus," is to be found every morning, not far from the "favoured abode of Themis," where he can be seen "inhaling ambrosia and sipping nectar in the shape of toast and tea," striving studiously "to look a man, but knowing within his breast that he was a god" (pp. 126-133).

When other characters enter the fray, they are also included in Trollope's mock-epic. Thus, Mr. Quiverful, the curate of Puddingdale, whom the archdeacon suggests as the new warden, is presented as a "wretched clerical Priam, who was endeavouring to feed his poor Hecuba and a dozen Hectors on the small proceeds of his ecclesiastical kingdom" (pp. 185-186). And Eleanor, who, unlike her father, is "not at all addicted to the Lydian school of romance," appears in the role of Iphigenia, once she determines on self-sacrifice in extricating her father from his miseries—though ultimately "the altar on the shore of the modern Aulis" reeks with no sacrifice, for John Bold agrees readily to abandon his attack (pp. 98-110).

Although Trollope's initial intent was to expose the "two opposite evils," the Bolds and the Grantlys, the radicals and the conservatives, obviously his own satiric techniques have blunted the lance of his polemical battle. The satire is humorous and sympathetic, more like Jane Austen's than Swift's or Pope's. It lacks the clarity of aim and virulence of manner so central to the great eighteenth-century satirists. In the final analysis, Trollope is just as sympathetic to Bold and Grantly, for all their excess, as he is toward the warden with his moral evasions. Clearly at work with Trollope, mitigating his efforts at exposing the two evils, is his own desire for quietude and decorum. This is what made it impossible to take up one side and cling to it, cudgeling the *Jupiter,* say, or the warden—"neither of these programmes recommended itself to my honesty," the novelist concedes in his autobiography.

Thus, satiric images surrounding John Bold are cushioned by Trollope's appraisal of Bold as "brave, eager, and amusing; well-made and good-looking; young and enterprising; his character is in all respects good" (pp. 14-15). In addition, Bold's impending marriage with Eleanor necessarily diminishes from the effectiveness of Trollope's original goal, for this demands a sympathetic portrayal of the reformer.

Similarly, the archdeacon, presented throughout as an object of ridicule, is described in the closing pages as "a gentleman and a man of conscience," one who "improves the tone of society of those among whom he lives," whose "aspirations are of a healthy, if not of the highest kind." The novelist continues with this apologetic for Grantly:

> We fear that he is represented in these pages as being worse than he is; but we have had to do with his foibles, and not with his virtues. We have seen only the weak side of the man, and have lacked the opportunity of bringing him forward on his strong ground. . . . On the whole, the Archdeacon of Barchester is a man doing more good than harm—a man to be furthered and supported, though perhaps also to be controlled; and it is a matter of regret to us that the course of our narrative has required that we should see more of his weakness than his strength [p. 187].

It is almost as if Trollope, anxious to avoid any semblance of political or ecclesiastical dissension, is carefully establishing his own system of checks and balances to enhance the peace and stability of the moment. Like the reigning political party, the novelist has as his responsibility securing and maintaining the peace within the microcosm of his art.

Professor Booth, viewing Mr. Harding as the center of the novel, projects the warden as the embodiment of integrity, incorruptibility and virtue. Still, we must recognize that "virtue" for the 1850's is to be distinguished from Shaftesburian benevolence, Paine's radicalism, or Mill's utilitarianism. For the warden, ethical principle is rather the essence of tranquillity, quietude and compromise. Trollope's gentle satire of the warden is no less apparent than his mock-heroics with Bold and Grantly. The whole situation is for Trollope a source of sympathetic humor. As with Bagehot's portrayal of the English constitution, large allowances must be made for stupidity, excessive zeal, and misplaced honor. What begins as ecclesiastical reform ends as a commentary on this whole "age of equipoise."

NOTES

1. Anthony Trollope, *The Warden* (New York, 1950), p. 51. Paginal references, included within the essay, are to this Modern Library edition.
2. Bradford A. Booth, *Anthony Trollope, Aspects of His Life and Art* (Bloomington, Indiana, 1958), pp. 34-39.
3. Asa Briggs, *Victorian People, A Reassessment of Persons and Themes, 1851-67* (Chicago, 1954), pp. 1-14, 87-115.
4. G. M. Young, *Victorian England, Portrait of an Age* (New York, 1954), pp. 131-138, 152-155.
5. For a fuller appraisal of shifting eighteenth-century standards toward St. Cecilia in particular and toward music in general, see Norman Maclean, "From Action to Image: Theories of the Lyric in the Eighteenth Century," in *Critics and Criticism,* ed. Ronald Crane (Chicago, 1952), pp. 408-460. Also, Jean H. Hagstrum, *The Sister Arts, The Tradition of Literary Pictorialism and English Poetry from Dryden to Gray* (Chicago, 1958), pp. 203-205.
6. Anthony Trollope, *An Autobiography* (Oxford, 1950), pp. 93-94.

ROBERT M. POLHEMUS

On *Barchester Towers*

In the early Barsetshire novels, *The Warden, Barchester Towers* and *Doctor Thorne,* written from 1853 to 1858, Trollope developed and became a master at the comedy of historical change. Barset may be, as Hawthorne wrote, "just as real as if some giant had hewn a great lump out of the earth and put it under a glass case, with all its inhabitants going about their daily business,"[1] but it is also a miniature England being hurled forward by the gigantic forces of history. The great transformation taking place in English life during the fifties was bringing hope and prosperity—especially to the middle classes[2]— and the changing times, with their inherently funny clashes between newfangledness and old fashions, provided rich opportunities for comedy.

Barchester Towers (1857) is Trollope's finest comic novel, and one of the best in English. In it, he helps define for us the special richness and value of mid-Victorian civilization. *The Warden* (1855), in which he had begun to discover and exploit the comic possibilities in the lives of churchmen and their families, is essentially about one

From *The Changing World of Anthony Trollope* (Berkeley and Los Angeles: University of California Press, 1968), pp. 35-50. Copyright © 1968 by the Regents of the University of California. Reprinted by permission of the Regents of the University of California and the author. The present version is slightly revised by the author.

man, Mr. Harding, but *Barchester Towers* is the story of a community. By expanding Barchester, he shapes a comic interpretation of his Victorian world. Outwardly calm and secure, Barsetshire seethes with ambition, passion, contradictions, idealism, banality, and pressures from changes of all sorts, just like a little Britain. It is, however, a place where the claims of the world and the individual conscience can be reconciled, where, in Crane Brinton's words, "Victorian civilization is more than mere struggle."[3]

I

The starting point of the comedy is the incongruity between the ideal of the Church as a spiritual entity and the reality of the Church as a temporal organization—a going concern, in fact, in which people like the Proudies and Mr. Slope can push their way to the top. Nothing is surer about the Victorian age than the power of religion and the church. Ecclesiastical affairs probably mattered more to a larger percentage of the people than they had for two centuries. Since organized religion was so important a part of the middle-class Victorians' search for meaning and stability, so interfused into the texture of national life, Trollope felt that the behavior of clergymen and the workings of Church institutions would inevitably reveal the tone and substance of English society.

Paradoxically his world was becoming more and more secular. There is a lot of fervor about religious decorum and policy in *Barchester Towers,* but none of that mystical force of faith which stabs into men's minds. A cleric dedicated to preserving the mysteries of religion remarks, " 'Everything has gone by I believe. . . . The cigar has been smoked out and we are the ashes.' " He then goes on to predict the workings of the modern secular state: " 'The Government is to find us all in everything and the press is to find the government.' "[4] Trollope wanted to show that the influential clerical establishment, like any other institution, was made up of comic and worldly people. As men and women came to understand the huge power that could be exerted through the various moral and theological establishments, they found a major outlet for their instinct to dominate others. Where there is power to be had, people will struggle, and though power struggles are sometimes frightening, they can be funny too. Self-important people trying to live up to a lofty position nearly always behave affectedly, and affectation, as Fielding says, is the mother of comedy.

Two comic figures, Archdeacon Grantly and Mrs. Proudie, domineer in the book. They seem to divide between them the effective worldly power—the power to move and influence other people. Though they battle each other for supremacy, they have a great deal in common. Each characterizes the era.

Trollope begins with a wonderful scene in which Grantly waits by the bedside of his dying father, the old bishop. Who the new Bishop of Barchester will be depends on whether the old man dies before or after the impending fall of a Conservative Ministry in "July in the year 185–" (Trollope carefully gives the book a realistic setting in moving time).[5] Grantly knows that if his father dies quickly the Conservatives will probably appoint him bishop:

> The ministry were to be out within five days; his father was to be dead—No, he rejected that view of the subject. . . . He tried to keep his mind away from the subject, but he could not. The race was so very close, and the stakes were so very high. . . . He knew it must be now or never. He was already over fifty, and there was little chance that his friends who were now leaving office would soon return to it. No probable British prime minister but he who was now in, he who was so soon to be out, would think of making a bishop of Dr. Grantly. Thus he thought long and sadly, in deep silence, and then gazed at that still living face, and then at last dared to ask himself whether he really longed for his father's death. . . . The proud, wishful, worldly man, sank on his knees by the bedside, and taking the bishop's hand within his own, prayed eagerly that his sins might be forgiven him.[6]

Trollope, in a short space, gets at the immense polarities and ambivalence in the single human personality and marvelously deepens Grantly's character. The novel opens with a son's wish for his father's death, a guilty conscience, and an example of that drive for power in human nature which can appear at any unseemly time. The longing for place overcomes, for the moment, the churchman's Christian principles. Grantly typifies a common Victorian state of mind: torn by the wish to rise high in the world's eye and the wish to live within the strict bounds of Christian decorum, he suffers from the knowledge that he fails to live up to his own ideals.

After this beginning, Trollope does what only a very skillful novelist could successfully do. Without denigrating the bishop's death or Grantly's emotion, he makes comedy out of the situation. When the old man finally dies, Grantly rushes to send a telegram to the government, hoping that the Conservatives will give him the job. But out of propriety, he makes Mr. Harding sign and send it. In the scene of this dutifully grieving son looking after his own bread-and-butter before he arranges the funeral, Trollope sees humor. This is a good instance of what Suzanne Langer calls comic rhythm—the amoral impulse of life asserting itself in the presence of death. Grantly represents one of the great comic paradoxes of nineteenth-century life, the extremely worldly man walking around in clerical garb. He does very well as a metaphor for the whole Victorian age.

Mrs. Proudie, that apostle of Evangelical thought and action, is a caricature of the age. Grantly's telegram is too late, and the new Liberal government sends the Proudies down from London to Barchester where they derange the old life. Mrs. Proudie, with her sense of moral duty, her reforming obsession, her Grundyism, her earnest certitude, and her utter lack of humor, also stands for a whole side of Victorian life. Like Grantly, she can rise to heights of moral indignation, but she has more kinetic force than he does—she wants to change more things.

The growing moral awareness of the nineteenth-century lay public was slowly but surely causing a secularization of morality. Trollope shows us the comedy in this when he imagines his virago, Mrs. Proudie, browbeating the clerical Barset society. In her unctuous language he parodies the Evangelical zeal: "'I fear there is a great deal of Sabbath travelling here . . . I see that there are three trains in and three out every Sabbath. . . . Don't you think Dr. Grantly, that a *little energy might diminish the evil?* Surely we should look at it differently. You and I, for instance in our position: surely we should do all that we can to control so grievous a sin . . . surely, surely,' continued Mrs. Proudie, 'Surely. . . .'"[7] And on she goes, turning morality into something petty. Moral awareness had been nurtured and guided by the Church. Mrs. Proudie lets us see how the Church itself was coming under the control of a secular society that was obsessed with institutionalizing virtue.

She and Grantly not only give us insights into their age, they also help us recognize the eternal human comedy of moral affectation in which earnestness and righteous posturing mask the aggressive will to dominate others. Especially in Mrs. Proudie, Trollope catches and makes ridiculous that insufferably offensive tone that always marks the smug proselyte of a "higher morality."

She also stars in Trollope's comic Victorian version of the Samson theme in *Barchester Towers*. Never before or since the Victorian age have strong, public-minded women so consistently been the butt of comedy in fiction. The reason is obvious: women were taking over more power and influence than they had ever had before, particularly in determining and judging moral conduct. In the age of Queen Victoria and Florence Nightingale the changing role of women was striking. From *The Pickwick Papers* to *The Way of All Flesh* comic Delilah avatars romp through English fiction, cowing men. In Barchester a formidable group of females, Mrs. Proudie, the Stanhope girls, Mrs. Quiverful, and others, shears away strength from docile male relatives. Nor is it accidental that all of these women have close ties with the Church; the evangelical spirit of nineteenth-century religion helped develop the moral insistence and will to power of Victorian females.

II

Trollope adds a whole new dimension to his comic anatomy of mid-Victorianism by bringing in the radical and provocative Stanhopes. Lacking earnestness and moral ambition, they just want to get through life as best they can. They are neither moral nor immoral but amoral, standing apart from the conventional morality and idealism of the age. Bertie and his sister Madeline do not take life seriously; they keep looking for comfort and amusement—mainly amusement. Since they will not conform, they affront Barchester and undermine its way of life. Trollope stresses their good nature, but he calls them "heartless," which means, as he uses it, that they cannot love or feel deeply. The Stanhopes are literary ancestors of Evelyn Waugh characters. Through them, Trollope went a long way toward making the scandalous frivolity and hollowness of upper-class life a major subject in British comic fiction.

Signora Madeline Stanhope Vesey Neroni, with her overt sexuality, contrasts sharply with the pure, relatively passive Eleanor and is one of the more intriguing females in Victorian literature. Trollope uses her as a highly intelligent antiheroine who knocks down sacred cows with her iconoclastic wit.

Through Madeline we can see the uncomfortably ambivalent attitudes that the Victorians were developing about sex. She is one of the most brazenly sexual creatures in a Victorian novel and one of the few characters before the last decades of the century who consciously sets out to trap men with her sex appeal (she insists on receiving her gentlemen callers while languishing, courtesan-like, supine on a sofa). She marries unhappily because a man got her pregnant: "Why she had chosen Paulo Neroni . . . need not now be told. When the moment for doing so came, she had probably no alternative. . . . After a prolonged honeymoon among the lakes, they had gone together to Rome. . . . Six months afterwards, she arrived at her father's house, a cripple and a mother."[8]

Madeline is neither a villainess, a pathetic victim, nor a social problem. For a popular Victorian novelist to impute the equivalent of a shotgun wedding to such a character was unheard of. The proper men of Barset love her ostentatious sexuality; Slope proposes to her, and Bishop Proudie, Arabin, and Squire Thorne all hover around her couch. But the fact that she is a cripple shows the pressure that Victorian efforts to repress sex could exert. An internal moral censor evidently told Trollope that the flaunting of sex must be punished, and so he imagined her with one leg shorter than the other. A robust Madeline who could get up off her couch and run off with some sex-starved parson would be too dangerous for Barchester's equilibrium. She had to be kept immobile and relatively harmless. Her letters, Trollope says, "were full of wit, mischief, love, latitudinarian philosophy, free religion, and sometimes, alas! loose ribaldry." That "alas!" has an ironical and plaintive quality, as if he envied her liberty to indulge in "ribaldry." But her freedom must be in her letters and not her life—she must be an invalid.

Madeline nevertheless cracks the rigid facade of Barchester's moral propriety, and Mrs. Proudie, the voice of codified prudery, immediately sees her as a deadly enemy: "Mrs. Proudie looked on the signora as one of the lost—one of those beyond the reach of Christian charity, and was therefore able to enjoy the luxury of hating her, without the drawback of wishing her eventually well out of her sins."[9] " 'Is she [Mrs. Proudie] always like this?' said the signora. 'Yes—always—madam,' said Mrs. Proudie, returning, 'always the same —always equally adverse to impropriety of conduct of every description.' " The signora's response to this speech—"She laughed loud, and set the sound of it ringing through the lobby and down the stairs after Mrs. Proudie's feet"[10]—shows the weakness of Proudieism, and the motive behind much of Trollope's comedy in the book becomes clear. People were beginning to resent the pleasure-denying tyrannies of people like Mrs. Proudie, and they found that comic ridicule could best express their feelings. When we see how easily Madeline can vamp the staid clerics of Barset, we see also how shaky Mrs. Proudie's hold on her society is getting to be and how ready human nature is to mock the claims of an absolute moral system.

Madeline plays the role of social outlaw. Trollope sees her as a kind of rebel. Not only does she reject Proudie propriety, she also makes fun of social rank and class. The meeting of the signora with the blood-proud Countess De Courcy, whose place in the aristocracy intimidates other characters, is extremely important:

> Lady De Courcy . . . taking her glass to investigate the Signora Neroni, pressed in among the gentlemen who surrounded the couch . . . and as she did so she stared hard at the occupant. The occupant in return stared hard at the countess. The countess who since her countess-ship commenced had been accustomed to see all eyes, not royal, ducal, or marquesal, fall before her own, paused as she went on, raised her eyebrows, and stared even harder than before. But she had now to do with one who cared little for countesses. It was, one may say, impossible for mortal man or woman to abash Madeline Neroni. She opened her large bright lustrous eyes wider and wider, till she seemed to be all eyes. She gazed up into the lady's face, not as though she did it with an effort, but as if she delighted in doing it. She used no glass to assist her effrontery, and needed none. The faintest possible smile of derision played round her mouth, and her nostrils were slightly dilated, as if in sure anticipation of her triumph. And it was sure: The Countess De Courcy, in spite of her thirty centuries and De Courcy castle, and the fact that Lord De Courcy was grand master of the ponies to the Prince of Wales, had not a chance with her. At first the little circlet of gold wavered in the countess's hand, then the hand shook, then the circlet fell, the countess's head tossed itself into the air, and the countess's feet shambled out to the lawn. She did not however go so fast but what she heard the signora's voice asking—
>
> "Who on earth is that woman, Mr. Slope?"
>
> "That is Lady De Courcy."

"Oh, ah. I might have supposed so. Ha, ha, ha. Well, that's as good as a play."

It was as good as a play to any there who had eyes to observe it, and wit to comment on what they observed.[11]

This is a perfectly achieved piece of drawing-room comedy (note, for example, the effects of the lustrous eyes, the dilated nostrils, the circlet of gold, the shaking hand, and the signora's use of the word "woman," in creating the comic intensity of the scene); but it is also revolutionary comedy. The target is the aristocracy's pretentious claim that other classes must automatically flatter its own pompous self-importance. Madeline behaves even more subversively than a character like Stendhal's Julien Sorel, who at least thinks the aristocracy of his world important enough to hate and envy. But her laughter is not the forced laughter of bitterness. She laughs genuinely at what she considers the ridiculous presumptions of a rude woman whose social rank matters not at all. The spirit of comedy in the signora's eye turns the countess into a silly and impotent old woman. A social hierarchy based on class and heredity was beginning to disintegrate because many people could no longer take it seriously. When Madeline chooses her name, Vesey Neroni, just because she likes the sound of it, and makes the claim that her child by the Italian is "the last of the Neros," she subverts polite society and turns the presumptions of gentility into a huge joke.

Trollope both loves and despises Madeline. He had that peculiar tendency of male Victorian novelists—a tendency which he, unlike Thackeray, was later able to throw off—to regard moral virtue and critical intelligence in a woman as somehow incompatible. He explicitly condemns the signora's lack of principle and religion and her neglect of her child. But he loves her when she strips away the hypocritical pretenses of his society and demolishes its cheap platitudes. When Chaplain Slope, for example, talks of love's sacredness, she shows him how often it is a passing whim based on sex and egotism. And when he, a self-righteous minister of the Church, makes love to her, a married woman, she makes him appear a foolish epitome of canting hypocrisy. At times she expresses the deepest urges of the mid-Victorian to rebel against the idealistic mythology of his age, declaiming, for instance, against the sentimental nonsense about the bliss of wedlock: "'I hate your mawkish sentimentality. . . . You know as well as I do in what way husbands and wives generally live together; you know how far the warmth of conjugal affection can withstand the trial of a bad dinner, of a rainy day, or of the least privation which poverty brings with it; you know what freedom a man claims for himself, what slavery he would exact from his wife if he could! And you know also how wives generally obey. Marriage means tyranny on one side and deceit on the other.'"[12] Trollope could never put a statement like this in his own voice, but a part of him obviously agrees with it.

When he reproves Madeline for exploiting her little daughter as a kind of pretty prop to win sympathy, he is interestingly ambivalent. She is a terrible mother, but through her he satirizes the gullibility of people who sentimentalize children. He saw in his age the growth of a child-cult which was to have its apotheosis in Freud. At one point he describes Eleanor Bold's baby-worship as she plays with her son: "'Diddle, diddle, diddle, diddle, dum, dum, dum,' said Eleanor. . . . 'H'm'm'm'm'm'm,' simpered the mama, burying her lips also in his fat round short legs. 'He's a dawty little bold darling, so he is.'"[13] Compare this with the signora's insincere outburst to Bishop Proudie about her child: "'Oh! my lord . . . you must see that infant—the last bud of a wondrous tree.'" The Madeline side of Trollope parodies the sentimentalization of childhood in both passages.

The signora speaks for the sophisticated, analytic Victorian intelligence that more and more came to detest the complacency, maddening provincialism, and simplistic morality in the culture. Madeline and Bertie, a generation younger than Grantly, Harding, and the Proudies, have a new outlook on life. They seem called into being in some dialectial fashion to give the old Barchester society what it lacks—a critical spirit of mind, a love of pleasure, and a touch of frivolity.

Bohemianism, that fascinating feature of modern life, really began to flourish in the nineteenth century. Bertie is even more bohemian than his sister. A charming, idle dilettante who flits about Europe dabbling in art and religious philosophy, he cuts a silly figure; and Trollope satirizes through him the latter-day British Romantics, pseudo-artists, and Pre-Raphaelite hangers-on who were always trotting off to Europe to waste time. But bohemianism, as the Stanhopes show, can mean comic gaiety, unexpected insight, and tolerance, as well as irresponsible arrogance and cultivation of the ego. Bertie conveys even more successfully than Dickens's Harold Skimpole the

siren-song appeal to the Victorians not to be moral and responsible.
The widow Eleanor Bold finds Bertie very attractive because he never
preaches sermons, and he dispels some of Barchester's stuffiness. The
funniest scene in the novel comes when he meets with the Proudies
and the other Barchester clerical dignitaries.[14] Ingenuously he asks
them about their salaries, tells the bishop "'On the whole I like the
Church of Rome best,'" starts recounting his religious experiences
"'I was a Jew once myself,'" tears Mrs. Proudie's dress, and makes
fun of a fat rector. A society which demands duty and moral earnestness must sooner or later discover in itself a hedonistic longing for
pleasure and jokes.

III

Trollope carefully balances the Stanhopes' rebellious modernity and
dismissal of traditional values with another brother-and-sister pair,
the pleasantly anachronistic Thornes of Ullathorne. Unashamedly
reactionary, the Thornes try to shut out all change by refusing to
acknowledge it. They link the changing present to the past and
show strong resistance to change in the Barsetshire world. Trollope
sympathizes with their fear of change and their love of security. He
treats them affectionately because he realizes that in any good civilization there must be people who dedicate themselves to preserving the
ideals of the past as the Thornes do. At the end of a slightly patronizing chapter on them Trollope writes, "Such, we believe, are the inhabitants of many an English country house. May it be long before
their number diminishes."[15] But he knew he was being nostalgic:
neither of the Thornes marries; they have no descendants.

He ironically uses one of Miss Thorne's attempts to revive feudal-
ism to get at the problem of social changes. She plans a Fête Cham-
pêtre for the neighborhood and decides to seat the upper classes in
one section and the lower classes in another. The trouble is that it is
not clear just where some people ought to sit: "It is in such definitions that the whole difficulty of society consists. To seat the bishop
on an arm chair on the lawn and place Farmer Greenacre at the end
of the long table in the paddock is easy enough; but where will you
put Mrs. Lookaloft whose husband, though a tenant on the estate,
hunts in a red coat, whose daughters go to a fashionable seminary in
Barchester, who calls her farm house Rosebank, and who has a piano-

forte in her drawing room?"[16] Miss Thorne learns that even a benevolent reactionary cannot escape the difficulties of a changing world.

Early in the book the atmosphere of change is unpleasant. Young, modern, ambitious Dr. Slope and the old, puzzled Harding have a gloomy interview:

> "You must be aware, Mr. Harding, that things are a good deal changed in Barchester," said Mr. Slope.
>
> Mr. Harding said that he was aware of it. "And not only in Barchester, Mr. Harding, but in the world at large. It is not only in Barchester that a new man is carrying out new measures and casting away the useless rubbish of past centuries. The same thing is going on throughout the country. . . . New men, Mr. Harding, are now needed, and are now forthcoming. . . . "

Trollope then comments:

> A man is nothing now unless he has within him a full appreciation of the new era; an era in which it would seem that neither honesty nor truth is very desirable, but in which success is the only touchstone of merit.[17]

This prediction comes true in Trollope's books such as *The Eustace Diamonds* (1873) and *The Way We Live Now* 1875), but in *Barchester Towers* he sees the possibilities for solving the problems of his world. The novel moves from the loss of equilibrium at the old bishop's death to a new equilibrium with the marriage of Eleanor and Arabin, Arabin's installation as Dean, and the tacit truce between Mrs. Proudie and Grantly that leaves them both with a share of the spoils of the diocese. Barchester in the end can assimilate and support a great variety of life without losing communal identity and integrity, and it becomes a better place for having accommodated itself to change.

IV

Trollope's key figure in achieving finally a harmony between worldliness and idealism is Mr. Arabin. He is even more important than Grantly and Mrs. Proudie in giving the novel shape and meaning. He is the one character who combines idealism, religious dedication, energy, and intellectual curiosity. If Barchester is to be anything more than an amusing but trivial place, he must flourish there. The book would be satirical and pessimistic if he did not thrive. It would say, in effect, that the best people could not live a good life in Barchester—or in Victorian England.

We need to see exactly what happens to Arabin. When Grantly brings him into Barset in order to counteract the Proudie influence, he is unhappy and discouraged with life. For religious reasons he has rejected the world, and his celibacy leaves him dissatisfied: "He was tired of his Oxford rooms and his college life. He regarded the wife and children of his friend with something like envy. . . . And now, if the truth must out, he felt himself disappointed. . . . The day-dream of his youth was over, and at the age of forty he felt that he was not fit to work in the spirit of an apostle. He had mistaken himself, and learned his mistake when it was past remedy."[18] He not only becomes happy, he becomes a better churchman by loving and winning Eleanor and accepting joy as a good in itself. When Harding learns his daughter is to marry Arabin, he arranges for him to be dean, thus increasing Arabin's moral influence. The way of the world in Barchester can further the cause of idealism.

Significantly, Madeline, the spirit of intelligence and radicalism, brings about the love match. In a funny and brilliantly penetrating conversation with Arabin—too long to quote in full—she teaches him to value the world and to understand his real feelings about Eleanor. She also expands his whole conception of life.

> "Is not such the doom of all speculative men of talent?" said she. "Do they not all sit apart as you now are, cutting imaginary silken cords with their fine edges, while those not so highly tempered sever the every-day Gordian knots of the world's struggles, and win wealth and renown? Steel too highly polished, edges too sharp, do not do for this world's work, Mr. Arabin. . . .
>
> "The greatest mistake any man ever made is to suppose that the good things of the world are not worth the winning. And it is a mistake so opposed to the religion which you preach. . . . You try to despise these good things, but you only try; you don't succeed. . . .
>
> "There is the widow Bold looking round at you from her chair this minute. What would you say to her as a companion for life."
>
> . . . "You cross-question me rather unfairly," he replied, "and I do not know why I answer you at all. Mrs. Bold is a very beauti-

ful woman, and as intelligent as beautiful. . . . One that would grace any man's house."

"And you really have the effrontery to tell me this," said she, "to tell me, who, as you very well know, set up to be a beauty myself, and who am at this very moment taking such an interest in your affairs, you really have the effrontery to tell me that Mrs. Bold is the most beautiful woman you know."

"I did not say so," said Mr. Arabin; "you are more beautiful—"

"Ah, come now, that is something more like . . ."

"You are more beautiful, perhaps more clever . . ."

"But Mr. Arabin, I am dying with hunger; beautiful and clever as I am, you know I cannot go to my food, and yet you do not bring it to me."[19]

Barchester needs Madeline's wit and critical detachment, and Trollope makes her his agent in overturning Arabin's stiffness. She draws out his humanity.

All the trends and factions in the community somehow finally work together for his good. The invasion of the Proudies causes Grantly to bring him to Barchester where such diverse forces as the signora's skeptical, scoffing intelligence and the quiet faith and traditional sentiment of Harding both favor him. Only half facetiously, Trollope calls Arabin at the end an "ornament of the age." The point is that the Barchester Victorian society has produced in him a man who can adapt to the world and still maintain high ideals.

Late in the novel, Arabin complains to Eleanor: " 'It is the bane of my existence that on important subjects I acquire no fixed opinion. I think, and think, and go on thinking; and yet my thoughts are ever running in different directions.' "[20] Arabin, Trollope, and the Victorians may have felt this state of mind to be a burden to them— *certainty* may be more comfortable than *uncertainty*—but it expresses again one of the glories of the age: the free play of the spirit of inquiry and "disinterested intelligence."[21] We ought to understand Arabin's statement in the context of the Barchester world and its background. Outwardly he lives a quiet life of clerical conformity. He seems to be a relatively tranquil member of a stable, solid institution, and yet his mind compulsively ranges everywhere looking for truth. In that seemingly stable Victorian England of the fifties, men like Darwin, Marx, and Mill were also thinking and looking for truth, though their thoughts were "running in different directions."

From behind the facade of conformity—out of all the silliness, the
squabbling, and the rich diversity of Barchester and nineteenth-
century England—ornaments of intelligence could emerge.

But Arabin, though crucial, is only one character, and the novel
is the comedy of a whole society. The title, *Barchester Towers,* symbolizes the double thrust of Trollope's human comedy. He wanted
his readers to get a detached view of this world, to look down on it—
from a tower, as it were—and see honestly its failings, its realities, its
hypocrisies, its ridiculousness, as well as its promise. From the detached point of view of comedy, or from a tower, people sometimes
look very small. Such a view helps dispel man's pride and his tendency to overestimate his own size and importance. But cathedral
towers not only look down, they point upward too, and they represent men's aspirations for moral purpose and meaning in life. The
Barchester towers, the expression of human idealism, give visible
continuity to the whole changing Barchester scene. Trollope, I think,
meant to show that as long as the citizens of Barchester and the Victorians recognized the moral as well as the physical reality of these
towers and, as best they could, tried to build their society around
them, they could, despite their worldly folly, sustain and increase the
value of their lives.

NOTES

1. See Anthony Trollope, *An Autobiography* (London, 1953), p. 125.
2. See G. M. Young, *Victorian England, Portrait of an Age* (London,
   1960).
3. *English Political Thought in the Nineteenth Century* (New York,
   1962), p. 87.
4. *Barchester Towers* (London, 1960), chap. xxxiv, p. 330.
5. Chap. I, p. 1.
6. Ibid., pp. 3-4.
7. Chap. V, pp. 33-34, italics mine.
8. Chap. IX, p. 67.
9. Chap. XXXVII, p. 360.
10. Chap. XI, p. 97.
11. Chap. XXXVII, pp. 356-357.
12. Chap. XV, p. 129.
13. Chap. XVI, p. 131.
14. Chap. XI, "Mrs. Proudie's Reception—Concluded."
15. Chap. XXII, p. 204.

16. Chap. XXXV, p. 334.
17. Chap. XIII, p. 106.
18. Chap. XX, p. 177.
19. Chap. XXXVIII, pp. 369-372.
20. Chap. XLVIII, p. 470.
21. "The function of the Nineteenth Century," said G. M. Young, "was to disengage the disinterested intelligence, to release it from the entanglements of party and sect . . . and to set it operating over the whole range of human life." *Victorian England*, p. 186.

MARIO PRAZ

Anthony Trollope

In Dickens the Victorian age seems to be reflected as it were in a
curved mirror. With its bold foreshortenings and queer perspectives,
a curved mirror gives a bewitched, preternatural image of the scene
it reflects. The colours are those of real life, but they are arranged
as if in a kaleidoscope, they are assembled and distributed, in that
motionless glass whirlpool, in such a way that the reflected scene
assumed the quality of a dream or nightmare. So it is with Dickens:
in Victorian society as we see it through his artist's eye, certain features are accentuated till they become positively surrealist; from
Dickens to the *collages* of Max Ernst, from the benevolence of the
Christmas Carols to the cruelty of *Une Semaine de bonté,* the step
is shorter than it might appear. Thackeray, at first sight, seems to
offer a more truthful image of the Victorian age, an image faithful
to the point of disenchantment; and yet there is something in this
image that disturbs us, that gives us the embarrassing feeling of being
looked at from behind: the photographer has photographed a mirror,
and, together with the people and the things in the room, has repro-
duced himself, behind his black cloth, intent on snapping his subject. This intrusion of the photographer's hooded figure is both awk-

Abridged from "Anthony Trollope" in *The Hero in Eclipse in Victorian Fiction,* trans. from the Italian by Angus Davidson (London: Oxford University
Press, 1956), pp. 261-318. Copyright © 1956 by Oxford University Press. Reprinted by permission of the author and publisher.

ward and upsetting, and sometimes suffices to take away all magic
of illusion from the adventures of the characters.

Now although Trollope, too, sometimes shares—as we shall see—
in this trick of Thackeray's, of obtruding himself into the scene with
his commentary, he does it in so discreet a measure that he does not
compromise his own essential quality, that of acting as the supremely
faithful mirror of the Victorian age between the years 1860 and
1880. It is due to this discreetness, and to his unruffled and benevo-
lently realistic estimate of human emotions, so full of shades and
subtleties, that Trollope, who had been declared "stupid" by the
wiseacre critics of the end of the last century, has come back into
fashion in our own day, whether because the society depicted by him
provides, in its relative quietness, a sharp contrast with modern times,
or because the reawakened interest in all things Victorian has found
more to nourish it in his calm, meticulous little pictures than in the
great canvases of Dickens. In Dickens, even when he is speaking of
things in everyday reality, there is often a kind of apocalyptic, cata-
clysmic atmosphere, just as there is in the paintings—the last phase
of the heroic landscape—of John Martin. . . . Trollope did not
choose to forsake the commonplace—so much so that someone, allud-
ing to him, has gone so far as to speak of "novels for young ladies."[1]
And anyone who considers his background of interested motives, of
love-affairs opposed by parents, of ambitions that go no farther than
a bishopric or a seat in Parliament, anyone who thinks of the usual
happy ending to the ups and downs of his plots, with a procession
of couples facing the altar, will feel that Trollope's volumes might
well form a part of the "bibliothèque rose."

But the very absence of too pronounced a character and style were
the salvation of this writer. The figure of the man may well disillusion those who seek originality or picturesqueness in an artist. Not
that a certain lack of balance was altogether absent in his early youth,
when he was oppressed by a sense of inferiority and unworthiness
which in other temperaments might have been a source of morbid
inspiration. A fixed job in the Post Office, and marriage, marked the
beginning of a better life; his restlessness, his continual postponements of the literary work in which, ever since he left school, he had
felt that his true career lay (discarding poetry, drama, history, and
biography, he decided very early to try the only way that seemed to
him profitable, the novel), his indecision, his laziness, were replaced
by an activity that has something of the miraculous about it, so that,

reviewing the period from 1850 to 1871, he was able to assert: "I feel confident that in amount no other writer contributed so much during that time to English literature." The miracle lies not so much in the quantity as in the method—a method which is thoroughly in harmony with the triumphs of industrial civilization and mass production. This is how he speaks of it in his *Autobiography*, which, with its candour and freshness, remains one of his best books:

> It was my practice to be at my table every morning at 5.30 a.m.; and it was also my practice to allow myself no mercy. . . . It had at this time become my custom,—and it still is my custom, though of late I have become a little lenient to myself,—to write with my watch before me, and to require from myself 250 words every quarter of an hour. I have found that the 250 words have been forthcoming as regularly as my watch went. . . . This division of time allowed me to produce over ten pages of an ordinary novel volume a day, and if kept up through ten months, would have given as its results three novels of three volumes each in the year.

Nor did the inspections and journeys that he had to undertake in his capacity as a postal official interrupt his activity:

> I always had a pen in my hand. Whether crossing the seas, or fighting with American officials, or tramping about the streets of Beverley, I could do a little, and generally more than a little. I had long since convinced myself that in such work as mine the great secret consisted in acknowledging myself to be bound to rules of labour similar to those which an artisan or a mechanic is forced to obey.

Whenever he heard people say that the correct thing for an artist was to wait for inspiration, he was unable to restrain his contempt. The idea appeared to him just as absurd as if a shoemaker had to wait to be inspired before starting to make a shoe, or a tallowchandler to wait for the divine moment of melting. This was the advice he gave to young writers: "Let their work be to them as is his common work to the common labourer. . . . I . . . venture to advise young men who look forward to authorship as the business of their lives . . . to avoid enthusiastic rushes with their pens, and to seat themselves at their desks day by day as though they were lawyers' clerks."

Not merely did he write during sea voyages, but even when he was seasick; not merely did he keep his eye on his watch, but he compiled a register of the pages written each day, and the two pages at the end of the *Autobiography* where he balances up the profits that had accrued to him from his work (profits amounting to a considerable sum, such as were attained by no other novelist of the time simply from novels) make one think of the profit and loss account drawn up by Robinson Crusoe. The recollection of Defoe might invite us to reflect upon the connexion between the puritan spirit and the mercantile spirit; but since such reflections have been made so often by others, a mere mention is all that is needed here. Of more interest to us is another relationship, that between Trollope's tireless bourgeois industry and the golden classic maxims to which it is allied. *Labor omnia vincit improbus, Gutta cavat lapidem, Nulla dies sine linea:*[2] Trollope never tires of repeating these Latin sayings, or of paraphrasing Horace's *utile et dulce.* "It is the first necessity of '[the novelist's] position that he make himself pleasant." Therefore his style must be correct, clear, intelligible without effort, and harmonious. "Honesty is the best policy." The first novel that impressed him was *Pride and Prejudice,* and if, later, he was inclined to consider that its position as the first among English novels was contested by *Ivanhoe,* the whole of Trollope's work is there to prove how Jane Austen, and not Scott, was his model.[3] From Miss Austen he learned the art of what may be called functional dialogue. "The dialogue," he wrote, "is generally the most agreeable part of a novel; but it is only so as long as it tends in some way to the telling of the main story." "The ordinary talk of ordinary people is carried on in short sharp expressive sentences, which very frequently are never completed—the language of which even among educated people is often incorrect. The novel-writer in constructing his dialogue must so steer between absolute accuracy of language—which would give to his conversation an air of pedantry, and the slovenly inaccuracy of ordinary talkers, which if closely followed would offend by an appearance of grimace—as to produce upon the ear of his readers a sense of reality. If he be quite real he will seem to attempt to be funny." He must therefore pursue a middle path. The *juste milieu,* the golden mean in all things. The precepts of Horace, underlined in England by Pope, find a belated follower in this bourgeois English novelist. Each man has his own method of work, and we shall not exclude, *a priori,* the possibility that the man who follows Trollope's method may be a great artist, just as we shall not agree that a man is necessarily a great artist because he has in front of him, for his

inspiration, an enchanting landscape rather than a timepiece, or derives stimulus from a drug instead of from the persistent repetition
of a maxim such as *Nulla dies sine linea.* In Trollope the method
of work is so completely in harmony with the work itself, and the
work so completely in harmony with its period, that we are not in
the least surprised at his now appearing to us as the most typical
representative of the Victorian spirit, or—to adopt a term of European
scope—of the Biedermeier spirit.

All he proposed to himself was to look at the world honestly and
to portray men exactly as they were, so that his readers should be
able to recognize themselves in his books and not feel that they had
been transported amongst divinities and demons. Through the mouth
of one of his characters, Brooke Burgess (in *He Knew He Was
Right*), he declared: "It is a great mistake to think that anybody is
either an angel or a devil." To these books the title of *novel* is suitable, but not that of *romance:* the elements of suspense, of mystery,
are lacking in them, as they are in the novels of Jane Austen. As
Henry James wrote about him (in *Portraits*): "There are two kinds
of taste in the appreciation of imaginative literature: the taste for
emotions of surprise and the taste for emotions of recognition. It is
the latter that Trollope gratifies." If, occasionally, the reader imagines he has discerned a theme of mystery, as in the secret nature of
George Vavasor's dwelling in *Can You Forgive Her?*, he is very
quickly brought back to the domain of ordinary reality: the mysterious figure received by Vavasor in this abode which is unknown
to his most intimate friends proves to be nothing more diabolical
than an election agent. It is like Charles Lamb dreaming of the
triumph of Neptune and Amphitrite; and then gradually the great
breakers sink down, the swell changes to flat calm and then to the
flow of a river, and the river is simply the gentle Thames which
lands him, rolling him up on one or two placid waves "alone, safe
and inglorious, somewhere at the foot of Lambeth Palace." A mysterious room like that of George Vavasor would have become, in
Dickens, the scene of some dark plot or other, directed, perhaps,
against an orphan whose life was bound up with the fate of a great
inheritance. And again, in *The Eustace Diamonds,* at a certain point
(chap. xliv) the course of the quiet narrative appears to be ruffled,
all of a sudden, by a sensational occurrence, the theft of the famous
necklace from Lizzie Eustace's bedroom. But all possible reasons for
mystery are dissipated in a few pages: Lizzie had taken the necklace

out of the jewel-box, and it was only the latter that the thieves had stolen. Had Lizzie then planned a faked robbery? Not at all! The robbery had been genuine enough; it was merely that Lizzie had at first been ashamed to say that, for fear of being robbed, she had brought the jewel-case empty and concealed the necklace about her person, then had at once seen, in a flash, that the circumstance might lead people to believe that the necklace really had been stolen, and only later had realized that this would create difficulties for her, but since she had not told the truth from the beginning, could not now retrace her steps. There is no suspense, no mystery: how differently matters would have turned out in Wilkie Collins! But Trollope says (chap. xlviii): "He who recounts these details has scorned to have a secret between himself and his readers." And again, in the case of the second, and genuine, theft of the diamonds (chap. lii), when the affair really seems to be becoming mysterious, Trollope states clearly in whose possession they are to be found, adding: "The chronicler states this at once, as he scorns to keep from his reader any secret that is known to himself."

On the question of suspense, Trollope expounds an important principle of his artistic technique at the end of the fifteenth chapter of *Barchester Towers*:

> And here, perhaps, it may be allowed to the novelist to explain his views on a very important point in the art of telling tales. He ventures to reprobate that system which goes so far as to violate all proper confidence between the author and his readers, by maintaining nearly to the end of the third volume a mystery as to the fate of their favourite personage. Nay, more, and worse than this, is too frequently done. Have not often the profoundest efforts of genius been used to baffle the aspirations of the reader, to raise false hopes and false fears, and to give rise to expectations which are never to be realized? Are not promises all but made of delightful horrors, in lieu of which the writer produces nothing but most commonplace realities in his final chapter? And is there not a species of deceit in this to which the honesty of the present age should lend no countenace?
>
> And what can be the worth of that solicitude which a peep into the third volume can utterly dissipate? What the value of those literary charms which are absolutely destroyed by their enjoyment? When we have once learnt what was that picture before which

was hung Mrs. Ratcliffe's[4] solemn curtain, we feel no further interest about either the frame or the veil. . . .

Nay, take the last chapter if you please—learn from its pages
all the results of our troubled story, and the story shall have lost
none of its interest, if indeed there be any interest in it to lose.
Our doctrine is, that the author and the reader should move along
together in full confidence with each other. Let the personages of
the drama undergo ever so complete a comedy of errors among
themselves, but let the spectator never mistake the Syracusan for
the Ephesian. . . .[5]

Honesty is the best policy. No deception with regard either to
events or characters. No mystery, and no hero. The abolition of the
hero is a salient feature in Trollope, no less—perhaps even more—
than in Thackeray. Neither are his likeable characters perfect, nor
do his scoundrels and wrongdoers lack some sympathetic traits; neither are the female protagonists of his love-stories dazzling beauties,
nor yet are his eminent statesmen geniuses. At the end of *The Three
Clerks* he declares:

> So much must be done in order that our readers may know
> something of the fate of those who perhaps may be called the hero
> and heroine of the tale. The author does not so call them; he pro-
> fesses to do his work without any such appendages to his story—
> heroism there may be, and he hopes there is—more or less of it
> there should be in a true picture of most characters; but heroes
> and heroines, as so called, are not commonly met with in our
> daily walks of life.

Doctor Thorne, in the novel of the same name, is a modest country
doctor, and "most far from perfect." Like many other of Trollope's
characters, he "had within him an inner, stubborn, self-admiring
pride . . . and he had a special pride in keeping his pride silently
to himself." As for Lord Lufton, with whom Lucy Robarts is madly
in love (in *Framley Parsonage*), "I know it will be said of Lord
Lufton himself that, putting aside his peerage and broad acres, and
handsome, sonsy face, he was not worth a girl's care and love":

> That will be said because people think that heroes in books
> should be so much better than heroes got up for the world's
> common wear and tear. I may as well confess that of absolute,
> true heroism there was only a moderate admixture in Lord Luf-

ton's composition; but what would the world come to if none but
absolute true heroes were to be thought worthy of women's love?
What would the men do? and what,—oh! what would become of
the women? [chap. xxi].

And in fact Lucy Robarts, in a moment of desperation, reproves
herself for having fallen in love with a "young popinjay lord." Another leading *amoroso*, Major Grantly, in the *Last Chronicle of
Barset*, may at one moment appear to be no more than a weak,
irresolute youth; and John Eames, a second constant lover in the
same novel, is excused for flirting with the usual announcement that
he was "certainly no hero,—was very unheroic in many phases of his
life; but then, if all the girls are to wait for heroes, I fear that the
difficulties in the way of matrimonial arrangements, great as they
are at present, will be very seriously enhanced. Johnny was not
ecstatic, nor heroic, nor transcendental, nor very beautiful in his
manliness; he was not a man to break his heart for love, or to have
his story written in an epic; but he was an affectionate, kindly, honest
young man; and I think most girls might have done worse than take
him" (chap. lxxvi). Another lover, Harry Gilmore, in *The Vicar of
Bullhampton*, "is not handsome, nor clever, nor rich, nor romantic,
nor distinguished in any way," observed Henry James; "he is simply
rather a dense, narrow-minded, stiff, obstinate, common-place, conscientious modern Englishman . . . he is interesting because he
suffers and because we are curious to see the form that suffering
will take in that particular nature."

Trollope's best ecclesiastics are far from faultless. Robarts, in
Framley Parsonage (chap. xlii),

> had within him many aptitudes for good, but not the strengthened
> courage of a man to act up to them. The stuff of which his man-
> hood was to be formed had been slow of growth, as it is with
> most men; and, consequently, when temptation was offered to
> him, he had fallen. But he deeply grieved over his own stumbling,
> and from time to time, as his periods of penitence came upon
> him, he resolved that he would once more put his shoulder to the
> wheel as became one who fights upon earth that battle for which
> he had put on the armour.

There is much of the heroic in another clergyman, Crawley, as
we shall see; but the character that comes closest to an ideal of

goodness, the purest clerical figure in Trollope, is Mr. Harding, the Warden; and he is a Biedermeier hero. The Archdeacon says of him, near the end of the book:

> "I feel sure that he never had an impure fancy in his mind, or a faulty wish in his heart. His tenderness has surpassed the tenderness of woman; and yet, when an occasion came for showing it, he had all the spirit of a hero. . . . He never was wrong. He couldn't go wrong. He lacked guile, and he feared God,—and a man who does both will never go far astray. I don't think he ever coveted aught in his life,—except a new case for his violoncello and somebody to listen to him when he played it."

At the end of *Barchester Towers* (chap. liii) Mr. Harding is recommended to readers:

> . . . not as a hero, not as a man to be admired and talked of, not as a man who should be toasted at public dinners and spoken of with conventional absurdity as a perfect divine, but as a good man without guile, believing humbly in the religion which he has striven to teach, and guided by the precepts which he has striven to learn.

. . . . . .

Trollope's anti-heroic point of view led him, as it did Thackeray, to see the other side of every situation, to prick every bladder he saw with a sharp pin: the self-sufficiency and the touchiness of doctors, the ordinariness of politicians and journalists, the melodramatic, romantic poses of heartless women—all these provided him with material for delectable scenes, flavored with the ironical bourgeois common sense which counts, in its tradition, such glorious names as those of Boccaccio, Chaucer, and Molière.

In Hawthorne's judgement upon Trollope . . . the American novelist confessed that his own individual taste was "for quite another class of works than those which I myself am able to write. . . . Have you ever read the novels of Anthony Trollope? They precisely suit my taste—solid and substantial, written on the strength of beef and through the inspiration of ale, and just as real as if some giant. . . ." &c.—and he continued with the comparison we have already quoted. I am not sure that the reference to beefsteaks and beer is the most obviously suitable one for emphasizing the "Old England" solidity that distinguishes Trollope's novels. Just as, with

Jane Austen, one is reminded of the functional elegance of certain English instruments and pieces of furniture—the kind of English furniture that has polished surfaces, strong, delicate joints and un-emphatic mouldings and that is adorned by the names of Hepple-white and Sheraton—so, with Trollope, one thinks of the solidity of English mahogany furniture of the nineteenth century—not the kind that displays the oddities of the fashion for Gothic, but the kind that honestly, if indeed weightily, carries on the noble tradition of functional beauty which had started a century earlier. For the rela-tionship that can be traced between Miss Austen and Trollope is exactly the same as that between a simple, slender piece of Hepple-white furniture and a Victorian piece, bare and massive: they are members of the same family, and they have the common qualities of honesty of workmanship, absence of emphasis, and fitness to their purpose. There is nothing showy about him, but much that is worthy of admiration for a practised eye. His qualities are rather like those of the statesman Plantagenet Palliser, who looked like a gentleman, but had nothing remarkable in his appearance, and a face that you might see and then forget; and yet when you looked at it bit by bit . . . "a face like a boot," to adopt an expression used by Sieg-fried Sassoon in his *Memoirs of a Fox-hunting Man* to describe cer-tain typical faces of English sportsmen. You may read Trollope and find, like Mr. Raymond Mortimer, that his characters are people you seem always to have known[6]; and you may fail to remember them with precision when you have turned your back upon them. For none of these characters will take you outside your ordinary everyday life; the impression of truth that they leave upon you is so profound that you will not be able to distinguish between them and the persons of your acquaintance any better than the birds in the story managed to distinguish between the real grapes and the ones painted by Zeuxis. His novels, said Henry James, are not so much stories as pictures: groups of people in everyday life, making them-selves known through dialogue. Just as the seventeenth-century Dutch painters, in their *genre* pictures, did not so much tell stories as present types of men and women who were in no way exceptional, just as they presented pictures of social life, constantly repeating themselves, so also does Trollope obtain his results through a slow accumulation of little pictures of ordinary life, with nothing spec-tacular about them—often, in fact, varied by only slight alterations. And both the Dutch painters and the English novelist knew how to make monotony lively, and how to bring a universal character into the portraiture of everyday things.

NOTES

1. Marco Lombardi (Aldo Camerino) in the *Corriere Padano* of Jan. 16, 1940.
2. "Persistent labour conquers all" (a time-hallowed misquotation from Virgil's *Georgics,* I. 145-6; the original reads *vicit,* "conquered," in allusion to the coming of the Age of Iron). "Drops of water hollow out the stone" (Ovid, *Epistles,* IV.x.5). "Never a day without a line" (said of the painter Apelles by Pliny the Elder). [Ed.]
3. There are many pages in Trollope that make one think of Jane Austen. Chapter xviii of *Doctor Thorne,* for example, with the exchange of letters between George de Courcy and Miss Dunstable. The latter often speaks like one of Miss Austen's sensible, "rational" girls (see, e.g. chapter xx of *Doctor Thorne*). Chapter xxxii of the same novel, with the figure of the clergyman Oriel and the conversations between Patience and Beatrice, seems also to be an echo of Miss Austen's world. And the remarks of Priscilla Stanbury on the subject of marriage (*He Knew He Was Right,* chap. xvi) to Mrs. Trevelyan, or the way in which Priscilla and Nora discuss the latter's refusal of Mr. Glascock's proposal (ib., chap. xviii), seem as it were like plaster casts of some of Jane Austen's pages. The limited horizon of parochial quarrels, of parochial love-affairs (see, for example, chapter iii of *Framley Parsonage*), the regular cycle of daily occupations, with breakfast marking the important moment of opening the letters (see *Can You Forgive Her?* chap. x), the misunderstandings which are so difficult to dispel (cf. *Barchester Towers,* chap. xxix), the dialogues between women (*Framley Parsonage,* chap. xxiv), the awkward wooings of clergymen (Dr. Slope in *Barchester Towers* is no more fortunate than the famous Mr. Elton in *Emma*), the absence of picturesque descriptions, the dry, unadorned page—these are some of the points of contact between the polished female novelist of the end of the eighteenth century and Trollope. Miss Austen too, be it noted, wrote in circumstances which to most people would seem highly unpropitious to artistic activity. For fuller details, see my introductory essay to the translation of *Emma,* reprinted in *La Casa della Fama,* Milan–Naples, Ricciardi, 1952.
4. This refers to a well-known incident in *The Mysteries of Udolpho.*
5. The allusion is to the plot in Shakespeare's *Comedy of Errors.*
6. In *The New Statesman and Nation,* Apr. 19, 1947.

ROBERT KIELY

Adventure as Boy's Daydream:
Treasure Island

Treasure Island is one of the most satisfying adventure stories ever
told primarily because it is the most unhampered. The great pleasure
in reading the first few chapters depends not only on the gathering
mystery, but on the exhilarating sense of *casting off* which Stevenson
gives us. I mean casting off both in the nautical sense of leaving port
and in the conventional sense of throwing off encumbrances. It is
the perennial thrill of the schoolboy tossing away his books on the
last day of the term or the youth flinging off his sticky clothes for
the first swim of the season. What this amounts to is a temporary
change of roles, a peeling down to what seems for the moment our
least complicated and perhaps our most essential self.

Stevenson begins the process in *Treasure Island* with shameless
dispatch by getting rid first of geographical place and time present
and all the demands that go with them. We are relieved of place in
the first sentence when Jim Hawkins explains that he will keep
"nothing back but the bearings of the island, and that only because
there is treasure not yet lifted." He then speaks of taking up his pen

From *Robert Louis Stevenson and the Fiction of Adventure* (Cambridge,
Mass.: Harvard University Press, 1964), pp. 68-89. Copyright 1964 by the
President and Fellows of Harvard College. Reprinted by permission of the
author and publishers.

to write the story "in the year 17—," but, like other "historical ro-
manticists," fails to fill in the last two numbers or to say how long
before 17— the adventure actually occurred. He says at the beginning
of the second paragraph, in introducing Billy Bones, "I remember
him as if it were yesterday," and here we have another notch in our
release from time. Not only are we well removed historically, but we
are offered as our only authority the imperfect memory of a boy who
assures us casually that he recalls past events as though they had all
happened the previous day.

We become aware almost at once that Jim Hawkins' memory is
anything but flawless. He recalls his first impression of Bones upon
his arrival at the Admiral Benbow:

> . . . a tall, strong, heavy, nut-brown man; his tarry pigtail falling
> over the shoulders of his soiled blue coat; his hands ragged and
> scarred, with black, broken nails; and the saber cut across one
> cheek, a dirty, livid white. [II, 3]

And, of course, the stranger immediately breaks into a chorus of
"Fifteen men on the dead man's chest." There seem to be a great
number of details here, but they would hardly help distinguish
Bones, tanned, scarred, and pigtailed, from the general run of disreputable seamen, especially as conceived in the mind of a child
who had never seen one. "Character to the boy is a sealed book,"
Stevenson wrote in "A Humble Remonstrance." "For him a pirate
is a beard, a pair of wide trousers, and a liberal complement of
pistols." Here then is the next item dismissed from the book. We
are early relieved of personality except as a costume or disguise which
may be put on and off at will.

Before the *Hispaniola* can sail in search of the treasure, the characters must all shed their old selves, determined up until then only
by the faintly vocational fact that one is an innkeeper's boy, one a
doctor, one a squire, and so forth, and assume the new roles required
by the nature of the adventure. As in any game, the assumed roles
should and do have some connection with the original talents or
inclinations of the character. Just as a strong arm and a straight eye
make the best "pitcher" and the smallest boy the best "cox," so the
characters of *Treasure Island* are assigned roles which best fit their
previously if sketchily established selves. Even the selecting is accomplished, as in a boy's game, by a self-appointed leader who achieves
the desired transformation merely by stating it:

> "Livesey," said the squire [to the doctor], "you will give up this wretched practice at once . . . we'll have the best ship, sir, and the choicest crew in England. Hawkins shall come as cabin-boy. You'll make a famous cabin-boy, Hawkins. You, Livesey, are ship's doctor; I am admiral." [II, 48]

Only Long John Silver takes on a role not befitting his pre-established character as buccaneer. When he becomes sea-cook aboard the *Hispaniola,* the first ominous rumblings begin which threaten to spoil the game, but really make it interesting.

Perhaps a corollary to the dismissal from the novel of historically measurable time and the complexity of human personality is Stevenson's cavalier casting off of the serious consequences of mortality. It is not that people do not die in *Treasure Island.* They drop on all sides throughout most of the book. There are, of course, the expected casualties among the pirates and the loyal but minor members of the crew, once the fighting gets under way on the island. But the fatalities before that are rather different and particularly indicative of the efficient purpose death serves in the story. The first demise, which takes place in Chapter III, is that of Jim's sick father, who we know is ailing somewhere in an upstairs bedroom, but whom we never meet face to face. Jim's account of the event is characteristically matter-of-fact and inaccurate. "But as things fell out, my poor father died quite suddenly that evening, which put all other matters on one side."

Actually, the death of Jim's father puts nothing aside at all. He is buried in the next paragraph and not mentioned again, while the incidents of the mystery continue to accumulate at the same headlong rate which had been established while he was still alive and ailing. The only thing the death of Jim's father puts aside is Jim's father. Critics are forever trying to read something of Stevenson's youthful difficulties with his own father into the recurring theme of filial isolation in his fiction.

It is true that Stevenson's early manhood was marked by several shattering disagreements with his father—especially on the subject of religion and the choice of a profession. Although the quarrels were usually smoothed over and Stevenson paid a moving tribute to his father's character in *Memories and Portraits,* the old contention undoubtedly left deep scars on the sensitive son of the "morbidly" orthodox, physically hardy, and professionally successful Thomas

Stevenson. But we need not reach very far into an author's private relationships to recognize the universal truth that boyish adventures, especially games involving danger, are possible only when the limiting authority symbolized by the male parent is absent. It might be mentioned in passing that both Robinson Crusoe and Frank Osbaldistone in *Rob Roy* are estranged from their fathers before embarking upon their adventures. The father of Amyas Leigh, the young hero of Kingsley's *Westward Ho!*, dies before the boy sets out for foreign seas; and H. Rider Haggard devotes considerable space at the beginning of *She* describing the last wishes and demise of Leo Vincey's father. Also the young heroes of Twain and Melville are often, for all practical purposes, fatherless. A mother may be overridden, convinced, left temporarily behind. But the father must give way altogether so that his place may be taken by a kind of romantic opposite, dusky and disreputable, a Nigger Jim, a Queequeg, a Long John Silver.

The next two deaths, occurring in fairly rapid succession before Treasure Island is reached and the main part of the story begins, efficiently eliminate characters who had served as narrative and psychological preliminaries to Long John Silver. Billy Bones and Blind Pew are the first to intrude seriously on the life of the inn at Black Hill Cove as representatives and messengers from a vast and mysterious other world where terror prevails; they also introduce separately the two apparently contradictory aspects of personality combined in Long John Silver.

One role we first see played by Billy Bones, the browned and burly pirate, lusty, loud, and frightening to behold, but basically good-natured and kind. His strong exterior hides not only a kind heart, but a weak one, which is the eventual cause of his death by apoplexy when he receives the black spot. This is the bogieman who turns out to be less of a threat than he had seemed, both kinder *and* *weaker* than he looked. When Bones dies of a stroke he has served the narrative purpose of bearing the seachest containing the chart of Treasure Island into the story and the psychological purpose of presenting Jim and the reader with half of what we can expect from Long John Silver. Jim dispenses with Bones quickly, and interestingly enough associates his tearful reaction to his death with leftover emotion from the death of his father.

The other half of Long John Silver and the next character to threaten the order of the Admiral Benbow Inn from a faraway renegade world is Blind Pew. He is the nightmare of every child, and perhaps of every adult—the deformed stranger, apparently harmless, even feeble, offering friendship and requesting help, and suddenly demonstrating unexpected reserves of cruel strength. Jim describes Pew as "hunched as if with age or weakness," obviously blind, and seemingly innocuous. He asks Jim,

> "Will you give me your hand, my kind young friend, and lead me in?" I held out my hand, and the horrible, soft-spoken eyeless creature gripped it in a moment like a vice. [II, 24]

This is a simple but classic example of the sudden horror of the realization of misplaced trust, the confusion and paralysis of being caught in a human trap. When Blind Pew has delivered the black spot, a warning of doom, to Bones, he too has served his narrative purpose and may die. He is stamped to death by horses, but the scene is too swift to be gory: "The four hoofs trampled and spurned him and passed by. He fell on his side, then gently collapsed upon his face, and moved no more." Hawkins does not even spare him the abbreviated sympathy he had given Bones; he mentions him only once more, "Pew was dead, stone dead," and passes busily on to other matters: "As for my mother, etc. . . ."

Death in *Treasure Island* is quick, clean, and above all, efficient for the rapid advancement of the plot. It never provokes a sense of real pathos even in the case of Jim's father, and it is not an impediment in the lives of the surviving characters. On the contrary, especially in the early part of the book, removal of characters by natural or "accidental" means is another step in the process of casting off the potential obstacles to free movement in the adventure to come. Bones and Pew could perhaps have wandered off, run away, disappeared from the plot without dying, when their respective missions were completed. But they would then have lurked in the background of the rest of the story, complicating its essential simplicity with minor but unanswered questions. It is appropriate anyway that these two advance guards from the pirate world, these two preludes to the character of Long John Silver, should die before that legendary and duplex buccaneer is born into the novel twenty pages later.

Long John Silver is the kind of character critics like to give hyphenated names to: villain-as-hero, devil-as-angel, and so forth. Certainly the duplicity of the man justifies these labels even if it does not seem adequately explained by the clichés they have be-

come. Silver appears to be physically weak because of the loss of one
of his legs, yet Jim repeatedly notes what a husky man he is and
how well he maneuvers even aboard ship. He is capable of being
generous, kind, and reasonable, as he demonstrates both on the
voyage out and at the end of the story when his position on the
island is weakened. But he is also capable of uncomplicated cruelty.
In both moods he holds a kind of parental sway over Jim. In the
early chapters Jim attaches himself to Silver and obeys him for much
the same reasons he obeyed Billy Bones, partly out of curiosity,
partly out of admiration, and partly out of pity for his physical dis-
ability. As for Long John, there is no doubt that he regards Jim
Hawkins with paternal affection. "'Come away, Hawkins,' he would
say; 'come and have a yarn with John. Nobody more welcome than
yourself, my son.'" And much later, on the island, Silver offers Jim
a kind of partnership in piracy in words not unlike those of a self-
made man inviting his son to join the family business: "I've always
liked you, I have, for a lad of spirit, and the picter of my own self
when I was young and handsome. I always wanted you to jine and
take your share" (II, 210).

But Jim has also seen Silver, like Pew, reveal startling physical
power in spite of his debility, and brutality, in spite of his previous
kindness. Jim is watching when Tom Morgan, a loyal member of
the crew, refuses Silver's invitation to mutiny. The sailor stretches
his hand out to Long John: "'Hands off,' cried Silver, leaping back
a yard, as it seemed to me, with the speed and security of the trained
gymnast." And when the sailor turns his back and begins to walk
away,

> John seized the branch of a tree, whipped the crutch out of his
> armpit, and sent that uncouth missile hurtling through the air.
> . . . Silver, agile as a monkey, even without leg or crutch, was
> on the top of him next moment, and had twice buried his knife
> up to the hilt in that defenceless body. [II, 107]

At moments like this it is obviously fear mixed with awe at the
athleticism of this supposed cripple that compels Jim. Stevenson, in
a letter to Henley (who had had a foot amputated in 1875), admits
that this combination of infirmity and power appealed to him: "It
was the sight of your maimed strength and masterfulness that begot
John Silver in *Treasure Island* . . . the idea of the maimed man,

ruling and dreaded by the sound, was entirely taken from you" (*Letters,* II, 138).

What, finally, are we to make of Long John Silver? Is he after all the heroic villain or the angelic devil? In a general way he is both. But this anxious reaching out for a permanent judgment over-emphasizes the moral dimension of Silver's character and of the whole novel. David Daiches, in an excellent essay, "Stevenson and the Art of Fiction," suggests that "all of Stevenson's novels have a highly sensitive moral pattern. . . . Consider even *Treasure Island,* that admirable adventure story. . . . What we admire is not always what we approve of. . . . That Stevenson was here consciously exploring the desperate ambiguity of man as a moral animal is perhaps too much to say."[1] I would agree that the structural design of Stevenson's later moral tales is visible in *Treasure Island,* but the "desperate ambiguity of man" seems to me to have been left deliberately—and successfully—unexplored. We should take Stevenson at his word when he explains to Henry James that the luxury in reading a good adventure novel, *Treasure Island* in particular, "is to lay by our judgment, to be submerged by the tale as by a billow."

Silver is a player with two faces, that of the blustering buccaneer with a good heart (like Bones) and that of the cripple with a vicious heart and almost superhuman strength (like Pew). For us to ask which is the "real" Silver, to push aside the whiskers and try to see which of the two roles is better suited to the countenance behind is unfair, irrelevant to the spirit of the novel, and not worth the trouble because it is impossible to do. It is also unconvincing to attempt integrating Bones and Pew in order to show Silver's double nature as springing from a single psychological source. The contradictory tendencies are not presented as part of a complex personality fraught with tension and paradox. Such a union of traits is not impossible for a novelist to achieve in a sea dog. Melville and Conrad both accomplish it. But Stevenson does not do it in *Treasure Island.* And that is another reason for questioning the value of the hyphenated labels. Not only do they stress moral issues where they barely exist, but they imply an integration of Silver's dual roles whereas Stevenson seems to have taken some pains to keep them apart.

One of the pleasures in reading *Treasure Island* is in observing Long John Silver making his repeated "quick-changes," alternating rather than growing or developing, bounding back and forth between "Bones" and "Pew." Stevenson again and again allows him to assume his most Pew-like part, unctuous and perfidious, only to be defied and shattered by a verbal barrage from a loyal member of the crew which transforms him into "Bones," a roaring but impotent husk. One of the best examples of Silver's capacity for rapid change is when Captain Smollett replies to his treacherous offer of "protection" if the pirates are given the treasure chart:

> "You can't find the treasure," [said Smollett]. "You can't sail the ship—there's not a man among you fit to sail the ship. You can't fight us—Gray, there, got away from five of you. Your ship's in irons, Master Silver . . . and they're the last good words you'll get from me; for, in the name of heaven, I'll put a bullet in your back when next I meet you. Tramp, my lad. Bundle out of this, please, hand over hand, and double quick." [II, 151-152]

Smollett speaks to Silver as though he were a bad boy, not only naughty, but bungling in his attempts at villainy. And at once, the fearsome and oleaginous enemy becomes a comic, almost pathetic, buffoon, bellowing hollow threats. Retreating without dignity, he literally "crawled along the sand" to safety.

Jim, too, gets in his verbal "licks" against the pirate chief when he falls into the enemy's hands and things are looking blackest for him. He pelts the Pew-disguise with a furious tirade and concludes by shouting: "I no more fear you than I fear a fly."

What self-respecting pirate would take this kind of talk from a child? None at all, of course, but then as we have pointed out, Silver is given no self to respect. There is no basic personality from which he may derive strength when challenged or to which the reader may assign responsibility when Silver himself is doing the threatening. He is a weed that flourishes in ideal conditions but shrivels almost without resistance at the first sign of opposition. The point of the story as well as the pleasure in reading it is in the active conflict, not in its cause or even its final result. To try to speak seriously of good or evil in *Treasure Island* is almost as irrelevant as attempting to assign moral value in a baseball game, even though a presumable requisite to enjoying the contest involves a temporary if arbitrary preference for one side or the other.[2]

The fuss that some critics have made over Silver's escape with a small part of the treasure at the end of the book as a sign of Stevenson's moral softness or of his "liberation" from strict Calvinist dogma seems rather foolish. Silver has murdered, robbed, and lied, but he has also been a good cook, a remarkable physical specimen in spite of his lost leg, and a rather affectionate if irresponsible replacement for Jim's dead father. Above all, he has been entertaining, and in a timeless, placeless, nearly conscienceless world, Stevenson seems justified in paying him off and sending him packing. To have killed him would have implied a punishment, a moral judgment Stevenson apparently did not want to make in this book. By the same token, to have rewarded him too generously or to have brought about his conversion would also have introduced a moral element not anticipated by anything earlier in the novel and therefore hardly appropriate at the conclusion.

If evil can be said to exist at all in one of the characters of Stevenson's early period, it is an illusion which wilts when exposed to daylight. Deacon Brodie, the two-faced "villain" of a play written with Henley in 1880, sees his own wickedness as a "blindness," a "nightmare," which vanishes when he awakes and his "eyes are opened." This prototype of Dr. Jekyll comes to an unhappy end, but not before absolving himself by declaring: "I see now that the bandage has fallen from my eyes; I see myself."

Later on, most obviously in *Dr. Jekyll and Mr. Hyde* and in *The Master of Ballantrae,* Stevenson returns to the theme of the double personality and tries with varying success to raise in the midst of melodrama serious moral and psychological questions. But it is important to see that his first impulse is to play a game and to teach us nothing more or less than how to play it with him. *Treasure Island* belongs not in the ironic mold of *Huckleberry Finn,* in which the adult world is seen through the eyes of a boy for what it really is. Without the transcendental overtones, it follows more closely in the tradition of Blake's *Songs of Innocence* and Wordsworth's "We Are Seven." The child is isolated from the adult world, protected from it by his own lack of experience, and does not really see it at all except in imperfect and distorted glimpses. We learn precious little about the psychology of evil from Long John Silver and nothing of real consequence about nineteenth-century morality from reading *Treasure Island.*

William Golding's *Lord of the Flies,* as a serious variation on the theme of boys' adventure, may make twentieth-century readers suspicious of the ingenuousness of a *Treasure Island* or a *Swiss Family Robinson.* In fact, it must have been intended, in part, as an anti-romantic antidote to that "escapist" genre. But it ought to be remem-

bered that, unlike *Treasure Island* and despite its popularity among
adolescents, *Lord of the Flies* depends almost entirely on adult
assumptions for its effectiveness as a novel. Moreover, one of the
ironies of the book is that, for any of the youngest participants, the
whole ghastly episode might have been regarded, even to the end,
as little more than an exciting (if bewildering) romp on a desert
island. It is this limited attitude toward reality, without benefit of
adult insinuation, which Stevenson sought to capture in *Treasure
Island*. His extraordinary success depended largely on his early conviction that, with respect to certain areas of experience, the child's
amoral view was perfectly valid.

In "A Gossip on Romance" Stevenson wrote:

> There is a vast deal in life and letters . . . which is not im-
> moral, but simply a-moral; which either does not regard the hu-
> man will at all, or deals with it in obvious and healthy relations;
> where the interest turns, not upon what a man shall choose to do,
> but on how he manages to do it; not on passionate slips and hesi-
> tations of the conscience, but on the problems of the body and of
> the practical intelligence, in clean, open-air adventure, the shock
> of arms or the diplomacy of life. [XIII, 329]

It is devotion to this principle of "clean" adventure virtually un-
blemished by good or evil which produces the novels that may be
placed in the category of boy's daydream, including *The Black
Arrow, Kidnapped, David Balfour,* and *St. Ives.*

Kidnapped (1886) and its sequel *David Balfour,* published as
Catriona seven years later, are usually taken as though they belonged
in an altogether different category from *Treasure Island.* Both novels
admit details of geographical locale and historical time which are
obviously missing from the earlier book, in which chronology is presented through the highly omissive mind of a child and an island
is a place where treasure is buried, not an actual piece of land a
given number of miles off the coast of England. There is also the
difference in the ages of the heroes. Jim Hawkins is only a boy
(though Stevenson, in keeping with his avoidance of particulars in
Treasure Island, does not give his precise age) whereas David Balfour, we are informed on page three of *Kidnapped,* is a youth of
seventeen when he first sets out on his adventures.

But in spite of these admittedly important differences, the basic impulse evident in the two later books, their primary value and interest to the reader, as well as Stevenson's apparent pleasure in writing them, places them with *Treasure Island* in the category of adventure fiction as boy's dream. At the center of the two books lies not psychology, or morality, or politics, or patriotism, or history, or geography, or romantic love, but "the problems of the body and of the practical intelligence, in clean, open-air adventure." Both *Kidnapped* and *David Balfour* are essentially amoral novels, aimless, hectic, and almost totally devoid of characters complex enough to experience the pleasures or pains of maturity.

Kidnapped, like *Treasure Island*, begins with the death of the young hero's father, and his departure from the familiar comforts and limitations of home to sections of Scotland previously unknown to him. The departure from home and the release from the conventional moral restraints associated with paternal authority is stated in the first sentence of the novel with almost scriptural economy as David recalls "the year of grace 1751, when I took the key for the last time out of the door of my father's house." David, like Jim Hawkins, is not plunged immediately into the unfamiliar world of buccaneers and Highland outlaws, but is given a hint of it by the eccentric and treacherous ways of parsimonious Uncle Ebenezer, his closest living kinsman, to whom he goes to claim a rightful inheritance. But Ebenezer, for all his wickedness (he makes several covert attempts on David's life and is eventually the cause of his being kidnapped), is physically vulnerable, like Blind Pew, the apoplectic Captain Flint, and one-legged John Silver.

When David returns alive from a supposedly fatal errand on which he was sent by his uncle up an unsafe staircase, in the dark, Ebenezer suffers a mild stroke. But neither in *Kidnapped* nor in *Treasure Island* is physical weakness necessarily an outer sign of inner moral decay as we often find it to be in Hawthorne and Melville. Nor does Stevenson, for all his borrowings from the Gothic, use physical deformity as Poe does, primarily as a macabre sign of insane depravity. Though the abnormalities of Pew, Silver, and Ebenezer obviously have in them elements of the grotesque, Stevenson generally insists upon employing them in their least symbolic and most literal sense. If an unnatural appearance frightens the boy-hero, it also gives him evidence of physical frailty in his enemy. In a genre which turns on "the problems of the body and the practical intelligence," that is a grave disadvantage indeed.

The weakness of the villain—or, more accurately, would-be villain since the skulduggery is rarely if ever carried out successfully—prevents evil from taking a permanent hold in the book. It should be remembered that in spite of the unexpected reserves of strength possessed by Pew and Silver their disabilities finally do them in. Pew is unable to see the horses bearing down upon him and Silver at his moment of humiliation is without a crutch and forced to crawl "hand over hand" like an infant. Nor does Stevenson really humanize his villains by making them vulnerable. It is simply his way of dissipating the threat of wickedness, of nipping evil in the bud, by reducing its physical power. Ebenezer Balfour is a bogieman like Bones and Pew and Silver, who can be depended upon to fall with a half-comic, half-pathetic, but very loud thud at the appropriate moment.

Uncle Ebenezer has sufficient strength and treachery, however, to have his nephew shanghaied by a disreputable crew of slave-traders under the leadership of the next potential "badman" of the story, Captain Elias Hoseason. After hearing several frightening tales of the captain from Ransome, the cabin-boy, David finally sees him. He turns out to be a "fine, tall figure with a manly bearing," which causes David to wonder "if it was possible that Ransome's stories could be true . . . they fitted so ill with the man's looks." Stevenson does not leave us very long with this puzzle, but offers an already familiar explanation:

> . . . indeed, he was neither so good as I supposed him, nor quite so bad as Ransome did; for, in fact, he was two men, and left the better one behind as soon as he set foot on board his vessel. [V, 45]

Here again, as in the case of John Silver, we have a character ready to play two roles, shedding one and assuming the other as the situation requires. Stevenson does not use the dual nature as an excuse to raise a subtle question of morality or to complicate the conscience of the captain, but rather as a way of neutralizing his character and side-stepping moral judgment of it altogether. By treating human nature as a kind of nonorganic particle in which positive and negative charges cancel each other, Stevenson denies that imbalance of properties which is the perennial source of moral conflict.

Even the natural landscape, for all its atmospheric importance in *Kidnapped,* is not permitted to pose an ultimate threat to the characters. Like Uncle Ebenezer and Captain Hoseason, it may *seem* frightening at first, but that is only because of imperfect perception on the part of David, and, as Stevenson has often explained, it is precisely this faultiness of vision which allows the child to become involved in adventures not possible for the more observant adult. Once the inadequate view has been corrected, the danger disappears and the young hero is able to control and toy with topography just as, with the help of Alan Breck, he overcomes Hoseason and his entire crew aboard the *Covenant,* and plays a practical joke at the end of the book on old Ebenezer.

One of the most interesting of David's various encounters with nature is his being washed ashore on the Isle of Earraid after the wreck of the *Covenant.* The episode is a kind of miniature *Robinson Crusoe* in the midst of a novel which is mostly set on the Scottish mainland. We enjoy observing the ingenuity by which David keeps himself alive on a diet of limpets and finds partial shelter between two boulders, but the incident reaches a most un-Defoe-like conclusion when two fishermen sail by and indicate to David that all along it had been possible for him to walk to the mainland.

> Earraid . . . [was] what they call a tidal islet, and except in the bottom of the neaps, can be entered and left twice in every twenty-four hours, either dry-shod, or at the most by wading. . . . The wonder was . . . that [the fishermen] had ever guessed my pitiful illusion. [V, 120]

The island is not a real island any more than Ebenezer and Hoseason are real villains. It, like its human counterparts, creates an *illusion* of danger until the hero is finally able to see all around it, and then it becomes innocuous, almost cooperative with the will of the protagonist. Even nature, then, has two selves, an illusive one which is unfriendly and threatening, and a "real" one which is bland and malleable.

For all the fatigue and discomforts caused by the rough terrain and the fickle Scotch climate during their flight in the heather, David and Alan have a rather whimsical time of it, whistling and joking and treating the dangers of man and nature with an air of casual disregard. Throughout their flight, while hotly pursued by semi-barbarous Campbells out for revenge, and troops of redcoats with a warrant for their arrest, the two heroes insist upon acting like vacationers on a walking tour of the Highlands:

> With a rivalry that much amused us, we spent a great part of
> our days at the waterside, stripped to the waist and groping about
> or (as they say) guddling for . . . fish. . . . They were of good
> flesh and flavour, and when broiled upon the coals, lacked only a
> little salt to be delicious. [V, 182]

A holiday mood of rough-and-tumble masculine playfulness per-
vades much of the novel. Near the end of the supposedly exhausting
and harrowing journey, while plotting to trick the maid of an inn
into giving them a boat, Alan turns to his friend:

> "Ye have a fine, hang-dog, rag-and-tatter, clappermaclaw kind
> of look to ye, as if ye had stolen the coat from a potato-bogle.
> . . ." I followed him, laughing. "David Balfour," said he, "ye're
> a very funny gentleman by your way of it, and this is a very funny
> employ for ye, no doubt." [V, 240]

Alan is referring to the immediate trickery at hand, but he might
as well be speaking of the entire adventure.

Kidnapped, we soon come to realize, is a "very funny employ"
indeed, another game not so very different in spirit from *Treasure
Island.* As in all games, at least two sides are required, though neither
has a profound moral advantage over the other. We are, of course,
expected to root for David and his Highland companion, Alan; we
hear the story told from their point of view, and as a result, they
seem to be friendlier company than Ebenezer, Hoseason, and the
redcoats. But we are often reminded that the members of the opposition have their better sides along with their weaknesses, and although
for the duration we agree to notice only their meanness, there is
always the possibility that in some future skirmish they might make
fairly respectable allies. "Our criminals are a most pleasant crew, and
leave the dock with scarce a stain upon their character," wrote
Stevenson in 1891. And though the specific reference is to *The
Wrecker,* it is applicable to a great many of his adventures.

One reason *Kidnapped* has been taken more seriously than *Treas-
ure Island* is that the alignment of opponents is more complex than
in the earlier book. We begin with David Balfour alone against
Uncle Ebenezer; then David, who is a Whig Lowlander, and Alan
Breck, a Tory Highlander, are against Hoseason and his pirates; then
David and Alan flee through the Highlands from the wrathful
Campbells and the King's redcoats. The infiltration into the game

of ancient rivalry between Highland and Lowland Scots and the historical enmity between Jacobite and Whig give the novel more weight than *Treasure Island,* and a point beyond the immediate conflict of characters engaged in tricking, battling, and escaping one another. But historical and geographical divisions, like the two halves of Hoseason's personality, also serve to accelerate and maintain motion, balancing each other with approximately equal resources, until one side eventually peters out, and gives the advantage to the other.

Stevenson set out to write a richer and more serious book than *Treasure Island* when he began *Kidnapped.* In many ways he succeeded. But if there is a tendency to expand the field of adventure and to complicate the action with historical and geographical association, there is, I think, a simultaneous and stronger tendency to remain in the relatively simple and limited world of child's dream.

Kidnapped has an authenticity which could not be claimed for *Treasure Island,* but when that authenticity threatens to intrude on the relatively carefree adventure with serious ethical and political questions, Stevenson withdraws from it. Undoubtedly his approval of the inclusion of a map of David's travels in the first edition of *Kidnapped* was a way of calling attention to the nationalist and topographical flavor of the story. But *Treasure Island* started with a map too, and it is difficult to read what Stevenson wrote about that cartographical invention without suspecting him of similar sentiments toward the genuine chart in *Kidnapped:*

> It contained harbours that pleased me like sonnets. . . . I am told there are people who do not care for maps, and find it hard to believe. The names, the shapes of the woodlands, the courses of the roads and rivers . . . the mills and the ruins . . . here is an inexhaustible fund of interest for any man with eyes to see, or twopence worth of imagination to understand with. [II, xii]

If the map at the front of *Kidnapped* is an aesthetic ornament even while it is serving as a fairly reliable guide to the Highlands, then it is a good symbol of the use to which Stevenson puts topography and political history in the novel. He takes them seriously enough to make the adventure turn on clan warfare between the north and south of Scotland, but not so seriously as to let them divert him from "the problems of the body and of the practical intelligence."

The quarrel between David and Alan is a typical example of the

extent to which history colors and intensifies a private conflict without ultimately lifting it above the level of an adolescent skirmish.
During their flight through the Highlands the two heroes, who in
spite of their friendship represent opposing political factions, have a
falling out. Alan, at one point, whistles a Jacobite ditty which mocks
David's Whiggery. They argue and each stands ready to duel, but
the two friends do not cross swords; David is too tired, and Alan too
sympathetic toward his young companion. The political differences
between them are in no way resolved or evaluated by Stevenson.
The quarrel amounts to little more than an entertaining interval of
name-calling, the Viking messenger berating Byrtnoth before the
Battle of Maldon or Unferth ridiculing Beowulf at the feast, with
the important difference that in *Kidnapped* the name-calling is not a
prelude to epic struggle.

David Daiches suggests that the reader of *Kidnapped* "provide
himself with sufficient background information to enable him to find
some satisfaction in the historical and topographical elements in the
novel."[3] His advice is good. It is true that much that at first appears
to be obscure local color makes better sense in the context of Scottish history. Nevertheless, it remains a fact that *Kidnapped* has continued to be popular with young readers who probably know almost
nothing about clan warfare in eighteenth-century Scotland. This
does not mean that the historical setting is not important in the
novel, but that it remains peculiarly detachable from the action in
the foreground. In reading *Kidnapped* a child can quite easily leave
"the bulk of the book unrealized," but fix on the rest and live it.
That is not true of the history and topography in *The Master of
Ballantrae* or *Weir of Hermiston;* and neither book has ever been
highly favored by Stevenson's younger admirers. The surface of
Kidnapped reveals an attempt by Stevenson to move away from the
self-contained world of *Treasure Island,* but the internal logic of the
narrative discloses again and again his compelling need to prolong
that inconsequential dream.

NOTES

1. David Daiches, *Stevenson and the Art of Fiction* (New York, 1951),
   p. 10.
2. John Conway discusses the athletic contest as a kind of "allegory,"
   "the type of all talent," in "Standards of Excellence," *Daedalus,* 90:

683-684 (Fall 1961). Though he is speaking specifically of athletics in American society, his point is relevant to Stevenson insofar as he describes the game as cutting across and avoiding moral and cultural complications by presenting "in its purest and most abstract form a skill and its simple realization . . . which can be appreciated by everybody, irrespective of education or background or individual gifts."

3. David Daiches, *Robert Louis Stevenson* (Norfolk, Connecticut, 1947), p. 72.

KATHERINE ANNE PORTER

Notes on a Criticism of Thomas Hardy

The Bishop of Wakefield, after reading Thomas Hardy's latest (and as it proved, his last) novel, *Jude the Obscure,* threw it in the fire, or said he did. It was a warm midsummer, and Hardy suggested that the bishop may have been speaking figuratively, heresy and bonfires being traditionally associated in his mind, or that he may have gone to the kitchen stove. The bishop wrote to the papers that he had burned the book, in any case, and he wrote also to a local M.P. who caused the horrid work to be withdrawn from the public library, promising besides to examine any other novels of Mr. Hardy carefully before allowing them to circulate among the bishop's flock. It was a good day's work; added to the protests of the reviewers for the press, and twenty-five years of snubbing and nagging from the professional moralists of his time, Thomas Hardy resigned as novelist for good. As in the case of the criticism presently to be noted, the attack on his book included also an attack on his personal character, and the bishop's action wounded Thomas Hardy. He seems to have remarked in effect "that if the bishop could have known him as he was, he would have found a man whose personal conduct, views of morality, and of vital facts of religion, hardly differed from his own."

This is an indirect quotation by his second wife, devoted apologist and biographer, and it exposes almost to the point of pathos the

From *The Southern Review,* VI, 1940, 150-61. Copyright © 1970 by Katherine Anne Porter. Reprinted by permission of Cyrilly Abels.

basic, unteachable charity of Hardy's mind. Of all evil emotions generated in the snake-pit of human nature, theological hatred is perhaps the most savage, being based on intellectual concepts and disguised in the highest spiritual motives. And what could rouse this hatred in a theologian like the sight of a moral, virtuous, well-conducted man who presumed to agree with him in the "vital facts of religion," at the same time refusing to sign the articles of faith? It was long ago agreed among the Inquisitors that these are the dangerous men.

The bishop threw the book in the fire in 1896. In 1928, Mrs. Hardy was happy to record that another "eminent clergyman of the church" had advised any priest preparing to become a village rector to make first a good retreat and then a careful study of Thomas Hardy's novels. "From Thomas Hardy," concluded this amiable man, "he would learn the essential dignity of country people and what deep and passionate interest belongs to every individual life. You cannot treat them in the mass: each single soul is to be the object of your special and peculiar prayer."

Aside from the comment on the social point of view which made it necessary thus to warn prospective rectors that country people were also human entities, each possessed of a soul important, however rural, to God, and the extraordinary fact that an agnostic novelist could teach them what the church and their own hearts could not, it is worth noting again that churchmen differ even as the laymen on questions of morality, and can preach opposing doctrine from the same text. The history of these differences, indeed, is largely the calamitous history of institutional religion. In 1934, a layman turned preacher almost like a character in a Hardy novel, runs true to his later form by siding with the bishop. Since his spectacular conversion to the theology and politics of the Church of England, Mr. T. S. Eliot's great gifts as a critic have been deflected into channels where they do not flow with their old splendor and depth. More and more his literary judgments have assumed the tone of lay sermons by a parochial visitor, and his newer style is perhaps at its most typical in his criticism of Thomas Hardy*:

> The work of the late Thomas Hardy represents an interesting example of a powerful personality uncurbed by any institutional attachment or by submission to any objective beliefs; unhampered

* In Eliot's *After Strange Gods: A Primer of Modern Heresy*, 1934 [Ed.].

by any ideas, or even by what sometimes acts as a partial restraint upon inferior writers, the desire to please a large public. He seems to me to have written as nearly for the sake of "self-expression" as a man well can, and the self which he had to express does not strike me as a particularly wholesome or edifying matter of communication. He was indifferent even to the prescripts of good writing: he wrote sometimes overpoweringly well, but always very carelessly; at times his style touches sublimity without ever having passed through the stage of being good. In consequence of his self-absorption, he makes a great deal of landscape; for landscape is a passive creature which lends itself to an author's mood. Landscape is fitted, too, for the purposes of an author who is interested not at all in men's minds, but only in their emotions, and perhaps only in men as vehicles for emotions.

After some useful general reflections on the moral undesirability of extreme emotionalism, meant as a rebuke to Hardy and to which we shall return briefly later, Mr. Eliot proceeds:

I was [in a previous lecture] . . . concerned with illustrating the limiting and crippling effect of a separation from tradition and orthodoxy upon certain writers whom I nevertheless hold up for admiration for what they have attempted against great obstacles. Here I am concerned with the intrusion of the *diabolic* into modern literature in consequence of the same lamentable state of affairs . . . I am afraid that even if you can entertain the notion of a positive power for evil working through human agency, you may still have a very inaccurate notion of what Evil is, and will find it difficult to believe that it may operate through men of genius of the most excellent character. I doubt whether what I am saying can convey very much to anyone for whom the doctrine of Original Sin is not a very real and tremendous thing.

Granting the premises with extreme reservations, Thomas Hardy was a visible proof of the validity of this disturbing doctrine. He had received early religious training in the Established Church, and by precept and example in a household of the most sincere piety, and of the most aggressive respectability. He remarked once, that of all the names he had been called, such as agnostic (which tag he adopted later, ruefully), atheist, immoralist, pessimist, and so on, a properly fitting one had been overlooked altogether: "churchy." He had once meant to be a parson. His relations with the church of his childhood had been of the homely, intimate, almost filial sort. His grandfather, his father, his uncle, all apt in music, had been for forty years the mainstay of the village choir. He felt at home in the place, as to its customs, feasts, services. He had a great love for the ancient churches, and as a young architect his aesthetic sense was outraged by the fashionable and silly "restorations" amounting to systematic destruction which overtook some of the loveliest examples of medieval church architecture in England during the nineteenth century. His devotion to the past, and to the history and character of his native Wessex became at times a kind of antiquarian fustiness. His personal morals were irreproachable, he had an almost queasy sense of the awful and permanent effects of wrong doing on the human soul and destiny. Most of his novels deal with these consequences; his most stupendous tragedies are the result of one false step on the part of his hero or heroine. Genius aside, he had all the makings of a good, honest, church-going country squire; but the worm of original sin was settled in his mind, of all fatal places; and his mind led him out of the tradition of orthodoxy into another tradition of equal antiquity, equal importance, equal seriousness, a body of opinion running parallel throughout history to the body of law in church and state: the great tradition of dissent. He went, perhaps not so much by choice as by compulsion of *belief,* with the Inquirers rather than the Believers. His mind, not the greatest, certainly not the most flexible, but a good, candid, strong mind, asked simply the oldest, most terrifying questions, and the traditional, orthodox answers of the church did not satisfy it. It is easy to see how this, from the churchly point of view, is diabolic. But the yawning abyss between question and answer remains the same, and until this abyss is closed, the dissent will remain, persistent, obdurate, a kind of church itself, with its leaders, teachers, saints, martyrs, heroes; a thorn in the flesh of orthodoxy, but I think not necessarily of the Devil on that account, unless the intellect and all its questions are really from the Devil, as the Eden myth states explicitly, as the Church seems to teach, and Mr. Eliot tends to confirm.

There is a great deal to examine in the paragraphs quoted above, but two words in their context illustrate perfectly the unbridgable abyss between Hardy's question and Mr. Eliot's answer. One is, of course, the word *diabolic*. The other is *edifying*. That struck and held my eye in amaze, for a moment. With no disrespect I hope to conventional piety, may I venture that in the regions of art, as of religion, edification is not the highest form of intellectual or spiritual experience. It is a happy truth that Hardy's novels are really not edifying. The mental and emotional states roused and maintained in the reader of *The Mayor of Casterbridge* or *The Return of the Native* are considerably richer, invoked out of deeper sources in the whole human consciousness, more substantially nourishing, than this lukewarm word can express. A novel by Thomas Hardy can be a chastening experience, an appalling one, there is great and sober pleasure to be got out of those novels, the mind can be disturbed and the heart made extremely uneasy, but the complacency of edification is absent, as it is apt to be from any true tragedy.

Mr. Eliot includes Lawrence and Joyce in his list of literary men of "diabolic" tendencies. Deploring Lawrence's "untrained" mind, he adds: "A trained mind like that of Mr. Joyce is always aware of what master it is serving. . . ."

Untrained minds have always been a nuisance to the military police of orthodoxy. God-intoxicated mystics and untidy saints, with only a white blaze of divine love where their minds should have been, are perpetually creating almost as much disorder within the law as outside it. To have a trained mind is no guarantee at all that the possessor is going to walk infallibly in the path of virtue, though he hardly fails in the letter of the law. St. Joan of Arc and St. Francis in their own ways have had something to say about that. The combination of a trained mind and incorruptible virtue is ideal, and therefore rare: St. Thomas More is the first name that occurs to me as example. Hardy's mind, which had rejected the conclusions though not the ethical discipline of organized religion (and he knew that its ethical system in essentials is older than Christianity), was not altogether an untrained one, and like all true Dissenters, he knew the master he was serving: his conscience. He had the mathematical certainties of music and architecture, and the daily, hourly training of a serious artist laboring at his problem over a period of more than half a century. That he was unhampered by ideas is therefore highly improbable. He wrote a few fine poems among a large number of poor ones. He wrote fifteen novels, of which a round half dozen are well the equal of any novel in the English language; even if this is not to say he is the equal of Flaubert or of Dostoievsky. His notebooks testify to a constant preoccupation with ideas, not all of them his own, naturally, for he inherited them from a very respectable race of thinkers, sound in heterodoxy.

He had got out of the very air of the nineteenth century something from Lucian, something from Leonardo, something from Erasmus, from Montaigne, from Voltaire, from the Encyclopaedists, and there were some powerful nineteenth-century Inquirers, too, of whom we need only mention Darwin, perhaps. Scientific experiment leads first to skepticism; but we have seen in our time, how, pursued to the verge of the infinite, it sometimes leads back again to a form of mysticism. There is at the heart of the universe a riddle no man can solve, and in the end, God may be the answer. But this is fetching up at a great distance still from orthodoxy, and still must be suspect in that quarter. Grant that the idea of God is the most splendid single act of the creative human imagination, and that all his multiple faces and attributes correspond to some need and satisfy some deep desire in mankind; still, for the Inquirers, it is impossible not to conclude that this mystical concept has been harnessed rudely to machinery of the most mundane sort, and has been made to serve the ends of an organization which, ruling under divine guidance, has ruled very little better, and in some respects, worse, than certain rather mediocre but frankly man-made systems of government. And it has often lent its support to the worst evils in secular government, fighting consistently on the side of the heavy artillery. And it has seemed at times not to know the difference between Good and Evil, but to get them hopelessly confused with legalistic right and wrong; justifying the most cynical expedients of worldly government by a high morality; and committing the most savage crimes against human life for the love of God. When you consider the political career of the church in the light of its professed origins and purposes, perhaps Original Sin *is* the answer. But Hardy preferred to remove the argument simply to another ground. As to himself, in his personal life, he had a Franciscan tenderness in regard to children, animals, laborers, the poor, the mad, the insulted and injured. He suffered horror and indignation at human injustice, more especially at the kind committed by entrenched authority and power upon the helpless. In middle age he remembered and recorded an early shock he received on hearing that, in his neighborhood, a young boy, a farm laborer, was found dead of sheer starvation in the fruitful field he had worked to cultivate. When he was planning *The Dynasts,* he wrote in his notebook: "The human race is to be shown as one great net-work or tissue which quivers in every part when one point is shaken, like a spider's web if touched." For Hardy, the death of that boy was a blow that set the whole great web trembling; and all mankind received a lasting wound. Here was a human fate for which human acts were responsible, and it would not serve Hardy at all to put the blame on Original Sin, or the inscrutable decrees of Divine Providence, or any other of the manifold devices for not letting oneself be too uncomfortable at the spectacle of merely human suffering. He was painfully uncomfortable all his life, and his discomfort was not for himself—he was an extraordinarily selfless sort of man—but the pervasiveness of what he considered senseless and unnecessary human misery. Out of the strange simplicity of his own unworldliness he could write at the age of 78: "As to pessimism. My motto is, first correctly diagnose the complaint—in this case human ills—and ascertain the cause: then set about finding a remedy if one exists. The motto or practise of the optimists is: Blind the eyes to the real malady, and use empirical panaceas to suppress the symptoms." Reasonableness: the use of the human intelligence directed towards the best human solution of human ills; such, if you please, was the unedifying proposal of this diabolic soul.

He himself in his few comments on public and practical affairs, had always been very reasonable. War, he believed, was an abomination, but it recurred again and again, apparently an incurable ill. He had no theories to advance, but wished merely that those who made wars would admit the real motives; aside from the waste and destruction, which he viewed with purely humane feelings, he objected to the immoralities of statecraft and religion in the matter. He was opposed to capital punishment on the simple grounds that no man has the right to take away the life of another. But he believed it acted as a material deterrent to crime, and if the judges would admit that it was social expediency, with no foundation in true morality, that was another matter. On the Irish question he was acute and explicit in expressing his view in this direction. "Though he did not enter it here [in his notebook] Hardy . . . said of Home Rule that it was a staring dilemma, of which good policy and good philanthropy were the huge horns. Policy for England required that it should not be granted; humanity to Ireland that it should. Neither Liberals nor Conservatives would honestly own up to this opposition between two moralities, but speciously insisted that humanity and policy were both on one side—of course their own." At another time

he complained that most of the philosophers began on the theory that
the earth had been designed as a comfortable place for man. He could
no more accept this theory than he could the theological notion that
the world was a testing ground for the soul of man in preparation for
eternity, and that his sufferings were part of a "divine" plan, or
indeed, so far as the personal fate of mankind was concerned, of any
plan at all. He did believe with a great deal of commonsense that
man could make the earth a more endurable place for himself if he
would, but he also realized that human nature is not grounded in
commonsense, that there is a deep place in it where the mind does
not go, where the blind monsters sleep and wake, war among themselves, and feed upon death.

He did believe that there is "a power that rules the world" though
he did not name it, nor could he accept the names that had been
given it, or any explanation of its motives. He could only watch its
operations, and to me it seems he concluded that both malevolence
and benevolence originated in the mind of man, and the warring
forces were within him alone; such plan as existed in regard to him
he had created for himself, his Good and his Evil were alike the
mysterious inventions of his own mind; and why this was so, Hardy
could not pretend to say. He knew there was an element in human
nature not subject to mathematical equation or the water-tight
theories of dogma, and this intransigent, measureless force, divided
against itself, in conflict alike with its own system of laws and the
unknown laws of the universe, was the real theme of Hardy's novels;
a genuinely tragic theme in the grand manner, of sufficient weight
and shapelessness to try the powers of any artist. Generally so reluctant to admit any influence, Hardy admits to a study of the Greek
dramatists, and with his curious sense of proportion, he decided that
the Wessex countryside was also the dwelling place of the spirit of
tragedy; that the histories of certain obscure persons in that limited
locality bore a strong family resemblance to those of the great, the ancient, and the legendary. Mr. Eliot finds Hardy's beloved Wessex a
"stage setting," such as the Anglo-Saxon heart loves; and Hardy's Wessex farmers "period peasants pleasing to the metropolitan imagination." Hardy was Anglo-Saxon; that landscape was in his blood. Those
period peasants were people he had known all his life, and I think
that in this passage Mr. Eliot simply speaks as a man of the town, like
those young vicars who need to be reminded of the individual dignity
and importance of the country people. Further, taking all the Hardy

characters in a lump, he finds in them only blind animal emotionalism, and remarks: "strong passion is only interesting or significant
in strong men; those who abandon themselves without resistance to
excitements which tend to deprive them of reason become merely
instruments of feeling and lose their humanity; and unless there is
moral resistance and conflict there is no meaning." True in part:
and to disagree in detail would lead to an endless discussion of *what*
exactly constitutes interest in the work of a writer; *what* gives importance to his characters, their intrinsic value as human beings or the
value their creator is able to give them by his own imaginative view
of them.

Hardy seems almost to agree with Mr. Eliot for once: "The best
tragedy—highest tragedy in short—is that of the WORTHY encompassed by the INEVITABLE. The tragedies of immoral and worthless
people are not of the best." My own judgment is that Hardy's
characters are in every way superior to those of Mr. Eliot, and for
precisely the reason the two writers are agreed upon. Hardy's people
suffer the tragedy of being, Mr. Eliot's of not-being. The strange
creatures inhabiting the wasteland of Mr. Eliot's particular scene are
for the most part immoral and worthless, the apeneck Sweeneys, the
Grishkins, and all. . . . They have for us precisely the fascination
the poet has endowed them with, and they also have great significance: they are the sinister chorus of the poet's own tragedy, they
represent the sum of the poet's vision of human beings without God
and without faith, a world of horror surrounding this soul thirsting
for faith in God. Mr. Forster has remarked that *The Waste Land* is
a poem of real horror, the tragedy of the rains that came too late—or
perhaps, never came at all. For how else can one explain the self-
absorbed despair of Eliot's point of view, even in religion? That uncontrolled emotion of loathing for his fellow pilgrims in this mortal
life? Was there not one soul worth tender treatment, not one good
man interesting enough to the poet to inhabit his tragic scene? It is
a curious paradox. Hardy feels no contempt for his characters at all;
he writes of them as objectively as if they existed by themselves,
they are never the background, the chorus, for the drama of his own
experience. Beside Eliot's wasteland, with its inhuman beings, Hardy's Wessex seems an airy, familiar place, his characters at least have
living blood in them, and though Mr. Eliot complains that Hardy
was not interested in the minds of men, still their head pieces are
not deliberately stuffed with straw by their creator.

Hardy's characters are full of moral conflicts and of decisions arrived at by mental processes, certainly. Jude, Gabriel Oak, Clem Yeobright, above all, Henchard, are men who have decisions to make, and if they do not make them entirely on the plane of reason, it is because Hardy was interested most in that hairline dividing the rational from the instinctive, the opposition, we might call it, between nature, and second nature; that is, between instinct and the habits of thought fixed upon the individual by his education and his environment. Such characters of his as are led by their emotions come to tragedy; he seems to say that following the emotions blindly leads to disaster. Romantic miscalculation of the possibilities of life, of love, of the situation; of refusing to reason their way out of their predicament; these are the causes of disaster in Hardy's novels. Angel Clare is a man of the highest principles, trained in belief, religion, observance of moral law. His failure to understand the real nature of Christianity makes a monster of him at the great crisis of his life. The Mayor of Casterbridge spends the balance of his life in atonement and reparation for a brutal wrong committed in drunkenness and anger; his past overtakes and destroys him. Hardy had an observing eye, a remembering mind; he did not need the Greeks to teach him that the Furies do arrive punctually, and that neither act, nor will, nor intention will serve to deflect a man's destiny from him, once he has taken the step which decides it.

A word about that style which Mr. Eliot condemns as touching "sublimity without ever having passed through the stage of being good." Hardy has often been called by critics who love him, the good simple man of no ideas, the careless workman of genius who never learned to write, who cared nothing for the way of saying a thing.

His own testimony is that he cared a great deal for *what* he said: "My art is to intensify the expression of things, as is done by Crivelli, Bellini, etc., so that the heart and inner meaning is made vividly visible." Again: "The Realities to be the true realities of life, hitherto called abstractions. The old material realities to be placed behind the former, as shadowy accessories." His notebooks are dry, reluctant, unmethodical; he seems to have spent his time and energies in actual labor at his task rather than theorizing about it, but he remarks once: "Looking around on a well selected shelf of fiction, how few stories of any length does one recognize as well told from beginning to end! The first half of this story, the last half of that, the middle of another . . . the modern art of narration is yet in its infancy." He made few comments on technical procedure, but one or two are valuable as a clue to his directions: "A story must be exceptional enough to justify its telling. We tale tellers are all Ancient Mariners, and none of us is warranted in stopping Wedding Guests . . . unless he has something more unusual to relate than the ordinary experiences of every average man and woman." Again: "The whole secret of fiction and drama—in the constructional part—lies in the adjustment of things unusual to things eternal and universal. The writer who knows exactly how exceptional, and how non-exceptional, his events should be made, possesses the key to the art."

So much for theory. Not much about the importance of style, the care for the word, the just and perfect construction of a paragraph. But Hardy was not a careless writer. The difference between his first and last editions proves this, in matters of style aside from his painful reconstruction of his manuscripts mutilated for serial publication. He wrote and wrote again, and he never found it easy. He lacked elegance, he never learned the trick of the whip-lash phrase, the complicated lariat twirling of the professed stylists. His prose lumbers along, it jogs, it creaks, it hesitates, he is as dull as certain long passages in the Tolstoy of *War and Peace,* for example. That celebrated first scene on Egdon Heath, in *The Return of the Native.* Who does not remember it? And in actual re-reading, what could be duller? What could be more labored than his introduction of the widow Yeobright at the heath fire among the dancers, or more unconvincing than the fears of the timid boy that the assembly are literally raising the Devil? Except for this; in my memory of that episode, as in dozens of others in many of Hardy's novels, I have seen it, I was there. When I read it, it almost disappears from view, and afterward comes back, phraseless, living in its sombre clearness, as Hardy meant it to do, I feel certain. This to my view is the chief quality of good prose as distinguished from poetry. By his own testimony, he limited his territory by choice, set boundaries to his material, focused his point of view like a burning glass down on a definite aspect of things. He practiced a stringent discipline, severely excised and eliminated all that seemed to him not useful or appropriate to his plan. In the end his work was the sum of his experience, he arrived at his particular true testimony; along the way, sometimes, many times, he wrote sublimely.

ALBERT J. GUERARD

On *The Mayor of Casterbridge*

Henchard, who is Hardy's Lord Jim, stands at the very summit of his creator's achievement; his only tragic hero and one of the greatest tragic heroes in all fiction. He takes his place at once with certain towering and possessed figures of Melville, Hawthorne, and Dostoevsky: a man of character obsessed by guilt and so committed to his own destruction. He anticipates not merely Lord Jim and the Razumov of *Under Western Eyes* but also the Michel of André Gide's *L'Immoraliste*. Fifty years before Karl Menninger, Hardy recognized —as Shakespeare did three centuries before him—that the guilty not merely flagellate themselves but also thrust themselves in the way of bad luck; *create* what appear to be unlucky accidents. Henchard's decline in Casterbridge was no more fortuitous than Lord Jim's in Patusan. These two "men of character" pursued strikingly similar destinies: forceful, conscientious, and proud, alike outcasts thanks to the unaccountable flarings of a moment's fear and anger, dedicating their lives to an impossible rehabilitation and a distant ideal of honor. They are isolated and obsessed by guilt even in their fat years of power and prestige; they are determined to bear yet face down the past. Both are men of character in a strangely double sense. They want to atone for the past through self-punishment; yet they resist, humanly, merely compulsive self-punishment. In the end both are paralyzed by "chance" reminders from the past (Brown and the fur-mity-woman)—reminders which, in fact, they had never ceased to carry about with them. They achieve death in solitude, each having one dull-witted uncomprehending native who remains failthful to the last. Of the two Henchard, whose will was a final self-condemna-tion, may have shown more courage than Lord Jim, who turned to his executioners and to the world with a last look of proud defiance. Henchard was a "man of character"; Lord Jim was "one of us."

There was nothing in Hardy's earlier novels to suggest that he would some day produce such a figure; there is no series of links and experiments leading from Springrove or Manston to Henchard. Ga-briel Oak, Diggory Venn, and many others seem to act perversely against their own interest, but this is owing to meditative impotence and a lack of normal aggressiveness. They are spectators rather than actors against themselves. Unlike them Henchard is a man of great force and destructive energy, which he turns outward occasionally but inward far more often. He has thus nothing in common with the irresponsible Wildeve, but a great deal in common with both Jude and Sue. There is little justification for the critic who sums up Henchard's tragic flaws as temper and addiction to drink; these were symptoms of the self-destructive impulse rather than its causes. Hardy himself was explicit enough:

> Thereupon promptly came to the surface that idiosyncrasy of Henchard's which had ruled his courses from the beginning, and had mainly made him what he was. Instead of thinking that a union between his cherished stepdaughter and the energetic thriv-ing Donald was a thing to be desired for her good and his own, he hated the very possibility.
>
> Among the many hindrances to such a pleading, not the least was this, that he did not sufficiently value himself to lessen his sufferings by strenuous appeal or elaborate argument.
>
> He had not expressed to her any regrets or excuses for what he had done in the past; but it was a part of his nature to extenuate nothing and live on as one of his own worst accusers.[1]

Henchard is simply incapable of acting consistently in his own in-terest. Captain Ahab, traveling the wide seas in pursuit of his own destruction, supposes cosmic hostilities in a whale. And so Henchard,

earthbound in Casterbridge, comes at last to think "some sinister intelligence bent on punishing him." Had someone roasted a wax image
of him? Was some power working against him? Unaware that the
power was wholly inward, he "looked out at the night as at a fiend."[2]

Thus Hardy, who had seldom troubled himself with crime and
punishment, at last explored the great nineteenth-century myth of the
isolated, damned, and self-destructive individualist—the more impressively because his Lara, Vautrin, Tito Melema, and Ahab was an
ordinary Wessex farmer-merchant. The particular myth was conceived in terms as grand as the Wessex environment would allow—
beginning with no less than the angry, drunken, and impulsive sale
of a wife on the fairgrounds of Weydon Priors, to which Henchard
would return a quarter of a century later in full circle. The tendency
to paranoia and self-flagellation must have had its origin, like that of
Sue Bridehead, in some part of an undisclosed childhood. At the very
beginning Henchard has already the "instinct of a perverse character"; he drinks too much and thinks he has ruined his chances by
marrying at eighteen. It is the crime of selling his wife which concentrates his energies, however; which both makes his character and
destroys it. (Here too he is exactly like Lord Jim, who might have
remained, in innocence, a fairly ordinary sea captain and trader.)
Henchard looks in vain for his wife; swears an oath not to drink for
twenty years; becomes mayor of Casterbridge, though equipped with
little more than energy—becomes a man of character. When Susan
finally reappears, he stolidly and conscientiously marries her; when
Lucetta reappears, he acts honorably, though long tempted to revenge
himself on Farfrae through her; when the furmity-woman reappears,
he publicly acknowledges his guilt. He is fair in his savage fashion,
and fights Farfrae with one hand tied behind his back. Ruined, he is
the most conscientious of bankrupts.

The Mayor of Casterbridge is a novel of temperament in action,
in minute action even; its distinction derives from a severe concentration on the self-destructive aspects of that temperament. The obligation to punish and degrade the self is at times fairly conscious.
Thus Henchard marries Susan not merely to make amends to her
and to provide Elizabeth-Jane with a home, but also "to castigate
himself with the thorns which these restitutory acts brought in their
train; among them the lowering of his dignity in public opinion by
marrying so comparatively humble a woman." He licks his wounds by
demanding that the journeymen sing the terrible One Hundred and

Ninth Psalm; he goes to work for Farfrae wearing the rusty silk hat of his former dignity; he humbles himself unnecessarily before Lucetta; he lingers on the second stone bridge where the failures and drifters of the town gather.[3] But Hardy recognized, intuitively at least, that the guilty may also punish themselves unconciously and cause their own "bad luck." The man who repeatedly cuts and burns himself is no mere victim of absurd mischance; he is compelled to cut and burn himself, though he may not understand his compulsion. Freud has documented the hidden psychology of errors; Menninger the motives of chronic failures and of those who suffer repeated "accidents." Psychologists have proved that the unfortunate are more often than not the guilty, who must pay daily hostages to their fear.

Henchard is such a man, for whom everything "goes wrong" once he has begun to struggle with his guilt. So his elaborate public entertainment fails dismally while Farfrae's modest one succeeds. Rain does not fall at the beck of the accusing conscience, but Henchard's party is ruined by more than rain. "A man must be a headstrong stunpoll to think folk would go up to that bleak place today." Later he gambles on disastrous rains to drive up the price of corn and is confirmed in his prophecy by the mysterious Mr. Fall; he buys enormous quantities of corn and is ruined by the blazing August weather. But the adverse force was his own lack of Wessex prudence. "He was reminded of what he had well known before, that a man might gamble upon the square green areas of fields as readily as upon those of a card-room . . . 'For you can never be sure of weather till 'tis past.'" Henchard's subconscious self-destructiveness shows itself far less equivocally at the time of the Royal Progress. He has a "passing fancy" to join in welcoming the royal visitor, though no longer a member of the town council. But what might have appeared a last conscious effort to reassert his dignity was in fact a half-conscious effort to degrade himself before the collected townfolk in the most humiliating way. "He was not only a journeyman, unable to appear as he formerly had appeared, but he disdained to appear as well as he might. Everybody else, from the Mayor to the washer-woman, shone in new vesture according to means; but Henchard had doggedly retained the fretted and weatherbeaten garments of bygone years." And he was drunk. When he resumed drinking after twenty years, a short time before this, he had committed himself to focal suicide and certain self-punishment. Character is fate; and Newson and the furmity-woman, those symbolic reminders, were part of his character and fate. Henchard would have destroyed himself even had they not returned. As a man of character he was morally obligated to do so. Yet he was also obligated to resist mere compulsive self-destructiveness. Here too, in fighting his suicidal destiny, he was a man of character.

Thus grandly and minutely conceived, Henchard might yet have remained as wooden as Farmer Boldwood. But he is very nearly the most personalized of Hardy's men: a voice and an unforgettable massive presence, with his twitching mouth and distant gaze, his "vehement" gloominess, his severe friendliness, and his businesslike bluntness even when proposing marriage. No doubt it is as a well-meaning man isolated by guilt that he makes his strongest appeal to our sympathy. Loneliness as well as guilt prompts him to hire Farfrae impulsively and to pour out his confession at once. And guilt as well as loneliness attaches him to Elizabeth-Jane: "He had liked the look of her face as she answered him from the stairs. There had been affection in it, and above all things what he desired now was affection from anything that was good and pure."[4] Finally, though his history is highly selective, we have the impression that we know Henchard's life in its every significant detail. The measure of the characterization's success is our unquestioning acceptance in its context of Henchard's stylized and symbolic will. It does not seem to us a gratuitous or merely ornamental offering of Hardy's pessimism, as a few of Jude Fawley's philosophical speeches do. Michael Henchard's excommunication of self is a reasoned one, for his life has actually so added up:

> That Elizabeth-Jane Farfrae be not told of my death, or made to grieve on account of me.
> & that I be not bury'd in consecrated ground.
> & that no sexton be asked to toll the bell.
> & that nobody is wished to see my dead body.
> & that no murners walk behind me at my funeral.
> & that no flours be planted on my grave.
> & that no man remember me.
> To this I put my name.[5]

"Let the day perish wherein I was born, and the night in which it was said, There is a manchild conceived"—Jude Fawley might have signed Henchard's will.

Jude is not, however, a tragic hero—if only because he is a "modern," Henchard's will is a final condemnation of self and of the "old mankind"; it is an achievement of the self-knowledge which tragedy compels. Jude's dying words are instead a condemnation of the cosmos in its dark and at last recognized absurdity. Not Jude but the cosmos is to blame. There are certain obvious links between the two characters: the common sensitiveness to music, the imprudent early marriages, the addiction to drink, the need to punish and degrade the self publicly. But the significant link occurs in the final paragraph of *The Mayor of Casterbridge;* in Elizabeth-Jane's observation "that neither she nor any human being deserved less than was given." The observation is pathetic and of course pessimistic in the commoner sense of that word. But it is not tragic, as all but the last pages of the novel are tragic. For the tragic attitude lays the blame not on the stars but on ourselves; it sees fate in character; its pessimism is grounded in the insufficiency of the human endowment; it insists, with Conrad's Marlow, that "nobody is good enough."[6] Jude is a victim of his society and inheritance and of a bad luck for which he is only in part responsible. He appeals to our sympathy more than Henchard does, but not merely because of his greater idealism and tenderness. For he appeals to our human indolence, our refusal to take the blame. . . .

NOTES

1. *The Mayor of Casterbridge,* Harper Thin-Paper Edition, Harper & Row, 1966, pp. 368, 396, 400.
2. *Ibid.,* pp. 151, 229, 151.
3. *Ibid.,* pp. 99, 281, 275, 332.
4. *Ibid.,* p. 347.
5. *Ibid.,* p. 404.
6. *Lord Jim,* Chapter 33.

TONY TANNER

Colour and Movement in Hardy's
Tess of the d'Urbervilles

> ". . . the discontinuance of immobility in any
> quarter suggested confusion."
> *(Return of the Native)*
> ". . . the least irregularity of motion startled
> her. . . ."   *(Tess of the d'Urbervilles)*

I

Every great writer has his own kind of legibility, his own way of
turning life into a language of particular saliences, and in Hardy
this legibility is of a singularly stark order. If we can think of a
novelist as creating, among other things, a particular linguistic world
by a series of selective intensifications of our shared vocabulary, then
we can say that Hardy's world is unusually easy to read. The key
words in his dialect, to continue the image, stand out like braille. It
is as though some impersonal process of erosion had worn away much
of the dense circumstantial texture of his tales, revealing the basic
resistant contours of a sequence of events which Hardy only has to
point to to make us see—like ancient marks on a barren landscape.
And Hardy above all does make us see. Just as he himself could not
bear to be touched, so he does not "touch" the people and things in
his tales, does not interfere with them or absorb them into his own

From *Critical Quarterly*, X, 1968, 219-39. Copyright © by Tony Tanner. Reprinted by permission of the author and publisher.

sensibility. When he says in his introduction to *Tess of the d'Urbervilles* that "a novel is an impression, not an argument," or in his introduction to *Jude the Obscure* that "like former productions of this pen, *Jude the Obscure* is simply an endeavour to give shape and coherence to a series of seemings, or personal impressions," we should give full stress to the idea of something seen but not tampered with, something scrupulously watched in its otherness, something perceived but not made over. Hardy's famous, or notorious, philosophic broodings and asides are part of his reactions as a watcher, but they never give the impression of violating the people and objects of which his tale is composed. Reflection and perception are kept separate (in Lawrence they often tend to merge), and those who complain about the turgidity of his thoughts may be overlooking the incomparable clarity of his eyes.

II

This illusion that the tale exists independently of Hardy's rendering of it *is* of course only an illusion, but it testifies to art of a rather special kind. For all Henry James's scrupulous indirectness, Hardy's art is more truly impersonal. He goes in for graphic crudities of effect which James would have scorned, yet, as other critics have testified, the result is an anonymity which we more commonly associate with folk-tale, or the ballads. By graphic crudity of effect I am referring, for instance, to such moments as when Tess, shortly after being seduced, encounters a man who is writing in large letters "THY, DAMNATION, SLUMBERETH, NOT." There are commas between every word "as if to give pause while that word was driven well home to the reader's heart." This is not unlike Hardy's own art which is full of prominent notations, and emphatic pauses which temporarily isolate, and thus vivify, key incidents and objects. On the level of everyday plausibility and probability it is too freakish a chance which brings Tess and the painted words together at this point. In the vast empty landscapes of Hardy's world, peoples' paths cross according to some more mysterious logic—that same imponderable structuring of things in time which brought the *Titanic* and the ice-berg together at one point in the trackless night sea. (See the poem "The Convergence of the Twain.") A comparable "crudity" is discernible in the characterisation which is extremely schematic, lacking in all the minute mysteries of individual uniqueness which a writer like James pursued. *Angel* Clare is indeed utterly ethereal; his love is "more spiritual than animal." He even plays the harp! On the other hand Alec d'Urberville is almost a stage villain with his "swarthy complexion . . . full lips . . . well-groomed black moustache with curled points," his cigars and his rakish way with his fast spring-cart. If we turn from character to plot sequence we see at once that the overall architecture of the novel is blocked out with massive simplicity in a series of balancing phases—The Maiden, Maiden No More; The Rally, The Consequence; and so on. Let it be conceded at once that Hardy's art is not subtle in the way that James and many subsequent writers are subtle. Nevertheless I think it is clear that Hardy derives his great power from that very "crudity" which, in its impersonal indifference to plausibility and rational cause and effect, enhances the visibility of the most basic lineaments of the tale.

III

I want first to concentrate on one series of examples which shows how this manifest visibility works. For an artist as visually sensitive as Hardy, colour is of the first importance and significance, and there is one colour which literally catches the eye, and is meant to catch it, throughout the book. This colour is red, the colour of blood, which is associated with Tess from first to last. It dogs her, disturbs her, destroys her. She is full of it, she spills it, she loses it. Watching Tess's life we begin to see that her destiny is nothing more or less than the colour red. The first time we (and Angel) see Tess, in the May dance with the other girls, she stands out. How? They are all in white except that Tess "wore a red ribbon in her hair, and was the only one of the white company who would boast of such a pronounced adornment." Tess is marked, even from the happy valley of her birth and childhood. The others are a semi-anonymous mass; Tess already has that heightened legibility, that eye-taking prominence which suggests that she has in some mysterious way been singled out. And the red stands out because it is on a pure white background. In that simple scene and colour contrast is the embryo of the whole book and all that happens in it.

This patterning of red and white is often visible in the background of the book. For instance "The ripe hue of the red and dun kine absorbed the evening sunlight, which the white-coated animals returned to the eye in rays almost dazzling, even at the distant eleva-

tion on which she stood." This dark red and dazzling white is something seen, it is something there; it is an effect on the retina, it is a
configuration of matter. In looking at this landscape Tess in fact
is seeing the elemental mixture which conditions her own existence.
In the second chapter Tess is described as "a mere vessel of emotion
untinctured by experience." The use of the word "untinctured" may
at first seem surprising; we perhaps tend to think of people being
shaped by experience rather than coloured by it—yet the use of a
word connected with dye and paint is clearly intentional. In her
youth Tess is often referred to as a "white shape"—almost more as a
colour value in a landscape than a human being. And on the night
of her rape she is seen as a "white muslin figure" sleeping on a pile
of dead leaves; her "beautiful feminine tissue" is described as "practically blank as snow." The historic precedent for what is to happen
to this vulnerable white shape is given at the start when we read
that "the Vale was known in former times as the Forest of White
Hart, from a curious legend of King Henry III's reign, in which the
killing by a certain Thomas de le Lynd of a beautiful white hart
which the king had run down and spared, was made the occasion
of a heavy fine." Against all social injunctions, white harts are
brought down. And in Tess's case the "tincturing"—already prefigured in the red ribbon—starts very early.

The next omen—for even that harmless ribbon is an omen in this
world—occurs when Tess drives the hives to market when her father
is too drunk to do the job. When she sets out the road is still in darkness. Tess drifts, sleeps, dreams. Then there is the sudden collision
and she wakes to find that Prince, their horse, has been killed by
another cart. "The pointed shaft of the cart had entered the breast
of the unhappy Prince like a sword, and from the wound his life's
blood was spouting in a stream and falling with a hiss on the road.
In her despair Tess sprang forward and put her hand upon the hole,
with the only result that she became splashed from face to skirt with
the crimson drops. Then she stood helplessly looking on. Prince also
stood firm and motionless as long as he could; till he suddenly sank
down in a heap." It is possible to say different things about this
passage. On one level the death of the horse means that the family
is destitute, which means in turn that Tess will have to go begging
to the d'Urbervilles. Thus, it is part of a rough cause and effect economic sequence. But far more graphic, more disturbing and memorable, is the image of the sleeping girl on the darkened road, bru-

tally awakened and desperately trying to staunch a fatal puncture, trying to stop the blood which cannot be stopped and only getting drenched in its powerful spurts. It adumbrates the loss of her virginity, for she, too, will be brutally pierced on a darkened road far from home; and once the blood of her innocence has been released, she too, like the stoical Prince, will stay upright as long as she can until, all blood being out, she will sink down suddenly in a heap. Compressed in that one imponderable scene we can see her whole life.

After this Tess is constantly encountering the colour red—if not literal blood, manifold reminders of it. When she approaches the d'Urberville house we read: "It was of recent erection—indeed almost new—and of the same rich red colour that formed such a contrast with the evergreens of the lodge." And the corner of the house "rose like a geranium bloom against the subdued colours around." Tess, with her red ribbon, also stood out against "the subdued colours around." Mysteriously, inevitably, this house will play a part in her destiny. And if this red house contains her future rapist, so it is another red house which contains her final executioner, for the prison where she is hanged is "a large red-brick building." Red marks the houses of sex and death. When first she has to approach the leering, smoking Alec d'Urberville, he forces roses and strawberries on her, pushing a strawberry into her mouth, pressing the roses into her bosom. Hardy, deliberately adding to the legibility I am describing, comments that d'Urberville is one "who stood fair to be the blood-red ray in the spectrum of her young life." On the evening of the rape, Tess is first aware of d'Urberville's presence at the dance when she sees "the red coal of a cigar." This is too clearly phallic to need comment, but it is worth pointing out that, from the first, d'Urberville seems to have the power of reducing Tess to a sort of trance-like state, he envelopes her in a "blue narcotic haze" of which his cigar smoke is the most visible emblem. On the night of the rape, at the dance, everything is in a "mist," like "illuminated smoke"; there is a "floating, fusty *debris* of peat and hay" stirred up as "the panting shapes spun onwards." Everything together seems to form "a sort of vegeto-human pollen." In other words it becomes part of a basic natural process in which Tess is caught up simply by being alive, fecund, and female. D'Urberville is that figure, that force, at the heart of the haze, the mist, the smoke, waiting to claim her when the dance catches her up (we first saw her at a dance and she can scarcely avoid being drawn in). It is in a brilliant continuation of this blurred narcotic atmosphere that Hardy has the rape take place in a dense fog, while Tess is in a deep sleep. Consciousness and perception are alike engulfed and obliterated. When Tess first leaves d'Urberville's house she suddenly wakes up to find that she is covered in roses; while removing them a thorn from a remaining rose pricks her chin. "Like all the cottagers in Blackmoor Vale, Tess was steeped in fancies and prefigurative superstitions; she thought this an ill omen." The world of the book is indeed a world of omens (*not* symbols) in which things and events echo and connect in patterns deeper than lines of rational cause and effect. Tess takes it as an omen when she starts to bleed from the last rose pressed on her by Alec. She is right; for later on she will again wake up to find that he has drawn blood—in a way which determines her subsequent existence.

After the rape we are still constantly seeing the colour red. The man who writes up the words promising damnation is carrying "a tin pot of red paint in his hand." As a result "these vermilion words shone forth." Shortly after, when Tess is back at home, Hardy describes a sunrise in which the sun "broke through chinks of cottage shutters, throwing stripes like red-hot pokers upon cupboards, chests of drawers, and other furniture within." (The conjunction of sunlight and redness is a phenomenon I will return to.) And Hardy goes on: "But of all ruddy things that morning the brightest were two broad arms of painted wood . . . forming the revolving Maltese cross of the reaping-machine." We will later see Tess virtually trapped and tortured on a piece of red machinery, and her way will take her past several crosses until she finds her own particular sacrificial place. When Tess is working in the fields her flesh again reveals its vulnerability. "A bit of her naked arm is visible between the buff leather of the gauntlet and the sleeve of her gown; and as the day wears on its feminine smoothness becomes scarified by the stubble, and bleeds." Notice the shift to the present tense: Hardy makes us look at the actual surfaces—the leather, the sleeve, the flesh, the blood. One of the great strengths of Hardy is that he knew, and makes us realise, just how very much the surfaces of things mean.

Of course it is part of the whole meaning of the book that there is as much red inside Tess as outside her. Both the men who seek to possess her see it. When Tess defies d'Urberville early on, she speaks up at him, "revealing the red and ivory of her mouth"; while when Angel watches her unawares, "she was yawning, and he saw the red interior of her mouth as if it had been a snake's." When Angel does just kiss her arm, and he kisses the inside vein, we read that she was such a "sheaf of susceptibilities" that "her blood [was] driven to her finger ends." Tess does not so much act as re-act. She would be content to be passive, but something is always disturbing her blood, and all but helplessly she submits to the momentums of nature in which, by her very constitution, she is necessarily involved. As for example when she is drawn by Angel's music "like a fascinated bird" and she makes her way through, once again, a misty atmosphere ("mists of pollen") of uncontrollable swarming fertility and widespread insemination. It is a place of growth, though not wholly a place of beauty. There are "tall blooming weeds" giving off "offensive smells" and some of the weeds are a bright "red." "She went stealthily as a cat through this profusion of growth, gathering cuckoo-spittle on her skirts, cracking snails that were underfoot, staining her hands with thistle-milk and slug-slime, and rubbing off upon her naked arms sticky blights which though snow-white on the apple-tree trunks, made *madder* stains on her skin. . . ." (my italics). In some of the earlier editions (certainly up to the 1895 edition) that final phrase was "blood-red stains on her skin"; only later did Hardy change "blood-red" to "madder," a crimson dye made from a climbing plant. This change clearly reveals that he intended us once again to see Tess's arm marked with red, though he opted for a word which better suggested something in nature staining, "tincturing," Tess as she pushes on through "this profusion of growth." And once again Hardy presents us with redness and snow-whiteness in the same scene—indeed, in the same plant.

After Tess has been abandoned by Angel and she has to renew her endless journeying the red omens grow more vivid, more violent. She seeks shelter one night under some bushes and when she wakes up: "Under the trees several pheasants lay about, their rich plummage dabbled with blood; some were dead, some feebly twitching a wing, some staring up at the sky, some pulsating quickly, some contorted, some stretched out—all of them writhing in agony, except for the fortunate ones whose torture had ended during the night by the inability of nature to bear more." There is much that is horribly apposite for Tess in these bloody writhings. (It is worth noting that Hardy uses the same word to describe the torments of the onset of sexual impulse; thus he describes the sleeping girls at Talbothays who are suffering from "hopeless passion." "They writhed feverishly under the oppressiveness of an emotion thrust on them by cruel Nature's law—an emotion which they had neither expected nor desired." The writhings of life are strangely similar to the writhings of death). Looking at the dying birds Tess reprimands herself for feeling self-pity, saying "I be not mangled, and I be not bleeding." But she will be both, and she, too, will have to endure until she reaches "the inability of nature to bear more." Like the white hart and the pheasants she is a hunted animal; hunted not really by a distinct human individual, but by ominous loitering presences like the cruel gun-men she used to glimpse stalking through the woods and bushes—a male blood-letting force which is abroad. Later when she makes her fruitless trek to Angel's parents she sees "a piece of blood-stained paper, caught up from some meat-buyer's dust heap, beat up and down the road without the gate; too flimsy to rest, too heavy to fly away, and a few straws to keep it company." It is another deliberate omen. Tess, too, is blood-stained, she, too, is beat up and down the road outside the gate (she has no home or refuge, no door opens to her); and she, too, very exactly, is too flimsy to rest, too heavy to fly away. (Cf. Eustacia Vye's envy of the heron. "Up in the zenith where he was seemed a free and happy place, away from all contact with the earthly ball to which she was pinioned; and she wished that she could arise uncrushed from its surface and fly as he flew then.") The blood-stained piece of paper is not a clumsy symbol; it is one of a number of cumulative omens. When Alec d'Urberville renews his pressure on Tess, at one point she turns and slashes him across the face with her heavy leather gauntlet. "A scarlet oozing appeared where her blow had alighted and in a moment the blood began dropping from his mouth upon the straw." (Notice again the conjunction of blood and straw.) The man who first made her bleed now stands bleeding from the lips. Blood has blood, and it will have more blood. We need only to see the scene—there, unanalysed, unexplained; a matter of violent movement, sudden compulsions. Hardy spends more time describing the glove than attempting to unravel the hidden thoughts of these starkly confronted human beings. Few other writers can so make us feel that the world is its own meaning—and mystery, requiring no interpretative gloss. Seeing the heavy glove, the sudden blow, the dripping blood, we see all we need to see.

At one point shortly before her marriage, Tess comes into proximity with a railway engine. "No object could have looked more foreign to the gleaming cranks and wheels than this unsophisticated girl, with the round bare arms. . . ." This feeling that her vulnerable flesh is somehow menaced by machinery is realised when she is later set to work on that "insatiable swallower," the relentless threshing machine. It is a bright red machine, and the "immense stack of straw" which it is turning out is seen as "the *faeces* of the same buzzing red glutton." Tess is "the only woman whose place was upon the machine so as to be shaken bodily by its spinning." She is beaten into a "stupefied reverie in which her arms worked on independently of her consciousness" (this separation, indeed severance, of consciousness and body is a crucial part of Tess's experience). Whenever she looks up "she beheld always the great upgrown straw-stack, with the men in short-sleeves upon it, against the grey north sky; in front of it the long red elevator like a Jacob's ladder, on which a perpetual stream of threshed straw ascended. . . ." There it is. We see Tess, trapped and stupefied in the cruel red man-made machine. Whenever she looks up in her trance of pain and weariness she sees— the long red elevator, the growing heap of straw, the men at work against the grey sky. It is a scene which is, somehow, her life: the men, the movement, the redness, the straw (blood and straw seem almost to be the basic materials of existence in the book—the vital pulsating fluid, and the dry, dead stalks). At the end of the day she is as a "bled calf." We do not need any enveloping and aiding words; only the legibility of vibrant, perceived detail.

The end of the book is sufficiently well known, but it is worth pointing out how Hardy continues to bring the colour red in front of our eyes. The landlady who peeps through the keyhole during Tess's anguish when Angel has returned reports that, "her lips were bleeding from the clench of her teeth upon them." It is the landlady who sees "the oblong white ceiling, with this scarlet blot in the midst," which is at once the evidence of the murder and the completion of a life which also started with a red patch on a white background, only then it was simply a ribbon on a dress. The blood stain on the ceiling has "the appearance of a gigantic ace of hearts." In that shape of the heart, sex and death are merged in utmost legibility. After this we hardly need to see the hanging. It is enough that we see Tess climb into a vast bed with "crimson damask hangings," not indeed in a home, for she has no home, but in an empty house to be

"Let Furnished." And in that great crimson closed-in bed she finds what she has wanted for so long—rest and peace. Apart from the last scene at Stonehenge, we can say that at this point the crimson curtains do indeed fall on Tess; for if she was all white at birth, she is to be all red at death. The massed and linking red omens have finally closed in on Tess and her wanderings are over.

Tess is a "pure woman" as the subtitle, which caused such outrage, specifically says. The purest woman contains tides of blood (Tess is always blushing), and if the rising of blood is sexual passion and the spilling of blood is death, then we can see that the purest woman is sexual and mortal. Remember Tess watching Prince bleed to death—"the hole in his chest looking scarcely large enough to have let out all that animated him." It is not a large hole that Alec makes in Tess when he rapes her, but from then on the blood is bound to go on flowing until that initial violation will finally "let out all that animated her." Hardy is dealing here with the simplest and deepest of matters. Life starts in sex and ends in death, and Hardy constantly shows how closely allied the two forms of blood-letting are in one basic, unalterable rhythm of existence.

IV

I have suggested that the destiny of Tess comes to us as a cumulation of visible omens. It is also a convergence of omens and to explain what I mean I want to add a few comments on the part played in her life by the sun, altars and tombs, and finally walking and travelling. When we first see Tess with the other dancing girls we read that they are all bathed in sunshine. Hardy, ever conscious of effects of light, describes how their hair reflects various colours in the sunlight. More, "as each and all of them were warmed without by the sun, so each of them had a private little sun for her soul to bask in." They are creatures of the sun, warmed and nourished by the source of all heat and life. Tess starts sun-blessed. At the dairy, the sun is at its most active as a cause of the fertile surgings which animate all nature. "Rays from the sunrise drew forth the buds and stretched them into stalks, lifted up sap in noiseless streams, opened petals, and sucked out scents in invisible jets and breathings." This is the profoundly sensuous atmosphere in which Tess, despite mental hesitations, blooms into full female ripeness. Hardy does something very suggestive here in his treatment of the times of day. Tess and Angel rise very early, before the sun. They seem to themselves "the first persons up of all the world." The light is still half-compounded, aqueous," as though the business of creating animated forms has not yet begun. They are compared to Adam and Eve. As so often when Tess is getting involved with the superior power of a man, the atmosphere is misty, but this time it is cold mist, the sunless fogs which precede the dawn. In this particular light of a cool watery whiteness, Tess appears to Angel as "a visionary essence of woman," something ghostly, "merely a soul at large." He calls her, among other things, Artemis (who lived, of course, in perpetual celibacy). In this sunless light Tess appears to Angel as unsexed, sexless, the sort of non-physical spiritualised essence he, in his impotent spirituality, wants. (At the end he marries a spiritualized image of "Tess.") But Tess is inescapably flesh and blood. And when the sun does come up, she reverts from divine essence to physical milkmaid: "her teeth, lips and eyes scintillated in the sunbeams, and she was again the dazzlingly fair dairymaid only. . . ." (That placing of "only" is typical of the strength of Hardy's prose.) Soon after this, the dairyman tells his story of the seduction of a young girl; "none of them but herself seemed to see the sorrow of it." And immediately we read, "the evening sun was now ugly to her, like a great inflamed wound in the sky." Sex is a natural instinct which however can lead to lives of utter misery. The same sun that blesses, can curse.

Tess drifts into marriage with Angel (her most characteristic way of moving in a landscape is a "quiescent glide"), because "every wave of her blood . . . was a voice that joined with nature in revolt against her scrupulousness," but meanwhile "at half-past six the sun settled down upon the levels, with the aspect of a great forge in the heavens." This suggests not a drawing-up into growth, but a slow inexorable downward crushing force, through an image linked to that machinery which will later pummel her body. It is as though the universe turns metallic against Tess, just as we read when Angel rejects her that there is in him a hard negating force "like a vein of metal in a soft loam." This is the metal which her soft flesh runs up against. Other omens follow on her journey towards her wedding. Her feeling that she has seen the d'Urberville coach before; the postillion who takes them to church and who has "a permanent running wound on the outside of his right leg"; the ominous "afternoon crow" and so on. I want to point to another omen, when the sun seems to single out Tess in a sinister way. It is worth reminding ourselves that when Angel finally does propose to Tess she is quite sun-drenched. They are standing on the "red-brick" floor and the sun slants in "upon her inclining face, upon the blue veins of her temple, upon her naked arm, and her neck, and into the depths of her hair." Now, on what should be the first night of her honeymoon we read: "The sun was so low on that short, last afternoon of the year that it shone in through a small opening and formed a golden staff which stretched across to her skirt, where it made a spot like a paint-mark set upon her." She has been marked before—first, with the blood of a dying beast, now with a mark from the setting sun. We find other descriptions of how the sun shines on Tess subsequently, but let us return to that crimson bed which, I suggested, effectively marked the end of Tess's journey. "A shaft of dazzling sunlight glanced into the room, revealing heavy, old-fashioned furniture, crimson damask hangings, and an enormous four-poster bedstead. . . ." The sun and the redness which have marked Tess's life, now converge at the moment of her approaching death. Finally Tess takes her last rest on the altar of Stonehenge. She speaks to Angel—again, it is before dawn, that sunless part of the day when he can communicate with her.

" 'Did they sacrifice to God here?' asked she.

'No', said he.

'Who to?'

'I believe to the sun. That lofty stone set away by itself is in the direction of the sun, which will presently rise behind it.' " When the sun does rise it also reveals the policemen closing in, for it is society which demands a specific revenge upon Tess. But in the configuration of omens which, I think, is the major part of the book, Tess is indeed a victim, sacrificed to the sun. The heathen temple is fitting, since of course Tess is descended from Pagan d'Urberville, and Hardy makes no scruple about asserting that women "retain in their souls far more of the Pagan fantasy of their remote forefathers than of the systematized religion taught their race at a later date." This raises an important point. Is Tess a victim of society, or of nature? Who wants her blood, who is after her, the policemen, or the sun? Or are they in some sadistic conspiracy so that we see nature and society converging on Tess to destroy her? I will return to this question.

To the convergence of redness and the sun we must add the great final fact of the altar, an altar which Tess approaches almost gratefully, and on which she takes up her sacrificial position with exhausted relief. She says (I have run some of her words to Angel together): "'I don't want to go any further, Angel. . . . Can't we bide here? . . . you used to say at Talbothays that I was a heathen. So now I am at home . . . I like very much to be here.'" Fully to be human is partly to be heathen, as the figure of Tess on the altar makes clear. (And after all what did heathen originally mean?—someone who lived on the heath; and what was a pagan?—someone who lived in a remote village. The terms only acquire their opprobrium after the advent of Christianity. Similarly Hardy points out that Sunday was originally the sun's day—a spiritual superstructure has been imposed on a physical source.) Tess's willingness to take her place on the stone of death has been manifested before. After she returns from the rape we read "her depression was then terrible, and she could have hidden herself in a tomb." On her marriage night, Angel sleepwalks into her room, saying "'Dead! Dead! Dead! . . . My wife—dead, dead!'" He picks her up, kisses her (which he can now only manage when he is unconscious), and carries her over a racing river. Tess almost wants to jog him so that they can fall to their deaths: but Angel can negotiate the dangers of turbulent water just as he can suppress all passion. His steps are not directed towards the movement of the waters but to the stillness of stone. He takes Tess and lays her in an "empty stone coffin" in the "ruined choir." In Angel's life of suppressed spontaneity and the negation of passional feeling, this is the most significant thing that he does. He encoffins the sexual instinct, then lies down beside Tess. The deepest inclinations of his psyche, his very being, have been revealed.

Later on, when things are utterly desperate for Tess's family and they literally have no roof over their heads, they take refuge by the church in which the family vaults are kept (where "the bones of her ancestors—her useless ancestors—lay entombed"). In their exhaustion they erect an old "four-post bedstead" over the vaults. We see again the intimate proximity of the bed and the grave. This sombre contiguity also adumbrates the ambiguous relief which Tess later finds in her crimson four-post-bed which is also very close to death. On this occasion Tess enters the church and pauses by the "tombs of the family" and "the door of her ancestral sepulchre." It is at this point that one of the tomb effigies moves, and Alec plays his insane jest on her by appearing to leap from a tomb. Again, we are invited to make the starkest sort of comparison without any exegesis from Hardy. Angel, asleep, took Tess in his arms and laid her in a coffin. Alec, however, seems to wake up from the tomb, a crude but animated threat to Tess in her quest for peace. Angel's instinct towards still-ness is countered by Alec's instinct for sexual motion. Together they add up to a continuous process in which Tess is simply caught up. For it is both men who drive Tess to her death: Angel by his spir-itualised rejection, Alec by his sexual attacks. It is notable that both these men are also cut off from any fixed community; they have both broken away from traditional attitudes and dwellings. Angel roams in his thought; Alec roams in his lust. They are both drifters of the sort who have an unsettling, often destructive impact in the Hardy world. Tess is a pure product of nature; but she is nature subject to complex and contradictory pressures. Angel wants her spiritual image without her body (when he finds out about her sexual past he simply denies her identity "'the woman I have been loving is not you'"); Alec wants only her body and is indifferent to anything we might call her soul, her distinctly human inwardness. The effect of this opposed wrenching on her wholeness is to induce a sort of inner rift which develops into something we would now call schizophrenia. While still at Talbothays she says one day: "'I do know that our souls can be made to go outside our bodies when we are alive.'" Her method is to fix the mind on a remote star and "'you will soon find that you are hundreds and hundreds o' miles away from your body, which you don't seem to want at all.'" The deep mystery by which consciousness can seek to be delivered from the body which sustains it, is one which Hardy had clearly before him. That an organism can be generated which then wishes to repudiate the very grounds of its existence ob-viously struck Hardy as providing a very awesome comment on the nature of nature. Tess is robbed of her integrated singleness, divided by two men, two forces. (This gives extra point to the various crosses she passes on her travels; the cross not only indicating torture, but that opposition between the vertical and the horizontal which, as I shall try to show, is ultimately the source of Tess's—and man's—sufferings in Hardy.) It is no wonder that when Alec worries and pursues her at the very door of her ancestors' vault, she should bend down and whisper that line of terrible simplicity—"'Why am I on the wrong side of this door?'" (A relevant poem of great power is "A Wasted Illness" of which I quote three stanzas which are very apt for Tess:

"Where lies the end
To this foul way?" I asked with weakening breath.
Thereon ahead I saw a door extend—
    The door to Death.

It loomed more clear:
"At last!" I cried. "The all-delivering door!"
And then, I know not how, it grew less near
    Than theretofore.

And back slid I
Along the galleries by which I came,
And tediously the day returned, and sky,
    And life—the same.)

Tess at this moment is utterly unplaced, with no refuge and no comfort. She can only stumble along more and rougher roads; increasingly vulnerable, weary and helpless, increasingly remote from her body. Her only solution is to break through that "all-delivering door," the door from life to death which opens on the only home left to her. This she does, by stabbing Alec and then taking her place on the ritual altar. She has finally spilled all the blood that tormented her; she can then abandon the torments of animateness and seek out the lasting repose she has earned.

V

This brings me to what is perhaps the most searching of all Hardy's preoccupations—walking, travelling, movement of all kinds. Somewhere at the heart of his vision is a profound sense of what we may call the mystery of motion. *Tess of the d'Urbervilles* opens with a man staggering on rickety legs down a road, and it is his daughter we shall see walking throughout the book. Phase the Second opens, once again, simply with an unexplained scene of laboured walking. "The basket was heavy and the bundle was large, but she lugged them along like a person who did not find her especial burden in material things. Occasionally she stopped to rest in a mechanical way by some gate or post; and then, giving the baggage another hitch upon her full round arm, went steadily on again." Such visualised passages carry the meaning of the novel, even down to the material burdens which weigh down that plump, vulnerable flesh: the meaning is both mute and unmistakable. At the start of Phase the Third, again Tess moves: "she left her home for the second time." At first the journey seems easy and comfortable in "a hired trap"; but soon she gets out and walks, and her journey again leads her into portents of the life ahead of her. "The journey over the intervening uplands and lowlands of Egdon, when she reached them, was a more trouble-some walk than she had anticipated, the distance being actually but a few miles. It was two hours, owing to sundry turnings, 'ere she found herself on a summit commanding the long-sought-for vale. . . ." The road to the peaceful vale of death is longer and harder than she thinks. Always Tess has to move, usually to harsher and more punishing territories, and always Hardy makes sure we *see* her. After Angel has banished her: "instead of a bride with boxes and trunks which others bore, we see her a lonely woman with a basket and a bundle in her own porterage. . . ." Later she walks to Emminster Vicarage on her abortive journey to see Angel's parents. She starts off briskly but by the end she is weary, and there are omens by the way. For instance, from one eminence she looks down at endless little fields, "so numerous that they look from this height like the meshes of a net." And again she passes a stone cross, Cross-in-Hand, which stands "desolate and silent, to mark the site of a miracle, or murder, or both." (Note the hint of the profound am-bivalence and ambiguity of deeds and events.) At the end of this journey there is nobody at home and there follows the incident of Tess losing her walking boots, another physical reminder that the walking gets harder and harder for her. "Her journey back was rather a meander than a march. It had no sprightliness, no purpose; only a tendency." Her movements do get more leaden throughout, and by the end Hardy confronts us with one of the strangest phenomena of existence—motion without volition. (Interestingly enough, Conrad approaches the same phenomenon in *The Secret Agent* where walk-ing is also the most insistent motif.) The only relief in her walking is that as it gets harder it also approaches nearer to darkness. Thus when she is summoned back to her family: "She plunged into the chilly equinoctial darkness . . . for her fifteen miles' walk under the steely stars"; and later during this walk from another eminence she "looked from that height into the abyss of chaotic shade which was all that revealed itself of the vale on whose further side she was born." She is indeed returning home, just as Oedipus was returning home on all his journeyings. Perhaps the ultimate reduction of Tess, the distillation of her fate, is to be seen when she runs after Angel having murdered Alec. Angel turns round. "The tape-like surface of the road diminished in his rear as far as he could see, and as he gazed a moving spot intruded on the white vacuity of its perspective." This scene has been anticipated when Tess was working at Flint-comb-Ash: "the whole field was in colour a desolate drab; it was a complexion without features, as if a face, from chin to brow, should be only an expanse of skin. The sky wore, in another colour, the same likeness; a white vacuity of countenance with the lineaments gone. So these two upper and nether visages confronted each other all day long . . . without anything standing between them but the two girls crawling over the surface of the former like flies." In both cases we see Tess as a moving spot on a white vacuity. And this extreme pictorial reduction seems to me to be right at the heart of Hardy's vision.

VI

To explain what I mean I want to interpose a few comments on some remarkable passages from the earlier novel, *Return of the Native*. Chapter One describes the vast inert heath. Chapter Two opens "Along the road walked an old man." He in turn sees a tiny speck of movement—"the single atom of life that the scene contained." And this spot is a "lurid red." It is, of course, the reddleman, but I want to emphasise the composition of the scene—the great stillness and the tiny spot of red movement which is the human presence on the heath. Shortly after, the reddleman is scanning the heath (Hardy's world is full of watching eyes) and it is then that he first sees Eustacia Vye. But how he first sees her is described in a passage which seems to me so central to Hardy that I want to quote at length.

> There the form stood, motionless as the hill beneath. Above the plain rose the hill, above the hill rose the barrow, and above the barrow rose the figure. Above the figure there was nothing that could be mapped elsewhere than on a celestial globe.
>
> Such a perfect, delicate, and necessary finish did the figure give to the dark pile of hills that it seemed to be the only obvious justification of their outline. Without it, there was the dome without the lantern; with it the architectural demands of the mass were satisfied. The scene was strangely homogeneous. The vale, the up-

land, the barrow, and the figure above it amounted to unity. Looking at this or that member of the group was not observing a complete thing, but a fraction of a thing.

The form was so much like an organic part of the entire motionless structure that to see it move would have impressed the
mind as a strange phenomenon. Immobility being the chief characteristic of that whole which the person formed portion of, the
discontinuance of immobility in any quarter suggested confusion.

Yet this is what happened. The figure perceptibly gave up its
fixity, shifted a step or two, and turned round.

Here in powerful visual terms is a complete statement about existence.
Without the human presence, sheer land and sky seem to have no
formal, architectural significance. The human form brings significant
outline to the brown mass of earth, the white vacuity of sky. But this
moment of satisfying formal harmony depends on stillness, and to
be human is to be animated, is to move. Hardy's novels are about
"the discontinuance of immobility"; all the confusions that make up
his plots are the result of people who perceptibly give up their fixity.
To say that this is the very condition of life itself is only to point to
the elemental nature of Hardy's art. All plants and all animals move,
but much more within the rhythms ordained by their native terrain
than humans—who build things like the *Titanic* and go plunging
off into the night sea, or who set out in a horse and cart in the middle
of the night to reach a distant market, in both cases meeting with
disastrous accidents. Only what moves can crash. Eustacia moves on
the still heath, breaking up the unity: there is confusion ahead for
her. Not indeed that the heath is in a state of absolute fixity; that
would imply a dead planet: "the quality of repose appertaining to
the scene . . . was not the repose of actual stagnation, but the
apparent repose of incredible slowness." Hardy often reminds us of
the mindless insect life going on near the feet of his bewildered
human protagonists; but to the human eye, which after all determines
the felt meaning of the perceptible world, there is a movement which
is like stillness just as there is a motion which seems to be unmiti-
gated violence. The "incredible slowness" of the heath, only serves
to make more graphic the "catastrophic dash" which ends the lives
of Eustacia and Wildeve. And after the "catastrophic dash"—"eternal
rigidity."

The tragic tension between human and heath, between motion and repose, between the organic drive away from the inorganic and, what turns out to be the same thing, the drive to return to the inorganic, provides Hardy with the radical structure of his finest work. The human struggle against—and temporary departure from—the level stillness of the heath, is part of that struggle between the vertical and the horizontal which is a crucial part of Hardy's vision. We read of the "oppressive horizontality" of the heath, and when Eustacia comes to the time of her death Hardy describes her position in such a way that it echoes the first time we saw her, and completes the pattern of her life. She returns to one of those ancient earthen grave mounds, called barrows. "Eustacia at length reached Rainbarrow, and stood still there to think . . . she sighed bitterly and ceased to stand erect, gradually crouching down under the umbrella as if she were drawn into the Barrow by a hand from underneath." Her period of motion is over; her erect status above the flatness of the heath terminates at the same moment: she is, as it were, drawn back into the undifferentiated levelness of the earth from which she emerged. At the same time, you will remember, Susan is tormenting and burning a wax effigy of Eustacia, so that while she seems to be sinking back into the earth Hardy can also write "the effigy of Eustacia was melting to nothing." She is losing her distinguishing outline and features. Hardy describes elsewhere how a woman starts to "lose her own margin" when working the fields. Human life is featured and contoured life; yet the erosion of feature and contour seems to be a primal activity of that "featureless convexity" of the heath, of the earth itself.

VII

This feeling of the constant attrition, and final obliteration, of the human shape and all human structures, permeates Hardy's work. Interviewed about Stonehenge he commented that "it is a matter of wonder that the erection has stood so long," adding however that "time nibbles year after year" at the structure. Just so he will write of a wind "which seemed to gnaw at the corners of the house"; of "wooden posts rubbed to a glossy smoothness by the flanks of infinite cows and calves of bygone years." His work is full of decaying architecture, and in The Woodlanders there is a memorable picture of the calves roaming in the ruins of Sherton Castle, "cooling their thirsty tongues by licking the quaint Norman carving, which glistened with the moisture." It is as though time, and all the rest of the natural order, conspired to eat away and erase all the structures and features associated with the human presence on, or intrusion into, the planet. Of one part of the heath Hardy says, in a sentence of extraordinarily succinct power, "There had been no obliteration, because there had been no tending." Tess working at Flintcomb-Ash in a landscape which is "a complexion without features," and Tess running after Angel, "a moving spot intruding on the white vacuity," is a visible paradigm of the terms of human life—a spot of featured animation moving painfully across a vast featureless repose. Like Eustacia, and like her wounded horse Prince, having remained upright as long as possible, she, too, simply "ceases to stand erect" and lies down on the flat sacrificial stone, as though offering herself not only up to the sun which tended her, but to the obliterating earth, the horizontal inertia of which she had disturbed.

Life is movement, and movement leads to confusion. Tess's instinct is for placidity, she recoils from rapid movements. Yet at crucial times she finds herself in men's carriages or men's machines. She has to drive her father's cart to market and Prince is killed. Alec forces her into his dog-cart which he drives recklessly at great speed. Of Tess we read "the least irregularity of motion startled her" and Alec at this point is disturbing and shaking up blood which will only be stilled in death. Angel, by contrast, takes Tess to the wedding in a carriage which manages to suggest something brutal, punitive, and funereal all at once—"It had stout wheelspokes, and heavy felloes, a great curved bed, immense straps and springs, and a pole like a battering-ram." All these man-made conveyances, together with the ominous train, and that "tyrant" the threshing machine, seem to threaten Tess. And yet she is bound to be involved in travelling, and dangerous motion, because she has no home. At the beginning the parson telling Tess's father about his noble lineage says an ominous thing. To Jack's question, "'Where do we d'Urbervilles live?'" he answers: "'You don't live anywhere. You are extinct—as a county family.'" Tess does not live anywhere. The one home she finds, Angel turns her out of. That is why she is bound to succumb to Alec. He provides a place but not a home. Alec takes her to Sandbourne, a place of "detached mansions," the very reverse of a community. It is a "pleasure city," "a glittering novelty," a place of meretricious fashion and amusement. "''Tis all lodging-houses here. . . .'" This is the perfect place for the modern, deracinated Alec. It is no place at all for Tess, "a cottage girl." But we have seen her uprooted, forced to the roads, ejected from houses, knocking on doors which remain closed to her; we have seen the process by which she has become an exhausted helpless prey who is finally bundled off to a boarding house. Her spell in this place is a drugged interlude; she seems finally to have come to that state of catatonic trance which has been anticipated in previous episodes.

Angel realises that "Tess had spiritually ceased to recognize the body before him as hers—allowing it to drift, like a corpse upon the current, in a direction dissociated from its living will." Tess has been so "disturbed" by irregularities of motion, so pulled in different directions, that she really is sick, split, half dead. Hardy was very interested in this sort of split person—for instance, people with primitive instincts and modern nerves, as he says in another book—and we can see that Tess is subjected to too many different pressures, not to say torments, ever to achieve a felicitous wholeness of being.

VIII

This brings me to a problem I mentioned earlier. We see Tess suffering, apparently doomed to suffer; destroyed by two men, by society, by the sun outside her and the blood inside her. And we are tempted to ask, what is Hardy's vision of the *cause* of this tale of suffering. Throughout the book Hardy stresses that Tess is damned, and damns herself, according to man-made laws which are as arbitrary as they are cruel. He goes out of his way to show how Nature seems to disdain, ignore or make mockery of the laws which social beings impose on themselves. The fetish of chastity is a ludicrous aberration in a world which teems and spills with such promiscuous and far-flung fertility every year (not to say a brutal caricature of human justice in that what was damned in the woman was condoned in the man). So, if the book was an attempt to show an innocent girl who is destroyed by society though justified by Nature, Hardy could certainly have left the opposition as direct and as simple as that. Social laws hang Tess; and Nature admits no such laws. But it is an important part of the book that we feel Nature itself turning against Tess, so that we register something approaching a sadism of *both* the man-made *and* the natural directed against her. If she is tortured by the man-made threshing machine, she is also crushed by the forge of the sun; the cold negating metal in Angel is also to be found in the "steely stars"; the pangs of guilt which lacerate her are matched by the "glass splinters" of rain which penetrate her at Flintcomb-Ash. Perhaps to understand this feeling of almost universal opposition which grows throughout the book, we should turn to some of Hardy's own words, when he talks of "the universal harshness . . . the harshness of the position towards the temperament, of the means towards the aims, of today towards yesterday, or hereafter towards today." When he mediates on the imminent disappearance of the d'Urberville family he says, "so does Time ruthlessly destroy his own romances." This suggests a universe of radical opposition, working to destroy what it works to create, crushing to death what it coaxes into life. From this point of view society only appears as a functioning part of a larger process whereby the vertical returns to the horizontal, motion lapses into stillness and structures cedes to the unstructured. The policemen appear as the sun rises: Tess is a sacrifice to both, to all of them. Hardy's vision is tragic and penetrates far deeper than specific social anomalies. One is more inclined to think of Sophocles than, say, Zola, when reading Hardy. The vision is tragic because he shows an ordering of existence in which nature turns against itself, in which the sun blasts what it blesses, in which all the hopeful explorations of life turn out to have been a circuitous peregrination towards death. "All things are born to be diminished" said Pericles at the time of Sophocles; and Hardy's comparable feeling that all things are tended to be obliterated, reveals a Sophoclean grasp of the bed-rock ironies of existence.

Tess is the living demonstration of these tragic ironies. That is why she who is raped lives to be hanged; why she who is so physically beautiful feels guilt at "inhabiting the fleshly tabernacle with which Nature had endowed her"; why she who is a fertile source of life comes to feel that "birth itself was an ordeal of degrading personal compulsion, whose gratuitousness nothing in the result seemed to justify." It is why she attracts the incompatible forces represented by Alec and Angel. It is why she who is a lover is also a killer. Tess is gradually crucified on the oppugnant ironies of circumstance and existence itself, ironies which centre, I have suggested, on the fact of blood, that basic stuff which starts the human spot moving across the white vacuity. Blood, and the spilling of blood; which in one set of circumstances can mean sexual passion and the creation of life, and in another can mean murderous passion and death— two forms of "red" energy intimately related—this is the substance of Tess's story.

And why should it all happen to her? You can say, as some people in the book say fatalistically, "'It was to be.'" Or you could go through the book and try to work out how Hardy apportions the blame—a bit on Tess, a bit on society, a bit on religion, a bit on heredity, a bit on the Industrial Revolution, a bit on the men who abuse her, a bit on the sun and the stars, and so on. But Hardy does not work in this way. More than make us judge, Hardy makes us see; and in looking for some explanation of why all this should happen to Tess, our eyes finally settle on that red ribbon marking out the little girl in the white dress, which already foreshadows the red blood stain on the white ceiling. In her beginning is her end. It is the oldest of truths, but it takes a great writer to make us experience it again in all its awesome mystery.

IX

Hardy specifically rejected the idea of offering any theory of the universe. In his General Preface to his works, he said "Nor is it likely, indeed, that imaginative writings extending over more than forty years would exhibit a coherent scientific theory of the universe even if it had been attempted—of the universe concerning which Spencer owns to the 'paralyzing thought' that possibly there exists no comprehension of it anywhere. But such objectless consistency never has been attempted. . . ." Hardy "theorizes" far less than Lawrence, but certain images recur which serve to convey his sense of life—its poignancy and its incomprehensibility—more memorably than any overt statement. Death, the sudden end of brilliance and movement, occupied a constant place in his thoughts. "The most prosaic man becomes a poem when you stand by his grave and think of him" he once wrote; and the strange brightness of ephemeral creatures is something one often meets in his fiction—pictorially, not philosophically. "Gnats, knowing nothing of their brief glorification, wandered across the shimmer of this pathway, irradiated as if they bore fire within them, then passed out of its line, and were quite extinct." Compare with that the description of the girls returning from the dance: "and as they went there moved onward with them . . . a circle of opalized light, formed by the moon's rays upon the glistening sheet of dew. Each pedestrian could see no halo but his or her own. . . ." Hardy is often to be found stressing the ephemeral nature of life—"independent worlds of ephemerons were passing their time in mad carousal," "ephemeral creatures, took up their positions where only a year ago others had stood in their place when these were nothing more than germs and inorganic particles"—and it often seems that the ephemeral fragments of moving life are also like bubbles of light, temporary illuminations of an encroaching darkness. One of the great scenes in all of Hardy is in *The Return of the Native* when Wildeve and Venn, the reddleman, gamble at night on the heath. Their lantern makes a little circle of light which draws things out of the darkness towards it. "The light of the candle had by this time attracted heath-flies, moths and other winged creatures of night, which floated round the lantern, flew into the flame, or beat about the faces of the two players." Much more suggestively as they continue to throw dice; "they were surrounded by dusky forms about four feet high, standing a few paces beyond the rays of the lantern. A moment's inspection revealed that the encircling figures were heath-croppers, their heads being all towards the players, at whom they gazed intently." When a moth extinguishes the candle, Wildeve gathers glow worms and puts them on the stone on which they are playing. "The incongruity between the men's deeds and their environment was great. Amid the soft juicy vegetation of the hollow in which they sat, the motionless and the uninhabited solitude, intruded the chink of guineas, the rattle of dice, the exclamations of the reckless players." Again, it is one of those scenes which seems to condense a whole vision of human existence—a strange activity in a small circle of light, and all round them the horses of the night noiselessly gathering at the very perimeter. And in *Tess of the d'Urbervilles* Hardy develops this scene into a metaphor of great power. He is describing how Tess's love for Angel sustains her: "it enveloped her as a photosphere, irradiated her into forgetfulness of her past sorrows, keeping back the gloomy spectres that would persist in their attempts to touch her—doubt, fear, moodiness, care, shame. She knew that they were waiting like wolves just outside the circumscribing light, but she had long spells of power to keep them in hungry subjection there. . . . She walked in brightness, but she knew that in the background those shapes of darkness were always spread."

I have singled out this image not only because I think there is something quintessentially Hardyan in it, but also because I think it is an image which profoundly influenced D. H. Lawrence. Here is a final quotation, taken from the culmination of perhaps his greatest novel, *The Rainbow.* Ursula is trying to clarify her sense of her own presence in the world.

> This world in which she lived was like a circle lighted by a lamp. This lighted area, lit up by man's completest consciousness, she thought was all the world: that here all was disclosed for ever. Yet all the time, within the darkness she had been aware of points of light, like the eyes of wild beasts, gleaming, penetrating, vanishing. And her soul had acknowledged in a great heave of terror only the outer darkness. This inner circle of light in which she lived and moved, wherein the trains rushed and the factories ground out their machine-produce and the plants and the animals worked by the light of science and knowledge, suddenly it seemed like the area under an arc lamp, wherein the moths and children played in the security of blinding light, not even knowing there was any darkness, because they stayed in the light.
>
> But she could see the glimmer of dark movement just out of range, she saw the eyes of the wild beast gleaming from the darkness, watching the vanity of the camp fire and the sleepers; she felt the strange, foolish vanity of the camp, which said "Beyond our light and our order there is nothing," turning their faces always inwards toward the sinking fire of illuminating consciousness, which comprised sun and stars, and the Creator, and the System of Righteousness, ignoring always the vast shapes that wheeled round about, with half-revealed shapes lurking on the edge. . . . Nevertheless the darkness wheeled round about, with grey shadow-shapes of wild beasts, and also with dark shadow-shapes of the angels, whom the light fenced out, as it fenced out the more familiar beasts of darkness.

Lawrence, more insistent as to the torments and sterilities of consciousness, confidently ascribes positive values to the shapes prowling around the perimeter of the circle of light. But Lawrence's *interpretation*—itself an act of consciousness—of the population of the dark, is only something overlayed on the *situation,* that irreducible configuration which is to be found, I suggest, at the heart of Hardy's work. "She walked in brightness, but she knew that in the background those shapes of darkness were always spread."

IRVING HOWE

On *Jude the Obscure*

. . . In Hardy's diary for 1888 there appears a note for "a short
story of a young man who could not afford to go to Oxford." It
would deal with "his struggles and ultimate failure. Suicide. There
is something this world ought to be shown, and I am the one to
show it. . . ." Six years later the projected story had grown into a
novel, Hardy's last and most bitter, *Jude the Obscure*. By 1895, the
year *Jude* came out, Hardy was in his mid-fifties, an established
writer who had composed two great novels and several of distinction.
But he was more than a famous or honored writer. For the English-
speaking world he had become a moral presence genuinely affecting
the lives of those who read him.

When Hardy first printed *Jude the Obscure* as a monthly serial in
Harper's Magazine between December 1894 and November 1895, he
agreed to cut some of its most vital parts: those which showed Jude
to be harried by sexual desire, others reporting that Jude and Sue
Bridehead did finally go to bed together, and still others displaying

From *Thomas Hardy* (New York: The Macmillan Company, 1967), pp.
132-46. Copyright © 1966 Irving Howe; 1967 The Macmillan Company and
George Weidenfeld and Nicolson, Ltd. Reprinted by permission of the
author and publishers. This selection is the second part of chapter six, "Let
the Day Perish," which also deals with *Tess of the D'Urbervilles*, and which
has the memorable beginning "As a writer of novels Thomas Hardy was endowed with a precious gift: he liked women."

Hardy's gift for a muted but humorous earthiness. In the serial Jude and Sue did not have a child; more demurely, they adopted one. Arabella, when she got Jude back and flooded him with liquor, ended the evening by tucking him into bed in a spare room. Today such mutilations by a serious writer would provoke an uproar of judgment; but Hardy, not being the kind of man who cared to languish in a garret, did what he had to do in order to sell the serial rights. In any case, he knew that his true novel, the one later generations would read and judge him by, was soon to appear in hard covers.

Some months later, when the book came out, it stirred up a storm of righteousness. Many of the reviewers adopted a high moral tone, denouncing Hardy's apparent hostility to the institution of marriage while choosing to neglect the sympathy he showed toward people caught up in troublesome relationships, whether in or out of marriage. One true-blooded Englishman, the Bishop of Wakefield, publicly announced that he "was so disgusted with [the book's] insolence and indecency that I threw it into the fire." To which Hardy added that probably the bishop had chosen to burn the book because he could not burn the author.

Later, writing to his friend Edmund Gosse, Hardy denied that the novel was "a manifesto on the marriage question, although, of course, it involves it." This is precisely the kind of distinction that most of the contemporary reviewers neither could nor wished to understand: they were, like most reviewers of any age, blunt-minded journalists who demanded from a work of art that it confirm the settled opinions they already had. What Hardy was getting at in his letter to Gosse is an idea now commonly accepted by serious writers: that while a work of fiction may frequently raise social and moral problems, the artist's main intention is to explore them freely rather than take hard-and-fast public positions. In his 1895 preface to *Jude the Obscure* Hardy made quite clear his larger purpose in composing the book:

> . . . to deal unaffectedly with the fret and fever, derision and disaster, that may press in the wake of the strongest passion known to humanity; to tell, without a mincing of words, of a deadly war waged between flesh and spirit; and to point the tragedy of un-fulfilled aims.

Nor were these new concerns for Hardy. In his earlier novels he had already shown what a torment an ill-suited marriage can be; he had known himself, through much of his first marriage, the dumb misery that follows upon decayed affections. By the 1890s, when England was beginning to shake loose from the grip of Victorian moralism, the cultivated minority public was ready for his gaunt honesty, even if the bulk of novel readers was not. That marriage had become a *problem,* that somehow it was in crisis and need of reform, was an idea very much in the air. During the 1890s the notorious Parnell case, involving an adultery suit against the leader of Irish nationalism, split the English-speaking world into hostile camps but also forced a relatively candid discussion of the realities of conjugal life. The plays of Ibsen were being performed in English translation during the years *Jude* was written, and their caustic inquiry into the evasions and repressions of middle-class marriage may have found an echo in Hardy's book. And through the late 1880s Hardy had been reading the work of Schopenhauer and von Hartmann, pessimistic German philosophers who had recently been translated into English; he did not need their help, or anyone else's, in order to reach his "twilight view" of man's diminished place in the universe, but he did find in their philosophic speculations a support—he might have said a confirmation —for his own temperamental bias.

Hardy's last novel was not quite the outcry of a lonely and embittered iconoclast that it has sometimes been said to be. *Jude* displeased official opinion, both literary and moral; it outraged the pieties of middle-class England to an extent few of Hardy's contemporaries were inclined to risk; but it also reflected the sentiments of advanced intellectual circles in the 1890s. Thus while it is true that *Jude* was not meant to be "a manifesto on the marriage question," the book could hardly have been written fifteen or twenty years earlier. Coming at the moment it did, *Jude* played a part in the modern transformation of marriage from a sacred rite to a secular and thereby problematic relationship—just as those nineteenth century writers who tried to salvage Christianity by scraping it of dogma and superstition unwittingly helped to undermine the whole structure of theism.

Jude the Obscure is Hardy's most distinctly "modern" work, for it rests upon a cluster of assumptions central to modernist literature: that in our time men wishing to be more than dumb clods must live in permanent doubt and intellectual crisis; that for such men, to whom traditional beliefs are no longer available, life has become inherently problematic; that in the course of their years they must face even more than the usual allotment of loneliness and anguish; that in their cerebral overdevelopment they run the danger of losing those primary appetites for life which keep the human race going; and that courage, if it is to be found at all, consists in a readiness to accept pain while refusing the comforts of certainty. If Hardy, excessively thin-skinned as he was, suffered from the attacks *Jude* brought down upon his head, he should have realized—as in his moments of shrewdness he did—that attack was precisely what he had to expect. For he had threatened his readers not merely in their opinions but in their deepest unspoken values: the first was forgivable, the second not.

In its deepest impress *Jude the Obscure* is not the kind of novel that compels one to reflect upon the idea of history, certainly not in the ways that Tolstoy's *War and Peace* or Stendhal's *The Red and the Black* do. Nor is it the kind of novel that draws our strongest attention to the causes, patterns and turnings of large historical trends as these condition the lives of a few centered characters. The sense *Jude* leaves one with, the quality of the pain it inflicts, has mostly to do with the sheer difficulty of human beings living elbow to elbow and heart to heart; the difficulty of being unable to bear prolonged isolation or prolonged closeness; the difficulty, at least for reflective men, of getting through the unspoken miseries of daily life. Yet to grasp the full stringencies of Jude's private ordeal, one must possess a strong historical awareness.

The English working class, coming to birth through the trauma of the Industrial Revolution, suffered not merely from brutality, hunger and deprivation, but from an oppressive snobbism, at times merely patronizing and at other times proudly violent, on the part of the "superior" social classes. By the middle of the nineteenth century a minority of intellectuals and reformers had begun to display an active sympathy for the workers: they could not live in peace while millions of country men lived in degradation. But meanwhile, and going as far back as the late eighteenth century, something far more important had begun to happen among the English workers themselves—the first stirrings of intellectual consciousness, the first signs of social and moral solidarity. Workingmen began to appear who sought to train their minds, to satisfy their parched imaginations, to grasp for themselves a fargment of that traditional culture from which Western society had coldly locked them out.

The rise of the self-educated proletarian is one of the most remarkable facts in nineteenth century English history. Frequently this new man discovered himself through the trade union and socialist movements, which brought to him a sense of historical mission, an assignment of destiny and role; but he could also be found else-where. Struggling after long hours of labor to master the rudiments of learning, he flourished in the dissident chapels which had shot up in England beyond the privileged ground of the Anglican Church; in the lecture courses and night schools that were started by intellec-tual missionaries; in little reading "circles" that were formed amidst the degradation of the slums. For some of these men education meant primarily a promise of escape from their cramped social position; for others, no doubt a minority, it could approximate what it meant to Jude Fawley—a joy, pure and disinterested, in the life of the mind.[1]

English fiction was slow to absorb this remarkable new figure, just as it was slow to deal with the life of the working class as a whole. There are glimpses of the self-educated worker in the novels of George Gissing; he appears a bit more fully in the "Five Towns" fic-tion of Arnold Bennett, and still more impressively in D. H. Law-rence's early novels; and in recent years, as he begins to fade from the social scene, he is looked back upon with nostalgia in novels about the early English Labor movement written by Raymond Wil-liams and Walter Allen.

Now Jude Fawley is not himself a character within this tradition. But he is close to it, a sort of rural cousin of the self-educated worker; and I think it can be said that unless the latter had begun to seem a significant type in late nineteenth century England, Hardy could not have imagined as strongly as he did the intellectual yearnings of Jude. That in his last novel Hardy should have turned to a figure like Jude is itself evidence of a major shift in outlook. The fixity of Hardy's rural attachments was, in the previous Wessex novels, so deep as to provide him with something equivalent to a moral abso-lute, a constant of moral security through which to set off—yet keep at a manageable distance—those of his characters troubled by unrest. But Hardy, by the point he had reached in *Jude the Obscure,* could no longer find in the world of Wessex a sufficient moral and emo-tional support. His feelings had come to a pained recognition that Wessex and all it stood for was slipping out of his fingers, changing shape beyond what he remembered from his youth, receding into his-tory. And as for Jude, though he comes from the country, he spends most of his life in the towns. The matters upon which Jude's heart and mind must feed, the matter which rouses him to excitement and then leaves him broken, is the intellectual disturbance of modern life—and that, for good or bad, can be found only in the towns. Not born a worker, and without the political interests which usually spurred the self-educated proletarian to read and study, Jude nevertheless shares in the latter's passion for self-improvement, as well as in the pathos of knowing that never can he really know enough. Jude is Hardy's equivalent of the self-educated worker: the self-educated worker transplanted into the Wessex world. So that when Hardy first conceived of Jude in that notable clause, "a young man who could not go to Oxford," he was foreshadowing not merely one man's deprivation but the turmoil of an entire social group.

Socially, Jude hovers somewhere between an old-fashioned artisan and a modern worker. The kind of work he does, restoring old churches, pertains to the traditional English past, but the way he does it, hiring himself out for wages, points to the future. His desire for learning, both as a boy trying to come by a Greek grammar and then as a man walking awestruck through the chill streets of Christminster (Oxford), is portrayed by Hardy with enormous sympathy. But to stress this sympathy is not at all to share the view of some critics that Hardy is so deeply involved with Jude's yearnings, he cannot bring to bear upon them any critical irony. What but somberly ironic is the incident in which Jude receives a crushing reply from the Christminster master to whom he has applied for advice, and what but devastatingly ironic is the scene in which Jude drunkenly flaunts his Latin before the good-natured uncomprehending artisans at the Christminster tavern? Jude is a thoroughly individualized figure, an achievement made possible by Hardy's balance of sympathy and distance; but Jude's personal drama is woven from the materials of historical change, the transformation and uprooting of traditional English life.

The same holds true for Sue Bridehead. She is a triumph of psychological portraiture—and to that we shall return. But the contours of her psychology are themselves shaped by a new historical situation. She could not possibly appear in a novel by Jane Austen or Dickens or Thackeray; her style of thought, her winsome charms and maddening indecisions, are all conditioned by the growth of intellectual skepticism and modernist sensibility. She is the first major anticipation in the English novel of that profoundly affecting and troublesome creature: the modern girl. If she could not appear in an earlier nineteenth century novel, she certainly could in a twentieth century one—the only difference would probably be that now, living in her

neat brownstone apartment in Manhattan or stylish flat in London
and working for a publishing house or television company, she would
have learned to accept a "healthier" attitude toward sex. Or at the
least, she would have learned to pretend it.

In the last third of the nineteenth century, the situation of women
changed radically: from subordinate domesticity and Victorian repression to the first signs of emancipation, leading often enough to
the poignant bewilderments of a Sue Bridehead. So that while Sue,
like Jude, is an intensely individualized figure, she is also characteristic of a moment in recent history; indeed, the force with which
Hardy has made her so uniquely alive depends a great deal on the
accuracy with which he has placed her historically.

Between Jude and Sue there is a special closeness, and this too has
been historically conditioned. It is the closeness of lovers, but more
than that. It is the closeness of intellectual companions, but more
again. In Jane Austen's *Pride and Prejudice* Elizabeth Bennet and
Mr. Darcy make their way past comic misunderstandings to a happy
marriage, for they share a sense of superior cultivation and, with the
additional advantage of status, can expect to keep themselves in a
semi-protected circle, a little apart from the dull but worthy people
surrounding them. At home in their society, they can yet maintain a
comfortable distance from it. In Emily Brontë's *Wuthering Heights*
Heathcliff and Cathy, in their moments of ecstasy, cut themselves off
from common life, neither accepting nor rebelling against society,
but refusing the very idea of it. In George Eliot's *Middlemarch* Dorothea Brooke and Lydgate, the two figures who should come together
but through force of circumstances and vanity do not, envision a
union in which they would struggle in behalf of those serious values
their society disdains. They know the struggle would be difficult, but
do not regard it as impossible. But by *Jude the Obscure* there is neither enclave nor retreat, evasion nor grasped opportunity for resistance. Jude and Sue are lost souls; they have no place in the world
they can cherish or to which they can retreat; their goals are hardly
to be comprehended in worldly terms at all. Lonely, distraught, rootless, they cling to one another like children in the night. Exposed to
the racking sensations of homelessness, they become prey to a kind
of panic whenever they are long separated from each other. The
closeness of the lost—clutching, solacing and destroying one another
—is a closeness of a special kind, which makes not for heroism or
tragedy or even an exalted suffering, but for that somewhat passive
"modern" sadness which suffuses *Jude the Obscure*.

Now it would be foolish to suppose that the social history of nineteenth century England can be neatly registered in this sketch of changing assumptions from Jane Austen to Thomas Hardy—though by 1900 there was, I think, good reason for cultivated persons to feel more estranged from their society than their great-grandparents might have felt in 1800. What can plausibly be assumed is that there were serious historical pressures behind the increasingly critical attitudes that nineteenth century English novelists took toward their society. Hardy comes at the end of one tradition, that of the solid extroverted English novel originating mostly with Henry Fielding; but he also comes at the beginning of another tradition, that of the literary "modernism" which would dominate the twentieth century. In personal background, novelistic technique, choice of locale and characters, Hardy remains mostly of the past; but in his distinctive sensibility, he is partly of the future. He moves somewhat beyond, though he does not quite abandon, the realistic social novel such as George Eliot and Thackeray wrote, and by *Jude the Obscure* he is composing the kind of fiction about which one is tempted to employ such terms as expressionist, stylized, grotesque, symbolic distortion and a portrait of extreme situations. None of these is wholly to the point, yet all suggest that this last of Hardy's novels cannot be fully apprehended if read as a conventional realistic work. Not by its fullness or probability as a rendering of common life, but by its power and coherence as a vision of modern deracination—so must the book be judged. It is not a balanced or temperate work; it will not satisfy well-adjusted minds content with the blessings of the wholesome; it does not pretend to show the human situation in its many-sidedness. Committed to an extreme darkness of view, a promethean resistance to fatality, *Jude the Obscure* shares in the spirit of the Book of Job, whose author seems also to have been a pessimist. In the history of Hardy criticism *Jude the Obscure* provides a touchstone of taste: the older and more traditional critics, loving Hardy for the charm and comeliness of his Wessex portraiture, have usually disparaged the book as morbid, while the more recent and modern critics are inclined to regard its very starkness as a sign of truth.

To present *Jude the Obscure* as a distinctively modern novel is surely an exaggeration; but it is an exaggeration I think valuable to propose, since it helps to isolate those elements which make the book seem so close to us in spirit. There is, in regard to *Jude the Obscure*, an experience shared by many of its readers: we soon notice its fragility of structure, we are likely to be troubled by its persistent de-

pressiveness and its tendency to prompt a fate already more than
cruel, yet at the end we are forced to acknowledge that the book has
moved and shaken us. This seeming paradox is almost impossible to
explain if *Jude* is regarded as a conventional realistic novel; it becomes easier to account for if the book is read as a dramatic fable in
which the traditional esthetic criteria of unity and verisimilitude are
subordinated to those of a distended expressiveness.

In Hardy's earlier novels, as in most of nineteenth century English
fiction, characters tend to be presented as fixed and synthesized entities, as knowable public events. They function in a social medium;
they form the sum or resultant of a set of distinguishable traits; they
act out, in their depicted conduct, the consequences and implications
of these traits; and their very "meaning" as characters in a novel derives from the action to which they are entirely bound. In a book like
The Mayor of Casterbridge the central figure, Michael Henchard,
becomes known to us through his action: what he does is what he is.
It would be impudent to suppose that in writing *The Mayor* Hardy
did not realize that human beings have a complex inner life, or that
there are discrepancies between one's inner and outer, private and public, experience. Of course he knew this, and so did such novelists as
Fielding, Jane Austen and Thackeray. But in their work, as a rule,
the inner life of the characters is to be inferred from their public behavior, or from the author's analytic synopses.

By *Jude the Obscure* Hardy is beginning to move away from this
mode of characterization. He is still quite far from that intense hover-
ing scrutiny to which James subjects his figures, nor does he venture
upon that dissolution of public character into a stream of psychic no-
tation and event which can be found in Virginia Woolf and James
Joyce. Yet we are made aware, while reading *Jude the Obscure,* that
human character is being regarded as severely problematic, open to
far-reaching speculative inquiry, and perhaps beyond certain knowledge; that the character of someone like Sue Bridehead must be seen
not as a coherent force realizing itself in self-consistent public action,
but as an amorphous and ill-charted arena in which irrational impulses conflict with one another; and that behind the interplay of
events occupying the foreground of the novel there is a series of distorted psychic shadows which, with some wrenching, can be taken to
provide the true "action" of the book.

Thinking, for example, of Jude Fawley, we are inclined to see him
as a man whose very being constitutes a kind of battlefield and who

matters, consequently, more for what happens within him than for what happens to him. He is racked by drives he cannot control, drives he barely understands. Powerfully sexed, drawn immediately to Arabella's hearty if somewhat soiled physical life, Jude is in constant revolt against his own nature. (That revolt comprises a major portion of the novel's inner action "behind" its visible action.) Jude responds far more spontaneously to Arabella than to Sue, for Arabella is unmistakably female and every now and then he needs a bit of wallowing in sex and drink to relieve him from the strain of his ambition and spirituality. At the same time Jude is forever caught up with Sue, who represents an equivalent or extension of his unsettled consciousness, quick and brittle as he is slow and cluttered, and therefore all the more attractive to him, as a vivid bird might be to a bear. The two of them are linked in seriousness, in desolation, in tormenting kindness, but above all, in an overbred nervousness. Theirs is a companionship of the nerves.

At least in part, Jude seems an anticipation of modern rationality struggling to become proudly self-sufficient and thereby cutting itself off from its sources in physical life. Though he is born in the country and lives mostly in towns, Jude could soon enough adapt himself to the twentieth century city: his mental life, in its creasing divisions and dissociations, is that of the modern metropolis. Destined to the role of stranger, he stops here and rests there, but without community, place or home. His frustration derives not so much from a denial of his desires as from their crossing and confusion; and as he struggles to keep in harmony his rumbling sensuality, his diffused ambition and his high ethical intent, one is reminded a little of St. Augustine's plaint to God: "Thou has counselled a better course than thou hast permitted."

Even more than Jude, Sue Bridehead invites psychological scrutiny; indeed, she is one of the great triumphs of psychological portraiture in the English novel. Sue is that terrifying specter of our age, before whom men and cultures tremble: she is an *interesting* girl. She is promethean in mind but masochist in character; and the division destroys her, making a shambles of her mind and a mere sterile discipline of her character. She is all intellectual seriousness, but without that security of will which enables one to live out the consequences of an idea to their limit. She is all feminine charm, but without body, without flesh or smell, without femaleness. Lacking focused sexuality, she casts a vaguely sexual aura over everything she touches. Her sensibility is kindled but her senses are mute. Quite without pride in status or self, she is consumed by vanity, the vanity of the sufferer who takes his suffering as a mark of distinction and bears a cross heavier than even fate might demand. Sue cannot leave anything alone, neither her men nor herself: she needs always to be tampering and testing, communicating and quivering. D. H. Lawrence, quick to see in Sue Bridehead the antithesis of his idea of the woman, writes of her with a fascinated loathing:

> She is the production of the long selection by man of the woman in whom the female is subordinate to the male principle. . . .
>
> Her female spirit did not wed with the male spirit. . . . Her spirit submitted to the male spirit, owned the priority of the male spirit, wished to become the male spirit. . . .
>
> One of the supremest products of our civilization is Sue, and a product that well frightens us. . . .
>
> She must, by the constitution of her nature, remain quite physically intact, for the female was atrophied in her, to the enlargement of the male activity. Yet she wanted some quickening for this atrophied female. She wanted even kisses. That the new rousing might give her a sense of life. But she could only *live* in the mind . . .
>
> Here, then, was her difficulty: to find a man whose vitality could infuse her and make her live, and who would not, at the same time, demand of her a return of the female impulse into him. What man could receive this drainage, receiving nothing back again? He must either die or revolt.

Yet one thing more, surely the most important, must be said about Sue Bridehead. As she appears in the novel itself, rather than in the grinder of analysis, she is an utterly charming and vibrant creature. We grasp directly, and not merely because we are told, why Jude finds himself unable to resist Sue. Hardy draws her with a marvelous plasticity, an affectionate yet critical attentiveness. She is happily charming when she first encounters Jude at the martyr's cross: "'I am not going to meet you just there, for the first time in my life! Come farther on.'" She is pathetically charming when she escapes the training school and, dripping wet, comes to Jude's chambers. And there is even charm of a morbid kind when she rehearses in church with Jude the wedding she is soon to seal with Phillotson. " 'I like to do things like this,' " she tells him, " 'in the delicate voice of an epicure in emotions' "—and in that remark lies a universe of unrest and perversity.

What has been said here about the distinctively "modern" element in *Jude the Obscure* holds not merely for its characterization but also for its narrative structure. The novel does not depend primarily on a traditional plot, by means of which there is revealed and acted out a major destiny, such as Henchard's in *The Mayor of Casterbridge*. A plot consists of an action purposefully carved out of time, that is, provided with a beginning, sequence of development and climax, so that it will create the the impression of completeness. Often this impression comes from the sense that the action of a novel, as given shape by the plot, has exhausted its possibilities of significant extension; the problems and premises with which it began have reached an appropriate terminus. Thus we can say that in the traditional kind of novel it is usually the plot which carries or releases a body of meanings: these can be profound or trivial, comic or tragic. *The Mayor of Casterbridge* contains a plot which fulfills the potential for self-destruction in the character of Henchard—but it is important to notice that in *this* kind of novel we would have no knowledge of that potential except insofar as we can observe its effects through an action. Plot here comes to seem inseparable from meaning, and meaning to inhere in plot.

When a writer works out a plot, he tacitly assumes that there is a rational structure in human conduct, that this structure can be ascertained, and that doing so he is enabled to provide his work with a sequence of order. But in "modernist" literature these assumptions come into question. In a work written on the premise that there is no secure meaning in the portrayed action, or that while the action can hold our attention and rouse our feelings, we cannot be certain, indeed must remain uncertain, as to the possibilities of meaning—in such a characteristically modern work what matters is not so much the plot but a series of *situations,* some of which can be portrayed statically, through tableaux, set-pieces, depth psychology, and others dynamically, through linked episodes, stream of consciousness, etc. Kafka's fiction, Joyce's novels, some of Faulkner's, like *The Sound and the Fury*—these all contain situations rather than plots. *Jude the Obscure* does not go nearly so far along the path of modernism as these works, but it goes as far as Hardy could. It is consequently a novel in which plot does not signify nearly so much as in his more traditional novels.

With a little trouble one could block out the main lines of a plot in *Jude the Obscure:* the protagonist, spurred by the dominant needs of his character, becomes involved in a series of complications, and these, in turn, lead to a climax of defeat and death. Yet the curve of action thus described would not, I think, bring one to what is most valuable and affecting in the novel—as a similar kind of description would in regard to *The Mayor of Casterbridge*. What is essential in *Jude,* surviving and deepening in memory, is a series of moments rather than a sequence of actions. These moments—one might also call them panels of representation—tend to resemble snapshots rather than moving pictures, concentrated vignettes rather than worked-up dramatic scenes. They center upon Jude and Sue at critical points of their experience, at the times they are together, precious and intolerable as these are, and the times they are apart, necessary and hateful as these are. Together, Jude and Sue anticipate that claustrophobic and self-destructive concentration on "personal relationships" which is to be so pervasive a theme in the twentieth century novel. They suffer, as well, from another "modern" difficulty: that of thoughtful and self-reflective persons who have become so absorbed with knowing their experience, they become unable to live it. Their predicament is "tragic" in that deeply serious and modern sense of the word which teaches us that human waste, the waste of spirit and potential, is a terrible thing. Yet a tragedy in any classical sense *Jude* is not, for it directs our attention not to the fateful action of a looming protagonist but to the inner torments of familiar contemporaries. In classical tragedy, the hero realizes himself through an action. In the modern novel, the central action occurs within the psyche of the hero. And *Jude,* in the last analysis, is a novel dominated by psychology.

It is not the kind of book that can offer the lure of catharsis or the relief of conciliation. It does not pretend to satisfy the classical standard of a composure won through or after suffering: for the quality it communicates most strongly is that of naked pain. Awkward, subjective, overwrought and embittered, *Jude the Obscure* contains moments of intense revelation, at almost any point where the two central figures come together, and moments of glaring falsity, as in the botched incident of Father Time's death. (Botched not in conception but in execution: it was a genuine insight to present the little boy as one of those who were losing the will to live, but a failure in tact to burden him with so much philosophical weight.) Such mixtures of psychological veracity and crude melodrama are characteristic of Hardy, a novelist almost always better in parts than the whole. Yet the final impact of the book is shattering. Here, in its first stirrings, is the gray poetry of modern loneliness, which Jude brings to apotheosis in the terrible words, *"Let the day perish wherein I was born, and the night in which it was said, There is a man child conceived."*

NOTES

1. In 1912 Hardy remarked, with forgivable pride, that "some readers thought . . . that when Ruskin College was . . . founded it should have been called the College of Jude the Obscure." Ruskin College at Oxford was the first English college designed to enable needy but gifted working-class boys to attend a university.

MORTON DAUWEN ZABEL

Samuel Butler:
The Victorian Insolvency

I

The Way of All Flesh is one of the milestones in the history of the English novel. The fact was recognized almost as soon as the book was published in 1903, but it is a fact that could have astonished no one more than its author. He was not a professional novelist. He wrote only one novel and never published it during his lifetime. To find it claiming a rank with the other books that set the dates and mark the progress of English fiction—*Robinson Crusoe, Pamela, Tom Jones, Tristram Shandy, Pride and Prejudice, Waverley, Pickwick, Vanity Fair, Adam Bede, Richard Feverel,* and their peers—could hardly have entered the calculations of his ironic mind. Yet this book, first issued two years after the death of Victoria, a year after Samuel Butler's own death, and about twenty after its completion, is not only the work by which Butler chiefly survives in literature but a book that marks as distinctly as any the point of division between the Victorian age and the Twentieth Century.

In its last pages its hero, Ernest Pontifex, having survived his or-

From *Craft and Character in Modern Fiction* (New York: Viking Press, 1957), pp. 97-113. Copyright © 1950 by Random House, Inc. Reprinted by permission of the publishers. The essay is a revised form of an Introduction to *The Way of All Flesh* (New York: The Modern Library, 1950).

deal to become a man of means and an author, says, in words that Butler certainly meant to apply to himself: "What can it matter to *me* whether people read my books or not? It may matter to *them*—but I have too much money to want more, and if the books have any stuff in them it will work by-and-by. I do not know nor greatly care whether they are good or not. What opinion can any sane man form about his own work?" And a moment later Ernest's publisher says that "Mr. Pontifex is a *homo unius libri*"—a man of one book. Butler appears to have believed that he himself might be remembered as a man of one book, but he thought the book would be *Erewhon,* his satirical fantasy of 1872, the only one of the seventeen volumes he published in his lifetime that had found any degree of popularity or touched the imagination of his contemporaries. Today *Erewhon* is still remembered as one of the most effective pieces of social criticism and prophecy the Nineteenth Century produced. And Butler is known and indexed in his age for a number of other reasons—for his notebooks and his advocacy of note-keeping as an indispensable habit of authorship; for his battle with Darwin and the theory of Natural Selection; for several eccentric theories of his own, such as his notion that the *Odyssey* was written by a woman in Sicily or his unorthodox interpretation of Shakespeare's sonnets; for his championship of then-neglected geniuses like Handel, Giovanni Bellini, Tabachetti, and Gaudenzio Ferrari, all of whom he used to challenge the father-images of their mightier contemporaries; for his promulgation of the ideas of "creative evolution," "life force," and "unconscious memory" that forecast the future thought of Shaw, Bergson, Freud, and Jung. But all these features of Butler's after-fame are known chiefly to specialists, to students of Victorian scientific controversy, to connoisseurs of English eccentricity, or to social and literary historians. It is as the author of *The Way of All Flesh* that he claims his place in the pantheon of English literature and among the forces that have shaped the modern novel and the Twentieth Century mind.

Its impact on the art and morality of our time has passed into common acceptance. One recent critic has epitomized its reputation by calling it "one of the time-bombs of literature":

> One thinks of it [says V. S. Pritchett] lying in Butler's desk at Clifford's Inn for thirty years, waiting to blow up the Victorian family and with it the whole great pillared and balustraded edifice of the Victorian novel. The book Thackeray failed to write in *Pen-*

dennis had at last been written. After Butler we look back upon
a scene of devastation. A spiritual slum has been cleared. . . .
Yes, says Samuel Butler, this was Heartbreak House.

Butler, he goes on to say, "opposed a system and its myth not with
another system but with the claims of the human personality.
Against Victorianism he placed himself; himself with both feet on
the ground, telescope to blind eye and in perverse self-possession,
against people whose dreary will to power—and whose hold on spiritual and material property as well—had dried the sap of sense and
life."[1]

No moment could have been more timely than 1903 for the appearance of such an attack. Butler's strategy of delay was justified.
His hour of deferred posthumous celebrity had, however, been long
prepared, anticipated as if by express plan and design. He had taken
his clue and much of his method from his great forerunners in Victorian satire and criticism—from Dickens, Thackeray, and Gilbert,
from Mill, Spencer, and George Eliot. His lineage as a satirist
reaches back farther still: to Fielding, Sterne, Byron, perhaps even
Jane Austen—all the critics who had impaled the cant, hypocrisy,
and sanctimony that form the dross of English habit and character.
Though he has been regarded at different times as an eccentric, a
pariah, an odd fish, a gadfly, a biological or spiritual "sport" in the
English moral tradition, he is firmly a part of that tradition—part of
its character and mentality, part of its divided intelligence, part of
the wit that competes with its self-esteem and parochialism, never so
effective as when he shows himself to contain its full ambivalence of
temperament and personality. Dickens, if a single name is to be emphasized, is his direct ancestor—the Dickens who both loved and pil-
loried the national character, who summed up in his lifework the
riddled self-delusion and spiritual dry rot at work in the social body
of his century, and whose families—Pecksniffs, Chuzzlewits, Chad-
bands, Smallweeds, Gradgrinds, Dorrits, Barnacles, Veneerings,
Wilfers—anticipate the Pontifexes. But neither Dickens nor Gilbert
nor Gissing, not even the iconoclasts of the nineties, not Shaw in his
early plays or Wells in his early novels, had so specifically fixed and
isolated the virus of Victorian fatuity and the special organism of its
most fruitful growth, the Victorian family, as Butler's novel did.

The Way of All Flesh classified this germ with the accuracy of a
bacteriologist. The English social novel found the fresh impetus it

was looking for. The Pontifexes became the case-history of a linger-
ing malady, coldly, remorselessly, almost passionlessly diagnosed. The
bourgeois ethos of the Victorian age had already died a dozen deaths,
but it was still alive and persistent in the mentality of the English
middle class. Not even the death of Queen Victoria herself in 1901
spelled its doom more decisively than Butler's novel did two years
later. Slow at first to win a public hearing, the book soon began to
stamp its imprint on the work of a new century—on Shaw, Wells,
Bennett, Forster, Beresford, D. H. Lawrence. "It drives one almost
to despair of English literature," said Shaw in 1905,[2] "when one sees
so extraordinary a study of English life as Butler's posthumous *The
Way of All Flesh* making so little impression that when, some years
later, I produce plays in which Butler's extraordinarily fresh, free,
and future-piercing suggestions have an obvious share, I am met with
nothing but vague cacklings about Ibsen and Nietzsche. . . .
Really, the English do not deserve to have great men." Bennett, youth-
fully eager to define a congenial paternity for his work, soon called
the tale "one of the greatest novels of the world." Another young
writer of the 1900s, then feeling his way toward authorship, was to
recall years later why the author of *Erewhon* struck his mind so
sharply. "For one thing," says E. M. Forster, "I have the sort of mind
which likes to be taken unawares. The frontal full-dress presentation
of an opinion often repels me, but if it be insidiously slipped in side-
wise I may receive it, and Butler is a master of the oblique. Then,
what he had to say was congenial, and I lapped it up. It was the food
for which I was waiting."[3] And when Shaw, at a later date, attempted to explain why he considered Butler a man of genius, he
said:

> A man of genius is not a man who can do more things, or who
> knows more things, than ordinary men: there has never been a
> man of genius yet who has not been surpassed in both respects in
> his own generation by quite a large number of hopeless fools. He
> is simply a man who sees the importance of things. . . . Butler
> saw the importance of what he had hit on, and developed it into
> a message for his age.

What that message was has become, in the half-century since Butler's death, something perhaps simpler than Butler intended. This is
doubtless the one unmistakable evidence of the factor of genius in a
talent whose authority is elsewhere debatable, or greatly confused by

erratic and perverse tendencies. One way of defining genius is by its
ability to make a certain idea or principle unmistakably its own, impossible to think of or employ except in the special form it has discovered for it. Butler's is a case of this order. He is celebrated as the
demolisher of Victorian moral sanctimony and the mentality it produced. This reputation, based on his criticism of religion in *The Fair
Haven*, on his satire on society in *Erewhon*, on his attack on the new
orthodoxy of science in *Evolution Old and New*, *Life and Habit*,
and *Luck or Cunning?*, but mainly on *The Way of All Flesh*, is
valid up to a point. It derives from the radical antinomianism in his
make-up. It issues from a fundamental impulse in all his work. "I
had to steal my own birthright," he once said. "I stole it and was bitterly punished. But I saved my soul alive." Yet the punishment, as
Edmund Wilson has pointed out, "affected him more permanently
than he knew. He had blasted Langar Rectory to eternity, but it had
left upon him its blight. His soul was alive; but, as Bernard Shaw
says, he had been maimed by his early training. Having begun as the
bad boy of a pious family, he was never to outgrow that state of
mind."[4] Another recent writer on Butler, G. D. H. Cole, has cor-
roborated this verdict:

> Acute critic as he was of many Victorian values, he was very
> much a Victorian himself. His perception seldom travelled far
> from the Victorian middle-class home and family; and when it did
> his view of things became superficial at once. Nothing could well
> be more thoroughly *bourgeois* than his picture of Erewhonian so-
> ciety; and it is not for being *bourgeois* that Butler mocks at it, for
> the way of living that he implicitly holds up beside it is not less
> *bourgeois*. No one ever insisted more firmly than Butler on the
> Victorian virtue of having enough money to live on securely in a
> comfortable *bourgeois* way; and no one ever upheld more strongly
> the importance of prudence—surely the most *bourgeois* of all the
> virtues. . . . Fiercely as he attacked the Victorian family, its spell
> was upon him, and he could not even try to throw it off. Nor
> could he ever stop worrying about God, even when he had become
> fully convinced that God was not worrying about him. He had
> most of the Victorian obsessions, though he had many of them
> upside down.[5]

This states Butler's predicament and the ambiguous cast of his legacy to his inheritors succinctly. It also indicates the complexity and

saving virtue of his case—the virtue of writing from deep inside the Victorian ethos—that gives his work its authenticity. The greatest satirists have written thus and perhaps only thus, from a profound involvement in their material. None of them was ever more inextricably involved than Butler was. To see how and why, a glance at his life is necessary, the more so since he transcribed that life so closely in his novel.

II

Butler was born in 1835 in the rectory of Langar in Nottinghamshire, son of the Reverend Thomas Butler and his wife Fanny Worsley. Thomas Butler was the son of Dr. Samuel Butler, headmaster of Shrewsbury School, later to become Bishop of Lichfield, one of the most formidable pedagogues and divines of his day and the subject of his grandson's one dull book, the biography the younger Samuel published in 1896 when, in an access of family conscience, he reversed the judgment on his grandfather that forms one of the most brilliant portraits in *The Way of All Flesh,* that of Ernest's grandfather George, the self-made, fatuously successful religious publisher. The family had advanced from the professional gentility of the Eighteenth Century, so deftly drawn in the first chapters of the novel with their picture of old Mr. Pontifex of Paleham, into the clerical class of the Nineteenth Century, custodian of English morality and education. As Mr. Cole has pointed out, the Butlers' class "was not the new *bourgeoisie* which had been created by the Industrial Revolution, but rather that middle class which had existed in the Eighteenth Century and had come through the Industrial Revolution almost unchanged, with a lively sense of its own gentility as contrasted with the vulgarity of many of the new rich, and with a steady allegiance to the Church of England as the church to which all really decent people belonged." This class prided itself on its associations with the liberal professions, with culture and religion in their official, class-vested character. It was not above making money: it made enough of it to provide the Butlers with substantial means and a reverence for means that remained one of Butler's own deepest convictions. "Money losses are the hardest to bear of any by those who are old enough to comprehend them," says the narrator of the novel, and money is in the book not only a mode of access to the pleasantest things in life but a refuge from vulgarity and indignity, a shield against ugliness and squalor, a weapon of tyranny, no doubt, but also an armor for the spirit. No novel of modern moral repute is more expressly a defense of the principle of property.

But Langar Rectory was more than an abode of rank and respectability. It was a fortress of religious sanctimony, with the Reverend Thomas its vested agent, a man of self-conceit and a bully, with an adoring wife to support his bullying discipline of their four children, Sam and Tom, Harriet and Mary. Of these Sam was the boy of sensitive nature, the child born to rebel. From the first he recognized his father as his enemy. "He never liked me, nor I him," he said years later; "from my earliest recollections I can call to mind no time when I did not fear him and dislike him. . . . I have never passed a day without thinking of him many times over as the man who was sure to be against me, and who would see the bad side rather than the good of everything I said and did." A regimen of lessons, hostile authority, and almost daily beatings was intermitted only once, when the family went on a carriage journey—how different from Ruskin's cushioned progresses in the family chariot—through France, Germany, Switzerland, and Italy, where Sam's love of nature, art, and the South found its first flowering. The rest of his childhood was a thralldom that bred his earliest resolution—to escape.

At ten he was sent to school at Allesley, and in 1848 to Shrewsbury School, where his grandfather's influence still prevailed and his shy, distrustful nature found a new kind of unhappiness. In 1854 he went on to Cambridge and knew happiness for the first time. But further distresses awaited him there too. He came to grips with the orthodox theology in which he had been bred and with the challenge of the profession his family had conceived for him, the ministry of the Church. He soon discovered that he was a natural skeptic, that he could never follow his father and grandfather into the clergy, that what he really wanted to be was a painter. He also discovered a will of his own capable of resisting his parents' effort to get him to enter, in default of the ministry, a respectable calling like the law or teaching. The upshot of the struggle was that when he finished Cambridge he decided, on the strength of a personal capital of two hundred seventy pounds and a promise of funds from his father, to emigrate to New Zealand and become a sheep farmer.

He sailed in 1859 at the age of twenty-three and stayed five years. He became, perhaps to his own surprise as much as to his family's, an efficient farmer. He made money. His health became robust. He delighted in the wild splendors of the southern wilderness (later to become the landscape of *Erewhon*). He found his first freedom of mind and spirit and returned to England a prosperous man, able at last to indulge his tastes and ambitions. But a new complication had entered his affairs and another confusion declared itself in his emotions. He returned with an incubus in the form of a friend, Charles Paine Pauli. Butler was fated to ill-advised or disappointing friendships all his life. They had their origins in his distracted and unresolved emotions, divided between romantic needs, uneasy suspicions, and a fear of giving himself freely that was dictated as much by social prohibitions as by the laming hostilities of his childhood. Pauli's was the most ill-fated of these. It clung to him, leechlike, money-draining, and nerve-sapping, for years.

In London Butler became a pupil at Heatherley's Art School, learned to paint, and before long was exhibiting at the Royal Academy. At Heatherley's he made another friendship, more tragic in its consequences even than Pauli's but the most fruitful of Butler's life. Eliza Mary Ann Savage, plain, lame, witty, one of the many pathetic wraiths of Victorian life and literature, was like himself a dissenter from Victorian smugness, and the one woman to whom Butler ever responded with a genuine spiritual sympathy. She may have loved him or she may not: her story is lost in silence and obscurity. Butler could never love her, but he also found it impossible to live without her lively response and encouragement. She became his modest Egeria. It was she who spurred him to write his novel, contributed much to its growth and detail, provided the model for its one bright spirit, Ernest's Aunt Alethea, and when she died in 1885 Butler was left with the remorse of having been unable to give her the love and marriage he came to realize she wanted. "The wrong I did in that I did no wrong": his sonnet to her memory speaks with the most intense poignance he ever permitted himself. The little lame lady who passed her courageous life between a depressing home and the various clubs or societies for emancipated women in which she served as secretary or manager remains the elusive sphinx of Butler's history. What is certain is that without her he would have missed the one creative relationship of his career and perhaps the stimulus for the writing of his novel.

He had made a tentative start in authorship with *A First Year in Canterbury Settlement*, put together by his father out of his letters from New Zealand in 1863. In New Zealand too he had begun to

cultivate the literary talent he had first discovered in essays and exercises at Cambridge, contributing to a local newspaper the fanciful
sketches that yielded the germ of the chapter of *Erewhon* called
"The Book of the Machines." Now in London the germ developed,
produced in 1872 the book of *Erewhon,* and brought Butler his first
notice as a writer. The next year he published *The Fair Haven,* a
satire on the historicity of the Scriptures and an argument for the
legendary, non-miraculous nature of Christianity. Having settled for
the moment his accounts with his inherited religion, he plunged into
the next of his lifelong battles, that against the mechanistic spirit of
Darwinism. The result was his first book on "creative evolution,"
Life and Habit, in 1878. Here he set Buffon and Lamarck against
Darwin and Huxley, whose hypotheses he believed to have "banished Mind from the Universe," creating a "soulless Determinism"
and "a vacuum which Nature abhors." Thus in three books he set
himself against the three great shibboleths of his age—material progress, religious orthodoxy, and scientific determinism. He took on
himself the task and odium of defying the gods of Victorian England, and systematically made himself a pariah of contemporary
culture.

Meanwhile, living in rooms in Clifford's Inn and with the help of
Pauli's cash-consuming parasitism, he was rapidly running through
his capital. A banker friend, Henry Hoare, hastened this process by
involving him in a series of wildcat promoting schemes that lost Butler most of his remaining fortune. He had to go to his father for
help, the bitterest concession he ever experienced. These experiences
left him with a dread of speculation and a passion for secure investments. His attempt to salvage what he could from Hoare's ventures
took him to Canada on two trips in 1874 and 1875. There he recovered about two thousand pounds (though he felt obliged to buy up
the defaulted shares of those whom he had influenced to invest),
and it was in Montreal that he profited by the colonial species of
British cant when he discovered that a plaster cast of the "Discobo-
lus" had been relegated to the basement of the local museum by the
city's prudes, thus inspiring the "Psalm of Montreal," his best-
known piece of invective. His financial troubles were over by 1886
when the inheritance due from his grandfather's estate came to him.
The final twenty years of his life were spent in Clifford's Inn, in
frequent trips to France and Italy (his love of mountains and the
South was recorded in *Alps and Sanctuaries* in 1882), in indulging
his love of music and Handel, in watching out the deaths of Miss

Savage and Pauli, in satisfying his sexual needs clandestinely through a Frenchwoman, Mme. Lucie Dumas, the seamstress who became his mistress, in finding a brief romantic friendship with a young Swiss called Hans Faesch and a new friend and Boswell in Henry Festing Jones, and in writing, composing music, translating Homer, and publishing a sequel to *Erewhon* called *Erewhon Revisited* in 1901, until death overtook him at sixty-six in June 1902.

It was a life that carried to its end the scars that had been stamped on it from birth and childhood. They show in its cautions and privations, in its perversities of intelligence and temperament, in its failure to love or give itself in love. In *The Way of All Flesh* Butler says that "accidents which happen to a man before he is born, in the persons of his ancestors, will, if he remembers them at all, leave an indelible impression on him; they will have moulded his character so that, do what he will, it is hardly possible for him to escape their consequences. If a man is to enter into the Kingdom of Heaven, he must do so, not only as a little child, but as a little embryo, or rather as a little zoosperm—and not only this, but as one that has come of zoosperms which have entered into the Kingdom of Heaven before him for many generations. Accidents which occur for the first time, and belong to the period since a man's last birth, are not, as a general rule, so permanent in their effects, though of course they may sometimes be so." The determinism he repudiated so violently in scientific theory claimed him in his personal fate. But against this belief his sense of justice enabled him to see also the plight of parents: that, as Edmund Wilson has pointed out, "parents have not chosen their children any more than their children have chosen them and that the plight in which the situation places us may be equally cruel for both"—thus the chapter called "The World of the Unborn" in *Erewhon*. This double burden of hurt and guilt never eased its weight in Butler. It came as close as it ever has among modern talents to inhibiting his gifts and canceling the liberty and birthright he won for himself through his harsh ordeal.

He has been accused by some critics—by Malcolm Muggeridge for one, in the most scathing of the indictments drawn against him[6]—of being a character essentially deformed who read his personal liabilities back into the age and conditions that produced him, of owning a nature dominated by defeatism and an egocentricity that could only hate. A share of this indictment is true: Butler never carried his resentment into a full intellectual or creative maturity like the greatest of the Victorian rebels. His books deny more effectively than they affirm. The worm of rancor and frustration gnaws their roots. Except in flashes he never won the vision of human suffering that animates the greatest satirists, from Aristophanes and Juvenal to Swift and Voltaire. The hurt he suffered was so much a part of himself that he could never disown it, never disengage himself from its injuries. He prized his wound and nursed his grievance; held the world at arm's length because he feared it; and protected himself with that world's own weapons—money, self-conceit, a protective suspicion of life. He knew himself a failure in compassion as much as in love, and he knew too much of great art—of Homer, Shakespeare, Handel, Bellini—to believe he had realized himself fully as an artist. He remained a Victorian—rebel and victim, agonist and apologist, radical and reactionary—to the end.

So much is evident. Butler does not stand in the highest rank of English or Victorian genius. He belongs to a radically limited order of English talent—it appears in such contemporaries as Beddoes, Lewis Carroll, Walter Pater, and Housman—that shows an ingrowth of imagination and spirit and that produces an art curtailed by doubt, self-indulgence, or eccentricity. His notebooks, with their flat cynicism, staled vituperation, and facile cheapness in deflationary witticism or crude raillery, show the sterility of emotion and moral insight that is betrayed when the mask of imagination is dropped. But such a talent can make its mark by a strategy of its own. It often appears on the scene of history at opportune moments to seize what more vigorous men may miss—the canker at the heart of human nature or society that inhibits the flowering of life. Its own defects become a clue to a prevalent malady of the human spirit. By recognizing that malady in itself, it sometimes gains its own definition of honor and justice. That, in the fact of the endemic cant and confusion of his age, is what Butler won for himself, for the contemporaries who gave him a hearing, and for the followers who took and assessed the cue he gave them. He used those least popular of keys, common sense, imagination, and justice, to unlock certain important secrets of moral energy and to make them available to the thought and art of a new century.

III

The Way of All Flesh maintains its importance, if for no other reason, because it records the ordeal necessary to such liberation in him-

self and his generation. *Life and Habit* is probably, as Clara G. Stillman argues in her excellent book on Butler,[7] his "most important
book from the point of view of his contribution to scientific and philosophic thought," and for what it and its sequels, *Evolution Old and
New* and *Luck or Cunning?*, gave to Shaw, Bergson, and a new age
of moral and ethical values. *Erewhon* is his most original work and
his real title to a place in the satirical tradition. His poetic gifts and
aesthetic capacities are best seen in *Alps and Sanctuaries*. But *The
Way of All Flesh* gives his conflict of spirit its substance of fact and
human actuality, of a tonic quality of wit and disillusioned insight
that will remain Butler's distinctive achievement in the art of words.
This gives it its rank among modern examples of the novel of initiation and education in life, the *Bildungsroman*, where its companions,
to name only English examples, are *Pendennis*, *Great Expectations*,
Feverel, *Adam Bede*, *Jude the Obscure*, Forster's *The Longest Journey*, Wells's *Tono-Bungay*, Bennett's *Clayhanger*, Lawrence's *Sons
and Lovers*, and Joyce's *Portrait of the Artist as a Young Man*.
Among these it is and will remain a landmark.

Reading it today we are able to see it as something more than the
pure polemic or indictment verging on caricature that its reputation
for iconoclasm and irreverence once made it appear. Butler's failure
to publish it in his lifetime is far from meaning that he did not write
it with all the seriousness in his power. He wrote it slowly, revised it
conscientiously, took to heart Miss Savage's acute criticisms, and kept
it in his desk as a kind of investment or insurance against the im-
permanence he felt his other books might suffer. He seems also to
have felt the difficulties under which a book that issued so intimately
from his own history labored. These are quite visible in its pages. By
dividing himself into two men—the callow victim and prig Ernest,
and the seasoned and disillusioned narrator Overton—he distanced
his ordeal but he also inhibited the imaginative reality of his hero.
Ernest is unfortunately the weakest part of the story. Compare him
with Dickens' Pip, with Forster's Rickie Elliot, with Lawrence's Paul
Morel or Joyce's Dedalus, all of them drawn with equal intimacy
from their authors' selves, and his blankness as a character is apparent. The agony of the boy is continuously attenuated by Overton's
mature wisdom. He lives too much after the fact to live convincingly
within the fact, and thus becomes one of the least impressive heroes
of his kind. For Ernest, says Mr. Pritchett, "one cares very little. Unlike Butler he does not act; because of the necessities of the book he

is acted upon. His indiscretions are passive. He has no sins; he has merely follies." But Pritchett's further argument that "the characters are dwarfed and burned dry by Butler's arguments," that he "chose them for their mediocrity and then cursed them for it," and that he did not sufficiently listen to Miss Savage when "she pointed out the dangers of his special pleading," is not so convincing. A close reading of the book shows that this special pleading yielded to a sound imaginative instinct in the best parts of it and permitted Butler to create certain characters that are triumphs of their sort.

These are old Mr. Pontifex of Paleham and his wife, Butler's tribute to the soundness in the older stock of his breed that came to suffer so sorry a decline in later generations; the grandfather of Ernest, George Pontifex, a portrait of canting hypocrisy that competes with Dickens' Pecksniff; Ernest's Aunt Alethea, briefly drawn but convincing as Butler's portrayal of the life-giving sympathy and generous instincts from which he felt genuine goodness to derive; and of course Ernest's parents, Theobald and Christina. Here Butler's sense of justice was put to its severest test. He knew them in all their meanness, self-conceit, and fatuity, their jealous smallness and niggardly complacency; he had not lost his sense of their enmity to him and the kind of life he valued; but some instinct—perhaps the very link of family attachment and tribal identity he never succeeded in breaking—kept him in sufficient sympathy with their misguided natures to permit a wholeness and complexity in the portraiture. He makes palpable their smugness, their selfish stratagems, the insinuating craftiness of their cruelty, but he shows where, in parental influence and social deceit, these originated, and before he has finished with them he makes us pity them as much as we blame them.

If, as Shaw said, Butler "actually endeared himself by parricide and matricide long drawn out," it is as much because he drew his dissection of these two characters out to its inevitable conclusion of pathos and tragedy as because he avenged himself and his generation for the blight they had suffered at the hands of Victorian parenthood. By the time we see Christina dying or Theobald in his comfortless old age we know how just but also how pitiful Christina's torturings of Ernest on the inquisitorial sofa or Theobald's fear of marriage on his ludicrous honeymoon make these scenes of their final despair. The lesser characters in the book—Ernest's sisters, the Cambridge evangelists, the Dickensian Mrs. Jupp, the sinister Pryer, even the ill-fated, vigorously drawn Ellen—show the lively realism of people taken directly from their moment in time. Here Butler's task was easier, though he met it with remarkable accuracy in comic invention. It was his more complex relations with his parents and grandfather that made his dealings with them difficult, and that saved him from facile caricature when he brought them to the bar of comic justice. That he did not shirk these difficulties is shown in the fact that he succeeded in lifting them to a level which makes possible not only a sound moral realism but the elements of tragedy.

By the time the book ends Ernest is saved. He is honest at last, a man of humanity and humor, a redeemed prig, a sane creature won over from the powers of ignorance to the side of life. He is not, however, oppressively or heroically edifying. He is happy to be well off, feels no scruples in leaving his children to be raised as wards of a Thames bargee, and means to live a life of modest effort and intelligent selfishness. His will has never recovered, will never fully recover, from its almost fatal testing. He will not impose or oppress, but he is unlikely ever to command and create. He mirrors, in this, his inventor. Both he and Butler have known too well what it means to be edifying in the wrong way to risk the dangers of becoming edifying in the right way. The book ends on a sigh of relief, a note of caution, an audible shudder of relaxation. The will has at last been cured of mania and excess. A soul has been saved and claimed its birthright.

Butler succeeded in putting the whole of himself into the novel. His shrewd if amateur scientific feeling is there; his sense of the conflict between conscious and unconscious forces in the human psyche is everywhere implicit; his hatred of mechanistic doctrine and the moral heartlessness it breeds is argued; his love of music and art is voiced by Overton's taste and Ernest's devotion to the organ; his contempt of the duplicity and inverted ethic of bourgeois morality suffuses the book, bringing the fantasy of *Erewhon* to terms with the realistic claims of fictional art. Overton's commentary, however intrusive and damaging to the imaginative freedom of the tale, nevertheless sums up the wisdom that Butler wrested from his personal history, and this is what makes the book, however short in the ultimate passion and vision of moral genius, a point of definition in the experience of its century. Osbert Sitwell has said that "the indictment against the Victorian age is not that it was not comfortable, or, in spite of its many cruelties, kindly; but that it left its debts, mental, moral, and physical, to be paid by a later generation." Butler, who missed in his age the greater vision and capacity for idealism that even critics as merciless and scathing, and as different, as Dickens and Baudelaire, Ibsen and Rimbaud, defined for it, was yet one man who determined to do his share in preventing that insolvency. It is for this reason—sufficient for his representative importance in modern experience and conflict—that the Twentieth Century has been grateful to him, has called *The Way of All Flesh* a classic among records of the human spirit in its struggle toward liberty and truth, and has granted him his honorable place among its benefactors.

NOTES

1. V. S. Pritchett, "A Victorian Son" in *The Living Novel* (1946), pp. 102, 104.
2. For Shaw on Butler see his review of *Luck or Cunning?* in the *Pall Mall Gazette,* May 31, 1887; his review of Henry Festing Jones's *Samuel Butler: A Memoir* in *The Manchester Guardian,* November 1, 1919; "Mr. Gilbert Cannan on Samuel Butler" in his *Pen Portraits and Reviews* (1932), and the prefaces to *Man and Superman* (1903), *Major Barbara* (1907), *Androcles and the Lion* (1913), and *Back to Methuselah* (1921, but especially in its new edition with postscript, 1946).
3. E. M. Forster, "Books That Influenced Me: Samuel Butler's *Erewhon,*" under the title "Books in General" in *The New Statesman and Nation* (London), July 15, 1944, now included in his *Two Cheers for Democracy* (1951), pp. 219-23. See also his "Butler Approached," a review of P. N. Furbank's *Samuel Butler,* in *The Spectator* (London), November 12, 1948.
4. Edmund Wilson, "The Satire of Samuel Butler" in *The Triple Thinkers* (1938); reprinted in *The Shores of Light* (1953), pp. 556–65.
5. G. D. H. Cole, preface to *The Essential Samuel Butler* (1949); see also his *Samuel Butler and The Way of All Flesh* (1947).
6. Malcolm Muggeridge, *The Earnest Atheist: A Study of Samuel Butler* (1936). ("A crosspatch of a book"—E. M. Forster.) This is the most inclusive attack on Butler and Butlerism that has appeared; for a shorter one see Graham Greene's in his *The Lost Childhood and Other Essays* (1951); and for three French studies written from outside the English situation see Madeleine L. Cazamian's in *Le Roman et les Idées en Angleterre* (Strasbourg, 1923), Valery Larbaud's *Samuel Butler* in *Les Cahiers des Amis des Livres* (Paris, 1920), and J. B. Fort's two-volume work, *Samuel Butler: 1835–1902* (Paris, 1935).

7. Clara G. Stillman, *Samuel Butler: A Mid-Victorian Modern* (1932). This is the best book on Butler produced in America and the best work to combine biography with a critical interpretation of Butler's work and ideas; it surpasses the earlier studies of Gilbert Cannan (1915), John F. Harris (1916), and C. E. M. Joad (1924) in this respect, as well as P. N. Furbank's later book (1948), and serves as a critical interpretation of the biographical material in the memoirs of Henry Festing Jones (1919) and Mrs. R. S. Garnett (1926).

JOHN HENRY RALEIGH
Victorian Morals and the Modern Novel

The life of the London poor in the nineteenth century was, for the
most part, miserable, and no one who has read Henry Mayhew, that
great sociologist, can ever forget his grim and heartbreaking people
and scenes. If man had set out consciously to fashion a hell for his
fellow men, he could not have done better than nineteenth-century
English culture did with the poor who "lived" off the streets of London. Indeed Mayhew's descriptions in *London Labour and the
London Poor* sometimes convey a kind of Pandemonium quality and
one can almost sniff the sulphur in the air. His description of a
crowd entering a "Penny Gaff"—a kind of temporary theater which
put on salacious performances—suggests some of the horror.

> Forward they came, bringing an overpowering stench with them,
> laughing and yelling as they pushed their way through the waiting
> room. One woman carrying a sickly child with a bulging forehead,
> was reeling drunk, the saliva running down her mouth as she
> stared about with a heavy fixed eye. Two boys were pushing her
> from side to side, while the poor infant slept, breathing heavily,
> as if stupified, through the din. Lads jumping on girls, and girls

From *Time, Place and Idea: Essays on the Novel* (Carbondale, Illinois, 1968),
pp. 137-63. Copyright © 1968 by Southern Illinois University Press. Reprinted
by permission of Southern Illinois University Press and the author. The essay
first appeared in *Partisan Review*, Vol. XXV, No. 2, 241-64.

laughing hysterically from being tickled by the youths behind
them, every one shouting and jumping, presented a mad scene of
frightful enjoyment.[1]

But if anything, as over against this evil of stench and noise, the
lonely pathos of individual tragedies is even more frightful: the
blind street-seller who had once been a tailor and had worked in a
room seven feet square, with six other people, from five in the morning until ten at night, the room having no chimney or window or
fire, though no fire was needed even in the winter, and in the summer it was like an oven. This is what it was like in the daytime, but
"no mortal tongue," the man told Mayhew, could describe what it
was like at night when the two great gaslights went on. Many times
the men had to be carried out of the room fainting for air. They told
the master he was killing them, and they knew he had other rooms,
but to no avail. The gaslights burned into the man's eyes and into
his brain until, "at last, I was seized with rheumatics in the brain,
and obliged to go into St. Thomas's Hospital. I was there eleven
months, and *came out stone blind*"; or the crippled streetseller of
nutmeg graters, who crawled, literally, out into the streets where he
stayed from ten to six eking out his pitiful existence, six days a week.
On wet days he would lie in bed, often without food. "Ah," he told
Mayhew, "It *is* very miserable indeed lying in a bed all day, and in
a lonely room, without perhaps a person to come near one—helpless
as I am—and hear the rain beat against your windows, all that with
nothing to put to your lips." Thus, if in what follows, the life of the
poor is shown to have some moments of joy, these are, it is remembered, only oases in an illimitable desert of misery.

And since the Victorian moral "code"—if there were such a thing—
will be subjected to equally large generalizations, these too should be
qualified in advance. Victorian "morality" is a very complex affair.
In the first place, what we call Victorian morality is only middle-class
morality. Above and below, in the relatively small aristocracy and in
the immense lower class, the puritanical code did not prevail; and
indeed, in many respects, the aristocrats and the poor had more in
common with one another, morally speaking, than either had with
the middle class. Noting the passion for card-playing, for example,
that prevailed among aristocrats and commoners, Mayhew remarked,
"It has been said that there is a close resemblance between many
of the characteristics of a very high class, socially, and a very low

class." Considering the life of the aristocracy as a whole, one cannot doubt but that life often ran high in those days, despite the decorous national examples of Victoria and Albert. Writing to Forster from Paris in 1856, Dickens relates an incident, given by a friend, of an experience with the English squirearchy. Dickens' friend, designated as "B," had, three years previously, been living near Gadshill and occupied himself with sketching in the outdoors. One day a gentleman stopped his carriage and invited "B" to come to his house and use his library. "B" accepted the invitation and stayed on at the house, as it turned out, for six months. The lady of the house aged twenty-five, was the squire's mistress. (He was married but separated from his wife.) The young lady, very beautiful, was engaged in drinking herself to death, while the squire, though "utterly depraved and wicked" was "an excellent scholar, an admirable linguist, and a great theologian." There were also two other "mad" visitors who stayed six months. Tea, coffee, even water, were seldom seen in this establishment: "Breakfast: leg of mutton, champagne, beer and brandy. Lunch: shoulder of mutton, champagne, beer and brandy. Dinner: every conceivable dish (Squire's income £7,000—a year), champagne, beer and brandy." The squire's wife, in her turn, was bringing up their one daughter in vice and in linguistic depravity, in order to spite the squire. At thirteen the daughter was "coarse" in conversation and always drunk. At last the mistress died, after which the "party" broke up. The squire himself later died of a "broken heart."[2] And similar concatenations, minus the £7,000 a year and the brandy and champagne, were abundantly evident in the lower class.

As for the middle class, it is by now quite clear that the later nineteenth century and the early twentieth century had considerably overestimated the nature and extent of its prudery and of its innocence. In their private and personal lives there is considerable evidence that the Victorians were much less inhibited and conventional than we are, generally speaking, today. By this assertion I do not refer only to the obvious facts of George Eliot's liaison with Lewes, or Dickens' with Ellen Ternan, or the involved ménage of John Chapman or the *ménage à quatre* of the Thornton Hunts and the George Henry Lewes, or any of the extralegal sexual relations which any Victorian worth his or her salt seemed to get himself or herself involved with. I mean that the general *attitude* toward the private, "unsanctified" relation, while in theory it might be rigorous, often turned out to be in practice remarkably tolerant. Especially was there tolerance among the Unitarians and Radicals. Thus when Harriet Taylor, after the birth of her second child, felt depressed and uncertain, and uncongenial in her intellectual relation to her hearty, businessman husband, went to see her pastoral counselor, the Unitarian William Johnson Fox, the minister, instead of advocating fasting and prayer, determined that she should meet John Stuart Mill, an event which took place and has since become a part of recorded history. Coincidentally Fox, although married and a father, was the lover of Harriet's best friend, Eliza Flower. Later Mrs. Fox, finding her position difficult, made a formal complaint to Fox's congregation, and Fox had to defend himself in "open church." Mill and Harriet Taylor, whose father was a prominent Unitarian and whose influence was used, rushed to his defense—Mill believing him "innocent"—and Fox was vindicated. One wonders how successfully a minister in our enlightened and psychological age would weather a similar situation or if the elders of his church would rush to his defense if he were once accused.

Yet it is true that the middle class exercised a far-reaching and vigorous moral censorship upon its chief entertainment, fiction, although even in this area some qualifications and provisos must be made. First there were differing degrees of censorship in differing decades of the century. In the forties, for example, there was much less squeamishness than in the sixties, by which time the habit of family reading had become firmly established, and by the eighties and nineties Hardy, Moore, and others had broken the familial tyranny. Thus it was only for a relatively brief period, after mid-century, that the censorship was in full operation.[3] In the earlier decades neither *Wuthering Heights* nor *Jane Eyre*, filled as they are with an intense sexuality, roused any general furor on this score. Furthermore, even within the conventions and in any decade, the Victorian novelists usually managed to convey the intended effect. No one was in doubt as to what Becky Sharp was up to in her days on the Continent, after her fall. There is, too, in many of Dickens' novels a kind of implicit bawdiness—a jeering crowd of urchins or elders, with smirks on their faces and, one may well imagine, profanity in their mouths. Mr. Pickwick, for example, in the company of a young lady, is called by someone in the crowd an "old ram." Even in later decades, when the censorship was real and rigorous, implication could serve with great effectiveness to circumvent the code. Dorothea Brooke's marriage to Casaubon is both a spiritual and a physical tragedy. The spiritual tragedy is fully and explicitly analyzed, but the physical tragedy, while never directly commented upon by the authoress, is concretely underlined by the characters in the novel, particularly by the remarks of Celia and Mrs. Cadwallader. By them we are reminded, again and again, that the magnificent Dorothea, with her great brown eyes and her powerful maternal hands and her immense vitality, is giving herself to a dried-up old pedant with two white moles—with hairs in them—on his cheek, who makes unpleasant noises when eating his soup, and who has one foot in the grave, although, as Mrs. Cadwallader says, he evidently intends to pull it back.

Still, with all these provisos admitted, Victorian morality was stringent, and it exercised a stringent censorship on the novel, and, partially anyway, upon life itself. But its historical irony consists in the fact that it broke down, in the novel, if not in life, in the direction of the morality and mores of the lower class, whose conduct and attitude the middle-class Victorians found so reprehensible and whose "lapsed" and unregenerate mode of life the bourgeoisie attempted to meliorate, usually without success. Mayhew reported that the costermongers said that tracts and sermons gave them "the 'orros," and, indeed, the poor were adamant in their unregeneracy in the face of the admonitions to "purity" that were administered to them. The classic instance in Victorian fiction is the impassioned retort of the workingman to the hectoring Mrs. Pardiggle in *Bleak House*: concluding a lengthy and aggressive list of his sins, he exclaims:

> "How have I been conducting of myself? Why, I've been drunk for three days; and I'd a been drunk four, if I'd a had the money. Don't I never mean for to go to church? No, I don't never mean for to go to church. I shouldn't be expected there, if I did; the beadle's too genteel for me. And how did my wife get that black eye? Why, I giv' it her; and if she says I didn't, she's a Lie!"

But the moral stance of the workingman, passive and helpless as he was in the context of the society of which he was more or less the creature, prevailed in a deep sense, and the revolt that occurred in English fiction in Butler and in Hardy and others, and later on pre-eminently in D. H. Lawrence, was in a sense an upsurge from below, an affirmation of the naturalistic and instinctive ways of life of the lower class, as against the theoretical and restrictive moral preconceptions of the middle class. And the history of the novel in the late nineteenth and early twentieth century is, in part, the story of how that workingman, whom Mrs. Pardiggle hectored, got up off the floor, and went, or perhaps staggered, to a writing desk, where he composed first *The Way of All Flesh* and *Jude the Obscure* and, later, such books as *The Rainbow, Women in Love,* and *The Man Who Died.*

The costermongers of the streets of London were without faith or hope, but, within the necessary limits, they practiced charity. They were, Mayhew tells us, scrupulously honest among themselves, although they could seldom indulge in the luxury of being honest with strangers. "Forgive us our trespasses, as we forgive them as trespass agin us," said a coster to Mayhew. "It's a very good thing, in coorse, but no costers can't do it." They were nevertheless surprisingly honest with the "deserving" rich. A certain Mrs. Chisholm, Mayhew reports, had let out at different times as much as £160,000 that had been entrusted to her for helping out the "lower orders," and the whole of this large amount had been returned, *"with the exception of £12."* They had no trust in banks or similar institutions, and although they had to pay usurious rates when forced to borrow from their own kind—sometimes at the rate of twenty percent per week, or no less than £1,040 a year for every £100 advanced—still their profound and unshakable distrust of all the institutions above them rendered them impervious to the whole idea of capitalism, investments, inheritances, and so on, although, it should be added, they passed on, like true entrepreneurs, the usurer's exorbitant rates to their benighted customers.

If the costers did not partake of the idea of capitalism that animated a great section of the middle class above them, neither did they bow down to the official Victorian deities of God, Home, and Country. Their nationalism was deep-grained in the sense that they disliked and distrusted foreigners—especially the omnipresent Irish whom they called the "Greeks"—yet they were completely skeptical, and rightly so, about the ecstatic chauvinism of part of the middle class. Like Matthew Arnold, they could be moved only to derisive laughter at Mr. Roebuck's Parliamentary encomiums on the beauties of being an Englishman in the nineteenth century. The popular song that was punctuated by the refrain, "Britons never shall be slaves," the costers rendered as "Britons always shall be slaves." For the detailed social structure of their society they had equal distrust and

ignorance. To be sure, Queen Victoria's granite-like moral eminence
was so towering that it cast a shade even over these lower depths.
Yet the costers would not be solemn about Her Majesty, and mock
love letters between her and Albert were hawked in the streets. Even
her philoprogenitiveness was not sacred. The combined respect and
irony in their attitude toward the Queen can be seen in the account
of the "patterers," who hawked literature in the streets. They never,
they told Mayhew, had much to say about the Queen: "It wouldn't
go down. . . . In coorse nothing can be said against her, and nothing
ought to, that's true enough." Yet one patterer, as it turned out, had
hawked "news" about the Queen during her most recent confine-
ment:

> I cried her *accouchement* [pronounced as in English without
> knowledge of French] of *three!* Lord love you, sir, it would have
> been no use crying *one;* peoples so used to that; but a Bobby came
> up and he stops me, and said it was some impudence about the
> Queen's *coachman!* Why look at it, says I, fat-head—I knew I was
> safe.

And the royal love affair seemed to have afforded them infinite
amusement. One street ballad, for example, had one quatrain:

> Here I am in rags
> From the land of All-dirt
> To marry England's Queen
> And my name is Prince Albert.

Of other eminent people they were liable to have more reserved
opinions. The hero of Waterloo was not much amiss, "if he lets
politics alone," but the name of a bishop was for them but another
name for Beelzebub. The aristocrats in general they regarded as
tricksters who somehow got something for nothing, although they
were completely nonplussed, literally, by the concept of living without working. As for the middle class, the patterers freely and cynically
exploited its prejudices, especially the anti-Roman one. One experienced patterer told Mayhew that although they peddled anti-Papal
literature during religious crises, as in the affair of Cardinal Wiseman, they had no feeling about the Pope one way or another: *"We
goes to it as at an election."* His favorite, the man said, was a ballad
called "The Pope and Cardinal Wiseman" whose chorus ran thus:

> Monks and Nuns and fools afloat,
>> We'll have no bulls shoved down our throat,
> Cheer up and shout down with the Pope,
>> And his bishop Cardinal Wiseman.

The over-all politics of the costermongers was simple and direct: it consisted simply in a hatred of the police; in fact, said Mayhew, the police *were* their politics. They were interested in Chartism, and they were mostly all Chartists, although they knew nothing of the six points and they could not understand why the Chartist leaders exhorted them to peace and quietness when they could just as well fight it out with the police at once. "I am assured," said Mayhew, "that in case of a political riot, every 'coster' would seize his policeman." And among themselves they did carry on a continuous civil war with the "Peelers." To "serve out" a policeman was the bravest act and the highest office to which a coster could aspire. They were implacable in this pursuit, motivated as they were by a simple revenge code, and would patiently shadow a policeman for months until, catching him at a disadvantage, they would "do him in." The ensuing jail sentence was regarded as a mere bagatelle, and well worth the status of a hero among the costers that also followed.

If the costers had no concept of nationality or law or politics, they were likewise devoid of any religious sentiment or understanding. Only among the most miserable of the street people—the lame, the halt, the blind—could Mayhew find any religious notions. The blind musicians were "a far more deserving class than is usually supposed—this affliction seems to have chastened them and to have given a peculiar religious cast to their thoughts." But among the main body of costers only three in a hundred had even been inside a church or knew what was meant by Christianity. Occasionally a sort of Hardy-esque feeling about the Deity emerged, as with an old sailor who told Mayhew that while there may have "once" been a God, He was either dead or grown old and diseased, for He obviously did not "fash" (trouble) himself with his creatures at all. But the bulk of the costers lived in cheerful ignorance of the facts of Christianity—"I don't know what the Pope is. Is he in any trade?"; "O, yes, I've heard of God; he made heaven and earth; I never heard of his making the sea; that's another thing, and you can best learn of that at Billingsgate"—and, moreover, out of the churches themselves they saw issuing forth only fashionable and well-dressed people. Although they hated the

Irish, they respected the Catholic Church because they actually saw the Sisters of Charity caring for the sick. Protestantism meant mostly tracts and sermons and although they respected some of the inferior orders of the Church of England, Mayhew was told that if they were to join any religion it would be the Catholic. But by and large they were freethinkers. The patterers hawked on the streets—and this sometimes took courage—Hone's notorious parodies of the catechism and the litany, and after Hone's trial and acquittal, he had become with them a "hero." Especially were the patterers, who were the intellectuals among the costers, skeptical and atheistical. Some of them had actually had a classical education and thus had the knowledge to back up their scoffing: "Most of them," said Mayhew, "scoffed at the Bible, or perverted its passages." The patterers possessed a high degree of sophistication generally and were, in politics, "liberal Tories" who hated the Whigs and lamented the death of Peel.

But what troubled Mayhew the most about the costers was their imperfect concept and practice of marriage and home life, which the middle class had enshrined at the apex of its system of values. Only one tenth of the couples living together were married, and none of them had any notion of "legitimate" or "illegitimate" children. They thought of the marriage ceremony as constituting a waste of time and money, and the women of illegal unions were as faithful as those of legal ones. But none of them, married or not, had strict notions about fidelity, and in hard times it was considered no crime for a woman to depart from the path of virtue in order to provide for a fire or a meal. Desertions, heavy drinking, and the accompanying brutality were, of course, frequent, but it didn't seem to matter much. As one informant told Mayhew:

> They sometimes take a little drop themselves, the women do, and get beaten by their husbands for it, and hardest beaten if the man's drunk himself. They're sometimes beaten for other things, too, or for nothing at all. But they seem to like the men better for their beating them. I never could make that out.

The whole idea of "home" was foreign to the costers. They worked in and often took their meals in the street. Leisure time was given over to the beer-shop, the dancing room, or the theater. The very word "home," according to Mayhew, was seldom used by them. The parent-child relation was likewise different from the one that prevailed in the middle class. Either it was established upon a non-authoritarian basis: "The costermongers are kind to their children, perhaps in a rough way, and the women make regular pets of them very often." Or, conversely, it plainly recognized and made explicit the latent hostility which is part and parcel of that delicate relation. It was very common for the father and son to quarrel by the time the boy reached adolescence, and for the boy, who knew business thoroughly by that age, to leave home and set out on his own. One of Mayhew's informants said of the coster boys, "If the father vexes him or snubs him, he'll tell his father to go to h—l, and he and his gal will start on their own account." Adolescent marriages were common; two or three out of every one hundred boys of thirteen or fourteen were either married to or living with a girl, who was usually a couple of years older.

The patterers, as might be expected, were the least legalistic and the most irregular of all the street people as concerns marriage. As they were itinerants, they often practiced polygamy, and, like the legendary sailor, had a wife in every town. Mayhew had heard of one "renowed" patterer who was married to four women and "had lived in criminal intercourse with his own sister, and his own daughter by one of his wives."

Yet this way of life—dirty and precarious and amoral—had immense attractions, the first of which was absolute freedom. There were in the streets, usually among the patterers, well-educated people from the middle class who had chosen to drop from that class into street life. Mayhew tells of two brothers, street patterers, who were "well-educated" and "respectably connected" who "candidly" confessed that they preferred that kind of life to any other and would not leave it if they could, and Mayhew remarked, somewhat ruefully, that it was an anthropological fact, always and universally true, that no one in any culture who has adopted the nomadic way of life ever abandons it, while, on the other hand, as in Indian country, the reverse is often true and the "civilized" people will often become nomads. According to Mayhew, the nomads are always characterized by twelve distinct habitual attitudes: a repugnance to regular and continuous labor; a want of providence in storing up for the future; a power for enduring privation; an immoderate love of gaming; a love of "libidinous" dances; a love of witnessing the suffering of sentient creatures; a delight in warfare and perilous sport; a desire for vengeance; a looseness of notions about property; an absence of chastity among females and a general disregard for feminine virtue; and a vague sense of religion and a crude notion of the Creator.

Mayhew, of course, considered these as the stigmata of immorality, but, obviously, the costermongers were "immoral" only in a relative sense; and they had their own moral code, which was based not upon the sanctity of property and home—the basis for middle-class morality —but upon the sanctity of the instincts of the blood. Like modern psychologists, they were the enemies of "repression," and like the upper class they believed in the idea of the "duel." An article of their faith was that a fight should never be stopped, and when one broke out in the streets, a ring was formed in order to insure its continuance, "for they hold it a wrong thing to stop a battle, as it causes bad blood for life; whereas, if the lads fight it out they shake hands and forget all about it." Their social code in general was based upon personal feelings rather than legal or moral sanctions. They boasted of always sticking together, and a coster could always leave his stall, as a shopkeeper never could, unprotected, knowing that his fellow costers would keep an eye on it and see to it that nothing was stolen. Their own code was based mainly on the idea of personal bravery. This code dictated, for example, that pain should be borne in silence and with pluck. They were all pugilists, and a good one was a local hero. All the pubs had gloves at hand, and fifteen-minute bouts were the order of the day. Their sports were generally dangerous, requiring both courage and dexterity. "They prefer," said Mayhew, "if crossing a bridge, to climb over the parapet, and walk along on the stone coping."

Above all there was no place in the code for the middle-class idea of "respectability." Indeed the more intelligent of the patterers mocked at the whole concept. And the impudence and wit that Dickens put at the disposal of the "Artful Dodger," especially in the trial scene when he directly confronts the forces of law and order, were evidently commonplace among the costers. Although most of them were completely uneducated—only one in ten was able to read— they were preternaturally acute, for only by their wits could they exist. One of the quickest-witted of the patterers was interviewed by Mayhew and recounted an experience that paralleled, with a happier ending, that of the Artful Dodger.

> I was once before Alderman Kelley, when he was Lord Mayor, charged with obstructing, or some humbug. "What are you my

man," he says quietly, and like a gentleman. "In the same line as yourself, my lord," says I. "How's that?" says he. "I'm a paper-worker for my living, my lord," says I. I was soon discharged and there was such fun and laughing, that if I'd a few slums in my pocket, I believe I could have sold them all in the justice-room.

And the great heavy Victorian morality overhead, which at its best produced such titans as John Stuart Mill, George Eliot, and Matthew Arnold, but which also produced, in lesser vessels, Theobald and Christina Pontifex, finally toppled over in the direction of lower-class morality, and *The Way of All Flesh* celebrates a way of life not far different from the life of the costers.

It hardly needs to be pointed out that Butler's attack upon official Victorian morality jibes, almost point by point, with the actual morality of the lower orders: freedom, or neglect, for children, an early exodus from the parental domain, no tie to formal religion or formal education, impudence, in general, about the sacred cows of the middle class, a wholesale rejection of the idea of "respectability," an over-all anarchism, and a belief in the instincts. Add a private income, some book learning, some notions—none too formal or precise—about a Deity, and subtract the love of brutality and the terrible suffering that often prevailed, and a street patterer would come close to being a Butlerian hero. It is no accident that Butler has his hero shed his last illusions about the middle-class outlook among the London poor (whom he is supposedly "converting" but who in actuality convert him) and that after his ultimate "fall"—the period spent in jail—he should, like a street patterer, have dropped out of his own class and joined the lower one. But the heart of the matter goes deeper than explicit ideas and institutions. What Butler was attacking, above all, was middle-class consciousness, that is, the way the middle-class mind operated, and he opposed this consciousness with another type or way of handling experience, which he associated with either the aristocracy or the lower class, for it was only these that had the famous Butlerian "grace," the ability to act by instinct and by the unconscious. Towneley, upper-class, and Mr. Shaw, the tinker of the lower-class, both have this faculty because they have not been brought up in what was for Butler the prison house of abstract moral codes and formulations and surrounded by all kinds of taboos and bugaboos which attempted anyway to repress instinct completely and to regulate all human conduct—even human thought—by acquired precepts. Butler thought that St. Paul was the real villain in Western history, for he represented formulated law.

If Butler embodies the comedy of this revolt against middle-class consciousness, Hardy embodies in his career as a whole, first, its antitype as pastoral and, second and finally, its antitype as tragedy. The world of *Far from the Madding Crowd* or *The Woodlanders* is the idyll from which, with some exceptions, the bugaboo of consciousness is absent, and where time has stopped and nature is benignly soft. There was a Hardy "mood," which all his admirers loved and which has no parallel in English literature. D. H. Lawrence, perhaps the best and most perceptive critic of Hardy, summed it up in a letter written in 1918 from a cottage in Berkshire: "It is very nice here—Hardy country—like *Woodlanders*—all woods and hazel copses, and tiny little villages, under the church, with fields slanting down, and a hazel copse almost touching the little garden wall."[4] Hardy himself described Little Hintock, the locale of *The Woodlanders,* as "one of those sequestered spots outside the gates of the world where may usually be found more meditation than action, and more passivity than meditation; where reasoning proceeds on narrow premises, and results in inferences wildly imaginative." Marty South and Giles Winterbourne, the real if not the titular hero and heroine, are Arcadian primitives, taciturn, in tune with the natural world—whose symbols they can decipher like hieroglyphs—instinctive, and personal: "Her [Marty's] face had the usual fullness of expression which is developed by the life of solitude. Where the eyes of the multitude beat like waves upon a countenance they seem to wear away individuality." Despite their mutual tragedy and Giles's death, they are outside the hell of consciousness. But as Hardy's career went on, the rustics got, in Henry James's phrase, squeezed into their "horrid age," with its formulations and conceptualized taboos. Tess is described as being surrounded by a host of "moral hobgoblins," false and contrary to her instincts, that harass her walking life and hound her to her death. Lawrence said that in Hardy none of the central characters ever really care about position or money or even immediate self-preservation. They are all struggling for that most passionate and most unself-conscious of relationships—love. They thus "explode out of convention"[5] and are destroyed, while those who remain safely and pallidly within the pale are saved. Critics of Hardy complained that his characters were always behaving in unexpected fashion and doing unexpected things, but that was just the point, according to

Lawrence: they were acting instinctively in a world where the instinctive was no longer allowable. In Hardy, as in Butler, the burden of consciousness and the legacy of St. Paul have become intolerable, and in Jude's terrible death and in Ernest Pontifex's final isolation, we see two prophecies as to its ultimate end-point: either it will drive people to their death or it will drive them into outlawry, however polite and genteel, as was Ernest's.

But Hardy and Butler, while in some respects they point in the same direction, are in other respects radically divergent. Butler quite clearly looks forward to E. M. Forster and D. H. Lawrence, with their instinctive ethic, their dynamic, purposive concepts of life, their disdain for and lack of concern with the minutiae of individual consciousness, and their sense of comedy. Hardy, on the other hand, while he has deep affinities with Lawrence, especially as the poet of nature and the apostle of the instincts, looks toward the stasis and tragedy, the entrapment of the individual in the hell of his consciousness, that is the province of the later James, of Conrad, of Woolf, of Joyce. The one tradition looks forward to *The Man Who Died;* the other to *Finnegans Wake.* Thus Lawrence and Joyce, the two indisputably great English novelists of the twentieth century, in whose "wake" the novel still wallows, are not so much the unique children of the twentieth century as they are the grandchildren of the nineteenth, the twin inheritors and summarizers of the great Victorian novel, which broke, split, and diverged in two directions in the late nineteenth century.

It all began with George Eliot; at least this is what D. H. Lawrence thought. As young readers, he and "E. T." were both wholehearted admirers of George Eliot, especially of *The Mill on the Floss.* Yet Lawrence has some reservations as to the direction, namely, the psychological, to which George Eliot's novels first pointed. "You see, it was really George Eliot who started it all," Lawrence was saying in that deliberate way he had of speaking when he was trying to work something out in his own mind. "And how wild they were with her for doing it. It was she who started putting all the action inside. Before, you know, with Fielding and the others, it had been outside. Now I wonder which is right?"[6] "E. T." promptly replied that of course George Eliot was right, but Lawrence demurred, if ever so slightly, "You know I can't help thinking there ought to be a bit of both."[7] For he faintly suspected then what he was to assert so vehemently later, namely, that the exploration of the minutiae of consciousness was finally, magnificent a subject though it might be, a cul-de-sac, as it has since proved to be. This is what he meant by his later and more famous statement that he was no longer interested in individuals and what he meant when he emitted one of his characteristic screeches at most modern novels: "They're all little Jesuses in their own eyes, and their 'purpose' is to prove it. Oh Lord! *Lord Jim! Sylvestre Bonard! If Winter Comes! Main Street! Ulysses! Pan!* They are all pathetic or sympathetic or antipathetic little Jesuses *accomplis* or *manqués*."[8] It is a rebellion against the intolerable "I," "I," "I," which is the signature of so many twentieth-century novels.

This subjective line that began with George Eliot and led to Henry James, to Conrad, to Virginia Woolf, to culminate in Joyce has certain marked characteristics both in content and form. Its content is the data of middle-class consciousness, usually described directly by the so-called stream of consciousness, or a variant thereof, with the exception of Conrad where narration is objective. Life is conceived of as static—nothing can change and nothing can really happen—and, with the exception of Joyce, tragic. But even in Joyce the major assumption is that we all are trapped in our own solitary cells, endlessly chewing the cud of moment-by-moment experience, slowly and sadly in James, abruptly and ironically in Conrad, poetically and wistfully in Virginia Woolf, rapidly and humorously in Joyce. The stasis, or entrapment, tragic in James and Conrad and Hardy, becomes wistful in Woolf and funny in Joyce. *Ulysses* leaves its hero in a perfect equilibrium—nothing ventured, nothing gained. When Leopold Bloom finally kisses the adulterous rump of which he is the adorer and falls off to sleep, dreaming of Sinbad the Sailor, he is certainly one of the most equanimous protagonists in all fiction, simply because he has accepted utterly the fact that life is what it is and nothing can be done. But the basic attitude of this genre is deeply pessimistic. Space is imprisonment, time a tyranny, and history a nightmare from which nobody can awake. The temporal is an obsession dominating all phases of life. Similarly the tone is nondidactic and seeks merely to describe, with no moral or lesson or thesis. Once more Joyce is the culmination and fullest expression of the genre, and *Ulysses* is the most scrupulously nonkinetic of novels. It moves to nothing but sheer contemplation, which was the author's primary and sole objective.

There are also formal resemblances in the Joyce tradition that set it off from the Butler-Forster-Lawrence line. Primarily the tradition is self-consciously "literary," both in structure and style. James, Conrad, Virginia Woolf, Joyce, whatever their great differences, were all united in a devotion to the carefully planned structure, from James's "point of view," through the looping narrative of Conrad and the artfully planned one of Virginia Woolf, to the gigantic battleship, with everything in place from the underwater bolts to the railing on the conning tower, of *Ulysses*. Likewise these authors were all magicians of "the word," not only the right words, but the right words in the right order. For each, language per se was a kind of daemon, almost an objective entity—a lovely goddess appearing to the breathless aging bachelor Henry James on a New Year's Eve, a divine instrument to Joyce for transforming that reality behind which existed a God in whom he still believed but could no longer serve.

None of these writers was connected to one another by any conscious lines of influence, with the exception of Virginia Woolf's recognizing the importance of *Ulysses* for the method and purpose of her own work. James was "The Master," *sui generis;* Conrad a foreigner working in a strange tongue; Virginia Woolf all alone in her room with a view; Joyce an Irishman living on the Continent and consciously disdainful of all that had preceded him in English fiction. Thus each thought of himself or herself as a new start, novelistically speaking. Seen in retrospect, they all prove to be culminative and evolutionary, but this evolution resulted from the workings of the *Zeitgeist* and not from the workings of their own minds, each of which saw itself as unique, precarious, and isolated.

The Butler-Forster-Lawrence tradition explicitly reverses all of these characteristics. In the first place it is quite consciously interdependent. Both Forster and Lawrence were admirers of Butler and his intellectual unconventionality. Forster once contemplated a book on Butler, and his own novels are filled with Butlerian echoes and attitudes. *The Longest Journey* is a repetition of the Butlerian thesis that the intellect is not supreme and that only common sense and instinct can make existence bearable, indeed liveable. Lawrence and Forster, of course, knew each other, and although Lawrence, as was his custom, was sparing in his praise of Forster's work, the tie between the two writers is manifest. Forster's admiration for Lawrence's work and his recognition of Lawrence's genius are specifically documented in *Aspects of the Novel,* where Lawrence is called the "one indisputable prophet" among modern writers. And the "natural man" who figures in Forster's early work, either an Italian like Gino or an

Englishman like Stephen Wonham, anticipate Lawrence's "dark game-keeper."

The Butler-Forster-Lawrence tradition likewise has its own form and content. Formally, it prides itself on being nonliterary, without involved manipulation of structure or scrupulously maintained "points of view" and without agonies over the *mot juste*. Forster thought that the sanctity of the device of the point of view, made into a holy of holies by James and Percy Lubbock, was an artificial shibboleth and very consciously in his own novels he violated it. Lawrence's disdain for the artifices of art was notorious. Whereas Joyce's method of rewriting was to complicate and complicate further, ever adding to a formal and precise structure, Lawrence's was to throw away the existing document and rewrite the original idea all over again.

In matters of content the Lawrencian tradition is equally divergent from the Joyce tradition. Stasis is replaced by dynamics, tragedy by comedy, and pessimism by hope. Space becomes freedom, time becomes growth, and history can be shed as the snake sheds its skin. Thus against the ending of *Ulysses* and its static entrapment, with Mr. Bloom accepting this entrapment, one can contrast the ending of *The Rainbow* where amid the thunder of the dark horses on the ground and under the splendor of the great rainbow in the sky, Ursula Brangwen sheds her own past and, by proxy, the past of her fellow human beings. This is a world which is organic and purposive; it is expressive of the anti-Darwinian argument that Butler had initiated, and Shaw had furthered. Studying botany Ursula rejects, solely on the basis of her own intuition, the mechanistic "purpose-less-ness" explanation of natural phenomenon that her professors give her, for she believes, against all reason and science, that everything has a "soul," even objects of nature, such as flowers. In her mind everything in the universe is potentially living and eternal, and time itself is no longer tyrannous. The earthly institution that most fully symbolized the victory over time of this Butlerian or Lamarckian universe was the medieval cathedral. Lincoln Cathedral in *The Rainbow* is described as:

> Away from time, always outside of time! Between east and west, between dawn and sunset, the Church lay like a seed in silence, dark before germination, silenced after death . . . potential with all the noise and transition of life, the cathedral remained hushed,

a great involved seed. . . . Spanned round with the rainbow, the jewelled gloom folded music upon silence, light upon darkness, fecundity upon death.

Other institutions, such as the great country house of Breadalby, that symbolize the dead and finished past but that still, anomalously, survive in the present are described as snares and delusions: "What a snare and a delusion, this beauty of static things."

Finally the Lawrencian tradition is avowedly, one might say frantically, kinetic; it has a "message," and the burden of this message, from Butler to Lawrence, is that the middle-class consciousness has become thin and neurotic, divorced from primal needs and instincts. According to Lawrence the middle class is "broad and shallow and passionless. Quite passionless. At best they substitute affection, which is the great middle-class positive emotion."[9] A corollary of this distaste for middle-class consciousness, which had been developed by a restrictive and absolutistic morality, was a distaste for all absolutes. Everything in the world is relative to everything else, and nothing had any value except insofar as it is related to the instincts—Butler's "grace" and Lawrence's "dark power."

What Lawrence represents, then, is the culmination in the novel of that upsurge from below which the "ethic" of the London proletariat had prefigured and which Butler had first embodied in the novel. Without getting into the argument between T. S. Eliot and F. R. Leavis about the "cultural resources" of Lawrence, it can certainly be said that he was, definitively and defiantly, of the lower class rather than of the middle class. There can be no doubt that if the bawdy, bearded, dying Lawrence of the later years were to rewrite *Sons and Lovers,* the scale of values would have been considerably altered, if not actually reversed, with the drunken, vulgarian, dominated father emerging as superior to the prim, powerfully-willed mother, and Paul becoming explicitly the priggish soul-mongerer, the "little Jesus," that he implicitly is in the novel itself. By the time he hit upon his true province, the world of *Women in Love* and *The Rainbow,* Lawrence had come to realize this himself. Completely unsatisfied with Skrebensky, the preeminent incarnation of the middle-class consciousness, Ursula Brangwen imagines that there must be another kind of consciousness, analogous to that of the workingman: "It doesn't matter. But a sort of strong understanding, in some men, and then a dignity, a directness, something unquestioned that there is in working men, and then a jolly, reckless passionateness that you see—a man who could really let go."

Joyce, then, represents the novel of middle-class consciousness in culmination and *in extremis,* and Lawrence represents the counter-attack from below. The question remains: where does the novel go from here? For certainly it has remained substantially in the doldrums since the deaths of Lawrence and Joyce. Good second-rank practitioners are of course abundant, but major talents, such as came in profusion from the 1830's to the 1920's, are indubitably lacking.

It is possible, of course, that the big novel is a thing of the past, a child of the special conditions of the nineteenth century. Even the writers whom one would tend to regard as the products of twentieth century, if only for chronological reasons, such as Proust, Mann, and Joyce, tend to look more and more, what with their preoccupation with ideas, their minute psychologizing, their grandiose architecture, like legacies of the nineteenth century and culminators of its particular ethos rather than new starts for the twentieth-century outlook, of which the early Hemingway is probably more representative. *The Sun Also Rises* is a functional twentieth-century house, while *Ulysses* or *Remembrance of Things Past* are Victorian mansions.

On the other hand, there is no reason per se for assuming that the novel is doomed. The very special conditions upon which the epic depended and which made its existence impossible once they disappeared have no real analogy in the history of the novel. Furthermore there have been in the past, in the history of the English novel, periods of stagnation, as, for example, in the late eighteenth century, before Scott and Austen, and in the early nineteenth century, before Dickens and the great Victorians. It is possible for two such giants as Lawrence and Joyce to exhaust momentarily the possibilities of a medium, for between them both they seem to say everything that can be said. Like Scott and Austen, a century before, they seem to have divided all human experience, and then, each in his own province, to have done everything that could be done. All of the Victorians were brought up on Sir Walter, and each thought in his youth that there was to be no "competing" with *this.* But compete with him they did, and in many cases surpassed him.

Just so, Lawrence and Joyce now look overpowering, and partly because of the antithetical nature of their talents: to abjure one is to compete with the other. Joyce is the great "artificer," Lawrence the great "natural"; Joyce celebrates the mystery of fatherhood and represents the male principle, while Lawrence is the voice of womanhood and her mysteries; Joyce describes the intricacies of the city, while Lawrence is the rhapsodist of nature; Joyce examines the illogicalities of conscious and unconscious life, Lawrence the wordless ways of the instincts; Joyce is the voice of Catholicism, Lawrence of Protestantism; Joyce is the cosmopolite, Lawrence the provincial; Joyce stands for history, Lawrence for futurity; Joyce is a Rabelaisian comedian, Lawrence a Puritan prophet; Joyce apotheosizes the family, Lawrence romantic love; Joyce describes, Lawrence evokes; for Joyce sex is of the devil, for Lawrence it is a religion; Joyce portrays the pathos of frustration, Lawrence prophecies an imagined release and fulfillment; Joyce thought language an ultimate reality, Lawrence thought it an ultimate sham. Psychologically, culturally, artistically, they are antithetical in every respect, and they stand like great roadblocks whose existence seems to imperil any fresh starts.

But they are roadblocks of a differing order, Joyce a real one, Lawrence only an apparent one. *Finnegan* is a literal "wake" for a certain kind of novel, but *The Man Who Died* is an allegory pointing to a prose fiction of the future. Joyce's work carries the exploration of the psyche, literary elaboration, the sense of human frustration, and linguistic experimentation as far as they can be carried, and *Finnegans Wake* is the point of no return. But Lawrence, for all his resemblances and indebtednesses to Butler and Forster, represents a fresh start, or better, a renewal.

Sociologically, he is a rebel against the individualism and the inhibitions of the middle class; artistically, he is the apostle of "naturalness," as opposed to "artifice"; psychologically, he is interested in instincts rather than the data of consciousness; ontologically, he stands for the idea of growth as against the idea of stasis; and, above all, he is perhaps the most striking representative of that late nineteenth and early twentieth century phenomenon: the reentry of the Bible into the main stream of European culture from which it had been excluded during most of the eighteenth century and most of the nineteenth century. All over the late nineteenth century, the Bible, supposedly permanently crippled by mid-nineteenth century science and rationalism, begins to reappear, as vigorous as ever. The major impulse behind Dostoevsky, as he himself said, was the Book of Job; for Tolstoy it was the New Testament; for Matthew Arnold the Bible as a whole; for Thomas Hardy the pessimistic parts of the Old Testament. Old Testament pessimism was likewise stamped into Melville's consciousness, and lies at the heart of *Moby Dick*.

Lawrence's interest in the Bible, however, and its force in his novels, lay in a different realm from any of these others, all of whom went to the Bible for philosophical or moral sustenance. In the first place, Lawrence did not like the climax of the Bible—the ending of the Four Gospels—and his last creative act was to rewrite Matthew, Mark, Luke, and John in *The Man Who Died*. The Bible that he loved was contained in the early books of the Old Testament, in Genesis, Exodus, Samuel, and Kings. Furthermore, it was not the didacticism of the Bible that attracted him, and he always insisted that, despite the fact that he was a "prophet," his own novels were nondidactic and simply represented life as fully and as deeply as possible.

Rather it was the *spirit* of the earlier parts of the Old Testament that attracted him and which he tried to inject into his own novels— the vigor, the fierceness, the elemental passions, and the closeness to the earth, from which the first Father and Mother had arisen in the opening chapters of Genesis. If any part of Christianity genuinely attracted him it was the militant aspect of Protestantism. In "Hymns in a Man's Life" he said that even deeper woven into his consciousness than such early literary influences as Wordsworth or Shakespeare or Keats were the banal Nonconformist hymns that dominated his childhood memories. He was proud of the fact that he was a Congregationalist, the oldest of the Nonconformist sects, because, in his childhood anyway, it had escaped the ghastly sentimentalism that had come in with Methodism and because it was vigorous and joyful.

So too it was the rapturously and rigorously physical depiction of life in the early parts of the Old Testament that fired his imagination and animated his novels, both in their content and in their style. The incantatory prose of Lawrence, at its best and at its worst, is purely Biblical, and a page of it could be put side by side with, say, "The Song of Solomon," and there would be no essential differences: there is the concreteness of everything, the short, rapt, bardic utterance, and the oracular repetitiousness. Characters likewise have their whole instinctual life motivated by Biblical imagery and utterance, particularly, generation by generation, in *The Rainbow-Women in Love* series. When Lydia and Tom Brangwen after two years of rather tense married life, finally come together in a deep sense, Lawrence describes it thus: "When at last they had joined hands, the house was finished, and the Lord took up his abode. And they were glad." And Anna, Lydia's daughter by her first marriage, at last feels confident in her parents: "She played between the pillar of fire and the pillar of cloud in confidence, having the assurance on her right hand and the assurance on her left. She was no longer called upon to up-hold with her childish might the broken end of the arch. Her father and her mother now met to the span of the heavens, and she, the child, was free to play in the space beneath, between." With Anna herself, as she grows up, the Biblical sense and utterance become more pronounced, and, at times, embarrassing. When pregnant, after her marriage to Will, she takes off her clothes and dances, for, "She liked the story of David, who danced before the Lord, and uncovered himself exultingly." With Ursula, their child, the Biblical sense becomes even more emphatic. Although she hates sermons, she loves Sundays; by day she sees in a vision the white-robed spirit of Christ passing between the olive trees and by night she hears a voice calling "Samuel, Samuel!" Her favorite book is Genesis and her favorite text, which motivates her whole life, is Genesis VI, 2-4, which begins: "The Sons of God saw the daughters of men that they were fair: and they took them wives of all which they chose." This passage stirs her like a call. There must be, she thinks, offspring of God, Sons of God, other than Jesus and Adam, men who had neither given up the life of the body nor been driven ignominiously from Paradise, and who "came on free feet to the daughters of men, and took them to wife, so that the women conceived and brought forth men of renown." Her whole instinctual life then is centered on finding for a mate a "Son of God." When she first sees Skrebensky, she imagines him as "one such as those Sons of God who saw the daughters of men, that they were fair"; she soon sees that he is Adamic and fallen. But in the sequel to *The Rainbow,* in *Women in Love,* Ursula finally finds, after much turmoil and struggle, her "Son of God" in Birkin. After they finally capitulate to one another, she thinks: "This was release at last. She had had lovers, she had known passion. But this was neither love nor passion. It was the daughters of men coming back to the sons of God, the strange inhuman sons of God who are in the beginning."

For the Bible, said Lawrence, was "in my bones."[10] He thought it was "a great confused novel" and that the novel itself was "the book of life." The Bible was not about God, but about "man alive." "Adam, Eve, Sarai, Abraham, Isaac, Jacob, Samuel, David, Bathsheba, Ruth, Esther, Solomon, Job, Isaiah, Jesus, Mark, Judas, Paul, Peter: what is it but man alive, from start to finish."[11]

The "man alive" that Mayhew, with disapproval, and Butler, with approval, saw in the upper and lower classes and that Lawrence saw in his own lower class had already been prefigured in the opening pages of the earliest and greatest of Western "novels," the Bible.

The saturation in the Bible, the feeling for the natural world, the passionate surge of impulse from the "lower orders" up into the world of educated-intellectualized consciousness, the opposition of "life" to "literature"—"storytelling" to "artifice," "speech" to "style"— the anarchist-instinctual rebellion against codes and restrictions and rationality and rules are obviously not unique with Lawrence. One or more or all of these characteristics calls up memories of Langland, Bunyan, Blake, Wordsworth, George Orwell—the whole anarchist tradition in English literature, a tradition that accounts for much of the strength of the greatest of the Western literatures which, because of this tradition, is forever renewing itself in the Bible, in the instinctual life and in the plangent organisms of its native soil. This is not to say that the anarchist tradition constitutes the primary strength of English literature; on the contrary, it is the Chaucers, Shakespeares, and Miltons who are its towering geniuses. But considered as historical forces, as influences, the supreme writers are positively baneful. Shakespeare helped to ruin the English verse drama just as surely as Milton helped to kill off the English verse epic, and just as surely did Joyce finish off the "psychological" and "literary" novel. There is no emulation of a genius and, historically, he serves only to create a moribund tradition.

On the other hand, the immense creative powers and accomplishments of the anarchist tradition must not be underestimated either. Its two most fierce and greatest representatives are Blake and Lawrence, and they must be accounted in the first rank of English poets and novelists. But good or bad, the anarchists are always movers and shakers, who constantly renew and revitalize literature and open doors to the future. And their existence is a constant reminder that every Milton needs his Bunyan, every Pope his Blake and Wordsworth, every Joyce his Lawrence.

NOTES

1. Henry Mayhew, *London Labour and the London Poor* (London, 1861), 1, 43.
2. *The Letters of Charles Dickens* [Bloomsbury, 1939], II, 767.

3. See Kathleen Tillotson's excellent *Novels of the Eighteen-Forties* (Oxford, 1954), pp. 54–58.

4. D. H. Lawrence, *The Letters of* . . . , ed. by Aldous Huxley (New York, 1932), p. 441.

5. D. H. Lawrence, *Phoenix* (New York, 1936), p. 410.

6. "E. T." *D. H. Lawrence* (London, 1935), p. 105.

7. *Ibid.*, p. 105.

8. *The Later D. H. Lawrence,* ed. by W. Y. Tindall (New York, 1952), p. 192.

9. D. H. Lawrence, *Selected Literary Criticism* (New York, 1956), p. 5.

10. *Ibid.*, p. 164.

11. *Ibid.*, p. 105.